Context in Computing

Patrick Brézillon • Avelino J. Gonzalez
Editors

Context in Computing

A Cross-Disciplinary Approach
for Modeling the Real World

Foreword by George A. Papadopoulos

 Springer

Editors
Patrick Brézillon
Laboratoire d'Informatique de Paris 6 (LIP6)
University Pierre and Marie Curie (UPMC)
Paris
France

Avelino J. Gonzalez
Computer Science Division
University of Central Florida
Orlando, Florida
USA

ISBN 978-1-4939-5576-3   ISBN 978-1-4939-1887-4 (eBook)
DOI 10.1007/978-1-4939-1887-4
Springer New York Heidelberg Dordrecht London

Foreword

The dimension of context has played an important role in many disciplines, such as Psychology, Philosophy, Sociology, Medicine and, indeed, Computer Science. In the latter, it has found applicability in many areas of contemporary Computer Science research, such as HCI, CSCW, Ubiquitous, Mobile or Distributed Systems, etc.

It is unavoidable and understandable that such a well researched, interdisciplinary and multidisciplinary notion has generated many definitions, based on what someone considers as being the most important facets of context. Probably the most acceptable definition is that by Dey (2001):

> Context is any information that can be used to characterize the situation of an entity. An entity is a person, place, or object that is considered relevant to the interaction between a user and an application, including the user and applications themselves.

The nature of context can be, for example, spatial (location, orientation or speed), temporal (date, time or season), environmental (temperature, light, noise), and social (people and their activities). It can have direct applicability to Computer Systems, such as context related to computation or network resources. It can also be of a different nature, such as physiological (blood pressure, body temperature or heart rate) and psychological (emotions, or preferences). Often context is being understood as being internal in nature and captured from a user's interaction activity (e.g. user's goals or emotions) or external and measured by sensors (e.g. location, light, or sound).

As a consequence of the involvement of context we have the so-called context aware systems. Dey (2001) gives the following definition:

> A system is context-aware if it uses context to provide relevant information and/or services to the user, where relevancy depends on the user's task.

Here it is worth pointing out that there is an ongoing debate as to whether a context-aware system is sufficient to simply record and use context or whether it should also be able to adapt itself to context (Ferreira and Alves 2014). In any case, a context-aware system will typically be able to present information to users augmented with contextual information, execute services based on the current context or associate digital data with the user's context.

Context-awareness is closely related to the vision of ubiquitous computing, as described by Weiser, who advocated a world where computing is available anywhere, anytime and for everybody but in such a way that computers themselves are « hidden » in the background and go unnoticed by the users. Other similar notions related to context and context-awareness are pervasive computing, proactive computing, adaptive computing and ambient intelligence.

There has been much research in context and context aware systems (see for instance the survey paper by Hong et al. 2009). However, this research area remains very active in the general field of Computer Science, due to recent developments in Advanced Software Engineering, Cloud and Service Oriented Computing, Intelligent Systems, CSCW and Social Computing. Consequently, this volume presents a contemporary view of state-of-the-art interdisciplinary and multidisciplinary research in many aspects of context-based systems. I therefore applaud the editors Patrick Brézillon and Avelino J. Gonzalez for having assembled and organized a number of high quality and divergent in topic papers, into this very exciting volume that promises to deliver to the readers a broad view of how context is used in computing.

Department of Computer Science   George A. Papadopoulos
University of Cyprus

References

Dey, A.K.: Understanding and using context. Pers. Ubiquit. Comput. **5**(1), 4–7 (2001)
Ferreira, P., Alves, P.: Distributed Context-Aware Systems. Springer (2014)
Weiser, M.: The Computer for the 21st Century. Scientific American (1991)
Hong, J., Suh, E., Kim, S.: Context-aware systems: A literature review and classification. Expert Systems and Applications. Elsevier (2009)

Preface by the Editors

The word *context* is used commonly in our vernacular. It is a concept that cuts across all the domains, cultures and languages. Context and our recognition of it have served to make communication among us efficient. Context, furthermore, can define expected behavior while one is in a particular context, as well as provide expectations of what may or may not happen. On the other hand, the absence of a shared or commonly accepted context between communicants can often lead to misunderstandings. For example, in the case of a person arriving on the first day of a new position with a new company, it is expected that he/she have the appropriate professional background to carry out the assigned duties. However, also important is that the person soon learns the corporate culture (i.e., strictly hierarchical, open communication, etc.) as well as the implicit social rules of the company, such as having a daily coffee break with colleagues, participating in golf or bowling leagues, after work happy hour, etc. Not understanding this social context can often make it difficult to carry out duties in spite of having professional competence.

Nevertheless, as familiar as the concept of context is to us, there is no single theory of context that crosses domains and applications. This is actually a good thing, as it allows each of us to define context in a way that best serves our specific real world application. This book illustrates the richness of this concept, and we hope takes us further towards the goal of using context as a modeling tool for a wider range of human activities. However, the concept of context as a modeling tool has not been well understood by the larger computing research community. It has not been extensively used possibly because the nature of context is continually misrepresented with respect to knowledge and reasoning. For example, in knowledge management, context is either (a) ignored, or (b) related strictly to "management", but practically never associated with knowledge. Context depends on the *focus* of an *actor* (one who experiences the context). That is, a piece of knowledge at one step may become a contextual element in a subsequent step. Nevertheless, the encouraging news for us who work with context is that the concept of context has been increasingly found in the computing research literature over the last several years. Context has been lately used to great advantage in computing, especially when human knowledge and/or behavior are to be modeled, represented and exercised. This may be because, while it may be hard to define, we can instantly recognize a context when we see it. Context has been associated with data, information, knowledge and reasoning, as well as in the fields of cognitive science and linguistics. More practically, context has been applied to managing data (*context awareness*), managing information (*context sensitivity*), managing knowledge (*contextual knowledge*), representing tactical agent behavior (*context driven*), intelligent reasoning (*context-based*), decision support, machine learning, and dialogue management for virtual humans, as well as for several other things.

As longtime friends, co-authors in several publications and now co-editors, our vision for this edited volume was to create, along with our outstanding contributing authors, what we hope will be the defining work in the field of context and computing. This field of research is relatively young (20–30 years), and encompasses many different and rich points of view. The volume compiles and describes the ideas, concepts, technology and research from the leaders in this field. The fundamental theme of this volume is how context has been and can be used in computing to model human behaviors, actions and communications as well as manage data and knowledge. This contributed volume, therefore, provides a broad as well as deep treatment of context in computing as well as in related areas that depend heavily on computing (e.g., cognitive science, medicine, engineering, law and many others). Its coverage is broad because of its cross-disciplinary nature and deep because each chapter treats its topic in sufficient depth to permit a reader to implement context in his/her computational endeavors. We hope it will be the defining work on context for computing.

The process used to invite, review the contributions, and publish what we have here now has been a long and effortful process, both on our parts as well as that of the contributing authors. We had conceived a proposed table of contents and published it at the outset of our effort to create this book. This began during the summer of 2013 when we requested two-page extended abstracts from our well known colleagues as well as several newly known ones. We asked our potential contributors to select a topic and address it in their extended abstracts. However, we also accepted abstracts from others who chose to focus on related topics that were not in the published ToC. As long as the topics described in these two pages were in line with our vision for the book, we accepted them and requested full-length manuscripts from the authors, offering some feedback as to how best direct their contributions to be in line with the objectives of this book.

Nearly six months later (February 2014), the full-length submissions were received. Each proposed contribution was carefully reviewed by us as well as by two outside reviewers. Many of the contributors served as reviewers and for that, we thank them. Their comments resulted in improved papers all throughout.

After receiving the comments by the reviewers as well as our own documented comments, we determined which of the submissions to accept and provided further feedback to the authors. Final manuscripts were received in late May and early June of 2014, which allowed us to meet the stringent deadline of July 15.

Lastly, the accepted papers you will see in this volume necessarily caused us to modify the table of contents to reflect the actual contents. In the Introduction (Chap. 1), we describe the classification of the contributions and the organization of the volume.

We thank the contributing authors for their participation in creation of this volume, both as authors as well as in many cases, reviewers. Without them, there would be no book. Secondly, we thank those other outside reviewers who, without compensation of any kind, agreed to help us in the review process and provided thoughtful and insightful reviews. Lastly, we thank the staff at Springer for making the publication process as easy as possible for us.

Finally, the wide applicability of context in the many disciplines makes it one of the most cross-disciplinary areas of research, especially in computing and all disciplines that depend on computing for critical support (i.e., a large number of domains, especially now with new personal communication technology growing at a rapid pace). It is exactly this usefulness and wide applicability of context that we hope that this volume emphasizes.

Contents

Contributors

Rami Alazrai School of Computer Engineering and Information Technology, German Jordanian University, Amman, Jordan

Miltiades Anagnostou National Technical University of Athens, Athens, Greece

Bruno Antunes CISUC, Department of Informatics Engineering, University of Coimbra, Coimbra, Portugal

Patrick Barlatier LISTIC/Polytech'Annecy-Chambéry, University of Savoie, Annecy-le-vieux cedex, France

Feras A. Batarseh Intelligent Systems Laboratory, University of Central Florida, Orlando, FL, USA

Luciana Benotti LIIS Team, FAMAF, Universidad Nacional de Córdoba, Córdoba, Argentina

Yolande Berbers iMinds-DistriNet, KU Leuven, Leuven, Belgium

Patrick Blackburn Department of Philosophy and Science Studies, Centre for Culture and Identity, Roskilde University, Roskilde, Denmark

Jacqueline Bourdeau Télé-université du Québec, Québec, QC, Canada

Patrick Brézillon Laboratoire d'Informatique de Paris 6 (LIP6), University Pierre and Marie Curie (UPMC), Paris, France

Sophie Chabridon Institut Mines-Télécom, CNRS UMR 5157 SAMOVAR, Télécom SudParis, Évry, France

Henning Christiansen Roskilde University, Roskilde, Denmark

Alan Colman School of Software and Electrical Engineering, Swinburne University of Technology, Melbourne, Australia

Richard Dapoigny LISTIC/Polytech'Annecy-Chambéry, University of Savoie, Annecy-le-vieux cedex, France

Thierry Desprats IRIT UMR 5505, Université Paul Sabatier, Toulouse, France

Bruce Edmonds Centre for Policy Modelling, Manchester Metropolitan University, Manchester, UK

Xiaoliang Fan Lanzhou University, Lanzhou, China

Thomas Forissier Université des Antilles et de la Guyane, Pointe-à-Pitre, Guadeloupe, France

Barbara Furtado CISUC, Department of Informatics Engineering, University of Coimbra, Coimbra, Portugal

Chiara Ghidini Fondazione Bruno Kessler, Trento, Italy

Paulo Gomes CISUC, Department of Informatics Engineering, University of Coimbra, Coimbra, Portugal

João Miguel Gonçalves Portugal Telecom Inovação S.A., Aveiro, Portugal

Avelino J. Gonzalez Computer Science Division, University of Central Florida, Orlando, FL, USA

Odd Erik Gundersen Verdande Technology AS, Trondheim, Norway

Department of Computer and Information Science, Norwegian University of Science and Technology (NTNU), Trondheim, Norway

Jun Han School of Software and Electrical Engineering, Swinburne University of Technology, Melbourne, Australia

Anneli Heimbürger University of Jyväskylä, Jyväskylä, Finland

Debra L. Hollister Valencia College, Lake Nona Campus, Orlando, FL, USA

Victor Hung Intelligent Systems Laboratory, University of Central Florida, Orlando, FL, USA

Mahmoud Hussein Menofia University, Menofia, Egypt

Vahid Jalali School of Informatics and Computing, Indiana University, Bloomington, IN, USA

Cynthia L. Johnson Georgia Gwinnett College, Lawrenceville, GA, USA

Muhammad Ashad Kabir School of Software and Electrical Engineering, Swinburne University of Technology, Melbourne, Australia

Nikos Kalatzis National Technical University of Athens, Athens, Greece

Malinda Kapuruge DiUS Computing Pty Ltd, Melbourne, Australia

Andrew Kinai Carnegie Mellon University, Rwanda and Pittsburgh, PA, USA

Yasushi Kiyoki Keio University SFC, Fujisawa, Kanagawa Prefecture, Japan

Stefan Werner Knoll Otto-von-Guericke University, Magdeburg, Germany

Pavlos Kosmides National Technical University of Athens, Athens, Greece

David Leake School of Informatics and Computing, Indiana University, Bloomington, IN, USA

Nicolas Liampotis National Technical University of Athens, Athens, Greece

Stephan G. Lukosch Delft University of Technology, Delft, The Netherlands

Pierrick Marie IRIT UMR 5505, Université Paul Sabatier, Toulouse, France

Pie Masomo Carnegie Mellon University, Rwanda and Pittsburgh, PA, USA

Yves Mazabraud Université des Antilles et de la Guyane, Pointe à Pitre, Guadeloupe, France

Yaser Mowafi School of Computer Engineering and Information Technology, German Jordanian University, Amman, Jordan

Roger Nkambou Université du Québec à Montréal, Montréal, Canada

Andrei Olaru Department of Computers, Faculty of Automatic Control and Computers, University "Politehnica" of Bucharest, Bucharest, Romania

Eliza Papadopoulou Heriot-Watt University Riccarton, Edinburgh, UK

Ioannis Papaioannou National Technical University of Athens, Athens, Greece

Jeanne E. Parker Intelligent Systems Laboratory, Department of EECS- CS Division, University of Central Florida, Orlando, FL, USA

Davy Preuveneers iMinds-DistriNet, KU Leuven, Leuven, Belgium

Arun Kishore Ramakrishnan iMinds-DistriNet, KU Leuven, Leuven, Belgium

Ioanna Roussaki National Technical University of Athens, Athens, Greece

Ana Carolina Salgado Centro de Informática, Universidade Federal de Pernambuco, Recife, Brazil

Hedda Rahel Schmidtke Carnegie Mellon University, Kigali, Rwanda and Pittsburgh, PA, USA

Luciano Serafini Fondazione Bruno Kessler, Trento, Italy

Alain Shema Carnegie Mellon University, Rwanda and Pittsburgh, PA, USA

Michelle Sibilla IRIT UMR 5505, Université Paul Sabatier, Toulouse, France

Efstathios Sykas National Technical University of Athens, Athens, Greece

Patrícia Tedesco Centro de Informática, Universidade Federal de Pernambuco, Recife, Brazil

Pieter J. Toussaint Department of Computer and Information Science, Norwegian University of Science and Technology (NTNU), Trondheim, Norway

Roy M. Turner School of Computing and Information Science, University of Maine, Orono, ME, USA

Hamed Vahdat-Nejad Pervasive and Cloud Computing Lab, Department of Computer Engineering, University of Birjand, Birjand, Iran

Vaninha Vieira Departamento de Ciência da Computação, Universidade Federal da Bahia, Salvador, Brazil

Leendert W. M. Wienhofen SINTEF ICT, Sluppen, Trondheim, Norway

Department of Computer and Information Science, Norwegian University of Science and Technology (NTNU), Trondheim, Norway

Haixia Yu Ricoh Innovations Corporation, Menlo Park, CA, USA

Ahmad Zmily School of Computer Engineering and Information Technology, German Jordanian University, Amman, Jordan

Chapter 1
Introduction

Avelino J. Gonzalez and Patrick Brézillon

Abstract The importance of context in reasoning about the world has been recognized by many researchers over the last several years. Its subsequent incorporation in models of human intelligent decision-making and behavior has facilitated the modeling problem manyfold. The co-editors hope that this volume will serve as the definitive guide to researchers and practitioners in this very important subject. This contributed volume contains a selection of the most current and advanced research on using context in modeling the real world in computers and computer systems. This chapter introduces the volume and provides the setting for the various chapters therein.

Context has always played an important, if little understood, role in human intelligence. This is especially true in human decision-making and communication. One's awareness of his/her context as well as that of others with whom she/he interacts permits many assumptions to be made about the discussion, the environment and/or the problem at hand. This allows many important aspects of human interaction to remain implicit when the communicants are in a common context, or alternatively, in different but mutually understood contexts. Otherwise, all assumptions would have to always be explicitly spelled out, a truly burdensome task for everyday communication.

Linguists often allude to conventions that exist among interlocutors that permit the meaning of a communication to be successfully captured by the communicating parties. These conventions in many ways involve context. For example, the word "skiing" has vastly different connotations in winter than in summer; in the mountains of Switzerland than in Miami Beach. Knowing the context in which the word "skiing" is being employed eliminates the need to further define it as alpine skiing or water skiing. Conversely, when a statement deviates from the expected context (say, when discussing skiing in the South of Brazil), the new context must be explicitly

A. J. Gonzalez (✉)
Computer Science Division, University of Central Florida, Orlando, FL, USA
e-mail: avelino.gonzalez@ucf.edu

P. Brézillon
Laboratoire d'Informatique de Paris 6 (LIP6),
University Pierre and Marie Curie (UPMC), Paris, France
e-mail: patrick.brezillon@lip6.fr

© Springer Science+Business Media New York 2014
P. Brézillon, A. J. Gonzalez (eds.), *Context in Computing*,
DOI 10.1007/978-1-4939-1887-4_1

announced in order to avoid confusing the other communicants. Many other similar examples can be given of the importance of context in correctly interpreting the meaning of otherwise ambiguous words.

The notion of context has been defined by several authors. See Bazire and Brézillon (2005) for an extensive discussion of these definitions. Webster's Dictionary defines context as "... the whole situation, background or environment relevant to some happening or personality." This definition suggests that the context is always tacit and is rarely mentioned explicitly. Another definition of context that is more operational in computing is "Context is what constrains a focus without intervening in it explicitly" (Brézillon and Pomerol 1999). Definitions that originate from researchers and practitioners in specific domains have singular and often narrow viewpoints, and focus on some aspects of context that can be identified from data, information or knowledge obtained through sensors that are specific to their domain or discipline. Indeed, we face the two opposite views on context, as pointed out by Brézillon and Abu-Hakima (1995), namely the engineering viewpoint and the cognitive-science viewpoint. This book is an attempt to reconcile these two views.

In problem solving, the context inherently contains much knowledge about the situation and environment of the problem. The context indeed constrains the focus, but conversely, the focus allows for the specification of the relevant contextual elements. For example, a dead battery in a car that has been parked overnight in freezing temperatures constrains the focus of a diagnostician, and specifies the contextual elements to the diagnostician. Thus, such a context has entirely different diagnostic implications than one where the car is in operation when the battery dies. Therefore, the effect of context on problem solving and decision-making can likewise be very significant.

Context also introduces an expectation of behavior that, by convention, goes along with a specific situation. Turner (1993) exemplifies this by alluding to the fact that when one enters a library, conversation is habitually reduced to a whisper. As the context changed (when the subject entered a library), new behaviors (whispers) were instantiated for use in the new context. Upon leaving a library, one's context changes again, and the prior behavior is no longer enforced.

Defining the exact scope of the context can be difficult to do. McCarthy (1987) asserts that context is of infinite dimension. While this may be theoretically true, humans seem to instinctively recognize the important aspects of a situation and identify the context and its bounds very quickly. Therefore, while context may indeed be of infinite dimension, it is clear that not all dimensions are necessary to define it in the practical world. In fact, we assert that relatively few dimensions are necessary. Some authors of this book distinguish contextual knowledge and external knowledge, and the latter is often excluded from the system during computation.

The notion of context can take on different meanings, depending on, well... the context. We now take a brief look at the significance of context in various disciplines.

Many misunderstandings in human discourse indeed take place when communicants are not in a common, or at least a shared, context. By shared, we mean to say that they are in different contexts but know and understand the context of the other party. Psychologists have long understood the influence of context on human behavior, specifically on memory recall (Godden and Baddeley 1975, 1980). In philosophy, *contextualism* is the opinion that human behavior "... always takes place in a context and can only be understood within that context. Therefore, any 'laws' which attempt to predict (for example) human behaviour will only ever be context-specific" (Grohol 1999).

Closer to home, in computer science and artificial intelligence, McDermott was one of the first to employ context in his work on R1 (McDermott 1982). McCarthy (1987) introduced context as a class, and defined a logic that can manage contexts. Guha (1991) makes significant use of context as a micro theory in the landmark CYC project. One of earliest expert system to be commercially viable, (GenAID (Gonzalez et al. 1986)) also employed contexts in a diagnostic task. More recently, Brézillon (2003) applied Contextual Graphs (CxG) to decision support in domains that rely on operational procedures to solve problems (subway line management). Turner (1993) developed Context-Mediated Behavior (CMB) to control robotic submarines. Gonzalez and Ahlers (1993, 1998) developed Context-based Reasoning (CxBR) for representing human tactical behavior in simulations. Finally, the field of context-aware systems employs context to facilitate user interfaces in complex devices (Dey et al. 2002).

The importance of context in our everyday lives is clear to any prospective reader of this volume. As co-editors, we have sought here to express how the elusive but quite real concept of context can be used to advantage when modeling or representing real world human activities. This volume, therefore, contains a broad and deep coverage of the rich subject of context. It's focus is on how it is/can be used to model the real world in a computer, as well as to assist us in our everyday tasks and activities. This volume contains contributions from an outstanding group of researchers and practitioners who collectively have many years of expertise in their domains in computing. With this in mind, we have divided the contributions of these authors into six major parts.

The chapters presented in Part I "Context in software and systems" show that it is possible to introduce context more intimately within software. This moves our concept of context from an initial view of context as a simple layer between the system and its environment (Vahdat-Nejad) to a view in which system and human jointly try to realize the task in a context-sensitive way (Brézillon; Viera et al.). Context can also enrich systems with an adaptive capability (Colman et al.) to react to changes in the environment. The contextual approach can also be applied to the design and development of the system itself (Batarseh; Antunes and Gomes; Vieira et al.).

In Part II "Context in the computing environment", another key feature of a context-based system is its potential to learn from its interaction with the user and its environment (Johnson) in order to be, on the one hand, more responsive to external stimuli, while on the other hand, improve its own behavior (through its algorithm). This feature becomes of paramount importance for mobile systems and modern ubiquitous computing environments (Ramakrishnan et al.). This is especially true with cloud computing (Hung; Fan), where, on the human side, one speaks of communities (of practice, of interest, etc. Liampotis et al.) as well as of social networks.

However, the quality of such systems as context managers must first be validated. This is treated by Marie et al.

The chapters in Part III "Context in an individual human dimension" and Part IV "Context in the collective human dimension" address the other side of the coin—the human dimension of context. Context in computing cannot be considered independent from the human with whom the system interacts. This is because we humans also have our own working context that must be reflected and attended to. Therefore, the context in computing must also be considered from the perspective of the human dimension. This is relevant to works in the cognitive sciences (Parker and Hollister). Furthermore, as the system becomes equipped with a learning functionality (see previous part and Forissier et al. in this part), context sensitivity opens the door for new techniques that allow humans to learn more effectively (tutoring systems), to express his/her needs relevant to the context, to make decisions that are contextually appropriate, etc. (Wienhofen et al.). Through new technology, context in computing also plays an important role in the interaction between humans, such as in collaborative works, social network, etc. This allows context-based systems to be merged within this collective human dimension through means such as social simulation (Edmonds), cross-cultural communication (Heimburger and Kiyoki), situational assessment (Gundersen), context evolution, context sharing, etc. Lastly, if new technologies have changed the way humans work together, conversely, our modern needs have required the development of new software to be able to include within the software, a part of context not yet considered, such as the social context (Kabir et al.; Knoll and Lukosch; Kalatzis et al.).

Part V "Context in modeling reasoning" and Part VI "Context in representing reasoning" discuss the building blocks of any system that uses context—its representation. We often cannot avoid speaking of context in an abstract way because context is always changing and depends heavily on the domain of application. Nevertheless, some formal approaches can open the door to a rigorous study of context. These include multi context logics (Ghidini and Serafini), constraint programming (Christiansen), implicatures (Bernotti and Blackburn), making explicit several different levels of granularity (Schmidtke), and expressive and clear semantics for context (Dapoigny and Barlatier). On the other hand, context in computing is already integral in such techniques as case-based reasoning (Leake and Jalali), context-based reasoning (Gonzalez), context-mediated behavior (Turner), multi-agent systems (Olaru), and contextual graphs for modeling human experience (Brézillon), etc. Furthermore, context in computing has found new interest in domains such as medicine (Schmidtke et al.) and law, where formalization remains difficult to this day.

We deeply thank the authors that contributed their outstanding work, ideas and systems to this volume. We are certain that it will represent a milestone in the progress we make in modeling the real world. Therefore, without further adieu, we now continue to the first of these sections, Context in Software and Systems.

Enjoy your reading!

References

Bazire, M, Brézillon, P.: Understanding context before to use it. Modeling and using context. In: Dey A., Kokinov, B., Leake, D., Turner, R. (eds.) Proceedings of CONTEXT-05 Conference. LNCS 3554, pp. 29–40. Springer, Heidelberg (2005)

Brézillon, P.: Context-based intelligent assistant systems: a discussion based on the analysis of two projects. In: Proceedings of the 36th Annual Hawaii International Conference on System Sciences, pp. 83–91, (2003)

Brézillon, P., Abu-Hakima, S.: Using knowledge in its context: Report on the IJCAI-93 workshop. AI Spring, **16**(1), 87–91 (1995)

Brézillon, P., Pomerol, J-Ch.: Contextual knowledge sharing and cooperation in intelligent assistant systems. Trav. Humain. **62**(3), 223–246 (1999)

Dey, A.K., Mankoff, J.G., Abowd, D., Carter, S.: Distributed mediation of ambiguous context in aware environments. In: Proceedings of the 15th Annual Symposium on User Interface Software and Technology (UIST 2002), Paris, France, pp. 121–130 (2002)

Godden, D., Baddeley, A.: Context-dependent memory in two natural environments: On land and under water. Br. J. Psychol. **66**, 325–331 (1975)

Godden, D., Baddeley, A.: When does context influence memory? Br. J. Psychol. **71**, 99–104 (1980)

Gonzalez, A.J., Ahlers, R.H.: Concise representation of autonomous intelligent platforms in a simulation through the use of scripts. In: Proceedings of the Sixth Annual Florida Artificial Intelligence Research Symposium, Ft. Lauderdale, FL (1993)

Gonzalez, A.J., Ahlers, R.H.: Context-based representation of intelligent behavior in training simulations. Trans. Soc. Comput. Simul. **15**(4), 153–166 (1998)

Gonzalez, A.J., Osborne, R.L., Kemper, C.T., Lowenfeld, S.: On-line diagnosis of turbine-generators using artificial intelligence. IEEE Trans. Energy Convers. **EC-1**(2), 68–74 (1986)

Grohol, www.psychcentral.com. This page is an extract from the LinguaLinks Library, Version 4.0, published on CD-ROM by SIL International (1999)

Guha, R.V.: Contexts: a formalization and some applications. MCC Technical Report ACT-CYC-423–91 December (1991)

McCarthy, J.: Notes on formalizing context. Knowledge Rep. **30**(12), 555–560 (1987)

McDermott, J.: R1: A rule-based configurer of computer systems. Artif. Intell. **19**(1), 39–88 (1982)

Turner, R.M.: Context-sensitive reasoning for autonomous agents and cooperative distributed problem solving. Proceedings of the 1993 IJCAI Workshop on Using Knowledge in Context, Chambery, France (1993)

Part I
Context in Software and Systems

Chapter 2
The CSS Design Process: On Supporting Context-Sensitive Systems Development

Vaninha Vieira, Patrícia Tedesco and Ana Carolina Salgado

Abstract A software process is a roadmap with predictable steps and guidelines related to the development of computer applications. It aims to support the creation of high-quality, timely products. Context-sensitive systems (CSS) belong to a special category of computer applications and consider new aspects and challenges related to context specific requirements. Including context into a system entails a different way of thinking about the system's engineering. When designing a CSS, a major emphasis should be given to the analysis of how users interact with the system and how these users expect the system to act on their behalf. This chapter discusses how Software Engineering techniques can be used to support context-sensitive system development. In particular, the authors present a software process named CSS Design Process (CDP). It details and provides a systematic way to execute the main activities related with context specification, management and usage on designing context-sensitive systems. To illustrate the process usage, the authors present its instantiation in two case studies in different domains and applications.

2.1 Context-Awareness

Providing applications with the ability to identify and understand the context of their interaction with users can greatly improve the communication between users and machines. Context appears as a fundamental key to enable systems to distil available information into relevant information, to choose relevant actions from a list of possibilities, or to determine the optimal method of information delivery. The ideal application should be able to provide information that is both accurate and

V. Vieira (✉)
Departamento de Ciência da Computação, Universidade Federal da Bahia, Salvador, Brazil
Tel no: +55.71.32836299
e-mail: vaninha@dcc.ufba.br

P. Tedesco · A. C. Salgado
Centro de Informática, Universidade Federal de Pernambuco, Recife, Brazil
Tel no: +55.81.21268430
e-mail: pcart@cin.ufpe.br

A. C. Salgado
e-mail: acs@cin.ufpe.br

© Springer Science+Business Media New York 2014   9
P. Brézillon, A. J. Gonzalez (eds.), *Context in Computing*,
DOI 10.1007/978-1-4939-1887-4_2

relevant without requiring the user to actively seek this information and determine its relevance.

The term Context-Aware Computing was first used in Schilit et al. (1994) to designate systems that are capable of examining the surrounding environment and reacting to changes in it. This view of context is mostly associated with Ubiquitous Computing, the area envisioned by Weiser (1991) where computing is available "anytime, anywhere from any device". Advances in technology, such as the broad usage of small devices, wireless communication, and more sophisticated sensors open a myriad of possibilities for context-aware systems (Hong et al. 2009).

The term *context-aware system* is used to refer to systems that use context to provide relevant information and/or services to the user, where relevance depends on the user's task (Dey et al. 2001). Other terms are used as synonyms to designate these systems, such as: *context-sensitive system, context-oriented system* and *context-based system*. In this chapter, we adopt the term *context-sensitive system* because we believe that it translates better the semantics of a system that *perceives* changes in its environment and *reacts* to those changes. We use the following definition (Vieira 2008): Context-Sensitive Systems (CSS) are those that manage and use context information to support an agent executing some task, where an agent can be a person or software. This support includes improving the agent's awareness about the task or providing system's adaptations to ease the task execution (Dourish, 2004).

Although there are several definitions of context, researchers agree that: context exists only when related to another entity (e.g. task, agent or interaction); context is a set of items (e.g. concepts, rules and propositions) associated to an entity; and an item is considered as part of a context only if it is useful to support the task at hand. For example, the proposition "it is raining" is considered as part of the context in a traffic jam support system, since rain has implications in visibility, speed and consequences in traffic. However, the same proposition is not contextual information in a museum guide system.

In our vision, there is a clear distinction between the concepts of context and contextual element (Vieira et al. 2007): **Contextual element (CE)** is any piece of data or information that enables one to characterize an entity in a domain, while the **Context** of an interaction between an agent and an application, in order to execute some task, is the set of instantiated contextual elements that are necessary to support the task at hand. We can observe that a CE is stable and can be defined at design time, while context is dynamic, and must be constructed at runtime, when an interaction occurs.

Developing a CSS is a complex and expensive task, since there are additional issues associated with it: which kind of information to consider as context, how to represent it, how to acquire and process it (considering several and heterogeneous sources), how to integrate the context usage into the system and how to present it since it is dependent on the recipient. In our research, we investigate the concept of context from the Conceptual Modeling and Software Engineering perspectives. The research is targeted, especially, to designers of CSS responsible for tasks such as knowledge engineering, requirements analysis and architecture design. We explore the idea that it is possible to modularize CSS development by separating application business domain elements from the specificities associated with context manipulation.

In this light, we propose (Vieira 2008) a conceptual framework to support context modeling and CSS design in a generic, domain-independent way, named CE-ManTIKA (Contextual Elements Modeling and Management through Incremental Knowledge Acquisition). CEManTIKA framework has three objectives: (1) to support the design of architectural elements related to context manipulation; (2) to assist designers in specifying and representing context in a generic domain-independent manner; and (3) to aid developers on modeling context and designing CSS. It is composed by four elements: a reference *architecture* context; a *metamodel* context, a set of *UML*[1] *profiles* context related to it and a *process* (CSS Design Process). This book chapter describes the proposed process. Further details about CEManTIKA can be found in Vieira et al. (2011b) and Vieira (2008).

2.2   Software Processes to Support CSS Development

Since context entails new requirements in the development of computer systems, researchers from Software Engineering perceived the need to provide specific methodologies and architectural support to aid the development of CSS. However, there is a growing need for software processes to support the design of CSS.

Henricksen and Indulska (2006) propose a Software Engineering methodology to guide the development of applications based on their Context Modeling Language (CML) and programming toolkit. This methodology specifies five main activities in CSS development: *Analysis* and specification of context fact types; *Design* of the triggering mechanisms for the application; *Implementation* of the application according to the programming toolkit; *Customization* of the abstract models (mapping of the CML model into relational models and identification of samples for testing); and *Testing* (modules, overall system and application acceptance with end users). The high-level process proposed contains only a flow of activities that should be followed to use their context modeling language and CSS programming abstractions. It does not mention the artefacts (input and output work products, guides or process roles) related to the activities, neither does it provide guidelines explaining how to perform each one.

Bulcão Neto et al. (2006) propose a Software Engineering approach to support the development of ontology-based context-sensitive systems, composed of three elements: a set of ontologies related to different dimensions of contextual information, an infrastructure to manipulate the ontologies and the *Process for Ontological Context-aware Applications* (POCAp). POCAp is a structured set of activities for developing ontology-based CSS. It is based on the SPEM notation and describes, at a high level, the activities related to building a CSS, as an instantiation of a common software process (according to the four main activities: *analysis and specification*, *design*, *development*, and *verification and validation*.). Its main drawback

---

[1] UML (Unified Modelling Language, http://www.uml.org/

is that it assumes an ontology-based solution for the CSS. In this sense, guidelines are focused on ontologies specification and manipulation instead of making context characteristics explicit.

Marco (2011) defines a framework to support a general lifecycle process for the development and the evolution of context-aware adaptive systems, focusing on requirements, design models and implementation mechanisms. He identified two different types of evolutions: foreseeable context variations by providing the required system evolutions at design-time; unpredictable context variations causing the change of user needs that can be expressed as a variation to the requirement set to satisfy. While in the predicted evolution the system evolves to keep satisfied a fixed set of system requirements in different known contexts, the unforeseen evolution is driven by new requirements arising from unforeseeable contexts. He proposes a software-centric approach, instead of developer-centric, with tools to support the development and evolution of the context requirements into implementations.

It is still the case that, in general, the related literature is either rather unspecific (i.e. it consists mostly of cases where methodologies proposed tend to adopt standard Software Engineering methodologies (Choi et al. 2011)) or it is rather dependent on representation techniques (ER models, Ontologies, e.g. (Hsu et al. 2010) Bauer (2012), (Bettini et al. 2010)) which constrains the types of CSS and CSS reasoning that can be designed.

The proposal of Vieira (2008), detailed in the next section, is original in the sense that it goes into detail about activities related to Context Specification and CSS Design and proposes a support tool for developers to reflect on the identification of context requirements and management. In particular, it argues that business models should be reused and extended to generate the context model.

2.3   The CSS Design Process (CDP) Specification

The *CSS Design Process* (CDP, for short) aims to guide a development team on modeling and designing context-sensitive systems. Three main roles are considered: *System Designer*, responsible for designing the system's architecture; *System Analyst*, responsible for identifying users' needs and translating business requirements into software specifications; and *Context Designer*, responsible for identifying context-related requirements and to design context-sensitive solutions. The context designer role demands expertise on multidisciplinary subjects related to human cognition, automatic acquisition technologies, artificial intelligence, software development and usability.

CDP follows the terminology, diagrams and notation provided by SPEM 2.0[2] (Software Process Engineering Metamodel), as illustrated in Fig. 2.1. SPEM is the OMG (Object Management Group) adopted standard for modeling software processes. It is a MOF-compliant metamodel and has an associated UML Profile. CDP

---

[2] http://www.omg.org/spec/SPEM/2.0/

Fig. 2.1 Notations and symbols of SPEM model used in CDP (Vieira 2008)

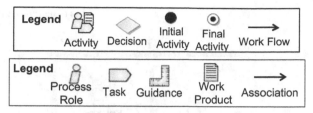

was modelled using SPEM Profile and two SPEM diagrams: *Workflow* (show how activities interact with each other and the execution order) and *Activity Detail* (present internal details of each activity, such as input/output artefacts and guidance). The process was defined with an overall indication of the sequence of activities to be performed. A detailed description of each activity presents its input and produced artifacts and guidelines that can be used to support its execution.

The following tasks are considered in CSS development (Vieira et al. 2011b) and were identified as the main activities of CDP (Fig. 2.2a). They are detailed in the next subsections.

- *Context Specification* (Fig. 2.2b) aims to identify possible variations in a CSS behavior affected by the context, and to define *what* should be considered as context to support the decision about a variation triggering;
- *Context Management* (Fig. 2.2c) is related to *how* context is implemented and used in the system; it is defined in terms of the main tasks it comprises: acquisition, storage, processing and dissemination (of contextual elements);
- *Context Usage* (Fig. 2.2d) refers to the employment of managed CEs to guide the variations in CSS behavior, either by enhancing users' awareness, influencing recommendations, or enabling adaptations of any kind.

2.3.1   Context Specification

This activity seeks to identify the context requirements based on the business requirements and to create two models: (1) *context conceptual model*, which describes the concepts related to the conceptual and structural elements of a CSS; and (2) *context behavior model*, which contains the concepts related to the behavioural aspects of a CSS. The models are created as instantiations of a context metamodel (Vieira et al. 2011b). This section will present the main tasks related to the Context Specification phase, which comprises the following ones:

a) *Identify Focus (S1)*: it aims to recognize from the business requirements which tasks and agents should be considered as foci in the CSS. It takes as input a Use Cases Model with the main business requirements for the CSS. It produces as output an extended version of the Use Cases Model enriched with the focus identification;

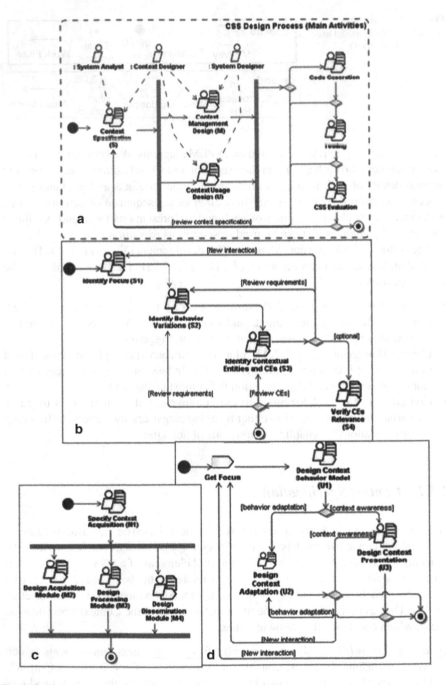

Fig. 2.2 CDP main activities and sub-activities (Vieira 2008)

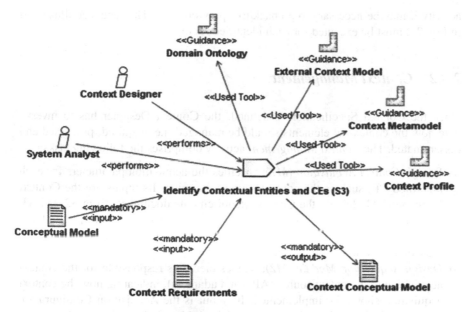

Fig. 2.3 Overview of the identify contextual entities and CEs activity (Vieira 2008)

b) *Identify Behaviour Variations (S2)*: a behavior variation indicates the different actions, related to a focus, that the CSS may execute, according to distinct contexts. S2 aims to identify, given a focus, which variations are expected in the CSS behavior and which factors affect them. It uses the extended Use Cases Model (from S1) and produces a Context Requirements document;

c) *Identify Contextual Entities and CEs (S3)*: aims to identify the entities related to the focus and the characteristics from those entities that influence each behavior variation. Figure 2.3 illustrates the detailed diagram for this activity. Its inputs are the Context Requirements document (S2), and a Conceptual Model from the CSS domain. The output artifact is a Context Conceptual Model. As guidance, it uses the concepts and stereotypes defined in the Context Metamodel and Context Profile. Optionally, other guidance can support this activity, such as domain ontologies and existing context models;

d) *Verify CEs Relevance (S4)*: the next step is to evaluate if the CSS end users and designers have the same understanding about the relevance of the identified CEs, and if the defined behavior variations reflect users' expectations. S4 uses as input the Context Conceptual Model (S3) and the Context Requirements document (S2), and produces a Relevance Evaluation document. It may also produce, as output, updated versions of the Context Conceptual Model and Context Requirements Document. As guidance, it may use evaluation guidelines (e.g. questionnaire samples).

These activities are performed by the context designer in collaboration with the system analyst. The activities are executed sequentially. While executing a given activity it may be necessary to go back to a previous one. The sequence illustrated in Fig. 2.2 must be executed for each identified focus.

2.3.2 Context Management

Once the Context Specification is defined, the Context Designer has to investigate how the contextual elements should be managed: i.e. acquired, processed and disseminated. The *Context Management* activity comprises the following tasks:

a) *Specify Context Acquisition (M1)*: specifies the acquisition parameters for each identified CE, such as the context sources mapping. Its inputs are the Context Conceptual Model and the Context Requirements document (from S2 and S3, respectively). Its output is an updated version of the Context Conceptual Model and an Acquisition Configuration document. It uses the Context Metamodel and the Context Profile as guidance;

b) *Design Acquisition Module (M2)*: defines elements responsible for the context acquisition (e.g. context sources APIs and adapters), indicating how the context acquisition should be implemented. Its input is the Acquisition Configuration document (M1) and it produces an Acquisition Module Specification. It uses the Context Architecture as guidance;

c) *Design Processing Module (M3)*: defines and designs the elements related to CE processing, i.e. derived CEs specification, CE knowledge base, inference rules and inference engine. Its inputs are the Context Conceptual Model (S3), the Context Requirements document (S2) and, optionally, the Context Behavior Model. Its outputs are the Contextual Rules, the specification of the Processing Module elements, and an updated version of the Context Behavior Model. It uses as guidance the Context Architecture;

d) *Design Dissemination Module (M4)*: defines the elements responsible for disseminating CEs to different context consumers. Its inputs are the Context Conceptual Model (S3) and the Context Requirements document (S2). It produces as output the Dissemination Module specification. Its guidance is the Context Architecture.

The last three tasks are independent from each other, and can be executed either in parallel or in any order.

2.3.3 Context Usage

This activity aims to design how context is effectively used in the CSS under development. Two main usages for context in a CSS were considered: to support behaviour adaptation (of any kind) and, to enrich a CSS agent's cognition with contextual information managed by the CSS (Bellotti and Edwards, 2001). It has three main activities:

a) *Design Context Behavior Model (U1)*: has the objective to produce the Context Behavior Model corresponding to the identified focus, as well as to design the associations between the CEs and the behavior variations. Its input is the Context Conceptual Model and the Context Requirements document (produced in S3 and S2, respectively). Its output is the Context Behavior Model for the focus, identified as a contextual graph (as presented in Brézillon (2007). As guidance, it uses the CxG Profile defined in the CEManTIKA approach (see Vieira (2008) for further details);

b) *Design Context Adaptation (U2)*: aims to specify how the CSS should adapt to the context. It uses as input the Context Conceptual Model (from S3), the Context Requirements document (from S2), and the Context Behavior Model (from U1). It generates the Adaptation Module Specification as output. To guide this activity, the designer may use specifications provided by the Context Architecture and guidelines with directives related to Adaptation and Usability Aspects;

c) *Design Context Presentation (U3)*: has the purpose of designing the presentation of the managed CEs to the CSS agents in order to enrich their knowledge about the task being executed. The inputs for this activity are the Context Conceptual Model (from S3), the Context Requirements document (from S2), and the Context Behavior Model (from U1). It generates the Presentation Specification document as output. To guide this activity, the designer may use specifications provided by the Context Architecture and guidelines with directives related to Interface and Usability Aspects.

These activities should be performed for each focus. The designer should decide how context affects the system's behaviour according to CSS requirements.

2.4 Case Studies

This section presents two case studies regarding CDP usage in two domains: Experts Recommendation and Public Transportation Information Systems.

2.4.1 Case 1: Experts Recommendation

A design project named ICARE (*Intelligent Context Awareness for Recommending Experts*) (Petry et al. 2008) was created in our research group. ICARE is an ERS (Expert Recommendation System) that considers contextual information about users (who are requesting the recommendation) and experts when processing recommendations.

ICARE maintains a *base of experts*. Users access ICARE through a *recommendation interface* and provide a set of keywords to receive a classified list of experts. This is the basic functionality of ICARE (*without considering context*). In order to provide experts that better match users' needs, ICARE uses a *context interface*. CEs related to the user performing the recommendation and to the recommended experts are considered in addition to the keywords. To modularize the context manipulation in ICARE the activities defined in the CSS Design Process were followed, as described below and summarized in Table 2.1.

Table 2.1 Context metamodel instantiation: ICARE

Concept	Examples of instances in ICARE
Focus	Agent *user* in task *search experts*
Contextual entity	*User*; *Expert*
Contextual element	Expert [*availability, .approachability, location, contactInfo, worksIn, organizationLevel, currentActivity, interests, expertiseDegree (expertise), reputation*]; User [*location, socialDistance(Expert), interests, organizationLevel, currentActivity*]
Context source	*Lattes database* (Brazilian curricula database); *GeoLite city* (location data related to IP addresses); *MSN* (instant messenger program); *User Profile* (form filled by users); *History cases* (previous recommendations)
Rules	*Rule1: Conditions* User.availability $> = 0.7$ AND User.organizationalLevel > 0.5 *Actions* CallBehavior("Solve keywords"); CallBehavior("Lookup experts"); CallBehavior("Set accessibility HIGH"); CallBehavior("Set expertise HIGH"); CallBehavior("Calculate fitness"); CallBehavior("Rank by fitness"); CallBehavior("Show experts")

- *S1*: the focus is the association between agent *User* and task *Search Experts*;
- *S2*: the specified behavior variation in ICARE is related to adaptations in experts' classification according to changes in the state of particular CEs;
- *S3*: the considered CEs related to entities *User* and *Expert* were: *availability* (indicates how busy the user or the expert is), *knows and socialDistance* (indicates, respectively, a social relation between two people and the number of people that separates them); *currentLocation* (physical location of experts and users); *contactInfo* (informs how a person can be reached); *worksIn and organizationalLevel* (identifies, respectively, the work relation between a person and an organization and the person's position in the organization); *currentActivity* (the activity the person is currently performing); *interest* (subjects a person has interest in); *expertise* and *expertiseDegree* (indicates, respectively, the subjects a person has expertise and the level of expertise in the subject); *approachability* (denotes how easy it is to contact the expert); reputation (points out the expert's overall quality as assessed by users who contacted her/him);
- *S4*: to evaluate the identified CEs, a survey was conducted with 50 participants from different research and development organizations. People were asked if they would consider the CEs identified in S3 when filtering and ranking experts. They were also asked to rank the CEs by relevance, according to their view. The results from this investigation are presented in (Petry et al. 2008). An interesting result refers to the CE *socialDistance*. It was considered irrelevant by 64 % of the participants. This result contradicts what was initially expected since the authors believed that recommendations could be more effective if the user already knows the recommended expert;

- *M1*: to model context acquisition, three external and two internal context sources were identified: *Lattes Database*[3] (a curricula database in Brazil); *GeoLite City*[4] (a database that supports the identification of location information according to IP addresses); *MSN*[5] (an instant messenger application); *User Profile* (a form filled by users when registering to ICARE); and *History Cases* (a base with previous recommendation cases);
- *M2*: the interaction interface between ICARE and the identified external context sources, using existent API, were designed. We used the design pattern Façade, which allows us to isolate the internal functionalities of ICARE; hence, changes in the context source do not impact its usage in ICARE;
- *M3*: we used the JEOPS[6] inference engine to process the managed CEs and the defined contextual rules. To identify the contextual rules, we used a machine learning software called Weka[7]. The questionnaire data (collected in S4) was used as input to Weka;
- *M4*: not performed since ICARE has only one context consumer;
- *U1*: in ICARE, context is used to change the relevance weight associated with the CEs used on experts ranking. According to the rules identified in M3, the conditions are associated with the CEs *availability* and *organizationalLevel*. A contextual graph was used to model the different paths associated with those CEs. Each path in the graph denotes a contextual rule, as indicated in Table 2.1;
- *U2*: ICARE adapts the returned experts list by changing the experts' classification according to the *fitness formula* described below. This formula separates elements directly proportional from those inversely proportional to the expert's fitness for the user's search. To better fit the recommendation to the user's expectation, each CE is associated with a corresponding relevance weight;

$$Fitness(e, u) = \frac{\alpha_1 \times ed_e + \alpha_2 \times (ap_e + av_e) + \alpha_3 \times p_e}{\alpha_4 \times socialDist(e, u) + \alpha_5 |OL_u - OL_e|}$$

Where:

αi = relevance weight for each CE;

ed_e = expert's expertise degree;

ap_e = expert's approachability;

av_e = expert's availability;

rep_e = expert's reputation;

socialDist (e, u) = Social distance (expert and user);

$|OLu - OLe|$ = Difference between the user's (OLu) and the expert's organizational level (OLe).

---

[3] http://lattes.cnpq.br
[4] http://dev.maxmind.com/geoip/legacy/geolite/
[5] http://www.microsoft.com/pt-br/download/details.aspx?id=13453
[6] http://sourceforge.net/projects/jeops/
[7] http://www.cs.waikato.ac.nz/ml/weka/

- *U3*: Context is also used to increase the user's awareness about the recommended experts. We believe that the perception about the appropriateness of an expert may change from user to user. In this sense, if ICARE provides contextual information about the experts, users themselves can identify which experts better fit what they need.

2.4.2 Case 2: Public Transportation Information Systems

In this instance, a context-aware system to support public transportation users, entitled "Your City on Time" (YCT), was proposed by our research group (Vieira et al. 2011a). YCT provides users with contextual information regarding buses they are waiting for on a bus stop, such as: the bus current location, its distance and estimated arrival time. While developing YCT, the guidelines, activities and steps defined in CDP (Vieira et al. 2011b) were followed.

For *Context Specification*, the main *focus* in YCT was an agent Passenger, and a task "visualizing information regarding buses on a bus station". The contextual entities are *Bus*, *BusStop* and *Stretch* (the path between two bus stations). The contextual elements defined for those entities, are:

- *installedAt (BusStop)*: indicates the bus stop location in which the YCT display is installed. It allows the CSS to filter which information should be exhibited in that station;
- *currentLocation (Bus)*: refers to the geographical position where the bus is in a given moment. It is used to infer the distance from a bus to a given bus station to support indicating the bus estimated arrival time;
- *allocatedTo (Bus)*: indicates the line for which the bus is allocated in a given time interval. It is used to filter the bus that stops in a station;
- *latestStopVisited (Bus)*: indicates the latest bus stop the bus passed by. It is used to indicate the bus location on its route;
- *distanceNextStop (Bus)*: refers to the distance from the bus location until the next bus stop. It is used to calculate the bus estimated arrival time;
- *averageSpeed (Bus)* and *averageSpeed (Stretch)*: indicate the average speed performed by a specific bus and the average speed performed by a set of buses in a specific stretch. They are used to achieve more accurate values for the arrival time;
- *weightedSpeed (Bus)* and *weightedSpeed (Stretch)*: indicate the weighted speed performed by a specific bus and the weighted speed performed by a set of buses in a specific stretch;
- *estimatedTimeNextStop (Bus)*: indicates the estimated time that a specific vehicle might take to arrive to the next stop. It is also inferred from the calculation of the weighted speed. It is used to calculate the bus estimated arrival time;
- *estimatedDuration (Stretch)*: identifies the estimated time that it might take to travel the stretch based on the weighted speed calculated. It is used to calculate the bus arrival time.

Regarding the *Context Management* phase, YCT considers two external context sources: GPS in a Bus (for CEs *currentLocation* and *averageSpeed*); and Google Maps (to provide directions and distance between a bus and the next bus station). It also considers four internal context sources: the *installation parameters*, which allows knowing the location for a bus station where the YCT application is installed; the *allocation itinerary*, which informs the lines and schedules for the buses; the *speeds history*, which supports inferring the traffic level; and the *central clock*, which provides temporal data for occurrences of certain scenarios. Processed data are stored in along with historical context and are used to calculate the bus estimated arrival time.

To infer the traffic level in a stretch (to calculate the bus estimated arrival time), we used two incremental weighted update formulas, proposed by Sananmongkhonchai et al. (2008):

$$VPn = [w1 \times Va] + [(1 - w1) \times VPu] \quad (1)$$

$$VPn = [w2 \times Vh(n)] + [(1w2) \times VPu] \quad (2)$$

Legend

   VPn = new weighted speed

   wi = attributed weight

   Va = received real − time speed

   VPu = last registered weighted speed

   Vh (n) = average of the historical registered speeds

Formula (1) must be applied in a scenario where new speed data is received from a vehicle that is passing by a stretch. It considers the previous weighted speed (VPu) with the received sample speed (Va). Formula (2) must be applied when no new speed data was detected for a vehicle or stretch in a period of time. In the experiments performed by Sananmongkhonchai et al. (2008) this waiting period was specified as 5 min long. In YCT we used 2 min as the waiting period, as the time for our back-end GPS data processing service execution. Formula (2) considers the last registered weighted speed along with the average of the historical speeds registered at that same week day and schedule. Each formula uses a weight that influences the final result. According to the experiments performed by Sananmongkhonchai et al. (2008), the weights that result in the smallest error between estimated and real data are w1 = 0.5 and w2 = 0.01.

According to CDP the next step is designing how context information should be *processed*. For instance, to process the contextual element *averageSpeed (Bus)*, the system first considers data related to *vehicle identification* and *registered locations*, extracted from the NMEA files; this data is combined with previous information encapsulated in the *latest stop visited rule* to generate the value for the *latestStopVisited;* this data is combined to data related to *vehicle identification, speed values and samples number* and the rule to *calculate the average speed* to provide value for the *averageSpeed (Bus)*. This reasoning is used to process all other contextual elements and to build the knowledge base.

In the third phase, *Context Usage*, we must define how acquired and processed context should be used to present information to the final user. To do so we build a contextual graph with a behavior model that defines how YCT should react to behavior variations. For instance, to display information to a passenger in a bus stop, YCT should follow these actions: *Identify Bus Stop, Search Lines* that passes on that bus stop and *Search Vehicles*. While performing the last action, the system faces a context-based decision and must verify the element *allocatedTo (Vehicle)*; if the vehicle is allocated to that bus stop, the system should perform the action *Calculate Distance* from the bus to the bus stop. Another context-based decision is affected by the *distanceToNextStop (Vehicle)*. For example, if the distance is less than 5 kms away, the system should perform the actions *Calculate Estimated Arrival Time* and *Display Vehicles Information*. In this phase, it is also important to define how context information will be presented to users. The YCT prototype interface was designed to provide easy understanding of presented information concerning a bus location, distance and estimated arrival time. A map is used to help with the location data, whereas a table is displayed in order to show the legend, the time and the distance of the buses to the bus stop.

2.4.3   *Evaluating CDP with CSS Designers*

To verify CDP usage in different projects, we conducted an experimental study involving distinct CSS designers. In this study, we had nine participants. Eight of them were students in a graduate course at our University. They used CDP to design their CSS projects for the course evaluation. Three projects were developed. The ninth participant was a master student from another university. She used the process to support context modeling for a *notification service*. The study was performed according to the following steps: (1) the overall proposal was explained to the participants; (2) they had two weeks to study the CEManTIKA framework and to develop a first version of their projects, following CDP steps and guidelines; (3) we had frequent interactions to clarify doubts about the process activities; (4) the three projects developed during the course were discussed in a debriefing session; and (5) the project developed by the master student was discussed in several virtual meetings, using a chat tool.

This experimental study gave us the opportunity to apply the process and the CEManTIKA approach on existing CSS projects and to observe its usage by different CSS designers involved in real projects. A participant, for instance, has declared that "the usage of CEManTIKA helped understanding how to map the context dynamics into a conceptual model; the CSS Design Process supported understanding that before thinking about context one need to analyze the system's behavior variations; by doing so, it become clearer the applicability of contextual information into the system". The observed results assured us about the relevance and potential of the presented approach. In particular, we observed that the process usage and the integration of context structure with behavior models helped designers to think about how context influences the system's behavior variations, making context more explicit. Participants also provided suggestions for improvements. For example, they suggested creating a context-sensitive version of CDP. In this sense, more examples and templates should be provided for novice designers while agile methods could be used for experts.

2.5 Final Remarks

This chapter presented CDP, a process to support context specification and the design of a CSS. Its main features are: (1) to provide a road map to support the CSS designer when starting a new CSS project; (2) to propose a clear separation of the context-related activities, creating a new role in the software development team, the *context designer*; (3) to emphasize the need to work with existing artifacts when designing a CSS (e.g. requirements, conceptual models, business logic), instead of starting from scratch; and (4) to cover the main activities related to CSS design, providing guidelines, indicating input/output artifacts and a systematic way to execute each activity.

CDP is useful both for guiding a CSS development team on designing new applications and also as a conceptual foundation to support teaching context and context-sensitive systems. Regarding the latter, instructors can use the process to introduce beginners with the concepts and activities on developing a CSS; guidelines and templates can assist them on learning how to accomplish each activity.

Its detailed view about context specification and CSS design activities represents a novelty in the context literature. Since context is a novel and not yet mature concept, and its applicability to computer systems is not a trivial task, we believe that the proposed process will be incrementally improved. To this end, it is necessary to conduct more complex projects and experiments, as well as to investigate technologies that could support CSS development. Other relevant improvements include analyzing the distinction between human and software agents and the impact on designing their interactions with a CSS as well as including design activities that cater for automatic learning computing the relevance of contextual elements. Currently, the process does not consider software agents.

Acknowledgments The authors thank the UbiBus research participants from UFPE, UFBA, UTFPR, UEM and CESAR. The authors also thank CNPq and CTIC-RNP for their financial support. This work was [partially] supported by the National Institute of Science and Technology for Software Engineering (INES)[8].

---

[8] http://www.ines.org.br

References

Bauer, C.: A comparison and validation of 13 context meta-models. In: Proceedings of the 20th European Conference on Information Systems (ECIS). http://aisel.aisnet.org/ecis2012/17.(2012)

Bellotti, V., Edwards, K.: Intelligibility and accountability: Human considerations in context-aware systems. Hum. Comput. Int. 16(2–4), 193–212 (2001)

Bettini, C., Brdiczka, O., Henricksen, K., Indulska, J., Nicklas, D., Ranganathan, A., et al.: A survey of context modelling and reasoning techniques. Pervasive Mob. Comput. 6, 161–180(2010)

Brézillon, P.: Context modeling: Task model and model of practices. In: Proceedings of the 6th International and Interdisciplinary Conference on Modeling and Using Context, Roskilde, Denmark. pp. 122–135 (2007)

Bulcão Neto, R.F., Kudo, T.N., Pimentel, M.G.C.: POCAp: A software process for context-aware computing. In: Proceedings of the International Conference on Intelligent Agent Technology, Hong Kong, China, pp. 705–708 (2006)

Choi, J., Arriaga, R.I., Moon, H., Lee, E.: A context-driven development methodology for context-aware systems. In: International Conference on Convergence and Hybrid Information Technology, Daejeon, Korea, pp. 429–436 (2011)

Dey, A.K., Salber, D., Abowd, G.D.: A conceptual framework and a toolkit for supporting the rapid prototyping of context-aware applications. Hum. Comp. Int. J. 16, 97–166 (2001)

Dourish, P.: What we talk about when we talk about context. Pers. Ubiquit. Comput. 8, 19–30(2004)

Henricksen, K., Indulska, J.: Developing context-aware pervasive computing applications: Models and approach. Pervasive Mob. Comput. J. 2(1), 37–64 (2006)

Hong, J., Suh, E-H., Kim, S.: Context-aware systems: A literature review and classification. Expert Syst. Appl. 36, 8509–8522 (2009)

Hsu, H., Wu, S., Wang, F.: A methodology to developing context-aware pervasive applications. In: Proceedings of the 5th IEEE International Symposium on Service Oriented System Engineering, pp. 206–213 (2010)

Marco M.: A software lifecycle process for context-aware adaptive systems. In: Proceedings of the 19th ACM SIGSOFT Symposium and 13th European Conference on Foundations of Software Engineering. ACM, New York, pp. 412–415 (2011)

Petry, H., Tedesco, P., Vieira, V., Salgado, A.C.: ICARE: A context-sensitive expert recommendation system. In: Proceedings of the Workshop on Recommender Systems, Patras, Greece, pp. 53–58(2008)

Sananmongkhonchai, S., Tangamchit, P., Pongpaibool, P.: Road traffic estimation from multiple GPS data using incremental weighted update. In: Proceedings of the 8th International Conference on ITS Telecommunications, Phuket, Thailand, pp. 62–66 (2008)

Schilit, B., Adams, N., Want, R.: Context-aware computing applications. In: Proceedings of the Workshop on Mobile Computing Systems and Applications. IEEE, Washington, pp. 85–90(1994)

Vieira, V.: CEManTIKA: A domain-independent framework for designing context-sensitive systems. Ph. D. Thesis. Informatics Center, Federal University of Pernambuco(2008)

Vieira, V., Tedesco, P., Salgado, A.C., Brézillon, P.: Investigating the specificities of contextual elements management: The CEManTIKA approach. In: Proceedings of the 6th International and Interdisciplinary Conference on Modeling and Using Context, Roskilde, Denmark, pp. 493–506(2007)

Vieira, V., Caldas, L., Salgado, A.C.: Towards an ubiquitous and context sensitive public transportation system. In: Proceedings of the 4th International Conference on Ubi-Media Computing, São Paulo-SP, pp. 174–179(2011a)

Vieira, V., Tedesco, P., Salgado, A.C.: Designing context-sensitive systems: An integrated approach. Expert Syst Appl. 38(2), 1119–1138 (2011b)

Weiser, M.: The computer for the 21st century. Scientific American 265(3), 66–75 (1991)

Chapter 3
Context-Driven Testing on the Cloud

Feras A. Batarseh

Abstract Context-Driven Testing (CDT) is the practice of validating and verifying software systems based on their most recent status. CDT is both an art and a science; ultimately, CDT is about *not accepting* a specific pre-defined set of best practices, it is about making decisions based on what the current context entails. This chapter introduces a context scheme deployed within a software engineering lifecycle; specifically through a testing method that utilizes a context-based philosophy for testing systems implemented on the cloud. The proposed method is called Context-Assisted Test Case Reduction (CATCR). In CATCR, the results of previous test cases are used to influence the selection of test cases in the next testing iteration. Using contextual inputs for reducing testing time/effort is the main goal of CATCR. Furthermore, through selecting appropriate cloud sites and automatically evaluating the situation, contextual testing helps the engineers make better timely decisions. To evaluate the proposed context-based method, an experimental assessment is performed using Amazon's Cloud. Experiment results are recorded and presented.

3.1 Introduction

Humans have the ability to perform the process of communication effectively; ideas could be conveyed in a comprehensible and quick manner. That is because humans use agreed-upon syntax (language) and that human brains can comprehend the context in which they are in, and accommodate their understanding of the events accordingly. Unfortunately, the same can't be said about computers, this "understanding of context" is a major Artificial Intelligence (AI) challenge—one of the most important ones in this age of technological transformations. With the latest massive diffusion of many new technologies such as smart mobile phones, tablets, and the cloud, AI applications such as context-aware software systems are gaining much attention. Context-aware systems have the advantage of dynamically adapting to current events and occurrences in the system and its surroundings. One of the main

F. A. Batarseh (✉)
Intelligent Systems Laboratory, University of Central Florida, Orlando, FL, USA
e-mail: fbatarseh@knights.ucf.edu

© Springer Science+Business Media New York 2014
P. Brézillon, A. J. Gonzalez (eds.), *Context in Computing*,
DOI 10.1007/978-1-4939-1887-4_3

25

characteristics of such systems (on mobile and the cloud) is to adjust the behavior of the system without user intervention. With all the new technologies, context is a suitable (and possible irreplaceable) candidate. The cloud is a specifically appropriate type of system in which to integrate context into its operations. That is a result of: (1) the dynamic nature of the technology (continuous resources allocation), (2) the cloud is a user-intensive and constantly changing environment, (3) it needs to be executed in a real time setup (4) it can't tolerate failures, (5) and it interacts with multiple external entities (Foster 2002).

Context awareness can be found across all levels of software development (Gonzalez et al. 2008). Nevertheless, this chapter is only concerned with the testing phase. Before getting into the details of context and its use within software development, it is appropriate to define context: *Context is all the information available to a software system that characterizes the situation it is running within.* Another important part to define is the traditional software engineering testing phase. Testing consists of Validation (building the right system) and Verification (building the system right) (Knauf et al. 2002; Smith and Kandel 1990, it aims to satisfy the following three main quality measures: (1) Functionality (exterior quality), which includes correctness, reliability, usability, and integrity. (2) Engineering (interior quality), which includes efficiency, documentation, and structure; (3) Adaptability (future quality), which includes flexibility, reusability, and maintainability (Knauf et al. 2007; Gonzalez et al. 2000). According to the traditional definition of software lifecycles, the main phases of software development include: (1) requirements, (2) specifications, (3) design, (4) development, (5) testing (V&V), (6) refinement, and (7) documentation (Shreiber et al. 2000; Herrmann et al. 1997; Abel and Gonzalez 1997). This is referred to as the waterfall model. Other models include the spiral model, reuse-oriented model, agile models, incremental model, and evolutionary development. Since the recent rise of agile software development and the continuous decline of classical life cycles, multiple customizations have been introduced and embedded into the different lifecycle phases. For the testing phase, one of the most important and novel approaches is Context-Driven Testing (CDT). CDT is a rapidly growing testing paradigm. It is part of the agile school of software development. It is based on the idea that the value of a software testing practice depends on its context, and that projects unfold over time in unpredictable ways that need to be handled in real time. CDT's philosophy influences the method proposed here. The seven basic principles of CDT include (Foster 2002; Knauf et al. 2002): (1) The value of any practice depends on its context. (2) Preferred practices exist in context, but there are no best practices. (3) People are an essential part of any software development context. (4) Software unfolds over time in ways that are not expected. (5) A product is a solution. If the problem isn't solved, the product doesn't work. (6) Good software testing is a challenging intellectual practice. (7) Only through judgment and skill, software engineers are able to perform the right actions at the right times to effectively test the product. Challenges of CDT include finding the means to figure out the relevant parameters and how to accommodate them in an appropriate manner. However, most importantly, it involves allocating the right resources to the right process, and to understand the context of these processes. Context and CDT are best suited for agile lifecycles, reasoning and related discussions are introduced next.

For the cloud, much information is available that needs to be considered for testing (e.g., size of the system, system modules and their communication, cloud design and number of users, to name a few). There has been much confusion regarding the term *cloud computing*, mostly because of the novelty of this branch of computer science. The following definition for cloud is adopted here—by Foster (2002)—"a system that coordinates resources that are not subject to centralized control using standard, open, general-purpose protocols and interfaces to deliver nontrivial qualities of service". Cloud context testing requires both validation and verification (V&V).

The persistent change of context in the cloud is part of its design and implementation. Cloud services change the way software is designed, how data are handled, and how testing is performed. In cloud computing, testing is delivered as a service (TaaS). Case testing—one of the most common testing approaches—could be used. However, executing test cases on a cloud system could be expensive and time consuming because of the number of test cases that needs to be executed (could reach the millions of test cases), the size of software deployed on the cloud (usually is gigabytes of data and programs), and the geographically distributed nature of a cloud computing software system. Therefore, test case reduction is performed to minimize the number of test cases to be executed on the system. Context is used to help achieve this goal. The method described seeks to find the *just right* number and set of test cases to execute, considering ideal coverage with no redundancies. Other testing methods (Shreiber et al. 2000; Herrmann et al. 1997; Abel and Gonzalez 1997; Smith and Kandel 1990) reduce the set of test cases a priori, and then begin the testing process. Inspired by the Context-Based Test Case Reduction (CBTCR) method in Abel and and Gonzalez (1997), this new method is based on the context of the testing process at any point in time. In problem solving, *context* would inherently contain much knowledge about the circumstances of the situation in which the problem is to be solved, or that serves as the environment of the problem (Smith and Kandel 1990). In validation and verification, context is also used that way. The test cases executed at each iteration depend on the *current* context. Context is defined by the state of the validation process while CDT drives most testing decisions.

Cloud computing is currently receiving much attention from the industry, government, and academia. It has changed the way computation is performed and how services are delivered to customers. In cloud computing, software is delivered as a service (SaaS). Similarly, data and testing are also delivered as services (thus the names, DaaS and TaaS). Although cloud computing provides new business opportunities, it also introduces new problems and challenges. Despite the bright side, there are some limitations; for instance, the lack of standards for cloud environments. Currently, there is no standard to incorporate cloud computing resources with companies' data sources, vendors have different models used as basis for their clouds, and customers face interoperability issues if they wish to switch vendors. Other challenges include security, performance, the need for a resilient infrastructure, managing big data, connectivity, geographical distribution of sites and cloud testing. CATCR aims to satisfy the quality of service (QoS) requirements (e.g., response time, availability) in a cloud environment. More specifically, for systems that include multiple users in different locations, CATCR addresses the challenge of deploying a cloud (including its VMs and Data) across different multiple geographical regions. The goal is to distribute software applications (components) among the VMs taking into account access to required data, and minimizing testing time. TaaS provides a pay-per-use type of service that eliminates upfront investments in many cases. Validation tools and services on the cloud are no exception. A testing method that addresses the constant context changes in a cloud environment is needed. More specifically, the new method proposed in this chapter tests systems that include multiple users in different locations. The focus is on the challenge of cloud testing across different multiple geographical regions (which is part of the information provided to define the current context) and providing TaaS within that context. Besides the fact that TaaS is increasingly gaining attention, it nonetheless begs the question of why perform testing on the cloud? The main reason is that it offers the opportunity to access test tools and test environments from anywhere around the world without the need to own these assets. Testing on the cloud however, is similar in many ways to conventional testing. The effectiveness of any testing method depends on how well the process can identify defects, errors and faults before releasing the system to the customer. This depends on the quality and quantity of the generated test cases used in testing. The steps of validating a system using test cases start with *test case generation* & *test case reduction*—two key steps that are treated in CATCR. Reduction happens when a subset of test cases is selected from the universal set of test cases to be executed on the system under test. Results are evaluated, and then the last step is *system refinement*, where actions toward fixing the errors and presenting the solutions are carried out (Knauf et al. 2002, 2007).

3.2 Background

This chapter discusses CDT, reviews the state of the art, and introduces a novel method to utilizing CDT for testing of systems built within a cloud environment. Multiple methods have been developed based on the philosophy of CDT (Knauf et al. 2002, 2007; Gonzalez et al. 2000). This section discusses the state-of-the-art of contextual testing.

3.2.1 Context Testing and Test Cases Reduction

Many methods have been proposed for test case reduction (Gonzalez et al. 2000; Shreiber et al. 2000; Herrmann et al. 1997; Abel and Gonzalez 1997), and they vary between random, contextual, formal and informal. The idea of testing every input to the system is impossible to design (or implement) in most cases. It is not feasible to run all possible test cases on the system—the exhaustive set of test cases (EST)— especially when some of these test cases may not even be physically possible in the real world. Therefore, Knauf et al. (2002, 2007) presented a formal method to validate systems using structural knowledge. They used formal approaches to reduce

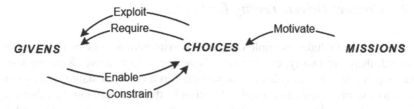

Fig. 3.1 Context testing philosophy

the exhaustive set of test cases in their testing method (Knauf et al. 2002). They did this by creating a *functionally exhaustive set of test cases (FEST)*, and from there built a *quasi-exhaustive set of test cases* (QUEST). This last set of test cases is meant to have the equivalent effect of testing all possible system cases, but with a reduced number of test cases. In the *quasi-exhaustive set of test cases,* it is sufficient to assume that if a specially selected subset of the test cases (T) is valid, then the whole set (S) is valid too. After test case sets are defined, for each set, a subset of test cases (T) will be executed. A set of mathematical classifiers is used to categorize the data into sets where an object can belong to one or more sets. The authors used statistical and formal means to show this (Knauf et al. 2002, 2007). Abel and Gonzalez (1997) and Smith and Kandel (1990) subsequently criticized the *quasi-exhaustive set of test cases* as still being impractical because of its large cardinality. The former (Abel and Gonzalez 1997) introduced another method to further reduce the number of test cases. Their method uses a criteria-driven reduction of test cases to generate a *reasonable set of test cases* (ReST). In ReST, all test cases need to be evaluated by the testing engineers. During the test case selection stage, a criterion is defined by answering the question: how well should the system be tested before it is considered valid? Answering this question requires looking at different criteria: domain related, user related, expert related, but most importantly context related. CATCR reduces the set of test cases to a number much lower than the *quasi-exhaustive set of test cases.*

As mentioned, the cloud is dynamic and the context of software running on it is constantly changing; therefore, the testing process needs to consider the context in which it being executed. Figure 3.1 illustrates how context influences testing. In that figure, testing is defined as a mission that motivates the choices (Kaner 2002). The context defines the missions that motivate the choice of test cases in each iteration. The context of the givens enable and more importantly constraint these choices. These givens are the requirements and specifications. Requirements enable the choices of the test cases as well, and so on.

The seven principles of CDT were introduced earlier, but as previously mentioned, besides being a science, CDT is also an art, one that requires experience and sound judgment from the software engineering team, and their management. Because the cloud is highly flexible and interactive, we believe that context testing and cloud testing could work together very well. We aim to establish that association. No testing method has been found that is solely based on context to validate software deployed on the cloud. Next section focuses on cloud's context-driven testing.

3.2.2   Context-Driven Testing for the Cloud

Testing software includes multiple conflicted considerations. For context testing in the cloud, there are two types of testing: Reactive and Proactive. Reactive testing includes practices such as rollbacks of software to a previous stable state, job migration to a stable machine or a stable location in the software. On the other hand, proactive testing includes incremental predictions of errors, creating copies of safe parts of the software, and creating models that can evaluate and measure software validity. An important question to drive the discussion here is: why is it difficult for computer systems to adopt context? One major reason is that there has been a general agreement that context is not essential for software systems, and the research community (at some point in the late 1990s and early 2000s) adopted an ideology that was *anti-context*. However, recent advances has pushed researchers in academia and industry to reconsider that ideology, and eventually, the idea of context (as well as other paradigms) floated to the surface again.

Therefore, most traditional testing methods for the cloud are based on the conventional performance testing (e.g., SOASTA CloudTest, CloudTestGo; Bach 2013), Integration testing (e.g., PushToTest and uTest; Rao 2014) automated testing (e.g., IBM cloud, Sauce Labs, Zephyr and STaaS; Bach 2013; Rao 2014), and lastly load testing (e.g., GCLOAD, Clap, LoadStorm and BlazeMeter; Kalliosaari et al. 2012). Although there have been efforts in introducing different contextual deployments in software engineering, there is still a crucial need for a testing method that is majorly driven by context. Moreover, no method or testing tool was found that provides a dynamic, context-based testing for the cloud.

This chapter is organized as follows: the next section introduces the CATCR method, including all the variables and the cloud's infrastructure. Section 3.4 introduces the step-by-step process, the experimental design, setup and results. Finally, Sect. 3.5 introduces the conclusions and the discussions.

3.3   Context-Assisted Test Case Reduction

CATCR seeks to reduce the number of test cases to be executed by finding the *just right* number of test cases to execute that provide ideal coverage with no redundancy. In testing, there is a context based upon what parts of the code have failed the most in the previous testing cycle. In other words, the test cases executed at each iteration depend only on the *current* context. Before we introduce the process, it is important to clearly state the cloud model that we assume for this method.

3.3.1 Contextual Cloud Variables

The deployment architecture of the cloud can have a large impact on its testing process. It is important to understand the cloud architecture in order to represent the variations among different testing setups. These basic modeling constructs are used in our cloud framework.

- A set *VM* of Virtual Machines and their associated parameters, *VMP* (i.e. availability, state, available memory... etc)
- A set of *S* of Sites and their associated parameters *SP* (i.e. number of VMs in the site, geographical location... etc)
- A set *C* of clients (such as users, PDAs, computers, and cell phones connecting to the cloud) and their parameters *CP* (i.e. location, criticality... etc)
- A set of *SC* software components (such as monitoring, collaboration, and communication applications)—in the experiment presented here (Lockwood and Chen 1995), a Knowledge-Based System is used as *SC*.
- A set *CloudDep* of all possible deployments of software components originating from different clients to different sites and VMs. 6– most importantly, a set *Q* of QoS and their associated functions *Qfn*. For consistency, we use all these constructs in the remaining of the chapter.

Other related cloud variables include:

- State of the *VM (SVM)*: *idle, busy* or empty queue (*EQ*)
- Number of *idle* or *EQ* machines in a site *S* (*NIS*). The presented variables are used in our method.

Some *factors* of contextual testing are: (1) testing the reliability, (2) ensuring that the system is available during the major times of usage, (3) software confidentiality, (4) testing the security and ensuring the safety of the system. Reducing the test cases in CATCR is partly based on a number of variables related to the *factors* mentioned above. At any iteration in the development process, the values of variables need to be modified while the system undergoes refinement (refer to Batarseh (2011) for more information). Context-assisted test case reduction is controlled by certain variables. More about the process and the variables is discussed in the next four sections/subsections.

3.3.2 Contextual Cloud Variables

For any software system, the users, administrators and vendors have different preferences about which QoS factor is more important. These factors are leveraged for the creation of a fair tradeoff for different scenarios. It is often very challenging, however, to provide complete high quality for all parameters, simply because they usually contradict each other. To define the QoS factors model in formal terms using the constructs defined previously, a set of system parameters needs to be defined, these parameters include:

- Number of *idle* or *EQ* machines in a site *S*
- Available site *S* to the client *C*
- The best Site (*S*) where VM is deployed on

It is important to distinguish between the decisions made and the problem we are trying to solve. As mentioned previously, the main goal is to reduce validation time. To address that, two main questions that our method aims to answer are: which *VM* is used for the software component (*SC*) testing? and which geographical site (*S*) to choose for validation in order to reduce testing time using the context of the validation process? CATCR determines whether testing is deployed in a certain site, such as:

$$T \in \{0,1\} \rightarrow \begin{cases} 1, if \text{ Testing } is \text{ } deployed \text{ } on \text{ } Sites \\ 0, otherwise \end{cases}$$

Within each site, only one Virtual machine is used for each test case. This represented by the following equation (For all sites, and all machines within that site, there needs to be one test case (from the universal set of test cases) executing on each machine):

$$\forall \text{ } testcase \in T \sum_{s \in S} \sum_{vm \in VM} s \times vm = 1$$

Figure 3.2 represents the cloud layers within the model that we assume for our method and the one we used for our experiments. It includes three main layers: a software applications layer, a virtual machines layer and a sites layer. The best site is selected using the Cloud Site Weight (**CSW**) variable presented in Sect. 3.5– after Local VM Importance and N.

3.3.3 Local VM Importance

Local VM Importance (LVMI) represents the importance of a test case within its own geographical site (*S*). LVMI is assigned by the engineer to every test case, to represent the priority of that test case and ensure the execution of the important ones. The local importance variable that falls between one and five. *Local importance = Average of (dependency + domain importance + criticality + occurrence).* Local importance is a factor of dependency (value assigned from 1–5), domain importance (value assigned from 1–5), criticality (value assigned from 1–5) and occurrence (value assigned from 1–5). The values of these four variables are set by the test engineer for each test case. For each iteration, these variables are used to define the context, that eventually controls CATCR.

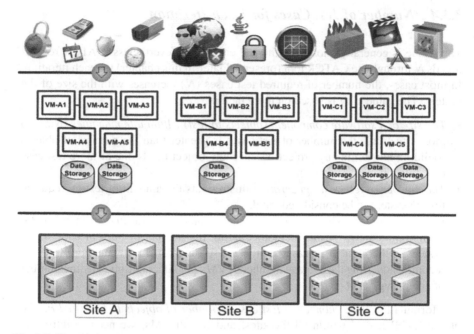

Fig. 3.2 Cloud infrastructure

- **Dependency:** In a cloud design, different virtual machines (*VM*) and software components (*SC*) are dependent upon each other, thus, the test cases extracted inherit this relation. Test cases are dependent on each other. Therefore, dependency is defined for each test case by the cloud engineer as part of the test case importance.
- **Domain importance**: Any test case represents a certain function in the system; some test cases have high importance because of their high representation of certain important functionality within the domain. Other test cases with less importance represent functions that are not strongly related to the domain.
- **Criticality:** In any organization, some tasks are more important than are others. Each test case is defined to partially or fully evaluate a specific functionality. Tasks (and thus, test cases) with greater criticality to the overall process have higher importance.
- **Occurrence:** In a process, some procedures occur more frequently than others. This variable reflects the level of a procedure occurrence in the system and how often is a certain software component (*SC*) used by a client (*C*).

3.3.4   Number of Test Cases for Each Iteration

This value is generally chosen by the test engineer. Nevertheless, CATCR recommends N through the CATCR tool (presented later in this chapter) for each iteration. In most cases, the number of required test cases (N) increases with the size of the system. The value of N is based on three factors:

- *The size of a software component (objects to test) within idle machines (NIS)*: In most situations, the number of test cases is greater than the number of objects (building blocks) in any project because any object needs one or more test case to validate it.
- *The number of test cases generated*: this reflects the amount of testing required for the system to be considered valid.
- *Project Size (PS)*: The size of the project could be measured in many ways. Common methods for this include counting the number of lines of code in the system or the number of cases in a use case diagram. In this method, CATCR recommends using the average number of *VM*s per site, multiplied by the number of sites (Avg. #VM × #S).

The formula for N is: *Number of test cases-Number of objects to be tested/PS*. To utilize LVMI and N within all the sites, and for all VMs, we need to introduce variables at the cloud level, Cloud Site Weight and Global Importance.

3.3.5   Cloud Site Weight

In CATCR, every model is assigned a weight after each iteration of development. Initially, all the sites have the same cloud site weight (CSW is set to 5), and the same significance. However, when the development starts, CSWs will constantly change based on the contextual outcomes of the test cases. The cloud site weight values fall between 1 and 10. CSW could be set to any value before the first iteration, 5 is the midpoint from 0 to 10 and therefore it was selected as the initial value. After the first validation iteration, the cloud system engineer has no control over the CSW, it is controlled by the results of previous validation results. Cloud site weight reflects the assurance level of the model. When the assurance of all models reaches 10 (100 %) and implementation is done, validation stops.

Another very important variable is *Global Importance (GI)*. GI is used to define the importance of any test case within the global set of test cases, across all cloud sites. *Global Importance = Local VM Importance * CSW*. As software is distributed across the cloud (different sites and VMs), the site with the highest importance is used for testing. We introduce the CATCR steps in the next section, which puts all these variables into perspective.

3.4 The Contextual Testing Process

The steps of context-assisted test case reduction that compose the testing of a system are discussed in this section. This algorithm is built into the CATCR tool (presented in the next section). The iterative process is applied on the software level (SaaS) of a cloud and not on the infrastructure or platform; different applications could be tested using this method. Context testing is applied on the cloud as a service for multiple clients (*C*) running the testing process. The **12** steps of CATCR are (For every CATCR step in process, it is indicated as to whether the step is manual or automated within the Java tool.):

1. Assign *local VM importance* for each test case. (Semi automated)
2. Set the size of test case subset: *N* based on the criteria discussed previously. (Automated)
3. Set all site *weights/assurance* to 5 (Automated)
4. Calculate *global importance* = local importance * model weight. Order test cases according to global importance (Automated)
5. Start iterative implementation, deployment of software on the cloud (Manual)
6. At the end of the first deployment iteration, select N number of test cases. Select test cases 1 to *N* from the ordered list. (Automated)
7. Execute the test cases on the system, and record the results, **for usage in next iteration's context definition** (Manual)
8. Based on **the context and the results** for each model test cases, re-assign assurance for each site. Ex: if 30 % of the test cases in a certain site are incorrect, that site's assurance will be 7 using the following formula: *100 − (% of successful test case)/10* (Automated)
9. Recalculate global importance for all test cases and reorder based on context (Automated). In CATCR, if a test case failed, the site from which this test case is from will have a very high importance site in the next iteration—and will be chosen as the site for testing.
10. Refine the system. This step includes refining the deployment of software within the cloud. This might lead to adding or deleting new test cases. This step is performed by the test engineer in a manual fashion. (Manual)
11. *Flag* test cases with a positive outcome (not to be picked again unless a change to their status was made). *Flag* test cases with unexpected outcomes (this is used to make sure that the test case is reselected before end of validation). *Flag* test cases that are affected by the refinements (to be selected again). Select different test cases and go to the next iteration (Automated)
12. Stop when assurance of all sites is equal to 10 (Automated)

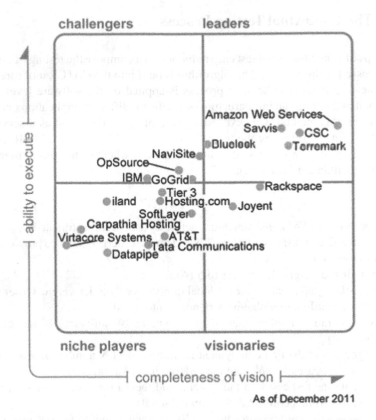

Fig. 3.3 Amazon cloud establishing itself as an industry leader (Gartner Research 2013)

The next section introduces the evaluation of CATCR. The experimentation is performed on the Amazon cloud and a Java tool that was developed in-house.

3.4.1 Experimental Process

Amazon cloud is used in this experiment. Although Amazon has been facing issues with their cloud, it has established itself as an industry leader when it comes to cloud computing; Amazon's cloud showed completeness of vision and execution (refer to Fig. 3.3). In Fig. 3.3, it is evident that Amazon leads among other vendors (including CSC, Terremark, Bluelock, IBM, GoGrid, OpSource, and NaviSite). A useful definition that was found on Amazon's Cloud website: "Amazon Cloud provides monitoring for cloud resources and the applications customers run on the cloud. Developers and system administrators can use it to collect and track metrics, gain insight, and react immediately to keep their applications and businesses running smoothly. Amazon *CloudWatch* monitors the cloud resources such as Amazon EC2"

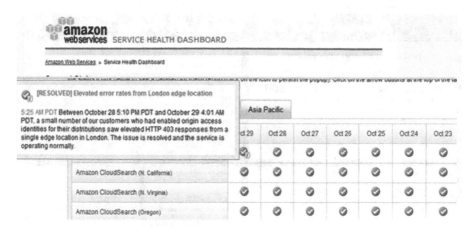

Fig. 3.4 Continuously changing context in the cloud (Amazon Cloud 2014)

(Amazon Cloud 2014). Developers and system administrators can use EC2 to collect and track metrics, gain insight, and react immediately to keep their applications and businesses running smoothly. Amazon CloudWatch can also monitor custom metrics generated by a customer's applications and services. With Amazon CloudWatch, users gain system-wide visibility into resource utilization, application performance, and operational health. Amazon CloudWatch provides a reliable, scalable, and flexible monitoring solution that users can take advantage of within minutes. Users no longer need to set up, manage, or scale their own monitoring systems and infrastructure. Using Amazon CloudWatch, users can easily monitor as much or as little metric data as you need. Amazon CloudWatch lets its users programmatically retrieve the monitoring data, view graphs, and set alarms to help with troubleshooting, spotting trends, and taking automated actions based on the state of the context of the environment. Although all these features were introduced as part of Amazon's offering, its cloud infrastructure still suffered from failures. In EC2's service health dashboard, users can see which sites are having issues, which days and which time of the day (among other information). The information provided on the dashboard changes constantly, as well as the context of the cloud infrastructure (refer to Fig. 3.4).

3.4.2 The CATCR Tool

The CATCR tool provides support for the context-assisted test case reduction. Test cases are entered into the tool's spread sheet with the following fields: *Test case ID* (an incremental integer that starts from zero and is incremented by one for every test case), *Local VM Importance* (an integer number from 1 to 5), *Number of Runs* (is set to zero, every time the test case is executed this number is incremented by one), *Site's Weight* (first is set to 5 for all sites then it is modified every iteration), *Global*

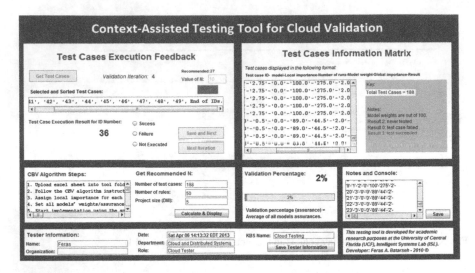

Fig. 3.5 Context-assisted test case reduction tool (Batarseh 2011)

Importance (the multiplication outcome of local importance and site weight), *Input Variables*, *Execution Steps*, *Expected Solution,System Result* (outcome displayed by the system) and an *Informal Description*. Based on the algorithm presented, when the iterative development starts, CATCR will recommend certain test cases for every iteration based on a major contextual input: *Result of previous iterations*. Initially, all test cases are set to 2 because none of the test cases is executed. When a test case is executed successfully, its *flag* value will be set to 1; if it failed, its value will change to 0. All this is picked up by the tool.

Panel 1 displays the selected test cases in a list where the test engineer can indicate the outcome of the test case, whether it is success or failure. This panel also displays the iteration number and the value of *N*. This is the main panel for the cloud engineer, where the test cases could be monitored and the results of the test cases after every iteration could be modified.

Panel 2 has two functionalities; it displays the algorithm's steps and explains how the tool works. Additionally, it is the panel to calculate the recommended *N* value. The test engineer enters the number of test cases, the number of rules in the project and the project size to get *N*.

Panel 3 displays all the test cases, each with its importance, execution results and the number of test cases in the database. In this panel, all the test cases changing statuses can be observed in real time, after every test case execution.

Panel 4 shows the testing percentage/assurance for the system. This is calculated by averaging of all the sites' assurances. A progress bar displays this percentage.

Panel 5 displays the console showing all the steps and all the actions performed. The console serves as a good documentation tool; it keeps all the test cases as well as all the models and their changing status. Everything is saved and displayed here, then saved to a file on the hard disk. A screen shot of the tool is shown in Fig. 3.5.

3.4.3 Experimental Setup

In this experiment, a Knowledge-Based System (KBS) is deployed on the cloud. The KBS used as test-bed is a housing application employed by the government of the Netherlands (for the less fortunate citizens) to assign apartments to applicants. The housing application had three users, the applicant, the Dutch government and a moderator. The applicants submit a request for an apartment, moderators assign them one based on their demographics, and then the government approves/disapproves the assignment. This housing KBS aims to replace the manual process of the moderator, and assign apartments automatically based on the moderator's knowledge. The housing KBS is a midsize project described in more detail in Batarseh (2011). While it is often very challenging to provide complete high quality for all parameters (simply because they may contradict each other), in the context of the cloud, users and vendors focus on two main aspects, the speed of the cloud (latency), and the cost. We configure the model based on scenarios that involve the following QoS factors:

- **Time**: elapsed between deploying a cloud and reaching a conclusion regarding its validity (testing time)
- **Cost**: it is the money spent per user, customer or institution.

In this experiment, and because it is rather difficult to calculate the cost of a cloud deployment without a real cloud system with actual users, the focus is on the QoS parameter of *Time*. CATCR is compared to two other methods. The three methods were deployed Amazon cloud. CATCR was used to select test cases for every testing iteration in CATCR. Test cases are manually executed on the system to detect theses errors. Amazon Cloud assigns geographical sites for its users. In most cases, the user doesn't have control over which site or which physical VM to use. They only can use the geographical area (such as southeast, southwest, northwest... etc). The goals of this experiment include: (1) compare Amazon's process for assigning sites to CATCR validation and context-driven cloud management process (2) measure validation time and compare between CATCR and other non-contextual validation methods. Each test case includes an "expected result" and a "system result". After executing any test case, if the system's result is different from the expected result, this indicates the existence of an error in the system. This experiment is only qualitative. After inspecting multiple testing methods and considering many candidates, we found that many of the methods were impossible to use because of different reasons. For example, some of the methods strictly required their development tools to be used and these tools were not readily available. Other methods provided no useful guidance on how to implement the testing method on a knowledge-based system. Yet other methods were only useable within a specific domain, such as testing methods for military or medical applications. Therefore, all these unsuitable methods were ruled out from consideration. Two methods were found to be the most suitable and had no constraints for being used in this testing experiment. These two methods claimed and reported positive outcomes for testing of KBS. They use two different testing methods that could be applied on the cloud. These two methods are VIVA (Gartner

Table 3.1 Time consumed using context testing (CATCR)

Stage name/description	Time consumed (h)
Cloud model deployment	6
Test cases extraction/definition	4
Assign local importance for each test case	4
Fill test cases into the sheet of the CATCR tool	11
Set all models' weights/assurance to 5	0 (Autonomous)
Calculate global importance and re-order	0 (Autonomous)
Defining the cloud variables, starting the VMs & cloning required VMs.	32 (Total)- On Amazon
Select N number of test cases	0 (Autonomous)
Execute test cases on the system	6 (Total for all iterations)
Recalculate global importance	0 (Autonomous)
Flag test cases based on results	0 (Autonomous)
Refine system and go to next iteration	8 (Total for all iterations)
Total # hours	71

Research 2013) and EMBODY (Wells 1993). These methods are used to validate the housing knowledge-based system test-bed described above on the cloud and their consumption of resources (time) is recorded and compared to CATCR's and its testing results. VIVA is a life-cycle-independent testing method while EMBODY validates the system by embedding knowledge testing into the knowledge acquisition process. EMBODY uses diagram-based testing while VIVA is based on traceability. VIVA uses transformational links for the transformation between the knowledge model to the code or the design, and between the design and the code and vice versa. VIVA uses structural links to link between objects within the knowledge model or the design. After this is done, testing specifications are derived such as: correctness, completeness and existence. For testing, the structure of the system is defined, the specifications are compared and mismatches are revised.

3.4.4 Experimental Results

The results of the experiments are illustrated in Tables 3.1, 3.2 and 3.3. Times consumed (in hours) for testing in the three methods are measured by summing their steps. First, the steps for CATCR are presented in Table 3.1, VIVA is in Table 3.2 and EMBODY is in Table 3.3. Results are in Fig. 3.6.

Figure 3.6 illustrates the results (compares setup vs. testing time spent for all three methods). Total for validating the housing KBS on the cloud using VIVA = **106 h.** Total for validating the housing KBS on the cloud using EMBODY = **97 h.**

Table 3.2 Time consumed using EMBODY and Amazon's sites distribution

Stage name/description	Time consumed (h)
Knowledge acquisition and organization	10 (Manual process)
Defining the cloud variables, starting the VMs among different locations, and cloning the appropriate machines.	32 (Total)- On Amazon cloud
Using EMBODY flow charts	17 (Manual process)
Representing the cloud in EMBODY's tabular format	12 (Manual process)
Validating the system	18 (Manual process)
Refine system	8 (Manual process)
Total # hours	97

Table 3.3 Time consumed using VIVA and Amazon's sites/VM distribution

Stage name/description	Time consumed (h)
Knowledge acquisition and organization	17 (Manual process)
Defining the cloud variables, starting the VMs among different locations, and cloning the appropriate machines	32 (Total)- On Amazon Cloud
Using VIVA defined methods	15 (Manual process)
Performing the VIVA link types for the cloud system	8 (Manual process)
Derivation of validation specification	10 (Manual process)
Validating the system	16 (Manual process)
Refine system	8 (Manual process)
Total # hours	106

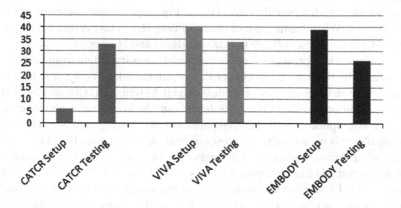

Fig. 3.6 Experimental results for CATCR (vs. VIVA and EMBODY)

Total for validating the same KBS on the cloud using CATCR = **71 h**. Although CATCR has the least total validation time, what we think is very important to note here, is that CATCR has an obvious difference in terms of setup. The setup time is very low when compared to the other two methods. Based on the projected results, CATCR consumes less time than the two other compared methods. Because time is an essential variable of quality, and because customers, users, and vendors pay close attention to the cost of time, CATCR is a strong candidate for contextual cloud testing.

3.5 Conclusions and Industry Examples

There is immense interest in recent context driven software engineering methods. For testing, a key phase in software development cycle, CDT has been the driving approach for recent agile validation and verification. A major exercise in testing is reducing the number of test cases. CATCR (presented here) does that. It is based on a specific contextual process. Agile development is currently very popular in industry. Besides Amazon, in a recent report published by SalesForce (A cloud computing provider in the US), they concluded that "cloud computing is the ideal environment for agile development". Certain contextual practices are implemented during testing. Such practices include: (1) Testing teams provide testing-related services; they do not run the development project. (2) It is correct for different test groups to have different missions. (3) A core practice in the service of one mission is independent of other services. (4) Different types of errors will be revealed by different types of tests. (5) Test artifacts are worthwhile to the extent that they satisfy their relevant requirements. Other major corporations such as Google and Microsoft are using context for software development projects. At Microsoft, 65 % of the teams used contextual agile development. However, they noted that at big corporations, context works only in small teams. When teams are more than 25 people, context driven development and agile testing become difficult to manage (Begel and Nagappan 2014).

To be able to use context in software engineering, it is important to understand the problem and the software system under development. Additionally, it is important to refer to the main principles of context-driven testing. CATCR addresses such concerns. Additionally, CATCR was evaluated, and had positive results in terms of resource consumption (*time*) when compared to other testing methods. Time spent in testing depends on assigning the most efficient and ready sites based on context, the size of software, number of test cases and the number of testing iterations. CATCR covered all of the mentioned aspects. Furthermore, CATCR has three main advantages: (1) Flexibility: the initial values of the weights and the models could be modified by the test engineer to cause a possibly quicker convergence. This gives the engineer full control. (2) Usage-oriented: this approach is based on the user needs and a real time testing feedback based on context. It is not a static function, rather a resilient one. More importantly, (3) Time reduction: reducing the number of test cases to be executed reduces time.

Some researchers have concluded that with current innovations in computing, context is still a poorly used source of information (Dey 2014). While it would be very useful to define a comprehensive lifecycle development process that uses context, in this chapter, only the testing phase if presented as an example. Other definitions of context are included in recent literature (Kaner 2002; Gill and Bunker 2013; White Paper by SalesForce 2014; Dey 2014). The reader is encouraged to review these references for more details, and other prospects that other researchers have presented. Other uses of context consider situation abstractions, the change in events, and ontological definitions. CATCR however, is concerned with the givens (requirements), the context, and current choices that are motivated by the testing missions. Finally, it is still up for debate whether context testing will be successful on the long run; and whether it will eventually contribute to the overall goodness of software.

References

Abel, T., Gonzalez, A.J.: Utilizing criteria to reduce a set of test cases for expert system validation. Proceedings of the 10th FLAIRS Conference, pp. 402–406 (1997)

Amazon Cloud: http://www.amazon.com/cloud (2014). Accessed 15 July 2014

Bach, J.: Heuristic test planning: Context model. Satisfice, Washington (2013)

Batarseh, F.A.: Incremental lifecycle validation of knowledge-based systems through CommonKADS. Doctoral Dissertation, University of Central Florida, May 2011

Begel, A., Nagappan, N.: Usage and perceptions of agile software development in an industrial context: An exploratory study. A paper published by Microsoft Inc. Research Institution, Redmond, WA. http://research.microsoft.com/pubs/56015/AgileDevatMS-ESEM07.pdf (2014)

Dey A.: Understanding and using context, a report. Georgia Tech Institute of Technology. Future Computing Environments Group (2014)

Foster, I.: What is the grid? A three point checklist. The Grid-Today (July 2002)

Gartner Research: Gartner magic quadrant for public cloud infrastructure as a service, a report. (2013)

Gill, A.Q., Bunker, D.: Towards the development of a cloud-based communication technologies assessment tool: An analysis of practitioners' perspectives. VINE **43**(1), 57–77 (2013)

Gonzalez, A.J., Gupta, U., Chianese, R.: Performance evaluation of a large diagnostic expert system using a heuristic test case generator. Eng. Appl. Artif. Intell. **9**, 275–284 (2000)

Gonzalez, A.J., Stensrud, B., Barrett, G.: Formalizing context-based reasoning: A modeling paradigm for representing tactical human behavior. Int. J. Intell. Syst. **27**, 822–847 (2008)

Herrmann, J., Jantke, K., Knauf, R.: Using structural knowledge for system validation. Proceedings of the 10th FLAIRS Conference, pp. 82–86 (1997)

Kalliosaari, L., Taipale O., Smolander, K.: Testing in the cloud: Exploring the practice. IEEE Software **29**(2), 46–51 (2012)

Kaner, C.: The context-driven approach to software testing. Notes from the Florida Institute of Technology (2002)

Knauf, R., Gonzalez, A.J., Abel, T.: A framework for validation of rule-based systems. IEEE Trans. Syst. Man Cybernet. **32**(3), 181–196 (2002)

Knauf, R., Tsuruta, S., Gonzalez, A.J.: Toward reducing human involvement in validation of knowledge-based systems. IEEE Trans. Syst. Man Cybernet. Part A Syst. Hum. **37**, 120–131 (2007)

Lockwood, S., Chen, Z.: Knowledge validation of engineering expert systems. Adv. Eng. Soft. **23**(2), 97–104 (1995)

Rao, R.: 10 cloud based testing tools. http://www.toolsjournal.com/testing-lists/item/404-10-cloud-based-testing-tools (2014). Accessed 15 July 2014

Shreiber, G., Akkermans, H., Anjewierden, A., De Hoog, R., Shadbolt, N., Van De Velde, W., Wielinga, B.: Knowledge engineering and management-the commonKADS methodology. MIT Press, Cambridge (2000)

Smith, S., Kandel, A.: Validation of expert systems. Proceedings of the Third Florida Artificial Intelligence Research Symposium (FLAIRS) (1990)

Wells, S.: The VIVA method: A life cycle independent approach to KBS validation. Proceedings of the IEEE AAAI Conference, pp. 102–106 (1993)

White Paper by SalesForce, Inc.: Agile development (the school of context) meets cloud computing for extraordinary results at SalesForce. http://www.developerforce.com/media/ForcedotcomBookLibrary/WP_Agile_112608.pdf (2014). Accessed 15 July 2014

Chapter 4
Context-Based Search, Recommendation and Browsing in Software Development

Bruno Antunes, Barbara Furtado and Paulo Gomes

Abstract With workspaces frequently comprising hundreds, or even thousands, of artifacts, developers spend a considerable amount of time navigating the source code or searching for a specific source code artifact they need to work. With the aim of helping developers during their work, the authors propose a context-based approach to search, recommend and browse source code in the workspace. The source code structure stored in the workspace of the developer is represented in a knowledge base, and a context model represents the source code elements that are more relevant for the developer in a specific moment. These structures are then used to improve the retrieval, ranking and navigation of source code elements. The experiments conducted with developers showed that the use of contextual information is of valuable importance to help identify the most relevant source code elements for the developer at each moment.

4.1 Introduction

The context of a developer can be viewed as a rich and complex network of elements across different dimensions. Although software development may include all the activities that result in a software product, from its conception to its realization, here we focus on the process of writing and maintaining the source code. This activity is usually conducted by developers in an IDE (Integrated Development Environment), which provide a set of tools aimed to help developers develop their work in an integrated workspace.

B. Antunes (✉) · B. Furtado · P. Gomes
CISUC, Department of Informatics Engineering, University of Coimbra,
Polo II, Pinhal de Marrocos, 3030-290 Coimbra, Portugal
e-mail: bema@dei.uc.pt

B. Furtado
e-mail: bfurtado@student.dei.uc.pt

P. Gomes
e-mail: pgomes@dei.uc.pt

© Springer Science+Business Media New York 2014
P. Brézillon, A. J. Gonzalez (eds.), *Context in Computing*,
DOI 10.1007/978-1-4939-1887-4_4

With the increasing dimension of software systems, software development projects have grown in complexity and size, as well as in the number of requirements and technologies involved. During their work, software developers need to cope with a large amount of contextual information that is typically not captured and processed in order to enrich their work environment. With workspaces frequently comprising hundreds, or even thousands, of artifacts, they spend a considerable amount of time navigating the source code or searching for a specific source code artifact they need to work (Murphy et al. 2006, Ko et al. 2006, Starke et al. 2009).

With regard to search, Starke et al. (2009) observed that most of the times the searches performed by developers are too generic, leading to a high number of search results. These searches are usually limited to the matching of specific patterns in the lines of code that comprise a software system. But the pattern matching approaches have several shortcomings, requiring a direct correspondence between the pattern and the text in the source code. The improvements achieved by the use of Information Retrieval (IR) techniques, encouraged researchers using these techniques to help developers finding relevant source code for their current task (Marcus et al. 2004; Lukins et al. 2008; Gay et al. 2009; Shao and Smith 2009). Despite the fact that context is argued to improve the effectiveness of IR systems (Jones and Brown 2004; Doan and Brézillone 2004), as far as we know, none of the previous approaches have used the contextual information of the developer to improve the retrieval and ranking of relevant source code in the IDE.

Having identified the potential of recommender systems for software development, researchers studied ways of using contextual information, either implicit or explicit, to recommend source code artifacts that are potentially relevant for the current task of the developer. For instance, the history of interactions between the developers and the source code was used to identify navigational patterns, which allowed the recommendation of relevant artifacts given a current artifact (Singer et al. 2005; DeLine et al. 2005; McCarey et al. 2005). With the same objective, the information stored in the project memory of a software product was used to identify relationships between source code artifacts (Ying et al. 2004; Zimmermann 2005; Cubranic et al. 2005). The context associated to the current task of the developer was used to help focus the information displayed in the IDE (Kersten and Murphy 2006), to improve awareness, and facilitate the exploration of source code (Parnin and Goeg 2006; Saul et al. 2007; Robillard 2008; Piorkowski et al. 2012).

Concerning the browsing of source code, different types of visualizations have been used to help developers navigate the source code structure. Some approaches allow developers to visualize and navigate through call graphs (Storey and Muller 1995; LaToza and Myers 2011; Karrer et al. 2011) or UML diagrams (Sinha et al. 2005). Other approaches replace the conventional interface of an IDE, providing an interface optimized to read and edit source code (Bragdon et al. 2010; DeLine 2010). Most of these tools do not make use of contextual information, and when they do it is in a simplistic manner, based only in the current location of the cursor in the source code editor. Also, they usually have little integration with existing IDEs, forcing developers to use external tools.

The work described here is focused on a context-based approach to search, recommendation and browsing of source code in the workspace of the developer. In our approach, the source code structure stored in the workspace of the developer is represented in a knowledge base. A context model represents the source code elements that are more relevant for the developer in a specific moment. These structures are then used to improve the retrieval, ranking and navigation of source code elements, such as classes, interfaces and methods, taking into account their relevance to the current context of the developer. We have implemented a prototype that integrates context-based search, recommendation and browsing features in the Eclipse [1] IDE. This prototype was then tested with a group of developers in order to validate our approach.

The remain of the paper starts with a description of the knowledge base and context model used. Then we present our approach to context-based search, recommendation and browsing of source code, as well as the mechanism used to adapt our approach to the developer behavior. Finally, we present the results of our validation and conclude with some final remarks.

4.2 Knowledge Base

The *knowledge base* represents the source code structure that is stored in the workspace of the developer. This knowledge base is unique for each developer, being built from the source code files with which the developer is working, and maintained as these files are changed. The source code structure is represented from a structural and a lexical perspectives, which are formalized using ontologies (Zuniga 2001). The structural perspective deals with the source code artifacts and the structural relations that exist between them, while the lexical perspective deals with the terms used to reference these artifacts and how they are associated.

The *structural ontology* represents a set of source code elements typically found in object-oriented programming languages, as well as a subset of their most relevant relations (see Fig. 4.1). The main source code elements represented in our structural ontology are Class, Interface and Method, which are the building blocks of an object-oriented programming language.

The *lexical ontology* represents the terms used to reference the source code elements, including two relations that are used to express how terms relate to each other and with the source code elements (see Fig. 4.1). The concrete *terms* used to compose the name, also known as *identifier*, of a source code element are represented as instances of the Term class. The terms used to reference a source code element become *indexed* by that element using the indexedBy relation. When two terms are used together to compose the name of a source code element, we create an associatedWith relation between them. This relation is used to represent the

---

[1] http://eclipse.org

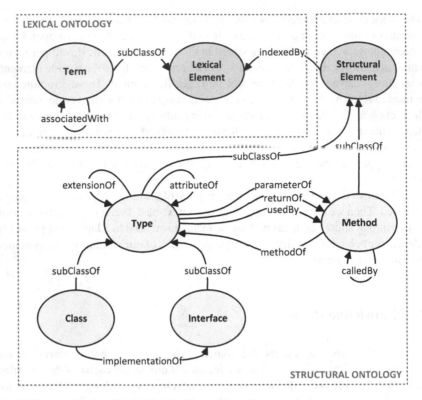

Fig. 4.1 The structural and lexical ontologies model

proximity between the terms, the same way co-occurrence is interpreted as an indicator of semantic proximity in linguistics (Harris 1954). We interpret co-occurrence of two terms in identifiers as an indication of some kind of relation between these terms. The terms that co-occur more often have a stronger relation than those that are rarely used together. Therefore, the number of times the two terms co-occur in the names of different structural elements is stored and used as the weight of the relation between these terms. For instance, a class named `DatabaseManager` would be indexed by the terms `database` and `manager`, and these terms would become associated because they were used together to name that class.

4.3 Context Model

The *context model* we have defined aims to represent the focus of attention of the developer in each moment and is based on the source code elements that are more relevant to her/his work in that moment. The model is built from the interactions of the developer with the source code elements and evolves over time, as the focus of attention of the developer changes. Similarly to the knowledge base, the context model comprises a structural and a lexical dimensions.

The *structural context* focuses on the structural elements and structural relations that are more relevant for the developer in a specific moment. The relevance of these elements and relations is derived from the interactions of the developer with the source code and is represented as an interest value. The structural context was inspired by the work of Kersten and Murphy (2006), that have used a similar model to represent the context associated to a task. The structural relations are not directly affected by the interactions of the developer, therefore their relevance is derived from the structural elements that exist in the structural context. When two, or more, structural elements are bound by one of these relations, that relation is added to the structural context. Associated with each relation is an interest value that represents the relevance of that relation in the context of the developer. The interest of a relation is computed as an average of the interest of all structural elements that are bound by that relation, so that it reflects the relevance of the structural elements that brought it to the structural context.

The *lexical context* focuses on the terms that are more relevant in the context of the developer. The terms are extracted from the names of the source code elements that are manipulated by the developer. Similarly to the elements and relations in the structural context, the relevance of each term is given by an interest value. The interest of a term is computed as an average of the interest of the structural elements from which the term was extracted. The more relevant a structural element is, the more relevant become the terms used to reference that element.

For the interested reader, a more comprehensive and detailed description of the context model is provided in (Antunes et al. 2013).

4.4   Context-Based Search

The *context-based search* process that we have defined allows the developer to search for source code elements, such as classes, interfaces and methods, stored in the workspace. The search results are retrieved using an Information Retrieval (IR) approach based on the Vector Space Model (VSM; Salton et al. 1975), which collects a set of source code elements that match a given query. These search results are then ranked according to their relevance to the query, but also taking into account their proximity to the context of the developer. We base our approach on the assumption that the source code elements the developer is looking for are likely to be related with the source code elements that are relevant in the current context. The approach presented here is an evolution of a preliminary version presented in (Antunes et al. 2012b).

The retrieved source code elements are ranked according to their relevance to the query and the context model of the developer, including the structural and lexical contexts. The relevance of a search result in relation to these components is given by a *retrieval score*, a *structural score* and a *lexical score*. The contribution of these components to the final score of the search result is given by a set of weights. The sum of the three weights is always 1 and the value of each score is always normalized in the interval [0, 1]. The final score of the search result is computed as a weighted sum of the three scores. The *retrieval score* represents the relevance of the search result in relation to the query provided by the developer. This score is computed using the TF-IDF (Salton and Buckley 1988) weighting approach used in the VSM.

The *structural score* represents the relevance of a retrieved search result in relation to the structural context. We define this relevance as the structural proximity between the source code element that was retrieved and the elements in the structural context. The structural proximity between two structural elements is inversely proportional to the structural distance between them. The task of measuring the structural distance between two source code elements is reduced to the problem of finding the shortest path between the two elements, by taking the structural ontology as a directed graph, where vertices are represented by structural elements and edges are represented by structural relations. The cost of a path is given by the sum of the cost of the relations that create the path. Instead of using a fixed cost for each relation, the cost of a relation is inversely proportional to the interest associated to that relation in the structural context. This way, we take into consideration the current relevance of the structural relations to the developer, assuring that the paths created with more relevant relations will have a lower cost. We only consider the top 15 elements with higher interest in the structural context and perform a search for the shortest paths with a maximum of three relations.

The structural distance between two structural elements is computed using (4.1), where sr_i is the ith relation of the n relations that create the shortest structural path between the elements se_a and se_b.

$$dist'_s(se_a, se_b) = \sum_{i=1}^{n} 1 - I(sr_i) \tag{4.1}$$

The structural distance between the source code elements is normalized using (4.2), so that this distance is always a real number in the interval [0, 1].

$$dist_s(se_a, se_b) = 1 - \left(\frac{1}{e^{dist'_s(se_a, se_b)}} \right) \tag{4.2}$$

As shown in (4.3), the structural proximity between a source code element se and an element in the structural context ce is inversely proportional to the structural distance between the two elements, given by $dist_s(se, ce)$, and is proportional to the interest of the element in the structural context, given by $I(ce)$. This way, the lower the interest of the element ce to the developer, the lower is the proximity of an element in relation to ce.

$$prox_s(se, ce) = (1 - dist_s(se, ce)) \times I(ce) \tag{4.3}$$

The structural proximity between a source code element and the structural context is computed as an average of the structural proximity between that element and the elements in the structural context. Therefore, the structural score of a retrieved element r is given by (4.4), where ce_i represents the ith element within the list of n context elements.

$$ss(r) = \frac{\sum_{i=1}^{n} prox_s(r, ce_i)}{n} \tag{4.4}$$

The *lexical score* represents the relevance of a retrieved search result in relation to the lexical context. We define this relevance as the lexical proximity between the terms associated with the source code element that was retrieved, which are extracted from its identifier, and the terms in the lexical context. This proximity is inversely proportional to the lexical distance between the terms. Similarly to the approach followed to compute the distance between two structural elements, the lexical distance between two terms is represented by the shortest path between them. Such paths can be found by taking the lexical ontology as a graph, where vertices are represented by terms and edges are represented by the co-occurrence relations (associatedWith). We use the co-occurrence frequency of the two terms to measure the weight of their relation. We are assuming that the more frequent the co-occurrence of two terms is, the stronger will be the relation between them. As shown in (4.5), the weight of a co-occurrence relation lr between terms t_a and t_b, is given by their co-occurrence frequency $cf(t_a, t_b)$, normalized by the maximum co-occurrence frequency in the knowledge base (cf_{max}).

$$w(lr_{t_a t_b}) = \frac{cf(t_a, t_b)}{cf_{max}} \tag{4.5}$$

This way, the cost of a relation is inversely proportional to the weight associated to that relation, so that more frequent relations connect terms with a lower cost. Accordingly, the cost of a path is given by the sum of the cost of the relations that create the path. By using the weight of the relations between terms to compute the cost of a path, we assure that the paths between terms that co-occur more frequently will have a lower cost. Again, we only consider the top 15 terms with higher interest in the lexical context and paths with a maximum of three relations. The lexical distance between two terms is computed using (4.6), where lr_i is the ith relation of the n relations that create the shortest lexical path between the terms t_a and t_b.

$$dist'_l(t_a, t_b) = \sum_{i=1}^{n} (1 - w(lr_i)) \tag{4.6}$$

The lexical distance between the two terms is normalized using (4.7), so that this distance is always a real number in the interval $[0, 1]$.

$$dist_l(t_a, t_b) = 1 - \left(\frac{1}{e^{dist'_l(t_a, t_b)}} \right) \tag{4.7}$$

As shown in (4.8), the lexical proximity between a term t and a term in the lexical context ct is inversely proportional to the lexical distance between the two terms, given by $dist_l(t, ct)$, and is proportional to the interest of the term in the lexical context, given by $I(ct)$. This way, the lower the interest of the term ct to the developer, the lower is the proximity of a term in relation to ct.

$$prox_l(t, ct) = (1 - dist_l(t, ct)) \times I(ct) \tag{4.8}$$

The lexical proximity between a term and the terms in the lexical context is computed as an average of the lexical proximity between that term and each one of the terms in the lexical context. The same way, the lexical proximity between a source code element and the terms in the lexical context is computed as an average of the lexical proximity between its terms and the terms in the lexical context. Therefore, the lexical score of a retrieved element r is given by (4.9), where t_i represents the ith term of the n terms associated to that element and ct_j represents the jth term of the m terms in the lexical context.

$$sl(r) = \frac{\sum_{i=1}^{n} \left(\frac{\sum_{j=1}^{m} prox_l(ti, ctj)}{m} \right)}{n} \tag{4.9}$$

4.5 Context-Based Recommendation

The *context-based recommendation* process we have defined uses the context model of the developer to retrieve and rank potentially relevant source code elements. This process is based on the assumption that most of the source code elements needed by the developer are likely to be structurally, or lexically, related with the elements that are being manipulated in that moment. This way, we want to help developers reaching the desired source code elements more easily and quickly, decreasing the effort needed to search for that elements in the source code structure. The context model plays a central role in this process, providing the mechanism needed to identify and evaluate the relevance of the source code elements that are being manipulated. We use the structural elements represented in the context model, along with their relations, to retrieve recommendations of elements that are potentially relevant for the developer. These recommendations are then ranked taking into account different components, representing both the retrieval process and the relevance to the context model. The context-based recommendation approach presented here is based on a preliminary version presented in (Antunes et al. 2012a).

The recommendations are retrieved using the source code elements in the context model by combining two different methods, one based on the interest of these elements and other based on the time elapsed since these elements were last accessed. The *interest* based method makes use of the relevance of the source code elements that have been manipulated by the developer to identify other potentially relevant elements. The recommendations include the top N elements with higher interest in the context model and all the elements that are structurally related with them. We call N the query size of the recommendation process, and the default value of N we have used in our approach is 3. The *time* based method uses the time, instead of the interest, to measure the relevance of the source code elements that are being manipulated by the developer. The interest of an element represented in the context model reflects the relevance of that element during a period of time. But, sometimes, the most relevant elements may not be those with an higher interest during that period of time, but the ones that have been accessed more recently. The time based method favors this aspect, retrieving source code elements that are related with the elements that have been manipulated more recently. The recommendations retrieved using this method include the top N elements of the context model that have been accessed more recently and all the elements that are structurally related with them.

The recommendations retrieved are ranked taking into account the retrieval process and their relevance to the context model of the developer. The retrieval process is represented by an *interest score* and a *time score*, while the relevance in relation to the context model is represented by a *structural score* and a *lexical score*. The contribution of these components to the final score of the recommendation is given by a set of weights. The sum of the four weights is always 1 and the value of each score is always normalized in the interval $[0, 1]$. The final score of a recommendation is given by a weighted sum of these scores.

The *structural* and *lexical* scores are computed the same way as for the context-based search ranking, see previous sub-section. Next, we describe in detail how the interest and time scores are computed.

The *interest score* represents the score of the elements that were retrieved using the interest based method. There are two types of elements retrieved, those that are in the list of the elements with higher interest in the structural context, and the ones that are structurally related with them. The elements that are retrieved in the list have a score that corresponds to their interest in the context model. The score of the elements retrieved through a structural relation with the elements in the list is computed using the interest of the relation and the interest of the element with which they are related. The interest of the element in the list is used to normalize the interest of the structural relation, so that the score of the retrieved element is proportional to the interest of the element in the list. This way, the score of the retrieved elements take into account the relevance of both the relation and the element that contributed to their retrieval. When an element has a structural relation with more than one of the elements in the list, the score is given by the average of the scores of all the relations. This way, the interest score is computed using (4.10), where $I(r)$ is the interest of element r in the structural context, while $I(se_i)$ and $I(sr_i)$ are the interest of the ith element and relation, respectively, that got element r retrieved.

$$
si(r) = \begin{cases} I(r) & \text{if retrieved directly} \\ \dfrac{\displaystyle\sum_{i=1}^{n} I(se_i) \times I(sr_i)}{n} & \text{if retrieved indirectly} \end{cases} \tag{4.10}
$$

The *time score* represents the score of the elements that were retrieved using the time based method. The score is computed in a way that is similar to that used to compute the interest score. The main difference is that the relevance of each element is computed using the time elapsed since it was last accessed, instead of using its interest. This time span (ts) is normalized by the minimum time span (ts_{min}) among the elements in the top N list.

Similarly to the interest score, the time score is computed using (4.11), where $T(r)$ is the normalized time span for element r, while $T(se_i)$ is the normalized time span for the ith element and $I(sr_i)$ is the interest of the ith relation, that got element r retrieved.

$$
st(r) = \begin{cases} T(r) & \text{if retrieved directly} \\ \dfrac{\displaystyle\sum_{i=1}^{n} T(se_i) \times I(sr_i)}{n} & \text{if retrieved indirectly} \end{cases} \tag{4.11}
$$

4.6   Context-Based Browsing

The *context-based browsing* approach we have developed is based on a visualization of the source code elements that are represented in our knowledge base. In this visualization, it is possible to browse the source code elements stored in the workspace of the developer, which are displayed in the visualization as nodes, with different colors and shapes according to their type. The relations that exist between the source code elements are represented in the visualization as edges connecting the nodes. When the developer expands a node, all the source code elements related with the expanded element are shown. In order to prevent the number of nodes in the screen from growing too fast, we have implemented a clustering mechanism that aggregates nodes connected by the same relation type inside a special type of node, the *aggregator node*. When the developer wants to explore the relations of a source code element, the *aggregator node* that represents the chosen relation type can be expanded and the aggregated nodes are added to the visualization.

In order to make the visualization more useful to developers, we make use of their contextual information to enhance the browsing of the source code elements and their relations. First, the size of the nodes in the visualization is dependent on their interest to the developer. Thus, the elements with higher interest values are more noticeable, so developers can easily distinguish the elements that are more relevant to their work and, for instance, start exploring other source code elements that are closely related with what they are working on. The same way, relations that connect source code elements that are in the context model have thicker edges than the others, becoming more explicit to the developer. Furthermore, the source code elements that are in the context model are automatically expanded from *aggregator nodes*, so developers do not have to expand all the relations to find the elements that are more relevant for them in that moment.

Additionally, developers can control the way the visualization behave as their context changes. The visualization automatically adapts to the changes in their context model according to three different modes of behaviour. The *clear mode* is the default mode and forces the visualization to focus in the source code element in which the developer is working in each moment. When the developer changes to a different class, interface or method in the source code editor, that source code element will appear in the center of the visualization, along with its relations, and the developer can start exploring the source code from there. This way, the visualization automatically adapts to the changes in the context of the developer as s/he manipulates the source code, so that the source code elements related with the one that is being manipulated are always accessible. If the developer is already exploring the source code structure in the visualization, s/he can block the visualization, by activating the *blocked mode*, and freely inspect the source code in the source code editor without loosing the state of the visualization. This mode is useful, for instance, when the developer is exploring the source code and open the source code element represented by a node to see more details about it, returning then to the visualization to continue exploring the source code structure. Developers may also choose the *add mode*, if they need to keep track of the source code elements which they are inspecting in the source code editor. In this mode, that elements will be added to the visualization, and developers can then start exploring each one of them in the visualization.

Finally, the context-based search and recommendation was integrated with the visualization, to allow an easier access to the source code elements stored in the workspace. This way, the developer is able to perform a search or select a recommendation and focus the visualization on the retrieved source code element. In addition to the selected element, the relations between that element and the source code elements that are part of the developer context model in that moment are also shown. This way, developers can better understand the relevance of the selected result for their work, by seeing how it relates with the source code elements they have been working.

4.7 Learning

As described in the previous section, the ranking of search results and recommendations, is computed using a set of different components. The contribution of each component to the final ranking is defined by a set of weights, one per each component. At first, these weights are equally balanced, so that each component contribute in the same proportion to the ranking of a result. We could not predict in advance which components would be more relevant in the ranking process. Furthermore, the relevance of each component could vary from developer to developer. Therefore, we have defined a learning mechanism to learn which components are more relevant for the developer, so that these components could be favored in the ranking process. This is done by learning the weights associated to each one of the components used in the ranking of the results.

This learning mechanism uses the results that have been selected by the developer to learn the weights that are associated to each component. This approach is based on the assumption that all the results selected by the developers can be considered useful. This way, the weights evolve based on the analysis of how each component contributed to rank the results that were useful for the developer. The objective is to increase the weights of the components that contributed to promote the selected results and decrease the weights of the components that contributed to demote them.

For the interested reader, a detailed description of the learning mechanism is provided in (Antunes et al. 2012a), which applies to the weights used in both the search and recommendation processes.

4.8 Validation

The context-based search, recommendation and browsing approaches described previously were integrated in the Eclipse IDE, using a prototype plugin named SDiC[2] (Software Development in Context). The plugin automatically builds and maintains the knowledge base, updating the structural and lexical ontologies whenever the source code base changes. The context model is automatically captured from the interactions of the developer in the IDE. The context-based search, recommendation and browsing of source code elements are accessible through specific views that were added to the Eclipse IDE, as shown in Fig. 4.2. In order to evaluate the context-based search and recommendation approaches, the prototype was installed and used during the daily work of 21 developers. The developers used the prototype during an average of 38 days, working with knowledge bases having an average of 3496 structural elements, 9370 structural relations, 679 lexical elements and 13,077 lexical relations.

4.8.1 Search

Concerning the context-based search we wanted to find evidence that the use of the context model was having a positive impact on the ranking of the search results. During the study, developers selected a total of 1120 search results. Among the searches with selected search results, the search queries used by the developers had an average size of 6.36 ± 0.26 characters. From our point of view, it is a reduced size for a search query, which may be indicative that the use of context reduces the need of using larger search queries. With regard to the ranking of the search results, the final ranking of each result depends on the combination of three components: retrieval, structural and lexical. The retrieval component represents a typical keyword-based

---

[2] http://sdic.dei.uc.pt

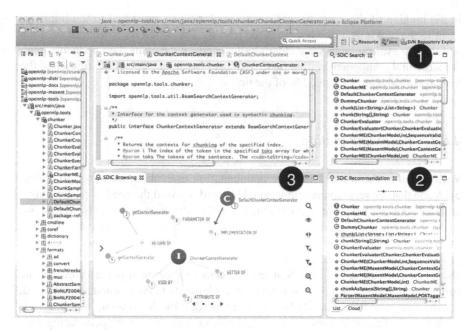

Fig. 4.2 A screenshot of the SDiC prototype showing the search view (*1*), recommendation view (*2*) and the browsing view (*3*) in the Eclipse IDE

search process, that is not influenced by the context model and can be used as a reference ranking. The other two components represent the influence of the context model in the final ranking of a search result. The best ranking would be 1 and the worst ranking would be 30, since only the top 30 search results are presented to the developer. The search results selected had, in average, a final ranking of 2.40 ± 0.16, a retrieval ranking of 8.03 ± 0.50, a structural ranking of 2.31 ± 0.19 and a lexical ranking of 5.34 ± 0.42. This means that if the search result was ranked using only one of the three components, in average, it would appear in eighth place with the retrieval component, in second place with the structural component, and in fifth place with the lexical component. These values clearly indicate that the search results that were relevant for the developer were frequently better ranked through the context components than through the keyword-based process. This behaviour shows evidence that the context components had a positive influence in the final ranking of these search results, which would be ranked in much lower positions if a simple keyword-based retrieval process was used.

Besides analyzing the average rankings for each component, we have also investigated if the search results were effectively getting better ranked by using the context model in the ranking process. In comparison with the retrieval component, the search results were better ranked in almost 60 % of the times, being worse ranked in only 11 % of the times. The average rankings difference when the search results were better ranked was 10.02 ± 0.68, being only 2.81 ± 0.54 when they were worse ranked. Although there were worse ranked results in 11 % of the times, the difference in the ranking of these results was much smaller when compared to the improvement in the rankings of the better ranked results. The differences between the final and the retrieval rankings were clearly influenced by the context components, with the structural component getting better rankings in about 71 % of the times and the lexical component in about 62 % of the times.

4.8.2 Recommendation

With regard to the context-based recommendation evaluation, we aimed to collect evidence that the recommendations could be used to avoid the need of performing a search or browsing the source code structure to find the needed elements. At first, we wanted to evaluate the capacity of the system in predicting the source code elements that the developers would need in the near future, so that these elements could be pro-actively recommended to them. Also, we wanted to discover what value of N should be used to achieve the best results. This evaluation was performed in the background, by verifying if the source code elements being opened, or accessed, for the first time were already being recommended by the system. This way, we were able to evaluate our approach using the behavior of the developers during their work, without requiring them to use our recommendations. We have implemented a mechanism to store the top 30 recommendations generated by the system with a random value of N (between 1 and 10). For each source code element opened, or accessed, for the first time, we have verified if that element was being recommended by the system in that moment. In average, considering all values of N, 41 % of the source code elements opened, or accessed, for the first time were already being recommended by the system. The best results were achieved with a value of 2 for N, with which the system has been able to predict the developer needs in 53 % of the times. As expected, the results showed that very lower values of N tend to have worse values, as the number of source code elements used to retrieve the recommendations is not enough to reach the desired element. The higher values of N also have worse results, which can be explained by the fact that when we increase the number of source code elements in the retrieval process, the recommendations became more dispersed and the probability of finding what the developer needs decreases. We believe that these results are very interesting and show that the context of developers has much to say about their immediate needs.

The average final ranking of the selected recommendations was 5.40 ± 0.55. Although it may still be subject to improvements, we consider that this is a good precision for this type of recommendation system. The average rankings of the individual components were 9.08 ± 0.77 for the interest component, 8.96 ± 0.80 for the time component, 8.03 ± 0.76 for the structural component and 7.41 ± 0.68 for the lexical component. These rankings do not show a significant difference between the four components. Although the context components have slightly better average rankings, the difference is lower than the difference obtained in the preliminary study. Interestingly, the lexical component achieves better rankings than the structural one, which depicts that the lexical relations between source code elements are contributing to improve the precision of the recommendations.

4.8.3 Browsing

In order to validate the context-based browsing approach, we have created an experiment with a total of 17 developers, which involved using the Eclipse IDE to perform a set of source code comprehension tasks in the Apache OpenNLP Java project. To evaluate the use of the contextual information of the developer in the visualization, we prepared a set of steps that would simulate the use of some classes during development. By following the provided guidelines, the accessed classes would become associated to the context model of the developer and it would affect the visualization in three different ways. First, the classes in the context model would auto expand from the aggregator nodes. Also, these classes would have bigger nodes than the source code elements that were not in the context model. Finally, the source code elements in the context model of the developer that were related with the selected search/recommendation results would be highlighted. During the walkthrough, the developers were asked to analyse the visualization and answer if they understand the three behaviours stated above. If the answer was positive, they were asked to write the reason why they think that happened and rate the utility of that behaviour in a scale from 1 (very low) to 5 (very high). The results show that about 94 % of the developers understood why specific nodes where being expanded from the aggregator nodes and rated that behavior with an average of 4.63 ± 0.50. The size of the nodes representing elements in the context model was understood by about 76 % of the developers and was rated with an average of 4.62 ± 0.51. The highlighting of source code elements related with the search/recommendation results was recognized by about 88 % of the developers and was rated with an average of 4.53 ± 0.52.

Despite being difficult to evaluate the use of context in browsing outside a real development environment, the results show that the developers considered it useful. They mentioned the utility of having the recently used source code elements more accessible in the visualization, as they browse through the source code structure. Although they also mentioned that its utility will depend on the performed task in a real situation, they think that by emphasing the recently used source code elements, and by not hiding them in the aggregator nodes, could help to better understand the connections between unknown parts of the source code with the part they are working. Furthermore, developers were asked to rate the utility of the three visualization modes of the tool (the clear, blocked and add modes). These modes adapt the visualization in different ways, according to the changes of context of the developer. All the modes were considered very useful, with an average rating of $4.82 \pm 0.0.39$ for the clear mode, 4.59 ± 0.62 for the blocked mode, and 4.41 ± 0.87. Most of the developers prefer the clear mode, because it allows to have the currently manipulated source code element always accessible.

4.9 Conclusions

We have presented an approach to context-based search, recommendation and browsing of source code in the workspace of a developer, which makes use of a context model to improve the retrieval, ranking and navigation of source code elements. The statistical information collected in a previous study (Antunes et al. 2013) shows that the source code elements manipulated by the developer are highly related, being structurally or lexically related with other elements already in the context model in more than 80 % of the times. This supports our claim that the relations that exist between source code artifacts can be used to measure the proximity between these artifacts and to compute their relevance in the current context of the developer. Also, we have verified that the context components have a clear contribution to improve the ranking of search results, which were better ranked in about 60 % of the times, and worst ranked in only 11 % of the times. With respect to recommendations, although the results are not so evident, we have shown that our context model could be used to retrieve relevant source code elements for the developer, being able to predict the needed source code element among the top 30 recommendations in about 53 % of the times. Finally, the use of context to improve the browsing of source code through our visualization was well received by developers and rated as very useful.

Acknowledgement Bruno Antunes was supported by a FCT (Fundação para a Ciência e a Tecnologia) scholarship grant SFRH/BD/43336/2008, co-funded by ESF (European Social Fund).

References

Antunes, B., Cordeiro, J., Gomes, P.: An approach to context-based recommendation in software development. In: Proceedings of the 6th ACM Conference on Recommender Systems (RecSys 2012), pp. 171–178. ACM Press, New York, NY, USA (2012a)

Antunes, B., Cordeiro, J., Gomes, P.: Context-based search in software development. In: Proceedings of the 7th Conference on Prestigious Applications of Intelligent Systems (PAIS 2012) of the 20th European Conference on Artificial Intelligence (ECAI 2012), pp. 937–942. IOS Press (2012b)

Antunes, B., Cordeiro, J., Gomes, P.: An approach to context modeling in software development. In: Cordeiro J., Hammoudi S., Sinderen M. (eds.) Software and Data Technologies, Communications in Computer and Information Science, vol. 411, pp. 188–202. Springer, Berlin (2013)

Bragdon, A., Zeleznik, R., Reiss, S.P., Karumuri, S., Cheung, W., Kaplan, J., Coleman, C., Adeputra, F., LaViola Jr., J.J.: Code bubbles: a working set-based interface for code understanding and maintenance. In: Proceedings of the SIGCHI Conference on Human Factors in Computing Systems, CHI '10, pp. 2503–2512. ACM, New York, NY, USA (2010)

Cubranic, D., Murphy, G.C., Singer, J., Booth, K.S.: Hipikat: a project memory for software development. IEEE Trans. Softw. Eng. **31**(6), 446–465 (2005)

DeLine, R., Khella, A., Czerwinski, M., Robertson, G.: Towards understanding programs through wear-based filtering. In: Proceedings of the ACM Symposium on Software Visualization (SoftVis '05), pp. 183–192. ACM, New York, NY, USA (2005)

DeLine, R., Venolia, G., Rowan, K.: Software development with code maps. Commun. ACM **53**(8), 48–54 (2010)

Doan, B.L., Brézillon, P.: How the notion of context can be useful to search tools. In: Proceedings of the World Conference E-learn 2004. Washington, DC, USA (2004)

Gay, G., Haiduc, S., Marcus, A., Menzies, T.: On the use of relevance feedback in IR-based concept location. In: Proceedings of the IEEE International Conference on Software Maintenance (ICSM 2009), pp. 351–360 (2009)

Harris, Z.: Distributional structure. Word **10**(23), 146–162 (1954)

Jones, G.J.F., Brown, P.J.: The role of context in information retrieval. In: Proceedings of the ACM SIGIR Workshop on Information Retrieval in Context. Sheffield, UK (2004)

Karrer, T., Krämer, J.P., Diehl, J., Hartmann, B., Borchers, J.: Stacksplorer: call graph navigation helps increasing code maintenance efficiency. In: Proceedings of the ACM UIST 2011 Symposium on User Interface Software and Technology (2011)

Kersten, M., Murphy, G.C.: Using task context to improve programmer productivity. In: Proceedings of the 14th ACM SIGSOFT International Symposium on Foundations of Software Engineering (SIGSOFT '06/FSE-14), pp. 1–11. ACM, New York, NY, USA (2006)

Ko, A.J., Myers, B.A., Coblenz, M.J., Aung, H.H.: An exploratory study of how developers seek, relate, and collect relevant information during software maintenance tasks. IEEE Trans. Softw. Eng. **32**(12), 971–987 (2006)

LaToza, T.D., Myers, B.A.: Visualizing call graphs. In: VL/HCC, pp. 117–124 (2011)

Lukins, S.K., Kraft, N.A., Etzkorn, L.H.: Source code retrieval for bug localization using latent Dirichlet allocation. In: Proceedings of the 15th Working Conference on Reverse Engineering (WCRE '08), pp. 155–164 (2008)

Marcus, A., Sergeyev, A., Rajlich, V., Maletic, J.I.: An information retrieval approach to concept location in source code. In: Proceedings of the 11th Working Conference on Reverse Engineering (WCRE'04), pp. 214–223 (2004)

McCarey, F., Cinnéide, M.O., Kushmerick, N.: Rascal: a recommender agent for agile reuse. Artif. Intell. Rev. **24**(3–4), 253–276 (2005)

Murphy, G.C., Kersten, M., Findlater, L.: How are Java software developers using the Elipse IDE? IEEE Softw. **23**(4), 76–83 (2006)

Parnin, C., Gorg, C.: Building usage contexts during program comprehension. In: Proceedings of the 14th IEEE International Conference on Program Comprehension (ICPC '06), pp. 13–22. IEEE Computer Society, Washington, DC, USA (2006)

Piorkowski, D., Fleming, S., Scaffidi, C., Bogart, C., Burnett, M., John, B., Bellamy, R., Swart, C.: Reactive information foraging: an empirical investigation of theory-based recommender systems for programmers. In: Proceedings of the ACM Annual Conference on Human Factors in Computing Systems (CHI '12), pp. 1471–1480. ACM, New York, NY, USA (2012)

Robillard, M.P.: Topology analysis of software dependencies. ACM Trans. Softw. Eng. Methodol. **17**(4), 18:1–18:36 (2008)

Salton, G., Buckley, C.: Term-weighting approaches in automatic text retrieval. Inf. Process. Manag. **24**(5), 513–523 (1988)

Salton, G., Wong, A., Yang, C.S.: A vector space model for automatic indexing. Commun. ACM **18**(11), 613–620 (1975)

Saul, Z.M., Filkov, V., Devanbu, P., Bird, C.: Recommending random walks. In: Proceedings of the 6th Joint Meeting of the European Software Engineering Conference and the ACM SIGSOFT Symposium on the Foundations of Software Engineering (ESEC-FSE '07), pp. 15–24. ACM, New York, NY, USA (2007)

Shao, P., Smith, R.K.: Feature location by IR modules and call graph. In: Proceedings of the 47th Annual Southeast Regional Conference (ACM-SE 47), pp. 70:1–70:4. ACM, New York, NY, USA (2009)

Singer, J., Elves, R., Storey, M.A.: NavTracks: supporting navigation in software maintenance. In: Proceedings of the 21st IEEE International Conference on Software Maintenance, pp. 325–334. IEEE, Budapest, Hungary (2005)

Sinha, V., Karger, D., Miller, R.: Relo: helping users manage context during interactive exploratory visualization of large codebases. In: Proceedings of the 2005 OOPSLA Workshop on Eclipse Technology eXchange, Eclipse '05, pp. 21–25. ACM, New York, NY, USA (2005)

Starke, J., Luce, C., Sillito, J.: Searching and skimming: an exploratory study. In: Proceedings of the IEEE International Conference on Software Maintenance (ICSM 2009), pp. 157–166. IEEE, Edmonton, Alberta, Canada (2009)

Storey, M.A.D., Muller, H.A.: Manipulating and documenting software structures using shrimp views. In: Proceedings of the International Conference on Software Maintenance, ICSM '95, pp. 275–284. IEEE Computer Society, Washington, DC, USA (1995)

Ying, A.T.T., Murphy, G.C., Ng, R., Chu-Carroll, M.C.: Predicting source code changes by mining change history. IEEE Trans. Softw. Eng. 30(9), 574–586 (2004)

Zimmermann, T., Zeller, A., Weissgerber, P., Diehl, S.: Mining version histories to guide software changes. IEEE Trans. Softw. Eng. 31(6), 429–445 (2005)

Zuniga, G.L.: Ontology: its transformation from philosophy to information systems. In: Proceedings of the International Conference on Formal Ontology in Information Systems, pp. 187–197. ACM Press (2001)

Chapter 5
Context Aware and Adaptive Systems

Alan Colman, Mahmoud Hussein, Jun Han and Malinda Kapuruge

Abstract Context aware software systems and adaptive software systems *sense* changes in their environments, and *respond* by changing their behaviour and/or structure appropriately. The perspective of these two approaches, however, tends to differ. Context aware systems focus on modelling and reasoning about the relevant environmental context often with aid of formal ontologies The system, however, can only respond to an *anticipated* change of configuration setting or a change of application mode. Adaptive systems in contrast focus on how the *system responds* to an *unanticipated* environmental change. However, adaptive systems typically lack sophisticated models of context. This chapter analyses the differences and similarities between context-aware and adaptive systems. It then describes an approach and framework called ROAD that supports the development of context-aware applications whose structure and behavior can be altered at runtime. ROAD provides mechanisms to acquire and record context information and provision a central store of 'facts' which are evaluated in rules. These rules mediate operational messages or trigger adaptations to the structure of the application.

A. Colman (✉) · J. Han
School of Software and Electrical Engineering, Swinburne University of Technology,
John Street, Hawthorn, PO Box 218, Melbourne, Australia
e-mail: acolman@swin.edu.au

J. Han
e-mail: jhan@swin.edu.au

M. Hussein
Menofia University, Menofia, Egypt
e-mail: mahmoud.hussein@ci.menofia.edu.eg

M. Kapuruge
DiUS Computing Pty Ltd, Melbourne, Australia
e-mail: mkapuruge@dius.com.au

© Springer Science+Business Media New York 2014
P. Brézillon, A. J. Gonzalez (eds.), *Context in Computing*,
DOI 10.1007/978-1-4939-1887-4_5

5.1   Introduction

Context-aware Software systems and Adaptive Software systems have many similarities. Both types of system *sense* changes in their environments, and *respond* by changing their behaviour and/or structure appropriately. The perspective of these two approaches, however, tends to differ. Context-aware systems focus on modelling and reasoning about the relevant environmental context often with aid of formal ontologies (e.g, Wang et al. 2004; Chen et al. 2003; Ranganathan et al. 2003; Bettini et al. 2010). While these context models may be rich and the reasoning complex, the context-aware system response typically tends to be simple—that is, an *anticipated* change of configuration setting or a change of application mode. Adaptive systems on the other hand focus on how the *system responds* to environmental context change or to changes in requirements. In adaptive systems the range of possible system configuration states is much larger. While some of these system states might be anticipated typically there being so many options available for configuration or regulation that not all configuration states can be anticipated. However, in general adaptive systems lack the sophisticated models of context apparent in context aware systems.

This chapter explores how the gap between context aware and adaptive systems, in particular adaptive service-based compositions, might be systematically bridged through a domain-specific language and framework that allows the rapid development of CAAS systems—Context-Aware Adaptive Systems (Nierstrasz et al. 2009; Hussein et al. 2011). To show how this gap can be bridged we will start from the perspective of adaptive systems, analyse the commonalities and differences between context-aware and adaptive systems, then discuss how richer models of context might be incorporated into such systems.

The structure of this chapter is as follows. In Sect. 5.2, we give an overview of approaches to adaptive software systems in terms of the goals of the adaptations, the environmental variables being monitored and modelled, the type of change enacted and how change is realised into the running system. In particular, we look at approaches that provide the potential to model more complex environments and user-focused adaptation. Section 5.3 presents a motivating scenario that shows the need for a system that is both context-aware and adaptive. Section 5.4 sets out the general requirements that we would need for models and a framework that can support the development of context-aware adaptive software systems—in particular adaptive service compositions. It also addresses some of the challenges faced in the development of such systems. Section 5.5 describes the approach for specifying the context, functional and adaptation properties of the system using the ROAD framework which is a model-driven approach to creating decoupled context-aware adaptive service compositions. We show how this approach meets the requirements identified in Sect. 5.4. Section 5.6 discusses related work in terms of our characterisation of context aware and adaptive systems, with Section 7 concluding the chapter.

5.2 Adaptive Systems

In the past decade or so there has been extensive research into how to create software systems that can change themselves in response to their environment (e.g. Cheng et al. 2008; Bradbury et al. 2004; Patikirikorala et al. 2012). Common with all these approaches is their aim to achieve some *goal* related to the system in its environment through definition of some form of loop whereby the environment and/or the system itself is *monitored*, the information gathered is *analysed*, a *decision* is taken as to what change is needed in the system in response, and these changes are then *enacted* in the system. For example, IBM in their vision of computer systems that behave 'autonomically' called this feedback loop a MAPE-K loop (Monitor, Analyze, Plan and Execute using a shared Knowledge base) (Kephart and Chess. 2003).

In this section, we will give a very brief overview of approaches to adaptive software systems based on the categories defined in a control loop (goal, monitoring and analysing the environment, making and enacting decisions) and contrast these approaches to work on context-aware systems.

5.2.1 Goal of Adaptation

Adaptive systems have some degree of self-management, for example self-configuring, self-optimizing, self-healing, and self-protecting—so-called *self-** properties. As well as varying goals, the definition varies as to scope of the 'system' that needs to be self-managed. In the case of IBM's autonomic initiative, the elements are typically regarded as assets within enterprise computing environment (e.g. servers, databases, network infrastructure, etc.) in order to reduce the amount of manual intervention required when components in the system fail or need to be changed. Other work has looked at lower levels of abstraction such as the allocation of server resources to optimise for energy efficiency. For example, cloud infrastructure providers continually need to automatically monitor and adapt the efficient provisioning of resources as user-demand and availability of servers change. Yet other work is focused on the software level, in particular managing service compositions in order to achieve service level objectives, or the changing availability/performance of constituent elements. In this case the systems goals and associated rules reflect real-world business relationships between service consumers and providers.

In contrast, in context-aware systems the goal has been typically to enable an application to adjust to its context of use or task, potentially taking into account user preferences (Dey et al. 2001). This adaptation may be restricted to the user interface level only, or may impact on the configuration of the functional system.

5.2.2 Model of the Environment and Reflective Representation of the System

In much of the work on adaptive systems, the aim is to change the behaviour and/or structure of the system in order to keep some monitored variable in line with a goal. These are typically performance variables such as response time, throughput, or reliability; or alternatively resource consumption variables such as memory used or energy consumed. As such, for adaptive systems the environmental context-in-focus is the *execution context* of the software application rather than just the *domain context* of the user (location, time, social situation etc.).The execution context can typically be well defined in terms of resource parameters, performance parameters, deployment or network topology, etc. In practice, it is therefore rare to see context ontologies used in adaptive systems as the environment is well defined in terms of what parameters are measured. Context-aware systems on the other hand often need to model and reason about the "messy" and perhaps uncertain domain context of the real world user.

While many software systems including context-aware systems exhibit various degrees of ability to adapt themselves, adaptive systems need to maintain a reflective runtime model (Bencomo 2009) of their own structure and/or behavior (Cheng et al. 2008). This reflective representation is used to reason about and trigger changes in the system. The 'self-awareness' of such systems means that changes can often be handled automatically compared with conventional systems that require off-line re-design, implementation and redeployment. The level of granularity of these models can vary greatly, from the code level (e.g. Wang et al. 2004) through to high level architectures or service compositions (e.g. Colman and Han 2007). Software architectural models are a course-grained view of the system as a set of components and connectors. Such models assume a closed computing environment. Service-oriented architectures, on the other hand, operate in much more open environments where the components or services that the application relies upon are not necessarily under the control of one organization. Such service-oriented compositions rely on the dynamic binding of services that are 'self-describing' using standards such as the Web Services Description Language (WSDL). The relationships between these 'loosely-coupled' services therefore need to be actively managed as requirements and service provisioning changes. The form of representation of models also varies from formal control models that model behavior (e.g. Patikirikorala et al. 2012) to structural models (e.g. Magee and Kramer 1996) that can automatically be composed, to more informal declarative representations (e.g.Bradbury et al. 2004; Garlan et al. 2004).

Context-aware systems in contrast do not necessarily maintain an explicit reflective model of the system. Rather, the system will have a number of predefined modes which are selected depending on the state of the sensed context. As context-aware systems become more adaptive their reflective models need to become commensurately more sophisticated.

5.2.3   *Making and Enacting Decisions*

Given a representation of the system and its environmental context, the nature of
the control loop in adaptive systems also varies greatly between approaches, and
depends on whether the system's behaviour is being *regulated*, or its structure *re-
configured*, or both. *Regulatory control* focuses on changing the *behavior* of the
system assuming a fixed composition structure. Two predominant forms of regulatory control are control-theoretic and rule-based. *Control-theoretic* approaches create
formal mathematical models of the behavior of the system and aim to maintain the
system at some desired set-point in the face of environmental perturbations. Such
approaches predominantly use blackbox feedback control where the perturbations
are unmodelled and there is no explicit model of context (see Patikirikorala et al.
2012 for a comprehensive survey). *Rule-based regulation,* on the other hand, can
explicitly reference contextual variables in the form of rule conditions that regulate
interactions over the program or composition structure. Challenges for rule-based
regulation include ensuring consistency of the rule-base both in their definition and
in application, and ensuring that valid, non-oscillatory desirable behavior results
from the application of complex rules sets (Cheng et al. 2008; Mannaert et al. 2012).
Adaptive reconfiguration on the other hand focuses on maintaining a model of the
architectural structure of the system, i.e., how the system is composed from components or services. Component based approaches (e.g. Magee and Kramer 1996) focus
on the compatibility and controlled composition of required and provided interfaces
(sometimes through connector components), whereas service-based compositions
typically model a variable business process that manages two levels of indirection:
(i) the relationships between abstract services and (ii) the binding of concrete services to those abstract services. Some of the key concerns that these compositional
approaches need to address include ensuring the functional correctness of each architectural configuration; monitoring and analysing the relative performance of various
configurations; coping with change in components/services bound to the composition; and safely transitioning between configurations at runtime. While some simple
forms of reconfiguration control rely on selection of an appropriate configuration
from a predefined set, more truly adaptive systems use rules, tactics, strategies or
other planning techniques to enable effective change while ensuring that structural
and behavioral constraints are not violated. The autonomic vision of adaptive systems (Kephart and Chess 2003) sees such systems as recursive compositions of
self-managing systems that can communicate with each other on both functional and
management levels.

   In adaptive systems changes occur at runtime. These changes must be reflected
both in the system model and in the runtime application itself. Many approaches
use a model checking mechanisms to ensure any planned changes are consistent
and beneficial, before any of the planned changes are committed to the runtime
system. Changes in the runtime system (e.g. unavailability of a service) need to be
reflected back in the model so that appropriate decisions can be made. Mechanisms
are therefore required to keep the model and the runtime in sync. In contrast, the

number of states in context-aware systems is typically more limited with a set number of configurations as such system contains no reflective model that can be manipulated. As these configurations have been predetermined, their validity can be checked at design time. Decision-making is therefore often a matter of simple switching of modes based on some in-built logic.

Depending on the type of system, the "intelligence" required to make a control decision can either be built into the system itself (for example through either rule design or through some reinforcement learning mechanism), or can be exogenous to the system (Colman 2007; Colman and Han 2005). In the latter case the adaptive system only provides the runtime model of the flexible system and the mechanisms for adapting the system while the decision about *what* to adapt is made by others. Approaches such as (Garlan et al. 2004) and (Kapuruge et. al. 2014) do a combination of both.

5.2.4   *Engineering Context-Aware and Adaptive Systems*

It is clear from the above discussion that there is no sharp distinction between context-aware and adaptive systems. Both need to continually monitor their runtime context in order to make appropriate changes. It is also clear that adding context-awareness or adaptivity to a basic functional software system adds considerable complexity to the development task. Supporting the engineering of such systems with appropriate methodologies, architectures, frameworks and tools therefore becomes necessary. In context-aware systems, it has been long recognised that the acquisition and management of context should be treated as a separate concern from the underlying functional system (Dey et al. 2001; Henricksen and Indulska 2004). Likewise, adaptive software frameworks typically maintain the separation at both the conceptual and implementation levels between the management of the system and the system's functionality, albeit within the autonomic element (Colman 2007). Another common approach that assists the control of the complexity inherent in both context-aware and adaptive systems is to use model driven frameworks that enable such systems to be defined at a higher level of abstraction and then (semi-) automatically generated.

In this chapter we will show how adaptive systems, based on a rules-based declarative service-composition approach, can incorporate some of the more complex aspects of context apparent in context-aware systems. This approach maintains a separation between functional, management, and contextual requirements and is supported by a set of tools and framework that enables the ready development of context-aware adaptive service compositions.

In summary, the table below characterizes some of the prototypical differences between context-aware systems and adaptive systems. In Sect. 5.6 on related work we discuss the extent to which various adaptive and context-aware approaches take these characteristics into account.

	Context-aware systems	Adaptive systems
Goal	Present appropriate interface or functionality based on context of use. Abstraction at the application level	Maintain system objective in response to environmental perturbation or changing requirements. Abstraction possibly at many levels (application, network, resource, . . .)
Model and analysis of the environment/user	Complex model of the domain and user context. Need to reason about domain semantics and user preferences	Simple representation of the environment in the form of parameters in the domain environment or the software system infrastructure
Representation of the system	Operational view of the system modes	Explicit behavioural or structural model of the system
Decision making and enactment	Selection of pre-defined configuration modes based on rules and utility models	Tuning system operational parameters or altering composition of system structure based on (multiple) objectives
Engineering models and modularity	Separation of functional aspects from context acquisition	Separation of functional aspects from adaptation management

5.3   Motivating Scenario for CAAS

Let us consider a travel guide application service that composes a number of other services to create travel itineraries based on user preferences. These services provided both the functionality of the system (e.g. route planners, user profile services, etc.) and the *domain context* information the system needs in order to function (e.g. weather and traffic information, attraction finder services and so on). Even application-specific functions like the derivation of inferred context might be outsourced as a service. In this scenario all functionality is provided by services external to the composition. The role of the composition is to define a process that takes user requests (e.g. plan itinerary given a set of attraction-types, time available, preferred transport modes etc.), obtains relevant contextual information (e.g. weather and road conditions), sends this information to a service that recommends to the user a set of attractions, which on selection is sent to a route planning service that creates the final itinerary given the user's current location. This scenario of the service composition with its functional and context services is illustrated in Fig. 5.1.

This application needs to adapt in a couple of ways. Firstly, during runtime operation the composition needs to be aware of its *execution context*. In the case of a service-oriented system this includes the availability or otherwise of services it already knows about. For example, moving between regions the application may have to switch between alternative traffic information providers. This management capability might be realised by rules embedded in the composition, or the capability

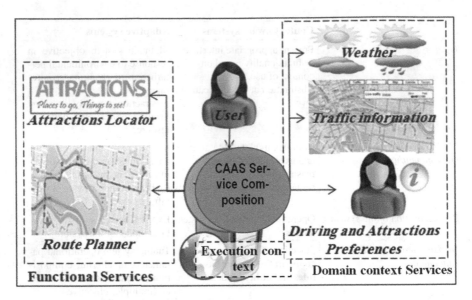

Fig. 5.1 Functional and context services

itself might be externalised in the service. Secondly, the provider of the travel guide
service wants to ensure that they can readily incorporate new *types* of service into
the composition (e.g. a transport disruptions service) without creating disruption to
users of the composite service. The composition needs to therefore be modifiable
without being taken off-line to go through another redesign/implementation-deploy
cycle.

5.4 Requirements for a CAAS Framework

The above scenario suggests a number of general requirements that need to be met
by any CAAS service composition framework. These include the ability to:

1. Mediate messages between functional services based on *domain context* information provided by context provider services.
2. Be able to alter the structure of the composition at runtime based on the *execution
   context*.
3. Be able to incorporate new types of behavior over a given structure by defining
   adaptable processes that can be changed at run time.
4. Readily incorporate not only new instances of services whose types are already
   known (service selection) but also incorporate new *types* of service (functional
   or context) into the composition without disruption to current process instances,
   and define the interactions between those new services and other services.

5. Incorporate new types of context information into the composition along with rules and make use of this information to mediate interactions or to handle changes in execution context.

As discussed in Sect. 5.2.4, given the complexity of CAAS systems, the engineering of such systems needs to be not only model-driven but maintain a reflective runtime model. On one hand, separation of concerns needs to be maintained between functional, context and management aspects while, on the other hand, facilitating the integration of these aspects into well-defined, deployable modules that have some degree of self-management.

5.5 A Model Driven Rules-based Approach to Implementing a CAAS Framework

To address the above requirements, in this chapter we propose a model-driven rules-based approach and framework for developing a CAAS applications. This approach is based on the clear separation between function, context, and management aspects as identified in Sect. 5.2, and incorporates these aspects into an integrated managed service composition. In a CAAS application, the structure and behaviour can be affected by not only changing state of the application but by changes in *domain* and *execution* contexts. What therefore is needed is a common format to represent this context information so that appropriate rules can be applied. To do this we adopt the event–condition–action (ECA) approach as:

- *Events* are generated as messages received by and passing through the composite. These messages can either be functional messages being mediated by the composite, or they may be messages indicating change of context which require updating of *facts* stored by the composite.
- *Conditions* are evaluated based on the stored facts. These facts can either be context acquired from external services, or be a reflection of the state of the process or composite itself.
- *Actions* arising from execution of rules can result in mediation of messages passing through the composite (e.g. message routing); generation of messages to services reflecting the state of the process or composite; generation of new facts either reflecting the internal state of the composite or its external context; firing of events which are then further evaluated by rules; automatic operational management actions (e.g. selection of an alternate to service based on availability); or generation of messages sent to management services/operators indicating need for re-configuration of the composite.

The following subsections describe how composite structure is defined, how the operational issues and adaptive behaviour is conditioned by context information, how this context information is acquired and provisioned, and how the development process is supported by a framework and tool chain.

Fig. 5.2 Functional
composite with domain
context providers

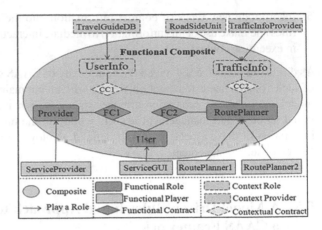

5.5.1 Composite Structure

To create the service composition that is both context aware and adaptive, we extend
our existing approach to creating adaptive service composites called ROAD (Role
Oriented Adaptive Design) (Colman and Han 2007; Kapuruge et al. 2011b). This
chapter will provide a very high level overview of the ROAD framework. A ROAD
composite structure is defined in XML along with associated rule files. These descriptions are deployed to a ROAD4WS container which contains a component called
ROADfactory that generates the run-time service. The interested reader is referred
to (Kapuruge et. al 2014; Kapuruge et al. 2012; Kapuruge et al. 2013a, 2004; Talib
et al. 2010; King and Colman 2009) for more details[1]. The purpose of this overview
is to show how context facts are acquired and how they are used in the operation and
adaptation of the service composite.

ROAD is based on an organisational paradigm which defines the service composite as a role structure. Roles represent an abstract service interfaces to which concrete
services ("role players") are dynamically bound (Kapuruge et al. 2011b). Role players can be functional services, context provider services, or management services.
Internally, the relationships between roles are represented by two types of contracts
(i.e. functional and contextual) which define permissible interactions between roles.
Figure 5.2 above illustrates a role structure based on our scenario with both external
functional and context provider services attached to the composite roles.

For example, a functional contract "FC2" exists between the user (role A) and
route planner (role B) roles as shown in Fig. 5.2. The contract has a set of permissible
interactions between the contracted roles as shown in Table 5.1. Each interaction has
(1) an identifier (e.g. i2); (2) an operation that needs to be performed by requesting
that interaction and the operation has a name (e.g. PlanRoutes2) and a set of input

---

[1] The ROAD schemas and framework can be viewed and downloaded from https://github.com/road-
framework.

Table 5.1 Part of the functional contract "FC2"

Functional Contract ID FC2: User_RoutePlanner
Parties: RoleA: User;   **RoleB**: RoutePlanner;
Interaction Clauses:
i1: {PlanRoute1 (Destination, CurrentLocation), AtoB, Routes};
i2: {PlantRoute2 (Destination, CurrentLocation, TrafficInformation), AtoB, Routes};
...

Table 5.2 The contextual contract "CC1"

Contextual Contract ID CC1: TrafficInfo_RoutePlanner
Parties:
Context Source: TrafficInfo;   **Context Consumer**: RoutePlanner;
Context Attributes:
a1:String: TrafficInformation;

parameters (e.g. destination, current location, and traffic information); (3) a direction to specify who is responsible for providing the operation included in that interaction; and (4) a return type (e.g. Routes).

Another type of contract is the contextual contract to define (represent) context information that is needed by the system roles (i.e. the context model). For example, the contract "CC1" shown in Table 5.2 specifies that the route planner role needs to know the live traffic information to calculate the routes effectively.

In addition to functional and context provider role interfaces, ROAD composites provide a management ("organiser") interface that allows the structure to be modified at run time. This interface provides a set of standard CRUD methods (a full list can be found in Appendix C of (Kapuruge et. al. 2014)) for monitoring and adapting the composite (e.g. adding and deleting roles and contracts, inject rules into contracts, etc.). Such methods enable the runtime adaptation of the context model by changing the system's contextual roles and contracts, and the system's functionality by adding, removing, and changing the functional services of the system (Hussein et al. 2013).

5.5.2 Operational Behaviour

Each composite has a global repository of facts (a "fact tuple space" or FTS). The FTS stores facts related to both the internal state of the composite *and* to any relevant execution or domain context acquired via context roles. The composite also contains a number of points on the role-contract-role path at which a message may be mediated. These points have rule evaluation mechanisms (implemented in Drools[2]) which evaluate patterns of events/facts stored in a local "working memory". Events

---

[2] http://www.jboss.org/drools/

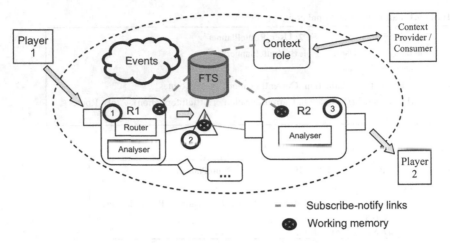

Fig. 5.3 Operational message flow

are triggered as messages pass through the composite. Facts in a working memory are obtained by it subscribing to relevant facts, including context facts, in the FTS. In the service composition behavioral mediation may be reactive (per message) or coordinated into a process. The flow of message through composite is illustrated in Fig. 5.3.

On receipt of a message at a role R1 ①, the message is transformed into the internal message format of the composite and routed to the relevant contract ②. This routing decision may be context dependent, for example a routing decision might depend on *execution-context* facts relating to the availability or loads on required services. A routing decision might be based on a *domain-context* rule that describes a particular user's preference for a service provider.

Likewise each contract contains a rule evaluation mechanism that can evaluate the messages against rules defined in the contract. These rules may be independent of context (e.g. is this type of message permissible) or maybe context-dependent (e.g. is the message permissable give the current location of the sender). Once the message has been processed by the contract it is passed to the outgoing role R2 ③ where it is transformed by the analyser object in that role to be sent to the player. This message transformation might (a) change the format/ordering of the message content and (b) incorporate extra information from other messages or facts from the FTS to make the message perceivable to the recipient.

Processes are implemented using Serendip (Kapuruge et al. 2012; Kapuruge et al. 2013b), which adds a coordination layer to the reactive message handling mechanisms of the ROAD framework. An example process is "plan route" shown in Fig. 5.4. Based on the live traffic information availability, a suitable route planning function is selected. Then, a set of routes are suggested to the user where she can select a route. In Serendip, processes can be viewed as event-process-chains (Kapuruge et al. 2013b) that compose units of behavior.

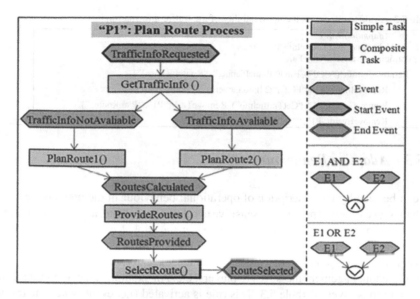

Fig. 5.4 An example behaviour process in the travel guide service

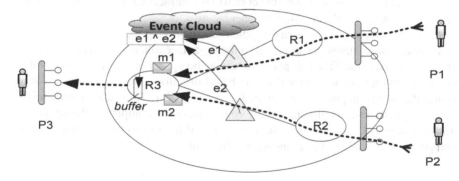

Fig. 5.5 Message coordination in an event driven process

At runtime, process instances are created from declarative process descriptions. The Serendip process engine enacts process instances in response to the events fed to the event-cloud. Typically, these events are published by the contracts into the event-cloud. Figure 5.5 illustrates a message being sent to a player P3 that requires prior receipt of messages from P1 and P2. Defining processes as a set of event-driven tasks with pre- and post-events not only makes the process much more readily adaptable but the evaluation of event conditions (e.g. $E1^{\wedge}E2$) readily enables context state to be included in those conditions.

Table 5.3 A rule to cope with the unavailability of the traffic information

Rule "AdaptationRule1": {
*When*ValueChanges (TrafficInfoAvailability);
*if*TrafficInfoAvailability == False;
*do*RemoveContract("CC2"), Bind("RoutePlanner", "RoutePlanner2"),
RemoveInteraction("FC2","i2"), RemoveRole("TrafficInfo"),
RemoveTask ("P1", "GetTrafficInfo"), RemoveTask("P1", "PlanRoute2"),
RemoveEvent("P1", "TrafficInfo Available")} ;

5.5.3   Adaptive Behaviour

As can be seen by the description of operational behaviour in the previous section, both message flow and process are sensitive to rules that evaluate, among other things, arbitrary context. Rules can also be defined at the global composite level which respond to anticipated changes in context to enact actions such as activation of role-player bindings, termination of a process instance, exception handling, generation of operational management messages to players, etc. An example adaptation rule from our scenario is given in Table 5.3. This rule is activated (i.e. event) when the traffic information is not available (i.e. condition). In response to this change, the service is adapted (i.e. action) by removing the contextual contract "CC2", binding the route planner role with the player "RoutePlanner2", etc.

For more complex decision-making potentially involving unanticipated situations, an external management player bound to the organizer role can subscribe to events and facts stored in the FTS. This player, who may be a program or a human controller, takes the appropriate adaptation decision based on information available, and then manipulates the composite as mentioned in section 5.5.1. This manipulation might be as simple as resetting the state of the system fact or as complex as the wholesale transformation of the composite structure. It is through this mechanism that the composite is also adapted to changing requirements.

5.5.4   Acquiring and Providing Context Information

Given that both operational and adaptive behavior can be conditioned by context information stored in the FTS, it remains to be described how such context information is acquired from external context providers. Or in the case where the composite self is a provider of context information to other services, how this information is made available to those services.

From an external point of view context roles and functional roles (as shown in Fig. 5.3 above) are identical. Both define provided and/or required service interfaces. The key differences between a context role and a functional role are that, firstly, context roles read and write from the FTS rather than passing a message to a functional contract. Secondly, the context role defines acquisition and provisioning regimes to either pull or push context information to the partner context provider/consumer service. These acquisition/provisioning regimes may be either periodic (e.g. update this context fact every 30 s) or event driven (e.g. notify this context consumer when this fact changes). It should be noted however that a single role can have both functional and context aspects given that its player may be sending/receiving both functional and context messages.

While it is possible to do some simple reasoning to derive/infer context using the rule mechanisms within the composite, a better strategy in terms of maintaining a clear separation of concerns and modularity of design is to externalise the reasoning about context to a separate computational entity/ service that is attached to the composite. Such entities subscribe to context facts using a standard context role, infer further facts from this information and return this derived context to the composite. Such inference might be as simple as calculating statistical information from facts obtained. More complex inference mechanisms using ontologies might also be implemented in such external entities, for example, inferring the situation (i.e. domain context) of a user based on facts about their interactions over the composite[3]. If this external entity is itself implemented as a ROAD composite then it can aggregate context information from multiple external sources.

5.5.5 Engineering CAAS Applications Using the ROAD Framework

Our approach has two main phases: development and runtime adaptation. The development phase is illustrated in Fig. 5.6. The service requirements are used for designing the service model using the ROADdesigner Eclipse plugin. The design transformed to an XML document and rules files following the ROAD schema. This model captures the service's functionality, context, and adaptive behavior. The service model is then transformed to an executable service using the ROADfactory component in ROAD4WS (Kapuruge 2011b; Kapuruge et al. 2013b). In particular, the generated runtime artifacts of the executable service are engineered to change at runtime (Step 2).

In the second phase, if there is a need to make unanticipated changes at runtime then the service's runtime model is adapted (Step 3). The differences between the running service's model and its adapted model are then computed. These differences are then used to generate a set of adaptation actions which are applied to the running composite service (Step 4). A more detailed description of this dynamic adaption process can be found in (Hussein et al. 2013).

The ROAD framework has applied in a number domains including adaptive business processes (Kapuruge et al. 2013b Kapuruge et al. 2011), personalised mobile phone call handling based on social context information obtained from social networks (Kabir et al. 2012) (see Chapter 19 of this book), context-aware access control

---

[3] See Chapter 19 "Socially-aware applications" for an example of such an approach.

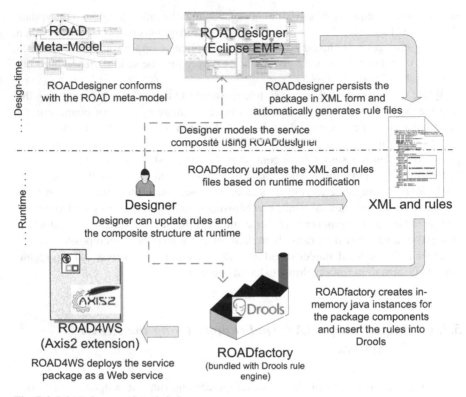

Fig. 5.6 ROAD framework tool chain

(Kayes et al. 2014), and multi-tenanted cloud applications (Kumara et al. 2013). Domain specific evaluations can be found in the above.

5.6 Related Work

A number of approaches support the development of context-aware adaptive software systems from self-adaptive and context-aware perspectives. In this section, we briefly analyze approaches in relation to the requirements we have identified.

Separation of Concerns   Existing approaches follow one of two ways for system modeling. Some separate system functionality from management but consider the context representation implicitly as found in self-adaptive systems research (Salehie and Tahvildari 2009). Other approaches have an explicit context representation but hard-code the system management with its functionality, as found in context-aware systems research (Baldauf et al. 2007). As such, they limit the system's runtime adaptation capability. In our approach, we separate the three aspects and keep them integrated from modeling to implementation and to runtime execution by capturing the system-context relationships explicitly (see Section 5). As such, we can clearly capture and manage the system model, the context model, and their relationships.

Runtime Changes of the Context Model   The context model needs to be changed at runtime to cope with unanticipated context changes such as new context information or changes in the number of context element instances unknown at design time, and to reduce the monitoring overhead by only selecting the context model elements that are needed by the functional system. Most of the existing approaches have only a design time context model (e.g. Bettini et al. 2010), and even those approaches that have a runtime context representation do not provide a method for dynamically managing the context model (Taconet et al. 2009; Sheng et al. 2009; Reichle et al. 2008). This makes it more difficult to deal with unanticipated runtime context changes. For example, in the MUSIC project (Rouvoy et al. 2009), the context model elements are represented at runtime and when an element is needed it is activated. But, they do not provide a method of managing the context model at the application level. Our approach has a runtime representation of the context model and its management (i.e. the organizer interface introduced in Section 5.1) enables its runtime changes.

Two Types of Contexts   There are two types of context information that need to be considered: (1) the *domain* context, which is the environment information that affects the system operation; (2) the *execution* context, which is the system states that the system management needs to know to initiate the adaptation process if needed. Current research considers either the domain context (Henricksen and Indulska 2004; Sheng et al. 2009; Gu et al. 2005; Mohyeldin et al. 2005; Serral et al. 2010), or the *execution* context (Garlan et al. 2004; Rouvoy et al. 2009). Our approach handles both in a generic and consistent way (see Section 5.2).

System-context Relationships   They can be classified into (1) operational relationships, where the system needs to know certain facts about its context to continue its operation; (2) management relationships, where the system needs to adapt itself in response to the context changes. Most of existing approaches consider these relationships implicitly (e.g. Garlan et al. 2004; Morin et al. 2009). Existing approaches do not maintain a runtime representation of the system-context relationships, and as such they cannot be changed at runtime. In our approach, we represent the two types of relationships explicitly and separately (as discussed in Sect. 5.1). Furthermore, we have a runtime representation of these relationships to enable their runtime change.

System realization   Many adaptive architectural approaches are based on dynamic component models that explicitly connect the required and provided functional interfaces of component (e.g. Acme Garlan et al. 1997, Darwin Magee et al. 1995). Any process is implicit in the behaviour of those components. In contrast, the approach described here provides an added level of indirection and mediation to the service composition. The downside of this mediated approach is that it requires message transformation that may be inherently more inefficient. The upside is that it allows a much greater the degree of flexibility in the definition of process and allows arbitrary mediators to be defined. In the case of ROAD this allows not only context and other business domain rules to be readily injected into the composition, but context acquisition and provisioning to be dynamically altered.

5.7 Conclusion

ROAD is an adaptive service composition framework that readily enables the incorporation of context information to facilitate both functional and management operations. It does this by providing mechanisms to acquire, record and provision a central store of 'facts' which are evaluated in rules that mediate operational messages or result in adaptations to the behavioral structure of the composite. These facts can include facts about the composite's domain and execution context.

Facts can be sourced either internally or from external context providers. The framework provides a standard way to generate role interfaces from declarative descriptions that can be injected dynamically into the composite. These interfaces can be for functional, context or management services. It also provides a way to inject new fact types and rules to adapt the behavior of the composite at run time.

This approach assists in the development of CAAS applications that integrate the explicit/sophisticated/separate context models of context aware system with the ability of adaptive systems to manage unanticipated change in their environments and requirements.

References

Baldauf, M. et al.: A survey on context-aware systems. Int. J. Ad. Hoc. Ubiquitous. Comput. **2**, 263–277 (2007)

Bencomo, N.: On the use of software models during software execution. In: Proceedings of the 2009 ICSE Workshop on Modeling in Software Engineering, pp. 62–67. IEEE Computer Society, Washington DC (2009)

Bettini, C. et al.: A survey of context modelling and reasoning techniques. Pervasive Mob. Comput. **6**, 161–180 (2010)

Bradbury, J.S. et al.: A survey of self-management in dynamic software architecture specifications. In: Proceedings of the 1st ACM SIGSOFT Workshop on Self-Managed Systems, Newport Beach, CA. ACM, New York (2004)

Chen, H., Finin, T., Joshi A.: An ontology for context-aware pervasive computing environments. Knowl. Eng. Rev. **18**(3), 197–207 (2003)

Cheng, B.H.C. et al.: Software engineering for self-adaptive systems: a research road map. In: Software Engineering for Self-Adaptive Systems. Schloss Dagstuhl—Leibniz-Zentrum fuer Informatik, Dagstuhl, Germany (2008)

Colman, A.: Exogenous management in autonomic service compositions. In: Proceedings of the Third International Conference on Autonomic and Autonomous Systems 2007 (ICAS 2007). IEEE Computer Society Press, Athens (2007)

Colman, A., Han J.: On the autonomy of software entities and modes of organisation. In: Proceedings of the 1st International Workshop on Coordination and Organisation (CoOrg 2005), Namur, Belgium (2005)

Colman, A., Han J.: Using Role-based Coordination to Achieve Software Adaptability. Sci. Comput. Program. **64**(2), pp. 223–245 (2007)

Dey, A.K., Abowd G.D., Salber D.: A Conceptual Framework and a Toolkit for Supporting the Rapid Prototyping of Context-Aware Applications. Hum. Comput. Interact. **16**(2–4), 97–166 (2001)

Garlan, D., Monroe R., Wile D.: Acme: an architecture description interchange language. In: Proceedings of the 1997 conference of the Centre for Advanced Studies on Collaborative research, p. 7. IBM Press, Toronto (1997)

Garlan, D. et al.: Rainbow: architecture-based self-adaptation with reusable infrastructure. Computer 37, 46–54 (2004)

Gu T.: A service-oriented middleware for building context-aware services. J. Netw. Comput. Appl. 28, 1–18 (2005)

Henricksen, K., Indulska J.: A software engineering framework for context-aware pervasive computing. In: The Second IEEE Annual Conference on Pervasive Computing and Communications (PERCOM 2004). IEEE Press, New York (2004)

Hussein, M., Han, J., Yu, J., Colman, A.: An approach to model-based development of context-aware adaptive systems. In: Proceedings of the 2011 IEEE 35th Annual Computer Software and Applications Conference (2011)

Hussein, M., Han, J., Yu, J.; Colman, A.: Enabling runtime evolution of context-aware adaptive services. In 10th International Conference on Services Computing (SCC), pp. 248–255. IEEE, Santa Clara (2013)

Kabir, M.A., Han, J., Yu, J., Colman, A.: SCIMS: a social context information management system for socially-aware applications. In: Ralyté, J., Franch, X., Brinkkemper, S., Wrycza, S. (ed.) Advanced Information Systems Engineering. Lecture Notes in Computer Science, vol. 7328, pp. 301–317 (2012)

Kapuruge, M., Han, J., Colman, A. "Service Orchestration as Organization;; Morgan Kaufmann (2014)

Kapuruge, M., Colman A., Han J.: Achieving multi-tenanted business processes in SaaS applications. In: Web Information System Engineering (WISE). Springer, Sydney (2011a)

Kapuruge, M., Colman A., King J.: ROAD4WS—extending Apache Axis2 for adaptive service compositions. In: IEEE International Conference on Enterprise Distributed Object Computing (EDOC). IEEE Computer Soc. Helsinki (2011b)

Kapuruge, M., Han J., Colman A.: Representing service-relationships as first class entities in service orchestrations. In: International Conference on Web Information System Engineering (WISE), Cyprus. Springer, Berlin (2012)

Kapuruge, M. et al.: Enabling ad-hoc adaptations through event-driven task decoupling. In: International Conference on Advanced Information Systems Engineering (CAiSE). Springer, Valencia (2013a)

Kapuruge, M. et al.: ROAD4SaaS: scalable business service-based SaaS Applications, In: Salinesi, C., Norrie, M., Pastor, Ó. (eds.), Advanced Information Systems Engineering, pp. 338–352. Springer, Berlin (2013b)

Kayes, A.S.M., Jun H., Colman A.: A context-aware access control framework for software services. In: Alessio Lomuscio S.N., Patrizi F., Benatallah B., Brandi I. (eds.) Lecture Notes in Computer Science: International Conference on Service-oriented Computing (ICSOC), pp. 569–577. Springer, Cham (2014)

Kephart, J.O., Chess, D.M.: The vision of autonomic computing. Computer. 36(1), 41–50 (2003)

King, J. Colman, A: A multi faceted management interface for web services. Australian software engineering conference, pp. 191–199. IEEE Computer Society, Los Alamitos (2009)

Kumara, I. et al.: Sharing with a Difference: realizing service-based SaaS applications with runtime sharing and variation in dynamic software product lines. In: Proceedings of the 2013 IEEE International Conference on Services Computing, pp. 567–574. IEEE Computer Society, Los Alamitos (2013)

Magee, J., Kramer, J.: Dynamic structure in software architectures. In: Proceedings of the 4th ACM SIGSOFT Symposium on Foundations of Software Engineering, pp. 3–14. ACM Press, San Francisco (1996)

Magee, J. et al.: Specifying distributed software architectures. Software Engineering—ESEC'95, pp. 137–153. Springer, London (1995)

Mannaert, H., Jan, V., Kris V, Towards evolvable software architectures based on systems theoretic stability. Softw. Pract. Exp. **42**(1) 89–116 (2012)

Mohyeldin, E. et. al.: A generic framework for context aware and adaptation behaviour of reconfigurable systems. In: Personal, Indoor and Mobile Radio Communications (PIMRC), pp. 1957–1963. IEEE, Piscataway (2005)

Morin, B. et. al.: Taming dynamically adaptive systems using models and aspects. In: Proceedings of the 31st International Conference on Software Engineering (2009)

Nierstrasz, O., Denker M., Renggli L.: Model-centric, context-aware software adaptation. Softw. Eng. Self-Adapt. Syst. **5525**, 128–145 (2009)

Patikirikorala, T. et al : A systematic survey on the design of self-adaptive software systems using control engineering approaches. In: Proceedings of the 7th International Symposium on Software Engineering for Adaptive and Self-Managing Systems, Zurich, Switzerland, 04–05 June 2012, pp. 33–42 (2012)

Ranganathan, A. et al.: Use of Ontologies in a Pervasive Computing Environment. Knowl. Eng. Rev. **18**(3), 209–220 (2003)

Reichle, R. et. al.: A comprehensive context modeling framework for pervasive computing systems. In: Meier, R., Terzis, S. (eds.) Distributed Applications and Interoperable Systems. Lecture Notes in Computer Science, vol. **5053**, pp. 281–295. (2008)

Rouvoy, R.: MUSIC: middleware support for self-adaptation in ubiquitous and service-oriented environments. In: Cheng, B.H.C., de Lemos, R., Giese, H., Inverardi, P., Magee, J. (eds.) Software Engineering for Self-Adaptive Systems, pp. 164–182. Springer, Berlin (2009)

Salehie, M., Tahvildari, L.: Self-adaptive software: landscape and landscape and research challenges. ACM Trans. Auton. Adapt. Syst. **4**, 1–42 (2009)

Serral, E. et al.: Towards the model driven development of contextaware pervasive systems. Pervasive Mob. Comput. **6**, 254–280 (2010)

Sheng, Q.Z. et al.: ContextServ: A platform for rapid and flexible development of context-aware Web services. In: Proceedings of the 31st International Conference on Software Engineering. (2009)

Taconet, C., et al.: CA3M: a runtime model and a middleware for dynamic context management. In: Proceedings of the Confederated International Conferences, CoopIS, DOA, IS, and ODBASE. Vilamoura, Portugal (2009)

Talib, M.A. et al.: A service packaging platform for delivering services. In: IEEE International Conference on Services Computing (SCC), pp. 202–209. IEEE Computer Society, Los Alamitos. (2010)

Wang, X.H. et al.: Ontology based context modeling and reasoning using OWL. In: Proceedings of the Second IEEE Annual Conference on Pervasive Computing and Communications Workshops (PERCOMW'04). IEEE, Orlando (2004)

Chapter 6
Context-Aware Middleware: A Review

Hamed Vahdat-Nejad

Abstract Over past years several studies have introduced the concept of "context-aware middleware", and also proposed solutions under this title; however, these systems are different in functionality. In this chapter, context-aware middleware is investigated from the standpoint of functional and non-functional requirements. Afterward, some well-known middleware systems are reviewed and, finally, open research directions as well as concluding remarks are presented.

6.1 Introduction

Context-aware applications have been considered as the building blocks of the pervasive computing paradigm. The main challenge involved with implementing a context-aware application is discovering and obtaining reliable contextual information from the environment. Designing and implementing a stand-alone context-aware application is a lengthy and sophisticated process, suffering from the following issues:

- The design and development procedure takes an excessive amount of time and cost.
- A majority of context-aware applications reside on devices with limited memory, computation, and communication capabilities such as mobile phone, PDA, tablet, and wearable computer. Hence, it is not reasonable to execute a massive program on them.

As a result, a research direction which spans design and deployment of a supporting system for developing context-aware applications has arisen. These systems, which are generally referred to as middleware, have been investigated under different titles including context acquisition and dissemination (Roussaki et al. 2010), distribution (Bellavista et al. 2013), management (Liao et al. 2004), toolkit (Dey et al. 2001)

H. Vahdat-Nejad (✉)
Pervasive and Cloud Computing Lab, Department of Computer Engineering,
University of Birjand, Birjand, Iran
e-mail: vahdatnejad@birjand.ac.ir; vahdatnejad@gmail.com

© Springer Science+Business Media New York 2014
P. Brézillon, A. J. Gonzalez (eds.), *Context in Computing*,
DOI 10.1007/978-1-4939-1887-4_6

83

and even engine (Carrizo et al. 2008). There are several reasons for the necessity of introducing middleware in pervasive systems:

- The Infrastructure of pervasive computing consists of many non-dedicated devices as well as sensors with limitations in memory, storage, computation and availability. Managing the vast number of devices and sensors and storing and processing the enormous volume of generated contextual data require extensive system support.
- In an environment with a variety of context-aware applications, many of single context elements are needed by different applications; each programmer may develop context provider software components for obtaining their required sophisticated context types. Therefore, designing stand-alone context-aware applications is inefficient in terms of reusability criterion.
- From the initial categorization of context types a decade ago, new dimensions of context have arisen such as social and urban context. Furthermore, context reasoning, mining and other techniques have led to the emergence of new sophisticated context types. These remarks motivate the design of an open cooperative system in which different entities could introduce new context elements and share their derived and estimated values.
- Finding and composing available context-aware services is difficult for application developers and needs system support (Raychoudhury et al. 2013).

In general, middleware is a software layer, which by residing between the operating system and the application layer in each node, provides new capabilities and facilitates the development of applications. Utilizing middleware leads to the design of well-architected distributed systems (Edwards et al. 2002). However, a middleware platform for pervasive computing or in particular, context-aware middleware, is different in certain aspects from traditional middleware in distributed systems.

To continue, Sect. 6.2 provides requirements of context-aware middleware. Sect. 6.3 is dedicated to surveying some well-known proposals for context-aware middleware, and finally, Sect. 6.4 discusses open research directions and concludes the chapter.

6.2 Requirements of Context-Aware Middleware

In general, requirements of a middleware platform are of two types (Loughran et al. 2005): (1) functional, which involves tasks that should be performed by the middleware, and (2) non-functional, which consists of the quality attributes (such as performance, availability, usability, extensibility, etc), which should be satisfied by the system. In the following subsections, functional and non-functional requirements of a general context-aware middleware are discussed.

6.2.1 Functional Requirements

Context-aware middleware should generally address the following functional requirements:

Context Acquisition Middleware should be able to discover context sources available in the environment. Usually, context-aware middleware systems provide registration mechanisms for context sources to declare their contextual capacities. Because most sensors and devices have a limited storage memory, it is the duty of middleware to gather and store contextual data.

Aggregation In wireless sensor networks, a diverse range of sensors produce a large amount of raw data. However, they aim to provide a few high-level pieces of contextual information. For example, numerous sensors may be set up inside a jungle to collaboratively detect fires and floods. Storing all these raw contextual data is not reasonable. Instead, context aggregation is utilized to obtain low-volume meaningful information for storage and transmission.

Quality of Context (QoC) Assessment Context is inaccurate and uncertain because of three aspects: inaccuracy of sensors, inaccuracy of reasoning algorithms, and dynamic and temporal nature of context. On the other hand, diverse applications require different levels of quality for their contextual needs. Inaccurate or unreliable values of context may result in serious problems for example, for applications available in the pervasive healthcare or elderly-care domain. In general, many applications need a specific minimum level of quality for their contextual requirements, with respect to which the context, produced by heterogeneous sources all over the environment, should be evaluated. Quality of context deals with assessing and measuring quality of a context element against application requirements. Besides, sometimes there is more than one source for a single context element and their provided values are different. In this case, middleware is responsible for resolving this conflict. Finally, the recently introduced "context provenance" (Riboni and Bettini 2012) notion, which consists of mechanisms for tracking the origin of context, lies in this part. Provenance can be used for assessing quality and reliability of context.

Modeling Raw contextual data produced by sources (e.g. sensors) should be modeled and transformed to meaningful information to be usable by applications. Because context (e.g. a moving person) involves multi-dimensional time series data, traditional approaches like key/value are not effective for modeling. Many prior studies have been performed on context modeling (Bettini et al. 2010). Main approaches to context modeling are object-role based, spatial models and ontology-based approaches (Bettini et al. 2010).

Reasoning Sensors can only measure simple context types. It is not possible to directly measure a high-level context such as activity or fall of a person through a sensor. In these situations, a reasoning component is exploited to derive the high-level context type from low-level ones.

Context Dissemination Interaction between context-aware middleware and applications is performed via context dissemination mechanism. In fact, a context-aware application uses context dissemination mechanism provided by the middleware to obtain its required context. Context dissemination mainly involves event-driven and query-based approaches. In the event-driven approach, when an event (context update) occurs, middleware publishes the new value to the interested applications. In the query-based approach, middleware provides a query-based language for disseminating contextual information.

Service Management In a smart environment, diverse types of basic services exist. A service can be a software/hardware service for controlling a device (such as starting fire alarm, showing daily news on the screen), or a basic context-aware service (such as turning off lights in a building after everyone has left for the day), or even a complex context-aware application. Application developers usually search for these miniature service components and try to build their context-aware applications by composing suitable available services. Context-aware middleware should provide the functionality for service discovery and composition. Directory-based and DHT-based approaches are popular for service discovery.

Privacy Protection Many of context types characterizing users are considered as private information by themselves and should not be openly disclosed (Hong and Landay 2004). However, a major part of context-aware applications rely on user's private information such as location, activity, health status, etc. The system should follow the policies of users when distributing their context among context-aware applications. Access control is widely used for protecting user's contextual information from unauthorized parties. Pseudo-nymity and anonymity (Beresford and Stajano 2003) are other solutions for privacy protection. In the first, users change their pseudonyms regularly to hide their identity. In the latter, for general location-based services users anonymously request for service.

6.2.2 Non-Functional Requirements

Each non-functional requirement is associated with a software quality attribute. In the IEEE scientific expressions definition (Recommended Practice for Architectural Description 2000), quality is the "degree of which the system satisfies requirements of its users". Quality attributes are the factors and parameters that influence overall quality of software. Each system is constructed to satisfy specific quality attributes, where many of these attributes such as usability are generally important for all systems. In this subsection, we focus on specific quality attributes that should be considered in the design stage of a context-aware middleware system:

Expandability A typical pervasive computing environment consists of several domains. Typically, the number of domains increases, by joining other homes, offices, organizations, hospitals, urban, social, and user personal domains, during the runtime of the system. Furthermore, over time, new entities and context types are introduced. Therefore, middleware should be expandable from the viewpoint of domain, entity, and context.

Transparency   Context-aware middleware should provide transparency for user's usage. Users typically interact with the middleware by utilizing context dissemination mechanisms. As a result, context dissemination should be transparent from two aspects: access and location. Context is provided and preprocessed by diverse programs, which are implemented using different languages, and residing on various platforms (e.g. mobile phone and Android OS, PC and Windows OS). Access transparency means that the programmer should utilize a common service, API or method for retrieving any of the context types. Location transparency indicates that the middleware should provide requested contextual information from anywhere (domain, server, etc) inside the environment without bothering the user with the location of the context provider, store, server, etc.

Reusability   Users normally develop software modules to acquire implicit and high-level contextual information. However, these modules may be needed by a diverse range of programmers. Another kind of reusability is concerned with sharing context-aware service components implemented by application programmers. Context-aware middleware should provide an open framework for facilitating component reuse and share between programmers. Providing a uniform understandability of the components and a systematic strategy for component retrieval are the most important challenges that the middleware should overcome to realize component reusability.

Reliability   Pervasive computing aims to help users in their daily tasks by offering everywhere every time services. Incorrect, inaccurate, early, and overdue services devastate the trust of the users in the system. According to the domain and aim of the middleware, different degrees of reliability are required. For some application domains, such as healthcare and collision avoidance in context-aware transportation systems, reliability is regarded as a critical factor. For example, an overdue detection of a person fall or an accident may result in loss of life.

6.3   A Survey on Context-Aware Middleware Systems

In this section, we review some well-known context-aware middleware systems. For this, at first a framework for systematically studying the projects is provided. Then in the subsequent subsections, results of reviewing each project are discussed according to the framework.

6.3.1   Reviewing Framework

We review middleware systems from the standpoint of three aspects:

- *Overview*: From this viewpoint, we review the scope of the assumed environment of each project and structure of their middleware system.

Table 6.1 Overview of the projects

Project	Scope of environment	Description	Structure
Context Toolkit	Single-domain	General	Centralized
Gaia	Multiple-domain	Active space involving homes, Offices, and meeting rooms	Centralized
Cobra	Single-domain	Meeting room	Centralized
SOCAM	Single-domain	Smart home	Centralized
Awareness	Multiple-domain	Mobile, home, office, and ad-hoc	Distributed
SM4ALL	Single-domain	Smart home	Centralized
Feel@home	Multiple-domain	Home, office, and outdoor	Hierarchal
CAMEO	Single-domain	Mobile domain	Distributed

- *Functional tasks*: Each middleware system supports some of the functional requirements that have been stated in the previous section.
- *Non-functional attributes*: Each middleware system satisfies some of the non-functional requirements that have been stated in the previous section.

From many projects related to context-aware middleware, we survey some well-known research studies including Context Toolkit (Dey et al. 2001), Gaia (Román et al. 2002), Cobra (Chen et al. 2004), SOCAM (Gu et al. 2005), Awareness (Pawar et al. 2009), SM4ALL (Baldoni et al. 2009), Feel@home (Guo et al. 2010), Open (Guo et al. 2011), and CAMEO (Arnabold et al. 2014).

6.3.2 Overview

Scope of the environment Context Toolkit, Cobra, SOCAM, SM4ALL, and CAMEO investigate a single-domain pervasive environment. Context Toolkit assumes a general domain, but Cobra, SOCAM and SM4ALL consider a specific domain. Cobra is proposed for a meeting room. SOCAM and SM4ALL propose middleware for smart home domain. CAMEO investigates the mobile domain in which every user holds a mobile phone.

Among multiple-domain projects, Gaia assumes an active space, which consists of homes, offices, and meeting rooms. Awareness assumes four domains: mobile, home, office, and ad-hoc, and Feel@home initially considers three domains: home, office, and outdoor. Table 6.1 summarizes scope of these middleware systems.

Architecture structure Structure of middleware architecture could be centralized, flat distributed, or hierarchal. Context toolkit is based on a central main component known as discoverer; therefore, the architecture of the middleware is centralized. Gaia is based on central context service component, which is responsible for the main context management tasks. Cobra is based on multi-agent systems, in which a central context broker is responsible for context management tasks and is regarded as the main component of the system. SOCAM's main component is service locating service, which is designed centrally. In the Awareness project, the architecture of the middleware of the mobile, home and office domains is centralized and the architecture of the middleware of the ad-hoc environment is peer to peer; however, bridges make a flat distributed architecture for the overall middleware. SM4ALL makes use of several central registries involving processor registry, context type registry and publisher registry. Feel@home utilizes a hierarchical architecture in which GAS is the vertex, and domain context managers are the branches. CAMEO is designed as a single software package, which is distributed on user's mobile phones. The mobile phones use peer-to-peer paradigm for communication.

6.3.3   Functional Tasks

In this subsection, we look through the context-aware middleware systems from the viewpoint of their functional capabilities. At the end, summary of the investigation is presented via Table 6.2.

Context Acquisition   Context Toolkit is based on context widgets. Each widget is a software component responsible for gathering a specific context type from sensors. Widgets register themselves to the discoverer component in order to declare their contextual capacities. Widgets store sensed context and can provide a history of them to the interested entities. In Gaia, the context service uses a registry component, for context discovery. The registry maintains the information about all context sources in the environment. In Cobra, Context source discovery is accomplished via sensing the presence of Bluetooth MAC addresses. It then stores XML-based contextual information in a relational database. In SOCAM, Context providers gather raw contextual data from sources. There is one logical context database in each domain, which stores a history of contextual information of that domain. The service locating component plays the role of context discovery by providing a mechanism for context providers and interpreters to advertise their contextual capacities. The mechanism needs context providers to be registered into a service registry. Awareness utilizes registration service for context source discovery. For this, context producers are required to register themselves to the context broker components. Awareness partially supports context storage by introducing context storage engine. Such an engine could subscribe to some context producers and store published context. In SM4ALL, each sensor has a wrapper, which serves as a context provider by representing the device as a web service. The wrappers register themselves to the Publisher Registry (discovery). Storage is supported by introducing context persistence as an optional plug-in. In Feel@home, Context Wrappers gather raw data from sources and send it to the context aggregator, which in turn triggers JENA operations to store it. CAMEO introduces Device Context Provider, which is in charge of collecting context data derived from internal components of the mobile phone. It also supports storage by introducing history as an enrichment parameter for context elements.

Table 6.2 Summary of Functional requirements

		Context Toolkit	Gaia	Cobra	SOCAM	Awareness	SM4ALL	Feel@home Open	CAMEO
Acquisition	Discovery	✓✓	✓	✓	✓	✓	✓	✓	✓
	Storage	✓	×	✓	✓	✓	✓	✓	✓
Aggregation in WSN		×	×	×	×	×	✓	×	×
QoC	QoC assessment	×	×	×	×	✓	✓	×	✓
	Conflict resolution	×	×	✓	✓	✓	✓	×	×
Modeling		✓	✓	✓	✓	✓	✓	✓	✓
Reasoning		×	✓	✓	✓	✓	✓	✓	✓
Dissemination		✓	✓	×	✓	✓	✓	✓	✓
Service management		×	×	×	×	×	×	✓	×
Privacy protection		×	×	✓	×	✓	✓	✓	×

Aggregation   Among the surveyed projects, only SM4ALL supports aggregating low-level context types over a long period by introducing various types of context processing paradigms. Summarization and aggregation are among them. In the summarization paradigm, a specific context type is gathered over a period and summarized into a single value, e.g. the power usage of a fridge for each hour. Aggregation pattern gathers some low-level contextual information and infers and aggregates it to a single high-level context element. The hybrid of summarization and aggregation is utilized for aggregating raw contextual data generated by several sensors over a time interval. An example is gathering data of several sensors, which are monitoring health status of a person, and publishing a periodic high-level context- "User Healthy".

Quality of Context Assessment   Among the projects, Awareness and SM4ALL provide functions for assessing QoC. In general, Awareness exploits the parameters of freshness, spatial resolution, temporal resolution and probability of correctness for assessing QoC. In SM4ALL, QoC has been considered as an optional attribute to all context types. It consists of three metrics: freshness, trust-worthiness, and precision. On the other hand, QoC evaluator is designed as an optional plug-in. CAMEO supports QoC by enriching the context model by several quality parameters including accuracy, freshness, cardinality, and dependencies between fact types.

Cobra and SOCAM only perform a kind of conflict resolution without assessing QoC. In Cobra, a kind of simple conflict resolution is performed by the context broker via detecting and resolving inconsistent knowledge stored in the shared context model (Chen et al. 2004). In SOCAM, the Context interpreter component, which involves a context Knowledge Base (KB), is responsible for performing conflict resolution by maintaining the consistency of context Knowledge Base and resolving conflicts.

Modeling   Context Toolkit makes use of an object-oriented modeling scheme, which is performed by widgets. In Gaia, context modeling is based on first order logic and Boolean algebra. A 4-ary predicate structure is adopted from simple English clauses to represent context. Cobra makes use of RDF for modeling and representing context. In SOCAM Context providers perform modeling using Web Ontology Language (OWL). There is one logical context database in each domain, which stores context ontologies of that domain. In Awareness, local middleware of domains provides different mechanisms for context modeling. In SM4ALL, a central Context Type component is responsible for context modeling. It makes use of an object-oriented scheme, which declares a unique name and list of attributes for each context type. In Feel@home, Context Wrappers perform modeling by transforming the obtained raw data into context markups. CAMEO makes use of Context Modeling Language (CML) as an extension of the object-role-based model. It provides formal representation for denoting object types and fact types. A fact type denotes a relationship between two object types.

Reasoning   Gaia supports limited context reasoning by using first order logic and Boolean algebra. Cobra utilizes OWL and rule-based inference for reasoning about high-level contextual information. In SOCAM the Context interpreter also involves reasoner component, which is responsible for deducing high-level context using logic reasoning. In Awareness context reasoning is performed by distributed context reasoners, which acquire low-level contextual information from various context producers and infer high-level contextual information. In SM4ALL aggregation pattern also plays the role of context reasoning by gathering some low-level contextual information and inferring it to a single high-level context element. Feel@home provides JENA component, which is based on the Jena Semantic Web package and OWL. It provides an inference engine that can infer high-level context. CAMEO makes use of CML reasoning technique, which is based on three valued logic.

Context Dissemination Context Toolkit provides a query-based mechanism for context dissemination. A context-aware application should query the discoverer to find the widget associated to the required context, and then should interact directly with the widget for subscribing to the context. In Gaia the context service provides a query-based dissemination approach for applications to query and register for their required context types. Cobra does not provide any context dissemination mechanism for independent context-aware applications. In SOCAM context dissemination is performed by service locating component via providing query mechanism for context-aware applications. Afterward, the context-aware applications find the context providers that present their contextual needs. Subsequently, they can directly obtain the required context via either query or event-driven (pull or push based) approaches. Awareness makes use of query and subscription approaches for context dissemination. In SM4ALL, context-aware applications acquire contextual needs by using context listeners. Each listener is associated with a context query and listens to the notifications of the middleware (dissemination). Feel@home utilizes publish-subscription paradigm for intra-domain context dissemination and query approach for global context dissemination. In CAMEO, each application should register to the middleware by specifying its required context element. During the registration, a unique identifier is assigned to the application. Afterwards, the middleware is responsible for notifying the application of context changes. In addition, CAMEO provides an application programming interface towards mobile social network applications. CAMEO also introduces the beaconing module, which implements periodical context exchange among one-hop neighbors.

Service Management Among the surveyed projects, only Open (Extension of Feel@home) supports service management. In the Open framework, a programming toolkit is provided, which supports three programming modes: incremental mode, composition mode, and parameterization mode. Several types of service sharing are supported by the toolkit. For this, applications are generally assumed to be composed of two parts: inference rules and actions. The incremental and composition mode allow using previously available inference rules for developing new context-aware applications. In the parameterization mode users utilize previously available applications by specifying new parameter values. Each developer introduces its developed inference rule or application as well as required parameters and publishes it to the resource-sharing module. Open provides keyword search and browsing for discovery of previously published inference rules.

Privacy protection Cobra involves policy-management module, which is responsible for considering user's policies when disseminating their contextual information. Awareness protects privacy of users by following and applying their policies in distributing their contextual information. In SM4ALL, each sensor has a wrapper, which implements access control. Privacy protection has been performed by designing "authorization" as an optional attribute to all context types. It enumerates services that are allowed to access a sensitive context type. In Feel@home, each domain context manager server involves a local access control component, which analyzes context requests against user privacy settings.

6.3.4 Non-Functional Attributes

In the following, middleware systems are analyzed for how well each satisfies the quality attributes. At the end, the result of surveying is summarized via Table 6.3:

Expandability None of the surveyed projects supports introducing a new domain to the environment; however, most of them support entity and context introduction. In Context Toolkit, discoverer provides a service for registering context widgets, interpreters and aggregators. This service supports expanding the environment by inserting new context types and entities. Similarly, SOCAM offers context provider and interpreter registration mechanisms. In the Awareness project, it is possible to introduce new entities and context types by registering new context producers. SM4ALL provides context type registration service for inserting new context types. It also provides publisher registry for introducing new context providers. CAMEO provides application registration service, which involves introduction of the application context types.

Transparency Transparency is considered from two aspects: access and location. In Context Toolkit, applications retrieve their contextual needs in two stages: At first, they issue a query to the discoverer to acquire handle to the widget and then subscribe for the context. This scheme is transparent from both of the aspects. SOCAM provides a uniform query mechanism for context retrieval. After receiving a query, the service locating server performs a semantic matchmaking and returns the reference to the corresponding context provider or interpreter. This scheme is transparent from both of the standpoints. In Awareness, different local context-aware middleware systems utilize different kinds of operators and syntaxes for context dissemination; however, bridges convert these mechanisms to each other. Therefore, users are unaware of this heterogeneity and make use of a uniform operator for context retrieval. Moreover, bridges roughly hide the difference of locations that the contextual information has come from. SM4ALL supports a general structure for queries and users acquire contextual needs by associating a listener to a query for a single context element. The approach is transparent from both of the aspects. Feel@home uses the same query mechanism for retrieving all global contextual information and does not need users to specify domain of the context; therefore, global query mechanism for context

Table 6.3 Summary of quality attributes

		Context Toolkit	Gaia	Cobra	SOCAM	Awareness	SM4ALL	Feel@home Open	CAMEO
Expandability	Domain	×	×	×	×	×	×	×	×
	Entity-context	✓	×	×	✓	✓	✓	–	✓
Transparency	Access	✓	–	–	✓	✓	✓	✓	✓
	Location	✓	–	–	✓	✓	✓	✓	✓
Reusability	Context providing components	✓	×	×	✓	✓	✓	–	✓
	Service components	×	×	×	×	×	×	✓	×
Reliability		×	✓	×	×	×	×	×	×

dissemination is transparent from both of the aspects. CAMEO provides uniform APIs to users, which are transparent from both of the aspects.

Reusability Reusability is investigated from two viewpoints: (1) Reusability of context provider (sensing, reasoning, mining, etc) components. (2) Reusability of context-aware service components. Among the surveyed projects only Open framework supports reusability of service components by supporting reusability of inference rule components among application developers. Context Toolkit supports reusability of context provider components through introducing widget concept. SO-CAM also supports context provider and interpreter reusability. By introducing the notion of context producer, Awareness supports reusability of context producer components. SM4ALL provides context processors (for aggregation, reasoning, etc) reusability by supporting registration of them to the context processor registry. It also supports context provider components reusability by registering them to the publisher registry. CAMEO also supports reusability of context provider by introducing Device Context Provider, which is in charge of collecting context data derived from internal components of the mobile phone.

Reliability Among the investigated projects, only Gaia provides a replication scheme for ensuring reliability. An event manager component is designed for de-coupling context providers and consumers. If a provider crashes, a replica continues its task to prevent from system crash.

6.4 Conclusion

In this chapter, context-aware middleware is investigated by proposing its functional and non-functional requirements and reviewing some well-known projects. According to this study, besides the traditional tasks of middleware, context discovery and storage, aggregation, modeling, reasoning, dissemination, QoC assessment, and service management as well as protecting privacy of the users are the specific tasks that should be supported by context-aware middleware. Moreover, context-aware middleware should satisfy expandability of the environment, transparency from the viewpoint of application programmers, reusability of components, and reliability for users. The most challenging step toward developing context-aware middleware is the architecture design. To support development of various kinds of context-aware applications, a multiple-domain environment should be considered. Designing context-aware middleware for such an environment envisages serious challenges including resource limitations of devices, dynamic nature of the environment, and mobility of entities. In addition to architectural design, there are independent open research directions in most of the other functionalities of the middleware.

References

Arnabold, V., Conti, M., Delmastro, F.: CAMEO: A novel context-aware middleware for opportunistic mobile social networks. Pervasive Mob. Comput. **11**(1), 148–167 (2014)

Baldoni, R., et al.: An embedded middleware platform for pervasive and immersive environments for all. Proceedings of the 6th annual IEEE communications society conference on sensor, mesh and ad hoc communications and networks workshops, pp. 1–3. IEEE Computer Society, Rome (2009)

Bellavista, P., Antonio, C., Fanelli, M., Foschini, L.: A survey of context data distribution for mobile ubiquitous systems. ACM Comput. Surv. **45**(1), 1–49 (2013)

Beresford, A.R., Stajano, F.: Location privacy in pervasive computing. IEEE Pervasive Comput. **2**(1), 46–55 (2003)

Bettini, C., Brdiczka, O., Henricksen, K., Indulska, J., Nicklas, D., Ranganathan, A., et al.: A survey of context modelling and reasoning techniques. Pervasive Mob. Comput. **6**(2), 161–180 (2010)

Carrizo, C., Hatalkar, A., Memmott, L., Wood, M.: Design of a context aware computing engine. Proceedings of IET 4th international conference on intelligent environments, pp. 1–4. IEEE Computer Society, Seattle (2008)

Chen, H., Finin, T., Joshi, A., Kagal, L., Perich, F., Chakraborty, D.: Intelligent agents meet the semantic web in smart spaces. IEEE Internet Comput. **8**(6), 69–79 (2004)

Dey, A.K., Abowd, G.D., Salber, D.: A conceptual framework and a toolkit for supporting the rapid prototyping of context-aware applications. Hum-Comput. Interact. **16** (2), 97–166 (2001)

Edwards, W.K., Bellotti, V., Dey, A.K., Newman, M.W.: Stuck in the middle: Bridging the gap between design, evaluation, and middleware. Intel research Berkeley. Intel Corporation, California (2002)

Gu, T., Pung, H. K., Zhang, D. Q.:. A service-oriented middleware for building context-aware services. J Netw. Comput. Appl. **28**(1), 1–18 (2005)

Guo, B., Sun, L., Zhang, D.: The architecture design of a cross-domain context management system. 8th IEEE international conference on pervasive computing and communications workshop, pp. 499–504. IEEE Computer Society, Mannheim (2010)

Guo, B., Zhang, D., Imai, M.: Toward a cooperative programming framework for context-aware applications. Pers. Ubiquitous Comput. **15**(3), 221–233 (2011)

Hong, J. I., Landay, J.A.: An Architecture for privacy-sensitive ubiquitous computing. Proceedings of the 2nd international conference on mobile systems, applications, and services, pp. 177–189. ACM, Boston (2004)

Liao, S. S., He, J. W., Tang, T.H.: A framework for context information management. J. Inf. Sci **30**(6), 528–539 (2004)

Loughran, N. et al.: Survey of aspect-oriented middleware. AOSD-Europe Project (2005)

Pawar, P., et al.: Bridging context management systems in the ad hoc and mobile environments. IEEE Symposium on Computers and Communications, pp. 882–888. IEEE Computer Society, Sousse (2009)

Raychoudhury, V., Cao, J., Kumar, M., Zhang, D.: Middleware for pervasive computing: A survey. Pervasive Mob. Comput. **9**(2), 177–200 (2013)

Recommended Practice for Architectural Description.: IEEE Standard. IEEE Standard Association, USA (2000)

Riboni, D., Bettini, C.: Context provenance to enhance the dependability of ambient intelligence systems. Pers. Ubiquitous Comput. **16**(7), 799–818 (2012)

Román, M., Hess, C., Cerqueira, R., Ranganathan, A., Campbell, R. H., Nahrstedt, K.: A middleware infrastructure for active spaces. IEEE Pervasive Comput. **1**(4), 74–83 (2002)

Roussaki, I., Strimpakou, M., Pils, C., Kalatzis, N., Liampoti, N.: Optimising context data dissemination and storage in distributed pervasive computing systems. Pervasive Mob. Comput. **6**(2), 218–238 (2010)

Chapter 7
Context-Centered Tools for Intelligent Assistant Systems

Patrick Brézillon

Abstract Modeling experts' experience requires an explicit consideration of the context and a uniform representation of elements of knowledge, reasoning and contexts. In a companion paper in this book (see Chap. 31) the author proposes the Contextual-Graphs formalism for representing expertise with practices. The exploitation of such experience bases is a new challenge for designing and developing context-based support systems able to tackle context in the same way as knowledge and reasoning. The author presents a conceptual framework for implementing management tools in intelligent assistant systems (IASs) that (1) work on experience described as practices, (2) deal with the process of decision-making and not the result only, and (3) build a context-specific model jointly with the decision-making process. Thus, an IAS can be equipped with domain-independent tools for managing the experience base, simulating practice development, explaining the rationale behind each practice, incrementally acquiring knowledge and learning practice. This chapter shows that functions like acquisition, learning and explanation, which were considered separately, become naturally integrated in IASs.

7.1 Introduction

Generally, support systems are designed and developed to help actors to realize their task. Such support involves data processing or contribution in problem solving (Brézillon 2011). In this paper, actors are experts that make critical decision. For example, the surgeon will rely on the anatomo-cyto-pathologist's decision to operate or not on a woman for breast cancer. Such experts rely on a highly compiled experience because the domain is complex and poorly understood, they generally act under temporal pressure and are very concerned about the consequences of their decision. Conversely to domain knowledge, expert knowledge results from a contextualization process and appears in a decision-making process as chunks of contextual knowledge. Thus, decision-making must be considered through its knowledge and information

P. Brézillon (✉)
Laboratoire d'Informatique de Paris 6 (LIP6), University Pierre and Marie Curie (UPMC), Paris, France
e-mail: patrick.brezillon@lip6.fr

© Springer Science+Business Media New York 2014
P. Brézillon, A. J. Gonzalez (eds.), *Context in Computing*,
DOI 10.1007/978-1-4939-1887-4_7

processing as well as its result. An important point is that reusing a practice requires a decontextualization followed by a recontextualization of the procedure in the new working context.

Hereafter, the paper is organized as follows. Sect. 2 discusses how context intervenes for representing experience, the Contextual-Graphs formalism and the resulting conceptual framework for IASs. Sect. 3 presents the two main tools needed for managing contextual graph by IASs, namely the CxG_Manager and the CxG_Simulator. Sect. 4 concludes this paper with perspectives.

7.2 Representation of Experience Within Contexts

7.2.1 Making Context Explicit

The essence of experience modeling is to understand and model how work actually gets done (i.e. the practice), not what is supposed to happen (i.e. the procedure). The effective transformation of a procedure into a practice assumes to account for the working context in which the task must be realized. Such a context concerns the way in which actors adapt a procedure based on their preferences, the particularities of the task to realize, the situation where the task is realized and the local environment where resources are available. The resulting practice expresses the actors' activity, while a procedure corresponds to a task model. As a consequence, there are as many practices (or activities) as there are actors and contexts.

The context constrains what must be done in the current focus (Brézillon and Pomerol 1999), but, conversely, the focus determines what is contextual knowledge and what is external knowledge in a context at a given moment. The key point here is to represent context as contextual elements. A contextual element corresponds to an information piece that must be analyzed. The value taken by the contextual element when the focus is on it—its instantiation—is taken into account as long as the situation is under the analysis.

The Contextual-Graphs (CxG) formalism (Brézillon 2007) proposes a representation of a task realization as a combination of diagnosis and actions. Diagnosis is represented by contextual elements, and paths correspond to practices developed by actors.

Figure 7.1 gives a contextual-graph representation of a task realization. Circles (1 and 2) represent contextual elements (CEs) with exclusive values $V1.1$ or $V1.2$, $V2.1$ or $V2.2$. Square boxes represent action, the building block of the representation at the chosen granularity. There are three paths representing three different practices for realizing the task. For example, in a working context where CE-1 is instantiated to $V1.2$, actor's activity corresponds to the execution of the action A6. CE instantiation only matters when the focus arrives on this contextual element during practice development. Because the instantiation of CE-1 is $V1.2$, the other contextual element CE-2 and its instantiation are not considered for the practice development. This means that CE instantiation needs to be considered in real time conditions.

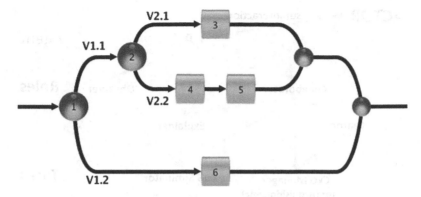

Fig. 7.1 Representation of a task realization as a contextual graph

We call *working context* the set of all the contextual elements of a contextual graph (CE-1 and CE-2) and their values (V1.1, V1.2, V2.1 and V2.2) and their instantiations (e.g. V1.2), i.e. the chosen values at the moment of the practice development.

7.2.2 *Conceptual Architecture of IASs*

The goal of an intelligent assistant system (IAS) is to intelligently help the expert in his decision-making process, not to provide an additional expertise in the domain. This expertise being stored in a contextual graph, the IAS works on a base of actors' experiences (See Chap. 31).

The IAS has to play different roles with the user. Figure 7.2 gives the general architecture of an IAS. This architecture is organized at three levels: agent, role and task. The IAS can take two roles: collaborator and observer. Each role corresponds to different tasks at two (sub-) levels and controlled by the CxG_Manager and the CxG_Simulator. The IAS exploits three bases. Firstly, the experience base corresponds to the contextual graphs representing domain expertise as actors' tasks. Thus this architecture can be applied in different domains with limited changes. Secondly, the base of external facts allows the transfer of some data or information between the different external applications and services triggered by an action in the contextual graph. The IAS manages this fact base because some information at the operational level may be relevant for managing practice development at the tactical level. For example, an action may cause a change of instantiation of a contextual element that leads the IAS to modify its practice building. Thirdly, IAS management can be described as a *personal experience base*. This base contains knowledge for managing tools.

The CxG_Manager helps the actor in the management of a contextual graph for acquiring incrementally new knowledge and for learning new practices for enriching the experience base. The CxG_Simulator automates, if possible, the development of a practice according to the working context, taking into account the consequences

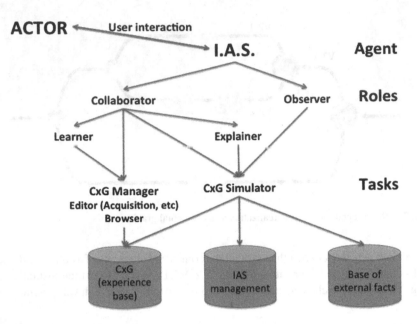

Fig. 7.2 Proposal of architecture for the IAS

of action execution. The modules working-context management and action management, which are discussed hereafter, are part of the "personal experience base" of the IAS and belong to the IAS management module. The personal-experience base also contains knowledge (described in a contextual graph too) about coordination of its different modules (action, working context) and a module for interaction management with the actor. Working on human experience, an IAS would behave similarly to a human and thus it is possible to have a description of tool management by the IAS in contextual graphs too.

7.3 Management Tools

In this section, we discuss different management tools needed by an IAS: the management of contextual graph by the CxG_Manager, and the management of the simulation by the CxG_Simulator.

7.3.1 Introduction

CxG formalism leads to a representation of an experience base described as practices structured by contextual elements. Each path in a contextual graph corresponds to the development of a practice effectively used by an actor for the task realizing in a given working context. Developing a practice corresponds to jointly building the practice and applying it. Practice building is led by the elaboration of a context-specific model (the proceduralized context). Applying a practice can be made either by the CxG_Manager and the actor, or by the CxG_Simulator (more or less) automatically.

An actor interacting with the IAS has the opportunity to browse a contextual graph for analyzing the different practices, alternatives, etc. An example is the reading of a recipe and its variants in a cookbook (a recipe being comparable to a task realization). The IAS can simulate practice development in a given context in which the actor may provide instances. In the recipe example, the "chef" (with the available ingredients in the kitchen) follows a recipe to prepare a dish according to an initial context (his taste, guests, social importance of the meal, available ingredients, equipment, etc.).

7.3.2   Contextual-Graph Management

7.3.2.1   Introduction

Design and development of an experience base depends on the human actor. Supporting the actor in this task is one of the roles of a CxG_Manager. The two main functions of the CxG_Manager are: (a) Edit a contextual graph, and (b) Browse the contextual graph. The CxG_Manager is implemented in the CxG_Platform (Brézillon 2012).

A CxG_Manager works at a tactical level where time is not considered explicitly (e.g. duration of an action and loop on routine action do not matter) because browsing concerns more comparison of practices than the effective development of a practice in a specific context (e.g. comparison of a given recipe in different cookbooks), while a specific recipe is used at an operational level). The focus is more on the realizability of the task than its effective realization.

In another application for the subway in Paris (Pomerol et al. 2002), operators used CxG-based browsing to replay how a colleague solved a given incident, look for alternatives, analyze the working contexts, and even study new practices.

7.3.2.2   Learning Management

The user that interacts with an IAS is an expert of high level (the term used in medicine is the *referent*). Conversely to the old image of an expert system as an oracle and the user as a novice (Karsenty and Brézillon 1995), the IAS must be in a position of assistant (like a "novice") with respect to the expert (as an "oracle"). Finally, the actor can support the IAS when the system fails. This occurs when the IAS does not know the practice developed by the actor because all the practices cannot be known in advance, the number of working contexts being large. Then, the actor provides the needed knowledge in its context of use and the IAS learns a new practice. The reason is often because, up to now, this contextual element kept the same value during all the task realization and, in the context at hand, the expert has identified a different instantiation. Thus, he decided to execute an action A2 (instead of action A1) in the new context. The IAS acquires the new piece of knowledge (A2) as well as the new contextual element with its two values (the old one leading to A1 and the new one leading to A2). Therefore it learns a new practice in a kind of practice-based learning and enriches its experience base.

Thus, the more the IAS is used, the more it learns and the more efficient it becomes. In the recipe example, this concerns the notes written by the "chef" to adjust the recipe next time according to the observed results (cooking, too salty or not, guests' feedback, etc.). There is an eventual more drastic change of the experience base when the expert decides that the learning of the new practice requires a re-organization of its experience base (i.e. the contextual graph).

An IAS may learn in two ways, (1) by assimilation (refinement of an existing practice); and (2) by accommodation of the CxG. Learning by assimilation is practice-based learning, while learning by accommodation is procedure-based learning. Note that the notions of "best practice" and of "business rule" result more of procedure-based learning than practice –based learning.

7.3.2.3   Explanation Management

A decision support system that exploits a contextual graph, applies a human expert's reasoning, and not an "automated reasoning" constrained by control knowledge hidden in the inference engine (e.g. fire the first rule on a list). Often, a contextual element is introduced to discriminate between an existing path and a new one. Thus, this contextual element is introduced before the existing path in the graph, but temporally after it: The justification of the CE introduction is after its use.

Trying to imitate human reasoning, the expert system (ES) presented the trace of its reasoning like a sequence of fired rules that was supposed to be an explanation of the way in which the expert system reached a conclusion. It was right, but (Karsenty and Brézillon 1995): (1) ES reasoning was built from "atoms" of the expert reasoning and the assembling of rules was not based on the expert reasoning, (2) explanations were generated at the implementation level because it was not possible to explain heuristics provided by human experts without additional knowledge (and not just domain knowledge), and (3) control knowledge was introduced by the knowledge engineer in the inference engine, not the domain expert (e.g. fire the first possible rule).

In Contextual Graphs, the explicit representation of context at the same level of knowledge and reasoning provides a new insight on explanation generation because we do not dissociate expert knowledge and expert reasoning like in expert systems. We show that a proceduralized context is attached to each item in a contextual graph. A proceduralized context is a compiled knowledge that appears as an ordered sequence of instantiated contextual elements that can be used for explanation generation. The IAS also is able to generate explanations for the training of a new actor by exploiting the properties of the experience base because the structure of a chunk of contextual knowledge—the ordered sequence of instantiated contextual elements—is known. In the recipe example, cooking separately meat and vegetables may be explained by the fact that one guest is vegetarian.

The uniform representation of elements of knowledge, reasoning and contexts allows the generation of different types of expressive context-based explanations (Brézillon 2012), such as visual explanations, dynamic explanations, user-based explanations, context-based explanations, micro- and macro-explanations, real-time explanations. These different types of explanation can be combined in different ways such as visual and dynamic explanations for presenting future alternatives and abandoned options.

7.3.3 Simulation Management

This section discusses the specificity of the *CxG-based Simulation* that is different from other types of simulation.

7.3.3.1 Introduction

Banks et al. (2001) presents the simulation as the imitation of the operation of a real-world process or system over time. The numerical simulation is based on a theoretical model of the real world (or at least a part of it). The act of simulating supposes that a model exists. The model contains the key characteristics or behaviors/functions of the selected physical or abstract system or process. The model represents the system itself, whereas the simulation represents the operation of the system over time.

Simulation is often used with scientific modeling of natural systems or human systems to gain insight into their functioning, especially when the real system is not to suppress accessible, or it may be dangerous or unacceptable to engage (Sokolowski and Banks 2009). Another use of simulation is training (Salas et al. 2009; Nembhard et al. 2009).

Simulation may also concern a cognitive activity like reasoning or task realization. Frequently, the simulation is conducted using software tools. For example, computer simulations is used to formally model theories of human cognition and performance like ACT-R (Anderson 2007).

Reasoning is more a simulation of the world fleshed out with all our relevant knowledge than a formal manipulation of the logical skeletons of sentences as also discussed in Johnson-Laird (2010). The term conceptual simulation is often used to refer to a type of everyday reasoning strategy commonly called "what if " reasoning (Trickett et al. 2007). Scientists use conceptual simulation in situations of informational uncertainty to make inferences from their data using a process of alignment by similarity detection. Brown (2002) proposed a three-step process of the "what-if" reasoning: (1) visualizing some situation; (2) carrying out one or more operations on it; and (3) seeing what happens by a causal reasoning. The process occurs at the conceptual level and it involves mentally playing out, or "running," a model of the visualized situation, so that changes can be inspected.

We build mental models of the world based on the meaning of the description and on our knowledge (Johnson-Laird 1983). Thus, the conceptual simulation obeys to the cycle of hypothesis–conceptual simulation–alignment. In conceptual simulation, new representations are generated by reference to a familiar situation and by taking what is known and transforming it to generate a future state of a system. Thus, conceptual simulation may be considered a form of model building, which is likely to occur when no easily accessible, existing source for analogy is available (Trickett et al. 2007).

Experts often generate conceptual simulations rather than retrieve solutions from memory. Experts use conceptual simulation when they are working either outside their immediate area of expertise or on their own cutting edge research—that is, in situations that go beyond the limits of their current knowledge. Novices are less capable of generating conceptual simulations because they lack domain knowledge, and that therefore they will use fewer conceptual simulations than experts.

7.3.3.2 Specificity of CxG-Based Simulation

In Contextual-Graphs formalism, we make a parallel between a practice and a model, except that the structure of the practice is not known initially but built progressively during practice development. A CxG_Simulator develops a practice by instantiating contextual elements and thereby choosing the path corresponding to a practice. Thus, a CxG-based simulation is, on the one hand, at the tactical level with an experience base containing all the practices developed for realizing a given task, and, on the other hand, at an operational level for developing a particular practice of the contextual graph in the working context. Time dependency appears because (1) an unpredicted event may modify the instantiation of a contextual element and thus the CxG-based simulation itself, and (2) the execution of an action may impact practice development in different ways independently of what is concerned by the execution of the action. For example, the execution of an action has a duration that may influence the reasoning, if unusual, at the tactical level, or may result in a change of instantiation of a contextual element.

A CxG_Simulator builds a practice (instantiation of contextual elements crossed) and develops it (accounting for the consequences of actions to execute or method to apply).

Building of the Practice A CxG_Simulator needs to know the instantiations of the contextual elements crossed, and the choice of the corresponding action to execute. The alteration of an instantiation implies a change of the working context. The CxG_Simulator has two options for reacting to a change of the working context. First, the altered instantiation involves a contextual element already crossed, and the CxG_Simulator must decide whether (1) to stop the development of the current practice and re-start the simulation; (2) to redo the part of the practice concerned (e.g. for a routine action); or (3) to finish the development of the practice at hand and then analyze the need for a new simulation in the new working context. The

CxG_Simulator will have to interact with the actor to make a decision on the strategy to apply. Second, the altered instantiation concerns a contextual element not yet crossed at the step of the practice development, and the CxG_Simulator can continue its simulation to progress in the contextual graph because this change of instantiation does not affect the part of the practice already built. The management of the working context can also be represented like a contextual graph.

Development of a Practice The CxG_Simulator needs to know the effects of action execution on the practice development. The execution of an action may modify the instantiation of a contextual element. In the recipe example, the "chef" may decide to replace pepper that is missing in the kitchen by paprika if the chef is in a hurry or, otherwise, she/he goes out and buy the pepper. In a CxG-based simulation, the execution of an action may put into question the simulation. The management of action execution also can be represented in the CxG formalism.

7.3.3.3 Working Context Management

The working context has two parts, a static part with the list of the contextual elements in the contextual graph and their known values (on the different branches), and a dynamic part with the known instances, i.e. the value taken by a contextual element for the problem solving at simulation time.

A contextual element allows the management of alternatives (each alternative corresponds to a value of the contextual element) for a part of the task realization by different methods or actions in the contextual graph. A contextual element, $CE°$, has as many (qualitative or quantitative) values as known alternatives:

$$\text{Value (CE }°) = V1°, V2°, V3°, \text{etc.}$$

Arriving to a contextual element, the CxG_Simulator looks for its instantiation in the working context to select the right path to follow and the action to execute. The instantiation can be known prior to the practice development, provided by the actor to the system during the practice development, or found by the CxG_Simulator in the local environment. In the example given Fig. 7.1, the list of contextual elements will be:

Contextual element CE-1	Contextual element CE-2
Values: $V1.1$, $V1.2$	Values: $V2.1$, $V2.2$
Instantiation: $V1.2$	Instantiation: N/A

During a CxG-based simulation, the instantiation of contextual elements may be altered by either an external or an internal event. The external event corresponds to an unpredicted event, i.e. not represented in the contextual graph. For example, an external resource ceases being available, such as an ingredient needed in the recipe is outdated. An internal event occurs as the result of an action execution. For example, the "chef" decides to prepare for more persons than there are guests to leftovers for someone that will come the next day.

The change of working context (change of instantiation of a contextual element) leads the CxG_Simulator to consider another practice. This may leads to stop the simulation (e.g. the required resource is no more available) with two options. First, the simulation must be restarted in the new working context and a new practice will be developed. Second, the change of working context corresponds to a routine action in the practice development that must be executed several times by the CxG_Simulator.

Working-context management is a key task of the CxG_Simulator for managing its interaction with actors, information received from external sources, the impact of action on the practice development, and the simulation itself.

7.3.3.4 Action Management

During a practice development, the CxG_Simulator executes actions and activities (e.g. execution of an external program or a service). It is not what an action is doing that is important, but how it is done and the conditions in which the action is realized. For example, going to a coffee machine to have a coffee assumes that there are coffee, cups, money back. Some consequences may impact the practice development as a side effect (e.g. the water does not reach the coffee machine). The most obvious consequence is the duration of the action execution that may delay the practice development. Other consequences may be indirect, such as a change of the instantiation of a contextual element (e.g. the coffee machine does not accept coins).

Some actions may express the wish of an actor to modify explicitly the instance of a contextual element. In an application in medicine, experts analyze a digital slide for cancer diagnosis from several criteria, and they make their decision according to the number of criteria that are verified. This is translated in contextual graph by an action "sum = 0" and actions "sum = sum + 1" when a criterion is present. Then, "sum" is considered as a contextual element. In the following, the contextual element "sum" is used to check a threshold to conclude whether it is a cancer or not. Thus, the instance of a contextual element is deduced by the reasoning described previously in the practice. The IAS also may benefit of two types of rules for selecting and instantiating contextual elements. For example, the integrity rules (if Value(Period_of_Day) = "night", then Value(Car_light) = "On") and rules about the expected driver's behavior (if Value(Weather) = "rainy", then the distance with the car before must be increased). See Chap. 31 for more details on this aspect.

The outputs of the action-management module (e.g. the alerts to the CxG_Simulator) are recorded in a base of external facts that will be exploited by the CxG_Simulator, which will decide to end the simulation or call for the context-management module.

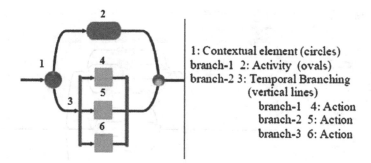

Fig. 7.3 Elements of a contextual graph

7.3.4   Implementation

A contextual graph (CxG) allows the representation of the different ways to solve a problem. It is a directed graph, acyclic with one input and one output and a series-parallel structure (Brézillon 2007). Each path in a CxG corresponds to a practice, a way to fix the problem. Figure 7.3 provides the definition of the four elements in a contextual graph. A more detailed presentation of this formalism and its implementation can be found in (Brézillon 2007).

A contextual graph is composed of the following elements: actions, contextual elements, activities and temporal branching.

An **action** is the building block of contextual graphs at the chosen granularity. An action can appear on several paths but it will be in different contexts.

A **contextual element** is composed of two nodes, a contextual node and a re-combination node. A contextual node has one input and N input branches [1, N], corresponding to the N values of the contextual element already encountered. The recombination node is [N, 1] and shows that, once items on the branch between the contextual and recombination nodes has been processed, it is not necessary to know which branch was followed (i.e. what was the instantiation). Contextual elements are used to represent and implement context about the different events occurring in a given situation.

An **activity** is a contextual graph by itself that is identified by participants because it appears on different paths and/or in several contextual graphs. This recurring sub-structure is generally considered as a complex action (i.e. a subgraph). An activity is a kind a contextualized task that can be aggregated in a unit or expanded in a sub graph according to the needs.

A **temporal branching** expresses the fact (and reduces the complexity of the representation) that several groups of actions (actions 4, 5 and 6 in Fig. 7.3) must be accomplished but that the order in which action groups must be considered is not important, or even could be done in parallel, but all actions must be accomplished before continuing the practice development. The temporal branching is the expression of a complex contextual element emerging from a lower granularity of the representation.

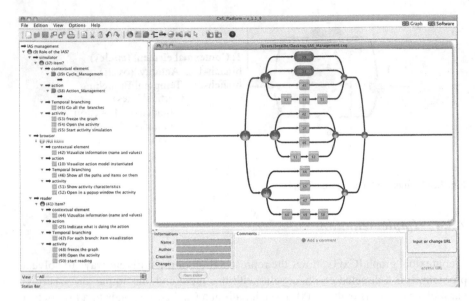

Fig. 7.4 A CxG_representation of the IAS management

The CxG_Platform (Brézillon 2007) contains an editor with the usual functions for managing a contextual graph and managing data. The piece of software is available at cxg.fr under GNU license and the screen display is shown in Fig. 7.4. It is an interface used by an actor wishing to edit a contextual graph, reading practices for selecting the best one in his working context, browsing alternatives of a practice, exploring a contextual graph at different granularity (by representing an activity by an item or by the contextual graph representing this activity), analyzing (contextual) information attached to each item (date of creation, comments, etc.). There also is the possibility to link an item in the CxG to an external document (Word, PDF, etc.), to run an external piece of software, etc.

A CxG_Simulator mimics an (human) actor's behavior. Thus, it is possible to represent the ≪ expertise ≫ of the CxG_Simulator in the same way. Figure 7.4 represents the contextual graph corresponding to the IAS management. The reason for this comes from the fact that if the IAS must deal with an expert's activity, we must represent the support systems' activities in the different modules of management instead of a simple description of the corresponding task.

7.4 Conclusion

Our goal is to develop an IAS to support a user that has a high level of expertise in a domain that is overly complex or not well understood. Users' expertise is highly compiled, such as chunks of contextual knowledge built mainly by experience. Such an expertise is generally used in a decision-making process leading to a critical and definitive decision. In one of the project on which we are working (the MICO project), the expert is an anatomo-cyto-pathologist that analyzes digital slides (coming from biopsies) to diagnose if a patient in a surgery has or not a breast cancer.

The six main consequences are the following. First, an intelligent assistant system must follow what the expert is doing, how he is doing it, anticipate potential needs. This assumes that the system possesses a representation of the experts' reasoning. The IAS must be an excellent secretary, fixing all the simple problems of human experts by itself, and preparing a complete folder on complex situations and letting experts make their decision.

Second, the IAS must work from the practices developed by experts with all the contextual elements used by the expert during practice development. The line of reasoning of the system is drawn from lines of experts' reasoning described in an experience base, which gives a user-centered representation of the domain.

Third, the IAS must be able to develop the decision-making process in real time to analyze the association diagnosis and action built by experts during their reasoning (Brézillon and Pomerol 1999). Indeed, the system simultaneously develops the decision-making process and its context-specific model.

Fourth, the decision-making process being highly contextual, the decision support system must benefit of its interaction with the expert to learn new practices by acquiring incrementally the missing knowledge, and thus enriching its experience base. In some sense, each practice of the contextual graph is the "best practice" for the corresponding working context. Thus, a contextual graph is a more powerful tool than the "best practice" considered in business.

Fifth, making context explicit in the experience base leads to the possibility of relevant explanations for:

- Presenting the rationale behind a practice with alternatives abandoned;
- Training (future) experts on the different practices developed;
- Facilitating experience sharing among experts;
- Proposing a dynamic corporate memory;
- Allowing a first step towards the certification of their protocol.

Sixth, the main tool of an intelligent assistant system is the CxG_Simulator, thanks to a uniform representation of elements of knowledge, reasoning and contexts. Its originality comes from building the practice and applying it at the same time. Indeed the CxG_Simulator is the key element of an IAS for real-time decision making because it is possible to account for unpredicted events, thank to an explicit modeling of context as contextual elements covering, the user, the task realization, the working situation, the local environment with its available resources. All the items are interdependent and also time-dependent. Thus, intelligent assistant systems cover a more general problematic than context-aware applications.

Acknowledgments   This work is supported by grants from ANR TecSan for the MICO project (ANR-10-TECS-015), and we thank partners (IPAL, TRIBVN, Service d'Anatomie Cytologie Pathologie at La Pitié, Thalès, Agfa) for the fruitful discussions, and from the TACTIC project funded by the ASTRID program of Délégation Générale aux Armées.

References

Anderson, J.R.: How Can the Human Mind Occur in the Physical Universe? Oxford University Press, New York ISBN 0-19-532425-0 (2007)

Banks, J., Carson, J., Nelson, B., Nicol, D.: Discrete-event System Simulation, p. 3. Prentice Hall, New Jersey ISBN 0-13-088702-1 (2001)

Brézillon, P.: Context modeling: Task model and model of practices. In: Kokinov et al. (eds.) Modeling and Using Context (CONTEXT-07), LNAI 4635, pp. 122–135. Springer, Heidelberg (2007)

Brézillon, P.: From expert systems to context-based intelligent assistant systems: A testimony. Knowl. Eng. Rev. 26(1), 19–24 (2011)

Brézillon, P.: Modeling activity management instead of task realization. In: Respício, A., Burstein, F. (eds.) Fusing DSS into the Fabric of the Context. IOS Press, Amsterdam (2012)

Brézillon, P., Pomerol, J.-Ch.: Contextual knowledge sharing and cooperation in intelligent assistant systems. Trav. Humain 62(3), 223–246 (1999)

Brown, J.R.: Thought experiments. The Stanford Encyclopedia of Philosophy Summer 2002 Edition (2002)

Johnson-Laird, P.N.: Mental Models: Towards a Cognitive Science of Language, Inference, and Consciousness. Harvard University Press, Cambridge (1983).

Johnson-Laird, P.N.: Mental models and human reasoning. Proc. Natl. Acad. Sci. U S A (PNAS) 107(43), 18243–18250 (2010)

Karsenty, L., Brézillon, P.: Cooperative problem solving and explanation. Expert Syst. Appl. 8(4), 445–462 (1995)

Nembhard, D., Yip, K., Shtub, A.: Comparing competitive and cooperative strategies for learning project management. Int. J. Eng. Educ. 98(2), 181–192 (2009)

Pomerol, J.-Ch., Brézillon, P., Pasquier, L.: Operational knowledge representation for practical decision making. J. Manag. Inf. Syst. 18(4), 101–116 (2002)

Salas, E., Wildman, J.L., Piccolo, R.F.: Using simulation-based training to enhance management. Education. Acad. Manage. Learn. Educ. 8, 559–573 (2009)

Sokolowski, J.A., Banks, C.M.: Principles of Modeling and Simulation, p. 6. Wiley, Hoboken ISBN 978-0-470-28943-3 (2009)

Trickett, S.B., Trafton, J.G.: "What if. . . ": The use of conceptual simulations in scientific reasoning. Cogn. Sci. 31, 843–875 (2007)

Part II
Context in the Computing Environment

Chapter 8
Context and Machine Learning

Cynthia L. Johnson

Abstract Machine learning is an ongoing research area in computing with multiple approaches and algorithms. Almost all machine learning is considered in the context of some application. However, most do not consider contextual features during the learning process. In this chapter, machine learning algorithms that are context-sensitive are reviewed. For this chapter, context-sensitive machine learning is defined as learning algorithms that use contextual features during the learning process. Several examples of context-sensitive machine learning algorithms are reviewed. However, the bulk of the chapter reviews context-sensitive applications designed to learn by observation of another entity. The machine learning approaches and algorithms in this chapter are related to, but not directly in the area of context-aware applications and middleware.

8.1 Introduction

This chapter discusses some of the trends in machine learning research combined with context-sensitive approaches. We look in detail at a subset of machine learning known as learning by observation and several recent applications that learned from observation to create a context-based intelligent agent. We look briefly at examples of context-sensitive machine learning applications as well as the background of machine learning and learning by observation. Context-sensitive machine learning has been used in researching multiple problems and a variety of machine learning algorithms.

Turney (1996) defines three different types of features in machine learning tasks: primary, contextual and irrelevant features. Primary features are those used most commonly in machine learning and are useful for classification when considered alone. Irrelevant features are not useful for classification purposes and should be disregarded. Contextual features are not useful when considered alone, but can be useful when combined with other features. Turney (1996) believes that primary features are often context-sensitive and learning algorithms will perform better when contextual features are included with the primary features.

C. L. Johnson (✉)
Georgia Gwinnett College, Lawrenceville, GA, USA
e-mail: cjohns25@ggc.edu

© Springer Science+Business Media New York 2014
P. Brézillon, A. J. Gonzalez (eds.), *Context in Computing*,
DOI 10.1007/978-1-4939-1887-4_8

The majority of the applications reviewed here test Turney's hypothesis. They share a goal of finding better performing machine learning algorithms by using contextual features as part of the learning process. Some other common goals of using context in machine learning are: maintaining learning through an unexpected change of context, and applying learning from one context to another (Edmonds 2002).

8.2 Background

8.2.1 Machine Learning

Machine learning describes a very large area of research involving computers. One definition is: "A computer program is said to learn from experience E with respect to some class of tasks T and performance measure P, if its performance at tasks in T, as measured by P, improves with experience E" (Mitchell 1997 p. 2). Machine learning techniques in the mid twentieth century originally focused on game playing programs. Currently, applications using machine learning techniques are varied and numerous.

In general, it can be said that machine learning algorithms create a computer system that improves with experience and time. Depending upon the application domain, these learning systems might also be called data mining, autonomous discovery, database update, programming by example and learning by example. Data points in machine learning algorithms are typically portrayed as feature-vectors that capture important information about the application at a point in time. The values of the features can be numerical or categorical. The number and types of features in the vector are going to vary greatly from task to task. The introduction of context into the application means that the feature-vector contents can vary from context to context within a single application (Grobelnik et al. 2011).

A variety of machine learning techniques and algorithms exist to train software agents. These techniques can be divided into two categories: supervised and unsupervised learning. Supervised learning consists of presenting the learning algorithm with training data reflecting the inputs and expected outputs. The learning technique must analyze or classify the data, and create a behavior function for the agent from the data. Examples of supervised learning are Gaussian mixture models, artificial neural networks, and support vector machines. Unsupervised learning, on the other hand, provides only input data, and the learning algorithm must explore the problem space, developing a behavior function based upon the results of that exploration. Reinforcement learning techniques typically fall into the unsupervised learning category although they are sometimes given their own category (Russell and Norvig 2009).

Almost all machine learning is carried out within the scope of at least one context. For example, moving a robotic arm in the context of playing air hockey (Bentivegna and Atkeson 2001), creating an agent to play soccer in context of the RoboCup competition (Floyd et al. 2008), learning to fly a flight simulator (Issac and Sammutt 2003) and learning inventory control (Jiang and Sheng 2009). Clearly limiting the machine learning to a single context limits the amount of data input into the learning algorithm. However, it doesn't necessarily address all possible contextual data.

8.2.2 Context-Sensitive Machine Learning

The applications of context-sensitive machine learning are not limited to a small amount of domains. In this section, an overview of some of those applications and a brief description of the learning algorithms are presented.

Natural Language Processing (NLP) is a domain where context has been used for many years. NLP applications are designed to allow a computer to understand human languages either spoke or written. Human beings are able to automatically and naturally process words that look or sound alike in the context of the speaker. In order to correctly interpret human speech, the computer must also understand the context of the speaker. Chapter 10 presents more detail on context and NLP. One tool used for NLP is a context-sensitive graph grammar. These graph grammars have costly construction and maintenance and are often error-prone. VEGGIE, A Visual Environment for Graph Grammar Induction and Engineering uses machine learning techniques to create these grammars. Contextual features are included in a reinforcement learning algorithm designed to extend existing technologies. Since the tool is context-sensitive, context is used in both parsing and inference of new graph grammars (Ates and Zhang 2007).

Empirical and statistical approaches to machine learning have been very popular in NLP since the 1990's. Knowing the context of the speaker greatly simplifies the task of determining the meanings of words with multiple meanings. Dinh et al. (2012) added context to help correct erroneously tagged words from a statistical machine learning model known as NB classification. As input into their learning algorithm, they used output from the NB classifier and a set of manually labeled ambiguous words with the correct context of the word. A transformation based learning algorithm was used to generate new rules for the classifier using this input data. Combining the NB classification with the additional transformation based learning increased the accuracy of their NLP application for the Vietnamese language by 4.8 % (Dinh et al. 2012).

The ability to determine context is often the subject of machine learning applications. Dekel et al. (2009) used a connectionist machine learning approach to build context trees. Context trees are a popular tool for tasks such as compression, sequential prediction and language modeling (Willems et al. 1995). The number of previous symbols they use to make a prediction is context dependent rather than being constant. The use of context makes them different from other types of sequential predictors. In this instance, context trees were built to address the problem of individual sequence prediction. The sequence prediction was recast in a Hilbert space and a neural network perceptron algorithm known as shallow perceptron learned context-tree predictors. This was an on-line learning algorithm and once each context tree was no longer making prediction mistakes, the tree was no longer updated (Dekel et al. 2009).

Researchers in the area of robotics control systems have also made advances by combining machine learning and context. In an attempt to have a robotic arm learn the correct movements, Petkos and Vijayakumar (2007) first formulated a probabilistic model to represent context as a variable. The context was estimated online using Markovian filtering. This context was continuously changing as the robotic arm moved. This changing context was fed as one of many inputs into an Expectation-Maximization clustering algorithm. The Expectation-Maximization algorithm is often used with a mixture of Gaussians. This approach worked well due to the fact the problem of context separation from context-unlabeled data in the control system was very similar to clustering problems using a mixture of Gaussians (Petkos and Vijayakumar 2007).

A similar approach to robotic control using context and machine learning is known as the Infinite Mixture of Linear Experts (IMLE) algorithm (Jamone et al. 2013). This algorithm learns a map described as a collection of local linear models coexisting in similar input locations. This potentially produces multi-valued estimates for the output. IMLE is a probabilistic algorithm that like the above problem uses an expectation-maximization procedure to update its parameter. This approach uses a discrete context estimation rather than attempt to discrete varying context and control (Jamone et al. 2013).

Context and machine learning also have a place in affective computing. One such application attempts to detect human emotion in the context of a human- computer interaction. This is a difficult problem because many human indicators of emotion such as crying could have a variety of emotions behind it. The online framework called the Emotional Machine uses an online version of an artificial neural network and k-nearest neighbor algorithm version called Distance-Weighted Nearest Neighbor to improve emotional predictions (Trabelsi and Frason 2010). The learning algorithm uses training sets from the Ortony, Close and Collins (OCC) (Ortony et al. 1988) model of emotions combined with a web-based anonymous questionnaire. The resulting learned algorithm was able to correctly distinguish among 23 different emotions approximately 65 % of the time (Trabelsi and Frason 2010).

The use of context also improved upon the ability to learn Markov network structure from datasets using independence-based learning. Algorithms that follow independence-based approaches use statistical test to learn conditional independence from data sets. These are encoded in an undirected graph. Edera et al. (2013) created CSPC an independence-based algorithm that encodes context-specific independences. This adaptation to use context in the algorithm and learn features rather than a graph allowed them to overcome some of the inefficiencies of traditional independence-based algorithms. (Edera et al. 2013)

Machine learning and context extend into the relatively new research area of expressive music performance research also known as the data mining of music. Grachten and Krebs (2014) extracted musical context using a variety of unsupervised feature learning algorithms. They used an opus of piano music composed by Chopin and played by the same pianist. Once the musical context is encoded, it is used to predict expressive dynamics in the music. They were able to compare the efficacy of the various feature learning algorithms which have been proven successful in image processing and other domains in this relatively new domain (Grachten and Krebs 2014).

While the works reviewed here are only a small sample, it is enough to see the variety of applications that combine context and machine learning. It is clear that the inclusion of contextual features in machine learning is not a passing trend. The majority of the reviewed works were able to show improved performance versus non-context-sensitive algorithms. As time goes by, more and more researchers embrace context-sensitive machine learning algorithms.

8.2.3 Learning by Observation

In this section, we review a subset of the machine learning research that embrace context to improve learning by observation. The research reviewed in this chapter all address the question of whether the inclusion of a context as part of a machine learning technique can accelerate the learning process or improve the performance of the resulting application.

Learning by observation falls into the supervised learning category although the inputs and outputs are not explicitly defined. They must be extracted from a sequence of data depicting correct behavior over time. The example behavior and its results are input into the learning algorithm and some sort of behavior function is output. The format of the behavior function will depend upon the type of agent being developed. A rule-based agent will develop a set of rules governing its behavior. An agent governed by a Markov decision process will develop a policy that maps state to action and state transitions. A Neural network based agent will develop connections and connection weights to each neuron. Some machine learning applications use a single algorithm; others combine two or more techniques to improve results.

Learning by observation or imitation has long been studied in humans and animals (Galef and Giraldeau 2001). It is debated whether or not the ability to imitate others is a sign of intelligence in animals (Byrne and Russon 1998), but there is little doubt that it could prove to be a time saving technique for training simulated agents and teams. It is particularly useful when opportunities to derive knowledge from the actual human experts are limited, such as when the expert or experts are usually absent or otherwise uncooperative (e.g., an opponent or enemy). Learning by observation also offers the opportunity to acquire implicit knowledge that is often not easily captured through other conventional knowledge acquisition techniques. Explicit knowledge includes facts, formulas and rules and is comparatively easy to obtain from an expert. Implicit knowledge, on the other hand, is more esoteric and difficult to articulate and represent. Also known as *tacit knowledge*, it encompasses habits that the expert may not even recognize. This type of knowledge is usually acquired through practice and experience and is often difficult to articulate. One definition of implicit knowledge defines it as knowledge that increases task performance without an accompanying increase in verbal knowledge about the task. Another definition is knowledge acquired without conscious knowledge of when and where it was acquired (Underwood and Bright 1996). It is sometimes referred to as unconscious memory. Learning by observation is one possible way to obtain this knowledge.

In addition to learning tacit knowledge, there are many advantages to learning by observation. These include (Fernlund 2004):

- Amount of expert's time needed is minimized. Expert need only demonstrate task, not talk about it.
- Software coding time is minimized as behavior function encoding is automated.
- Development of agent is quicker.
- It is possible to incorporate demonstrations from multiple experts.

Several techniques exist that use learning by observation to train a simulated entity. Applications exist that have trained agents to drive a car simulator (Fernlund 2004), teach planning application operators (Wang 1995), and learn to fly Isaac and Sammutt 2003) drive a simulated tank in formation (Fernlund et al. 2009) and many others.

A related area of study in robotics is known as learning by demonstration. This is similar to learning by observation and uses many of the same machine learning techniques. The primary difference is that in learning by demonstration the examples or demonstrations are generated by a teacher specifically for learning purposes. Demonstrations are often repeated to improve the learning of the robotic (Chernova and Veloso 2010). Learning by observation is done using data collected while the expert or experts perform the task or tasks being learned. The data collection is typically done so that the expert is not actively involved in the collection.

8.3 Learning by Observation with Context

In modeling and simulation, machine learning is often used to train intelligent agents to operate independently within a simulation. Context-based paradigms have proved particularly useful in this domain, as it is rare for this type of simulated entity to act in a single context. One context-based paradigm for the development of this type of agent is known as *context-based reasoning*. Context-based reasoning (CxBR) is the contextual-based paradigm used in a number of machine learning approaches. Because CxBR is a paradigm rather than a framework, it offers flexibility in implementation not always available with the other human behavior representation frameworks. CxBR simulates human behavior without simulating all of the human thought processes. The life of a software agent typically consists of processing information and making a decision on the next action or state. By knowing the current context, an agent can limit expectations as to what is normal in the current context. When the situation is changed, environmental or internal events can trigger a transition to a new context (Gonzalez et al. 2008).

A CxBR agent categorizes rules and function hierarchically. The top level of the hierarchy is known as the Mission Context. Each CxBR agent has a single Mission Context. The Mission can be defined as the process of interacting with the environment and making decisions while trying to accomplish a goal or objective. The Mission Context is responsible for maintaining that objective, defining the criteria for ending the mission, and maintaining the plan. Within a particular Mission, various situations are categorized into Major Contexts that can contain Sub-Contexts. The Mission contains universal rules that are applicable to all contexts and contains a list of all the possible Major Contexts applicable to the mission. These universal rules, sometimes called *universal transition rules*, are typically a set of actions triggered by a particular state or data transition. These universal transition rules are checked by all the contexts because they define conditions that should result in a particular action regardless of the current context. Each context contains additional rules and functionality specific to that context, also known as *action rules*, and rules governing the transition from one context to another, known as *transition rules*. Sub-contexts represent a lower level of abstraction than the Major Contexts, but operate in essentially the same manner with the exception that context transitions are only between Sub-contexts of the active Major Context or back to the Major Context. Each context is an object-oriented class with its own set of attributes and methods relevant to that context. The flexibility and encapsulation of the contexts make CxBR agents lightweight and easy to implement. A more formal and detailed description of CxBR is presented in Chap. 30.

Several techniques have been used to develop a CxBR agent from observed behavior using a variety of machine learning techniques. In order for a CxBR agent to function properly, it must know how to behave in a certain context (action functions and rules) and when it is appropriate to switch to a new context (transition rules). Any learning strategy used with CxBR must evolve both types of knowledge in order to be effective. Because CxBR is a paradigm rather than specific implementation, the action rules and transition rules need not be literal rules in a production system. The very nature of CxBR can facilitate learning behaviors from observation.

Fernlund (2004) created a CxBR agent capable of driving a simulated car through an urban setting using learning by observation. He used genetic programming as his learning strategy. Fernlund modeled human driving behaviors after observing them in a simulated car. The driving simulation was instrumented to allow the human drivers' action to be logged for use in training. The contexts for the driving tasks were predetermined and the data partitioned to match the predetermined context. A Genetic programming algorithm was created called Genetic Context Learning or GenCL. GenCL was used to evolve the rules controlling the activation of the contexts and the actions of the driver within each context. A population of instruction trees that could be translated into C code was developed. Crossover and mutation operators were created to combine the instruction trees in various configurations. The instruction trees were converted into compilable source code. A simulator known as the MicroSimulator was used a fitness function. It contained minimal operational requirements to evaluate the performance of an evolving agent. Each individual in the population was run through the MicroSimulator and the fitness score was generated based on a comparison with the original observed data in the same situation. The resulting agents performed the initial task well and were able to generalize the skills learned in similar scenarios (Fernlund 2004).

Fernlund was able to show the flexibility of GenCL by creating CxBR agents from observed live military training data. (Fernlund et al. 2009) The data were collected from two opposing tank platoons using a Deployable Instrumentation Training System (DITS). In DITS, each tank was instrumented with GPS to accurately record its location and firing events were simulated with laser attachments to the weapons. The information collected by DITS instrumentation was transmitted to a central server where it was logged for future analysis. Using the DITS data and GenCL, Fernlund et al. (2009) were able to create CxBR agents able to simulate the tank platoons' movements. These simulations were used to aid in the assessment or after-action review of future live training exercises (Fernlund et al. 2009).

Trinh and Gonzalez (2013) expanded upon Fernlund's work by learning the context structure by observation in addition to the action function and transition rules. Trinh actually created two version of an observer module that automatically parsed the observed data into contexts. The observed data were the same logs from the human drivers observed in Fernlund's work. (Fernlund 2004) Using the same simulated car and virtual world as Fernlund, he merged his work with GenCL to create an agent capable of navigating the simulated car through the virtual world. The first approach named Contextualized Fuzzy ART (CFA) used the data point clustering technique known as Fuzzy ART. The clustering technique grouped the observational data into contexts using instances of time as the basis for clustering. This provided a benchmark against which the second approach could be evaluated (Trinh and Gonzalez 2013).

The second approach known as the Context Partitioning and Clustering (COPAC) method consisted of a combination of clustering and partitioning algorithms. The first partitioning algorithms were known as standard sequence partitioning and fuzzy partitioning. Two clustering algorithms, k-means and similarity clustering were used in conjunction with the partitioning to create four unique algorithm combinations. The resulting contexts are then fed into GenCL to complete the development of the final agent. The generated contexts were quite different from the original human generated contexts, but were still meaningful and usable by the GenCL algorithm. Although, the process of creating the agents was computationally expensive and time-consuming, the algorithms produced agents that behaved nearly as well as the original driving agents developed by Fernlund (Trinh and Gonzalez 2013).

Stensrud and Gonzalez (2008) used learning by observation to learn the criteria for context transitions in a CxBR agent. Their system observed a player in a computerized game of strategy. Sequences of observations were associated with the human action taken and grouped into training data. These observations were mapped by the FAM/Template-based Interpretation Learning Engine (FAMTILE). FAMTILE combines the Fuzzy ARTMAP (FAM) neural network clustering technique with template-based interpretation (Stensrud and Gonzalez 2008).

FAMTILE is able to infer the context of the observed human actor and then map that context to the environment. The inference of context is done by the template-based interpretation and the mapping utilizes the FAM clustering network. The input and output patterns governing context switches is generated and used to train a neural network to recognize observation patterns and map them to contexts. The algorithm was tested on maze navigation games and Texas Hold'Em Poker computerized games. The authors concluded that FAMTILE is an adequate technique for learning high-level behavior. It also proved to have an excellent track record for predicting subjects' actions. This could be useful in gaining a perspective of why the human actor is doing what he/she is doing (Stensrud and Gonzalcz 2008).

8.4 Multi-agent Machine Learning with Context

After the successful development of CxBR agents using machine learning, the next logical step was to create teams of agents using machine learning algorithms. Machine learning techniques relevant to single agents are often difficult to implement in a multi-agent scenario (Sycara 1998). It is possible to individually train agents that are part of the team independently from other teammates. This can be a useful first step in a multi agent system, but agents trained in this manner often do not work well together (Stone 2007). The effort is analogous to putting a group of human strangers in a team and expecting them to immediately behave and communicate effectively.

Before attempting to learning collaborative behavior, a multi-agent framework capable of modeling collaborative behavior was needed, preferably one incorporating context. Collaborative Context-based Reasoning (CCxBR) was developed to create a team of CxBR agents. Barrett (2007) formalized CCxBR in terms of joint intention and related it to the popular Belief-Desire-Intention (BDI) model (Georgeff et al. 1999). In CCxBR, an agent is always aware of its current Mission and the current context, whether it is a Major Context or a Sub-context (Barrett 2007).

CCxBR builds upon the work of Johansson, who implemented collaborative behavior between CxBR agents using a shared Mission context (Johansson 1999). This Mission Context is a form of joint intention as the Mission Context contains the high level goal of the agent. However, this did not provide any sense of shared situational awareness or means of coordination between the agents. To address this issue, a teamworking class was introduced to the framework that focused on communication between collaborating agents (Johansson 1999). Johansson's incorporation of the team working class included the creation of a team mission known as the team mission context shared by the group of collaborating agents. This team mission included the specification of sub-goals for the team members. This addition made more of the information needed for effective teamwork available to each of the team members. Among the information included was team member status, team mission, status of the mission objective, and the role of individual team members. It also provided a means of communicating status changes and mission objective changes that could change individual sub-goals (Johansson 1999).

CCxBR implements Johansson's teamworking class using a Team Context. This Team Context is shared among the CxBR agents functioning as a team. It contains information about each agent's context as well as the joint goal and status of the joint goal. The basic concept behind CCxBR is that team members can easily maintain coordination by communicating their current context to each other via the Team Context. By virtue of knowing the context of another agent, an agent can reasonably predict its actions.

Barrett built three separate CxBR prototypes designed to perform the same basic plays in a simulated soccer game. The first prototype consisted of a team of basic CxBR agents with no accommodation for teamwork. This version simply added a shared team context containing the current context of the mission. The second prototype called "CxBRwithJIT" used the same basic agent, but added reasoning to allow each agent to infer their teammate's context based upon position and state of the game. The third prototype implemented CCxBR and implemented explicit communication of each agent's context among the teammates. Experimentation showed that while the CxBRwithJIT prototype performed better than CxBR with shared Mission, the CCxBR prototype was the most effective at teamwork (Barrett 2007).

This dissertation uses the third prototype as the paradigm of choice for a team displaying collaborative behavior in this dissertation. The shared Mission and team context will provide the necessary shared mental model and link to JIT needed to effectively duplicate human teamwork behavior. The individual agents will have the ability to learn and duplicate individual task skills by developing their own Major Contexts.

Johnson (Johnson and Gonzalez 2014) used CCxBR as a multi-agent framework in COLTS (Contextually-based Observational Learning of Teamwork System). COLTS is an approach to training multi-agent systems using observational learning techniques. While COLTS is based on existing single agent learning algorithm, it adds several non-trivial novel elements that allow it to function acceptably for learning team behaviors. The goal of the COLTS process is to acquire the basic knowledge needed by CxBR agent automatically and build the behavior function for each of the team members from observation.

At the core of the COLTS behavior function is a memory-based policy approach called *behavior maps* that was inspired by the learning-by-demonstration work of Bentivegna (2004) and the case-based reasoning techniques used by Floyd et al (2008). The case base in case-based reasoning provided the inspiration for behavior maps. The primary difference is that rather than a single case base, there is a behavior map for each context of the agents. The individual agents assess their current context based on situational data, team context, and previous context. The same collected data is used to determine the appropriate behavior in the current time step of the discrete simulation and a determination of whether or not the context has changed since last assessed. The COLTS toolkit contains a basic system capable of being (relatively) easily adapted to various types of teams (Johnson and Gonzalez 2014).

COLTS consists of an observer module, a learning module and a run-time module. Figure 8.1 shows a block diagram of the components. The observer module is responsible for acquiring the observed data from the entity or entities being learned

Fig. 8.1 Block model of the
COLTS system

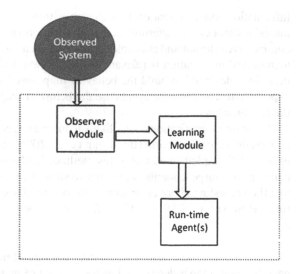

from. It is responsible for taking the observations and converting them into a format
readable by the learning module. The learning module translates the observed data
into some learned function usable by the software agent or agents replicating the
behavior of the observed entity or team. The learned function is then made available
to the run-time agents in the run-time module (Johnson and Gonzalez 2014).

Behavior maps drive the behavior of the COLTS team. A behavior map is analogous to the case base in case-based reasoning. The behavior map is different from
these approaches by the inclusion of collaborative data in the state vector. The inclusion of collaborative data enhances the traditional approaches for use in emulating an
entire team. Additionally, both of the fundamental approaches used a single policy or
case base for each entity. Because CCxBR breaks the behavior of the team and team
members into contexts, there will be a behavior map for each identified context in
an application. This is vital to creating a scalable application. Limiting the number
of state vectors to compare against to those relevant to a particular context keeps the
size of the behavior map small enough to execute more quickly than a single case
base or policy (Johnson and Gonzalez 2014).

The behavior of the observed agent or agents can be thought of as a series of situations and actions. The situation can be represented by a state vector S containing the
available information about each agent's environment. For use in learning collaborative behavior, this vector must be expanded to include information about teammates
and team goals. The behavior maps are built from observed data that contains both
environment information and collaborative information. The situation vector S will
contain m items of environment information, E, and n items of collaborative information, C. At run-time, the environment information is derived from agent sensors
and communications and the collaborative information is provided from the team
context. The values of m and n will vary based upon the application domain. The
actual collaborative information stored in S may be specific contexts of teammates or

information about the teammate such as position and bearing from which the team-mates' context can be determined. It is also important to determine if all teammates' contexts are relevant and available at run-time. In many team situations, only certain teammates' information is relevant to determining behavior. The COLTS learning module is designed to build the behavior map based upon observed data from the expert team. The run-time agents use the behavior maps to determine the actions of the run-time agents.

A teamwork application is very likely to have a larger situation vector and choice of actions than the robotic arm (Bentivegna et al. 2006) and single soccer player (Floyd et al. 2008) implemented using this method. Without modification, this approach can consume large amounts of memory to store the mappings of situation and action and the nearest neighbor algorithm could potentially consume excessive processing time. However, COLTS uses CCxBR to break the problem down using the natural contextual partitioning of the problem. This breakdown of the problem into contexts enables the development of a separate behavior map for each context making the use of behavior maps feasible by limiting the size of the behavior maps. The size of each behavior map is determined by the number of mappings of situations to actions stored in the map. The use of contextually-based behavior maps will also address the possibility that the expert might encounter very similar situations in different contexts that result in differing actions.

The COLTS concept was tested on two separate applications of increasing complexity. The first prototype tested the ability to teach individual members of a simulated fire-fighting bucket brigade. As expected, the trained team members learned the behavior of the example team members with high precision. This was expected because the bucket brigade team members had a limited number of contexts and behaviors. The second prototype was a more sophisticated pursuit-evasion game with a single evader and a team of four pursuers. The COLTS system attempted to learn the behavior of the team of four pursuers. While the results were not exact, the method shows promise for expansion into ever more complex simulations and agents. Additional work to expand the technique into a simulated soccer game is underway (Rekabadar et al. 2012).

8.5 Conclusion

As stated in the introduction, the goal of machine learning is to create programs that are able to perform a new learned task and/or continue to improve their performance on a task. The works reviewed combine tried and true machine learning algorithms that include contextual features in the learning process. Almost all showed that the inclusion of context had a positive effect upon the performance of the resulting program. In a few cases such as COLTS, the use of context enabled the use of an algorithm that would have otherwise been overwhelmed by the amount of data available. In none of the research was the use of context found to hinder or slow down the performance of the machine learning algorithm. The variety in the types of machine learning algorithms among the various applications is also noteworthy. The results from each were consistent with or better than applications of the algorithm without using context. This trend seems to indicate that the use of context-sensitive paradigms can only increase the effectiveness of machine learning algorithms. It also indicates that the use of context-sensitive paradigms does not limit the type of machine learning algorithm available for use. Research in machine learning is ongoing and active, and the works discussed in this chapter indicate that the inclusion of context as a factor in these works can only lead to new applications for this research.

References

Ates, K., Zhang, K.: Constructing VEGGIE: Machine learning for context-sensitive graph grammars. 19th IEEE International Conference on Tools with Artificial Intelligence, vol 2. IEEE (2007)

Barrett, G.C.: Collaborative context-based reasoning. Doctoral dissertation, University of Central Florida, Orlando, FL (2007)

Bentivegna, D.C.: Learning from observation using primitives. (Doctoral Dissertation) (2004)

Bentivegna, D.C., Atkeson, C.G.: Learning from observation using primitives. IEEE International Conference on Robotics and Automation, pp. 1988–1993. Seoul (2001)

Bentivegna, D.C., Atkeson C.G., and Cheng G.: Learning similar tasks from observation and practice. In: Intelligent Robots and Systems, 2006 IEEE/RSJ International Conference on, pp. 2677–2683. IEEE (2006)

Byrne, R.W., Russon, A.E.: Learning by imitation: A hierarchical approach. Behav. Brain Sci **21**, 667–684 (1998)

Chernova, S., Veloso, M.: Confidence-based multi-robot learning from demonstration. Int. J. Soc. Robot **2**, 195–215 (2010)

Dekel, O., Shalev-Schwartz, S., Singer, Y.: Individual sequence prediction using memory-efficient context trees. IEEE Trans. Inf. Theory **55**(11), 5251–5262 (2009)

Dinh, P.-H., Ngyuen, N.-K., Le, A.-C.: Combining statistical machine learning with transformation rule learning for Vietnamese word sense disambiguation. 2012 IEEE RIVF International Conference on Computing and Communications Technologies, Research, Innovation, and Vision for the Future. IEEE (2012)

Edera, A., Bromberg, F., Schlüter, F.: Markov random fields factorization with context-specific independences. arXiv preprint arXiv:1306.2295 (2013)

Edmonds, B.: Learning and exploiting context in agents. Proccddings of the 1st International Joint Conference on Augonomous Agents and Multiagent Systems, part 3. ACM (2002)

Fernlund, H.K.: Evolving models from observed human performance. Doctoral dissertation, University of Central Florida, Orlando (2004)

Fernlund, H., Gonzalez, A.J., Ekblad, J., Rodriguez, A.: Trainee evaluation through after-action review by comparison. J. Def. Model. Simul Appl. Methodol. Technol. **6**(3), 135–150 (2009)

Floyd, M.W., Esfandiari, B., Lam, K.: A case-based reasoning approach to imitating RoboCup players. Proceedings of the Twenty-First International FLAIRS Conference, pp. 251–256 (2008)

Galef, J.B., Giraldeau, L.: Social influences on foraging in vertbrates: Causal mechanisms and adaptive functions. Anim. Behav **61**, 3–15 (2001)

Georgeff, M., Pell, B., Pollack, M., Tambe, M., Woolridge, M.: The belief-desire-intention model of agency. Proceedings of Agents, Theories, Architectures and Languages (ATAL) (1999)

Gonzalez, A.J., Stensrud, B.S., Barrett, G.: Formalizing context-based reasoning: A modeling paradigm for representing tactical human behavior. Int. J. Intell. Syst **23**(7), 822–847 (2008)

Grachten, M., Krebs, F.: An assessment of learned score features for modeling expressive dynamics in music. IEEE Trans. Multimed **PP**(99) (2014)

Grobelnik, M., Mladenic, D., Leban, G., Stajner, T.: Machine learning techniques for understanding context and process. In: Warren, P., Davies, J., Simperl, E. (eds.) Context and Semantics for Knowledge Management, pp. 127–146. Springer, Berlin (2011)(editor)

Isaac, A., Sammut, C.: Goal-directed learning to fly. Proceedings of the International Conference on Machine Learning, pp. 258–265. Washington, D.C (2003)

Jamone, L., Santos-Victor, B., Takanishi, A.: Online learning of humanoid robot kinematics under switching tools contexts. 2013 IEEE International Conference on Robotics and Automation, pp. 4811–4817. IEEE (2013)

Jiang, C., Sheng, C.: Case-based reinforcement learning for dynamic inventory control in a multi-agent supply-chain system. Expert Syst. Appl 36, 6520 6526 (2009)

Johansson, L.: Cooperating AIPs in the context-based reasoning paradigm. Master's thesis, ECE Dept. University of Central Florida, Orlando (1999)

Johnson, C.L., Gonzalez, A.J.: Learning collaborative team behavior from observation. Expert. Syst. Appl 41(3), 2316–2328 (2014)

Mitchell, T.: Machine Learning. McGraw-Hill, New York (1997)

Ortony, A., Clore, G.L., Collins, A.: The Cognitive Structure of Emotions. Cambridge University Press, New York (1988)

Petkos, G., Vijayakumar, S.: Context estimation and learning control through latent variable extraction: From discrete to continuous contexts. 2007 IEEE International Conference on Robotics and Automation. IEEE (2007)

Rekabdar, B., Shadgar, B., Osareh, A.: Learning teamwork behaviors approach: Learning by observation meets case-based planning. In: Ramsay, A., Agre, G. (eds.) Artificial Intelligence: Methodology, Systems and Applications, pp. 195–201 (2012)

Russell, S., Norvig, P.: Artificial Intelligence: A Modern Approach. Prentice Hall, New Jersey (2009)

Stensrud, B.S., Gonzalez, A.J.: Discovery of high-level behavior from observation of human performance in a strategic game. IEEE Trans. Syst. Man Cybern. Cybern 38(3), 855–874 (2008)

Stone, P.: Multiagent learning is not the answer. It is the question. Artif. Intell 171: 402-405 (2007)

Sycara, K.: Multiagent systems. AI1 Mag. 19(2), 79 (1998)

Trabelsi, A., Frasson, C.: The emotional machine: A machine learning approach to online prediction of user's emotion and intensity. 2010 IEEE 10th International Conference on Advanced Learning Technologies. IEEE (2010)

Trinh, V.C., Gonzalez, A.J.: Discovering contexts from observed human performance. IEEE Trans. Hum. Mach. Syst 43(4), 359–370 (2013)

Turney, P.: The management of context-sensitive features: A review of strategies. Proceedings of the ICML-96 Workshop on Learning in Context-sensitive Domains, pp. 53–69 (1996)

Underwood, G.D., Bright, J.E.: Cognition with and without awareness. In: Underwood, G.D. (ed.) Implicit Cognition, pp. 1–40. Oxford University Press, Oxford (1996)

Wang, X.: Learning by observation and practice: An incremental approach for planning operator acquisition. Proceedings of the 12th International Conference on Machine Learning. The International Machine Learning Society, Tahoe City, CA (1995)

Willems, F.M., Shtarkov, Y.M., Tjalkens, T.J.: The context-tree weighting method: Basic properties. IEEE Trans. Inf. Theory 41(3), 653–664 (1995)

Chapter 9
A Bayesian Framework for Life-Long Learning in Context-Aware Mobile Applications

Arun Kishore Ramakrishnan, Davy Preuveneers and Yolande Berbers

Abstract This chapter focuses on multi-view learning, incremental learning and meta-learning, highly relevant yet understudied machine learning principles that enable life-long learning in context-aware mobile applications. The authors present a Bayesian framework to realize them in modern ubiquitous computing environments that are characterized by dynamic and ever-evolving contexts inferred from heterogeneous sensors with varying churn rates. These techniques enable life-long learning in the context-aware applications to meta-learn their learning principles and continuously adapt the context models in-tune with their environments. This chapter studies the benefits of the proposed techniques and demonstrate their advantages for context-aware mobile applications.

9.1 Introduction

Fuelled by the recent developments in the field of micro-electronics and mobile computing, modern context-aware applications are seeking to provide personalized, real-time user-centric services. As a result, many smart applications are shifting focus from utilizing simple and static contexts (e.g. user profile data) towards more dynamic and complex contexts (e.g. user activity recognition).

Due to this paradigm shift in the modern smart environments, the simple and rigid rule-based context reasoners are being replaced by more flexible and sophisticated probabilistic machine learning algorithms that can automatically learn the user contexts from a multitude of sensors.

These machine learning models have not only simplified the development of the context-aware applications but also have taken them to the masses (Kwapisz et al. 2010a) by minimizing the tedious task of creating complex and often hand-coded

A. K. Ramakrishnan (✉) · D. Preuveneers · Y. Berbers
iMinds-DistriNet, KU Leuven, Celestijnenlaan 200A, 3001 Leuven, Belgium
e-mail: arun.ramakrishnan@cs.kuleuven.be

D. Preuveneers
e-mail: davy.preuveneers@cs.kuleuven.be

Y. Berbers
e-mail: yollande.berbers@cs.kuleuven.be

© Springer Science+Business Media New York 2014
P. Brézillon, A. J. Gonzalez (eds.), *Context in Computing*,
DOI 10.1007/978-1-4939-1887-4_9

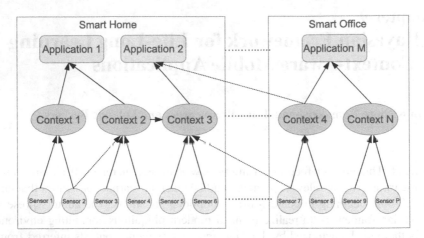

Fig. 9.1 A conceptual overview of interactions between context-aware applications and modern Ubiquitous Computing environments (Ramakrishnan et al. 2013)

knowledge bases of inference and adaptation rules. Nevertheless, collection and representation of training data, and model learning are still non-trivial tasks that are being aggravated by the dynamic, heterogeneous and ever evolving modern ubiquitous computing environments.

As illustrated in Fig. 9.1, modern smart environments (like SmartHome, SmartOffice, etc) sense, interpret and anticipate multiple user contexts (both simple and complex contexts) simultaneously, often by using resource constrained devices connected in a distributed software systems.

Note that Fig. 9.1 is a simplified representation of smart environments with focus on user context inference. In practice, the smart applications take multiple streams of data as input and user contexts usually act as a control parameter enabling intelligent behaviour of these applications.

Moreover, with mobile applications tapping into their environments, the operating conditions are continuously changing, giving rise to other non-trivial challenges such as sensor ambiguities (e.g., sensor failures and missing data). The dashed arrow lines in the Fig. 9.1 illustrate one such challenge, i.e., location dependent sensor availability. Therefore, these ubiquitous applications have to cope with heterogeneity, context drifts and continuous changes in operating conditions with minimal input from the end-users. This chapter highlights the need for various life-long learning principles and presents a Bayesian framework, HARD-BN (Ramakrishnan et al. 2013) to realize them.

The life-long learning techniques such as incremental, multi-view and meta learning we explore are realized on top of HARD-BN and validated in the scope of BUTLER[1], a EU FP7 project on the Internet of Things. The aim of BUTLER is to

---

[1] http://www.iot-butler.eu/

develop a horizontal platform for context-awareness cutting across multiple smart domains (e.g., smart home, smart city, smart health, etc.), necessitating applications to have mechanisms to handle the emerging heterogeneity and dynamicity in such open environments.

9.2 Related Work on Modelling and Inferring User Contexts for Mobile Applications

There is a great deal of literature available on machine learning based context modelling and recognition. In line with our use case described in the next section, we discuss a few prominent works on semantic location and user activities recognition using inertial sensors readily available in modern mobile devices.

Location has been an important contextual information primitive for intelligent applications. Nowadays, semantic localisation has an indisputable place not only to provide personalized user-centric services but also to infer other contexts such as the activity of the user (Liao et al. 2005). Although most of the earlier works has been focussing on accurately inferring semantic location from highly informative sensors such as GPS (Xin et al. 2010), the recent trend is to infer energy efficiently by utilizing less-informative yet energy efficient sensors such as ambient sensors (Martin et al. 2009).

Another important contextual information is activity awareness—especially the physical activity of the user—which can be readily inferred by analysing accelerometer data embedded in today's smart mobiles (Mannini and Sabatini 2010). For instance, (Mannini and Sabatini 2010; Kwapisz et al. 2010b) have studied the possibility of detecting physical activities of a user directly using low-level signals from tri-axial accelerometers. In (Mannini and Sabatini 2010), the high-level user activities such as standing, walking, running, etc., are modeled as latent state variables of a Hidden Markov Model (HMM) and are trained and inferred directly from the probability distribution of observable sensor readings i.e., a body-worn accelerometer. Contrarily, in (Yin et al. 2008; Liao et al. 2005), the authors have inferred activities indirectly through user location which in turn were estimated from other low-level sensors (e.g. signal strengths from wireless LAN beacons).

Today's smart phones come with an increasing range of sensing, communication, storage and computational resources, but an ill-informed usage of information rich contextual sensors and resource hungry machine learning techniques would adversely affect the normal function of those devices (Aaron et al. 2010). Recent works in ubiquitous mobile computing have considered device energy efficiency and explored various mitigation techniques: selecting a optimal set of sensors (Piero et al. 2008), dynamically switching on-off certain high-cost sensors (Dawud et al. 2012) and dynamically adapting the sensor sampling frequency (Zhixian et al. 2012). These performance-efficiency trade-offs not only necessitates the presence of various heterogeneous context sources but can also benefit from the heterogeneity of the modern smart environments by dynamically selecting appropriate context sources depending on the application's objectives. These trade-off can exist either while choosing an inference method (i.e., machine learning algorithms) or while choosing an appropriate context source. For example, if an entertainment application with no critical requirement on performance requests user activity information, it can be inferred from location information instead of switching on dedicated sensors (e.g., accelerometers).

9.3 A Novel Bayesian Framework for Context-Aware Applications

Based on the literature study in the previous section, we can conclude that the recent works are successful in modelling and inferring user contexts from low-level sensors with fewer input from the user by using various machine learning algorithms. Nevertheless, most works assume that ideal conditions are available (e.g., availability of sufficient training data, availability of data sources at run time, etc.). Although the presence of correlations among user contexts is identified and their benefits are emphasized, we are unaware of any work on mobile context-aware applications which make use of multi-view learning or meta learning techniques to leverage the inherent dynamism and heterogeneity of the mobile sensing infrastructures for their benefits. In this section, we present a typical use case for ubiquitous computing and present our Bayesian framework to model the user contexts for such use cases.

9.3.1 Motivating Use Cases and Requirements

As a running example, consider a loosely coupled context recognition framework that can support multiple Personal Assistant application scenarios that rely on the same sensor/inference infrastructure.

Two personal assistant applications that rely on such a framework are described below.

Smart notifier: A smart notification system that seamlessly alters the medium (voice/text/mail) of notification based on the current location and activities of the user. As a major problem to realize such a system is the inability of a single sensor device to recognize multiple location cues relevant for the application at hand, we propose to utilize multiple heterogeneous context sources distributed spatially across different ubiquitous infrastructures (e.g., wearable devices, a home/office wireless sensor networks, smart phones, etc.). Various location cues inferred are: at home, work, outdoors-alone, outdoors-public place, car, public-transport.

Activity monitor: Monitor and measure the current physical activity levels of the user using the accelerometer embedded in smart phones and periodically inform the user to motivate him to achieve a minimal physical activity on a regular basis.

The significant high-level functional and non-functional requirements of the framework for these application scenarios are:

1. Be able to model different types of heterogeneous contexts and context sources.
2. Have the flexibility to add and remove contexts at run-time.
3. Support performance-efficiency trade-offs w.r.t. application specific requirements.
4. Be resilient to sensor ambiguities such as temporary unavailability of context sources or missing data to maintain a given quality of service.

For instance, when the primary sensor of a localization module (i.e., GPS) is unavailable, the system should still be able to reasonably predict the user location of interest using secondary sensors or other co-related contexts. For example, active variations in the CPU load of the computer at the office can suggest the presence of the user at work whereas the detection of multiple unrecognised Bluetooth enabled devices and GPS readings can overrule and predict the presence of the user in a public place and travelling. Note that these applications have certain Quality of Service requirements i.e., minimal prediction accuracy limits for an acceptable performance, say an accuracy of 90 % is sufficient for user activity whereas 95 % for semantic location context and the framework can thrive to be energy-efficient provided it has achieved this minimum performance limits.

9.3.2 HARD-BN: A Heterarchical, Autonomic, Recursive and Distributed Bayesian Network

As there is a need for representing various contexts of interest and their sources, along with the meta-data such as possible co-relations and associated performance-efficiency trade-offs, we have developed a graphical Bayesian framework (HARD-BN) to model user contexts.

Technically, HARD-BN is a collection of naive Bayesian networks where each individual Bayesian network models high level contexts (see Fig. 9.2).

As stated in the Sect. 9.3.1, the application scenarios require only the continuous monitoring of current physical activity of the user (i.e., 'staying still', 'walking' and 'running') and the semantic location of the user, namely home, work, outdoors-alone, outdoors-public place, car, public-transport. The available context sources are two physical sensors—accelerometer and GPS—and a set of soft sensors such as IP address and WiFi ssid monitors, Bluetooth enabled device discovery module and CPU load monitors for the devices.

As shown in Fig. 9.3, the high level contexts—location and activities of the user—are modelled as parent nodes with their respective context sources. Note that two different Bayesian networks are used here to model the location information as the context sources are available in different platforms (say GPS, WiFi ssid and Bluetooth device discovery on smart mobile, and IP address and CPU load on desktop computers).

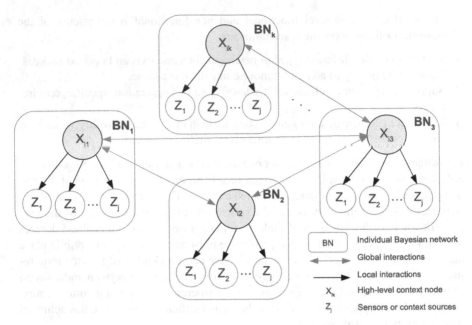

Fig. 9.2 A conceptual overview of an heterarchical autonomic recursive distributed Bayesian network (Ramakrishnan et al. 2013)

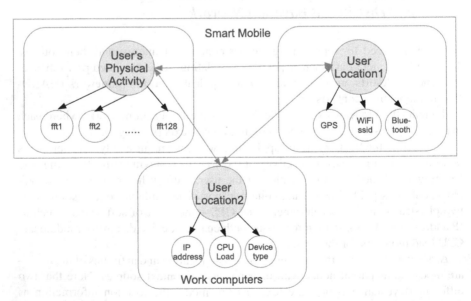

Fig. 9.3 An instance of HARD-BN framework realizing a scenario from the personal assistant case study (Ramakrishnan et al. 2013)

The application components for the smart phone are compatible with Android 4.0—Ice Cream Sandwich. Hence, two versions of the framework are developed (in Java): one for Android and another one for desktop computers. The learning and inference techniques are implemented using Weka[2], a collection of machine learning algorithms suitable for Java based learning and inference applications. Data is collected from four users (all male in the age group of 25–35) over a week covering different user locations and activities. The ground truth is collected in real time using an Android application and later correlated manually with the sensor data.

9.4   Incremental Learning and Self-Adaptation

Learning or training is an important step in any supervised machine learning algorithms and most classical algorithms assume that sufficient training data are available prior to classification. As outlined in Sect. 9.1, the characteristics of modern environments do not guarantee this assumption for context-aware applications.

Hence, there is a need to design machine learning algorithms to learn from new training examples even after deployment of the models and to add/remove a new context or sensors at run-time. For instance, in HARD-BN the likelihood values (measurement model) of the context sources are incremented with each new instance and the updated values are used to predict the class value probabilistically for the new instance, i.e.:

$$P(Z_j | X_{ik}), \ \forall \ i = 1, \ldots, n; \ k = 1, \ldots, m \text{ and } j = 1, \ldots, p$$

where Z_j is the observation of the jth sensor source information conditioned on the ith context value in kth Bayesian network as shown in Fig. 9.2. In our running example, the likelihood values of energy in the accelerometer readings (fft values) corresponding to each class value of the *User's Physical Activity* context node will be incremented according to the new example. Similarly the measurement model of the individual Bayesian networks that is incremented when observing the other high-level context nodes i.e.,

$$P(X_{ik} | X_{ab}), \ \forall \ i, a = 1, \ldots, n; \ k, b = 1, \ldots, m \text{ and } ik \neq ab$$

where Z_{ik} is the observation of the ith context value in kth Bayesian network conditioned on the ath context value in bth Bayesian network with a constrain that kth Bayesian network and bth Bayesian network are not the same network.

In our running example, a distribution over semantic locations corresponding to each context value of the *User's Physical Activity* node is learnt incrementally at this step. As the learning in HARD-BN involves estimating the likelihoods described above in the individual BNs, they can be easily parallelized as concurrent tasks

---

[2] http://www.cs.waikato.ac.nz/ml/weka/

to reduce the overall training time. As a result, HARD-BN can accommodate the context drifts in long-term such as learning new Device types for User Location2 context node and new WiFi ssid for the User Location1 node in Fig. 9.3.

In addition to incremental parameter learning, HARD-BN also supports self-adaptation of the network structure in response to addition or deletion of context sources by modifying the inference algorithm at run-time. If any particular context value is not available, then its likelihood value is omitted while calculating the posterior. For instance, while calculating the posterior of User's physical activity based on other high-level contexts in Fig. 9.3, if the User Location3 context node (localisation based on ambient sensors) is not available any more because user switched to another smart phone which does not support those sensors, then the likelihood of that node will be omitted while calculating the posterior. For addition of new context nodes, the corresponding likelihood value is included after evaluating the stability of the node's prediction on the last n data.

9.5 Multi-View Learning: Leveraging Data Heterogeneity

In general, co-training and multi-view learning leverage the consistency among multiple views in a dataset to improve the prediction rate. The primary idea is to bootstrap the learning with different classifiers for distinct data views (either different feature sets or data sets) where pseudo-labeled data are used iteratively for training when atleast one of the classifiers is confident enough (Xu et al. 2013). HARD-BN leverage multi-view learning not only to improve the prediction performance but also to introduce robustness in ubiquitous application by creating redundant views of different context information without compensating much on performance.

Inference in HARD-BN is done in bootstrap mode by recursively executing two steps to combine the global and local views of the individual Bayesian networks. First, a global view on the estimate of each high-level context nodes is generated by combining objective prior probabilities (uniform distribution) and evidences from other high-level contexts. Later, in order to generate a local view from dedicated sensors, the posterior estimated from the global view is used as an informed prior to determine the most probable value for each of the high-level contexts.

9.5.1 Generating a Global View on Context Nodes

The advantages of the informed prior is well known in the literature, but often paid less attention to because of the practical difficulties in acquiring them for highly dynamic systems. The objective of this inference step is to utilize the global influence of a context on other co-related context information to update the uniform prior distribution for improved prediction.

$$P'(X_{ik}) = P''(X_{ik}) \prod P(X_{ab}|X_{ik}),$$

$\forall\, i, a = 1, \ldots, n;\ k, b = 1, \ldots, m$ and $ik \neq ab$

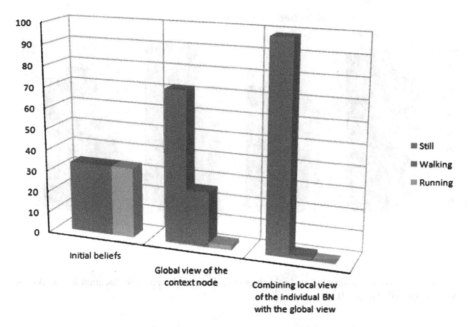

Fig. 9.4 Multi-view learning in HARD-BN for *User's Physical Activity* node in the running example

In our running example, an estimate of the current physical activities of the user is inferred from the location information. For example, if the location of the user is outdoors, then the probability of him/her being active is higher.

9.5.2   Generating a Local View in Individual Bayesian Networks

This step acts as a correction step where the estimated context values from the previous step are adjusted according to the evidence from the local observations.

$$P(X_{ik}) = \arg\max_{i} P'(X_{ik}) \prod P(Z_j|X_{ik}),$$

$$\forall\, i = 1,\ldots,n;\; k = 1,\ldots,m\; j = 1,\ldots,p \text{ and } ik \neq ab$$

In this final step of inference, the informed prior is combined with the local evidence from dedicated sensors (i.e, features from the accelerometer) to mitigate the influence of errors from the other high-level contexts (i.e., location node).

Figure 9.4 illustrates the influence of different inference steps on the probability distribution of *User's Physical Activity* node of the running example. Initially, all the class values *staying still, walking, running* had the same probabilities. At the end of the first step, contextual information from other high-level context nodes

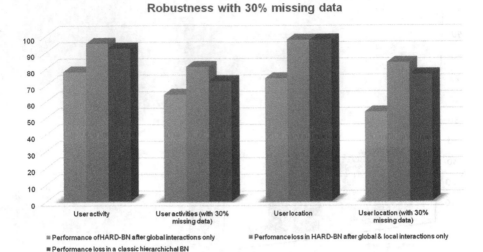

Fig. 9.5 Multi-view learning induced robustness to missing values for user location and activities contexts modelled in HARD-BN

(i.e., semantic location of the user is office) is used by the framework to modify the distribution favouring *staying still and walking* over *running*. In the next step, the accelerometer readings are combined with the informative priors to arrive at the final estimate of the probability distribution for the *User's Physical Activity* node.

To summarize, the term $P''(X_{ik})$ is the objective prior for the context variables with equal probability distribution for the possible values of a context node and $P'(X_{ik})$ is the informed prior obtained from the global view of the framework. Note that the likelihood estimates used while generating the global view is the latest likelihood estimates of the other high-level context nodes available from previous iteration or time step. This is understood to provide a good approximation of temporal dependencies of the context nodes on its own value in the previous time step. Furthermore, in general, the local view can be related to causality whereas global view estimates the co-relations among various loosely coupled high-level contexts.

Another major objective of combining multiple views of context in HARD-BN is to create robustness for contexts to missing values. Most of the existing works (Maytal and Foster 2007; Sagha et al. 2010) handle the missing data issue at prediction by imputation of raw data through various statistical methods, imputation decision trees, k-means methods, etc. In this chapter, HARD-BN imputes the data at the classifier level where the global view generates an estimate of the possible context values of the BN (based on the other co-Bayesian networks) for which the low-level sensor data are missing. Figure 9.5 illustrates the robustness resulting from multi-view learning in HARD-BN in the presence of 30 % missing data.

Also note that under the minimal performance requirement criteria in HARD-BN, combining global and local views show improvement in realizing non-functional

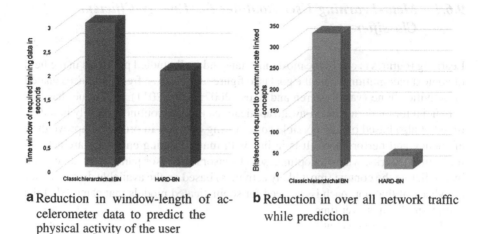

a Reduction in window-length of accelerometer data to predict the physical activity of the user

b Reduction in over all network traffic while prediction

Fig. 9.6 Reduction in data required for prediction due to multi-view learning

requirements such as response time and network traffic. Figure 9.6 shows the reduction in time for context sensing due to reduction in window size of accelerometer data for predicting user physical activity and amount of data required for predicting with the required minimum confidence compared to a typical hierarchical Bayesian network. Note that the energy and memory efficiency of the framework can vary widely depending on the configuration of the framework, and application specific pre-processing, learning and inference techniques being used. Hence, a thorough evaluation will be carried out as part of our future works.

9.6   Meta-Learning: Learning to Learn

The definition of meta-learning has been ever-expanding since its introduction by (Rice 1976), where its initial scope was restricted to a formal abstract model that can explore and select the best algorithm for a specific domain. Later works in the machine learning community have broadened the scope of meta-learning by including works on algorithm ranking, combination of individual classifiers/algorithms, self-adaptive algorithms and incremental life-long learning.

Despite the varying definitions, the central question to meta-learning has been: how to improve the performance of machine learning algorithms for a particular domain (over time) by exploiting the (meta-)knowledge about the learning and the problem domain?

Despite the efforts, the goal of meta-learning remains far from being achieved because no single algorithm can work well on all domains. Hence, we take the more pragmatic approach for meta-learning i.e., utilizing domain knowledge to improve the machine learning models both at design and run-time.

9.6.1 Meta-Learning User Routines for Energy-Efficient Classifiers

Learning routines is one of the most important and well-studied problems in the field of context recognition where the goal is to figure out the most frequent places visited or activities done (van Kasteren and Krose 2007; Sadri 2011). We argue that it is beneficial for modern context-aware applications to learn routines not only based on time but also based on any possible co-occurring contexts in order to improve their efficiency and performance. It is in line with many existing energy-aware activity recognition works, where an optimal set of sensors or sensor parameters are chosen by predicting the context (most likely activities) based on the available data. A major drawback of that approach is the need for sophisticated models that can predict the evolution of states over time.

Hence, we propose to utilize the other co-occurring contexts in order to isolate the sub-space of concern out of all possible contextual state space which in turn can be used to activate selected set of sensors for improved energy efficiency. This approach takes advantage of the nature of the probability distribution of user contexts i.e., not all context values are equally probably, but each context (say user activity or location) can have only a small subset of all its possible values depending on other co-related user contexts. For example, if the user location is known (e.g., home/office), the set of all possible activities of the user can be reduced to smaller set specific to the location which, in turn would help to not switch on energy-consuming but information rich dedicated sensors. The idea is to give a 'warm start' for contextual sensing instead of completely starting from scratch. HARD-BN inherently supports multi-view routine learning for the users by generating the global view of the context nodes. The meta-learning module in HARD-BN is then used to discover such user and environment specific patterns in the co-related context nodes and utilize it to improve the overall energy efficiency. For instance, we found that the user 3 is not at all active while at his desk late at night. This meta-knowledge is utilized to dynamically switch-off the accelerometer to save considerable energy.

9.6.2 Meta-Learning for Detecting View-Disagreement

Although using multiple Bayesian networks to model a single context type (say location) works well for distributed infrastructures, it might create a consensus problem where different networks have conflicting belief about the same context type. The view-disagreement can occur because of multiple reasons: failure of sensors, temporary unavailability of the sensors, anomaly in user routines contradicting application's knowledge base the inability of an individual classifier to learn a context value, etc. For instance, Fig. 9.7 shows a typical view-disagreement problem where the user location suggests the user to be active (global view) whereas the faulty accelerometer predicts that the user is *being still* in the next step while combining accelerometer data.

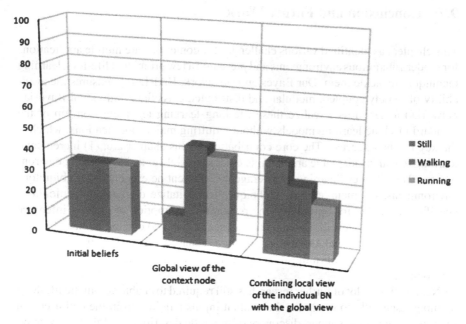

Fig. 9.7 The distribution of the context values of the *User's Physical Activity* showing view-disagreement

Identifying these view disagreements is as important and difficult as it is to resolve them.

In HARD-BN, these view disagreements are handled in an elegant way as shown in Fig. 9.7, i.e., the final inference results on a well-trained classifier will be (approximately) a uniform distribution indicating zero gain in knowledge about the corresponding contextual node even after reasoning with global and local views.

HARD-BN incorporates meta-learning to handle the view-disagreement resulting from the inability of an individual classifier to learn a context value by monitoring whether different Bayesian Networks are active and they belong to the same context types. For instance, a GPS based location inference Bayesian Network can suggest the user is travelling by car (based on the velocity estimates) and the Bluetooth device discovery Bayesian Network can suggest the user is in a public place whereas in reality the user might be in a public transport. The meta-learning module will detect these view disagreements and resolve it based on certain pre-defined rule-based domain knowledge. Note that the above example is a special case of view-disagreement resulting from the distributed nature of the HARD-BN, where we chose to model the distributed context sources using individual Bayesian networks.

9.7 Conclusion and Future Work

This chapter has identified various challenges for context-aware mobile applications for modern ubiquitous environments and presented a few prominent life-long learning techniques to tackle them. Our Bayesian framework, HARD-BN, ensures the availability of loosely coupled, modular and distributed classifiers (individual Bayesian networks) to seamlessly realize these life-long learning techniques on top of the standard machine learning models without requiring major modifications, which is the key for their success. The core contribution of this chapter are, (1) incremental learning to realize adaptable and flexible context models to tackle dynamic environments, (2) multi-view learning to leverage the inherent heterogeneity of ubiquitous environments, (3) meta-learning techniques to capitalize domain/application/user specific knowledge for optimizing the resource consumption of context inference tasks and to detect view disagreements between distributed context models. Our experiments on the Personal Assistant application scenarios demonstrate the advantages of these techniques confirming their applicability for dynamic modern ubiquitous environments.

Nevertheless, a lot of further research is still required to enable automatic life-long learning, especially to minimize the explicit inputs required from the end users. In the future, we plan to support discovery of semantic descriptions of the newly arriving contexts and their sources in order to assist incremental learning and automate self-adaptation in HARD-BN. Moreover, another important aspect of meta-learning which will be investigated in the future is transfer learning, i.e., to transfer models for tasks learned under certain conditions to tasks under other conditions. For instance transferring the classifiers learned for existing users to the new users easing the latter's training requirements. Such transfer learning techniques will not only minimize the training required at the beginning but also result in smaller knowledge bases (especially in HARD-BN) as classifiers can be shared between users.

Acknowledgements This research is partially funded by the Research Fund KULeuven, and by the EU FP7 project BUTLER.

References

Aaron, C., Gernot, H.: An analysis of power consumption in a smartphone. In: Proceedings of the 2010 USENIX Conference on USENIX Annual Technical Conference (2010)

Dawud, G., Jurgen, C., Takashi, M., Michael, B.: Energy-efficient activity recognition using prediction. In: 16th Annual International Symposium on Wearable Computers (ISWC), pp. 29–36 (2012)

Kwapisz, J.R., Weiss Gary, M., Moore Samuel, A.: Activity recognition using cell phone accelerometers. SIGKDD **12**(2), 74–82 (2010a)

Kwapisz, J.R., Weiss, G.M., Moore, S.A.: Activity recognition using cell phone accelerometers. In: Proceedings of the Fourth International Workshop on Knowledge Discovery from Sensor Data, pp. 10–18 (2010b)

Liao, L., Fox, D., Kautz, H.: Location-based activity recognition. In: Advances in Neural Information Processing Systems (NIPS), pp. 787–794. MIT Press, Cambridge (2005)

Mannini, A., Sabatini, A.M.: Machine learning methods for classifying human physical activity from on-body accelerometers. Sensors **10**(2), 1154–1175 (2010)

Martin, A., Ionut, C., Romit, R.C.: SurroundSense: mobile phone localization via ambience fingerprinting. In: Proceedings of the 15th Annual International Conference on Mobile Computing and Networking, pp. 261–272 (2009)

Maytal, S.-T., Foster, P.: Handling missing values when applying classification models. J. Mach. Learn. **8**, 1623–1657 (2007)

Piero, Z., Clemens, L., Thomas, S., Elisabetta, F., Daniel, R., Luca, B., Gerhard., T.: Activity recognition from on-body sensors: accuracy-power trade-off by dynamic sensor selection. In: European Conference on Wireless Sensor Networks, pp. 17–33 (2008)

Ramakrishnan, A., Preuveneers, D., Berbers, Y.: A loosely coupled and distributed Bayesian framework for multi-context recognition in dynamic ubiquitous environments. In: IEEE International Conference on Ubiquitous Intelligence and Computing, December 2013

Rice J.R.: The algorithm selection problem. In: Advances in Computers, vol. 15, pp. 65–118 (1976)

Sadri, F.: Ambient intelligence: a survey. ACM Comput. Surv. **43**(4), 36:1–36:66 (2011)

Sagha, H., Millán, J.d.R., Chavarriaga, R.: A probabilistic approach to handle missing data for multi-sensory activity recognition. In: Workshop on Context Awareness and Information Processing in Opportunistic Ubiquitous Systems, September 2010

van Kasteren, T., Krose, B.: Bayesian activity recognition in residence for elders. In: 3rd IET International Conference on Intelligent Environments, 2007, IE 07, pp. 209–212 (2007)

Xin, C., Gao, C., Christian, S.J.: Mining significant semantic locations from GPS data. In: Proceedings VLDB Endow, vol. 3, issue 1–2, pp. 1009–1020, September 2010

Xu, C., Tao, D., Xu, C.: A survey on multi-view learning. CoRR, vol. abs/1304.5634 (2013)

Yin, J., Yang, Q., Shen, D., Li, Z.-N.: Activity recognition via user-trace segmentation. ACM Trans. Sen. Netw. **4**(4), 19:1–19:34 (2008)

Zhixian, Y., Vigneshwaran, S., Dipanjan, C., Archan, M., Karl, A.: Energy-efficient continuous activity recognition on mobile phones: an activity-adaptive approach. In: 16th Annual International Symposium on Wearable Computers (ISWC), pp. 17–24 (2012)

Chapter 10
Context and NLP

Victor Hung

Abstract Early Natural Language Processing (NLP) endeavors often employed contextual cues as supplemental assistive measures—secondary sources of data to help understand its users' linguistic inputs. Context was used more as a tie-breaking tool rather than as a central component in conversational negotiation. Recent work in context-based reasoning has inspired a paradigm shift from these context-*assisted* techniques to context-*centric* NLP systems. This evolution of context's role in NLP is necessary to support today's sophisticated Human-Computer Interaction (HCI) applications, such as personal digital assistants, language tutors, and question answering systems. In these applications, there is a strong sense of utilitarian, purpose-driven conversation. Such an emphasis on goal-oriented behavior requires that the underlying NLP methods be capable of navigating through a conversation at the conceptual, or contextual level. This chapter explores the natural bond between NLP and context-based methods, as it manifests itself in the context-centric paradigm. Insights and examples are provided along the way to shed light on this evolved way of engineering natural language-based HCI.

10.1 Introduction

Natural Language Processing (NLP) encompasses the internalization of linguistic constructs into data structures that can be manipulated and analyzed by machines. NLP systems are designed to process a user's spoken utterance or text input to render a conversationally appropriate response. The overarching challenge here is the development of effective tools that enable a computer to "understand" a human user's linguistic input, whether in text or speech form.

Early attempts at mastering NLP envisioned a word-for-word collection of user responses, followed by an extensive analysis of each sentence-capture to determine a proper machine retort. With rampant semantic and syntactic ambiguities caused by the general complexity of spoken language, along with the limited computing

V. Hung (✉)
Intelligent Systems Laboratory, University of Central Florida, Orlando, FL 32816, USA
e-mail: victor@knights.ucf.edu

© Springer Science+Business Media New York 2014   143
P. Brézillon, A. J. Gonzalez (eds.), *Context in Computing*,
DOI 10.1007/978-1-4939-1887-4_10

power of the time, contextual cues were integrated into NLP algorithms as an assistive resource. Researchers saw the need to add context to a machine's ability to disambiguate meaning for the words voiced by its human users. For example, a system could identify the proper meaning of a user's intention of the word "pitcher," depending on if the speaker was already talking about orange juice or the New York Yankees baseball team.

Context, however, was simply a secondary tool to help make these semantic judgments. As NLP technology began to expand its horizons beyond parlor tricks in the form of quirky computerized chatting services, to useful instruments of human-computer interaction (HCI), the role of context also began to mature beyond its roots as an assistive device.

This chapter documents the evolution of context from its supporting role to the full-blown mechanisms of context-centric systems. The next section examines the necessity of context in linguistic systems, followed by a discussion of context-assisted NLP. The final section presents the next generation of context-based linguistic systems with an exploration in the state-of-the-art in context-centric NLP systems.

10.2   The Need for Context in NLP

NLP deals with developing algorithms to understand a human user's language-based responses. The primary obstacle in developing these systems is overcoming the multiple sources of linguistic ambiguity. (Wilks 2005) These ambiguities cause complications in syntactic processing and semantic understanding. (Baker et al. 1994) Such ambiguities can be easier resolved when the context of the user input is taken into consideration. This section examines the need for contextual awareness for the sake of linguistic disambiguation.

10.2.1   Syntactic Ambiguity

NLP may be employed to perform a simple examination of word-for-word text inputs. This syntactic dissection of word groupings may undergo Parts of Speech (POS) tagging as a means to further a machine's understanding of a user's input.

In dealing with syntax in NLP, ambiguities crop up when sentence parts can be interpreted in a variety of permutations. The sentence "the man bought the car with the check" may be interpreted as a person purchasing a vehicle with a cashier's check, or it could also mean a man buying a particular automobile adorned with a checkmark decal. Each of these meanings has different POS tagging signatures. It is up to the listener to determine the speaker's intent.

Enabling contextual awareness within a conversation proves to be an important asset in clarifying a speaker's meaning. Context allows the listener to incorporate any surrounding environmental cues to helps resolve syntactic ambiguity. For a machine, this process of identifying meaning from syntax through POS tagging can be aided by an a priori word database, such as WordNet. (Miller et al. 1990) Pairing POS tagging with machine learning (ML) techniques, the task of syntactic disambiguation can also be facilitated through probabilistic modeling. (Roth 1998)

Adding contextual data to these ML-based disambiguation systems improves the reliability of the POS tagging for a given user input. (Kübler et al. 2010) Knowing a sentence's parts of speech, however, does not necessitate enough conceptual understanding of the user's input for a machine to provide an appropriate response. The next step in linguistic understanding entails semantics processing, including overcoming the ambiguities associated with its practice.

10.2.2 Semantic Ambiguity

Once the POS structure for a user input is established, a linguistic system must drill further into determining its semantics. Phrase chunks may be identified between adjacent words to help with these semantics. "Red car," or "dog in the cage," or "wooden picture frame" are all chunks derived from the sentences "He drove the red car," "I waved to the dog in the cage," and "That is a wooden picture frame," respectively. An NLP system can now represent each of these phrases as a single-serving idea. A collection of these phrases could be processed to potentially produce a cohesive understanding.

Semantic ambiguity is caused when the meanings of the sentence parts may be interpreted in several ways, and much of this type of ambiguity is encountered when dealing with phrase chunks. (Wilks 2005) The sentence "the pitcher put the batter in the refrigerator" is one such example. Here, the listener must discern whether "batter" is a baseball player or a food item. To complicate things even further, the words "pitcher" and "refrigerator" each fall into a food-related context, while "pitcher" and "batter" are both baseball terms. This is where context would greatly enhance a linguistic system's ability to discern semantic meaning. Thusly, contextual cues would be necessary to soundly choose one meaning over the other.

Given this discussion on ambiguities in linguistic systems, it is clear that an additional dimension to resolve competing meanings must be provided for NLP to be effective. Researchers have tinkered with the idea of incorporating context as that extra edge to performing disambiguation more effectively. The next section further explores the notion of employing context as an assistive disambiguation tool in NLP systems.

10.3 Context-Assisted NLP

To better direct an NLP system's ambiguity resolution process, its search space can be dramatically pruned by incorporating clues from the ambient conversational surroundings. Such contextual assistance reduces the entirety of a machine's knowledge base to only a fraction of this data. This subset of the knowledge base is known as a context.

The use of contexts effectively adds an extra layer of knowledge-based input to any reasoning system. ML-based semantic analysis methods have been enhanced by introducing context-based information into their training routines. (Mooney 2006) In general, NLP problems can easily be enhanced through context-based methods (Porzel and Strube 2002), such as those found in spoken language translation (Levin et al. 1995) and knowledge modeling (Porzel et al. 2006). By adding a sense of context to assist an NLP system, the ability of the machine to accurately establish its users' intent becomes more probable.

Context-assisted NLP was also featured in the works of Gonzalez et al. (1991) and Towhidnejad et al. (1993), both of which presented techniques for automatic semantic clarification in a knowledge base. Each incorporated context-based solutions for determining missing or erroneous details in component descriptions found in computer-aided design (CAD) drawings, relying on narrowing down the list of possible candidates using constraints induced by the contextual cues inferred from the surrounding information.

The remainder of this section furthers the discussion on the use of context assistance for two specific NLP applications: speech recognition systems and dialog management.

10.3.1   Context-Assisted Speech Recognition

The underlying algorithms involved in NLP's processing of syntax and semantics are realized in the realm of Automated Speech Recognition (ASR). These systems are designed to transform sounds from a user's voice into a textual representation. The machine must not only decipher a user's syntax, but it also must endure any of the physical signal-related nuances associated with ASR technology, usually caused by speaker accent and/or excessive background noise. Before reaching any concept-level decisions on a user's speech, ASR software must first capture the raw syntax of a user's voice.

The accuracy of an ASR system, however, is often hampered by the linguistic ambiguities that also plague human-to-human conversations. Speech recognition ambiguities appear when a speaker's original input can be easily replaced with words that are phonetically similar. For example, the phrase "wreck a nice beach" could be a viable replacement for the similar-sounding phrase "recognize speech" (Lieberman et al. 2005).

Resolution of speech recognition ambiguities often employ the extra dimension of contextual cues to constrain the number of possible matching words for the user's utterances. The expectation for an NLP machine to be competent of speech-based input further complicates this quest for understanding the user.

ASR researchers saw the use of context as an opportunity to improve their systems. Early work, such as the MINDS project (Young 1989) utilized context to make predictions and expectations on user's speech input. Contextual information was gathered from a list of goals, sub-goals, and domain subjects that MINDS deemed as significant for the conversation. Additional knowledge sources were augmented to build up this sense of context. Young's findings did indeed support the notion that context improved semantic accuracy, citing an improvement with using a context-assisted algorithm over a non-predictive grammar policy.

Serridge's (1997) phoneme-driven speech recognition utilized contexts from domain information. A Viterbi search was modified to traverse a search space pruned by a context-dependent speech model. This research served as an example that context-dependent models can be used as inexpensive methods to reduce speech recognition errors. Fügen et al. (2004) reduced speech recognition errors through the use of a knowledge-based dialog manager. Their coupling of a domain-specific dialog manager with a speech recognizer saw statistically significant reductions in word errors. In both of these efforts, the addition of contextual domain information allowed for improved performances in ASR.

Yan and Zheng (2004) used contexts to serve as dialog constraints for better speech recognition. Their approach emphasized a user goal-centered architecture, where conversation topics exist as expected foci, in essence, contexts. Each expected focus brings forth a set of associated constraint words to facilitate the understanding of the dialog. Yan and Zheng's work would eventually be implemented in the EasyFlight airline booking system.

Eisman et al. (2012) developed a natural language-based virtual assistant framework that allows for omissions of words in conversations. Inaccurate ASR systems often cause gaps in the user's speech. Eisman et al.'s work heavily relied on context cues in lieu of this missing syntax. Anzalone et al.'s (2012) human-robot interaction research also dealt with ASR inaccuracies. They concluded that ASR difficulties are mission critical challenges when dealing with speech-based robot-human interfaces. Their use of context mitigated the complications caused by ASR errors.

10.3.2   Context-Assisted Dialog Management

Dialog management refers to the NLP technology that negotiates a human-computer conversation. These discourse mechanisms are found in the heart of every chatbot, interactive avatar, or embodied conversation agent (ECA).

Context assistance and dialog management was instantiated in the ProBot (Sammut 2001) chatbot. User inputs were matched to fire off resulting output responses from a Prolog expression rule base. When unexpected utterances were received, a contextually-organized hierarchy of information sought to assist Probot for an appropriate response. An activation level triggered by user interest shaped the hierarchical form. The top-level context provided the relevant rules for interaction. The basic idea here is that Sammut's work provided a glimpse into utilizing relevant contexts to provide appropriate behavior to a user.

The context-based techniques in this section exemplify how context assistance can be utilized to enhance NLP, especially when dealing with semantic disambiguation. In these examples, context established itself as an impactful factor in improving NLP systems, even if it only served as a supporting function. The natural evolutionary step up in context's role in NLP systems entertains the notion that context can play a primary role in driving natural language interactivity—this is what is known as context-centric NLP (Hung and Gonzalez 2013).

10.4 Context-Centric NLP

The previous discussion on context-assisted NLP framed context as a support mechanism for ambiguity resolution in NLP. Context-centric NLP takes context's importance a step further, where it exists as a processing centerpiece, alongside the user's linguistic input itself. Under this paradigm, the conversational input-output loop becomes a feedback system centered on the state of the context parameter during a linguistic human-computer interaction. In these context-centric systems, the driving behavioral force shifts from the linguistic level to that of the conceptual level. The next sections describe the methods and technologies involved in identifying and manipulating contexts to drive NLP applications.

10.4.1 Context Identification

The key task in a context-centric architecture is context identification. (Gonzalez et al. 2008) The general infrastructure for such a process is very similar to identifying words in ASR. In ASR, the collective input phonemes are converted to a list of matches from a dictionary of known words, and that list is further pruned using a variety of methods to provide the resultant recognized speech string. Likewise, context identification processes a raw collection of phrase chunks or the input text itself into a possible context list from existing contexts. To further refine this list of context possibilities, fine-tuning methods have been devised to determine the best matching context. The remainder of this section expands upon the context identification process for context-centric NLP endeavors.

Researchers have tackled context identification using both knowledge-based and data-driven methods. Knowledge-based context identification often takes the form of a rule-based state machine, offering full control of context's boundary definitions. The specialized hand-modeling of this method, however, can be time-consuming and tedious.

Mahmoudi et al.'s (2012) research paper indexer uses a knowledge-based context identifier. In their work, an a priori domain ontology defines the contextual boundaries for each research topic, and an NLP processing of the papers using this knowledge base performs the indexing. Weichselbraun et al. (2014) devised an opinion mining system that also relied on a contextual database derived from a domain-specific training corpus. This work has implications in improving methods for affective computing, such as those found in SenticNet (Cambria et al. 2014). The KnowCIT project (Breuing 2010) equipped an ECA, Max, with Wikipedia as its context knowledge base. Early work with Max revealed the importance of context identification when single utterances are being exchanged in a dialog.

Data-driven context identification uses ML to produce relationship models between inputs and contexts. These methods yield more generalizable solutions, but their effectiveness is only as good as the quality and quantity of training data. Varges et al. (2011) incorporated such a method by using Partially Observable Markov Models (POMDP) to assist a dialog manager with conceptual disambiguation. While data-driven methods are becoming more prevalent, there still exists a need for the expertise-based modeling of knowledge-based systems, especially in NLP. (Dethlefs 2014) An optimal context identification method would combine the advantages of both knowledge-based and data-driven methods.

Angrosh et al. (2010) tackled context identification with conditional random fields. Their work consisted of categorizing research articles using the body of sentences found in related works sections. These sections provided two opportunities for context identification: ML processing of the citation content and knowledge-based NLP sentence analysis. The combination of these tasks provides a hybrid solution for performing context categorization using data-driven and knowledge-based methods. Waltinger et al. (2012) also employ a hybrid context identification method in their question-answering systems. Their work utilizes both an ML-based question classifier with a human-in-the-loop context definition process. Nie et al. (2013) and Dong et al. (2011) use knowledge-based contextual information to enhance the results of their data-driven systems. Specifically, Nie et al. identify segmentations in Chinese news transcripts using context-enhanced ML methods. Dong et al. exploit context-centric ontologies meant to detect semantic similarities.

Context identification remains the key mechanism for any context-centric system. In NLP, this identification process can be accomplished through data-driven means such as ML, knowledge-based methods such as rule-based detection, or a mix of these two techniques. Following this discussion on the mechanics of context identification, the rest of this section will present an applied look at context-centric NLP, beginning with context-centric dialog management.

10.4.2 Context-Centric Dialog Management

The Flycht-Eriksson and Jönsson (2000) dialog manager model consists of two parts: a discourse model and a knowledge base. The discourse model is the blueprint on how output responses will be chosen given a user input. The knowledge base provides the foundation of facts, rote rules, quips, or any generally useful information that the dialog manager may use at its disposal to build its output response. In contrast to the earlier mentions of context-assisted dialog management, a context-centric dialog manager utilizes context as the central driving force of both the discourse model and the knowledge base. (Hung and Gonzalez 2013)

By feeding context into the discourse model, the dialog manager can now provide a response with strong relevance to the content matter without jeopardizing the conversational focus. The heavy use of context in a dialog manager's discourse helps to enhance conversational cohesiveness, and thus the realism of an HCI experience. Kunc et al.'s (2013) work sought to incorporate turn behavior into their discourse model, where environmental context was a pivotal input into outcome of the dialog manager's turns. Gardent et al. (2013) used contextual awareness as the determining factor into their discoveries on the differences between open dialog cues versus tightly constrained expectation-based discourse model interaction.

A context-driven knowledge base blends seamlessly with a context-centric discourse model, as the shared identified context can immediately prune the knowledge base down to an easily manageable subset of information to be used by the dialog manager. Skillen et al. (2012) advocated the use of context-centric knowledge bases with their findings on personalized, user-specific contexts. The Semantic-Driven Context Aware System (SDCAS) (Sakirulai et al. 2011) relies on temporal contexts to aid in its information management dialog management. Griol et al. (2014) conceived a context-based dialog management framework that was reusable for different domains. Their work exemplifies the idea that context-centric architecture lends itself to easily interchangeable knowledge bases.

Context-centric architecture decouples NLP technology from its syntax-dependent roots. Empowering machines with contextual awareness neutralizes the linguistic ambiguities that were once a stumbling block for conversation agents. This paradigm shift towards concepts, rather than parts of speech, elicits a more pragmatic approach to NLP, where the goals and tasks of the user supersede the importance of the actual words she or he is saying. The next section presents a set of recent development in applied NLP agents that utilize context-centric dialog management.

10.4.3   Context-Centric NLP Agents

Today's most accessible and useful NLP conversation agents rely on this basic mantra of context-centric architecture: there is a finite number of contexts for any given agent, and each context is relative distinct and mostly useful in nature. This section explores a variety of context-centric NLP agents, all of whom share this aforementioned technological philosophy.

Assistive systems remain one of the most populous groupings of NLP-based agents. Context-centric architectures work very well in these assistance-based environments because of the tightly constrained context set often found in their subject matter expertise knowledge bases. One such assistive system exists in the Project LifeLike ECA, based on the CONCUR context-centric dialog manager. (Hung and

Gonzalez 2013) This agent manifested itself as a fully animated 3-D avatar interactive information deployment tool for the U.S. National Science Foundation.

Latorre-Navarro and Harris (2014) developed another assistive context-centric agent, an academic schedule planning chatbot. The narrow knowledge base (course descriptions, instructor names, class schedules, user account information) for this conversation agent lends itself to a directed contextual identification effort.

Some other context-centric assistive agents include: the MobileSage agent (Røssvoll 2013) whose immediate contextual awareness of the physical world was designed to help its elderly users via natural language, and Shinozaki et al.'s (2013) ELIZA-based system that assisted in information technology counseling by exploiting a domain-specific corpus to drive the interaction dialog.

Language tutoring also lends itself to context-centric NLP implementations. The Dialog-based Computer Assisted Language Learning (DB-CALL) system (Lee et al. 2010) emulated human tutor behavior by cross-referencing a student's actual utterance against her or his intentions. These intentions were matched with the expected fluent response that the learner desired to attain. By limiting the context of the conversation to an expected response pairing with the verbal cues of the tutor, Lee et al. were able to provide an effective dialog system for the purposes of automating language learning feedback. Lee et al. (2012) extended DB-CALL's capabilities to robot platforms (Mero and Engkey) and a virtual 3-D learning game (Pomy).

Perhaps the most ubiquitous examples of context-centric NLP exist in the realm of Personal Assistant (PA) technology. PA agents allow human users to speak into a handheld device, such as a mobile phone to control features on the phone, or to ask for information. Examples of PA's include Apple's Siri and Google Now. (Mehra 2012)

As these PAs almost always exist within a smart phone platform, the reach of NLP is suddenly empowered with direct and speedy access to the Internet, combined with geographical location sensors via global positioning system (GPS) hardware. These sources of data formulate an enormous vault of knowledge, as well as provide contextual cues (as is the case with the GPS features). This enables devices to couple the powerful combination of contextual awareness (from location and person-specific usage profiling) with the immense data delivery services and off-loaded processing power provided by the Internet. These multimodal context identification systems suddenly make mobile devices powerful vehicles for context-centric applications. (Janarthanam et al. 2012)

Now companies such as Google and Apple can use powerful cloud-based ASR services to provide speech-based transcriptions, thus shifting the HCI experience focus back to the user's goals. The goals of a mobile PA user, however, are naturally contextually constrained, as there is a relatively limited number of actions to be done on a smart phone.

The existence of useful modern-day NLP agents has been made possible through the use of context-centric architectures. User intent is the basic drive in the discourse model for each of these agents, where the NLP system is in a constant state of fulfilling whatever requests are being communicated. The bounded number of request contexts helps to narrow down the contextual scope of a conversation, and the requests themselves provide clues into what pieces of information in the knowledge base are relevant for an appropriate response.

10.5 Conclusion

The major goal of an NLP input system is to accurately understand a user's response. There are two ways to define success in achieving this goal. The first deals with the accuracy of the mechanical translation of the response, or how well a system can transcribe each detected word. The other definition of success in understanding is a bit more abstract, as it deals with how well a machine can detect the user's intent, or conversational goals in his or her response.

A context-assisted system will focus its attention on the former description of success, making contextual information simply a tool to help disambiguate literal representations. The context-centric architecture, on the other hand, provides a more holistic approach at conversation. The calling card of any context-centric approach is the explicit use of user goals rather than the users' words. These goals translate directly into contexts that clue into the appropriate conversational discourse and the relevant knowledge needed for an NLP machine to give reasonable responses.

The engineering of context-centric NLP systems yields its own practical challenges. Specifically, the design should only support a manageable set of contexts, each of which is easily distinguishable from one another, for the sake of context identification purposes. Secondly, each context is generally associated with a purposeful action, so as to maintain the pragmatic relevance of the NLP system itself.

This chapter has presented the general challenges of NLP technology in the light of HCI applications. One effective tool to overcome these challenges is the incorporation of contextual awareness. As improvements in context-aware methods continue, the role of contexts in NLP continues to evolve from context-assisted algorithms to context-centric systems.

References

Angrosh, M.A., Cranefield, S., Stanger, N.: Context identification of sentences in related work sections using a conditional random field: towards intelligent digital libraries. Annual Joint Conference on Digital libraries, vol. 10, pp. 293–302 (2010)

Anzalone, S.M., Yoshikawa, Y., Ishiguro, H., Menegatti, E., Pagello, E., Sorbello, R.: A topic recognition system for real world human-robot conversations. Intell. Auton. Syst. **194**, 383–391 (2012)

Baker, K.L., Franz, A.M., Jordan, P.W.: Coping with ambiguity in knowledge-based natural language analysis. FLAIRS-94 (1994)

Breuing, A.: Improving human-agent conversations by accessing contextual knowledge from Wikipedia. WI-IAT Doctoral Workshop, in Conjunction with the 2010 IEEE/WIC/ACM International Conference on Web Intelligence and Intelligent Agent Technology, vol. 3, pp. 428–431 (2010)

Cambria, E., Olsher, D., Rajagopal, D.: SenticNet 3: A common and common-sense knowledge base for cognition-driven sentiment analysis. AAAI-14 (2014)

Dethlefs, N.: Context-sensitive natural language generation: From knowledge-driven to data-driven techniques. Lang. Linguist. Compass **8**(3), 99–115 (2014)

Dong, H., Hussain, F.K., Chang, E.: A context-aware semantic similarity model for ontology environments. Concurr. Comput.: Pract. Exp. **23**(5), 505–524 (2011)

Eisman, E.M., López, V., Castro, J.L.: A framework for designing closed domain virtual assistants. Expert Syst. Appl. **39**(3), 3135–3144 (2012)

Flycht-Eriksson, A., Jönsson, A.: Dialogue and domain knowledge management in dialogue systems. Proceedings of the 1st SIGdial Workshop on Discourse and Dialogue, vol. 10, pp. 121–130 (2000)

Fügen, C., Holzapfel, H., Waibel, A.: Tight coupling of speech recognition and dialog management—dialog-context dependent grammar weighting for speech recognition. INTERSPEECH-2004, pp. 169–172 (2004)

Gardent, C., Lorenzo, A., Nancy, L., Perez-Beltrachini, L., Rojas-Barahona, L.: Weakly and strongly constrained dialogues for language learning. SIGDIAL, pp. 357–359 (2013)

Gonzalez, A.J., Myler, H.R., Towhidnejad, M., McKenzie, F.D., Kladke, R.R.: Automated knowledge generation from a CAD database. Knowledge Discovery in Databases, pp. 383–396. AAAI, Menlo (1991)

Gonzalez, A., Stensrud, B., Barrett, G.: Formalizing context-based reasoning: A modeling paradigm for representing tactical human behavior. Int. J. Intell. Syst. **23**(7), 822–847 (2008)

Griol, D., Molina, J.M., de Miguel, A.S.: Domain and subtask-adaptive conversational agents to provide an enhanced human agent interaction. Advances in practical applications of heterogeneous multi-agent systems. The PAAMS Collection Lecture Notes in Computer Science, vol. 8473, pp. 134–145. Springer International, Switzerland (2014)

Hung, V., Gonzalez, A.: Context-centric speech-based human-computer interaction. Int. J. Intell. Syst. **28**(10), 1010–1037 (2013)

Janarthanam, S., Lemon, O., Liu, X., Bartie, P., Mackaness, W., Dalmas, T., Goetze, J.: Conversational natural language interaction for place-related knowledge acquisition. Place-Related Knowledge Acquisition Research Workshop, Spatial Cognition Conference (2012)

Kübler, S., Scheutz, M., Baucom, E., Israel, R.: Adding context information to part of speech tagging for dialogues. International Workshop on Treebanks and Linguistic Theories, vol. 9 (2010)

Kunc, L., Mikovec, Z., Slavík, P.: Avatar and dialog turn-yielding phenomena. Int. J. Technol. Hum. Interact. **9**(2), 66–88 (2013)

Latorre-Navarro, E.M., Harris, J.G.: A natural language conversational system for online academic advising. International Florida Artificial Intelligence Research Society Conference, vol. 27, pp. 186–189 (2014)

Lee, S., Lee, C., Lee, J., Noh, H., Lee, G.G.: Intention-based corrective feedback generation using context-aware model. International Conference on Computer Supported Education, vol. 1, pp. 11–18 (2010)

Lee, S., Noh, H., Lee, J., Lee, K., Lee, G.G.: Foreign language tutoring in oral conversations using spoken dialog systems. IEICE Trans. Inf. Syst. **95-D**(5), 1216–1228 (2012)

Levin, L., Glickman, O., Qu, Y., Gates, D., Lavie, A., Rose, C.P., Van Ess-Dykema, C., Waibel, A.: Using context in machine translation of spoken language. Proceedings of Theoretical and Methodological Issues in Machine Translation (TMI-95) (1995)

Lieberman, H., Faaborg, A., Daher, W., Espinosa, J.: How to wreck a nice beach you sing calm incense. International Conference on Intelligent User Interfaces (2005)

Mahmoudi, M.T., Taghiyareh, F., Rajavi, K., Pirouzi, M.S.: A context-aware framework for semantic indexing of research papers. International Conference on Information, Process, and Knowledge Management, vol. 4 (2012)

Mehra, P.: Context-aware computing: Beyond search and location-based services. IEEE Internet Comput. **16**(2), 12–16 (2012)

Miller, G., Beckwith, R., Fellbaum, C., Gross, D., Miller, K.: Introduction to WordNet: An on-line lexical database. Int. J. Lexicogr. **3**(4), 234–244 (1990)

Mooney, R.J.: Learning language from perceptual context: A challenge problem for AI. Proceedings of the 2006 AAAI Fellows Symposium (2006)

Nie, X., Feng, W., Wan, L., Xie, L.: Measuring semantic similarity by contextualword connections in Chinese news story segmentation. IEEE ICASSP, pp. 8312–8316 (2013)

Porzel, R., Strube, M.: Towards context-dependent natural language processing in computational linguistics for the new millennium: Divergence or synergy. Proceedings of the International Symposium, pp. 21–22 (2002)

Porzel, R., Zorn, H., Loos, B., Malaka, R.: Towards a separation of pragmatic knowledge and contextual information. ECAI-06 Workshop on Contexts and Ontologies (2006)

Røssvoll, T.H.: The European MobileSage project—situated adaptive guidance for the mobile elderly: Overview, status, and preliminary results. International Conference on Advances in Computer-Human Interactions, vol. 6 (2013)

Roth, D.: Learning to resolve natural language ambiguities: A unified approach. AAAI-98, vol. 15, pp. 806–813 (1998)

Sakirulai, O., Osman, I.T., Peytchev, E.: Managing contextual information in semantically-driven temporal information systems. IEEE SUKSim, pp. 451–456 (2011)

Sammut, C.: Managing context in a conversational agent. Electron. Trans. Artif. Intell. **5**(B), 189–202 (2001)

Serridge, B.: Context-dependent modeling in a segment-based speech recognition system. M. Eng. thesis, MIT Department of Electrical Engineering and Computer Science (1997, Aug)

Shinozaki, T., Yamamoto, Y., Tsuruta, S.: Context-based counselor agent for software development ecosystem. Computing pp. 1–26, Springer, Vienna (2013)

Skillen, K. L., Chen, L., Nugent, C. D., Donnelly, M. P., Burns, W., & Solheim, I.: Ontological user profile modeling for context-aware application personalization. In Ubiquitous Computing and Ambient Intelligence (pp. 261–268). Springer Berlin Heidelberg. (2012)

Towhidnejad, M., Myler, H.R., Gonzalez, A.J.: Constraint mechanisms in automated knowledge generation. Appl. Artif. Intell. **7**(2), 113–134 (1993)

Varges, S., Riccardi, G., Quarteroni, S., Ivanov, A.V.: POMDP concept policies and task structures for hybrid dialog management. IEEE ICASSP, pp. 5592–5595 (2011)

Waltinger, U., Breuing, A., Wachsmuth, I.: Connecting question answering and conversational agents: Contextualizing German questions for interactive question answering systems. Künstl. Intell. **26**(4), 381–390 (2012)

Weichselbraun, A., Gindl, S., Scharl, A.: Enriching semantic knowledge bases for opinion mining in big data applications. Knowledge-Based Systems. Elsevier, Amsterdam (2014)

Wilks, Y.: The history of natural language processing and machine translation. Encyclopedia of Language and Linguistics, Kluwer, Amsterdam (2005)

Yan, P., Zheng, F.: Context directed speech recognition in dialogue systems. International Symposium on Tonal Aspects of Languages with Emphasis on Tone Languages, pp. 225–228 (2004)

Young S.: The MINDS system: Using context and dialog to enhance speech. Human Language Technology Conference Workshop on Speech and Natural Language, pp. 131–136 (1989)

Chapter 11
The QoCIM Framework: Concepts and Tools for Quality of Context Management

Pierrick Marie, Thierry Desprats, Sophie Chabridon and Michelle Sibilla

Abstract In the last decade, several works proposed their own list of quality of context (QoC) criteria. This chapter relates a comparative study of these successive propositions and shows that no consensus has been reached about the semantic and the comprehensiveness of QoC criteria. Facing this situation, the QoCIM meta-model offers a generic, computable and expressive solution to handle and exploit any QoC criterion within distributed context managers and context-aware applications. For validation purposes, the key modelling features of QoCIM are illustrated as well as the tool chain that provides developers with QoCIM based models editor and code generator. With the tool chain, developers are able to define and use their own QoC criteria within context and quality aware applications.

11.1 Introduction

The expansion of the Internet of Things (the extension of the Internet to objects of the real world), cloud computing, big data and mobile technologies foster the development of new ubiquitous, context- and situation-aware applications. These situations are computed from ambient data, profiles of users and information collected from heterogeneous and spatially distributed sources. Context-aware applications become more and more usual. These applications require a fine and efficient management of the quality of the context information (QoC) they rely on. QoC is related to any

P. Marie (✉) · T. Desprats · M. Sibilla
IRIT UMR 5505, Université Paul Sabatier, 31062 Toulouse, France
e-mail: Pierrick.Marie@irit.fr

T. Desprats
e-mail: Thierry.Desprats@irit.fr

M. Sibilla
e-mail: Michelle.Sibilla@irit.fr

S. Chabridon
Institut Mines-Télécom, CNRS UMR 5157 SAMOVAR,
Télécom SudParis, 91011 Évry, France
e-mail: Sophie.Chabridon@telecom-sudparis.eu

© Springer Science+Business Media, New York 2014
P. Brézillon, A. J. Gonzalez (eds.), *Context in Computing*,
DOI 10.1007/978-1-4939-1887-4_11

information that describes the quality of context data as stated by the seminal definition proposed by Buchholz et al. (2003). QoC specializes the general notion of Quality of Information (QoI) for context information.

A relevant behaviour of the QoC-aware applications strongly depends on the QoC they receive. However, according to the business objectives of these applications, some QoC criteria may appear more important than others. Sometimes the freshness criterion is sufficient, sometimes it is the precision criterion and other times both are necessary. A solution to handle this need is to use context managers. They support context information throughout their life cycle. The life cycle of a piece of context information begins at its creation by a sensor and ends at its consumption by a context-aware application. Between these two events, context data are aggregated, filtered, deduced or transformed many times (Bellavista et al. 2012). These data are intrinsically incomplete and inaccurate (Henricksen and Indulska 2004). A bad quality of context information could lead to wrong decisions and irrelevant reactions. That is why context managers must take into account QoC at each step of the context information life cycle. This challenge logically remains in the case of the next generation of multi-scale distributed context managers.

The extension of the scope of context managers from local ambient environments to the Internet of Things (IoT) leads to a spatio-temporal decoupling between context providers like raw data producers close to RFID readers or sensors networks, and context consumers that are context-aware applications running, for example, on mobile devices close to users. This kind of middleware must be deployed over various devices or servers, spread across various networks or clouds, and we name them *Multiscale Distributed Context Managers* (MDCM).

Several solutions have already been proposed. In 2007, the AWARENESS project (Sheikh et al. 2007) proposed a middleware to manage context information and offered a way to manipulate the QoC. In 2009, the COSMOS project (Abid et al. 2009) proposed mechanisms for the efficient management of QoC for ambient intelligence. In 2011 (Hoyos et al. 2011) proposed a DSL (MLContext) and a process to easily develop context-quality aware applications. With the DSL developers are able to create new context and QoC aware applications. MLContext offers the benefits of considering the QoC in terms of guarantees for the producers of context and in terms of QoC requirements for the consumers of context. Finally, one of the objectives of the INCOME project (Arcangeli et al. 2012), started in 2012, is to design solutions able to handle QoC as well as to preserve privacy within a new MDCM.

We intend to provide future context managers with a *generic*, *computable* and *expressive* way to manipulate and exploit QoC simply and efficiently. *Generic*, because our solution has to model complex and heterogeneous QoC criteria. *Computable*, because the estimation of the quality level of context information is based on treatments and operations on QoC criteria. Lastly, *expressive*, because context-aware applications must be able to express their QoC requirements to different context managers.

This paper is organized as follows. Section 11.2 compares the lists of QoC criteria that have been proposed over the last decade. Section 11.3 illustrates with a fictional scenario what kind of services the new generation of context manager have to fulfil. After having found, in Sect. 11.2, no standard list of criteria to measure QoC and illustrate, in Sect. 11.3, the necessity to handle the QoC within MDMC, we propose the *Quality of Context Information Meta-model* (QoCIM) in Sect. 11.4. It brings a *generic*, *computable* and *expressive* solution to manipulate and manage QoC. The modelling key points of QoCIM are illustrated in Sect. 11.5. Finally, Sect. 11.6 presents the software tool chain we have built to produce and to manage libraries of QoCIM-based QoC criteria models and Sect. 11.7 concludes this paper.

11.2   Comparative Study of Existing QoC Criteria Lists

We study in this section the existing works about QoC measurement. Many authors have already established their own list of QoC criteria to measure QoC. We first enumerate the main proposals published over the last decade, and finally we compare the proposed criteria with regard to their semantics. The study highlights the existing variations in terms of name and meaning of QoC criteria. Different authors define a same meaning but associate it with a different denomination. On the contrary, a same denomination defined by different authors may correspond to different meanings.

11.2.1   Overview of QoC Criteria Lists

Buchholz et al. (2003) proposed the first list of QoC criteria for context-aware services. This list is composed of five criteria: *precision*, *probability of correctness*, *trust-worthiness*, *resolution* and *up-to-dateness*. All of them are defined through a textual description. No computation method is formulated for their estimation, but the authors provide examples to illustrate each of them.

Kim and Lee (2006) proposed a new list of QoC criteria built by confronting Buchholz et al.'s QoC criteria to generic criteria to measure quality. The authors provided five criteria associated to a definition from the point of view of the end-users of the context information. The end-user is the last entity which consumes context information. The proposed criteria are *accuracy*, *completeness*, *representation consistency*, *access security* and *up-to-dateness*. Then, they defined a mathematical formula to estimate the value of their first two criteria: *accuracy* and *completeness*.

Sheikh et al. (2007) formulated their own list of QoC criteria for the AWARE-NESS project. These criteria are *precision*, *freshness*, *temporal resolution*, *spatial resolution*, and *probability of correctness*. Although these criteria are textually described, no method is provided to estimate their value. Like Buchholz et al., Sheikh et al. gave examples to illustrate the definitions of their criteria. The descriptions of the criteria adopt successively the points of view of the consumer and of the producer of the context information. Producers are entities that create and provide context information such as sensors, while consumers are context-aware applications.

Filho (2010) studied the lists of QoC criteria that had been previously listed in Buchholz et al. (2003), Kim and Lee (2006) and Sheikh et al. (2007) and proposed a new list of QoC criteria for the access control security domain. Filho redefined *up-to-dateness, sensitiveness, access security, completeness, precision* and *resolution* criteria. For each criterion, Filho offered an example to illustrate the notion which is measured. He also provided a mathematical formula or a sample Java program that he used to estimate these criteria.

Neisse (2012) suggested adapting the ISO standard used in metrology to define QoC criteria. He established that the concepts of *accuracy* and *precision* used as QoC criteria are just an approximative definition of the precision criterion used in metrology. In the same way, Neisse estimated that the concepts of *spatial resolution* and *temporal resolution* defined by Sheikh et al. (2007) are just a redefinition of the ISO standard of precision applied to spatial and temporal information. Neisse suggested measuring the QoC with only two criteria: the *age* and the *precision* of the context information. The *age* is the elapsed time since the production of the information. The *precision* criterion applies the ISO standard of measurement precision to other kinds of information depending on the needs of the application. So, this *precision* criterion could be applied to the location of the source of the information, for example.

Manzoor et al. (2012) offered the most complete list of QoC criteria. They defined seven high level QoC criteria which depend on other lower level QoC criteria. For each of these high level QoC criteria, the authors associates a mathematical formula. The proposed criteria are *reliability, timeliness, completeness, significance, usability, access right, representation consistency*. The definition of some criteria, like the significance, adopts the point of view of the context producer. The significance "indicates the worth or the preciousness of context information in a specific situation" where the context producer is a sensor. Whereas the definition of other criteria adopts the point of view of the context consumer. For example, the criterion *representation consistency* is computed with information coming from requirements expressed by the context-aware applications in terms of QoC. The criterion "depends upon the amount of effort that is needed to transform that context object according to the data model presented by context consumer".

11.2.2 Discussion

The study of the semantics of the QoC criteria listed above shows some divergences. The same name of a criterion appears in several lists with a different meaning. Conversely, a same meaning appears in several lists with different denominations. There are also meanings associated with denominations that appear only once into all the lists. Table 11.1 groups together the studied criteria by author and highlights the differences that exist between all of these criteria.

The different lists of QoC criteria are represented vertically. The name and the year of the first author of each list are mentioned on the first line and are sorted

Table 11.1 Comparison of different lists of QoC criteria

		Buchholz et al. 2003 [4]	Kim and Lee 2006 [11]	Sheikh et al. 2007 [17]	Filho 2010 [7]	Manzoor et al. 2012 [12]	Neisse 2012 [14]
1	Probability context is free of errors	Correctness	Accuracy		Precision	Accuracy	
2	Max. distance to get context					Sensor range	
3	Location of the real world entity					Entity location	
4	Location of the sensor					Sensor location	
5	Time between production of contexts			Temporal resolution	✓	Time period	
6	Date of collection of context	✓	✓	✓	✓	Measurement time	Timestamps
7	Granularity of location			Spatial resolution	Resolution		
8	Rate the confidence of the provider	Trust worthiness					
9	Critical value of context					Significance	
10	Closeness, Repeatability of measurements (ISO)						Precision
11	Granularity (detail level) of context	Precision		Precision	Sensitiveness	Usability	
12	Context consumer have access to context		✓			Access right	
13	Context transfers restricted, secured		Access security (12)		Access security		
14	Format respects consumer needs		Consistency			Consistency	
15	Validity of context based on freshness	Up to dateness (6)	Up to dateness (6)	Freshness (6)	Up to dateness (5, 6)	Timeliness (5, 6)	
16	All aspects of entity are available	Resolution	Completeness		Completeness (15)	Completeness	
17	Belief in the correctness of context			Correctness		Reliability (1, 2, 3, 4)	

Meaning	Meaning used by all authors
Name	Criterion (name + meaning) only defined by one author
Name	Name only defined by one author
Name	Name defined by different authors with different meanings
Name	Name defined by different authors with the same meaning
Name (X)	The definition of this criterion depends on the criterion number X
✓	Criterion not defined by author but another criterion depends on it

chronologically. We associate a number to each criterion, which is indicated in the first column of the table. The second column summarizes the meaning of each criterion. The cells of the table which contain a name correspond to criteria proposed by the authors. An empty cell indicates that the authors did not propose the criterion on this line. A cell with a check-mark represents a criterion implicitly used by the corresponding author but not clearly defined in its list of QoC criteria. Grey cells represent criteria defined by only one author. The lightgrey color indicates that there is one common meaning used by all authors. The criteria written in italic are names used only once. The criteria written in bold are names used by at least two different authors with different meanings. Some names of criterion are followed by numbers. For example, on line 17, the reliability criterion defined by Manzoor (Manzoor et al. 2012) is followed by the numbers 1, 2, 3 and 4. These numbers reference the numbers in the first column and indicate that this criterion is composed of other criteria. For this example, the criterion is computed using the first four criteria listed in this table.

Lastly, QoC criteria are sorted in the table by following a specific order. Criteria extracted directly from raw sensor data and which do not need computation or statistical analysis are placed on the top of the table. Whereas criteria at the bottom of the table require historical analysis or data from many sensors to be estimated. The more a criterion requires computations and data, the lower it is placed in the table. Manzoor (Manzoor et al. 2012) classifies criteria into two categories, objective and subjective criteria; an objective criterion does not depend on the final application whereas a subjective criterion depends on the purpose of the final application. Table 11.1 orders criteria as a function of the effort that is required to estimate them.

Table 11.1 highlights that there is no consensus about which QoC criteria have to be used to measure the QoC of context information. This supports the idea of Bellavista et al. (2012) indicating that a consensus about the definition of a common list of QoC criteria is still an open problem. Moreover the table provides a way to compare different lists of QoC criteria. This makes it possible to compare new specific lists between them. Indeed, with the development of context-aware applications, if a new high level criterion appears, Table 11.1 offers a method to classify lists of QoC criteria relatively to one another.

Despite the plethora of QoC criteria, MDCMs still have to handle the QoC all along the life cycle of context information. Using MDCMs implies that it is no longer possible to establish a kind of "one-to-one QoC-based contract" between context data producers and respective consumers. Nevertheless, QoC requirements subsist and MDCMs have to match the quality of the context information that is delivered to a consumer with its expectations. Symmetrically, MDCMs have to know about the guarantees that a context data producer claims about some related QoC criteria. Lastly, because one of the main functionalities of context managers is to apply some processing to context information (aggregation, inference and so on), they also have to tackle the QoC during the execution of these operations. Consequently, MDCMs should be extensible by enabling the definition of any QoC criterion including their associated computation algorithm. A solution to supply QoC management within MDCM is to use a common way to model QoC criteria, to compute the value of the QoC and to express requirements and guarantees. The next Section presents an example to illustrate the services that new generation of context managers have to fulfil.

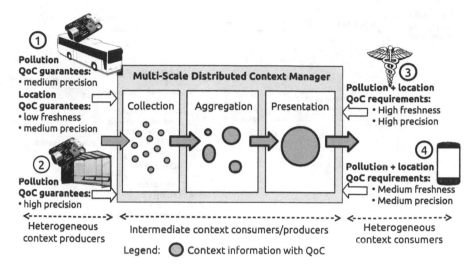

Fig. 11.1 QoC for the pollution measurement scenario

11.3 Scenario

This section describes a fictional scenario inspired from an existing concern: the urban pollution. We plan to develop the scenario in the future to experiment our solution. The future experimentations may be based on real pollution measurements realised with sensors networks or with simulated and random measurements. In our scenario, a city installs on its public transportation buses a pollution sensor and a location sensor like a GPS to inform users about the most polluted streets. The city also installs more sophisticated pollution sensors in each bus station. To improve the performance and increase the utility of the offered services, an embedded software is associated to the pollution and location measurement sensors. The software uses both the precision, criterion number 10 defined by Neisse (2012), and the freshness, criterion number 15 defined by Sheikh et al. (2007), to qualify the location of the buses, and it only uses the precision to qualify the pollution measured on the buses and the bus stations. The MDCM provides different QoC-aware applications with context information about the pollution measured by the buses and the bus stations in the city. The MDCM also provides information about the quality of the context information. The QoC is presented to the QoC-aware applications as meta-data associated to the context information.

In this example, as shown on Fig. 11.1, the buses (1) are committed to providing their location with at least low freshness and medium precision and their pollution measurements with at least medium freshness. The bus stations (2) are committed to providing their pollution measurements with at least high precision. Context-aware applications will receive information concerning the location of the most polluted streets. The health care application (3) requires context information with at least

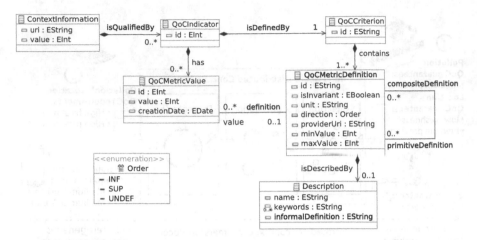

Fig. 11.2 QoCIM: QoC Information Model

high freshness and high precision. The application is used by asthmatic people to avoid the most polluted streets when they walk in the city. A general mass-market mobile application (4) requires context information with at least medium freshness and medium precision. This application is used by healthy people to get news about the pollution in the city.

In the case where the health care application does not receive context information with the expected QoC, the application will stop its services and display a message to indicate it does not have enough information to provide its services. Indeed, the health care application is critical for asthmatic people. It is preferable to not provide any service instead of providing erroneous indications. For the second application, if it does not receive the QoC that it expected, the application will continue to provide its services but a warning will be displayed. It indicates the users have to momentarily decrease their confidence into the instructions of the application. This architecture highlights the necessity to use a common model of QoC criteria to: (i) measure the QoC of a context information, (ii) express QoC requirements and guarantees, (iii) help context manager to deal with the QoC. The next section presents QoCIM, our solution to answer these problems.

11.4 QoCIM: A New QoC Meta-model

QoCIM is our proposed meta-model for designing and representing QoC. According to Open Geospatial Consortium (2005) a meta-model "is used to refer to a model of some kind of meta-data" and meta-data "is used to refer to data whose purpose is to describe other data". As described in the next section, we use QoCIM to build other models of QoC indicators, that is why we consider QoCIM as a meta-model. QoCIM is not dependent on any QoC criterion. It offers a unified solution to model, at design time, heterogeneous QoC criteria. The key modelling points of QoCIM are inspired from interesting concepts or modelling patterns used in several existing models studied in Marie et al. (2013). Thus, models based on QoCIM could be used, at runtime, by both MDCM and QoC-aware applications, for the dynamic handling of QoC. This section briefly describes the QoCIM meta-model introduced in Marie et al. (2013).

11.4.1 Presentation of QoCIM

Figure 11.2 presents the QoCIM meta-model. QoCIM qualifies context information represented with the class ContextInformation. An indicator is represented with the class QoCIndicator, it contains the quality of context information and is defined by one criterion, with the class QoCCriterion. Indicators and criteria are identified uniquely with the attribute id. At runtime, a valuation of the QoC is available with instances of the class QoCMetricValue, identified with the attribute id. Its value attribute provides a valuation of the QoC. The date of creation of a value is contained into the attribute creationDate. The attributes of the class QoCMetricDefinition define the production of instances of QoCMetricValues:

- isInvariant indicates whether the produced value is a constant, neither editable, nor dynamically computed.
- unit represents the unit of the produced value. It could be, for example, one of the units of the International System.
- direction compares different QoCMetricValues based on their attribute value from the point of view of the consumer of context information. The possible values of this attribute are *INF*, *SUP* and *UNDEF*:
  - *INF* means that a high value induces a worse QoC level. For example, the freshness, or age, of a piece of context information is usually computed with the following formula:

    freshness = current date − date of the production of the context.

    The result of this operation increases with the time whereas the quality of the information decreases.
  - *SUP* means that a high value induces a better QoC level. For example, the spatial reliability of a piece of context information, that indicates how much we can trust a sensor according to its distance to the observed entity, could be computed with the following formula:

    $$spatial\ reliability = 1 - \frac{distance\ between\ sensor\ and\ observed\ entity}{maximum\ distance\ for\ sensor\ to\ get\ context}$$

If the sensor is close to the context, the result of this operation and the quality of context will be greater than if the sensor is far to the context.

– *UNDEF* is used when neither *INF* nor *SUP* can be expressed.

• providerUri identifies the resource that provides the QoCMetricValue. This attribute brings a way to filter the QoC based on the entity which computed it at runtime.

• minValue and maxValue respectively define the minimum and the maximum allowed value of the attribute value of the class QoCMetricValue.

The class Description brings semantics for the class QoCMetricDefinition. The attribute name contains the name of the description. The attribute keywords is a list of keywords. Finally, the attribute informalDefinition is a text that informally describes the QoCMetricDefinition. For the purpose of building composite indicators, the recursive association set on the class QoCMetricDefinition supports the ability to model and use a resulting indicator based on other indicators. Therefore, QoCIM authorizes QoCMetricDefinition depending on other classes QoCMetricDefinition.

11.4.2   Discussion

The analysis of existing models presented in Marie et al. (2013) highlights interesting concepts of modelling patterns used in QoCIM. The first concept comes from the meta-model of the IoT-A (Internet of Thing Architecture Project 2012) project. It proposes to associate meta-data with context information. QoCIM also uses this technique with the classes ContextInformation and QoCIndicator. Like the DMTF CIM metrics model (Distributed Management Task Force 2009), QoCIM separates the metrics definition, QoCMetricDefinition, from the metrics value, QoCMetricValue. QoCIM reuses a few attributes of the Object Management Group (OMG) QoS meta-model (Object Management Group 2008) like isInvariant, direction and unit. QoCIM adds other attributes, like providerUri, and the class Description which are not specified in the OMG QoS meta-model. The DMTF CIM metrics model and the OMG QoS meta-model build higher level complex definitions of metrics based on other definitions of metrics. With the same objective, QoCIM also gives designers of context-aware applications the ability to specify new composite QoC indicators thanks to the recursive link set on the class QoCMetricDefinition.

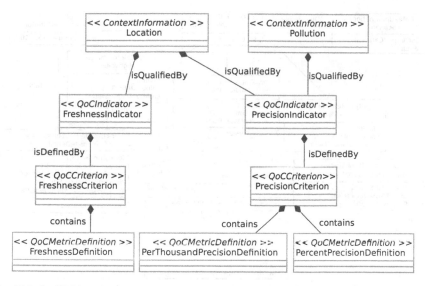

Fig. 11.3 QoCIM based model of multiple QoC criteria definitions

11.5   The Key Modelling Features of QoCIM

The following paragraphs describe Figs. 11.3 and 11.4 and illustrate the six main modelling features of QoCIM. The figures are two UML[1] class diagrams based on QoCIM. Figures 11.3 and 11.4 have been built with a "QoCIM models editor" that we present in the next section.

Feature 1: Qualifying Information with Several QoC Indicators With the example of two pieces of context information, the pollution measurement and the location, Fig. 11.3 exhibits how QoCIM qualifies context information. In this example, the location information is qualified with two QoC indicators, the freshness and the precision. Freshness corresponds to the 15th definition referenced in Table 11.1. According to Sheikh et al. (2007), freshness "is the time that elapses between the determination of context information and its delivery to a requester". Precision corresponds to the tenth definition referenced in Table 11.1. According to Neisse (2012) and CEI and ISO (2004), precision "is defined as how close together or how repeatable the results from a measurement are". Qualifying a piece of context information with different QoC indicators allows to analyse the information from different points of view. It is thus possible to get a complete opinion of the real quality of the information and provides QoC-aware applications with all they need to deliver relevant services to end-users.

---

[1] Unified Modeling Language: www.uml.org .

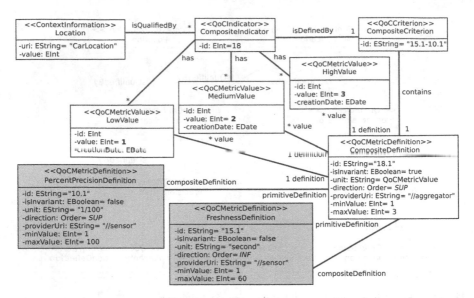

Fig. 11.4 QoCIM based model of a QoC composite indicator

Feature 2: Reusing a QoC Indicator Offering a way to reuse already defined QoC indicators eases the development of QoC-aware applications. This feature is supported by QoCIM. It enables developers of QoC-aware applications to reuse already defined QoC indicators for their needs. As illustrated in Fig. 11.3, the precision indicator qualifies two pieces of context information at the same time, the pollution measurement and the location. With a collection of QoC indicators, developers indeed just have to pick-up what indicators they need for their QoC-aware applications.

Feature 3: Defining a QoC Criterion with One Definition In Fig. 11.3, the definition of freshness provided by Sheikh (2007) is evaluated in a single way. Only one definition, `FreshnessDefinition`, is used to measure the freshness of the location context information. This is the simplest way to define a QoC criterion with QoCIM, with only one definition per criterion. The next paragraph describes a more complex way to define a criterion.

Feature 4: Defining a QoC Criterion with Multiple Definitions In Fig. 11.3, the definition of precision provided by CEI and ISO (2004) can be evaluated in multiple ways. In our example, we illustrate this plurality by providing two different definitions associated to the precision criterion. One definition expresses the precision in percent while the other definition expresses the precision in per thousand. They still have the same semantics but their implementation will differ. Providing multiple definitions for a same criterion allows different sensors with different capabilities to choose which definition is more appropriate to qualify their measurements according to their properties. For example, in the scenario described in Sect. 11.3, sensors placed on bus stations are more sophisticated than sensors placed on buses. A consequence of this difference could be a different definition used to compute the value of the precision. The precision of the measurements made with the sensors placed on the buses will be express in per-hundred while the precision of the measurements made with the sensors placed on the bus stations will be express in per-thousand.

Feature 5: Composing Multiple Definitions Figure 11.4 presents the definition of a composite indicator. The composite indicator depends on the classes `PercentPrecisionDefinition` and `FreshnessDefinition`. These classes are the implementation of the freshness and the precision indicator presented previously and adapted from the class `QocMetricDefinition` described in Sect. 11.4. The id of the composite indicator is 18 because it could be classified into Table 11.1 as a new indicator, that is to say the eighteenth indicator. The value of the id of the class `CompositeCriterion` is "15.1 − 10.1". This value corresponds to the concatenation of the value of the id of the classes `FreshnessDefinition`, which is "15.1", and `PercentPrecisionDefinition`, which is "10.1". The value of the attribute id of the class `CompositeDefinition` is "18.1", because the `CompositeDefinition` is the first definition of the eighteenth indicator. As for the precision indicator, the value of the attributes `direction` of the class `CompositeDefinition` is *SUP*. It means that the more the value of this indicator increases, the more the quality of the context information increases. The computation of these values depends on the combined evaluation of the two primitive indicators, precision and freshness.

Feature 6: Producing Discrete Values In Fig. 11.4, the high level indicator may take three different `QoCMetricValues`: `HighValue`, `MediumValue` and `LowValue`. These `QoCMetricValues` are respectively associated to a default value: 1, 2 or 3. The computation of these values are specified with the Object Constraint Language (OCL)[2]. As an example, listing 11.1 shows the mandatory constraints to produce a `HighValue`. With few OCL constraints, QoCIM allows to create discrete values based on two continuous values, in this example: the values of the precision and freshness.

```
context CompositeDefinition::value (): HighValue
   pre: self.PerCentPrecisionDefinition.QoCMetricValue.value >=
      85 % self.PrecisionDefinition.maxValue
   pre: self.FreshnessDefinition.QoCMetricValue.value <=
      15 % self.FreshnessDefinition.maxValue
```

Listing 11.1 OCL constraints to define HighValue for the composite indicators

Figures 11.3 and 11.4 illustrate the six most important modelling features of QoCIM. However, manipulating a meta-model to build new models without dedicated tools

---

[2] Object Constraint Language: www.omg.org/spec/OCL .

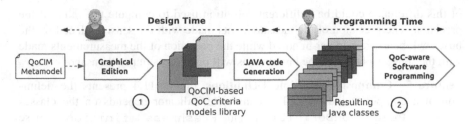

Fig. 11.5 Software tool chain process

rapidly becomes complex and error prone. If the developers of QoC-aware applications cannot easily handle models based on QoCIM, they will prefer to build their own QoC solution to the detriment of the interoperability with MDCMs or with the other QoC-aware applications.

11.6 QoCIM Software Engineering Tool Chain

This section presents the software tool chain that we developed to build a library of QoCIM-based QoC indicator models. The purpose of the tool chain is a first step to easily defining new primitive or composite models of QoC indicators. As examples, Figs. 11.3 and 11.4 have been produced with the tool. In a second step, the tool chain can automatically generate the source code corresponding to the models previously defined. Figure 11.5 illustrates the two steps of this process to build a library with the source code of QoC indicator models.

Step 1, Designing New QoCIM-Based QoC Indicator Models With the graphical tool, the designers define new QoC indicators based on QoCIM. The graphical tool is a dedicated software that aims to graphically produce new UML class diagrams of QoC indicators. It is possible to edit the indicators models by adding new definitions, new descriptions or new discrete values. With the tool, it is also possible to define new composite indicators depending on other already defined indicators. The designers are able to create and handle their own library of QoC indicator models. The tool offers a unified way to create QoCIM-based indicators model and manage them within libraries. The graphical models handled by the editor are stored into XML files, enabling sharing and maintaining a library of QoC indicators. Then, the designers may share their library of QoC indicators models with others by using an online repository of models, for example. The other designers just have to use the tool to pick-up, modify or complete the models according to their needs. Using a graphical tool is a solution to easily handle a collection of QoC indicator models.

Step 2, Generating the Source Code of QoC Indicators At the end of the first step, designers will possess a set of QoC indicator diagrams. At programming time, developers choose from the set of QoC indicator diagrams what they desire for their QoC-aware applications and with the tool generate the code corresponding to the

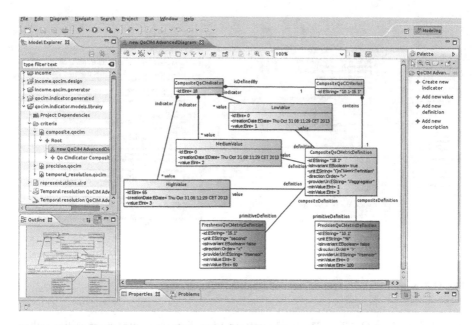

Fig. 11.6 Screenshot of the part of the tool dedicated to edit models

indicators. The generated code will handle the QoC within QoC-aware applications or MDCMs. Currently, the software is able to generate Java code but, for future works, the QoC indicator diagrams could be translated into many different programming languages. We use the strength of the Object-oriented paradigm supported by Java to manipulate the generated classes through the factory method pattern. This provides developers with an easy way to manipulate the classes of the models within their applications. Then, computing the right value of QoC according to the definition of the indicator is based on the delegation pattern and isolated into an empty method. Once the code corresponding to the QoC indicators is produced, the developers just have to complete this empty method to evaluate the QoC within QoC-aware applications.

Figures 11.6 and 11.7 are two screenshots of the tool. Figure 11.6 shows the graphical editor used to design new QoC indicators diagrams. Figure 11.7 represents a sample of the Java code generated with the editor from a QoC indicator diagram.

The QoC indicator manipulation tool that we developed is built with the Open Source Obeo technology[3]. It is a software based on the Eclipse Modelling Framework (EMF) technology[4]. With the Obeo software, it is possible to easily create and configure new software dedicated to the manipulation of models based on a meta-model. The resulting software that we configured is able to graphically create new

---

[3] Obeo Designer v6.2: www.obeodesigner.com/download.
[4] Eclipse Modelling Framework: https://www.eclipse.org/sirius/index.html

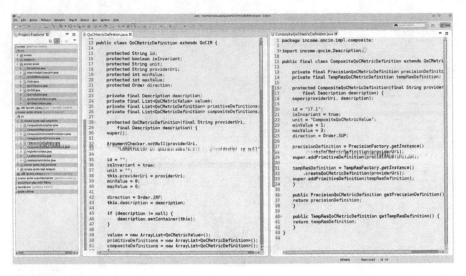

Fig. 11.7 Screenshot of the part of the tool dedicated to the code generation

models based on QoCIM. The configuration files that we wrote are specific to the Obeo technology. We also wrote template files that are used by our graphical editor to generate source code corresponding to models based on QoCIM. The editor analyses the models and applies instructions contained in the template to generate new text files. We configured the template files to generate new Java classes.

Four steps are necessary to develop a QoC-aware application with the DSL and the process proposed by Hoyos et al. (2011): (1) describe the observed context entities, (2) express the capabilities of the context sources, (3) specify the QoC attributes of the providers of context, (4) identify the QoC requirements of the applications. MLContext handles the QoC in the steps 3 and 4 but with "the most commonly used quality attributes in the literature" and a key-values system. Our solution is focused on QoC management and is able to defining and handling a large collection of QoC criteria. That is why, to extend the usability of QoCIM and improve its expressiveness to develop QoC-aware applications, future works could consist to integrate QoCIM within MLContext to express QoC requirements and guarantees with a generic model of QoC criteria instead of using a pre-defined list of criteria.

11.7 Conclusion and Perspectives

In the last decade, several works have addressed QoC modelling and management. This article presents the result of our analysis of some of the QoC criteria lists proposed by different authors. The analysis explicitly demonstrates the existence of divergences and concludes on the difficulty to converge to a unique and exhaustive QoC criteria list. Facing this situation, we propose the QoCIM meta-model. QoCIM is dedicated to exploit and manipulate any QoC indicator within MDCM and QoC-aware applications. This article introduces the informational core of QoCIM. Then, it presents the key modelling elements of QoCIM that ease the definition of QoC indicators and the qualification of context information. Because reasoning with a meta-model is not convenient, the article describes a graphical model editor that helps developers to build and integrate QoC models within their QoC-aware applications. We are currently working on identifying and defining QoC processing functions that occur all along the life cycle of context information. The purpose is to find the potential relationships that exist between the functions of context information transformation (fusion, aggregation, interpretation, inference) and QoC processing functions. Identifying QoC processing functions will allow us to build graphs, such as coloured Petri nets, to visualize and formalize the construction of high level context information delivered to context consumers.

Acknowledgements   This work is part of the French National Research Agency (ANR) INCOME project (ANR-11-INFR-009, 2012-2015, http://anr-income.fr).

References

Abid, Z., Chabridon, S., Conan, D.: A framework for quality of context management. First International Workshop on Quality of context. Lecture Notes in Computer Science. Stuttgart, Germany (2009)

Arcangeli, J.P., et al.: INCOME - Multi-scale context management for the internet of things. Conference Ambient Intelligence (AmI). LNCS 7683, Pisa, Italy (2012)

Bellavista, P., Corradi, A., Fanelli, M., Foschini, L.: A survey of context data distribution for mobile ubiquitous systems. ACM Comput. Surv. (2012)

Buchholz, T., Kupper, A., Schiffers, M.: Quality of context information: What it is and why we need it. 10th International Workshop of the HP OpenView University Association. Geneva, Switzerland (2003)

CEI and ISO: International vocabulary of metrology—Basic and general concepts and associated terms (VIM). http://www.bipm.org/utils/common/documents/jcgm/JCGM_200_2008.pdf (2008). Accessed October 2014

Distributed Management Task Force: DSP1053 : Base metric profile. http://www.dmtf.org/sites/default/files/standards/documents/DSP1053_1.0.1.pdf (2009). Accessed October 2014

Filho, J.B.: A family of context-based access control models for pervasive environments. Ph.D. thesis, University of Grenoble Joseph Fourier (2010)

Henricksen, K., Indulska, J.: Modelling and using imperfect context information. Proceedings of 1st PerCom Workshop CoMoRea. Orlando, Florida (2004)

Hoyos, J., Preuveneers, D., García-Molina, J., Berbers, Y.: A dsl for context quality modeling in context-aware applications. Ambient intelligence—software and applications, advances in intelligent and soft computing. In: Paulo Juan M. C. (eds.) Novais, Davy Preuveneers. Springer, Salamanca (2011)

Internet of Things Architecture: Deliverable 1.3, reference model for iot v1.5. http://www.iot-a.eu/arm/d1.3 (2012). Accessed October 2014

Kim, Y., Lee, K.: A quality measurement method of context information in ubiquitous environments. Proceedings of the International Conference on Hybrid Information Technology (2006)

Manzoor, A., Truong, H.L., Dustdar, S.: Quality of context models and applications for context-aware systems in pervasive environments. Knowledge Engineering Review Special Issue on Web and Mobile Information Services (2012)

Marie, P., Desprats, T., Chabridon, S., Sibilla, M.: QoCIM: a meta-model for quality of context. CONTEXT'13 : Eighth International and Interdisciplinary Conference on Modeling and Using Context. Annecy, France (2013)

Neisse, R.: Trust and privacy management support for context-aware service platforms. Ph.D. thesis, University of Twente, Enschede (2012)

Object Management Group: Uml profile for modeling quality of service and fault tolerance characteristics and mechanisms specification. http://www.omg.org/spec/QFTP/1.1 (2008). Accessed October 2014

Open Geospatial Consortium. Topic 20: Observations and measurements. http://portal.opengeo spatial.org/files/?artifact_id=41579 (2007). Accessed May 2013

Sheikh, K., Wegdam, M., Van Sinderen, M.: Middleware support for quality of context in pervasive context-aware systems. Fifth Annual IEEE International Conference on Pervasive Computing and Communications Workshops. White Plains, New York, USA (2007)

Chapter 12
Contextualized Scientific Workflows in the Cloud

Xiaoliang Fan

Abstract Scientific workflow allows automating the workflow procedure through a compilation of known sequences of actions in distributed environments such as the cloud. Preliminary benefits have been seen in realizing scientific workflows on the cloud. However, there is a notable absence of a holistic view in current scientific workflow systems that, on one hand, capture the evolving context when designing workflow models; and on the other hand, help a specific user interact with the system during QoS prediction and dynamic selection of the relevant cloud services. In this chapter, recent works on designing scientific workflows are first reviewed by discussing the opportunities and challenges respectively. The author then proposes a contextualized approach and research directions to improve the designing of scientific workflows in the user-oriented paradigm. Finally, a case study in drug design process is presented to evaluate the contextualized methodology. The contextualized approach could be considered as an effective way of addressing the socio-technical issues in designing scientific workflows in the cloud.

12.1 Introduction

Scientific workflow technology has merged over the last decade to automate the composition and execution of complex computational and data analyses tasks in science domain. With the paradigm-shifting technology, especially cloud computing (Buyya et al. 2008), more and more scientists are migrating their scientific workflows in the cloud. Such migration is advanced to enable a utility-oriented computing model in terms of elastic size of data center on-demand resource provisioning mechanism. Cloud projects (Buyya et al. 2008) are widely applied in genome informatics, nano science, drug discovery process, etc.

Preliminary benefits have been seen in realizing scientific workflows on the cloud (Fan et al. 2013). The scientific workflow implemented in the cloud is supposed to enable the dynamic choice of datasets, parameters and workflow components in

X. Fan (✉)
Lanzhou University, Lanzhou, China
e-mail: fanxiaoliang@lzu.edu.cn

© Springer Science+Business Media New York 2014   173
P. Brézillon, A. J. Gonzalez (eds.), *Context in Computing*,
DOI 10.1007/978-1-4939-1887-4_12

the cloud. Thus it is not possible to design it in advance. Furthermore, the explorative nature of scientific results in a large number of alternative scientific workflow components (i.e., cloud services) which could provide equivalent functionalities but with different service quality. Thus, scientists who are about to adopt the usage of scientific workflow systems begin to take into account the differences in quality of services (QoS) when selecting cloud services with similar functionality (Kuang et al. 2012). This issue is extremely challenging in the cloud computing environment, because the elastic nature of cloud further boosts the increase of alternative services. To address this problem, early research works mainly deal with the QoS constraints (Liu et al. 2012), such as time, cost, fidelity, reliability and security. More recently, the QoS-aware methodology has been used in dealing with the issue of dynamic service selection in scientific workflows.

Furthermore, when manipulating contextual constraints for QoS prediction and service recommendation, those works above (Kuang et al. 2012; Liu et al. 2012) only take into account the contextual information about the physical world (such as network bandwidth and IP address which indicate the location of the user), while neglecting the user-oriented context constraints (such as user preference, user behavior and user mood). With such limitation, we could foresee potential failures of the system where a cloud workflow recommended with services of good quality will not satisfy the individual scientist who may not know how to manipulate the service at all.

We believe that it is worthy of presenting a novel paradigm to design scientific workflows in a socio-technical perspective. We coin the term "contextualized scientific workflows in the cloud", featuring: (1) a user-/context-oriented approach in the center of the system to allow making contexts explicit in designing workflows with the dynamic selection of cloud services; (2) the abstract model of cloud workflows, contextualized to a set of concrete models by the user who faces the workflow execution in a specific context; (3) the special focus on the social and human factors of designing scientific workflows.

Hereafter, this chapter is organized as follows. Section 12.2 introduces the possibilities of migrating context to cloud workflows. Section 12.3 discusses potential opportunities in the design of contextualized workflows in the cloud. Section 12.4 presents a group of major challenges when designing scientific workflows with contextual constraints. Section 12.5 proposes suggestions on research directions to which we could put our research efforts. A case study is presented in Sect. 12.6. Finally, the general conclusion and perspective in Sect. 12.7 closes this paper.

12.2 Making Context Explicit in Cloud Workflows

Context has long played a well acknowledged role in a number of domains, such as natural language processing, problem solving, machine learning, knowledge acquisition, and databases and ontology. In this chapter, we use the definition of context

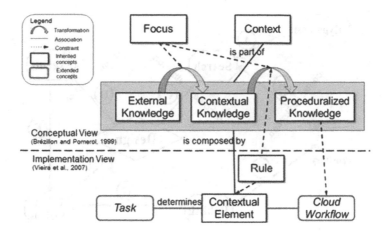

Fig. 12.1 Our framework for modeling context in cloud workflow

described in (Brézillon and Pomerol 1999). They declared that *context* is "what constrains the resolution of a problem without explicit intervention in it".

In order to introduce the context methodology in scientific workflows, we first propose our working definition of context, which is divided into two parts (see Fig. 12.1): (1) the conceptual view of context uses the view in (Brézillon and Pomerol 1999); and (2) the implementation view of context is inherited from (Vieira et al. 2007) applied in cloud workflows. In general, the representation in Fig. 12.1 illustrates the relationship among task, contextual element, rule and cloud workflow.

The major differences between our definition and Vieira et al. (2007) embrace the following two extended concepts (see Fig. 12.1): (1) we use the concept of "task" instead of "entity" in a broader view of context that does not appear explicitly in the task, not limited to the context of which depends on static attributes from pre-defined entities, as mentioned in context-aware applications (Henricksen and Indulska 2006); and (2) we introduce the concept of "cloud workflow" in order to describe the relationship among context-related concepts and information in scientific workflows in the cloud.

Furthermore, we propose that the usual approach for scientific workflow lifecycle is to consider explicitly three contextualized processes (see Fig. 12.2):

- *Contextualization process* identifies the published cloud workflow from the repository in a context close to the context at hand (Point A & B in Fig. 12.2);
- *Decontextualization process* extracts the part of published cloud workflow—the abstract model—to be reused for the problem at hand (Point C in Fig. 12.2); and
- *Recontextualization process* designs the cloud workflow concrete model before the cloud workflow is executed to adapt to the current context (Point D in Fig. 12.2).

Compared with (Fan et al. 2011), the major characteristics of cloud workflow lifecycle is that after the execute phase (see Fig. 12.2), the lifecycle enters the result

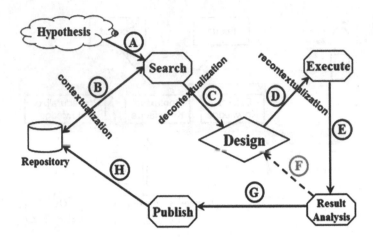

Fig. 12.2 The contextualized scientific workflow lifecycle in the cloud

analysis process, after which the scientist potentially re-designs the current cloud workflow concrete model (Point F in Fig. 12.2). In this evolving cloud workflow lifecycle, scientists cycle through this process until they are satisfied with the result. Finally, the new cloud workflow concrete model has proved its worth and is to be published to the repository for the purpose of sharing (Point G & H in Fig. 12.2).

12.3 Opportunities

The roles of context during the design phase of scientific workflows in the cloud are: (i) context is considered as the key component of cloud workflow design; (ii) context is capable of managing constraints to validate the cloud workflow design model before execution; and (iii) context enables the solution to drive programmable-level specification when the use of workflow specification or language presents an interest for users.

We believe that context could bring potential benefits between the scientific workflow design and the user-oriented need. More specifically, context modeling would be the ideal tool for recording provenance information. Using context-based provenance information, scientists could debug workflow execution, validate scientific results, and guide the workflow design and execution with explicit contextual cues. It is in harnessing this possibility, by encouraging scientists to collaborate with the cloud workflow system through interactivity, that contextualized approach could act as one of possible solutions to leverage this gap.

In the implementation level, we aim to utilize the Contextual Graphs, or CxGs (Brézillon 2005), for representing the assembling of a cloud workflow in context at the conceptual level. A contextual graph is a directed graph, acyclic with one input and one output and a general structure of a spindle. A path in a contextual graph is

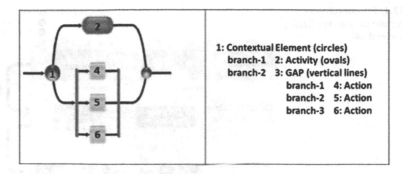

Fig. 12.3 Elements of a contextual graph [22]

composed of elements of reasoning and contexts, which corresponds to a specific way for problem solving. Figure 12.3 provides the definition of the elements in a contextual graph (actions, contextual elements, sub-graphs, activities and parallel actions grouping). A CxG can improve the process by proposing the known practices (i.e., ways to build the specific cloud service) to explore. Thus it could be assimilated to a simulation leading to the best specific workflow component (i.e., a cloud service) in the user's query context.

The role of CxG could be considered as: (1) the production of workflow models according to the quality of service constraints (time, cost, fidelity, reliability and security) and contextual constraints (i.e., type of contextual elements); (2) the translation of workflow candidates according to both contextual clues (i.e., instantiations of contextual elements). The Contextual Graphs (CxGs) software is available at http://www.cxg.fr.

12.4   Challenges

Contextualized workflow system is a novel type of workflow management system implemented in the cloud, thus its system architecture is consistent with the cloud computing paradigm and its functionalities contain the general workflow functionalities and new components extended for cloud computing. Additionally, because of the market-oriented and the dynamic nature of cloud computing, quality of service (QoS) management plays an important role in cloud workflow systems. Therefore, we consider the main challenges of designing contextualized workflow systems in the dimension of architecture, functionality and QoS management.

12.4.1   Architectural Challenges

The system architecture decides how the system components are organized and how they communicate with each other. For contextualized cloud workflow systems, the architecture should not only follow the general architecture of cloud computing

Fig. 12.4 The conceptual
architecture of contextualized
cloud workflow

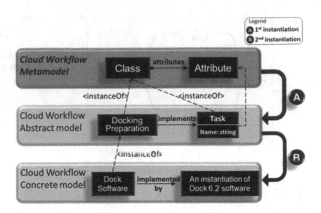

paradigm, but also should be adapted according to the contextual requirements of the users.

As discussed before, the real use of cloud workflow systems requires the introduction of the concept of "context". Current failures are mainly attributed to the lack of explicitness of contexts in cloud workflow design and its contextualization process (Fan et al. 2013). We propose a conceptual architecture of contextualized cloud workflow in Fig. 12.4 to make contexts explicit in three layers of cloud workflow models, as a trade-off between the global (workflow-level recommendation) and local (service-level selection) optimization to enable a "Workflow as a Service".

The conceptual architecture in Fig. 12.4 features in the abstraction of a high-level layer, called *Cloud workflow Metamodel* (the upper layer in Fig. 12.4), from the underlying layers. We propose that the metamodel should represent: (1) general steps of the experiment; (2) initial descriptions of scientists' requests for the experiment, such as requirements for the generation of cloud workflow; (3) constraints that must be satisfied by a cloud workflow model in order for it to be validated. For example, dataflow is consistent with the software constraints. Otherwise, it provides suggestion to make other software substituted to achieve the similar function while complying with the constraints; and finally (4) the contextual correlation between cloud workflow abstract model and its corresponding cloud workflow concrete models.

Point A in Fig. 12.4 shows the first instantiation in the conceptual framework. The contextualized cloud workflow metamodel is instantiated to an abstract one in a specific domain to address the particular focus and requirement in this domain. The first instantiation leads to defining the domain that is relevant for the current focus. For example in Fig. 12.4, the cloud workflow metamodel class is instantiated in the domain of docking preparation.

The cloud workflow abstract model (the intermediate layer in Fig. 12.4) corresponds to the cloud workflow abstract model. This model is specified without identifying the specific resource or service for cloud workflow execution. The scientist makes a simulation before running the cloud workflow concrete model without paying attention to the instances of contextual elements for the current problem. For example, it is shown in Fig. 12.4 that the class of "Docking Preparation" implements a "Task" activity.

Point B in Fig. 12.4 highlights the second instantiation that cloud workflow abstract model is instantiated to address a given situation and the scientist's current understanding of the experiment, combining with the scientist's focus and services or resources available for cloud workflow execution.

The cloud workflow concrete model (the lowest layer of Fig. 12.4) describes the concrete model, which combines the abstract model with specific resources or services. In this layer, the instances of contextual information are chosen to address the specific situation at a given context. Each abstract model represents a separate thread of execution of activities and actions to be controlled independently to the individual enactment. For example in Fig. 12.4, the "docking software" is instantiated to "an instantiation of Dock 6.2 software". Similarly, "actor's preference" will be instantiated to "familiarity of the software", "skill" could be instantiated to "expertise", and "user's mood" is expected to instantiate as "normal".

12.4.2   Functionality Challenges

System functionality is the set of system functional components that are designed and developed to meet the system functional requirements. The major challenge to system functionality of contextualized cloud workflow systems can be classified to two categories (Liu et al. 2012): (1) functional components to realize the basic functionalities of cloud workflow systems (integration of cloud services, such as cloud resource management and QoS management); (2) functional components to enable the management of context and system reasoning (modeling and representation of contextual information in cloud workflows, dynamic selection of cloud services, etc.).

12.4.3   QoS Management Challenges

QoS management focuses on non-functional requirements which are the constraints on the system functionality such as time, cost, reliability and security (Liu et al. 2012). The main challenge here is how to combine the traditional QoS constraints with user-oriented contextual constraints (user preference, user behavior, etc.).

A user may ask for a specific scientific workflow model, and then the subsequent steps would be:

- The system recommends the cloud services corresponding to the demand;
- The system builts a contextual process by assembling elementary services according to both QoS constraints (time, cost, fidelity, reliability, security, etc.) and contextual elements (size of the problem, estimated time for the building of the service, cost estimation of this building, etc.);

- QoS constraints and contextual elements constitute the contextualized workflows for the specific user.
- The contextual constraints mentioned above may come from several sources (Fan 2011):
- *Task at hand* (i.e., urgency of the task, and the budget for computation): If it is a urgent task and the budget is adequate, scientist could choose a more powerful and expensive cloud services;
- *Situation in which the task is realized* (i.e., availability of resources): such as availability of virtual machines, cloud services, storage and instruments;
- *User's preference, skill and familiarity of the service*: when a scientist is going to choose one cloud service from multiple candidates with similar functionality, he might choose the secondary choice instead, in order to escape the long-time learning curve of manipulating the first-choice method that he doesn't know how to use at all.

12.5   Research Directions

As mentioned in the previous section, various challenges are foreseen in designing cloud workflows with context constraints. However, those are also prospective areas to which we can put our research efforts and make breakthroughs towards contextualized workflows. We aim to discuss the research directions of contextualized workflows in the socio-technical dimension, such as user-system interaction, decision supporting system, context-based intelligent assistant system, etc.

However, we are not recommending designing a contextualized workflow from ground up. Middleware technologies that can bridge existing workflow systems with the cloud would seem more cost effective. Plus, to better utilize the mutual approach of designing workflows, we will put contextualized and user-oriented approach as top priority by discussing the research interests within the framework of workflow reference model (WfMC 1995) and well-known taxonomy of workflow management systems (Yu and Buyya 2005). By implementing the building blocks in the workflow reference architecture, we could also leverage existing cloud technologies, such as data management, resource provisioning, etc.

There are many existing cloud workflow systems, but it is difficult to involve the user in the design process, because of the lack of making context explicitly and exposing the system's reasoning to a specific user. However, transitioning into the cloud gives an opportunity for scientists to implement the various key components of workflow that need to be designed in portions. Thus, looking at the actual results of a portion helps decide how that portion should be and once it is settled, then the next portion can be designed.

Context-aware Workflow QoS prediction has been identified as promising research directions in real-world web services (Zheng et al. 2012) and cloud workflows (Kuang et al. 2012), especially when choosing a certain cloud workflow component (i.e., a cloud service) according to contextual information. QoS predication aims at providing personalized QoS value prediction for service users, employing the historical QoS values. Recent works mainly consider two kinds of QoS properties: (1) service-side QoS properties (e.g., price, popularity, etc.), which are given by the service providers and identical for different users; and (2) user-observed QoS properties (e.g., response-time, through-put, failure probability, network bandwidth, user location, etc.), which can vary widely for different users because of unpredictable Internet connections and the heterogeneous user environment. However, there is a lack of personalized QoS properties that depend on the user-oriented information (e.g., user behavior, user preference, user experience, etc.). Furthermore, methods for evaluating the prediction accuracy of different prediction approaches would benefit both cloud service providers and end users.

Dynamic cloud service selection combining the QoS with context constraints would become a necessity for modeling the correlations between QoS values (e.g., time, cost, fidelity, reliability, security, etc.) and user-oriented information (e.g., user preference, user behavior and user experience, etc.). Besides dealing with QoS constraints such as time and cost, it is necessary to consider the context constraints as well to expose the system's reasoning to a user for intelligent workflow design (Gil et al. 2011). For example, a user may want a justification for why a parameter was set to a certain value or the reason why an algorithm is not appropriate for his data management. This would involve both extending the system to record the contextual reasoning behind its decisions as well as designing the representation of such information. In addition, it is interesting to investigate the types of user satisfactory in cloud workflows.

The automatic composition of cloud workflow model has been considered as one of the main concerns for the adoption of human factors in designing cloud workflows (Gil et al. 2011). The proposed roadmap of designing scientific experiment as cloud workflows would be: (1) maximizing all possible workflow compositions; (2) eliminating invalid compositions according to the user-oriented contextual information; (3) predicting the effectiveness and efficiencies of the recommended workflow model with both context and QoS constraints; and finally (4) learning from the failure of dynamic service selection and workflow recommendation by the process of incremental knowledge acquisition.

Realizing elastic requirement of the users could also be an interesting and powerful direction. The design phase of cloud workflows may be heavily reliant on professional knowledge and customized preference of the specific user. Thus how to model the interactivity between the user and the system becomes a necessity for incremental knowledge acquisition (Brézillon 2005), especially when the iterative sub-process such as result analysis process is considered.

12.6   Case Study

We introduce a case study in the field of drug discovery process called "virtual screening research on avian influenza H5N1 virus". Virtual screening is about selecting *in silico* the best candidate drugs acting on a given target, by docking millions of small molecules separately on the target, which is the initial step in the drug discovery

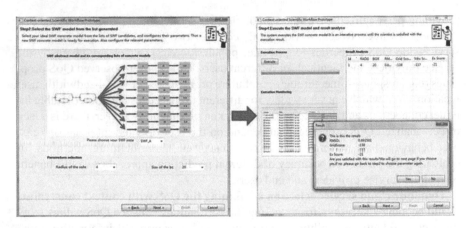

Fig. 12.5 Implementation of making contexts explicit in the design phase of cloud workflow

process (Chen and Shoichet 2009). This case study aims to find dozens of drug candidates for H5N1 virus, by docking millions of small molecules separately on H5N1 protein. Normally, describing a complete set of "all possible execution paths" during docking process might be undesirable. As a result, the strategy of incremental acquisition could enable the cloud workflow or its portions to be dynamically defined during workflow execution through the interactivity between the user and the system.

The result is shown in a prototype called CxCloudFlow (Contextualized Cloud Workflow Systems). CxCloudFlow prototype was developed by an open source package Eclipse Helios Sr2[1] and Java Development Kit 1.6.0[2]. The cloud workflow model was orchestrated by ActiveBPEL engine[3].

As what we discussed in Sect. 12.2, the system interactively builds a workflow model with the user in result analysis and workflow publication phase as recontextualization and decontextualization process. Figure 12.5 shows the CxCloudFlow prototype implementing our contextualized methodology in the design phase of cloud workflows. The prototype illustrates (see Fig. 12.5): (1) in the left part, the system makes available parts of contextual information while the role of the user is to select his/her choice from the possibilities (nine cloud workflows in parallel generated by Contextual Graphs in Fig. 12.5) suggested by the system; (2) in the right part, after the selection of the user and result analysis process, the system needs collaboration with the user by asking questions. For example, in right part of Fig. 12.5, system askes the question "Are you satisfied with the result?"

If the answer is "Yes", the system directs the scientist to see the final result. Otherwise, the system receives the values of contextual elements from the scientist

---

[1] Eclipse Helios Sr2 Packages. Available via: http://www.eclipse.org/downloads/packages/release/helios/sr2.

[2] Java Development Kit 1.6.0. Available via: http://www.java.com/en/download/manual.jsp.

[3] ActiveBPEL engine. Available via: http://www.activevos.com.

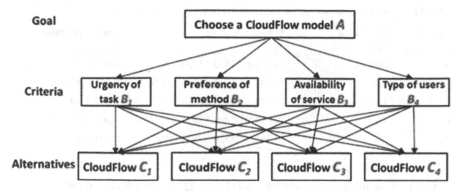

Fig. 12.6 The AHP model for the case study

that "NO, I need to modify the parameter of the radius of the spheres". Then the consequent action is taken to drive the iterative process by modifying the parameters. Once satisfied, the system adds new workflow concrete model to the cloud workflow repository for the sake of sharing.

Furthermore, we use a multi-criteria methodcalled the analytic hierarchy process (AHP) model (Phillips-Wrena et al. 2007) to evaluate our prototype. AHP model could incorporate both qualitative and quantitative criteria into a single metric. An advantage of the AHP model for our evaluation is that contributions of the contextualized methodology used in the system to individual criteria can be determined.

We first set up the AHP model for our application (see Fig. 12.6). The goal of the evaluation is that system recommends the best cloud workflow model according to inputs from the scientists (i.e., instances of contextual elements) when they are choosing from multiple candidate models. There are four cloud workflow alternatives (C_1, C_2, C_3, C_4) for reaching the goal, and four criteria (B_1, B_2, B_3, B_4) to be used in choosing among alternatives.

Then we make comparative judgments of the criteria on single pairwise comparisons. Thus, five matrices are built: A–B, B_1–C, B_2–C, B_3–C, B_4–C. Furthermore, linear-based synthesis of priorities where alternatives are evaluated in pairs with respect to the criteria on the next level of the hierarchy, and criteria are given a priority expressed as a weight in the AHP matrix, according to the following equation:

$$\lambda = \frac{1}{n} \sum_{i=1}^{n} \frac{(AW)_i}{w_i}$$

Table 12.1 shows the maximized eigenvalue λ that we calculated from the equation. And the feature vector is also given as parameters. Then, the consistency ratio proves that the deviation of the calculation is within a minimized value.

Finally, the weights of four alternatives illustrate that the recommended choice by the AHP model is C_2, which is in accord with the result generated by the CxCloudFlow prototype.

Table 12.1 Eigenvalue, feature vector and consistency ratio of five matrices

Matrix	Maximized eigenvalue λ	Feature vector w	Consistency ratio
A–B	4.008	$[0.230, 0.518, 0.122, 0.130]^T$	$0.003 < 0.1$
B_1–C	4.004	$[0.105, 0.258, 0.362, 0.170]^T$	$0.015 < 0.1$
B_2–C	4.014	$[0.592, 0.117, 0.092, 0.199]^T$	$0.005 < 0.1$
B_3–C	4.019	$[0.149, 0.058, 0.522, 0.063]^T$	$0.007 < 0.1$
B_4–C	4.080	$[0.367, 0.288, 0.085, 0.260]^T$	$0.003 < 0.1$

$$\text{Weight of } C_2 = 0.230 \times 0.592 + 0.508 \times 0.117 + 0.122 \times 0.092 + 0.130 \times 0.199 \approx 0.342$$

$$\text{Weight of } C_3 = 0.230 \times 0.149 + 0.508 \times 0.058 + 0.122 \times 0.522 + 0.130 \times 0.063 \approx 0.144$$

$$\text{Weight of } C_4 = 0.230 \times 0.367 + 0.508 \times 0.288 + 0.122 \times 0.085 + 0.130 \times 0.260 \approx 0.285$$

$$\text{Weight of } C_1 = 0.230 \times 0.105 + 0.508 \times 0.258 + 0.122 \times 0.362 + 0.130 \times 0.170 \approx 0.229$$

In summary, we use two approaches to evaluate our methodology: (1) the CxCloud-Flow prototype; (2) a Multi-criteria DSS evaluation method (AHP model). The former one could be considered as a qualitative approach, while the latter one is a quantitative approach. Contextualized approach especially in design phase of cloud workflows would bring the significance in: (1) enhancing the ability of interactivity between the user and the system to improve the decision-making process for each cloud workflow; and (2) providing the assistance for the social and human preferences of end-users to represent the knowledge, reasoning and contexts of the user.

12.7 Conclusions

Scientific workflow technology has been evolving over the last decade to automating the composition and execution of complex computing and data analysis in science domain. However, the challenge for a large use of workflow is the failure in addressing both the dynamic execution environment (i.e. cloud) and the elastic requirement of users (i.e., logic of use rather than logic of functioning). Two lines of research emerged to address this problem. Upstream, researchers try to make explicit the contextualization process in scientific workflows building to facilitate the reuse of contextualized cloud workflow components or services. Downstream, cloud computing is a technology that would bring a better orchestration of workflows but support an on-demand provisioning of workflow resources.

Thus, we proposed a user-oriented system called "contextualized scientific workflow in the cloud" to make the user in the center of cloud workflow orchestration and provisioning that contexts are made explicit in designing cloud workflows. The motivation is to help users to select the best cloud service, datasets and parameters from a vast amount of functionally equivalent cloud services. Thus how to construct the best cloud workflow candidate (i.e., the combination of best services) for a specific user under a specific context remains an open issue.

The common approach is to use the QoS expectation of the current user as a filter to select the ideal cloud service from the existing service catalog. However, the QoS itself ignores the role of the user. Furthermore, recent works begin to take into account the context constraints. However, they only consider the "objective" and static part of context (time, network bandwidth, location, etc.), but exclude the "subjective and cognitive" part of context, that is user-oriented context (preference, mood, level of skill, etc.). We believe that a hybrid method combining the context (user preference, user behavior, user experience, etc.) and QoS constraints (time, cost, reliability, etc.) will be a feasible approach to enable the intelligent design assistance for scientists.

As with any other new paradigm, there are concerns about cloud workflow. For example, the lack of context, such as what kind of contextual reasons is attributed to the unavailability of service in the current situation. By increasing the overlapping on the three communities (i.e., workflow, context, cloud), we expect that each community will benefit from other communities to collectively reach the socio-technical perspective in designing scientific workflows in the cloud.

Acknowledgments   This work is supported by the grants from Natural Science Foundation of China (61300232), Natural Science Foundation of Gansu Province in China (1208RJZA278), and the Fundamental Research Funds for the Central Universities (lzujbky-2013-40).

References

Brézillon, P.: Task-realization models in contextual graphs. In: Proceeding of Modeling and Using Context: 5th International and Interdisciplinary Conference (CONTEXT'05). Lecture Notes in Computer Science, vol. 3554/2005, pp. 55–68. Springer, Heidelberg (2005)

Brézillon, P., Pomerol, J.-C.: Contextual knowledge sharing and cooperation in intelligent assistant systems. Le Trav. Hum. **62**(3), 223–246 (1999). doi:10.1.1.33.1224

Buyya, R., Yeo, C.S., Venugopal, S., Broberg, J., Brandic, I.: Cloud computing and emerging IT platforms: Vision, hype, and reality for delivering computing as the 5th utility. Future Gener. Comput. Syst. **25**(6), 599–616 (2008). doi:10.1016/j.future.2008.12.001

Chen, Y., Shoichet, B.K.: Molecular docking and ligand specificity in fragment-based inhibitor discovery. Nat. Chem. Biol. **5**(5), 358–364 (2009). doi:10.1038/nchembio.155

Fan, X.: Context-oriented scientific workflow and its application. Ph.D Thesis, University Pierre and Marie Curie, France (2011)

Fan, X., Zhang, R., Brézillon, P.: Contextualizing workflow in cooperative design. Proceeding of 15th International Conference on Computer Supported Cooperative Work in Design (CSCWD'11), IEEE Computer Society Press, IEEE, pp. 17–22 (2011)

Fan, X., Zhang, R., Brézillon, P.: Investigating the feasibility of making contexts explicit in designing cloud workflow. Proceeding of 2013 IEEE 27th International Parallel and Distributed Processing Symposium (IPDPS'13) Workshop on CloudFlow, Boston, Massachusetts, USA, pp. 2121–2128 (2013)

Gil, Y., Ratnakar, V., Jihie, K., Moody, J., Deelman, E., Gonzalez, P.A., Groth, P.: Wings: Intelligent workflow-based design of computational experiments. IEEE Intell. Syst. **26**(1), 62–72 (2011). doi:10.1109/MIS.2010.9

Henricksen, K., Indulska, J.: Developing context-aware pervasive computing applications: Models and approach. J. Pervasive Mob. Comput. **2**(1), 37–64 (2006). doi: 10.1109/MPRV.2003. 1203753

Kuang, L., Xia, Y., Mao, Y.: Personalized services recommendation based on context-aware QoS prediction. Proceeding of IEEE 19th International Conference on Web Services (ICWS'12), IEEE Computer Society press, IEEE, pp. 400–406 (2012)

Liu, X., Yang, Y., Yuan, D., Zhang, G., Li, W., Cao, D., He, Q., Chen, J.: The design of cloud workflow systems. Springer, New York (2012). ISBN: 978-1-4614-1932–7

Phillips-Wrena, G., Morab, M., Forgionnec, G.A., Gupta, J.N.D.: An integrative evaluation framework for intelligent decision support systems. Eur. J. Oper. Res. **195**(3), 642–652 (2007) doi:10.1016/j.ejor.2007.11.001

Vieira, V., Tedesco, P., Salgado, A.C., Brézillon, P.: Investigating the specifics of contextual elements management: The CEManTIKA approach. In: Kokinov, B., et al. (eds.) Modeling and Using Context (CONTEXT'07), pp. 493–506. Springer-Verlag, Berlin (LNAI 4635) (2007)

WfMC: The workflow reference model. Workflow management coalition technical report. WFMC-TC-1003. http://www.wfmc.org/standards/docs/tc003v11.pdf (1995). Accessed 1 Jan 2014

Yu, J., Buyya, R.: A taxonomy of workflow management systems for grid computing. J. Grid. Comput. **3**(3–4), 171–200 (2005). doi:10.1.1.59.8378

Zheng, Z., Zhang, Y., Lyu, M.: Investigating QoS of real-world web services. IEEE Trans. Serv. Comput. **99**, 1–10 (2012). doi:10.1109/TSC.2012.34

Chapter 13
Context-Sensitive Trust Evaluation in Cooperating Smart Spaces

Nicolas Liampotis, Ioanna Roussaki, Nikos Kalatzis, Eliza Papadopoulou, João Miguel Gonçalves, Ioannis Papaioannou and Efstathios Sykas

Abstract Social networking is a dominant computing paradigm of the last decade that enables users to virtually interact and socialise, to collaborate and to share any kind of content. A drawback in current social networking systems is that they integrate poorly with the wealth of hardware and software resources that the users have access to locally or remotely. To overcome this, the Cooperating Smart Spaces (CSSs) notion has been introduced that couples the advantages of social computing with those of pervasive systems. However, as this promising merging is largely based on the collection and exploitation of various user-related information, and enables the discovery and interaction among users, groups of users and resources that are not necessarily trustworthy, a reliable trust management and evaluation system needs to be established. This chapter elaborates on such a system that has been prototyped, tested and evaluated via real user trials, in order to address the needs of CSSs. It considers context information in the trust evaluation process and it enables trust-sensitive community lifecycle and membership management; automated discovery of trusted entities; and trust-based control of personal data disclosure.

N. Liampotis (✉) · I. Roussaki · N. Kalatzis · I. Papaioannou · E. Sykas
National Technical University of Athens, 9 Heroon Polytechneiou Str, Athens 15773, Greece
e-mail: nicolas.liampotis@cn.ntua.gr

I. Roussaki
e-mail: ioanna.roussaki@cn.ntua.gr

N. Kalatzis
e-mail: nikosk@cn.ntua.gr

I. Papaioannou
e-mail: jpapai@cn.ntua.gr

E. Sykas
e-mail: sykas@cn.ntua.gr

E. Papadopoulou
Heriot-Watt University Riccarton, Edinburgh EH14 4AS, Edinburgh, UK
e-mail: E.Papadopoulou@hw.ac.uk

J. M. Gonçalves
Portugal Telecom Inovação S.A., Rua Eng. José Ferreira Pinto Basto,
Aveiro 3810-106, Portugal
e-mail: joao-m-goncalves@ptinovacao.pt

© Springer Science+Business Media New York 2014
P. Brézillon, A. J. Gonzalez (eds.), *Context in Computing*,
DOI 10.1007/978-1-4939-1887-4_13

187

13.1 Introduction

The integration of social networking services (Kietzman et al. 2012; Lin and Lu 2011) with current pervasive computing systems (Hansmann et al. 2003; Obaidat et al. 2011) has the potential to support users to identify and interact with other individuals that share common interests, preferences or expectations, and in general, demonstrate similar context. This can eventually lead to enhancing the overall user experience, to optimised assistance of their communication and socialisation, as well as, to proactively facilitate their everyday activities with minimal effort. In order to bridge the gap between current pervasive systems and social networking services, the notion of Cooperating Smart Spaces (CSSs; Doolin et al. 2012) has been introduced. CSSs aim to extend pervasive systems beyond the individual to dynamic communities of users and are the building blocks for enabling pervasive computing in physical or virtual social communities. CSSs enable groups of users that share commonalities to join together in pervasive communities. A Pervasive Community, once constituted, forms a Community Interaction Space (CIS; Doolin et al. 2012). There is a one-to-one mapping between pervasive communities and CISs. Individuals may belong to any number of pervasive communities, and thus CISs, at the same time.

The functionality of CSSs entails three broad phases, namely, Discover, Connect and Organise (Doolin 2013), each of which contributes to the formation of CISs. More specifically, the system enables the Discovery, Connection and Organisation of relevant people, resources and things, crossing the boundary between the physical and the virtual world. The role of trust in all three phases is evident given, on one hand, the plethora and diversity of available resources and, on the other hand, the sensitivity of information that is disclosed, communicated and processed. Thus, the various resources provided should be accessible on top of a trust-enabled layer, designed to prevent abuse of resources and to preserve user privacy. In this context, the role of trust is threefold: (i) to support automatic discovery of trusted people, communities, services and resources in general; (ii) to assess what data to disclose to whom and when; and (iii) to facilitate trust-based community membership management, as well as, sub-community formation based on the trust relationships among members of parent communities.

Most trust evaluation systems assume that trust ratings of resources are available, as in the case where users are given the option to rate items, for instance, through like/dislike or star classification schemes. Relying on a rating system that is averaged across all users aiming at a global trust calculus (reputation) cannot be personalised, and is particularly poor in tasks where there is large variation in the items of interest, as in the case of CSSs where the available resources span from individuals to communities and a multitude of services. Contrary to the artificial behaviour imposed by any rating system, trust evaluation should be based on unobtrusive observations of actual user behaviour. Context-awareness (Roussaki et al. 2012), which is a key feature of CSSs, may significantly contribute to this task as a plethora of context data about users and their environment is made available. For example, the user's current activity, interests, preferences, biological/emotional state, agenda, social interconnections can be used to evaluate the user's interactions with individuals, communities and resources. In order to support this, a context-aware trust management and evaluation system must be established. Such a system should enable user interaction monitoring, which heavily relies on a robust context model incorporating all the necessary concepts for efficiently representing the contextual information of both individuals and pervasive communities.

Trust assessment should be based not only on the experiences and evaluation of a user's own interactions, but also on those of other trustworthy individuals and communities. Existing collaborative filtering systems allow making automatic predictions with regards to the interests of a user by collecting preferences or taste information from a multitude of users (Su and Khoshgoftaar 2009). Thus, these systems aim to predict the ratings of individuals based on their past ratings, as well as, based on a set of ratings collected from other users. It should be noted that these predictions are user-specific, as opposed to the simpler approach of assigning an average global reputation score for each item of interest that is applicable for the entire set of users considered.

The trust management and evaluation system presented in this chapter, is suitable for Cooperating Smart Spaces, and is able to infer the user-perceived trust of parties (individuals, communities, or services) based on the user's own interactions (direct trust evidence), as well as, on the trust perceptions of other users (opinions or indirect trust evidence). The collection, processing and evaluation of direct and indirect trust evidence data associated with each party is context-sensitive and inherently personalised aiming to support interconnections with trusted people and resources in a privacy-aware manner.

This chapter is structured as follows. After the introductory section, a literature review on context-aware trust management systems is presented. Section 13.3 describes example use cases where trust information can be exploited by CSSs. Section 13.4 elaborates on the context-based modelling approach that has been adopted to infer user interactions which provide the basis for assessing the trustworthiness of the entities that the user directly engages with. Subsequently, the designed trust management architecture is described, along with the respective trust model employed. Section 13.6 provides an overview of the implemented trust evaluation mechanisms with emphasis on the context-related aspects. Finally, the chapter's conclusions are drawn and the respective future plans are presented.

13.2   Related Work

Trust management has been defined as the "activity of collecting, encoding, analyzing and presenting evidence relating to competence, honesty, security or dependability with the purpose of making assessments and decisions regarding trust relationships" (Grandison 2003). Based on the categorisation proposed in (Beth et al. 1994), trust can be either *direct* or *indirect*. A trust relationship formed from direct experience or interactions can be characterised as direct trust, while a trust relationship built from recommendations by trusted third parties is called indirect trust. While several trust management and evaluation systems have been proposed in the litera-ture, the remainder of this section, focuses on those which utilise context. On the one hand, as context incorporates personal and thus, sensitive user information, trust can facilitate the privacy-preserving mechanisms. On the other hand, exploiting context information can greatly improve the efficiency of the trust evaluation facilities.

In the context-aware trust management system presented in (Abdul-Rahman 2005), each node decides which peers are trustworthy based on information col-lected from the interactions with other nodes. Furthermore, the model supports trust recommendations, meaning that a third node can be considered trustworthy if it is "proposed" by other trusted nodes. The evaluation is based on specific context parameters but faces scalability issues that restrict its application.

The model proposed by (Wang et al. 2008), is based on a Bayesian network integrating context information from reliable entities in order to decide on the trust-worthiness of a new entity or an existing one upon changes in its behaviour. The model is updated periodically based on observations and the system evaluates each (new) entity in due time. Similarly, in (Uddin et al. 2008), context information is collected and specific trust attributes are extracted either directly or indirectly, while context similarity criteria are applied aiming to improve indirect trust calculations. Furthermore, in (Sydow 2008), machine learning approaches are employed in social networking platforms in order to predict the trust levels of entities; however, context parameters are faced statically and are, therefore, difficult to be applied in real and rapidly changing environments.

The design of a context-aware trust management system, suitable for an Internet of Things environment consisting of wireless sensors, is presented in (Chen et al. 2011). More specifically, the trustworthiness for a specific packet forwarding service is evaluated, where trust computation is performed on entity level and disseminated among adjacent entities. This allows for the employment of recommendations to entities which do not perform trust computations, while the context parameters that affect the results include the resources available and other qualitative and quantitative parameters, such as mobility, availability, location.

Metrics to compute the trust level of a node, based on various context parameters, such as cooperativeness as a service provider, community interests and evaluation of trust level recommendations, are proposed in (Bao and Chen 2012). The described system defines a weighting factor to evaluate the trust level received from other nodes. This factor increases proportionally with the global trust level of the node and characterises the entity in its interactions with other entities as well.

The authors in (Ben Saied et al. 2013), propose a system that calculates and periodically reevaluates dynamic trust scores of the entities (nodes) that are bound in some way, taking into account different context attributes, such as status, preferences and past behaviour. The calculations lead to a recommendation score that reflects the trustworthiness of the entity, while the other nodes can either accept or reject the score based on their own thresholds.

In (Kim and Park 2013), a trust management approach for reliable data inte-gration and management in mobile cloud computing environments is proposed. Trustworthiness is measured based on the information collected from the phone call interactions among users and the information is flooded among mobile peers upon request. However, as the authors note, their model needs to be integrated with social and personal information, as well as, environmental data for each user, apart from the basic attributes they have considered.

Finally, trust management in web-based social networks is discussed in (Sherchan 2013). The authors argue that the large number of online social networks emerging on the Web extend the concept of trust with various elements originating from the personal and digital characteristics of each user. Therefore, trust management models designated for social networking should incorporate context information, independently of its dynamic (e.g. preference for a specific status/location/time of day) or static (e.g. the user's hobbies) nature.

Based on the context-aware trust management and evaluation approaches previously discussed, it is evident that many of them have been designed for very specific application domains; others consider only a restricted number of mostly static context attributes, often neglecting the richness of information that can be obtained from existing social networking services. To address these limitations, we propose a Trust Management and Evaluation system which is suitable for a wide range of applications and, by means of the pervasive and social computing facilities of the CSS platform, provides a trust computational model that is context-aware and fully personalised aiming to support interconnections with trustworthy people, communities and resources, while safeguarding user privacy.

13.3   Exploitation Use Cases of Trust Information

A CSS can interact, communicate, or share its resources with other CSSs, communities of CSSs, or services. The degree of collaboration with a given entity should be determined by the trustworthiness of that particular entity. The context-aware Trust Management and Evaluation system presented in this chapter, provides the necessary infrastructure for assessing dynamically changing trust levels of entities with respect to different domains of collaboration. Example use cases, where the assessed level of trust can be exploited, are discussed hereafter.

Trust-Based Grouping CSSs can form groups, i.e. CISs, for sharing context information, services and other resources. This raises substantial privacy considerations as a member of a CIS does not only share personal information with a service, but, at the same time, provides access to this information to other members of the group. From the point of view of a non-member, its decision whether to join a CIS relies on the trustworthiness of group members, as well as, that of the services that are shared among CIS members. On the other hand, the trustworthiness of a CSS requesting to gain membership is also considered prior to acceptance.

Trust-Based Privacy Policy Negotiation Privacy policy negotiation is required in order to define the privacy practices of service providers with respect to user context data. More specifically, the privacy policy associated with a service is evaluated against the privacy preferences of the user and the two parties negotiate on the personally identifying information that needs to be made available to the service in question. The evaluation process relies on the trustworthiness of both the service provider and the service itself.

Trust-Based Service Recommendations The recommender system of a CSS can provide its owner with suggestions on a particular type of service based on their previous choices or those of other CSSs. The factor of trust is crucial in collecting and evaluating these suggestions. Therefore, the Trust Management and Evaluation system supports the assignment of a confidence level to each service recommendation based on the trustworthiness of the party that provides the specific service.

13.4 Context-Based User Interaction Modelling

This section describes the modelling scheme employed by the presented Trust Management and Evaluation system in order to represent user interactions. Trust assessment is not an one-off process; it is rather a continuous activity, whereby an individual reevaluates their experience regarding the entities with which they interact over the course of time. Similarly to the human process of identifying, analysing and assessing interactions with surrounding entities and the environment, a CSS is able to monitor user behaviour with respect to other individuals, communities and services. This heavily relies on a robust context model incorporating all the necessary concepts for efficiently representing the identified user interactions.

The CSS context model, which is suitable for characterising the situation of both individuals and communities, has been detailed in (Kalatzis et al. 2014). Nevertheless, it is worth outlining the main concepts, namely, the CtxEntity, the IndividualCtxEntity, the CommunityCtxEntity, the CtxAttribute, and the CtxAssociation. These classes comprise the core of the model, which is further enriched by additional meta-data, such as quality characteristics, that mainly address context management requirements. A CtxEntity is used to represent an object of the physical or conceptual world, such as a "person" or "service". The two specialisations of the CtxEntity, i.e. the IndividualCtxEntity and the CommunityCtxEntity, correspond to the notions of CSS and CIS, respectively. The various properties of a CtxEntity are modelled as key-value pairs referred to as CtxAttributes. For instance, the "name" and the "location" of a "person" CtxEntity can be represented as CtxAttributes. Furthermore, CtxEntities may be interrelated via CtxAssociations, such as "isFriendsWith" or "isMemberOf". All the aforementioned model classes are associated with a timestamp denoting their most recent time of modification.

After having sketched the main CSS context model concepts, we present an example demonstrating how the represented information can be exploited in order to infer the interactions of a user with other individuals, communities and services. The main character in this example is Alice; the context information maintained in her CSS is illustrated in Fig. 13.1. It should be emphasised that this is a highly abstract view of the

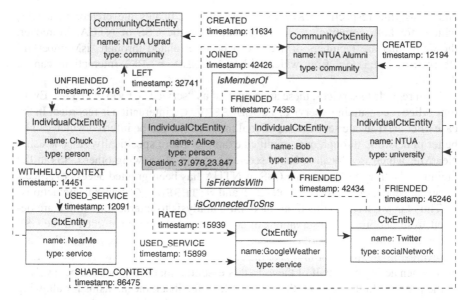

Fig. 13.1 A simplified example of context-based interaction modelling in Cooperating Smart Spaces

actual data. More specifically, the identifiers which are required to uniquely address context data items have been omitted from the depicted CtxEntities, while only a minimal set of the accompanying CtxAttributes and CtxAssociations is included in the diagram. Apart from Alice (highlighted in grey), the illustrated example involves three additional CSSs which, as already mentioned, are represented as IndividualCtxEntities. The "type" CtxAttribute indicates the type of the CSS owner, thus, Alice, Bob and Chuck are of type "person", while the National Technical University (NTUA) is denoted as "university". The "location" CtxAttribute holds the geographic coordinates of Alice's last known location.

Friend relationships among CSSs are modelled via "isFriendsWith" CtxAssociations, the modifications of which, are interpreted as (UN)FRIENDED interaction events escorted by the respective timestamp. In our example, once the CSS of Alice befriended that of Bob, an "isFriendsWith" CtxAssociation was established between them, hence the recorded FRIENDED interaction; conversely, when Alice removed Chuck from her list of friends, their "isFriendsWith" CtxAssociation was eliminated, leading to an UNFRIENDED event. It should be noted that the system is also able to detect friendships, which have been established through external Social Networking Services (SNS). Thus, based on the information from Alice's Twitter account that has been connected to her CSS profile (see the "isConnectedToSns" CtxAssociation), two additional FRIENDED interactions have been automatically inferred by the system: one with Bob and another with the CSS of NTUA.

In addition to the interactions related to CSSs, Fig. 13.1 depicts two CISs represented as CommunityCtxEntities. The "isOwnerOf" CtxAssociation and, thus, the respective CREATED interaction indicates the creator of a CIS, which, for both communities in our example, is the CSS of NTUA. Moreover, the CSSs that are members of a CIS can be interrelated through "isMemberOf" CtxAssociations, from which, either JOINED or LEFT interactions can be derived.

With regards to services, these are modelled as "service" CtxEntities. Every time Alice is consuming a service, a USED_SERVICE interaction is recorded. In the case of context-aware services, additional interactions can be inferred which can be better understood through our simplified example. More specifically, Alice is using NearMe, which is a location-based service capable of showing other CSSs in the vicinity. Contrary to Chuck, the CSS of NTUA has been granted access to Alice's location, hence, the SHARED_CONTEXT and WITHHELD_CONTEXT interactions.

Thus far, we have confined our modelling analysis to interactions which are derived from unobtrusive observations of actual user behaviour recorded in the CSS context repository. As described in Sect. 13.6.1, these interactions serve as the basis for evaluating the trustworthiness of the entities which the user engages with. However, when acting on behalf of the user, it is essential that they, too, can be involved in the process. In this respect, the CSS employs feedback mechanisms for allowing the user to rate the entities they interact with. The resulting RATED interactions are not extracted from context information, nevertheless, they have been included in this section to provide a more complete picture of the interaction modelling scheme.

13.5 Context-Aware Trust Management and Evaluation Architecture

This section presents the components of the Trust Management and Evaluation architecture. The functional view of this architecture is illustrated in Fig. 13.2, where the interconnections with Context Management (CM) components have also been depicted. It should be noted that this architecture diagram only includes the CM components which pertain to the functionality of the Trust Management and Evaluation system. A full description of the CM architecture is provided in (Roussaki et al. 2012).

The *Direct Trust Engine* is responsible for evaluating the trust evidence that result from direct interactions among the CSS owner (trustor) and the trusted entities (trustees), in order to estimate the trust level of the latter. A number of factors influence the (re)evaluation of the trustor's direct trust in a certain entity, such as the history of their interactions which includes the number of previous interactions, as well as, the frequency of interactions and their duration. The *Direct Trust Engine* retrieves such information from the *Trust Evidence Repository*, processes it, estimates the direct trust and stores the estimated value in the *Trust Repository*.

It should be highlighted that in many cases there is no direct trust relation between the trustor and the trustee, or the history of direct interactions is limited. However, with the use of trust values from other CSSs, the trustor is able to infer trust. This

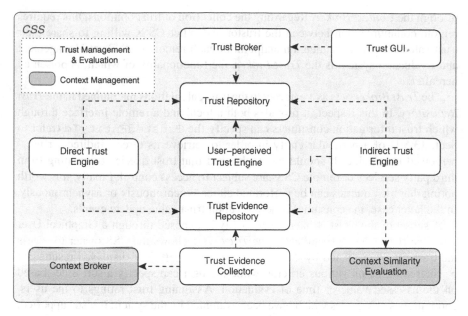

Fig. 13.2 Context-aware Trust Management and Evaluation architecture of Cooperating Smart Spaces

is the responsibility of the *Indirect Trust Engine* which retrieves the indirect trust evidence (trust opinions) from the *Trust Evidence Repository*, processes it, estimates the indirect trust and stores the estimated value in the *Trust Repository*. As detailed in Sect. 13.6.2, each trust opinion is weighted based on the context similarity between the trustor and the entity providing that particular opinion. Thus, the *Indirect Trust Engine* relies on the *Context Similarity Evaluation* component which is capable of quantifying this similarity.

The *User-perceived Trust Engine* is then responsible for fusing the direct and indirect trust values of an entity in order to assess the aggregate value as perceived by the CSS owner. The direct trust value generally outweighs the indirect one in this fusion process. However, the weight of each factor also depends on the confidence level with which it has been estimated. For instance, when the direct trust evidence is not sufficient, the opinions from other CSSs have a greater effect in assessing the aggregate trust value.

As already described, the evaluation of direct and indirect trust in an entity is based on trust evidence. This information can be of various forms and originate from diverse sources, including trust opinions from other CSSs (indirect trust evidence), as well as, locally collected data from direct interactions with services, CSSs and CISs (direct trust evidence). The *Trust Evidence Collector* is responsible for obtaining such information and storing it in the *Trust Evidence Repository*. As far as direct trust evidence are concerned, the respective interactions are modelled as context information (refer to Sect. 13.4) which the *Trust Evidence Collector* is able to access through the *Context Broker*. Regarding the collection of trust opinions, this requires remote communication between the trustor and other CSSs willing to share their trust values. The communication endpoint of each remote CSS Trust Management and Evaluation system is the *Trust Broker*, the functionality of which, is presented hereafter.

The *Trust Broker* acts as a gateway to the trust calculations maintained in the *Trust Repository*. In this respect, it provides both a local and a remote interface through which trust information consumers can specify the `TrustedEntityId` (refer to Sect. 13.5.1) of a particular entity in order to retrieve its direct, indirect or user-perceived trust value. It should be emphasised that trust queries originating from third party services or remote CSSs are subject to access control. Finally, it is worth noting that trust queries can be performed either synchronously or asynchronously. In the latter case, the consumer is notified upon trust value update events.

A subset of the Trust Broker functionality is exposed through a Graphical User Interface (GUI). More specifically, the *Trust GUI* allows the CSS owner to access the trust values evaluated by the system on their behalf. The displayed results can be filtered based on various criteria, while the user can specify a sort order based on the assessed value or time of evaluation. Assigning trust ratings to the users, communities or services which have been evaluated by the system is also supported.

13.5.1 Trust Model

This subsection elaborates on the Trust Model which has been designed in order to allow for the efficient management and exploitation of trust information. As illustrated in Fig. 13.3, the `TrustedEntity` is the core concept upon which the Trust Model is built. This class is used to represent an entity trusted by the trustor, i.e. the owner of a CSS. Each `TrustedEntity` can be referenced by its `TrustedEntityId`, which uniquely identifies the trusted entity. Trusted Entity Identifiers (TEIDs) are formatted as Uniform Name Numbers (URNs).

In addition, every `TrustedEntity` is associated with three trust value representations, namely the `DirectTrust`, `IndirectTrust` and `UserPerceivedTrust`. The `DirectTrust` class is used to represent the direct trust value in a `TrustedEntity`. This value is evaluated based on the experiences from direct interactions between the trustor and the `TrustedEntity`. On the other hand, the `IndirectTrust` class is used to model the indirect trust in a `TrustedEntity`. This value is evaluated based on the recommendations or trust opinions originating from other `TrustedEntities`. Finally, the `UserPerceivedTrust` class represents the trust in an entity as perceived by the trustor. In this respect, its value is evaluated based on an accumulation of the `DirectTrust` and `IndirectTrust` in that entity.

Considering the main types of entities with which a CSS may interact, we have extended the `TrustedEntity` class in order to model their interrelations. More specifically, the `TrustedCis` class is used to represent a CIS and is assigned a set of

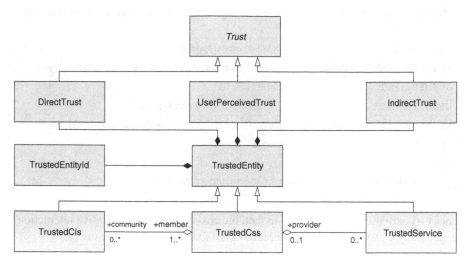

Fig. 13.3 Trust model of Cooperating Smart Spaces

`TrustedCss` objects which correspond to its members. The `TrustedCss` class is, in turn, associated with a set of `TrustedService` objects which correspond to the services provided by the modelled CSS.

13.6   Context-Sensitive Trust Evaluation

The trust evaluation mechanisms that have been designed to support CSSs are described in this section with emphasis on the context-related aspects. More specifically, Sect. 13.6.1 presents the evaluation process regarding the direct interactions extracted from context, while Sect. 13.6.2, elaborates on the role of context in the assessment of trust recommendations from which indirect trust can be inferred.

13.6.1   Direct Trust Evaluation

User interactions with another individual, community, service or resource in general, serve as the basis for evaluating the direct trust in that particular resource. These interactions, as already described in Sect. 13.4, can be inferred through context information which is enriched by the pervasive and social computing facilities of the CSS platform.

The main interactions, along with the related context types, have been included in Table 13.1. Depending on their impact on the evaluated trust, interactions can be classified as either *positive* or *negative*. More specifically, positive interactions (denoted with +) tend to increase the trustworthiness of an entity, while negative

Table 13.1 Context-based interactions and their impact on evaluating direct trust in Cooperating Smart Spaces

Interaction type	Related context type(s)	Impact
FRIENDED/UNFRIENDED	isFriendsWith[a], isConnectedToSns[a]	+/−
JOINED/LEFT	isMemberOf[a]	+/−
USED_SERVICE	usesService[a], lastAction[b]	+
SHARED/WITHHELD_CONTEXT	The type of context that was shared or withheld	+/−
CREATED	isOwnerOf[a]	+
RATED	n/a	+/−

Context Model Types: [a] CtxAssociation, [b] CtxAttribute (cf. Sect. 13.4)

ones (−) have the opposite effect; in fact, the cost incurred by a negative interaction is generally considered higher compared to the gain from a positive one.

Each of the aforementioned interactions is assigned a numeric score and is associated with a timestmap expressing the time it was recorded. Thus, if $\mathbf{x_{u,r}}$ denotes the vector of interactions $x_{u,r}$ recorded between user u and resource r over time, then the direct trust value $d_{u,r}$ assigned to resource r by user u can be calculated as follows:

$$d_{u,r} = \kappa \; f(\mathbf{x_{u,r}}) \qquad (13.1)$$

where function f aggregates the scores which correspond to each interaction and κ is a normalising factor, such that $d_{u,r}$ lies in the range [0, 1]. The highest value in this range denotes full trust, while the lowest one indicates complete distrust.

13.6.2 Indirect Trust Evaluation

The indirect trust value $e_{u,r}$ which is inferred on behalf of user u for resource r, can be calculated as an aggregation of *similar* users' direct trust values $d_{u',r}$ for that particular resource. Thus, indirect trust can be generally expressed as $e_{u,r} = f_{u' \in U}(d_{u',r})$, where f is the aggregation function and U denotes the set of users u' that are most similar to user u and have assigned a direct trust value to resource r. Key in the above calculation is, therefore, determining the similarity between the reference user u and all available users in order to extract the top N relevant users. To acieve this, existing collaborative filtering systems employ various mechanisms, such as Pearson correlation or vector cosine-based similarity (Linden et al. 2003), whereby the user's direct trust values are compared against those of other users. Our system has adopted the cosine-based similarity, the evaluation of which is more efficient in the case of sparse vectors where only non-zero dimensions need to be considered. We will henceforth refer to this notion of user similarity, as *trust-based user similarity*, as it pertains to the users' trust preferences.

However, user similarity evaluation can be significantly improved by exploiting context information, which leads to the notion of *context-based user similarity*. There are many context-related criteria that can be used to evaluate the commonalities of users, such as the following: sharing the same geographic location; having the same or similar preferences; sharing a common belief, idea, or goal; sharing common interests, experiences, background or knowledge; sharing ties of friendship, kinship, membership in physical/virtual communities, or other forms of social relationships, etc. The component responsible for quantifying the level of similarity with regards to the aforementioned context attributes is Context Similarity Evaluation, presented in Sect. 13.5. A detailed description of the context similarity evaluation process is provided in (McGovern 2013).

In addition to trust- and context-based similarity discussed previously, we also consider the direct trust relationship $d_{u,u'}$ between two users as a factor for inferring indirect trust. More specifically, let $\mathbf{d_u}$ denote the vector of all direct trust values assigned by user u, then we express the trust-based similarity with user u' as $simt(\mathbf{d_u}, \mathbf{d_{u'}})$. Likewise, if $\mathbf{c_u}$ is the vector of the context attributes of user u, let $simc(\mathbf{c_u}, \mathbf{c_{u'}})$ represent the context-based similarity. The formula for inferring the indirect trust on resource r can, thus, be rewritten as:

$$e_{u,r} = f_{u' \in U}(d_{u,u'},\ simt(\mathbf{d_u}, \mathbf{d_{u'}}),\ simc(\mathbf{c_u}, \mathbf{c_{u'}}),\ d_{u',r}) \tag{13.2}$$

13.7 Conclusions

This chapter presented the Trust Management and Evaluation system employed by Cooperating Smart Spaces, which combine social network computing with pervasive features aiming to facilitate the discovery, connection and organisation of relevant people, communities and things across the physical and digital worlds. The context information that needs to be collected and processed in such a framework, is by nature highly sensitive, as it comprises profile data, preferences, interests, social interconnections, as well as, past, current, and even future activities. Thus, one compelling reason for evaluating the trustworthiness of the involved parties, is to assess what data to disclose to whom and when, and thereby to support user privacy.

In addition, the trust evaluation process itself can benefit from the plethora of context data about users and their environment. The literature review provided in this chapter, substantiates the need to consider context throughout the entire lifecycle of trust information, ranging from the collection of trust evidence to the processing and dissemination of the derived trust levels. The presented architecture is able to incorporate the wealth of context information made available through the pervasive and social computing facilities of the CSS platform. More specifically, it exploits this information in order to extract user interactions which provide the basis for assessing the trustworthiness of the entities that the user directly engages with. Furthermore, when inferring indirect trust based on recommendations made by other users, context information is utilised to identify commonalities with the sources of these recommendations. Thus, the overall trust assessment considers not only the experience and evaluation of a user's own interactions, but also those of other trustworthy and, at the same time, similar individuals, leading to a trust computation model that is inherently personalised and context-aware.

It should be noted that a prototype implementation of the presented system has been evaluated through a series of trials by users from three different domains: a Student community, an Enterprise community, and a Disaster Management community. User trials were conducted in realistic environments and, despite the prototype nature of the implementation and the restricted number of participants, the analysis of the recorded data along with the feedback captured, indicate that the Trust Management and Evaluation system is able to perform well in a variety of CSS usage situations.

The authors plan to further evaluate and test the prototyped system aiming to identify any scalability problems that may arise. The goal is to address such issues, while enabling rapid and reliable trust assessment, even in cases where the number of users considered in the indirect trust evaluation is very large and the number, nature, experience and rating of their respective interactions greatly vary across time. Finally, it is planned to extend this system to support community-assisted trust learning and prediction to be applied for entities that have minimal interactions.

Acknowledgements The research leading to these results has received funding from the European Community's Seventh Framework Programme [FP7/2007-2013] under grant agreement no. 257493 of the *SOCIETIES* (Self Orchestrating CommunIty ambiEnT IntelligEnce Spaces) Collaborative Project

References

Abdul-Rahman, A.: A framework for decentralised trust reasoning. PhD thesis, University College London (2005)

Bao, F., Chen, I.R.: Dynamic trust management for Internet of Things applications. In: Proceedings of the 2012 International Workshop on Self-aware Internet of Things, ACM, New York, NY, USA, Self-IoT'12, pp. 1–6 (2012). doi:10.1145/2378023.2378025

Ben Saied, Y., Olivereau, A., Azzabi, R.: COACH: A context aware and multi-service trust model for cooperation management in heterogeneous wireless networks. In: Proceedings of The 9th International Wireless Communications and Mobile Computing Conference, IWCMC'13, pp. 911–918 (2013). doi: 10.1109/IWCMC.2013.6583679

Beth, T., Borcherding, M., Klein, B.: Valuation of trust in open networks. In: Proceedings of the 3rd European Symposium on Research in Computer Security. Springer, London, UK, ESORICS'94, pp. 3–18 (1994)

Chen, D., Chang, G., Sun, D., Li, J., Jia, J., Wang, X.: TRM-IoT: A trust management model based on fuzzy reputation for internet of things. Comput. Sci. Inf. Syst. **8**(4), 1207–1228 (2011). doi:10.2298/CSIS110303056C

Doolin, K.: Societies Magazine—Issue 1 Feb 2013. http://www.ict-societies.eu/magazine/ (2013). Accessed 14 May 2014

Doolin, K., Roussaki, I., Roddy, M., Kalatzis, N., Papadopoulou, E., Taylor, N., Liampotis, N., McKitterick, D., Jennings, E., Kosmides, P.: SOCIETIES: Where Pervasive Meets Social. Lecture Notes in Computer Science, vol. 7281. Springer, Heidelberg, pp. 30–41 (2012)

Grandison, T.: Trust management for internet applications. PhD thesis, Imperial College London (2003)

Hansmann, U., Merk, L., Nicklous, M.S., Stober, T.: Pervasive Computing: The Mobile World, 2nd edn. Springer, Berlin (2003)

Kalatzis, N., Liampotis, N., Roussaki, I., Kosmides, P., Papaioannou, I., Xynogalas, S., Zhang, D., Anagnostou, M.: Cross-community context management in cooperating smart spaces. Pers. Ubiquit. Comput. 18(2), 427–443 (2014). doi:10.1007/s00779-013-0654-2

Kietzman, J.H., Silvestre, B.S., McCarthy, I.P., Pitt, L.F.: Unpacking the social media phenomenon: Towards a research agenda. J. Public Aff. 12(2), 109–119 (2012)

Kim, M., Park, S.: Trust management on user behavioral patterns for a mobile cloud computing. Cluster Comput. 16(4), 725–731 (2013). doi:10.1007/s10586-013-0248-9

Lin, K.Y., Lu, H.P.: Why people use social networking sites: An empirical study integrating network externalities and motivation theory. Comput. Hum. Behav. 27(3), 1152–1161 (2011). doi:10.1016/j.chb.2010.12.009

Linden, G., Smith, B., York, J.: Amazon.com recommendations: Item-to-item collaborative filtering. IEEE Internet Comput. 7(1), 76–80 (2003). doi:10.1109/MIC.2003.1167344

McGovern, J.: Context similarity evaluation: Inferring how users can collectively collaborate together in a pervasive environment. In: Proceedings of The 2013 International Conference on Cloud and Green Computing, IEEE Computer Society, pp. 553–557 (2013). doi:10.1109/CGC.2013.93

Obaidat, M.S., Denko, M., Woungang, I. (eds.): Pervasive Comput and Networking, 3rd edn. Wiley, Chichester (2011)

Roussaki, I., Kalatzis, N., Liampotis, N., Kosmides, P., Anagnostou, M., Doolin, K., Jennings, E., Bouloudis, Y., Xynogalas, S.: Context-awareness in wireless and mobile computing revisited to embrace social networking. IEEE Commun. Mag. 50(6), 74–81 (2012). doi:10.1109/MCOM.2012.6211489

Sherchan, W., Nepal, S., Paris, C.: A survey of trust in social networks. ACM Comput. Surv. 45(4), 47:1–47:33 (2013). doi:10.1145/2501654.2501661

Su, X., Khoshgoftaar, T.M.: A survey of collaborative filtering techniques. Adv. Artif. Intell. 2009, 4:2–4:2 (2009). doi:10.1155/2009/421425

Sydow, M.: Towards context-enriched trust prediction: A proposal. In: Proceedings of the 2008 International Workshop on Combining Context with Trust, Security and Privacy, Trondheim, Norway (2008)

Uddin, M.G., Zulkernine, M., Ahamed, S.I.: CAT: A context-aware trust model for open and dynamic systems. In: Proceedings of The 2008 ACM Symposium on Applied Computing, ACM, New York, NY, USA, SAC'08, pp. 2024–2029 (2008). doi:10.1145/1363686.1364176

Wang, Y., Li, M., Dillon, E., Cui, L.G., Hu, J.J., Liao, L.J.: A context-aware computational trust model for multi-agent systems. In: Proceedings of The IEEE International Conference on Networking, Sensing and Control, ICNSC'08, pp. 1119–1124 (2008). doi:10.1109/ICNSC.2008.4525384

Part III
Context in the Individual Human Dimension

Chapter 14
The Cognitive Science Basis for Context

Jeanne E. Parker and Debra L. Hollister

Abstract Cognitive Science is a diverse field composed of an amalgamation of re-search in subject areas such as philosophy, psychology, neuroscience, and artificial intelligence. Through these fields there are several unifying factors which emerge as necessary building blocks for cognition, both human and artificial. One of these necessary components is context and its consideration and involvement in all facets of cognition, from language to reasoning to memory. This work examines the theories and implementations of contextual involvement in cognition through the viewpoints of the aforementioned disciplines which make up the field of cognitive science. This analysis will highlight its importance and significance as an invaluable cognitive tool and a unifying factor within the field.

14.1   Introduction

Cognitive Science is a diverse area of study containing fields such as philosophy, cognitive psychology, neuroscience, and artificial intelligence. Within these fields exist many differing perspectives and theories as to how effective cognition can be accomplished. However, upon analysis there are unifying themes which emerge and point to necessary ingredients for a successful view of cognitive operation. One such theme is the necessity of context.

This work will investigate the ways in which contextual processing is used as a tool by a successful working cognition, and conversely how it can act as a force to shape cognition, both human and artificial. Context is an integral aspect of the human capability to process stimuli and information, and to maintain the brain's incredible intellectual ability. To define that which will be included in the discussion of context, we feel that it would be beneficial to begin with a brief discussion of

J. E. Parker (✉)
Intelligent Systems Laboratory, Department of EECS- CS Division,
University of Central Florida, Orlando, FL, USA
e-mail: jeanne13@knights.ucf.edu

D. L. Hollister
Valencia College, Lake Nona Campus, Orlando, FL, USA
e-mail: dhollister@valenciacollege.edu

© Springer Science+Business Media New York 2014
P. Brézillon, A. J. Gonzalez (eds.), *Context in Computing*,
DOI 10.1007/978-1-4939-1887-4_14

what we mean by the term context. It is important to note that there is an infinite dimension to the depth and breadth of context, as it can be derived from a vast myriad of sources (McCarthy 1993). To provide clarity on the subject Bazire and Brézillon (2005) conducted an analysis of a corpus of 166 definitions of context found in a number of domains. The subsequent conclusion they reached from this assessment is that context can be derived from anything that is significant in a given moment and may potentially include the environment, an item within that environment, a user, or even an observer. The interaction of these four elements provides a definition of context that can easily be broken down and related to different elements of cognitive theory in order to illustrate the respective strengths and weakness of the different perspectives we will discuss herein. This inclusive, multifaceted, definition will be used throughout the chapter as an operational definition and, as such, will serve as a baseline to which the discussion of other contextual elements can be drawn and related.

The main areas of interest in this chapter will be philosophy, cognitive psychology, neuroscience, and artificial intelligence. The focus in the literature selected for discussion will be on those topics which illustrate the ways in which context unifies the field of cognitive science and the ways in which the different disciplines within the field can build upon each other with context as a central point of relation. The organization will move from the most abstract discussions, philosophy, to the most concrete, neuroscience, and finally, artificial intelligence with each section building on previous information to highlight the interconnected and essential nature of context in cognitive science. Finally, the concepts discussed in the earlier sections will be related to discussions of highly contextually involved artificial intelligence systems to complete the discussion of context as a unifying theme of cognitive science.

14.2 Philosophical Foundations

The philosophy of cognitive science and context is the most fundamental level for the beginning of the discussion of the pivotal role of context in cognition, whether human or artificial. Clark (1998) states that an accurate definition of cognition presents it as the interconnected bond of perception, action, and thought. This description demonstrates the diversity of cognition and the necessity for contextual consideration as perception, action, and thought relate to all of the differenct aspects of contextual influence in the assessment offered by Bazire and Brézillon (2005).

The British Empiricist John Locke (1970/1690) contributed a theory of learning which emphasized the *environment* and *item within the environment* aspects of contextual information as it was based on the contextual information that could be accumulated from the environment. In an Essay concerning Human Understanding, Locke alluded to ideas on how humans understand the world around them. In the four books of the Essay, Locke considers the sources and nature of human knowledge. In the first Book, Locke argues that humans have no innate knowledge at birth; that the human mind is essentially a blank slate ready to be written upon as experiences occur. In the second Book, Locke claims that all ideas come from the experiences that one has. The term 'idea,' Locke tells us, ". . . stands for whatsoever is the Object of the Understanding, when a man thinks" (Essay I, 1, 8, p. 47). He felt that all experience comes from either sensation or reflection. Sensation explains the things and processes in the external world while reflection tells us about the operations of our own minds. As we reflect on our internal state we become conscious of the mental processes in which we are engaged. Some ideas may be gained only from sensation, some only from reflection and some from both. Knowledge was defined as the perceptions of the connection and agreement or disagreement of ideas (IV. I. 1. p. 525). Locke's ideas on knowledge acquisition allowed him to decide that an individual could become trapped in their ideas by trying to define what they know based on what they see, touch or hear.

Another argument regarding the acquisition of cognitions must take into consideration the demands placed on an individual by the culture that the individual has been exposed to throughout life (Haste and Abrahams 2008). What is acceptable in one culture (context) may not be acceptable in another. There are many different institutions in a society that range from the formal to the informal and each rule system has different assigned rules and roles. Aspects of functioning within these different institutions constitute social, cultural and psychological processes, and context. It must be taken into consideration that every person is an active agent in their environment rather than simply a passive agent in their culture.

The Genevan Romantic Jean-Jacques Rousseau (1947) [1762] emphasized the other two aspects of contexual information by focusing on the *user* and *observer*, the more cultural aspects, in contextual influence by arguing that human experience is based on more than the accumulation of sensory experiences. According to Rousseau, social context and the rules and restrictions imposed thereby are the most influential aspects of the human experience, as a sort of cost/benefit analysis emerges as the individual gives up some freedoms, or preferences, in order to partake of the beneficial aspects of social interaction (Rousseau 1947 [1762]). With the combination of the sensory emphasis of Locke's Empiricism and the free will action and thought of Rousseau's Romanticism a complete picture of cognition can emerge with full involvement of all four contextual information sources; *environment, item, user*, and *observer*.

Linguistic philosophy points to contextual involvement in linguistic development and comprehension as well. Nye (1998) points out that meanings are, necessarily, shared among speakers of a certain language; however, the ideas behind the meanings are not necesarily. Thus, language is a mix of the public meaning and the private idea. The question then becomes how the public meaning of language has the ability to adequately represent the private meaning. The answer lies with context.

Wittgenstein (1958) argued that meaning in language is derived entirely from the social context in which it is used. Furthermore, he stated that language has no internal value of its own; it is not intrinsically meaningful. As such, meaning can never be private because there is no way to assign public meaning to private ideas and all formal relations between words are rendered meaningless in and of themselves. In short; meaning is use (Wittgenstein 1958). This idea of the public use and definition of meaning in language is further supported by the ideas of Malinowski (1965), an anthropological linguist who studied methods of translating languages. He determined that direct translation of meaning is quite often impossible, even between some relatively similar European languages. Instead, he argues for a contextually guided interpretation of concepts. He argues that the only way for the meanings of words to be understood between languages is to also understand the "contexts of cultural reality" as well (Malinowski 1965).

Within the philosophy of cognitive science there emerges an evident necessity for contextual involvement in successful cognition, whether in reference to a theory of learning, mind, or language. At the most abstract, fundamental contemplations of what cognition is and what is required of it, we see a dependence on contextual integration.

14.3 Cognitive Psychology and Context

Cognitive psychology concerns the assessment of the theories and processes involved in successful human cognition, evaluating areas such as language, memory, and reasoning. In this section we will highlight evidence of contextual involvement in the human psychological process, drawing upon the philosophical foundations and leading into neuroscience and artificial intelligence considerations.

There is significant research pointing to the interaction of different types of contexts in the development of the human cognition. Historically, there has been considerable focus placed on the role of the environmental contexts in influencing cognition, but not as much on the ways in which internal contexts are crucial to the developing mind. The individual can, to a degree, regulate their environment through their activities and as such can be considered at least partially responsible for using their internal contextual information, such as preferences and desires, to produce the experiences that will be influential in the developing cognition. This recalls Locke's ideas on reflection and sensation (1970/1690). By reflecting upon internal preferences and desires, the individual can influence the sensations that will be encountered in the environment and what experiences will be gained.

It is the nature of these experiences that is dependent on the types of not only physical, but also social environments that the individual selects and constructs. An agentic perspective can promote research that will provide new insights into the social construction of the functional structure of the human brain (Eisenberg 1995). Individuals must select which behaviors that are modeled by others are important to integrate into their own behavioral systems. Bandura felt that the competence of the model performing a behavior would help the individual determine if it was behavior that should be integrated into their own behavioral schemata (Bandura 1977). This self-efficacy is a major determinant of self-regulation and has been a central focus of Bandura's research since the late 1970s. Bandura felt that cognitions would change over time as a function of maturation and experience. The social cognitive approach finds the source of this change in maturation, exploratory experiences, and, most importantly, in the imparting of information by social agents in the form of guided instruction and modeling from the "models" in the environment. This internal construction of schemata from models and the agentic action make up the contexts of the more internal elements of the *user* and *observer* aspects.

A classic study conducted by Godden and Baddeley (1975) provides evidentiary support for the incorporation of contextual information along with learning. In the case of this study, specifically information regarding the *environmental* context. A consequence of this phenomenon, called state dependent learning, specifies that creating a consistent environment between learning and recall will facilitate increased efficacy in recall. In a memorization and recall test Godden and Baddeley (1975) asked a group of SCUBA divers to split in half and study a list of simple words on dry land and in the water, respectively. After one week, the groups were split again, with half of the water group remaining on land and half of the land group going in the water. All participants were then issued a recall test for the words they had learned the previous week. Those divers who had been kept in consistent environments for study and recall scored significantly higher on the recall assessment, with higher volume and accuracy of words recalled. State dependent learning and the resulting increase in efficacy of recall are largely because of the involvement of the environmentally based facets of contextually facilitated cognition. Since the contextual information was kept constant, it served as a basis from which raw informational recall could be facilitated.

Context is also heavily involved in the linguistic aspects of cognitive psychology. The Spreading Activation Model proposed by Meyer and Schvaneveldt (1971) is an example of a heavily contextual theory of linguistic processing. This model, which follows the premise of representation activation in cognitive processing of language, uses contextual similarity and familiarity as a baseline for spreading concept activation. According to this model, if a root word such as, "kitchen" is activated, then the activation will spread along contextual lines of familiarity to associated words and concepts in order to provide a contextual frame for understanding. The evidence for this theory was derived from a study using a lexical decision task wherein participants were asked to state whether or not two words displayed on a screen were both proper English words. The decision making response times were recorded and the results indicated that the decision was significantly expedited when the two words displayed were contextually related to one another (Meyer and Schvaneveldt 1971).

Another significant study in the area of contextually engaged linguistic processing comes from Treisman (1960). Somewhat related to the Meyer and Schvaneveldt (1971) study, Treisman investigated semantic activation within linguistic processing. The study involved a dichotomous listening task in which the participants were asked to shadow, or listen to and repeat, the audio signal received by one ear. Meanwhile, the other ear would be receiving random words, to which the participants were not to attend. The participants were largely successful in their task; except when the words in the unattended channel were more contextually relevant to the message in the attended channel. To clarify, if the message in the attended channel was, "I sang a. . ." the participant would shadow the contextually relevant word, "song" even if it was presented in the unattended channel. After deviating and shadowing the unattended channel for the more relevant word, the participant returned to shadowing the attended channel as instructed.

Following this study, Treisman developed a theoretical framework, called the Attenuation Model, to explain why the participants made the switch even though they were not attending to the information in the second channel. According to the Attenuation Model, there is a selective filter in the brain which selects which channel should receive attention and processing resources based on contextual cues. After receiving a ranking of importance from the filter, both channels proceed to a mental dictionary. It is in this dictionary that the words are sorted and the correct meanings of words are activated for the message. According to Treisman, it is this activation process that caused the participants to switch channels. As such, within this model the probability that an incoming word will be activated and have meaning assigned to it by the dictionary is dependent upon the context of the situation in which the word is received. If a word in a sequence is contextually relevant, then the probability that it will be recognized and that its meaning will be activated is increased, resulting in a lower activation threshold (Treisman 1960). In the example from the study, the reason the word "song" received spontaneous attention was because its activation threshold was lowered as a result of its contextual relevance to the statement, "I sang a..."

When considering these two theoretical frameworks, the Meyer and Schvaneveldt (1971) Spreading Activation Model and the Treisman Attenuation Model (1960) in relation to the linguistic philosophies of Wittgenstein (1958) and Malinowski (1965) there emerge relationships between the linguistic philosophy and the cognitive psychology of linguistic processing. In the Spreading Activation Model, the meaning of the activation word dictates which representations will be activated and, subsequently, what contextual information will be provided to the individual. Since, according to Wittgenstein, the meanings of individual words are entirely based upon the context in which they are used, it further stands to reason that the entire linguistic processing system in human cognition can be considered to be entirely dependent on contextual meaning. Furthermore, in relation to the Treisman model, when Malinowski is considered, the "contexts of cultural reality" define which words will be appropriate where. In order to understand that which is being said by another it is necessary to consider the cultural context. Both the Meyer and Schvaneveldt and Treisman models would be ineffective if not for the publicly shared, contextual meanings of words having considerable influence over the internal mental representations that are activated in linguistic processing.

14.4   Neuroscience and Context

Context is at work in the human brain, both as a tool for optimizing function and as a shaping process from birth. From birth, the human brain is adapting to stimuli and changing according to the different contexts that the individual encounters (Pfefferbaum et al. 1994; Zillmer et al. 2008). Humans are born with significantly more neuronal connectivity than is necessary. However, the brain then evolves in structure with emphasis on neural economy; connections that aren't reinforced are pruned away. Context is what determines that which will and will not be eliminated (Zillmer et al. 2008). For example, there is evidence that at 6 months of age the human infant is capable of distinguishing between individual primate faces, but 9 month old infants and adults are not (Pascalis et al. 2002). The ability to distinguish between primate faces is not contextually reinforced and is subsequently pruned away. The same phenomenon occurs with language. There is extensive research indicating that it becomes difficult to learn non-native sounds- i.e. a second language, and in some cases any language, after a critical learning period has passed (Birdsong 1999; Johnson and Newport 1991; Mayberry 2010; Zillmer et al. 2008). This demonstrates that there is a time sensitive affordance for language in the developing brain that must be taken advantage of by the developmental context.

It is important to remember that by context we indicate not only the external environmental factors imposed upon the individual, but also the internal contexts of the individual, or user. The cerebral system, as well as the sensory and motor systems, allows individuals to give meaning and direction to their lives (Bandura 1977; Harre and Gillet 1994). Predicting what an individual's preferences and patterns are or will be is often difficult because of the numerous options by which one is often challenged. As individuals, we frequently base our activities on our interests and these interests can change based on experiences and interactions with others. This ongoing development involves not only physical but emotional and cognitive development as well. This is important because it implies that our cognitive development is undergoing changes that allow one to perceive changes in the environment that one is able to manipulate.

There is significant research on brain development that has focused on the influential role that agentic action plays in shaping the brain and the neuronal and functional structure of the brain. Many researchers feel that it was not just exposure to stimulation that made the changes, but agentic action in exploring, manipulating, and influencing the environment that led to change in brain behavior (Diamond 1988; Kolb and Whishaw 1998). Agentic action can be defined as behavior that is performed with intentionality, forethought, self-reactiveness, and self-reflection (Bandura 2001). Agentic factors that also have explanatory, predictive value may be translatable and modeled (Rottschaefer 1985, 1991).

As previously stated, there is research on brain development that emphasizes how much influence agentic action exerts in shaping the development of the neuronal and functional structure of the brain (Diamond 1988; Kolb and Whishaw 1998). Stimulation is important in brain development, but the importance of agentic action in exploring, manipulating, and influencing the environment should not be overlooked in developing the brain function. Since each individual helps to regulate their environment through their activities, they hold a portion of the responsibility in producing the experiences that form the neurobiological foundation of symbolic, social, psychomotor, cognitive and other skills.

Information processing concerns the relationship between encoding and retrieval of material that has been read or heard. These two memory processes greatly influence our cognitive behaviors including perception, attention, learning, and cognition. This formation of associations must take into account memory storage and transference from one type of memory system to another (Atkinson and Shriffin 1971). The human memory system contains a distinction in memory specifying a type of memory that is used for the storage of contextual information as opposed to raw factual knowledge. This distinction, first posited by Tulving (1972), differentiated between the knowledge based semantic memory and the contextual episodic memory. The episodic memory specializes in recollection of experiences which occur within specific contexts (Tulving 1972, 1983, p. 123). To reflect back on the Godden and Baddeley (1975) SCUBA experiment, the semantic memory would have been involved in the knowing of the word lists, whereas the episodic memory would go further and store and later recall the context in which the words were learned. As such, the success of the context consistent group seems to come from the involvement of not only the semantic, but also the episodic memory in successful recall. There have been studies illustrating that this distinction in types of memory is further neurologically supported, as the right side of the prefrontal cortex has been shown to be active in the successful retrieval of contextual episodic memories (Shallice 1988; Shimamura 1995).

A study by Wagner et al. (1998) used fMRI scanning to further demonstrate that there is a context-dependent aspect to memory at the neurological level. They confirmed that certain regions in the right prefrontal cortex were activated when an attempt was made by the subjects to retrieve a piece of episodic information. Furthermore, the findings demonstrated that the context in which the retrieval attempt is made will affect the probability that the regions of the prefrontal cortex associated with episodic memory retrieval will activate. Namely, consistent contexts were correlated to increased probability of prefrontal cortex activation in the observed episodic memory retrieval areas.

The ability to access internally generated or remembered contexts, via the episodic memory, and relate them to outside information is also evidenced at the neurological level in humans. The rostrolateral prefrontal cortex has been found to be highly active and argued to be quite necessary in the relating of internally generated information, whether largely declarative or emotional in nature to external environmental information (Christoff et al. 2003; Damasio et al. 2000; Gusnard et al. 2001). When the inclusive definition of context posited by Bazire and Brézillon (2005) is taken into account this ability accrues even more value, as it represents the ability to synthesize contextual information offered by both the *user* and the *environment* facets of context.

As these studies demonstrate, context is not only involved in conceptually framing cognition, but also physically within the neurological structure and function of the brain. The neuroscience aspect of cognitive science can and does provide physical support for the interconnectivity of context within cognition. Furthermore, this support can be seen as the practical expression of some of the more abstract theories proposed in philosophy and psychology.

14.5   Interpretations in Artificial Intelligence

It is clear that artificial cognition, like its human counterpart, requires the integration of contextual information in order to become fulfilled in its conception. This section will investigate the ways in which the contextual paradigms of the previously discussed fields are present in two heavily contextually involved computational systems and assisting the goals of a fully functional artificial intelligence. However, McCarthy (1993) states that there can be inherent difficulties in directly translating ideas on context from a more abstract field such as philosophy to the concrete realm of computation. To address this difficulty, we are not always arguing for an exact translation, but rather an interpretation of ideas, as Malinowski (1965) would advocate; a contextually guided inheritance of ideas rather than an attempt at directly grafting one field onto another.

The first system we will discuss is Context Based Reasoning, or CxBR. This system is a tactical knowledge representation system, which has the capability to successfully complete tasks in both simulated and physical agents (Gonzalez et al. 2008). In order to accomplish the tasks set before it, CxBR dissects and itemizes large behaviors into categories of contexts and sub-contexts. Within each context is a compilation of behavioral and environmental information relevant to the situation specified by the context. The environmental information specifies what situations and conditions it must encounter in the world for that context to take control of the agent. Once the environment has been deemed a contextual match, the behavioral information dictates appropriate actions for the agent to take in conjunction with the environmental cues. During a tactical event the situation may change or evolve. In which case, a contextually aware component activates and the system must evaluate whether another context would be more appropriate for the new stimuli it is receiving. If the CxBR determines that this is the case then it adapts and transitions from the currently active context to one that would better suit the present situation.

Genetic Context Learning, or GenCL, uses Context Based Reasoning in conjunction with genetic programming. GenCL utilizes the tactical contextual map employed by Context Based Reasoning with the addition of state dependent learning principles (Fernlund et al. 2006). This is accomplished by the GenCL architecture by drawing upon the predetermined context and sub-context architecture of CxBR within a first generation of agents. However, while the contexts and sub-contexts have been arranged, they are empty of both the appropriate environmental information and behavioral protocols which define their use. The agents then begin attempting to perform a certain tactical event, such as the proper operation of a motor vehicle, and are compared to a human expert for proficiency. The agents with the highest level of proficiency are then selected and "breeded" to create the subsequent generation. Not only are the environmental and behavioral protocols within the different contexts evolved, but also the transition specifications for moving between one context and another. This process is then replicated for each successive generation to achieve the most favorable results (Fernlund et al. 2006). As stated previously, all of the contexts used by GenCL are predetermined, defined by the user a priori. As such, despite the advances this architecture represents with regard to state dependent learning and contextual awareness, at the time of its completion in this 2006 study, the system was unable to produce and define new contexts for environments and situations that did not fit into those already defined.

Context Based Reasoning, and its associated system, Genetic Context Learning, can be related to numerous other context dependent methods of learning in cognitive science including the sensation and reflection method of gathering knowledge of Locke, the state dependent learning of Godden and Baddeley, and subsequently the Semantic and Episodic Memory considerations of Tulving. In relation to Locke, the system gains initial knowledge via sensation by the decomposition of behaviors into contexts and sub-contexts and associating the appropriate environmental information. Reflection is then employed in the genetic programming aspect of GenCL with the selection of the best performance as compared to a human expert. By employing this cycle of contextual sensation and reflection a level of tactical competence can be achieved that is competitive with human actors (Fernlund et al. 2006). Additionally, as the contextual information is encoded with, and indeed determines, appropriate tactical information, CxBR and GenCL incorporate the concepts of state dependent learning from Godden and Baddeley. The success of which is based on the incorporation of both semantic and episodic memory in correct recognition and recall.

Another highly contextually involved system is the Contextual Graph which is not only a form of computational architecture, but also a conceptual framework for the study of context (Brézillon 2005). According to this framework, the analysis of context may only occur within the consideration of a specific focus. Furthermore, a parsing of knowledge occurs so that only the contextual information, which bears at least some relevance to the focus, is stored within the CxG. The external information which is unrelated to the focus of assessment is not considered by the CxG and remains with the user.

Context Based Reasoning, and its associated system, Genetic Context Learning, can be related to numerous other context dependent methods of learning in cognitive science including the sensation and reflection method of gathering knowledge of Locke, the state dependent learning of Godden and Baddeley, and subsequently the Semantic and Episodic Memory considerations of Tulving. In relation to Locke, the system gains initial knowledge via sensation by the decomposition of behaviors into contexts and sub-contexts and associating the appropriate environmental information. Reflection is then employed in the genetic programming aspect of GenCL with the selection of the best performance as compared to a human expert. By employing this cycle of contextual sensation and reflection a level of tactical competence can be achieved that is competitive with human actors (Fernlund et al. 2006). Additionally, as the contextual information is encoded with, and indeed determines, appropriate tactical information, CxBR and GenCL incorporate the concepts of state dependent learning from Godden and Baddeley. The success of which is based on the incorporation of both semantic and episodic memory in correct recognition and recall.

Another highly contextually involved system is the Contextual Graph which is not only a form of computational architecture, but also a conceptual framework for the study of context (Brézillon 2005). According to this framework, the analysis of context may only occur within the consideration of a specific focus. Furthermore, a parsing of knowledge occurs so that only the contextual information, which bears at least some relevance to the focus, is stored within the CxG. The external information which is unrelated to the focus of assessment is not considered by the CxG and remains with the user.

By applying this framework, the Contextual Graph is used to model the process of making decisions by utilizing relevant contextual information (Brézillon 2003). In order to accomplish this task, context is represented in branching format, with each successive level representing contextual knowledge at a more fine grained level. Then, once all of the contextual information is clearly represented and identified, a decision can be made in a straightforward manner. The CxG is capable of continuous refinement and augmentation, allowing it to be highly adaptive in the face of varying contexts because it employs not only raw knowledge, but also experience, which Brézillon argues is what is produced when context is added to raw knowledge.

Brézillon (2013) further elaborates on how such a continually enriched decision making paradigm may be accomplished through the use of a base of experience rather than the traditional knowledge base that is used in many approaches to intelligent computing. The conception of the practical application of an intelligent assistant system was used to demonstrate the necessary components of such an experientially based system (Brézillon 2013). Specifically, this model demonstrates the necessity of modeling practices over procedures. To elaborate, much as Wittgenstein (1958) argues that words derive meaning from their use in context, so Brézillon (2013) argues that practices are the ideal models of an experience as they are derived from the implementation of rule based procedures with the addition context. It is also reminiscent of the Dreyfus model of skill acquisition as situations are decomposed, reconstituted, and adapted to fit the evolving needs of the practice. The work of Dreyfus and Dreyfus (1980) supports the contextual involvement and experiential base for decision making and task proficiency as they state that the ideal learning method is for the student to depend less and less on the abstract rules, or procedures, and instead rely on their developing base of experiences with the task, or practices, in order to achieve expert level proficiency.

These two examples of contextual utilization in artificial intelligence highlight the interconnected nature of ideas in cognitive science with context as the unifying principle. The next question to consider in contextual computing then becomes what occurs when one considers the idea of ubiquitous computing; of one user having a plethora of instances, and devices, with which they interact all with contextual consideration (Hansmann 2003; Schmidt 2003). The discussion then progresses to that of the question of the source from which contextual meaning may be derived when a computational system is in reality an amalgamation of a number of devices and subsystems (Dey 2001; Greenfield 2006). In order to address this question we must discuss the idea of contextually aware computing. In contextually aware applications the intention is that these systems may be aware of their surroundings, whether that is a physical environmental consideration or one of state of being, and can react appropriately often without consulting the user (Dey 2001). A contextually aware application may decide that which is important for active processing based upon past circumstances and the frequency of application use by the user.

This type of computing, wherein the user may be relegated to a secondary role in the larger scope of contextual processing, is reminiscent of the ways in which the human brain prunes unused, or bolsters heavily relied upon, neurological resources in order to increase efficiency. The conscious mind, or cognitive user so to speak, is unaware of this process, but the subconscious function is none the less contextually aware of the needs of the system to the point that it is able to typically accurately predict that which will not be useful for further development (Pfefferbaum et al. 1994; Zillmer et al. 2008). Furthermore, a context aware application would have use in the employment of contextual continuity recognition and economic allocation of resources. This ability for contextual awareness would function much like episodic memory in the Godden and Baddeley (1975) SCUBA study, facilitating faster, more efficient overall operation of the systems and subsystems involved in ubiquitous computing. The employment of contextual awareness would significantly increase the efficacy and efficiency of the system, as contexts would be remembered in conjunction with information and processes.

Although in an optimum contextually aware system the user may not dictate the function of that system directly, this is not to say that the user should be discounted. The optimal condition would be to employ as many aspects of the derivation of contextual information as possible to define in the most refined manner what is relevant to the focus at hand (Brézillon 2005). All aspects of contextual resources are necessary for the most effective system. Recalling the agentic perspective discussed earlier, the user is capable of selecting and influencing their environment both directly and indirectly. As such, for context aware applications to be truly successful there need to be avenues as well for the user to be able to move between a more secondary role to a primary one and vice versa. As in GenCL, the human expert may be considered the *user* for a time, with the learning, evolving agent acting in the *observer* capacity of contextual assessment. However, once the observer obtains sufficient contextual awareness by properly populating its contexts and sub-contexts the user is no longer strictly necessary and can allow the system to analyze and act upon the outward aspects of context, the *environment* and *item within the environment* facets of context, leaving the user largely uninvolved and thus unencumbered for the completion of other tasks.

As evidenced by the systems discussed and the employment of contextual awareness, there is much to be gained when the interdisciplinary approach is taken to the fruition of a fully functioning artificial cognition. Similarly, the lessons learned in computing can shed new light onto the implications of ideas in the other fields discussed.

14.6   Conclusion

The literature included above points to the importance of context in the realms of human and artificial cognition. The findings illustrate the dynamic nature of context and its interconnected nature within all processes of cognition. The study of context in human cognition sheds numerous insights into the expansion of the field of artificial intelligence.

Despite the interdisciplinary nature of the diverse field of cogntive science, when context is used as a center point to which other ideas can be drawn and compared, many parallels and congruous elements can be highlighted within the different disciplines that make up the field. By drawing theses parallels and considering fields such as philosophy, psychology, neuroscience, and artificial intelligence side by side, a more complete picture of seccessful cognition can begin to emerge with contextual processing and understanding at its core. This type of interdiciplinary analysis can shed light on the validity of numerous theories in cognitive science. Ideas from philosophy, psychology, and neuroscience support the directions that research in artificial intelligence has taken. Conversely, research in artificial intelligence can provide insight through the application of theories in the other disciplines. The overall, unchanging, conclusion that can be drawn through this analysis is that context is necessary for successful cognition no matter what type of approach is taken.

References

Atkinson, R.C., Shriffin, R.M.: The control of short term memory. Sci. Am. **225**, 82–90 (1971)

Bandura, A.: Social Learning Theory. Prentice Hall, Englewood Cliffs (1977)

Bandura, A.: Social cognitive theory: An agentic perspective. Annu. Rev. Psychol. **52**, 1–26 (2001)

Bazire, M., Brézillon, P.: Understanding context before using it. In: Modeling and Using Context, pp. 29–40. Springer, Berlin (2005)

Birdsong, D. (ed.): Second Language Acquisition and the Critical Period Hypothesis. Psychology, Oxford (1999)

Brézillon, P.: Representation of procedures and practices in contextual graphs. Knowl. Eng. Rev. **18**(2), 147–174 (2003)

Brézillon, P.: Task-realization models in contextual graphs. In: Modeling and Using Context, pp. 55–68. Springer, Berlin (2005)

Brézillon, P.: Context-based development of experience bases. In: Modeling and Using Context, pp. 87–100. Springer, Berlin (2013)

Christoff, K., Ream, J.M., Geddes, L., Gabrieli, J.D.: Evaluating self-generated information: Anterior prefrontal contributions to human cognition. Behav. Neurosci. **117**(6), 1161–1168 (2003)

Clark, A.: Being There: Putting Brain, Body, and World Together Again. MIT Press, Cambridge (1998)

Damasio, A.R., Grabowski, T.J., Bechara, A., Damasio, H., Ponto, L.L., Parvizi, J., Hichwa, R.D.: Subcortical and cortical brain activity during the feeling of self-generated emotions. Nat. Neurosci. **3**(10), 1049–1056 (2000)

Dey, A.K.: Understanding and using context. Pers. Ubiquit. Comput. **5**(1), 4–7 (2001)

Diamond, M.C.: Enriching Heredity. Free Press, New York (1988)

Dreyfus, S.E., Dreyfus, H.L.: A five-stage model of the mental activities involved in directed skill acquisition (No. ORC-80–2). University of California Operations Research Center, Berkeley (1980)

Eisenberg, L.: The social construction of the human brain. Am. J. Psychiatry **152**, 1563–1575 (1995)

Fernlund, H.K.G., Gonzalez, A.J., Georgiopoulos, M., DeMara, R.F.: Learning tactical human behavior through observation of human performance. IEEE Trans. Syst. Man Cybernet. **36**(1),128–140 (2006)

Godden, D.R., Baddeley, A.D.: Context-dependent memory in two natural environments: On land and underwater. Br. J. Psychol. **66**(3), 325–331 (1975)

Gonzalez, A.J., Stensrud, B.S., Barrett, G.: Formalizing context based reasoning—a modeling paradigm for representing tactical human behavior. Int. J. Intell. Syst. **23**(7), 822–847 (2008)

Greenfield, A.: Everyware: The Dawning Age of Ubiquitous Computing, vol. 7. New Riders, Berkeley (2006)

Gusnard, D.A., Akbudak, E., Shulman, G.L., Raichle, M.E.: Medial prefrontal cortex and self-referential mental activity: relation to a default mode of brain function. Proc. Natl. Acad. Sci. **98**(7), 4259–4264 (2001)

Hansmann, U. (ed.): Pervasive Computing: The Mobile World. Springer, Heidelberg (2003)

Harre, R., Gillet, G.: The Discursive Mind. Sage, Thousand Oaks (1994)

Haste, H., Abrahams, S.: Morality, culture and the dialogic self: taking cultural pluralism seriously. J. Moral Educ. **37**(3), 377–394 (2008)

Johnson, J.S., Newport, E.L.: Critical period effects on universal properties of language: The status of subjacency in the acquisition of a second language. Cognition. **39**(3), 215–258 (1991)

Kolb, B., Whishaw, I.Q.: Brain plasticity and behavior. Annu. Rev. Psychol. **49**:43–64 (1998)

Locke, J. (ed.) with critical apparatus, Nidditch, P.H.: An Essay Concerning Human Understanding. Scholar, Menston (1970/1690)

Malinowski, B.: The Language of Magic and Gardening. Indiana University Press, Bloomington (1965). (Original work published 1935)

Mayberry, R.I.: Early language acquisition and adult language ability: What sign language reveals about the critical. In: Marschark, M., Spencer, P.E. (eds.) The Oxford Handbook of Deaf Studies, Language, and Education, vol. 2, p. 281. Oxford University Press, Oxford (2010)

McCarthy, J.: Notes on formalizing context In: Proceedings of 1993 International Joint Conference on Artificial Intelligence. Morgan Kaufmann, Los Altos (1993)

Meyer, D.E., Schvaneveldt, R.W.: Facilitation in recognizing pairs of words: Evidence of a dependence between retrieval operations. J. Exp. Psychol. **90**(2), 227–234 (1971)

Nye, A. (ed.): Philosophy of Language: The Big Questions. Blackwell, Oxford (1998)

Pascalis, O., de Haan, M., Nelson, C.A.: Is face processing species-specific during the first year of life? Science. **296**(5571), 1321–1323 (2002)

Pfefferbaum, A., Mathalon, D.H., Sullivan, E.V., Rawles, J.M., Zipursky, R.B., Lim, K.O.: A quantitative magnetic resonance imaging study of changes in brain morphology from infancy to late adulthood. Arch. Neurol. **51**(9), 874–887 (1994)

Rottschaefer, W.A.: Evading conceptual self-annihilation: some implications of Albert Bandura's theory of the self-system for the status of psychology. New Ideas Psychol. **2**, 223–230 (1985)

Rottschaefer, W.A.: Some philosophical implications of Bandura's social cognitive theory of human agency. Am. Psychol. **46**, 153–155 (1991)

Rousseau, J.J.: The Social Contract (trans. C. Frankel). Macmillan, New York (1947) (Original work published 1762)

Schmidt, A.: Ubiquitous computing—computing in context. Dissertation, Lancaster University (2003)

Shallice, T.: From Neuropsychology to Mental Structure. Cambridge University Press, Cambridge (1988)

Shimamura, A.P.: Memory and frontal lobe function. MIT Press, Cambridge (1995).

Treisman, A.M.: Contextual cues in selective listening. Q. J. Exp. Psychol. **12**(4), 242–248 (1960)

Tulving, E.: Episodic and semantic memory. In: Tulving, E., Donaldson, W. (eds.) Organization of Memory, pp. 381–402. Academic, New York (1972)

Tulving, E.: Elements of Episodic Memory. Clarendon, Oxford (1983)

Wagner, A.D., Desmond, J.E., Glover, G.H., Gabrieli, J.D. Prefrontal cortex and recognition memory. Functional-MRI evidence for context-dependent retrieval processes. Brain. **121**(10), 1985–2002 (1998)

Wittgenstein, L.: Philosophical Investigations (trans. G.E.M Anscombe). Blackwell, Oxford (1958)

Zillmer, E., Spiers, M., Culbertson, W.C.: Principles of neuropsychology. Cengage Learning, Stamford (2008)

Chapter 15
User-Centered Approaches to Context Awareness: Prospects and Challenges

Yaser Mowafi, Rami Alazrai and Ahmad Zmily

Abstract Context awareness has gained increasing recognition as one of the emerging technologies for the next generation of personal ubiquitous computing. Recent advancements in mobile computing technologies have paved the way for alternative frameworks that enabled the embedding or cueing of user context into the design and development of context-aware applications. This chapter contributes to the current understanding of the role of the user context in the acquisition and presentation of context information. In particular, it explores proposed approaches and methods for representing the user context in defining context awareness. Ultimately, coupling context awareness with user context of interest may provide a promising approach to the development and deployment of effective context-aware applications.

15.1 Introduction

Proliferations of mobile handheld devices in humans' everyday life combined with the significant advancement in mobile technologies have taken Human Computer Interaction (HCI) beyond the desktop level. Fueled by remarkable market growth and promising potential, mobile devices manufacturers are working around the clock on enhancing their products with a wide variety of value added and rich content applications. Amid this evolving trend, context-awareness, which refers to computational systems that can sense clues about users' context and enable desired interaction between those systems and users, has gained increasing recognition as one of the emerging technologies for the next generation of mobile devices. Context awareness represents the future vision of intelligent computing where devices can recognize and interpret the user's surrounding environments and react proactively and intelligently (Aarts and Ruyter 2009; Sadri 2011).

Y. Mowafi (✉)· R. Alazrai · A. Zmily
School of Computer Engineering and Information Technology,
German Jordanian University, PO Box 35247, Amman 11180, Jordan
e-mail: yaser.mowafi@gju.edu.jo

© Springer Science+Business Media New York 2014
P. Brézillon, A. J. Gonzalez (eds.), *Context in Computing*,
DOI 10.1007/978-1-4939-1887-4_15

Context awareness focuses on the acquisition and successful interpretation of the wealth of contextual information obtained from users' surrounding environment, and the adaptation of context-aware systems to the user needs in a transparent and non-obtrusive manner. A context-aware system is particularly characterized by the following characteristics:

- Awareness of the surrounding and situational context information.
- Personalized and tailored to the users' needs and context of interest.
- Adaptive to the continuous changing of users' needs and ongoing tasks.
- Ubiquitous to fit with the dynamic and mobile nature of users' activities and tasks.

In addition to the above characteristics context awareness embarks on sensing, reasoning, decision-making, and ambient intelligence. Nowadays, we are surrounded by various mobile computing devices such as smart phones, tablets, various sensors ranging from RFID, infrared motion sensors, as well as biometric identification sensors. These sensors are capable of providing high precision, accurate raw data that can be used to make inference about user context. In addition, advances in mobile computing and devices have sparked ambitious attempts to bring context awareness one step closer to mobile users.

This chapter attempts, first, to provide a state-of-the-art overview of context awareness approaches and methods. Secondly, it contributes to the current understanding of these proposed methods towards representing the user context of interest in defining context awareness. Ultimately, coupling users' context of interest with their surrounding context can bring more insights into effective design and implementation policies of context awareness in users' daily lives.

15.2 Fundamental Concepts and Motivation of Context Awareness

15.2.1 What Is Context?

According to Oxford Dictionaries, the term context is the circumstances that form the setting for an event, statement, or idea, and in terms in which it can be fully understood and assessed. The vibrant nature of the circumstances that surround the context setting has granted the notion of context with a "slippery" characteristic that kept the context schema subject to the researchers' scope and intention of context utilization. There are many definitions of context in the literature; amongst these definitions, we present the following:

- Context encompasses more than just the user's location, because other things of interest are also mobile and changing. Context includes lighting, noise level, network connectivity, communication costs, communication bandwidth, and even the social situation (Schilit et al. 1994).

- Context is the set of environmental states and settings that either determines an application's behavior or in which an application event occurs and is interesting to the user (Chen and Kotz 2000).
- Any information that can characterize the situation to an entity that is considered relevant to the interaction between the user and the application. An entity is a person, place, or object that is considered relevant to the interaction between user and the application, including the user and applications themselves (Dey and Abowd 2000).
- Context is not simply the state of a predefined environment with a fixed set of interaction resources. It is part of a process of interacting with an ever-changing environment composed of reconfigurable, migratory, distributed, and multi-scale resource (Coutaz et al. 2005).

The unconstrained boundaries of context have also led to a taxonomy approach to context categorization in the literature. Of the earliest classifications is the one that categorized context based on the source of context information like users' context, physical or environment context, and computing context (Schilit et al. 1994). Other categorizations boil down context into: environment (e.g., physical and social states), user (e.g., device, physiological, and cognitive states) and activity (e.g., behavior and tasks) (Schmidt et al. 1999). Additionally, context has been classified into conceptual or abstraction at the user level (e.g., location, time, identity, and activity), and measurement categories at the environmental or physical level (e.g., light, noise, and proximity objects) (Salber et al. 1999; Schmidt et al. 1999; Barkhuus 2005). The aforementioned classifications of context have been amalgamated within a two-tier hierarchy classification, namely primary context, such as location, time, identity, and activity, and secondary context attributes of the primary context (Dey and Abowd 2000).

Despite the fact that context domain is nearing a state of abundance of potentially available context data, little is known about the relevancy of the collected context data to the user context of interest in reality. For example, many argue that the main challenge that renders context awareness services lies not so much in recording context data, but in acquiring context information that is relevant to the user (Barnard et al. 2007; Nwiabu et al. 2011; Rogers et al. 2012).

15.2.2   Context Sensing

Key to context and context awareness is sensing and the sensing tools or sensors. The word "sensor" refers not only to physical context, such as location, light, sound and movement, but also to any sensing source and/or device that can provide usable context information mostly captured by the users or by monitoring users' interactions, such as tasks and activities. Context sensing can be generally categorized as physical sensors, virtual sensors, and logical sensors:

- Physical sensors (e.g., Gyroscopes and accelerometers which are typically used for physical movement monitoring) are normally associated with specific devices and communication infrastructure for their operations.
- Virtual sensors usually represent an abstraction of context information (e.g., user's activities) extracted from users' network IP address that can be used to infer the location of that device.
- Logical sensors often infer context information from a hybrid of both physical and virtual information to provide a higher level of information abstraction, such as logical deduction of whether a user will be able to attend an event scheduled in his appointment calendar on time based on his current location and the time it would take to reach the appointment location at a reasonable speed.

Recent advances in computing and sensing technologies have paved the way for the adoption of multimodal sensing technologies (e.g., vision, speech recognition, gesture-based detection), which enables the possibility of recognizing peoples' activities, with some accuracy and sensitivity, and deliver instrumental support to those peoples' needs and tasks. For example, researchers have explored the usage of RFID tags (Tan et al. 2007; Parry and Narayanan 2010), and accelerometers or gyroscopes for tagging and using the data for activity recognition (Clough 2010). Other modalities that have been researched for activity recognition include video cameras, microphones, and motion detection sensors (Aarts and Ruyter 2009; Balandin et al. 2010; Hollosi et al. 2010; Thyagaraju and Kulkarni 2010; Meetoo-Appavoo 2011).

15.2.3   Context Abstraction

To make sense of the wide variety of the low level context sensors, context must be abstracted (Han et al. 2008). For example, GPS sensor data that provides geographical coordinates of an object need to be abstracted to make better use of detailed location information such as street or building names for a context-ware tour guide mobile applications.

An operational functionality of context abstraction embodies two notions: context aggregation and context interpretation. Whereas context aggregation refers to selecting and integrating context data that is relevant to an application, context interpretation refers to transforming low-level context data into a high-level with a purpose of obtaining the semantics behind correlative context features (Zhang et al. 2009). While the latter is perceived for transforming context sources into a new form of context information, the former is contemplated as the process of logically collecting only the context information that is relevant to context applications' needs (Chen and Kotz 2002). Given the wide variety of sensors that provide broad range of the context data, it became imperative to aggregate the low-level context sensors data to provide a high-level abstraction of these data that can be used by context-aware systems. In turn, a multi-layer context abstraction architecture has been suggested in the literature (Dey 2001; Ranganathan and Campbell 2003; Patterson et al. 2005; Hong et al. 2009). Context abstraction consists of the following layers: (1) sensors network layer to collect the context information; (2) middleware layer to aggregate

Table 15.1 Context modeling methods

Context modeling	Description
Markup scheme	Using a hierarchical data structure that consists of markup tags with attributes and content to model context (Chen and Mohapatra 2005; Soldatos et al. 2007)
Tagged-based	Contexts and their corresponding actions are modeled as tags, in a form of Standard Generic Markup Language (SGML) or unified modeling language (UML). Access to contextual information is provided through specified interfaces only (Blake et al. 2007; Rost et al. 2008)
Ontology-based	Specifying different types of context and their relationships in a form of concepts and sub-concepts and facts, such as users' daily life, and present it into data structure that can be used by context computing applications (Korpipaa et al. 2004; Preuveneers et al. 2004; Strang and Popien 2004; Qin et al. 2007)
Rule-based	Defining context as facts, expressions, and rules using logic representation (Ranganathan and Campbell 2003; Dey and Mankoff 2005; Kwon et al. 2006; Blake et al. 2007; Kaptein et al. 2010; Jung and Park 2013)

and interpret the context information; (3) application layer to provide users with the appropriate service; and (4) presentation layer to offer suitable interface to users. (Clough 2010)

15.2.4   Context Modeling

Conceptually, context modeling aims to describe a situation or the environment of the device or the user, where each context model is described by a set of features with a range of values that are determined (implicitly or explicitly) by the context. Whereas the explicit approach is broadly based on users' direct input and setting commands, the implicit approach is based on providing users with some certain awareness behaviors over time and place (Schilit et al. 1994; Pascoe 1998; Dey and Abowd 2000). Existing context modeling approaches can be classified into categories based on the scheme of data structures used for exchanging contextual information (Chen and Kotz 2000; Strang and Popien 2004), as shown in Table 15.1.

A major challenge in context modeling is the mobile and dynamic nature of context, which is normally acquired from multiple and heterogeneous context sources. Hence, context data needs to be disambiguated and integrated into sensible information. One approach is to provide a mediation technique that allows users to manually disambiguate it, which is often burdensome. For example, (Dey and Mankoff 2005) suggest some guidelines for user mediation techniques in order to achieve a level of interactivity in a manageable way to (a) provide redundant mediation techniques that enable natural and smooth interactions between the user and the context-aware systems; and (b) provide interpretations of ambiguous context defaults to minimize user mediation.

The past few years have witnessed a shifting trend towards incorporating user preferences within the context modeling. Thyagaraju and Kulkarni (2010) present a model for representing and capturing user's interaction preferences into context-aware TV-recommender system. The model aims at defining and representing context from users' perspective by aggregating users' TV watching behavior that would offer users greater services without any explicit requests and at the same time resolve conflict among multiple users. Similarly, (Durán et al. 2010) propose a user metadata model that combines user personal information, user related context information, and user preference information dependent on contextual information. The model aims at increasing users' experience in ubiquitous environments and satisfying their needs based on their circumstances.

For a context-aware system to signal context information of interest to the user, the system is required to obtain an accumulated knowledge about the user's interests and some details about user's social situations (Aknouche et al. 2012). For example, (Nwiabu et al. 2011) present an awareness approach that combines user situation and context awareness. The system provides the capability to handle uncertain knowledge and predict the state of the environment in order to solve specific awareness domains.

15.2.5   Context-Aware Systems

A context-aware system is a system that uses context to provide relevant information and/or services to the user, where relevancy depends on the user's task (Dey and Abowd 2000). Context-aware systems have been developed in academia and industry, as summarized in Table 15.2. The classification criteria used in categorizing these systems is based on the context awareness domain, goal, and context sensing and context modeling presented earlier, along with the context awareness approaches presented in the Sect. 15.3.

15.3   User-Centered Context Awareness Approaches

Much of research on context and context awareness has broadly focused on the technical aspects of context acquisition and interpretation of users' surroundings, also called physical or sensor-based context. Such an approach suffered from the limitation of reconciling the perception of real-world context exhibited by users, or the so-called user context. First, separating user context of interest from the context captured by sensors might result into irrelevant inputs unintentionally included in the context-aware system trained data, leading to a mismatch between the user anticipation and the context-aware system interpretation of that context. Second, neglecting the relevancy link between the users and their surroundings may hinder context-aware systems from connecting users with their context of interest. For example, the exact GPS coordinates may not be of any value to inform about the user current location and corresponding context. Nevertheless, the name of the place may be.

Table 15.2 Context-aware systems' classifications

Context awareness domain	Context awareness goal	Context sensing type	Context modeling	Context awareness approach
Place awareness	Tourist guide (Hagen et al. 2005; Schwinger et al. 2007)	Physical sensors	Tagged-based	Decision support
	Place-aware services (Rost et al. 2008; Clough 2010; Hwang et al. 2010; Chen and Huang 2012)	Physical sensors; logical sensors	Tagged-based	Decision support
	Place-aware and motion presence (Sohn et al. 2006; Bentley and Metcalf 2007; Seppänen and Huopaniemi 2008; Skubic et al. 2009; Meetoo-Appavoo 2011)	Physical sensors; logical sensors; virtual sensors	Tagged-based; rule-based	Decision support; activity recognition
Social networking	Social networking association and interaction (Persson and Jung 2005; Håkansson et al. 2007; Häkkilä et al. 2009; Jensen et al. 2010)	Physical sensors; logical sensors; virtual sensors	Tagged-based; ontology-based; rule-based	Decision support
User activity inference	Inferring users' presence and availability (Perttunen and Riekki 2004; Horvitz et al. 2005; Papliatseyeu and Mayora-Ibarra 2008)	Logical, virtual sensors	Ontology-based; rule-based	Activity recognition
	Inferring user interaction habits with PCs and mobile devices (Papliatseyeu and Mayora-Ibarra 2008; Tsang and Clarke 2008; Durán et al. 2010; Hartmann 2010; Hollosi et al. 2010; Nwiabu et al. 2011)	Logical, virtual sensors	Ontology-based; rule-based	Decision support; activity recognition
	Inferring users' access role (Kulkarni and Tripathi 2008; Kirkpatrick and Bertino 2009; Jung and Park 2013)	Physical, logical, virtual sensors	Ontology-based; rule-based	Decision support; sensors modalities

Different themes and initiatives have been proposed to incorporate the relevant dependencies between users' context and their surrounding environments. Following is a review of the main initiatives that have been entertained in the literature to bring users and context-aware systems closer in defining a user-centered context awareness approach driven by the users' context of interest.

15.3.1 Activity Recognition

Pivotal to context awareness is the recognition of the user activity and ongoing task, which is a challenging and well-studied problem. The goal of activity recognition is to identify users' activities as they occur based on data collected by sensors and machine learning techniques in inferring the users' activities.

Aggarwal and Ryoo (2011) suggest a four-level, complexity-based taxonomy of human activities: gestures, actions, interactions, and group activities. Gestures are a set of primitive human-body-parts movement including arms, legs, fingers and head movements. Actions can be thought of as a composition of multiple gestures, such as walking and running. When human activities involve two entities of person and/or objects, they are classified as interactions (e.g., handshaking). Finally, activities performed by a set of multiple persons and/or objects are called group activities. A typical example is a group of people interacting with a robot.

An approach-based taxonomy classifies human activity recognition methodologies into two categories: single-layered and hierarchical approaches. Single-layered approaches consider inferring human activities by analyzing each frame in a sequence of video images. Hierarchal approaches (or multi-layered approaches) consider recognizing complex activities by describing them in terms of other simpler activities, which are usually called sub-events. Aggarwal and Ryoo (2011) suggest a further level of classification for both single layered and hierarchal approaches based on the methodology used to model human actions. Single-layered approaches can be classified into two types based on the representation model of human actions: spatial-temporal approach (Masoud and Papanikolopoulos 2003; Schuldt et al. 2004; Laptev et al. 2008) and sequential approach (Oliver et al. 2000; Lublinerman et al. 2006; Lv and Nevatia 2007). In the spatial-temporal approach, human activities are modeled as a 3D volume in a space-time dimension, while sequential approaches recognize human activities based on analyzing sequences of features. Similarly, hierarchal approaches can be classified based on the recognition methodology used into three types: statistical approaches, syntactic approaches, and description based approaches. A detailed description and definition of these approaches can be found in (Aggarwal and Ryoo 2011), and a quick review of the human activity recognition approaches is shown in Fig. 15.1.

Existing methods that are used in modeling and recognizing users' activities can be categorized into template matching techniques, generative, and discriminative approaches (Acampora et al. 2013). Template matching techniques deploy a nearest-neighbor classifier based on Euclidean distance (Patterson et al. 2005; Stikic and Schiele 2009). Generative approaches utilize Bayesian classifiers where activity samples are modeled using Gaussian mixtures for batch learning (Im and Cho 2006; Mowafi et al. 2008). Generative probabilistic graphical models, such as Markov models (Zhu et al. 2002; Cook et al. 2013), are used to model time sequenced activities. Finally, discriminative approaches, such as support vector machines (Brdiczka et al. 2009), are used in users' activities clustering.

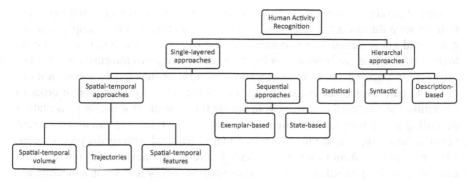

Fig. 15.1 Tree structure of the approach-based taxonomy of human activity recognition methodologies. (Adapted from Aggarwal and Ryoo (2011))

Several research efforts (Fogarty et al. 2004; Perttunen and Riekki 2005; Lo et al. 2008) have explored activity recognition of users' presence and availability status from users' interaction with their daily communication tools, such as Instant Messaging (IM) tools and Groupware Calendar Systems (GCS's). For example, (Perttunen and Riekki 2005) used Lotus Notes calendar information and the Lotus Same time collaboration system to infer users' availability. Others (Mynatt and Tullio 2001; Tullio et al. 2002; Weiß et al. 2008) developed probabilistic inference models of user's activities recognition. Similarly, (Horvitz et al. 2005; Bentley and Metcalf 2007) study users' willingness to accept/deny the incoming phone calls based on their availability and busyness status.

In addition, (Tsang and Clarke 2008) devise a personalized and dynamic run-time to user context adaptation that enables selecting relevant information from users' behavior history for mining usage patterns and selecting the appropriate adaptation behavior that matches users' context. Similarly, (Hartmann 2010) explores an intelligent user interface gathered from the environment (e.g. user current location) and users' interaction behavior. The work aims at supporting the user's navigation by reducing the user interface input by presenting the next relevant interaction to the user for mobile use according to the user's current location.

15.3.2   Sensors Modalities

Advances in computing and sensing technologies have opened the way for sensor modalities sensing technology, which enables the possibility of predicting and delivering, with some accuracy and sensitivity, peoples' needs and tasks (Rogers 2006). Today's smart phones are equipped with various built-in sensors that are capable of collecting and providing high precision and accurate data, such as location, motion, acceleration, rotation, and environmental conditions. Applications can then use that information for activity recognition (Gyorbiro et al. 2009; Skubic et al. 2009; Parry and Narayanan 2010).

One of the key challenges to sensors modalities is mainly attributed to the connection between the collected contextual information and users. For example, sensors can record a user's environment context that can be inferred into a rich array of contextual information, such as the user location, and relating this information to his/her information retrieval for a certain location or point of interest. However, a more difficult context inference is the aggregation of the sensors information in order to determine the user current activity is to devote the context information presentation according to the user level of attention that is mostly related to the user's current activity. An example is the mobile device that is featured with media presentation, such as switching from ring tone to silent. However, the device does not have the capability of distinguishing whether a user specific indoor activity is a meeting activity, in which he/she prefers not to be interrupted, or browsing the internet while sitting in the office, in which the user does not mind to be interrupted by phone calls or messages. One approach that has been investigated broadly ponders on using context data from multiple sensors, also called sensor fusion, to remove the noise of the context data when it exists (Sadri 2011). An example of sensor fusion techniques are the location-aware mobile devices that use GSM positioning systems to offset GPS service which tends to work poorly indoors.

15.3.3 Decision Support

Context awareness dynamically combines a variety of heterogeneous contexts involves multiple, sometimes conflicting, measures of context. Some measures, like those of user surrounding context measures, and those of mobile human interaction context measures. Moreover, because some of the measures are tangible and objectively measured, it will be necessary to consolidate the various measures into a single comprehensive and integrated context awareness value for those approaches. From this perspective, context awareness becomes a multi-criteria decision making problem (MCDM) (Dyer et al. 1992).

MCDM has been widely used in a variety of policy selection, decision making, adaptive learning and recommendation systems (Chen et al. 2002; Rokach et al. 2008; Wu 2008; Mowafi and Forgionne 2011). For example, (Ahmed et al. 2006) present a context-aware decision algorithm for wireless network handover), which takes into account information from both terminal side (i.e., mobile device capabilities and running applications quality of service requirements) and network side (i.e., available access points and their addresses). Other researchers (Cocea and Magoulas 2009) use MCDM for personalized learning mechanism and recommendation depending on the user's learning mode (i.e. individual or collaborative), the context within a task (i.e. specific or general) and the learner's characteristics. Additionally, (Koumoto et al. 2009) apply in prioritizing mobile devices' notification service (i.e., display, speaker and vibrator) based on users' awareness of incoming calls and appropriation preferences.

15.4   Future Research Directions

15.4.1   Context Personalization

User modeling is broadly geared towards user preferences, which do not change dramatically with change of user's place and surroundings (e.g., users' interests in certain news or favorite music, sports, and books normally do not change based on the user's place of search, home or office). In contrast, context personalization is a mix of dynamic and continuously changing surrounding environments (i.e., locations, surrounding objects and people, users' tasks and activities). Therefore, context personalization is not only about how to capture users' interests from past or historical events, but also about how to generalize such historical events in order to include the future as well as the past. For example, (Fischer 2012) proposes a context awareness architecture that aims to record users' actions and store this information for future reference in order to adapt it with future context-aware retrieval. Similarly, (Tsang and Clarke 2008) devise a personalized, dynamic, run-time approach to context adaptation. The proposed approach enables selecting relevant information from users' behavior history for mining usage patterns, and for generating, prioritizing, and selecting the appropriate adaptation behavior that matches users' context.

15.4.2   Situated Action in Context

The concept of situated action, which was first introduced by Suchman (1987), is based on the elucidation of the relation between humans' structure and resources of actions and constraints afforded by environmental and social circumstances. According to Suchman (1987), users' plans and goals are considered as maps to their actions. By abstracting uniformities across situations, plans allow us to bring past experience and projected outcomes to bear on our present actions. Given the difficulty of determining what information is necessary to infer from the surrounding context, the contribution of situated action comes from its relevance in defining user's unique context from his/her actions (Brdiczka et al. 2009).

Context-aware systems need not only to provide intelligibility of system behavior, but also to support accountability of users and the system by enabling users to understand how a system is interpreting the state of the world around them. For example, a context-aware system must inform the user of current contextual system capabilities and understandings, and provide control and defer to the user over the system.

15.5   Summary

The separation between context-aware application interpretation of users' environment and users' aspect of their context has caused a mismatch between context awareness and its relevancy to users' needs and tasks. Such a gap has hindered context aware systems from connecting users' context of interest with their context.

Recent advances in mobile computing devices along with the improvement in connectivity and innovative sensing capabilities have paved the way for cueing and embedding user context into the design and development of context-aware applications. As mobile computing is getting increasingly tied to humans' everyday life, today mobile devices are getting increasingly equipped with adaptive, personalized, and intelligent context-aware features.

Based on the literature presented in this chapter, we have identified a number of important issues that need to be addressed in context awareness future research. First, we believe that context awareness research needs to focus on anticipating user's needs of context information acquisition and presentation. Second, context awareness research needs to emphasize on advising and guiding users through their daily-life in a manner more like to personal assistant rather than a traditional computer.

References

Aarts, E., Ruyter, B.d.: New research perspectives on ambient intelligence. J. Ambient Intell. Smart Environ. **1**(1), 5–14 (2009)

Acampora, G., Cook, D.J., et al.: A survey on ambient intelligence in health care. Proc. IEEE. **101**(12), 2470–2494 (2013)

Aggarwal, J., Ryoo, M.: Human activity analysis: A review. ACM Comput. Surv. **43**, 16:1–16:43 (2011)

Ahmed, T., Kyamakya, K., et al.: Design and implementation of a context-aware decision algorithm for heterogeneous networks. SAC'06, Dijon, France (2006)

Aknouche, R., Asfari, O., et al.: Integrating Query Context and User Context in an Information Retrieval Model Based on Expanded Language Modeling, vol. 7465, pp. 244–258. Springer, Berlin (2012) (Lecture Notes in Computer Science: Multidisciplinary Research and Practice for Information Systems)

Balandin, S., Dunaytsev, R., et al.: Smart spaces and next generation wired/wireless networking. Third Conference on Smart Spaces, SMART 2010, and 10th International Conference, NEW2AN. Springer, St. Petersburg, Russia (2010)

Barkhuus, L.: The Context Gap: An Essential Challenge to Context-Aware Computing. Computer Science. Copenhagen, The IT University of Copenhagen (2005)

Barnard, L., Yi, J.S., et al.: Capturing the effects of context on human performance in mobile computing systems. Pers. Ubiquitous Comput. **11**(2), 81–96 (2007)

Bentley, F.R., Metcalf, C.J.: Sharing motion information with close family and friends. SIGCHI Conference on Human Factors in Computing Systems, San Jose (2007)

Blake, M., Kahan, D., et al.: Context-aware agents for user-oriented web services discovery and execution. Distrib. Parallel Databases. **21**(1), 39–58 (2007)

Brdiczka, O., Crowley, J., et al.: Learning situation models in a smart home. Syst. Man Cybernet. Part B: Cybern. IEEE Trans. **9**(1), 56–63 (2009)

Chen, C.-C., Huang, T.-C.: Learning in a u-museum: Developing a context-aware ubiquitous learning environment. Comput. Educ. **59**, 873–883 (2012)

Chen, G., Kotz, D.: A survey of context-aware mobile computing research. TR2000-381, Department of Computer Science, Dartmouth College (2000)

Chen, G., Kotz, D.: Context aggregation and dissemination in ubiquitous computing systems. Proceedings of the Fourth IEEE Workshop on Mobile Computing Systems and Applications, IEEE Computer Society (2002)

Chen, H., Mohapatra, P.: A context-aware HTML/XML document transmission process for mobile wireless clients. World Wide Web. **8**(4), 439–446 (2005)

Chen, J.-N., Huang, Y.-M., et al.: Adaptive multi-agent decision making using analytical hierarchy process. Australian Joint Conference on Artificial Intelligence, London (2002)

Clough, G.: Geolearners: Location-based informal learning with mobile and social technologies. IEEE Trans. Learn. Technol. **3**(1), 33–44 (2010)

Cocea, M., Magoulas, G.: Context-dependent personalised feedback prioritisation in exploratory learning for mathematical generalisation. User Modeling, Adaptation, and Personalization, 17th International Conference, UMAP (2009)

Cook, D., Feuz, K.D., et al.: Transfer learning for activity recognition: A survey. Int. J. Knowl. Inf. Syst. **36**(3), 537–556 (2013)

Coutaz, J., Crowley, J., et al.: Context is key. Commun. ACM. **48**(3), 49–53 (2005)

Dey, A.K.: Understanding and using context. Pers. Ubiquitous Comput. **5**(1), 4–7 (2001)

Dey, A.K., Abowd, G.D.: Towards a better understanding of context and context-awareness. Workshop on the What, Who, Where, When, and How of Context-Awareness, as part of the 2000 Conference on Human Factors in Computing Systems (CHI 2000), The Hague, CHI (2000)

Dey, A.K., Mankoff, J.: Designing mediation for context-aware applications. ACM Trans. Comput.-Hum. Interact. **12**(1), 53–80 (2005)

Durán, J.I., Laitakari, J., et al.: A user meta-model for context-aware recommender systems. HetRec'10, Barcelona, Spain, ACM (2010)

Dyer, J.S., Fishburn, P.C., et al.: Multiple criteria decision making, multiattribute utility theory: The next ten years. Manag. Sci. **38**(5), 645–654 (1992)

Fischer, G.: Context-Aware systems-the 'right' information, at the 'right' time, in the 'right' place, in the 'right' way, to the 'right' person. AVI '12, Capri Island, Italy (2012)

Fogarty, J., Hudson, S.E., et al.: Examining the robustness of sensor-based statistical models of human interruptibility. SIGCHI Conference on Human Factors in Computing Systems, Vienna (2004)

Gyorbiro, N., Fabian, A., et al.: An activity recognition system for mobile phones. Mob. Netw. Appl. **14**(1), 82–91 (2009)

Hagen, K.T., Modsching, M., et al.: Context based navigation by a dynamic tour guide. The 2nd Workshop on Positioning, Navigation and Communication (WPNC'05) & 1st Ultra-Wideband Expert Talk (UET'05) (2005)

Håkansson, M., Rost, M., et al.: Facilitating mobile music sharing and social interaction with Push!Music. HICSS-40, Hawaii (2007)

Häkkilä, J., Mäntyjärvi, J., et al.: Context-aware mobile media and social networks. MobileHCI'09, Bonn, Germany, ACM (2009)

Han, L., Jyri, S., et al.: Research on context-aware mobile computing. 22nd International Conference on Advanced Information Networking and Applications, GinoWan, Okinawa, Japan (2008)

Hartmann, M.: Context-aware intelligent user interfaces for supporting system use. Ph.D. thesis, TU Darmstadt (2010)

Hollosi, D., Schroder, J., et al.: Voice activity detection driven acoustic event classification for monitoring in smart homes. Applied Sciences in Biomedical and Communication Technologies (ISABEL), 3rd International Symposium on IEEE (2010)

Hong, J.-y., Suh, E.-h., et al.: Context-aware systems: A literature review and classification. Expert Syst. Appl. **36**, 8509–8522 (2009)

Horvitz, E., Koch, P., et al.: Bayesphone: Precomputation of context-sensitive policies for inquiry and action in mobile devices. User Modeling Edinburgh, Scotland (2005)

Hwang, G.J., Kuo, F.R., et al.: A heuristic algorithm for planning personalized learning paths for context-aware ubiquitous learning. Comput. Educ. **54**, 404–415 (2010)

Im, S.-B., Cho, S.-B.: Context-based scene recognition using Bayesian networks with scale-invariant feature transform. Advanced Concepts for Intelligent Vision Systems (ACIVS 2006), Antwerp, Belgium (2006)

Jensen, B.S., Larsen, J., et al.: Predictability of mobile phone associations. Proceedings of the 21st European Conference on Machine Learning, Mining Ubiquitous and Social Environments Workshop, Barcelona, Spain (2010)

Jung, K., Park, S.: Context-aware role based access control using user relationship. Int. J. Comput. Theory Eng. **5**(3) (2013)

Kaptein, M., Markopoulos, P., et al.: Persuasion in ambient intelligence. J. Ambient Intell. Humaniz. Comput. **1**(1), 43–56 (2010)

Kirkpatrick, M., Bertino, E.: Context-dependent authentication and access control. iNetSec 2009—Open Research Problems in Network Security, IFIP Advances in Information and Communication Technology, Springer, Berlin (2009)

Korpipaa, P., Hakkila, J., et al.: Utilising context ontology in mobile device application personalisation. Proceedings of the 3rd International Conference on Mobile and Ubiquitous Multimedia, ACM, College Park, Maryland (2004)

Koumoto, Y., Nonaka, H., et al.: A proposal of context-aware service composition method based on analytic hierarchy process. New Advances in Intelligent Decision Technologies, The First KES International Symposium on Intelligent Decision Technologies (KES IDT'09), Himeji, Japan (2009)

Kulkarni, D., Tripathi, A.: Context-aware role-based access control in pervasive computing systems. SACMAT'08, Estes Park (2008)

Kwon, O.B., Shin, J.M., et al.: Context-aware multi-agent approach to pervasive negotiation support systems. Expert Syst. Appl. **31**(2), 275–285 (2006)

Laptev, I., Marszalek, M., et al.: Learning realistic human actions from movies. IEEE Conference on Computer Vision and Pattern Recognition (CVPR) (2008)

Lo, S.-C., Chiang, J.-L., et al.: Design of a context-aware mobile guiding application. 22nd International Conference on Advanced Information Networking and Applications-Workshops (AINA Workshops 2008), IEEE Computer Society, Los Alamitos, CA, USA (2008)

Lublinerman, R., Ozay, N., et al.: Activity recognition from silhouettes using linear systems and model (in)validation techniques. International Conference on Pattern Recognition (ICCV) (2006)

Lv, F., Nevatia, R.: Single view human action recognition using key pose matching and viterbi path searching. IEEE Conference on Computer Vision and Pattern Recognition (CVPR) (2007)

Masoud, O., Papanikolopoulos, N.: A method for human action recognition. Image Vis. Comput. **218**, 729–743 (2003)

Meetoo-Appavoo, A.: SmartSense: A novel smart and intelligent context-aware framework. Int. J. Comput. Sci. Netw. Secur. **11**(8), 53–62 (2011)

Mowafi, Y., Forgionne, G.: Determining decision values of context awareness in ubiquitous computing environments. J. Multi-Criteria Decis. Anal. **18**(3–4), 203–218 (2011)

Mowafi, Y., Zhang, D., et al.: Examining a Bayesian approach to personalizing context awareness in ubiquitous computing environments. 4th International Conference on Collaborative Computing: Networking, Applications and Worksharing. ColloborateCom 2008., IEEE, Orlando, Florida (2008)

Mynatt, E., Tullio, J.: Inferring calendar event attendance. 6th International Conference on Intelligent User Interfaces, ACM, Santa Fe, New Mexico, USA (2001)

Nwiabu, N., Allison, I., et al.: Situation awareness in context-aware case-based decision support. IEEE First International Multi-Disciplinary Conference on Cognitive Methods in Situation Awareness and Decision Support (CogSIMA) (2011)

Oliver, N., Rosario, B., et al.: A bayesian computer vision system for modeling human interactions. IEEE Trans. Pattern Anal. Mach. Intell. **22**(8), 831–843 (2000)

Papliatseyeu, A., Mayora-Ibarra, O.: Mobile Habits: Inferring and predicting user activities with a location-aware smartphone. 3rd Symposium of Ubiquitous Computing and Ambient Intelligence (UCAMI'08), Springer, Salamanca, Spain (2008)

Parry, D.T., Narayanan, A.: RFID enabled smartcards as a context-aware personal health nod. Healthc. Inform. Rev. Online. **14**(2), 10–16 (2010)

Pascoe, J.: Adding generic contextual capabilities to wearable computers. ISWC '98: Proceedings of the 2nd IEEE International Symposium on Wearable Computers, IEEE (1998)

Patterson, D.J., Fox, D., et al.: Fine-grained activity recognition by aggregating abstract object usage. Ninth IEEE International Symposium on Wearable Computers, IEEE (2005)

Persson, P., Jung, Y.: Nokia sensor: from research to product. Proceedings of the 2005 Conference on Designing for User Experience, AIGA: American Institute of Graphic Arts, San Francisco, California (2005)

Perttunen, M., Riekki, J.: Inferring presence in a context-aware instant messaging system. 2004 IFIP International Conference on Intelligence in Communication Systems (INTELLICOM 04), Bangkok, Thailand (2004)

Perttunen, M., Riekki, J.: Introducing context-aware features into everyday mobile applications. International Workshop on Location- and Context-Awareness (LoCA 2005), Oberpfaffenhofen Munich, Germany (2005)

Preuveneers, D., Bergh, J.V.d., et al.: Towards an extensible context ontology for ambient intelligence. Ambient Intelligence: Second European Symposium, EUSAI 2004, Springer, Eindhoven, The Netherlands (2004)

Qin, W., Shi, Y., et al.: Ontology-based context-aware middleware for smart spaces. Tsinghua Sci. Technol. **12**(6), 707–713 (2007)

Ranganathan, A., Campbell, R.H.: An infrastructure for context-awareness based on first order logic. Pers. Ubiquitous Comput. **7**(6), 353–364 (2003)

Rogers, Y.: Moving on from Weiser's vision of calm computing: Engaging UbiComp experiences. In: Dourish, P., Friday, A. (eds.) Ubicomp 2006 Procccdings, LNCS 4206. Springer, Berlin (2006)

Rogers, Y., Sharp, H., et al.: Interaction Design: Beyond Human Computer Interaction. Wiley, New York (2012)

Rokach, L., Meisels, A., et al.: Anytime AHP method for preferences elicitation in stereotype-based recommender system. ICEIS. **2**, 268–275 (2008)

Rost, M., Bergstrand, F., et al.: Columbus: Physically exploring geo-tagged photos. UbiComp 2008, Seoul, South Korea (2008)

Sadri, F.: Ambient intelligence: A survey. ACM Comput. Surv. **43**(4), 36:1–36:66 (2011)

Salber, D., Dey, A.K., et al.: The context toolkit: Aiding the development of context-enabled applications. Proceedings of the SIGCHI Conference on Human Factors in Computing Systems: The CHI is the Limit, ACM, Pittsburgh, Pennsylvania, USA (1999)

Schilit, B., Adams, N., et al.: Context-aware computing applications. IEEE Workshop on Mobile Computing Systems and Applications, IEEE Computer Society, Santa Cruz, CA (1994)

Schmidt, A., Aidoo, K.A., et al.: Advanced interaction in context. Proceedings of the 1st International Symposium on Handheld and Ubiquitous Computing, Springer, Karlsruhe, Germany (1999)

Schmidt, A., Beigl, M., et al.: There is more to context than location. Comput. Graph. **23**(6), 893–901 (1999)

Schuldt, C., Laptev, I., et al.: Recognizing human actions: A local SVM approach. International Conference on Pattern Recognition (ICPR) (2004)

Schwinger, W., Grün, C., et al.: Context-awareness in mobile tourism guides. IOS. **3**(2), 71–88 (2007)

Seppänen, J., Huopaniemi, J.: Interactive and context-aware mobile music experiences. 11th International Conference on Digital Audio Effects (DAFx-08), Espoo, Finland (2008)

Skubic, M., et al.: A smart home application to eldercare: Current status and lessons learned. Technol. Healthc. **17**(3), 183–201 (2009)

Sohn, T., Griswold, W.G., et al.: Experiences with place lab: An open source toolkit for location-aware computing. 28th International Conference on Software Engineering, Shanghai, China, ACM, New York (2006)

Soldatos, J., Stamatis, K., et al.: Semantic web technologies for ubiquitous computing resource management in smart spaces. Int. J. Web Eng. Technol. **3**(4), 353–373 (2007)

Stikic, M., Schiele, B.: Activity recognition from sparsely labeled data using multi-instance learning. In: Choudhary, T., Quigley, A., Strang, T., Suginuma, K. (eds.) Location and Context Awareness, pp. 156–173. Springer, Heidelberg (2009)

Strang, T., Popien, C.: A context modeling survey. Workshop on Advanced Context Modelling, Reasoning and Management as part of UbiComp 2004. The Sixth International Conference on Ubiquitous Computing, Nottingham/England (2004)

Suchman, L.: Plans and Situated Actions: The Problem of Human-Machine Communication. Cambridge University Press, New York (1987)

Tan, T.-H., Liu, T.-Y., et al.: Development and evaluation of an RFID-based ubiquitous learning environment for outdoor learning. Interact. Learn. Environ. **15**(3), 253–269 (2007)

Thyagaraju, G.S., Kulkarni, U.P.: Modeling user context for interactive context aware TV. IEEE International Conference on Computational Intelligence and Computing Research (ICCIC) (2010)

Tsang, S.L., Clarke, S.: Mining user models for effective adaptation of context-aware applications. Int. J. Secur. Appl. **2**(1), 214–221 (2008)

Tullio, J., Goecks, J., et al.: Augmenting shared personal calendars. ACM Symposium on User Interface Software and Technology (UIST 2002), Paris, France (2002)

Weiß, D., Helas, S., et al.: Context-aware adaptation of mobile multimedia presentations. First International DisCoTec Workshop on Context-aware Adaptation Mechanisms for Pervasive and Ubiquitous Services (CAMPUS) (2008)

Wu, T.-T.: Utilizing analytic hierarchy process to support adaptive learning navigation in a ubiquitous learning environment. The 2008 International Conference on Business and Information (BAI2008), Seoul, South Korea (2008)

Zhang, D., Adipat, B., et al.: User-centered Context-Aware Mobile Applications-The Next Generation of Personal Mobile Computing. Communications of AIS. Accepted for publication on Dec. 4, 2008 (2009)

Zhu, J., Hong, J., et al.: Using Markov models for web site link prediction. Proceedings of the Thirteenth ACM Conference on Hypertext and Hypermedia, ACM, College Park, Maryland, USA (2002)

Chapter 16
Event Quality Awareness for Contextualized Decision Support in e-Health Applications

Leendert W. M. Wienhofen, Davy Preuveneers, Pieter J. Toussaint and Yolande Berbers

Abstract This chapter introduces contextualization of events as a means to improve decision support systems in clinical environments. Modern hospitals are full of technology producing electronic records of events and activities, each meaningful in their specific context. This creates the opportunity to culminate these events into a wealth of information that we can tap into to make better informed decisions and facilitate coordination. By means of a problem frame analysis of a use case in a hospital setting, the importance of event contextualization is presented. The authors explain and evaluate how the quality of these events impact decision making when changes to a pre-set patient trajectory occur.

16.1 Introduction

This chapter focuses on context-awareness in the e-health domain with a case study on the patient trajectory as a clinical process in a hospital setting. We define a patient trajectory as a timeline-oriented representation of what actually has occurred and will happen with the patient during encounters with clinicians. Through inspecting a patient trajectory, a clinician can see how far the plan concerning a patient has progressed, and also whether there have been deviations from the original plan. Based on this information, he can decide if he needs to make any adjustments to his own activities. Given the distributed nature of many hospital systems, the events

L. W. M. Wienhofen (✉)
SINTEF ICT, P.O. Box 4760, Sluppen, 7465 Trondheim, Norway
e-mail: leendert.wienhofen@sintef.no

D. Preuveneers · Y. Berbers
iMinds-DistriNet, KU Leuven, Celestijnenlaan 200 A, 3001 Leuven, Belgium
e-mail: davy.preuveneers@cs.kuleuven.be

Y. Berbers
e-mail: yolande.berbers@cs.kuleuven.be

P. J. Toussaint · L. W. M. Wienhofen
Department of Computer and Information Science, Norwegian University of Science and Technology (NTNU), Sem Sælandsv 7–9, 7489 Trondheim, Norway
e-mail: pieter@idi.ntnu.no

© Springer Science+Business Media New York 2014
P. Brézillon, A. J. Gonzalez (eds.), *Context in Computing*,
DOI 10.1007/978-1-4939-1887-4_16

they produce, and the lack of their contextual relevance on an overall level, it is hard for a clinician to gain an overview over the current overall patient status.

In this chapter we introduce a notion on the quality of the context information that these events carry as this is of vital importance to make well-informed decisions. However, as the events are meant to be used within their set context, combining events from different sources and different contexts will have an impact on the quality of the information upon which decisions are based. Furthermore, hospitals are required to cope with an assortment of compliance regulations that constrain the way patients and healthcare professionals can be tagged and tracked to collect information about their whereabouts and circumstances. One of the challenges is to infer the location of the stakeholders by the events generated in the various underlying systems instead of simply being able to tap into a location service. Events from the same source and even with the same value can have different interpretations depending on more or less implicit context.

To crisply identity the main problems to be solved, we carried out a domain analysis using the *problem frame* method (Jackson 2001). Jackson describes it as follows: *"problem analysis considers a software application to be a kind of software machine. A software development project aims to change the problem context by creating a software machine and adding it to the problem context, where it will bring about certain desired effects. The particular portion of the problem context that is of interest in connection with a particular problem - the particular portion of the problem context that forms the context of the problem - is called the application domain."*

Through observations in the field and various discussions with medical stakeholders, we found that a system for helping to get an accurate overview of the situation was very desirable and we elicited the following key concerns:

1. **Non-deterministic occurrence of events:** With some systems operating in isolation, not every event in the real world can be represented with a digital event. The order of events is often undetermined, and from a medical point of view the exceptions are more interesting than common fixed patterns.
2. **Context-dependent meaning of events:** Two similarly looking events produced by the same system can have a totally different meaning. Their interpretation is subject to the current context, previous events and those that are about to occur.
3. **Quality awareness in events:** The inference of complex events should account for the quality of information of its constituents. The quality of an event (probability of occurrence, reliability, relevance, etc.) may vary over time and influence the confidence in the value of an encompassing complex event.

We define a contextualized event as a complex event semantically enriched through situational refinement. The quality of a contextualized event can be justified by detecting patterns based on historical data, or gather additional information from pseudostatic sources such as calendar or planning systems. Contextualized events can continuously be upgraded or degraded based on new knowledge affecting the quality indicator. Our goal is to contextualize events to make sure that event streams are correctly interpreted. We therefore introduce the notion of *Quality of Event*:

Quality of Event: is a quality measure for the validity of events of how well they characterize activities in the real world. The measure combines the following quality attributes: (1) q_p, the *probability* that the related activity has occurred, (2) q_r, the *reliability* that the order and the information the individual events carry are correct, (3) q_c, the *contextual relevance* (e.g. time, space, semantics) for being retained as a significant constituent in a complex event pattern (representing an activity).

For a more detailed description of the Quality of Event, we refer to our previous work (Wienhofen et al. 2011). After a short background about the field, this chapter will first introduce a real-world case study of several diagnostic activities in a patient's trajectory taking place at a Norwegian hospital. This case stems from the COSTT[1] project. Tackling the challenge of the non-deterministic nature of healthcare processes is instrumental to realizing a system that can cope not only with the majority of regular cases - but also recognize the minority of cases with deviations in event values. The main contributions of this chapter can be summarized as follows:

- Insights into applying context in an a-typical application domain
- Demonstration with a real-world use case on patient trajectories at a hospital
- Reusable concepts and lessons learned for context quality management

The feasibility and effectiveness of our framework for contextualized decision support system has been tested on top of the SAMURAI system[2], a *Streaming Architecture for Mobile and Ubiquitous RESTful Analysis and Intelligence*. This system was partly developed and evaluated in the frame of the FP7 BUTLER[3] project.

16.2   Background and Related Work

Variability is a key characteristic of clinical work (Tucker 2004; Bardram and Hansen 2010; Aaserud et al. 2001). This variability is a result of hospitals becoming larger, as well as the growing complexity in the organizational structure, new technology and treatments. Furthermore, with incoming emergency cases pre-empting planned work as well as the outcome of treatments not going according to expectations, hospitals need to deal with a continuous stream of unforeseen, though somehow expected interruptions to their routine work. To cope with these challenges, health care professionals need up-to-date information about the state of the processes in their immediacy. The increased use of technology enables a growing availability of streams of system events that can be tapped into for better informed decisions and coordination, though the ambiguous nature of raw data taken out if its context makes this a challenging endeavor.

  Lee et al. (2008) investigated data fusion in pervasive healthcare monitoring systems (PHMS), and identified similar challenges regarding collecting and aggregating

---

[1] http://www.ntnu.no/nsep/costt.
[2] https://butler.cs.kuleuven.be/samurai/.
[3] http://www.iot-butler.eu.

events from body sensor networks, wireless sensor networks and mobile devices. The rate of collected data in medical sensor networks is increasing, and so is the complexity to produce high confidence data for medical diagnosis and treatment. They address the reliability of measured data by body sensors and communicating the data over heterogeneous wireless networks. Wasserkrug et al. (2008) carried out similar work on uncertainty in complex event streams. They confirm that most contemporary event composition systems are unable to handle incomplete or uncertain information. Their framework not only handles uncertain events, but also the uncertainty in the inference process. They consider a temporal context and which events are relevant to the inference of other events.

Context-aware applications depend on the availability of context information at the right time and place and in the right quality. Buchholz and Schiffers (2003) argued on the importance of Quality of Context (QoC) for real-life applications to make effective use of provided context information. The QoC is any information that describes the quality of the information that is used as context information. As such, it is a quality parameter that more relates to the precision, the probability of correctness, the accuracy and up-to-dateness of context information. Intensive research has been carried out in the domain of modeling quality of context information. Work by Buchholz and Schiffers (2003), Henricksen and Indulska (2004) and Manzoor et al. (2008) defined several quality metrics for context information and other authors like Krause and Hochstatter (2005), Sheikh et al. (2007) and Abid et al. (2009) have further added to these parameters. In our work, we introduce a similar notion, specifically for events and event-based information systems.

16.3 Use Case Scenario of Patient Assessment Activities

The domain knowledge and the concrete use case behind this article was acquired through observations of a pre-operative medical evaluation for cardiac patients in a Norwegian University Hospital Clinic (though do note that we have tried to keep the scenario at a level understandable for an audience without any form of medical training and therefore we needed to make some simplifications or minor changes to the scenario). To reduce the inconvenience for the patients, what used to be seven or eight examinations over several visits to the hospital has been compressed into one full day of examination activities. While this is beneficial to the patient, it increases the complexity on behalf of the hospital by increasing the need for timely coordination and communication in order to execute this plan. Problems that earlier could be sorted out between visits, will now have to be coordinated on the spot.

As patients in our scenario undergo the same examinations by the same medical stakeholders, a variation in the time used versus the time planned will impact the consultation of the other patients. General event patterns can be created, though the temporal order may vary from patient to patient. As each of the activities generate events that map to the temporal ordering and the pattern, one can get a fair impression of the progress of a patient while he/she traverses all activities.

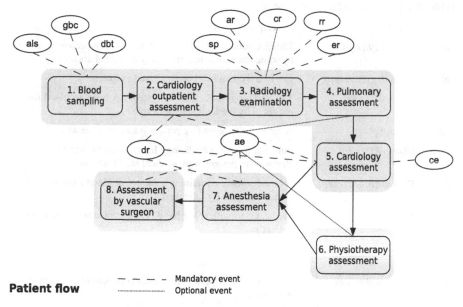

Fig. 16.1 Typical flow of patient activities and corresponding events

During the examination day, the patient has to undergo a number of standardized tests (e.g. laboratory tests, radiologic exam, ECG) in a more or less pre-determined chronological order, see Fig. 16.1. The list in Table 16.1 is a non-exhaustive list of events, though rather a selection of reasonably reliable and obtainable events that can be captured in order to be able to detect that this particular activity is going on. In Table 16.2 we have described the main activities and corresponding events over the course of such a day. In our notation, the ";" operator denotes a sequence of events, and "?" the presence of an optional event.

The order in which events occur often follows a predefined workflow path, which could be seen as an event pattern. The order in which events occur can differ based on the workflow path chosen. The ideal ordering of standard tests a patient typically has to undergo during the examination day can be represented as follows:

$$A_2; A_5 \tag{16.1}$$

$$\{A_1, A_2, A_3, A_4, A_5\} \quad (; A_6)? \quad ; A_7 \quad ; A_8 \tag{16.2}$$

It shows that the first five activities can be carried out in any order, except for step 2 (*cardiology outpatient assessment*) that must precede step 5 (*cardiology assessment*). The sixth step (*physiotherapy assessment*) is optional, and the flow ends with steps 7 (*anesthesia assessment*) and 8 (*assessment by vascular surgeon*) in that order. The ordering of activities in the patient workflow may change because of to resource constraints or interference with other patients. For example, whereas the logical consequence of activities would be A_1, A_2, A_3, A_4, A_5, the order of activities A_2 and

Table 16.1 Description of associated events

	Event	Description
ae	AccessEPR(r, p)	The Electronic Patient Record of patient p has been accessed by someone with role r (typically a medical doctor)
als	AccessLabSystem(p)	The Lab System has been accessed for patient p
ar	AccessRIS(r, p)	The Radiology Information System has been accessed for patient p by medical staff with role r
ce	CardioEcho(p)	A cardio echo regarding patient p has been stored
cr	ChangeRIS(r, p)	Information in the Radiology Information System has been changed for patient p by medical staff with role r
dbt	DispatchBloodTest(p)	A blood sample containing a sample of blood from patient p has been sent by tube mail
dr	DictateResult(r, p)	Medical staff with role r has dictated a voice note regarding patient p
er	ExaminationReady(r, p)	A staff member with role r at the radiology department has finished the examination of patient p
gbc	GenerateBarCode(p)	A bar code with patient information of patient p has been generated
rr	ReportReady(r, p)	A staff member with role r at the radiology department has finished the report regarding patient p
sp	StoreInPACS(r, p)	Information regarding patient p has been stored in the picture archiving and communication system by medical staff with role r

A_3 for a particular patient might be altered if there is currently no free slot in the radiology department.

16.4   Problem Frames Analysis

Following the problem frame method (Jackson 2001), we have contained the scenario in an overall context diagram (see Fig. 16.2), showing how the machine to be built fits in the problem world (meaning the hospital, including all technology that is already available as well as the people that work there and the patients).

The solid lines depict interfaces between the domains. Event patterns is a domain that is not given but needs to be designed (hence the single line on the left side of the box) and the coordination support machine is the machine to be developed (hence the double lines on the left side of the box). The other squares depict other domains that we cannot change.

In Fig. 16.2 shared events between the domains are an abstraction, the actual elaborate dialogues are not important for this context diagram. The syntax, adopted from (Jackson 2001), denotes that at interface "a" domain "CSM" is responsible "!" for phenomena "[notification]".

Table 16.2 Activities during a patient assessment and associated events

	Activity	Description	Pattern
A_1	Blood sampling	are obtained for screening blood values, which could indicate patient conditions that need to be controlled to mitigate risk and ensure safe surgery	als; gbc; dbt
A_2	Cardiology outpatient assessment	to assess the suitability of the patient for surgical intervention with respect to the functioning of the patient's circulatory system. This includes an income interview and an *echo-Doppler* examination	ae; dr
A_3	Radiology examination	where x-ray imagery is used to help assess the suitability for operation. This also serves as input for the anaesthetist assessment later in the day	ar (; cr?); sp; er; rr
A_4	Pulmonary assessment	including a spirometry test. This is in essence a measurement of the amount (volume) and/or speed (flow) of air that can be inhaled and exhaled, and used to assess lung function. This is input for the anesthetists and vascular surgeon's assessment	(ae)?
A_5	Cardiology assessment	to assess the heart function of the patient for suitability for operation	ac; ce; dr
A_6	Physiotherapy assessment	is undertaken for some specific diagnoses. The patient sees a cardiopulmonary physiotherapist for an assessment	(ae)?
A_7	Anesthesia assessment	is conducted to evaluate and score, the patient according to a standardized set of criteria, partly based on the information collected throughout the day. It is also meant to give the patient an opportunity to ask questions to ease any discomfort the patient has about being anesthetized and allow the anesthesiologist to make an evaluation of which form of anesthesia is to be used	ae; dr
A_8	Assessment by vascular surgeon	is the final point of the day where the patient has a consultation with a vascular surgeon. This gives the surgeon a last opportunity to make any additional examinations and the final evaluation based on all the data gathered during the day as well as an opportunity for the patient to ask questions about his or hers own illness and any discomfort about undergoing surgery	ae

Catch value is a generic description as we do not know what values we can catch, nor what they represent. It can be anything from a stream from an indoor positioning system, to a trigger in an access log or the saving of a dictation. Both the patients and the medical staff create digital traces generated by different digital event generators and these traces are intended to be caught by the coordination support machine.

The relations in Table 16.3 are in general one-way. The reason lies in the nature of the intended system. It is meant to help medical staff to self-coordinate based on situational awareness. This self-coordination is based on getting an overview of the problem world at a glance, the system is not meant to send reminders or use other forms of intrusive communication. At first glance it might seem odd that medical

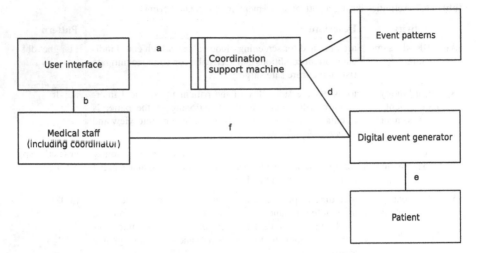

Fig. 16.2 Overall context diagram

Table 16.3 Interfaces on the context diagram

Interface	Description
a	CSM! [Notification]
b	UI! [View], MS! [Read]
c	EP! [Pattern, Range]
d	DEG! [Generate Event], CSM! [Catch Value]
e	PA! [Factor Evidence]
f	MS! [Factor Evidence]

staff has no link to the patients, however, the machine can only capture digital events generated by either the medical staff or the patients and therefore the relation between the two, from a machine point of view, is irrelevant.

Being a type of socio-technical system, the social aspect cannot be neglected. The machine to be built must be able to cope with changes and non-causal and non-deterministic behavior. The main issue is to provide stakeholders with information that has been gathered from multiple systems that each in their way try to represent a piece of the "real world". The information to be displayed leads only to biddable interaction, it is always up to a human to decide whether to act upon the displayed information or not.

16.4.1 Problem Diagrams

The problem itself is not located in the context diagram and this section will shed some light on the actual problem and the requirements. In this section we loosely follow the approach for mapping role activities to problem frames as described

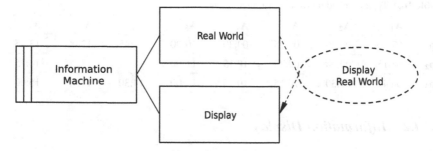

Fig. 16.3 Information display problem diagram. (Adopted from Jackson 2005)

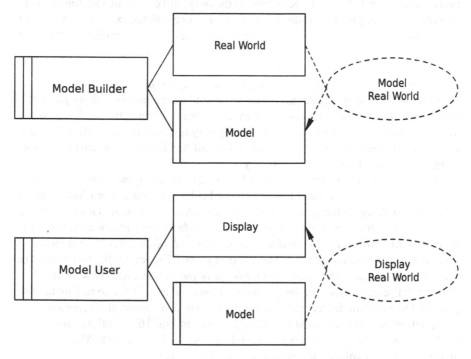

Fig. 16.4 A decomposed view. (Adopted from Jackson 2005)

by Cox et al. (2005). By following this approach, we take into consideration the three main factors identified in the case, namely: non- and in-deterministic occurrence of events, context-dependent meaning of events and quality awareness in events. The outcome of the elicitation process is that the coordination support machine is in fact an information display, much like the one described in (Jackson 2005). In short "In an Information Display problem the Information Machine is required to monitor the state and behavior of a Real World and to display information about it on a Display". Figures 16.3 and 16.4 are copies of the figures provided in Jackson's paper and depict a generic decomposed view of the information display.

Table 16.4 Typical schedule for the examination day

	A$_1$	A$_2$	A$_3$	A$_4$	A$_5$	A$_6$	A$_7$	A$_8$
p$_1$	07:50	08:30	09:15	09:30	10:00	11:45	12:00	13:45
p$_2$	08:15	09:00	09:45	10:15	11:00	–	13:00	14:15
p$_3$	08:45	09:30	10:15	10:45	13:00	14:30	14:45	15:00

16.4.2   Information Display

In short, while the patient traverses the activities according to the plan, the information dependencies between the activities are the only hard constraints for the ordering of work. For example, an anesthesiologist cannot conclude his examination without the results of a cardio echo. For some of these activities it is both crucial that the right information be tied to the right patient, but also that the information from prior steps be available for later activities to proceed. Table 16.4 presents a typical schedule of an examination day of three different patients. It represents three patient flows p_i with various activities A_j (i.e. the assessments and examinations) taking place at a pre-defined timeslot. Though each activity can generate events, the clinical systems triggering events are not integrated and are largely unaware of each other. Hence it is not directly possible to automatically gather all this information across multiple sources, let alone display it appropriately.

Displaying a (partial) representation of the real world is a typical information display problem, and fits the Information Display Problem Frame pattern. Wirfs-Brock et al. (2006) describe the pattern in slightly different words than Jackson: *"there is some part of the world about whose states and behavior certain information is needed... the problem is to build a machine that will obtain this information and present it at the required place in the required form."* Especially the last words are important for our case, *the required place in the required form.* Ideally we would like to give a 1:1 representation of the real world. However, as we have to rely on incomplete and to a certain degree, unreliable information as a source, this representation is not achievable. We represent the frame concern in Fig. 16.5. Both the figure and the frame concern explanation below are taken from Jackson (2001), Wirfs-Brock et al. (2006) as this explanation fits very well with our case.

The key concern of the Information Display problem frame is that the Information Machine must ensure the Displays output is derived from the values in the Real World. Though again, as we at best can give a partial representation of the real world, we need to represent it as well as we can based on the information at hand. We understand that the case caters to at least four flavors of frame variants, as we have description problems, operator problems, connection problems and control problems, each of which each could be represented by its variant. However, as we cannot gain control over many of the factors, as described in earlier sections, we instead propose to accept that we cannot represent the real world in a 1:1 manner and instead we need to represent an $x : 1$ relation where the x needs to be as high as possible (on a 0 to 1 scale). We call this the quality of the representation of the activity. In order to be

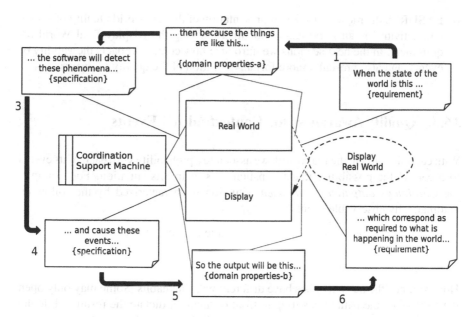

Fig. 16.5 The information display frame concern. (Adopted from Wirfs-Brock et al. 2006)

able to classify the quality of the activity, we need to assign quality attributes to the underlying events as well. The quality of the events is again impacted by the context surrounding the events. The frames concern, illustrated in Fig. 16.5, can be stated as follows:

1. When the Real World is in a particular state
2. THEN because the Real World domain contains particular values
3. AND the Machine will detect those values from the Real World domain
4. AND it causes events to the Display domain
5. AND the Display domain produces some output in response to those events
6. ENSURES the Display can be interpreted as corresponding (as required) to the Real World.

Referring to the case, we can say that the Coordination Support Machine always ensures that the Display responds to the state of the Real World according to the Display Real World requirement:

1. When a digital event generator sends an event
2. THEN the coordination support machine includes this new event
3. AND the events pattern will detect the event and assign it to one or more specific activities
4. AND it adjusts the quality values for all impacted events and activities
5. AND the updated quality is represented on the display per activity

6. ENSURES the most up-to-date representation of the real world Quality of events and activities is an important factor for satisfying the Display Real World requirement. In the next sections we introduce how context impacts the validity of events, and also present a more formal definition of the quality of events.

16.5   Quality Awareness for Contextualized Events

With each situation in the real world, we associate a probability with each of its events to ascertain the possibility that the patient is still in this situation. For example, the *Cardiology outpatient assessment* situation is characterized by the following automatically observable events:

- *ae*: the cardiologist opens the electronic patient record (EPR)
- *dr*: the cardiologist dictates the results of the assessment into the speech recognition software

However, healthcare specialists have different working habits. Some may only open the EPR while the patient is sitting in front of them, or dictate the results while the patient is still present, while other ones open all the patient files in the morning or dictate the results after the patient has left. Hence, the occurrence of a particular event is not a guarantee that the patient is (still) at this location. So, in order to be able to represent the real world for the purpose of serving as a decision support system, we need to introduce a notion of quality to the event. We associate a prior probability of each event in each situation to characterize the possibility that the patient is at this location when this event occurs. These prior probabilities are derived through discussions with the medical stakeholders. For the *Blood sampling* situation this has led to a prior probability of 100 % for the *als* and *gbc* events, and a prior probability of 70 % for the *dbt*. This means that the patient is surely at this location when either of the two first events is recognized. However, there is a slight chance that the patient has already left when the last event is triggered.

Ideally, we would use proven probabilistic reasoning techniques like Bayes' probability theory, Zadeh's fuzzy logic or Dempster–Shafer's evidence theory. We investigated each of these techniques but none of them turned out suitable because of pragmatic reasons, such as the maintenance of the knowledge for non-technical experts. With Bayes' theorem, we can compute the probability for a situation S given the events E knowing the probability of the events given the situation.

$$P(S|E) = P(S \cap E)/P(E) = P(E|S) * P(S)/P(E)$$

However, each situation is usually characterized by a set of events:

$$P(S|E_1, E_2, E_3, \dots) = P(E_1, E_2, E_3, \dots |S) * P(S)/P(E_1, E_2, E_3, \dots)$$

This means that for any set of events we need to know their probability in every situation, and this is guess work without a proper data set from which we can obtain these probabilities.

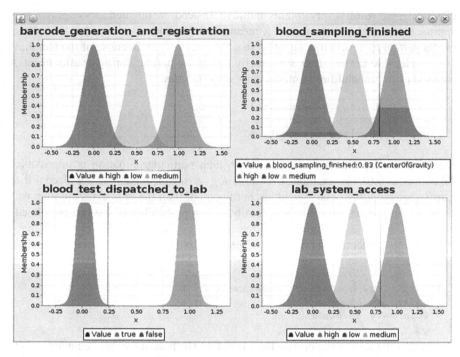

Fig. 16.6 Fuzzy Logic for the Blood Sampling situation

Zadeh's fuzzy logic has the advantage that it allows you to express domain knowledge with linguistic terms rather than with crisp values. However, various arbitrary choices have to be made, such as the shape of each fuzzy variable (triangle, trapezoid, bell, . . .), the modeling of fuzzy sets and rules, as well as the defuzzification into crisp values. Figure 16.6 illustrates this concern for inferring the *blood_sampling_finished* event based on the occurrences of the other observable events (*als, gbc, dbt*), based on fuzzy rules like the following:

if (dbt is false) **then** *blood_sampling_finished is low;*

if (als is medium) **and** *(dbt is not true)* **then** *blood_sampling_finished IS low;*
. . .

The evidence theory from Dempster-Share is a generalization of Bayes based on belief and plausibility, but without going into details, experiments with Dempster's combination rule of evidence have shown that it can sometimes lead to counter-intuitive results. Zadeh himself used the following example to illustrate this concern:

```
Doctor A:                       99% brain tumor,    1% meningitis
Doctor B:                       99% concussion,     1% meningitis
Dempster's combination rule: 100% meningitis
```

Obviously, this result is very counter-intuitive. Instead, we pursued a more pragmatic approach. Remember that situation X means that the patient is at location X. Various events pertain to a particular situation (e.g. ae, cr, dr, ...). Because of the fact that events related to the situation can actually take place before, during or after events, we used prior probabilities to model these uncertainties:

```
P(ar | Radiology examination)    = 1.0
P(ae | Pulmonary examination)    = 0.6
P(dr | Cardiology examination)   = 0.6
```

If predicates of a situation are false, then then particular situation is impossible (likelihood is 0.0). For example, the *Cardiology assessment* cannot take place if the *Cardiology outpatient assessment* has not finished. If all the predicates are true, we compute the probability of the situation based on probability of the last correlated event, and infer the possibility of all the remaining situations. However, this may lead to some mathematical nonsense. Given the likelihoods of the following possible situations:

```
P(Cardiology outpatient assessment) = 0.7    // rr
P(Radiology examination)            = 0.5    // ae
P(Pulmonary assessment)             = 0.5    // ar
```

We see that the sum of the probabilities is not 1. The reason for this behavior is that the related events do not occur all at the same time. If P(X) would be 1.0, we would be absolutely sure that the patient is at that location. However, if it would be 0.95, then there is room for doubt. To solve this problem, we implemented a function $f(x_i)$ (with x_i being the values above) with the following properties:

- $\Sigma\, f(x_i) = 1.0$
- $f(1.0) = 1.0$ and $f(0.0) = 0.0$ *(What is absolutely true or false, remains so)*
- Partial ordering of x_i is the same as partial ordering of $f(x_i)$

The solution is a value z with $f(x_i) = (x_i)^z$ and z such that $\Sigma(x_i)^z = 1.0$. The value z is not easy to compute directly, so we use an iterative method to find the right value.

```
P(A) = 0.99                      f(P(A)) = 0.948
P(B) = 0.5     with z = 5.265    f(P(B)) = 0.026
P(C) = 0.5                       f(P(C)) = 0.026
```

The property of the proposed function maintains the weight of the most likely situation while ensuring the transformed values add up to one. We compared our approach with the fuzzy logic method, by capturing the impact for each situation using fuzzy rules like those for the blood sampling event. Our approach classified the location of the patient (by selecting the one with the highest probability) in some cases up to 31 % better than with the fuzzy rules. However, we should point out that the outcome of the comparison to some extent depends on set of event traces being used. We also compared the mathematical output and color coding with the experience of medical stakeholders, and while stepping through the trace of events the likelihood of the outcomes were similar to their expectations. Furthermore, the results and methodology were more intuitive and therefore easier to understand by these healthcare professionals. We elaborate more in depth on our approach as well as on the visualization support in our previous works (Wienhofen et al. 2011; Preuveneers et al. 2012).

While testing, we found that cross-cutting work flows greatly impact the handling of events. For the blood sampling activity for example, for coordination purposes one only needs to know if the sample has been taken and if the patient is done with this activity. However, the outcome of the actual lab results is an input for later activities, but it does not impact the flow of the patient though the day.

16.6   Conclusions, Lesson Learned and Further Work

Event processing systems are becoming more and more mainstream to continuously monitor behavior and progress in human-in-the-loop systems. For real world decision support in healthcare applications, these systems must account for the inherent uncertain and non-deterministic nature of event occurrences. The major cause of this uncertainty is the gap that exists between the events that happen in real life, and their often incomplete or inaccurate representation with digital event patterns that are being processed by the event based systems.

We found it very useful to apply the problem frame method in order to get a good understanding of the underlying problem of the system. In a typical requirement elicitation we would look into system details and the technical solutions to these problems rather than the actual problem that the *real world* poses. By defining the problem context, we found the need to identify the notion of event quality and an underlying principle for the support system. This clearly sets the boundaries for the technical requirements and our proof-of-concept.

Lessons learned for event quality management and contextualized decision support in the e-health use case are:

- The problem frame methodology is very well suited to identify the gap between the real situation and the digital counterpart.
- We bridged this gap by introducing Quality of Events as a way to measure the trustworthiness of the aggregated information upon which decisions are based.
- The overhead of the probabilistic approach to quality management is negligible with respect to the benefits it brings to ascertain the value of context information.
- In our case study, our approach has shown it can handle different events causing ambiguity because of disagreement about the most likely situation.
- The suggested approach is simple to understand and intuitive so that it can be used by end users without a background in Artificial Intelligence techniques.

Our notion of Quality of Event characterizes how well digital events represent events in the real world. The analysis presented in this chapter provides insight into the diversity of quality requirements that we have to deal with when implementing such a system in medical pre-operative environment. These assessments and requirements are based on real life use cases obtained through various observations and discussions with medical stakeholders in the field.

Additionally, further research should lead to continuous improvements of the quality metrics through feeding the correctness of the inference engine back into the system as input to the original quality metrics. Certain situations can confirm or refute previously recognized situations, thus leading to an improved set of quality metrics based on empirical data, improving upon any statically assigned quality metrics.

References

Aaserud, M., Trommald, M., Boynton, J.: Elective surgery-cancellations, ring fencing and efficiency. J. Nor. Med. Assoc. **121**(21), 2516–2519 (2001)

Abid, Z., Chabridon, S., Conan, D.: A framework for quality of context management. In: Proceedings of the First International Conference on Quality of Context, QuaCon'09, pp. 120–131. Springer, Berlin (2009)

Bardram, J.E., Hansen, T.R.: Why the plan doesn't hold: A study of situated planning, articulation and coordination work in a surgical ward. In: CSCW '10: Proceedings of the 2010 ACM Conference on Computer Supported Cooperative Work, pp. 331–340. ACM, New York (2010)

Buchholz, T., Schiffers, M.: Quality of context: What it is and why we need it. Proceedings of the 10th Workshop of the OpenView University Association, Switzerland (2003)

Cox, K., Phalp, K., Bleistein, S.J., Verner, J.M.: Deriving requirements from process models via the problem frames approach. Inf. Softw. Technol. **47**(5), 319–337 (2005)

Henricksen, K., Indulska, J.: Modelling and using imperfect context information. In: Proceedings of the Second IEEE Annual Conference on Pervasive Computing and Communications Workshops, PERCOMW '04, pp. 33–37. IEEE Computer Society, Washington, DC (2004)

Jackson, M.: Problem Frames: Analyzing and Structuring Software Development Problems. Addison-Wesley, Boston (2001)

Jackson, M.: Problem frames and software engineering. Inf. Softw. Technol. **47**(14), 903–912 (2005)

Krause, M., Hochstatter, I.: Challenges in modelling and using quality of context. In: Magedanz, T., Karmouch, A., Pierre, S., Venieris, I.S. (eds.) MATA, Lecture Notes in Computer Science, vol. 3744, pp. 324–333. Springer, Germany (2005)

Lee, H., Park, K., Lee, B., Choi, J., Elmasri, R.: Issues in data fusion for healthcare monitoring. In: Proceedings of the First International Conference on Pervasive Technologies Related to Assistive Environments, PETRA '08, pp. 3:1–3:8. ACM, New York (2008)

Manzoor, A., Truong, H.-L., Dustdar, S.: On the evaluation of quality of context. In: Proceedings of the Third European Conference on Smart Sensing and Context, EuroSSC '08, pp. 140–153. Springer, Berlin (2008)

Preuveneers, D., Landmark, A.D., Wienhofen, L.W.M.: Probabilistic event processing for situational awareness. In: Lecture Notes in Informatics (LNI)—12th International Conference on Innovative Internet Community Systems (I2CS 2012), vol. P-204, pp. 96–107. Köllen Druck+Verlag GmbH, June 2012

Sheikh, K., Wegdam, M., van Sinderen, M.: Middleware support for quality of context in pervasive context-aware systems. In: Proceedings of the Fifth IEEE International Conference on Pervasive Computing and Communications Workshops, PERCOMW '07, pp. 461–466. IEEE Computer Society, Washington (2007)

Tucker, A.L.: The impact of operational failures on hospital nurses and their patients. J. Operat. Manag. **22**(2), 151–169 (2004)

Wasserkrug, S., Gal, A., Turchin, Y., Etzion, O.: Efficient uncertainty management in complex event systems: Saving the witch from henzel & gretel. In: Proceedings of the Second International Conference on Distributed event-based systems, DEBS '08, pp. 305–308. ACM, New York (2008)

Wienhofen, L.W.M., Preuveneers, D., Landmark, A.D., Toussaint, P.J., Berbers, Y.: A notion of event quality for contextualized planning and decision support systems. In: Proceedings of the 7th International and Interdisciplinary Conference on Modeling and Using Context, CONTEXT'11, pp. 307–320. Springer, Berlin (2011)

Wirfs-Brock, R., Taylor, P.R., Noble, J.: Problem frame patterns: an exploration of patterns in the problem space. In: Proceedings of the 2006 Conference on Pattern Languages of Programs, PLoP '06, pp. 21:1–21:19. ACM, New York (2006)

Chapter 17
Computing the Context Effect for Science Learning

Thomas Forissier, Jacqueline Bourdeau, Yves Mazabraud
and Roger Nkambou

Abstract In science learning, context is an important dimension of any scientific object or phenomenon, and context-dependent variations prove to be as critical for deep understanding as are abstract concepts, laws and rules. The hypothesis presented is that a context gap between two students can be illuminating to highlight the respective general-particular aspects of an object or phenomenon. Furthermore, provoking a perturbation during the learning process to obtain the emergence of such an event could be a productive tutoring strategy. The authors introduce the emergence of context effects as a problem space, to be modeled in the system, and propose a model of the contextual dimension (MazCalc) associated with an analytical view of its modeling, based on a metaphor in physics. A Learning Scenario (Gounouy) has been designed and tested with two groups of learners in Guadeloupe and in Quebec, and MazCalc has been instantiated for this pilot study. Finally, an architecture of a Context-Aware Intelligent Tutoring System is presented, with services to learners, teachers and researchers.

17.1 What Is the Role of Context in Science Learning?

Is the role of context in science learning an obstacle to learning or an essential component for authentic learning? Our claim is that context, and more specifically context effects, can be instrumental in stimulating deep and robust learning among students from different regions of the world. It can be modelled in order to predict the

T. Forissier (✉) · Y. Mazabraud
Université des Antilles et de la Guyane, Pointe-à-Pitre, Guadeloupe, France
e-mail: tforissi@espe-guadeloupe.fr

Y. Mazabraud
e-mail: mazab@espe-guadeloupe.fr

J. Bourdeau
Télé-université du Québec, Québec, QC, Canada
e-mail: jacqueline.bourdeau@licef.ca

R. Nkambou
Université du Québec à Montréal, Montréal, Canada
e-mail: Nkambou.Roger@uqam.ca

© Springer Science+Business Media New York 2014
P. Brézillon, A. J. Gonzalez (eds.), *Context in Computing*,
DOI 10.1007/978-1-4939-1887-4_17

potential effects of context on the learning process, and to orient or test instructional scenarios.

In science learning, context is an important dimension of any scientific object or phenomenon, and context-dependent variations prove to be as critical for a deep understanding as abstract concepts, laws or rules. To our knowledge, a state of the art on context in science education has not yet been carried out, but several studies in science education have explore the issue of context. These studies can be classified into three groups based on their objectives. The first group, stemming from the sociology of education, focuses on various aspects of context (e.g. socio-economical status, gender, etc.) and their impact on students' choice of discipline and later academic achievement in science. It has been shown that the number of students in scientific programs is influenced by social class (Duru-bellat and Van Zanten 2009) and gender (Weinburgh 1995). The second group, constituted mostly of educational psychologists, study the impact of mental representations (as internal contexts) on learning processes. What they consider as context in this case is students' mental representations and the process of contextualization-decontextualization-recontextualization, and they propose instructional strategies which take these processes into account (Van Oers 1998). The third group advocates a *context-based approach* to science education (Schwartz et al. 2004; King et al. 2011; Van Eijck and Roth 2010). Here, the context is considered external to the learner and the learners conduct their enquiries in natural environments, based on authentic situations. The goal of our study is to connect the viewpoints of the last two groups: the mental representations of students and the natural environment of the authentic learning situation. The limitation of the second approach lies in the difficulty to predict the contextual parameters that will be relevant in a specific learning situation (Bazire and Brézillon 2005). We agree with the context-based approach in the importance of constructing representations based on inquiries and we propose to exploit the confrontation of several contexts, both internal and external, to foster learning.

Our hypothesis is that a context gap can be illuminating to highlight the respective general-particular aspects of an object or phenomenon. Provoking a perturbation during the learning process to obtain the emergence of such an event can be a productive tutoring strategy.

In this chapter, we first introduce the notions of context and context effects, as well as the reasons for modeling them. The following section, entitled "The CLASH Model", provides the reader with the theoretical background and justification for our hypothesis and an overview of our project, which aims to test it. This includes a description of the computing component called MazCalc which computes the frequency of the emergence of context effects. It also contains a justification of Design Based Research (DBR) (Barab and Squire 2004; Sandoval and Bell 2004) as the methodology which supports our experimentations as well as the evolution of the design of the system. Section 17.4, describes the pilot study, entitled Gounouy (with participants from Quebec and Guadeloupe). Section 17.5 (CAITS), provides an insight into an architecture of a Context-Aware Intelligent Tutoring System that is envisioned in the near future. In the last section, future work is briefly described, followed by a conclusion.

17.2 Modeling the Context and the Context Effect

Why model a context? The first reason is to have a scientific tool in science learning that is a representation of a shared understanding of what context is made of. Therefore, the modeling implies a specification and a structure with entities and categories that can be manipulated and computed, as well as instantiated and extended. The second reason is to use context as an instructional tool for learners and teachers in order to design field or laboratory activities to collect observation and measurement data that can be imported and computed. A third reason is to be able to integrate the context model into a technological platform that can connect with sensors and captors (via the Web of objects) in mobile learning situations. A fourth reason is to target situational awareness which allows the sharing of situations between computers and humans (Kokar and Endsley 2012). The fifth and last reason is to enable the design of a Context-Aware Intelligent Tutoring System (CAITS), with the full capacity of understanding the learner's actions and guiding them.

Modeling the context can facilitate the identification and description of a phenomenon. The model possesses a predictive value in the fact that by implementing the parameters of the contexts studied, it indicates the likelihood of the emergence of a context effect. Measuring the scientific objects in terms of levels of '*contextuality*' may bring valuable information for the understanding and interpretation of the object of study. The objective is to highlight the comparison of learners' conceptions in response to observed results that are different but linked to a single theoretical concept. In biology and geology, but also in other domains of science, contexts are an integral part of the concepts studied.

In their paper, Bazire and Brézillon (2005) in 2005 analyse 150 different definitions of context. We adopted the definition in which they distinguish a situation (composed of an environment, an item, a user and an observer) from its context, whose parameters are not directly identifiable. We also adhere to the definition of shared context as understood by Zimmermann et al. (2007) but applied to scientific understanding. As Van Wissen et al. (2013), we study the interaction between two levels of context, internal and external. For us, these three definitions are perfectly compatible and highly complementary. In science learning, the internal context of the learner consists of previous knowledge and skills, conceptual models, metacognitive capabilities, motivation, conception and value systems. The external context is linked with location and spatial and ecological environments.

A context effect (Leurette and Forissier 2009) is an event that is produced via tension between two internal contexts in a pedagogical situation (Fig. 17.1). This event is challenging for learners, particularly for their existing mental models. Suddenly, the existing representations they have, while previously correct, no longer account for the new context, and the learners are challenged to carry out a conceptual change or to accommodate multiple representations. From a scientific viewpoint, each context effect can be isolated to allow for the study, control and manipulation thereof. However, this would mean to study it out of its context, similar to *in vitro* investigations. From a more naturalistic viewpoint, we wish to study the process of the emergence of these events, and consequently the position of an event either on a timeline or in

Fig. 17.1 Predicting the emergence of context effects

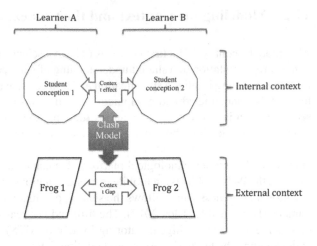

space. We also wish to analyze the correlations among a set of co-occuring events. Measuring the scientific objects in terms of levels of 'contextuality' might bring valuable information for the understanding and interpretation of the object of study. Our intent is to understand the conceptual change (internal) by analyzing the context effect produced by the context gap (external) (Fig. 17.1).

Our approach is based on the measurement of the gap between external contexts, with a calculator that predicts the themes and time of the occurrences of a context effect in a learning scenario which will be presented and used here as an example.

17.3   Context Effect in Science Learning: The CLASH Model

Science teaching is designed to take into account observations of what is real, as well as the results of lab experiments. Authentic teaching aims to foster the construction of conceptions by students based on real situations both in the laboratory (Roth 1995) and in the field, to incorporate the naturalistic dimensions of the sciences in the learning process. Authentic approaches based on contexts (King et al. 2011) fit into this vein and entail investigations based on the study of environments familiar to the students. The gaps between the contexts of the various actors can lead to misunderstandings, and there are times, in particular when these gaps are significant and when the teaching situation lends itself thereto, where an "event" emerges that renders the gaps explicit. These incidents are called "context effects" (Leurette and Forissier 2009); we call them 'clashes'. In a classroom, different actors, each with their own conceptions, are involved. It may be the case between a teacher and a student, two students or a student and a manual, but in all cases, their conceptions have contextual dimensions that are not necessarily shared. In experimental science education, numerous examples can be given: the conception of the cycle of water of Bedouin kids is very rich but completely different compared to the Israeli curriculum (Assaraf et al. 2012); teaching temperate climatic seasons to children living in a tropical area is not coherent with their environment; the reaction of a child raised in a religious household upon learning the theories of evolution can cause confusion, etc.

The emergence of a context effect can take different forms: misunderstanding, questioning, neglecting, rejection, contradiction. The teacher does not necessarily perceive these effects for what they are. In the learning process, the context effect highlights the presence of contextual factors, their influence on the phenomenon observed, and the eventual variations depending on a specific context. As it happens, the context effect becomes the focus of attention, and the learners are guided to understand it and to differentiate the notions that are context-independent (species, nutrition, reproduction, etc) from the variations due to contextual parameters (temperature, ecosystems, etc). As a result, when learning life sciences, learners become aware of the relative values of the features of living creatures depending on context, and they can change their mental models to reach a more exact and more precise level of knowledge.

The model we propose here, the CLASH model, aims to facilitate the identification and description of this phenomenon. Our model possesses a predictive value in that by implementing the parameters of the contexts studied, it indicates the likelihood of the emergence of a context effect.

The objective is to highlight the comparison of learners' conceptions in response to observed results that are different but linked to a single concept. In biology and geology, the contexts are an integral part of the concepts studied. The concept may be considered as a straight line of which the contexts would be the segments. Situating this context amounts to defining its specificity and representability. The comparison of two unique contexts may be carried out in two ways: (1) through resemblance, which makes it possible in particular to specify the level of generalization of the characteristics observed to all or a part of the concept; and (2) through differentiation, which is useful for specifying limitations, singularities and false interpretations. In order to test the CLASH model and, more specifically, our hypotheses regarding the context effect, we adopted a methodology that allows for producing, implementing and testing new research ideas, through iterative design.

17.3.1 The Design Based Research (DBR) Methodology

The methodology selected for this project is inspired by Design Based Research (DBR) (Barab and Squire 2004), which is relevant for working on theoretical issues while designing a solution for an educational problem and testing it *in situ*. This methodology consists of iterations including analyzing the problem, designing and developing a solution, and testing the various aspects or stages of the solution in a realistic situation. It differs from a developmental methodology in that DBR's goal is to contribute to learning theories with new ideas or results. The solution designed can be an instructional strategy, an interactive learning environment or another kind of innovation. Each iteration can vary in terms of specific objectives and research techniques. The output of one iteration becomes the input for the next. DBR emerged in the late 1990s as a new paradigm for testing both human interventions

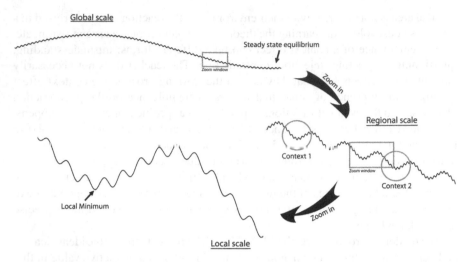

Fig. 17.2 The metaphor for context modeling in the Mazcalc

and technology-enhanced learning environments. Sandoval and Bell (2004) adopted DBR and specified this methodology in the study of science education. In this project, the first iteration corresponds to the pilot study named Gounouy, where the context effect hypothesis is studied via the implementation of the learning scenario. The results of this iteration will be instrumental for the second one, which aims mainly to develop and test the MazCalc component. The third iteration will see the design of the tutoring system components and their integration with MazCalc. The fourth will focus on the design of the authoring system components and their integration with the previous components; it will be tested with instructional designers. The fifth and last iteration consists in testing the Context-Aware Intelligent Tutoring System as a whole, with learners and teachers.

17.3.2 Modeling the Context Effect

In the CLASH model, context effects are modeled based on a metaphor taken from signal processing (Fig. 17.2). In the case of a multi-frequency signal, which corresponds to a sinusoidal curve with various wavelengths, the law selected by the observer to describe the signal may be different in comparison with her observation thereof. According to the observation scale, she is likely to concentrate her analysis on the wavelength that is the most visible at this scale. Much smaller and much larger variations in wavelength will not be perceived, even though they affect the signal in its entirety. Another parameter, the sample size, influences the effect of the various wavelengths in the general representation. When we attempt to describe the evolution of a measured value by comparing it to a theoretical value, indicators such as the Root Mean Square (RMS) are classically used to quantify the error. It is therefore a question of minimizing the RMS and increasing precision in the course of the process.

If the observation scale or the sample size is inappropriate, the minimum RMS value might not correspond to the best overall solution. In such a case, the solution is likely to be specific but inexact. This is known as a local minimum. To avoid this possibility, the scales of analysis have to be varied and the sample size increased. Unfortunately, it is not always possible to adjust the scale (technical constraints) or to have a comprehensive view (outcroppings available in geology, for example). In this case, it is best to make observations of the same type but in different contexts through context gap jump-over. By making observations of the same system in different contexts, it is possible to understand how the system evolves (in space, time, society, etc.).

Derived from this model is the Maz-Calculator (MazCalc), the component which computes the frequency of appearance of context effects based on the gaps of different parameters in two educational contexts. Each context is described in terms of the parameters associated with the observed phenomena, objects or species. Though describing context in this way is sufficient (for determining context effect) in some natural sciences such as Biology, organizing the parameters in different scales of observation is sometime needed in order to avoid the local minima problem. In the Magma project (Geology), it has been found that changing the observation scale could significantly change the probability of a context effect. For instance, observing a *plagiogranite* and a *continental granite* at the 'sample scale' will lead to a low probability of context effect (little difference between the values of parameters in both contexts) while the same observation at another scale may lead to a higher probability.

The MazCalc operates using a database of given contexts structured by scales of observation, each scale containing a number of observation parameters. As mentioned previously, the database can be projected in one scale only to support observations where multiple scales is not necessary. The database is filled with measurements gathered by the learners, which act as either qualitative or quantitative values of parameters (Galliker and Weimer 1997). Data can be collected in two ways depending on the learning mode in which learners are involved: (1) using appropriate user interface to import or enter measurement data or (2) importing them directly from sensors and other measurement instruments in the case of mobile learning. More details about the tools associated with the MazCalc are given in the Sect. 17.4 of this chapter.

For each learning scenario, MazCalc first computes the contexts of each site. This is done through a meta-projection operation in the database structure using observation items and parameters involved in the scenario. The resulting data structure (database schema) is then used as the input for (1) collecting observation data; (2) computing the gap between contexts at several scales and (3) computing a context effect prediction model (a set of prediction rules learned from data) which may evolve when new data arrive in the system. These rules form the basis for predicting the context effect in a specific situation. A first instantiation of MazCalc has been specified for the pilot study, Gounouy, which can be found in Table 17.1. It shows a single scale, with more than 20 parameters divided into five families in accordance with the five student teams. A second instantiation is under preparation, for the learning of magmatism in geology.

Table 17.1 Measurement of context gap can be qualitative or quantitative

Family	Data	Scale	Number of data	Species A		Species B		Quantification	Unit	% of gap vs data	Context gap (from 1 to 5)
				data 1	data 2	data 1	data 2				
Call	Frequency	1	4	2	4	1.2	1.2	1.8	kHz	60	3
Call	Calling months	1	2	12		4		8	NaN	67	3
Call	vocal sac	1	2	Y		Y		NaN	NaN		1
Morphology	weight	1	2	4		280		−276	grams	−6900	5
Morphology	length	1	2	11		190		−179	mm	−1627	5
Morphology	color	1	2	brown		green		NaN	NaN		4
Frog vs Human relation	IUCN status	1	2	LC		LC		NaN	NaN		1
Frog vs Human relation	social perception	1	2	neutral		positive		NaN	NaN		3
Frog vs Human relation	distribution	1	2	anywhere		near pounds		NaN	NaN		4
Frog vs Human relation	Phylogeny	1	6	Anura	Eleuthéro dactylidae	Anura	Neobatrachia	NaN	NaN		1
Nutrition	preys on	1	5	insects	small fish	insects	arthropods	NaN	NaN		4
Nutrition	predators	1	2	reptiles	mammals	reptiles	mammals	NaN	NaN		1
Development	Free larvae	1	2	N		Y		NaN	NaN		5
Development	Nb of eggs	1	3	50		3000	5000	−3950		−7900	5
Development	Larvae life length	1	2	2		50		−48	weeks	−2400	5
Development	Larvae length	1	2	4		45		−41	mm	−1025	5
Development	seasonal variation	1	2	always active		Hibernates		NaN	NaN		3

17.4   The "Gounouy" Learning Scenario

When you ask someone to describe a frog, the answer invariably sounds like this: an animal of about 10 cm, green, with webbed feet, with a call that sounds like "ribbit ribbit" and living in a pond where tadpoles grow in the spring. In Quebec or Guadeloupe, this description is false in many ways. For example, in Guadeloupe, the most common frog is called whistling (*Euleutherodactylus sp.*) which is brown or yellow, very small (less than 3 cm), does not have webbed paw, lays eggs in the ground, from which small frogs (and not tadpoles) emerge and whistle every night, making a sound similar to "tweet tweet" all year long. In Quebec, the largest frog in North America is called a bullfrog (*Lithobates catesbeianus*), has a call that sounds like a bull and is well adapted to the winter season (bullfrog tadpoles are big and can live up to 2 years). Apart from these specificities, the scientific concepts acquired by students during the learning scenario are numerous: the adaptation of the species to its environment, phylogenetic homology and homoplasy, the methodology used to study frog calls, the biology of frog development (stages of development and metamorphosis) and their ecological niche.

Both of these highly contrasting external contexts are used in a learning scenario specially designed to allow the emergence and observation of the context effect in order to test our hypothesis on the benefits of context effects.

17.4.1   Scenario Design

The scenario in biology named 'Gounouy' (which means 'frog' in Antillean Creole) is designed in such a way that the learners are stimulated by the contrasting results of their observations and the common ground of the biological concepts. It involves two groups of students, one in Guadeloupe, a tropical area in the French West Indies, and one in Quebec, in Canada. Both have French as a common language.

The scenario is based on collaborative learning, direct observation, lab investigation, information exchange, expertise sharing, collaborative reflection and discussions. It is organized in three phases; the first one, entitled "organization" (Fig. 17.3) mainly consists of a group discussion between all students through videoconferencing. After each presentation, teachers ask each group to investigate the subject by observing their frogs in the wild in order to present the definition of a frog via a synthesis of their observations. Homologous teams working on different themes (frog call, systematic and morphological characteristics, sustainable development and relationship with humans, development, and nutrition) are constituted in each school.

The Gounouy scenario is based on external context gaps and on various interactions that allow the observation of context effects. During the investigation, which is conducted in the field and in the classroom, each student is required to communicate with those of her team and with those of the homologous team through videoconferencing and with her entire class group by developing the presentation synthesis. A context effect may emerge in each interaction phase.

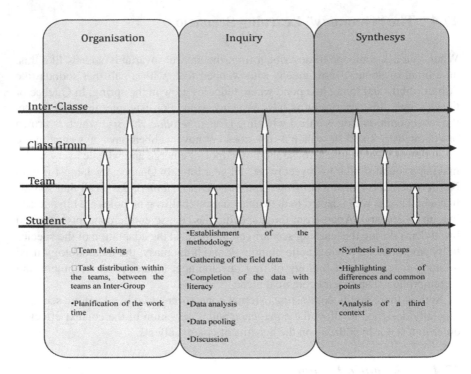

Fig. 17.3 The three phases of the Gounouy Scenario

17.4.2   Testing and Evaluation

According to the DBR methodology described in Sect. 17.3, the first iteration was conducted in 2013. It involved two groups of students. The first one was from "College de Guenette", (Le Moule, Guadeloupe) and the second one from the school "Henri-Bourassa et Soleil de l'Aube" (Repentigny, Québec). The acquisition hardware and the data processing tools available to the students for their observations consisted of various instruments for capture and measurement, and of sensors for collecting data (temperature, weight, video, sound). They also used mobile tools for data recording, as well as tablets for communication with homologous teams and data analysis and visualization.

Student communications were numerous throughout the scenario but structured in a framework for the collection of research data to identify themes and places of emergence of context effects according to the scenario implemented in a digital workspace (Moodle). Various tools allowed student peer groups to communicate with each other, through chat, forum and document sharing tools. Two inter-group and five intra-group videoconferences were organized. Various direct and indirect observations (Table 17.2) have been conducted to enable the observation and characterization of the emergence of context effects.

Table 17.2 Direct and indirect data from scenario analysis

Phases	Data elaborated by student	Recorded data
Organization	Presentation of each class group including school presentation	Pre-test: questions about what is a frog Video conference recording
Inquiry	Document sending and sharing on Moodle Forum and homologuous team video conference Field video recordings Field notebooks Data sensors	Field recordings Researchers observation
Synthesis	Synthesis documents Oral presentation	Post-test: questions about what is a frog Video record during video conference Explicatory interview

The qualitative analysis of these data is compared with the results from the Maz-Calculator. Actually, it is a comparison between the external context gap (MazCalc) and internal contexts (didactic analysis of the emergence of context effect). For these two scenarios, a simple learning environment has been implemented through a Learning Management System, *Moodle*, to provide access to documents and services (communication, sharing), as well as to capture the data needed to test our hypothesis.

Preliminary results indicate that, according to our hypothesis, a context gap-based learning scenario produces context effects, which in turn produce conceptual changes among the learners. Comparisons between pre- and post-test results reveal significant conceptual changes. Sixty video clips with a total of 4 h 15 min illustrate several context effects. With the documents filed by the students mainly via Moodle, the overall context effects have been characterized both in terms of educational content and in terms of the project timeline. These results allow the adjustment of MazCalc.

Moodle has been instrumental for the collection of field data and multiple video-conferences. A digital platform has been designed and structured to meet the specificity of this learning scenario. It includes common work areas for each of the two groups so that students can interact within their class in the preparation of the final presentations. Team spaces (Fig. 17.4) are also used to enable thematic exchanges between homologous teams. Both teachers had access to all areas, where they provided the teams with work sheets, answers to questions as well as access to experts on specific issues.

17.5 Towards a Context-Aware Intelligent Tutoring System

In parallel, the modeling of a Context-Aware Tutoring System is under elaboration. Several components can provide a structure for the modeling of a Context-Aware Tutoring System (CAITS): domain, scales, competencies, and context of the animal, the learner and the teacher. The role of an Intelligent Tutoring System (ITS) is

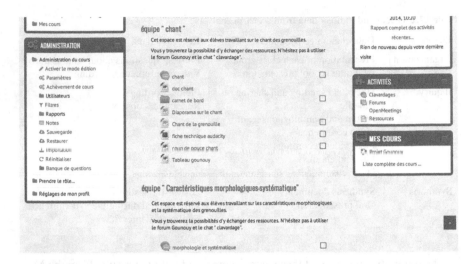

Fig. 17.4 Moodle space of homologous Frog call teams

envisioned to provide guidance to learners with an awareness of the context in which the learners are making their investigations. The system will be knowledgeable about the learning scenario, including the learning activities expected, and the instruments to be used for observations and measurements. It connects to the MazCalc component to capture the actual state of the data (values) captured by the learners and can reason about those to diagnose the eventual learning difficulties encountered by learners. Consequently, it provides adaptive guidance to support learning by doing and from errors (Nkambou et al. 2010).

The architecture of a context-aware tutoring system with its 'authoring services' is proposed as illustrated in Fig. 17.5. One key issue in developing successful learning environments or tutoring systems is to provide the system with a valid learning scenario. In this authoring system, the Maz-Calculator is a key service, used not only for estimating the context effect frequency but also for highlighting the context parameters that are involved. The author could then use this information to revise the learning scenario. She can be assisted in this adaptation task using Context Effects Manager (CEM) tools combined with three scenario management tools: Context-Aware Scenario Editor (CAS-Edit), Context-Aware Scenario Vizualizer (CAS-Viz) and Context-Aware Scenario Simulator (CAS-Sim), as illustrated in Fig. 17.5. In this way, it would be possible to iteratively quantify the importance/influence of each context parameter, provided by the Maz-Calculator, and adjust the scenario accordingly. The resulting scenario is stored in the database named Context-Sensitive Learning Scenario (CSLS). As shown in Fig. 17.5, the Intelligent Tutoring System itself (CAITS) comprises three main components, and is connected to the contexts pool in three ways. The first connection is implemented by the interaction between the Maz-Calculator and the Context-Sensitive Domain Model (CSDM); this connection makes it possible to provide the ITS with context effect information which will drive

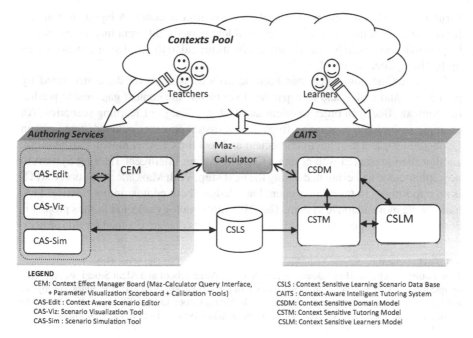

Fig. 17.5 CAITS architecture with its authoring services

the domain model behavior. The second connection is a direct link to the context pool, which gives access to other contextual parameters to be considered during learner/system interactions; this includes contextual information about the learners' profiles, as well as instructional/learning strategies. The third connection is done through the Context-Sensitive Learner Model (CSLS) database, allowing the CAITS to load relevant instructional scenarios that will drive the tutor behavior.

In summary, the envisioned Context-Aware Intelligent Tutoring System extends the classical ITS modules (domain, learner, tutor), with two components related to context: MazCalc and Context Pool. Furthermore a set of specific authoring services is provided for the instructional designer or teacher to adapt or adjust their strategy, and for researchers to test their hypotheses.

17.6   Conclusion

Modeling the context can leverage science learning when used for provoking context effects that are productive for the understanding of basic concepts in life sciences. This chapter introduced the CLASH Model that makes it possible to validate experimental hypotheses on the emergence of context effects in science teaching. A context effect is defined as a sudden revelation that the facts observed are attributable to context elements and relative to the natural environment of the learner. Consequently, learners can distinguish between basic (context-independent) notions and contextual variations, and build conceptual models that are more accurate. Adapting this model for research on similar teaching at different levels or for different themes appears to be possible and would be particularly useful as an aid to the choice of contexts taken up by the teacher.

The MazCalc component has been described, with its database structured by parameters and scales, and its capability to compute the context gaps and to predict the context effects, in order to orient and test the design of learning scenarios. An example in biology, comparing frogs in contrasted contexts in Guadeloupe and in Quebec, illustrates the plan to implement and test the CLASH model. Furthermore, another plan presented is to design a Context-Aware Intelligent Tutoring System to be implemented and evaluated during the next step. With MazCalc at its core, CAITS is an opportunity to take into account knowledge about context into a classical ITS, making it a more adaptive system. The DBR methodology selected for this project is described, with a specialization of the five iterations that are planned for this project.

Acknowledgments   Sophie Fecil, science teacher at Collège de Guenette, Guadeloupe, France; Julie Poulin, teacher at Henri-Bourassa et Soleil de l'Aube school and Alain Stockless, ICT pedagogical advisor at Commission scolaire des Affluents, Québec, Canada; Alexandra Vorobyova for English révision; Rectorat de l'académie de Guadeloupe; the LICEF research center, Tele University, Quebec and the CRREF research center, University of The French West Indies.

References

Assaraf, O.B.Z., Eshach, H., Orion, N., Alamour, Y.: Cultural differences and students' spontaneous models of the water cycle: a case study of Jewish and Bedouin children in Israel. Cult. Stud. Sci. Educ. **12**, 1–27 (2012)

Barab, S., Squire, K.: Design based research: putting a stake in the ground. J. Learn. Sci. **13**(1), 1–14 (2004)

Bazire, M., Brézillon, P.: Understanding context before to use it. LNAI **3554**, 29–40 (2005). doi:10.1007/11508373_3

Duru-bellat, M., Van Zanten, A.: Sociologie du système éducatif. Les inégalités scolaires: PUF 237 (2009)

Galliker, M., Weimer, D.: Context and implicitness: consequences for qualitative and quantitative context analysis. In: Proceedings of (CONTEXT-97), Federal University of Rio de Janeiro (ed.), pp. 151–163 (1997)

King, D.T., Winner, E., Ginns, I.: Outcomes and implications of one teacher's approach to context-based science in the middle years. Teach. Sci. **57**(2), 26–30 (2011)

Kokar, M.M., Endsley, M.R.: Situation awareness and cognitive modeling: intelligent systems. IEEE Intell. Syst. **27**(3), 91–96 (2012). doi:10.1109/MIS.2012.61

Leurette, S., Forissier, T.: La contextualisation dans l'enseignement des sciences et techniques en Guadeloupe. Grand N. **83**, 19–26 (2009)

Nkambou, R., Bourdeau, J., Mizoguchi, R. (eds.): Advances in Intelligent Tutoring Systems. Springer, Heidelberg (2010)

Roth, W.M.: Authentic School Science: Knowing and Learning in Open-Inquiry Science Laboratories. Kluwer, Dordrecht (1995)

Sandoval, W., Bell, P.: Design-based research methods for studying learning in context: introduction. Educ. Psychol. **39**(4), 199–201 (2004)

Schwartz, R.S., Lederman, N.G., Crawford, B.A.: Developing views of nature of science in an authentic context: an explicit approach to bridging the gap between nature of science and scientific inquiry. Sci. Educ. **88**, 610–645 (2004). doi:10.1002/sce.10128

Van Eijck, M., Roth W.M.: Towards a chronotopic theory of "place" in place-based education. Cult. Stud. Sci. Educ. **5**(4), 869–898 (2010). doi:10.1007/s11422-010-9278-2

Van Oers, B.: From context to contextualizing. Learn. Instr. **8**(6), 473–488 (1998). doi:10.1016/S0959-4752(98)00031-0

Van Wissen, A., Kamphorst, B., Van Eijk, R.: A constraint-based approach to context. LNAI **8175**, 171–184 (2013). doi:10.1007/978-3-642-40972-1. (Heidelberg).

Weinburgh, M.: Gender differences in student attitudes toward science: a meta-analysis of the literature from 1970 to 1991. J. Res. Sci. Teach. **32**, 387–398 (1995). doi:10.1002/tea.3660320407

Zimmermann, A., Lorenz, A., Oppermann, R.: Citations an operational definition of context. LNAI **4635**, 558–571 (2007). doi:10.1007/978-3-540-74255-5_42

Part IV
Context in the Collective Human Dimension

Chapter 18
Contextual Cognition in Social Simulation

Bruce Edmonds

Abstract This chapter looks at the modelling of cognition in social simulation with respect to its context-dependency. After making some conceptual clarifications, it briefly reviews existing attempts to include context-like elements into social simulations. It then proposes a principled way, using cognitive context, of integrating machine learning and reasoning processes into a single cognitive model suitable for use in social simulation. This approach is not only particularly suitable for social agents and their coordination but solves several problems at once, including: the feasibility of learning and reasoning, and avoiding over- and under-determination of practical reasoning. Using an example model of an artificial stock market, it shows how context-dependency can make a substantial difference to the outcomes from such models.

18.1 Introduction

This chapter looks at the role of context when modelling human behaviour for social simulation. Models of human behaviour in social simulation vary from very simple cellular automata, where there is usually no cognition represented, through to simulations with relatively detailed cognitive models. In order to capture social dynamics, one needs enough agents to make a meaningful society. This means that it is infeasible to include all the features of a rich cognitive model. However, in order to capture this interplay (where social behaviour influences individual behaviour, and vice versa), it is important to incorporate at least some aspects of cognition into models of human behaviour if one wants to capture many kinds of social phenomena.

For example, the phenomenon of social norms involves both a cognitive dimension (for example what people believe is the norm) as well as the social dimension (for example what patterns of behaviour are most common). There is both an emergent process, from the "bottom up", whereby the beliefs of people interact and aggregate to result in a social regularity (e.g. which side of a corridor to walk down), as well as a process of "downward causation" where the dominant norms constrain the individual

B. Edmonds (✉)
Centre for Policy Modelling, Manchester Metropolitan University, Manchester, UK
e-mail: bruce@edmonds.name

© Springer Science+Business Media New York 2014   273
P. Brézillon, A. J. Gonzalez (eds.), *Context in Computing*,
DOI 10.1007/978-1-4939-1887-4_18

behaviour (Conte et al. 2013). Here a social norm *is* a complex that arises from the interplay of both cognitive and social processes—if one only considered one of these one would miss essential properties (Xenitidou and Edmonds 2014). Here, I argue that contextual cognition and behaviour is a similar case.

Contextual cognition is simply the idea that much of the cognitive processes we might need to include within the agents in a simulation are, in fact, highly context-dependent. In other words, that the very context-dependency of these cognitive processes can be important because it results in a different set of social outcomes (to the case where the processes are context-free).

The next section will look at the nature of this context-dependency and the various concepts of context that this might involve. This will be followed by a brief review of how contextual cognition has been used in social simulation, followed by an abstract model of how such a cognitive model might be built illustrated with an example.

18.2   Context and Context-Dependency

Context pervades the human social and cognitive realms but due to its very nature it is often unnoticed or left implicit. However, when one is involved in trying to understand and model these realms it becomes an important factor. How one attempts to understand any kind of phenomena depends upon its properties. The implicit nature of context means that attempts to label it are often "over-loaded", with the result that the word "context" seems to have a variety of related, but distinct, meanings. Here I do not want to enter the debate concerning the "right" meaning of this word, since that has turned out to be a fairly fruitless enterprise. However it is necessary to clear away some of the confusions that can arise from its use and to make clear my meaning.

Unfortunately, "Context" is used in many different senses and has many different analyses. It is somewhat of a "dustbin" concept, in that if a theory or idea does not work the reason may be assigned to "the context". Thus to many (e.g. linguists) context is a subject that is to be avoided due to its difficulty. "Context" is closely related to (but not identical to) a number of other concepts, including: tacit knowledge (Polanyi 1966), the frame problem in AI (McCarthy and Hayes 1969), framing in psychology (Goffman 1974), and the "situation" (Barwise and Perry 1983).

The situation context is the particular situation where some events or other described phenomena takes place. This could include the time and location, but could include all that is the case about that situation. In this sense the context is indefinitely extensive, it notionally includes all the circumstances in which an event or utterance occurs. Such a context may be able to be specified adequately (if rather uninformatively) by giving the time and place of the events, but the relevant details might not be effectively retrievable from this. Thus when talking about the situational context it is almost universal to abstract from this to what is relevant about that context, or what might be commonly understood (and hence safely not described but left implicit). Thus the phrase "the context" (as in the question "what was the context?") may mean "those factors that are relevant to understand this particular occurrence" even though it may refer to the situational context in general.

Whilst the situational context could include anything, at least in theory, the linguistic context is composed of the words that surround an utterance or phrase. Here we are taking a broader view since I am considering other aspect of cognition than linguistic communication.

Clearly many aspects of human cognition are context-dependent, including: visual perception, choice making, memory, reasoning and emotion (Tomasello 1999; Kokinov and Grinberg 2001). Much of the recall, learning and inference is only done *with respect to* a recognised kind of situation. That is, some knowledge is acquired in a particular situation and then made available in similar situations. This abstraction of a situation in the brain—the recognised kind of a situation in which packages of knowledge etc. are relevant—is sometimes called the *"cognitive context"* (Hayes 1995). This is the cognitive correlate of the situational or linguistic context. Humans seem to have an innate ability to recognise the cognitive contexts of others (Tomasello 1999). It is this conception of context that I will be using in this chapter. This relates to the idea of framing in psychology (Goffman 1974). I do not have space to discuss this in detail but the action of framing can be seen as one effect of considering something within a particular cognitive context—it is the result of cognitive context on opinion and choice. The two concepts are very close but the idea of Cognitive Context is more general—it encompasses other areas, such as how and when these patterns of salience are acquired and how it affects the acquisition of knowledge as well as its application.

Some of the cognitive contexts we have learnt seem to correspond to recognisable kinds of social situation. Examples include: greeting, lecturing, and a political discussion. Once established these seem to be self-perpetuating, in that habits, conventions, norms, terms etc. can be developed by people who recognise the context, but in turn this might mean that the context is more recognisable as an important kind of situation which has its own characteristics. Thus *social contexts* can be co-constructed over time and passed-on (in terms of experience and social artefacts) to others and progressively entrenched in society and thus easily and explicitly identifiable.

18.3 Approaches to Cognitive Contextuality in Social Simulation

Given that context-dependency seems to be fundamental to human cognition and human social behaviour, it is a notable fact that very few social or cognitive simulations represent any of the processes for dealing with such context-dependency. That is to say, the agents in social simulations tend to be endowed with cognitive processes which are not sensitive to, recognise or use context. In other words, agents in social simulations tend not to have anything that might act as a cognitive context. If the situation in which the agents are being represented can be considered as a single and fairly simple set of situational contexts, then this is reasonable since one only has to capture the behaviour and interactions within that.

However many simulations are intended not as a representation of something more general than those corresponding to a single cognitive context but aspire to be a more general theory of social interaction. In this case, one has to assume that either the simulation is to be taken only as an analogy or that the simulator does not think people's behaviour, norms etc. will be sufficiently similar between situational contexts so the context-free representation is adequate (even when using very charitably assumptions).

In the former case where the simulation is used only as an analogy, then this is valid because humans are experts at applying analogy in a context-dependent manner, adjusting its assumptions and form to be appropriate to its domain of application.

In the later case, where an essentially context-independent algorithm is used to represent a highly context-dependent process must, at least, be the legitimate target for doubt. Whilst the psychological realism that is necessary in a social simulation does depend upon the purpose of the simulation and the level of aggregation (Gilbert 2006), it is certainly not the case that the results of a simulation are robust against changes in the cognitive model being used (e.g. Edmonds and Moss 2001).

There are not many simulations which represent some aspects of context-dependency in their agents, but there are a few: (Edmonds 1998) used a cognitive learning model specifically because it included some aspects of context-dependency; Schlosser et al. (2005) argue that reputation is context-dependent, Edmonds and Norling (2007) looks at the difference that context-dependent learning and reasoning can make in an artificial stock market, Andrighetto et al. (2008) shows that learning context-dependent norms is different from a generic adaption mechanism, and Tykhonov et al. (2008) argue that the definitions of trust mean that trust is also context-dependent. These show that, at least in some cases, that context-sensitive cognition can make a difference. The fact that it can make a difference is not very surprising given the apparently important role it plays in human cognition, means that there is a burden of justification on those who claim it is unnecessary—explaining why it *can* be safely ignored in their simulations.

There are approaches to including cognitive context within the learning and decision-making of agents. (Edmonds 2001b) which suggests a particular algorithm and approach to learning appropriate cognitive context (but did not achieve the co-development of cognitive context due to the anti-cooperative environment they were embedded within. (Andrighetto et al. 2008) use an approach based on social norms, whereby some of the habits and knowledge of agents are dependent upon the social context, in the sense of which group they are part of. Alam et al. (2010) uses an endorsement mechanism to implement a kind of context-sensitive learning/decision-making mechanism in agents within a simulation of some of the power structures within Afghanistan. In particular they relate this to folk psychological accounts of how reasoning works and is of a form that relates better to available observational and participant evidence. Knoeri et al. (2011) look to Gidden's structuration theory and structural agent analysis. Within this framework they implement what they call a context-dependent Agent-based model using an analytical hierarchy process as the basis for the agent decision-making process in a model of mineral construction in Switzerland. Dignum et al. (2004a, b) describe a multi-layered system for specifying agents in simulations that explicitly includes the context-specific interpretation of social norms. Antunes et al. (2000) and Nunes et al. (2013) look at context specificity in terms of the context of different social networks, with switching between them in terms of different social influence operating in each.

18.4   A Model of Contextual Cognition

In this section I look at the outlines of a lightweight cognitive model that allows for context dependent cognition to be implemented within social simulation models. This model integrates Machine-learning type of learning with an AI kind of reasoning via a context-structured memory.

Both learning and reasoning are far more feasible when their scope is restricted to a particular context because this means that only the relevant knowledge needs to be dealt with. However if any significant degree of generality is to be obtained in this manner (McCarthy 1971) then an intelligence must be able to appropriately change this focus as the external context, that is the context we inhabit in (Barwise and Perry 1983), changes. In other words there needs to be some internal correlate of the external context that allows an intelligence to identify which set of beliefs apply. We will call this internal correlate the cognitive context—this is the "internal" approach identified in (Hayes 1997). There are (at least) two tasks necessary for this: identifying the appropriate cognitive context from the perceptions of the environment; and accessing the appropriate beliefs given the identified cognitive context.

The success of this strategy of assessing the relevance of knowledge via identifiable "contexts" depends upon whether the environment is usefully divided up in such a manner. This is a contingent matter—one can imagine (or devise) environments where this is so and others where it is not. The "pragmatic roots" of context, i.e. why context works, depends upon the underlying pattern of commonalities that occur in an environment or problem domain (Edmonds 1999). A cognitive context indicates the boundaries of what might be relevant in any situation.

Context serves not only to make it feasible to deal with our knowledge at any one time but also, at a more fundamental level, to make our modelling of the world at all feasible. The efficacy of our limited learning and inference in dealing with our complex world is dependent on the presumption that many of the possible causes or affects of events that are important remain relatively constant (Zadrozny 1997). Otherwise we would need to include all possible causes and affects in our models and decision making processes, which is clearly infeasible. It is the existence of relative constancy of many factors in particular situations that makes our limited modelling ability useful: we can learn a simple model in one circumstance and successfully use it in another circumstance that is sufficiently similar to the first (i.e. in the same "context").

It is the possibility of the transference of knowledge via fairly simple models from the circumstances where they are learnt to the circumstances in which they are applied that allows the emergence of context. The utility of "context" comes from the possibility of such transference. If this were not feasible then "context", as such, would not arise. For such a transference to be possible a number of conditions need to be met, namely that: some of the possible factors relevant to important events are separable in a practical way; a useful distinction can be made between those factors that can be categorized as foreground features and the others (the constant, background features); similar background factors are capable of being reliably recognized later on as the same "context", the world is regular enough for such models to be learnable; and that the world is regular enough for such learnt models to be useful where such a context can be recognized.

While this transference of learnt models to applicable situations is the basic process, observers and analysts of this process might identify some of these combinations of features that allow recognition and abstract them as "a context". Note that it is not necessarily possible that such an observer will be able to do this as the underlying recognition mechanism may be obscure, too complex or difficult to analyze into definable cases.

Such a strategy answers those of the "frame problem" (McCarthy and Hayes 1969). Firstly, although the frame problem may be unsolvable in general it is learnable in particular contingent cases. Secondly, the identification of appropriate contexts are not completely accessible to reasoning or crisp definition—rather it is an unreliable, information-rich, and imprecise process. Thus knowing B in context A, is not translatable into statements like $A \rightarrow B$, because the A is not a reified entity that can be reasoned about.

The power of context seems to come from this combination of "fuzzy" and fluid context identity and crisp, relatively simple context "contents". Thus context straddles the fields of Machine Learning and Artificial Intelligence. Machine learning seems to have developed appropriate methods for complex and uncertain pattern recognition suitable for the identification of context. Artificial Intelligence has developed techniques for the manipulation of crisp formal expressions. Context (as conceived here) allows both to be used for different functions in an coherent way.

Context in Reasoning In 1971, in his ACM Turing Award lecture, John McCarthy suggested that the explicit representation and manipulation of context might be a solution to the effective lack of generality in many AI systems; these ideas were later developed and written up in (McCarthy 1971). McCarthy's idea was to reify the context to a set of terms, i, and introduce an operator, ist, which basically asserts that a statement, p, holds in a context labeled by I, thus $c{:}ist(i, p)$, reading "p is true in context i" which is itself asserted in an outer context c. ist is similar to a modal operator but the context labels are terms of the language. Reasoning within a single context operates in a familiar way and in addition one needs a series of 'lifting' axioms, which specify the relation between truth in the different contexts. This framework is developed in McCarthy and Buvac (1998) and there are now many formal systems which are closely related to the above structure, including, notably: the situations of Barwise and Perry (1983); Gabbay's fibered semantics (Gabbay 1999); and the local semantics of the Mechanized Reasoning Group at Trento (Ghidini and Giunchiglia 2001).

One of the problems with this sort of approach is that it is likely that trying to apply generic reasoning methods to context-dependent propositions and models, will be either inefficient or inadequate (Greiner et al. 2001). The generic approach forces a choice of the appropriate level of detail to be included, so that it is likely that either much information that is irrelevant to the appropriate context will be included (making the deduction less efficient) or much useful information that is specific to the relevant context may be omitted (and hence some deductions will not be possible).

Another problem is that, in practice, this type of approach requires a huge amount of information to be explicitly specified: contexts, contents of each context and bridging rules.

Context in Learning The use of context in machine learning can be broadly categorized by goal, namely: to maintain learning when there is a hidden/unexpected change in context; to apply learning gained in one context to different context; and to utilize already known information about contexts to improve learning. There are only a few papers that touch on the problem of learning the appropriate contexts themselves. Included in those that do, Widmer (1997) applies a meta-learning process to a basic incremental learning neural net; the meta-algorithm adjusts the window over which the basic learning process works. Here it is an assumption that contexts are contiguous in time and so a time-window is a sufficient representation of context. Harries et al. (1998) employ a batch learner as a meta-algorithm to identify stable contexts and their concepts; this makes the assumption that the contexts are contiguous in the "environmental variables" and the technique can only be done off-line. Aha describes an incremental instance-based learning technique which uses a clustering algorithm to determine the weight of features and hence implicitly adjust context (Aha 1989).

Contextual knowledge has been used to augment existing machine learning techniques in a number of instances. Turney (1993) used explicit identification of what the contextual factors would be, but others have used implicit features (e.g. Aha 1989). Turney (1996a) discusses the problem of the effects of context on machine learning and surveys some heuristics used to mitigate these effects (Turney 1996b).

Combining Context-Dependent Learning and Reasoning Restricting both reasoning and learning to an appropriate context makes both more feasible. However, as usual, there are a number of difficulties with applying a context-dependent approach to reasoning. *Firstly*: explicitly specifying a set of knowledge appropriate for a whole set of potential contexts is both time-consuming and labor-intensive.

Thus with a few honorable exceptions (e.g. CYC (Lenat 1995)), most systems of context-dependent learning or reasoning are only tried out with a few contexts. A possible answer to this (and the one employed here) is to learn the contexts and the context-dependent knowledge. The second is easier than the first; for, as indicated above, there are a number of techniques to learn the knowledge associated with contexts.

The learning of the contexts themselves (i.e. how to recognize when a set of beliefs learnt in a previous situation are again applicable) requires a sort of meta-learning. As documented above, there are such techniques in existence. However most of these either require reasonably strong assumptions about the particular nature of the contexts concerned. An exception is Edmonds (2001) which describes how contexts can be co-learnt along with the knowledge associated with those contexts. This applies an evolutionary learning algorithm where the knowledge is distributed across a space, where different positions in that space are associated with different set of perceptions or different parts of a problem. This can be clearly understood via the following ecological analogy. If the space can be thought of as a landscape where different parts of the landscape have different properties, and different plants require different properties (some might thrive in marshy land, others sunny and dry etc.). The set of solutions can be seen as varieties of a plant. The different varieties propagate and cross with others in each locality so that, eventually, each variety adapts and, at the same time, spreads across the areas that it is best adapted for. The patches where different sets of varieties thrive define the different ecological niches—corresponding to the different contexts via this analogy.

The ability to learn context allows us to move beyond the 'loose' loop of:

repeat
    learn/update beliefs
    deduce intentions, plans and actions
until finished

to a more integrated loop of:

repeat
  repeat
    recognise/learn/choose context
    induce/adapt/update beliefs in that context
    deduce predictions/conclusions in that context
  until predictions are consistent
    and actions/plans can be determined
  plan & act
until finished.

Such a co-development of cognitive contexts along side their "contents" gives rise to a new problem when the knowledge in these contexts is used to infer predictions and decisions. Thus a *second* problem is this: *When some of the contents turn out to be wrong, how can one tell when it is the context that is wrong and when it is the contents that are wrong?*

There is no universal answer to such a question—it will, in general, depend upon the nature of the domain and hence the appropriate contexts in that domain. However there is a heuristic, as follows: if only a few of the elements of knowledge associated with a context are disconfirmed, it is likely that these are wrong (update the set); if many of the elements are disconfirmed then it is likely that the context is wrong (change it and learn).

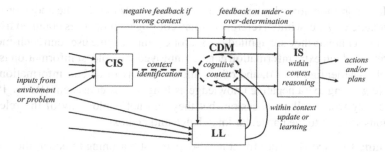

Fig. 18.1 How the context-identification system (*CIS*), the context-dependent memory (*CDM*), the local learning algorithm (*LL*), and inference system (*IS*) work together

Thus in the proposed architecture there are four modules: (1) the context identification system; (2) the context-dependent memory; (3) the local learning/induction algorithm; and (4) the inference system, as shown in Fig. 18.1.

The *context identification system* (CIS) takes a rich range of inputs and learns in a flexible and imprecise way an indication of the context (which it outputs to the memory). The CIS learns as the result of negative feedback when too much of the knowledge in the cognitive context is disconfirmed. The *context-dependent memory* (CDM) takes the indication given by the CIS and identifies all those memory items stored within that context. It evaluates the (current) truth of these and if too many are false it returns negative feedback to the CIS, which will identify another context. If a sufficient number of indicated contents are true, then the local learning updates the items within that context. Those items that are (currently) true are passed to the inference system. The *local learning algorithm* (LL) performs a local update of the knowledge in the memory. It may include the propagation of successful items towards the focus, but may also include the deletion/correction of items that were false and the possible insertion of new induced/learned. Finally the *planning/inference system* (IS) tries to deduce some decisions as to the actions or plans to execute. It could do this in a number of ways, but this could include trying to predict the future states of the world given possible actions and comparing the predictions using its goals.

Two common problems with inference systems that attempt to deduce predictions or decisions from an arbitrary collection of knowledge are under- and over-determination. Under-determination is when there is not enough information to come to a conclusion or decision that needs to be reached. In other words there may be a key proposition, α, such that neither α nor $\leftarrow \alpha$ can be inferred. Over-determination is when there is contradictory information, i.e. when there is an α such that both α and $\leftarrow \alpha$ can be deduced.

This architecture allows a useful response in these two situations. In the case of under-determination the context can be expanded so that more knowledge can be made available to the IS so that it may make more inferences. In the case of over-determination the context can be reduced so that some of the knowledge can be excluded, those peripheral to the context.

Many non-monotonic logics can be seen as attempts to solve the above problems in a generic way, i.e. without reference to any contingent properties obtained from the particular contexts they are applied in. So, for example, some use 'entrench-ment' to determine which extra information can be employed (e.g. oldest information is more reliable (Gärdenfors 1984)), and others allow a variety of default information to be used (e.g. using extra negative knowledge as long as it is consistent (Reiter 1980)). These may work well on occasion, but they can not exploit any of the relevance relations specific to the particular knowledge and context.

Learning Context In order for context-dependent reasoning to occur, the context-dependent information (or beliefs) need to be captured. If the relevant contexts are already known by the designer (and there is some effective way of recognizing when they apply), then either the relevant information can be entered or a context-enhanced learning algorithm can be employed to learn the information with respect to each context. The former case can be onerous because one not only has to enter the relevant facts as well as specifying each fact's domain of application, but one also has to define all the 'lifting-rules' to allow the integration of the context-dependent information. In the later, the context-dependency of the learning means that one needs correspondingly more information within each context for the learning to be complete. Thus in order for the desired efficiency in terms of context-constrained reasoning to occur (without a laborious entry of information) for each appropriate context, this information (that is the contexts *and* the content in the contexts) should be learned by the agent, at least to some extent.

The basic idea is to simultaneously learn the models and the circumstances in which they work best. If there is sufficient regularity in the environment to allow it this will allow some clusters of similar circumstances to be identified and the corresponding models to be induced. However the clustering and induction parts of the algorithm can not work independently; i.e. clusters of like circumstances being identified and then models induced for these clusters. The reason for this is the contexts are identified by those circumstances where particular models work best. These may correspond to a neat (i.e. humanly identifiable) cluster but this is not inevitable—they may be (to the human eye) inextricably intertwined or overlapping.

There is a population of candidate beliefs, each of which is composed of two parts: a crisp model in a formal language (the content) and some information that specifies the model's domain of application (the domain). In the examples given here the designer specifies what inputs will be used for context recognition and which can be referred to in the model content (some may be in both). Repeatedly a particular circumstance is chosen (for example, these are the ones that simply occur to the agent), and those beliefs who are recognized as most probably relevant (or 'closer') are selected. Out of these the ones that work best are preferentially selected and crossed into future generations of the population. Beliefs that are never anywhere near occurring circumstances are, over time, forgotten.

The basic learning algorithm is as follows:

```
Randomly generate candidate models
Place them randomly about the domain, D
for each generation
  repeat
    randomly pick a point in D, P
    pick n models, C, biased towards those near P
    evaluate all in C over a neighbourhood of P
    pick random number x from (0,1)
    if x < propagation probability
      then propagate the fittest in C to new generation
      else cross two fittest in C, put result into new
           generation
  until new population is complete
next generation
```

A biological analogy makes this clear. Imagine that each belief is an plant. These plants exist in a space defined by the factors that allow context recognition. They compete locally, and those that are better replicate themselves into a neighbourhood (by propagation and sexual reproduction). Thus slowly the successful plants adapt and spread to fill all of the space in which they are relatively successful. Different plants will occupy different areas in the space. The contexts correspond to the ecological niches. Following are examples of the some more general heuristics (Edmonds 2001).

- *Formation*: A cluster of models with similar or closely related domains suggests these domains can be meaningfully abstracted to a context.
- *Abstraction*: If two (or more) contexts share a lot of models with the same domain, they may be abstracted (with those shared models) to another context. In other words, by dropping a few models from each allows the creation of a super-context with a wider domain of application.
- *Specialisation*: If making the domain of a context much more specific allows the inclusion of many more models (and hence useful inferences) create a sub-context.
- *Content Correction*: If one (or only a few) models in the same context are in error whilst the others are still correct, then these models should either be removed from this context or their contents altered so that they give correct outputs (dependent on the extent of change needed to "correct" them)
- *Content Addition*: If a model has the same domain as an existing context, then add it to that context.
- *Context Restriction*: If all (or most) the models in a context seem to be simultaneously in error, then the context needs to be restricted to exclude the conditions under which the errors occurred.
- *Context Expansion*: If all (or most) of the models in a context seem to work under some new conditions, then expands the context to include these conditions.
- *Context Removal*: If a context has only a few models left (due to principle 2) or its domain is null (i.e. it is not applicable) forget that context.

18.5   Example: An Artificial Stock Market Model

In order to demonstrate this approach to learning, I needed an environment that was sufficiently complex yet having emergent contexts (i.e. ones difficult to predict in advance). I have chosen a stock market model, composed of many trading agents and one market maker (roughly following the form and structure of Palmer et al.1994). The traders can choose to buy or sell one of a number of shares (if this is possible for them) from or to the market maker. The only fundamental in the market is a dividend rate for each of the shares which slowly change in a random walk. There are only a limited amount of each stock available to the market as a whole. The market maker sets prices as a result of the demand—if there is net demand for a stock it raises the price and if there is a net negative demand it lowers the price. There is a small transaction cost to the traders for every trader, so rapid random trading is unlikely to benefit it.

The goal of the traders is to maximise the total value of their assets (cash plus shares at current value). Thus the traders are in competition with each other—one trader tends to gain at another's expense. However this is not a zero-sum game due to the dividends paid on stocks and the possibility of making money at the market maker's expense.

Each time period the traders simultaneously buy or sell each of the stocks, assuming they have enough cash to fund the net price, the stocks to sell, and the market maker has the stocks to sell. Traders do not have to trade in any stock. Thus the decision that each of the traders has to make is how much to attempt to buy or sell of each stock each time period.

Traders can observe the following: the current and past prices of all stocks; the past actions of all traders; and the current and past dividend rates. In addition the traders are provided with primitives for: the current and past market index (average of all prices); recent trend of the index; recent total volume of trading; recent market volatility; and the maximum historical price of any stock. The operators available to the agents to build models with are: basic arithmetic $(+, -, \times, \div)$; and the ability to refer back in time (last and lag operators). They also have some constants, namely: the names of the other traders, the names of the stocks; and a selection of random constants.

Basically the traders try to learn to predict what each of the stocks will be in the next time period and then buy or sell if they predict it will rise or fall sufficiently for this to be worthwhile.

This sort of set-up produces a rich series of dynamics as the traders participate in sequences of modelling 'arms-races' and imitation 'games'. Any successful prediction schema will not last forever as the other traders will soon spot your trading pattern and exploit it to your disadvantage. However, as with real stock markets, there are definitely patterns and market 'moods' (if there are enough traders and stocks), for example bull markets and speculative bubbles. There will be periods of relative quiet as traders sit on stock and so effectively prevent trading and periods of high volatility as subgroups of traders engage in bouts of activity trying to exploit each other. The dynamics are related to those of the "minority game" (Arthur 1994), and similar (Akiyama and Kaneko 1995) but are more varied and complex. Thus, although this is an artificial setting, it goes way beyond a "toy" problem in terms of both scope and complexity.

There are two types of traders: which I will call generic and context traders. Both types maintain a population of 20 models, each of which is composed of a separate expression to predict the future price of each stock. All models are initially randomly generated to a depth of 5 using the inputs, primitives, operators and constants already listed. Both kinds of agent use an evolutionary learning algorithm which evaluates fitness by the profit the agent would have made over the past three time periods had it used these models to predict prices. The generic traders use a genetic programming learning algorithm to evolve their predictive models and the context traders have an adapted version of this algorithm to allow the simultaneous learning of context for its models. The types are otherwise identical. Their learning algorithm is:

> Randomly generate initial population of candidate models
> **tor** each generation
>   **for** each model
>   evaluate what the total wealth of the agent would be if it had used this
>   model in trading over the past few time periods, this is the model's fitness
>   **next** model
>   repeat
>   randomly pick two models with a probability proportional to their current
>   fitnesses
>   pick random number x from (0,1)
>   **if** x < propagation probability
>   **then** propagate them to new generation
>   **else** cross them and put results into new generation
>   **until** new population is complete
> **next** generation

The context trader's algorithm differs a little from the basic version outlined in the last section. This is because from an agent's point of view the only relevant circumstances (in terms of the space of possible ones) are those that actually occur. Therefore instead of randomly picking a sequence of circumstances until the new population is generated, we use only the present circumstance repeatedly and we propagate the rest into the next population with a bias against those that are furthest from any circumstance that has occurred. Also in this model, I have associated with each model content a set of positions, so that its domain of application is indicated by a small cloud of points, not a sharply defined region.

It is not obvious that the context trader is a better learner than the generic trader. The context algorithm restricts which models can be crossed to produce new variants to those that are in the same neighbourhood of an occurring circumstance, whilst the generic algorithm allows a more global search for solutions. Thus one might

Fig. 18.2 Difference of
average asset values between
context vs. generic traders,
scaled by current asset spread

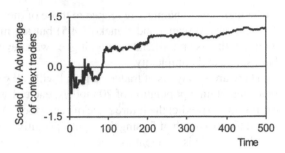

Fig. 18.3 Growth in agents'
assets over time (context
traders in *black*, generic in
white)

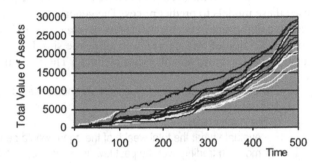

expect that the context traders do better only if there is a context-dependency in the
environment to exploit. As we shall see this appears to be the case in this model.

The model was run with 7 of each type of agent (thus 15 including the market
maker) trading 5 different stocks over 500 time periods. The model was implemented
in SDML (Moss et al. 1998).

For the first 80 periods one of the generic traders was doing substantially better
than the others, but after this the context traders clearly did better, on the whole
(see Fig. 18.3). To make clear the significance of the difference between context and
generic traders I have plotted the difference between the average value of context
traders' assets minus the average value of the generic trader's assets, scaled by the
current standard deviation of the spread of total asset values (Fig. 18.2). It is notable
that the generic traders did better if there were only two or three of each type of
trader—the context traders only reliably out-perform the generic traders (on the
whole) with larger populations of traders. The context traders do particularly well
if they are in a minority among many generic traders. It is postulated that it is only
with larger numbers of the same type of trader that learnable contexts appear in
the trading patterns for the context traders to learn and exploit. To show that the
context traders are, in fact, identifying meaningful contexts (at least sometimes), I
have taken a snapshot of the positions indicating the domain of the six of the models
in one agent for one stock at one time (the best performing agent halfway through
the run). These clusters are shown in Fig. 18.4. The contents of these six model are
shown in Table 18.1.

Fig. 18.4 Snapshot of
clusters of positions of six
action models within the
memory of a context trader
indicating three distinct
emergent contexts

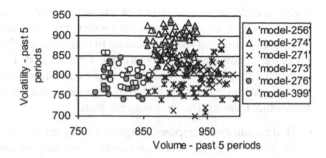

Volatility - past 5 periods
Volume - past 5 periods

Table 18.1 The action
models (for stock 3) in
Fig. 18.4

Model-256	priceLastWeek (stock-4)
Model-274	priceLastWeek (stock-5)
Model-271	doneByLast (normTrader-5) (stock-4)
Model-273	IDidLastTime (stock-2)
Model-276	IDidLastTime (stock-5)
Model-399	Minus (divide (priceLastWeek (stock-2)) (priceLastWeek (stock-5))) (times (priceLastWeek (stock-4)) (priceNow (stock-5)))

For this agent at this time there seem to be three regions that might correspond to
different contexts: one for lower volatility and higher volume, one for lower volatility
and lower volume and one for higher volatility and middle volume. It is notable that,
even within each of these there are a mixture of two models that are appropriate. Thus,
even given the circumstances, the model selected for will be determined by recent
predictive performance: for example, in the case of stock 3 in the above snapshot its
price may be modelled best by either the price of stock 4 or stock 5 last time period.

The point of this example is two-fold: that implementing a context-dependent
cognitive model within a social simulation is feasible, and that it makes a difference—
there is an observable difference in behaviour between the context and generic traders
in this simulation. The point is *not* that context-dependent cognition will be perform
better in all circumstances, since as with all cognitive processes (Edmonds 2008),
context-sensitivity will be helpful in some circumstances and not in others.

18.6   Conclusions

The lack of agents endowed with the cognitive ability to recognise social context must
limit or change the social complexity that results when they interact. In particular,
the co-development of social contexts will be lacking, where the recognisability of a

distinct social context will allow new and specific habits, norms etc. to be developed for that situation, enabling that social context to become more recognisable etc. This will limit the ability of such simulations to capture some classes of social phenomena where the co-development of social context is a key part. Thus it may be, for example, that such things as a "jittery market" might correspond to a co-developed cognitive context, recognised and reinforced by the market traders in that market (as well as many other factors). Thus this suggests that:

- That a simulation composed of agents with essentially non-context cognitive models might be giving deceptive results, especially in cases where the agents are learning and/or making decisions in a variety of situations.
- Sometimes less "smooth" learning and inference algorithms in the agents in a simulation, that mimic some aspects of context-dependency, as observed in the humans that are being modelled, might well produce a simulation that matches the observed outcomes better.

In other words, the cognitive model encoded in the agent can matter. One can not hope that an "off-the-shelf" model based on something from another context, like AI or machine learning, will be good enough.

Context-dependency pervades the subject matter of social phenomena, with feasible modelling possible only within specific varieties of context. At the very beginnings of sociology Max Weber did point out the inherent context-dependency of social phenomena, also pointing out that this does not stop a scientific study of it (Coser 1977). These roots seem to have been somewhat forgotten.

Acknowledgments The author acknowledges funding from the EPSRC, grant number EP/-H02171X/1, as well as discussion with Emma Norling and a great number of people at the Using and Modelling Context conference series.

References

Aha, D.W.: Incremental, instance-based learning of independent and graded concept descriptions. In: Proceedings of the 6th International Workshop on Machine Learning, pp. 387–391. Morgan Kaufmann, Burlington (1989).

Akiyama, E., Kaneko, K.: Evolution of cooperation, differentiation, complexity, and diversity in an iterated three-person game. Artif. Life **2**, 293–304 (1995)

Alam, S.J., Geller, A., Meyer, R., Werth, B.: Modelling contextualized reasoning in complex societies with "Endorsements". J. Artif. Soc. Soc. Simul. **13**(4), 6 p. (2010) (http://jasss.soc.surrey.ac.uk/13/4/6.html)

Andrighetto, G., Campennì, M., Conte, R., Cecconi, F.: Conformity in multiple contexts: Imitation vs norm recognition. In: World Congress on Social Simulation 2008 (WCSS-08) George Mason University, Fairfax, USA (2008)

Antunes, L., Nunes, D., Coelho, H., Balsa, J., Urbano, P.: Context switching versus context permeability in multiple social networks. In: EPIA 2009, 547–559 (2000)

Arthur, B.: Inductive reasoning and bounded rationality. Am. Econ. Assoc. Pap. **84**, 406–411 (1994)

Barwise, J., Perry, J.: Situations and Attitudes. MIT Press, Cambridge (1983)

Conte, R., Andrighetto, G., Campennì, M. (eds.): Minding Norms-Mechanisms and Dynamics of Social Order in Agent Societies. Oxford University Press, Oxford (2013)

Coser, L.A.: The Sociology of Max Weber. Vintage, New York (1977)

Dignum, V., Vazquez-Salceda, J., Dignum, F.: A model of almost everything: Norms, structure and ontologies in agent organizations. In: Proceedings of the Third International Joint Conference on Autonomous Agents and Multiagent Systems-Volume 3 (AAMAS '04), vol. 3, pp. 1498–1499. IEEE Computer Society, Washington (2004a)

Dignum, V., Vazquez-Salceda, J., Dignum, F.: OMNI: Introducing social structure, norms and ontologies into agent organizations. In: PROMAS 2004, 181–198 (2004b)

Edmonds, B.: Modelling socially intelligent agents. Appl. Artif. Intell. **12**, 677–699 (1998)

Edmonds, B.: The pragmatic roots of context. In: CONTEXT'99, Trento, Italy, Sept 1999. Lecture Notes in Artificial Intelligence, vol. 1688, pp. 119–132 (1999)

Edmonds, B.: Learning appropriate contexts. In: Akman, V., et al. (eds.) Modelling and Using Context-CONTEXT 2001, Dundee, July 2001. Lecture Notes in Artificial Intelligence, vol. 2116, pp. 143–155 (2001)

Edmonds, B.: The social embedding of intelligence: How to build a machine that could pass the Turing test. In: Epstein, R., Roberts, G., Beber, G. (eds.) Parsing the Turing Test, pp. 211–235. Springer, Dordrecht (2008)

Edmonds, B., Moss, S.: The Importance of Representing Cognitive Processes in Multi-Agent Models, Artificial Neural Networks—ICANN'2001, Aug 21 -25 2001, Vienna, Austria. In: Dorffner, G., Bischof, H., Hornik, K. (eds.) Lecture Notes in Computer Science, vol. 2130, pp. 759–766. (2001)

Edmonds, B., Norling, E.: Integrating learning and inference in multi-agent systems using cognitive context. In: Antunes, L., Takadama, K. (eds.) Multi-Agent-Based Simulation VII, vol. 4442, pp. 142–155. Springer, Berlin (2007)

Gabbay, D.M.: Fibring Logics. Clarendon, Oxford (1999)

Gärdenfors, P.: Epistemic importance and minimal changes of belief. Australas. J. Philos. **62**(2), 136–157 (1984)

Ghidini, C., Giunchiglia, F.: Local models semantics, or contextual reasoning = locality + compatibility. Artif. Intell. **127**(3), 221–259 (2001)

Gilbert, N.: When does social simulation need cognitive models? In: Sun, R. (ed.) Cognition and Multi-Agent Interaction: From Cognitive Modeling to Social Simulation, pp. 428–432. Cambridge University Press, Cambridge (2006)

Goffman, E.: Frame Analysis: An Essay on the Organization of Experience. Harvard University Press, Cambridge (1974)

Greiner, R., Darken, C., Santoso, N.I.: Efficient reasoning. ACM Comput. Surv. **33**(1), 1–30 (2001)

Harries, M.B., Sammut, C., Horn, K.: Extracting hidden contexts. Mach. Learn. **32**, 101–112 (1998)

Hayes, P.: Contexts in context. Context in knowledge representation and natural language. Paper presented at AAAI Fall Symposium, MIT, Cambridge, Nov 1997 (1995)

Knoeri, C., Binder, C.R., Althaus, H.-J.: An agent operationalization approach for context specific agent-based modeling. J. Artif. Soc. Soc. Simul. **14**(2), 4 p. (2011) (http://jasss.soc.surrey. ac.uk/14/2/4.html).

Kokinov, B., Grinberg, M.: Simulating context effects in problem solving with AMBR. In: Akman, V., Bouquet, P., Thomason, R., Young, R.A. (eds.) Modelling and Using Context, vol. 2116, pp. 221–234. Springer, Berlin (2001)

Lenat, D.B.: CYC-A large-scale investment in knowledge infrastructure. Commun. ACM **38**(11), 33–38 (1995)

McCarthy, J. (1971) Generality in Artificial-Intelligence—Turing Award Lecture. Commun ACM. **30** (12), 1030–1035

McCarthy, J., Buvac, S.: Formalizing context (expanded notes) (1997). In: Aliseda, A., van Glabbeek, R., Westerståhl, D. (ed.) Computing Natural Language, pp. 13–50. CSLI, Stanford (1998)

McCarthy, J., Hayes, P.J.: Some philosophical problems from the standpoint of artificial intelligence. Mach. Intell. **4**, 463–502 (1969)

Moss, S., Gaylard, H., Wallis, S., Edmonds, B.: SDML: a multi-agent language for organizational modelling. Comput. Math. Organ. Theory **4**(1), 43–69 (1998)

Nunes, D., Antunes, L., Amblard, F.: Dynamics of relative agreement in multiple social contexts. In: EPIA 2013, 456–467 (2013)

Palmer, R., Arthur, W.B., Holland, J.H., LeBaron, B., Taylor, P.: Artificial economic life—a simple model of a stock market. Physica D **75**, 264–274 (1994)

Polanyi, M.: The Tacit Dimension. Doubleday, New York (1966)

Reiter, R.: A logic for default reasoning. Artif. Intell. **13**, 81–132 (1980)

Schlosser, A., Voss, M., Brückner, L.: On the simulation of global reputation systems. J. Artif. Soc. Soc. Simul. **9**(1), 4 p. (2005) (http://jasss.soc.surrey.ac.uk/9/1/4.html)

Tomasello, M.: The Cultural Origins of Human Cognition. Harvard University Press, Cambridge (1999)

Turney, P.D.: Robust classification with context-sensitive features. In: Industrial and Engineering Applications of Artificial Intelligence and Expert Systems, IEA/AIE-93, Edinburgh, 1993, pp. 268–276. Gordon and Breach, Newark (1993)

Turney, P.D.: The identification of context-sensitive features: A formal definition of context for concept learning. In: ICML-96 Workshop on Learning in Context-Sensitive Domains, (Bari, Italy, 1996), pp. 53–59. (1996a)

Turney, P.D.: The management of context-sensitive features: A review of strategies. In: ICML-96 Workshop on Learning in Context-Sensitive Domains, (Bari, Italy, 1996), pp. 60–66 (1996b)

Tykhonov, D., Jonker, C., Meijer, S., Verwaart, T.: Agent-based simulation of the trust and tracing game for supply chains and networks. J. Artif. Soc. Soc. Simul. **11**(3), 1. (2008) (http://jasss.soc.surrey.ac.uk/11/3/1.html)

Widmer, G.: Tracking context changes through meta-learning. Mach. Learn. **27**, 259–286 (1997)

Xenitidou, M., Edmonds, B.: The Complexity of Social Norms. Springer, Heidelberg (2014)

Zadrozny, W.: A pragmatic approach to context. Context in knowledge representation and natural language, AAAI Fall Symposium, Nov 1997, MIT, Cambridge (1997)

Chapter 19
SocioPlatform: A Platform for Social Context-Aware Applications

Muhammad Ashad Kabir, Alan Colman and Jun Han

Abstract With an explosive growth in the popularity of social media and increasing prevalence and features of advanced mobile devices, interest has grown significantly in applications that are aware of users' social context and are able to assist them in their daily activities. A key requirement of developing social context-aware applications is the platform support to reduce the complexity of engineering such applications. In this chapter, the authors present such a platform, namely *SocioPlatform*, to aid the development of social context-aware applications by acquiring, reasoning, storing and provisioning different types of social context information, and managing their runtime interactions and adaptation. The platform hides the complexity of managing social context, and thus assists the development of social context-aware applications. The authors demonstrate the feasibility and applicability of the platform by developing two different types of such applications.

19.1 Introduction

Context-Aware Computing is a paradigm that aims to make pervasive applications more intelligent and accessible, and is increasingly gaining attention in the research community. The notion of context is widely appreciated today, and usually refers to information about systems, entities, and their environments. Software applications that adapt their behaviour with the changes of context information (e.g., location, temperature, and time) are called *context-aware* applications. A context-aware application uses context to provide relevant information and/or services to the user, where relevancy depends on the user's task (Dey 2001).

M. A. Kabir (✉) · A. Colman · J. Han
School of Software and Electrical Engineering,
Swinburne University of Technology, John Street, Hawthorn,
PO Box 218, Melbourne, Australia
e-mail: akabir@swin.edu.au

A. Colman
e-mail: acolman@swin.edu.au

J. Han
e-mail: jhan@swin.edu.au

© Springer Science+Business Media New York 2014
P. Brézillon, A. J. Gonzalez (eds.), *Context in Computing*,
DOI 10.1007/978-1-4939-1887-4_19

Humans, however, are social beings. Hence, the notion of social context-awareness (in short *social awareness*) extends the vision of context-aware computing. An application is socially-aware if it uses social context information (e.g., social relationships, social roles, social interactions and situations) to adapt its behaviour (Ferscha 2012).

While early context-aware applications relied on ad hoc architectures and representations, it has already been recognized that separating the process of acquiring contextual information from actual applications is key to facilitating application development and maintenance (Dey et al. 2001; Henricksen and Indulska 2006). Therefore, a number of software architectures, frameworks and platforms have been proposed for developing and managing context aware applications (see Raychoudhury et al. 2013 for a survey). Existing software architectures and platforms for context-aware applications, however, mostly address contexts of a physical nature such as location, time, and activity, and so on.

Taking account of social context poses additional challenges for application developers as they must define or collect social context information from various sources, mediate/coordinate social interactions across parties and manage them in a consistent manner. There has been comparatively only limited work investigating contexts of a social nature such as social roles, interaction- and connection-oriented social relationships and social situations (Kabir 2014b). Even though recently some works have attempted to manage social context (e.g., Kourtellis et al. 2010), they are limited in representing different aspects of social context. Furthermore, there is a lack of support for managing the acquisition, changes and provision of various types of social context.

In this chapter, we present a platform, called *SocioPlatform*, to aid the development of socially-aware applications. The essence of our approach is to hide the complexity of acquiring, classifying, inferring, storing and managing social context by providing a supporting platform, and thus assist the development of socially-aware applications. The platform provides a number of functionalities. It acquires social context information from various sources; classifies, integrates and stores such information into a knowledge base. It supports the specification of reasoning rules and the derivation of a richer set of social context information. The platform also enforces users' privacy preferences in accessing their social context information and allows users to specify their privacy preferences in a consistent manner. The platform provides efficient access of social context information by implementing a query interface so that application developers can use the interface to access users' social context information. The platform also provides runtime environment for mediating social interactions based on interaction-oriented social relationships and supports their runtime adaptation.

The chapter is organized as follows. Section 19.2 describes social context and key requirements of developing socially-aware applications. After giving an overview of our SocioPlatform in Sect. 19.3, Sects. 19.4 and 19.5 present the two key components of the SocioPlatform architecture followed by the presentation of a prototype implementation in Sect. 19.6. Section 19.7 reviews related work and Sect. 19.8 concludes the chapter.

19.2   Social Context and Socially-Aware Applications

19.2.1   Social Context

In context-aware computing area, early works on context-awareness referred to context as primarily the location of people and objects (Schilit and Theimer 1994). In recent works, context has been extended to include a broader collection of factors, such as physical and social aspects of an entity (Dourish 2004).

Schmidt et al. (1999) present a model of context with two distinct categories: human factors and physical environment. *Human factors* consist of three categories: information about the user (*e.g.,* profile, emotional state), the user's social environment (*e.g.,* presence of other people, group dynamics), and the user's tasks (*e.g.,* current activity, goals). *Physical environment* also consists of three categories: location (*e.g.,* absolute and relative position), infrastructure (*e.g.,* computational resources), and physical conditions (*e.g.,* noise, light). This model gives a classification according to specific contextual factors, but does not provide a formal definition. Dey (2001) presents a survey of alternative view of context, which are largely imprecise and indirect, typically defining context by synonym or example. Finally, he offers the following definition of context, which is perhaps now the most widely accepted: *"Context is any information that can be used to characterise the situation of an entity. An entity is person, place or object that is considered relevant to the interaction between a user and an application, including the user and the application themselves"*. Henricksen (2003) relates context to tasks, rather than to interactions between users and applications, as in the definition of Dey. She separates the concepts of context, context modelling and context information. Henricksen argues that context represents a nebulous concept, is difficult to define and bound, where as context models and context information are well defined and understood, and are primary interest in constructing context-aware systems.

Several studies have attempted to define and represent social context from different perspectives. Han et al. (2008) define social context as the user's social surroundings, that is to say, the social relationships of the user. Eugster et al. (2009) rely on a more restricted definition of social context. They consider distributed objects as peers and the social context of a peer represents its awareness of the existence of other peers. Zheng et al. (2007) identify social context as one of the essential elements of the context space for online social interaction. They consider social context as social, cultural, psychological, and emotional influences on online social interactions. Wang et al. (2010) analyse the role of the social group in a ubiquitous computing environment as a source of contextual information. They define social context as: *"Information relevant to the characterisation of a situation that influences the interactions of one user with one or more other users"*. Biamino (2011) views social context as social aggregations or social groups, and defines social context using 3-tuple expression (<number of nodes, number of connections between them, nature of relations between the nodes>) that characterises a social network. Endler et al.

(2011) introduce the term "situated social context" to enable location-based spontaneous interaction among people and define the term as: "*Situated Social Context of an individual is the set of people that share common spatio-temporal relationship with the individual, which turn them into potential peers for information sharing or interacting in a specific situation*". Schuster et al. (2012) combines the concept of social context with pervasive context and introduce the term "pervasive social context" which they define as: "*Pervasive Social Context of an individual is the set of information that arises our of direct or indirect interaction with people carrying sensor-equipped pervasive devices connected to the same Social Network Service*".

As can be seen from the above discussion, the term "social context" can have many meanings or definitions, but most of the above works view social context as possible forms of *relationships* and *interactions* among people. Taking this insight, the following interpretations are adopted in this chapter:

- *Social Context* characterises social milieu[1] of an individual with respect to another individual or a group of individuals.
- A *Social Context Model* represents a subset of the social milieu, which we define in terms of social roles, relationships, interactions and situations, of an individual with respect to another individual or a group. The social context model is employed by a given socially-aware application, is usually explicitly specified by the application developer but may evolve over time.
- *Social Context Information* is a set of data, gathered from various sources (*e.g.,* social media) or explicitly specified by human, that conforms to a social context model. It provides a snapshot that approximates the state, at a given time, of the subset of the social context encompassed by the model.

19.2.2 Socially-Aware Applications

Based on the factors that dominate the applications' behaviour, we categorize socially-aware applications as data-centric and interaction-centric applications.

In *data-centric* socially-aware applications, data on social context information such as social roles, social situations and connection-oriented social relationships, are the basis of the applications' behaviour. The *connection-oriented* relationships represent users' relational *ties* which can be further categorised as object-centric and people-centric relationships (Kourtellis et al. 2010). An *object-centric* relationship is identified between people who have shown common interests or participated in common activities or become members of similar groups. This type of relationship has been used in applications to infer preferences (Gummadi et al. 2006) and incentives of resource sharing (Li and Dabek 2006). The *people-centric* relationship is a formal and declarative definition of a direct relationship between people. For example, a

---

[1] Refers to the social setting or environment in which people live or something happens (Bauer and Gaskell 1999)

person identifies other persons as father, supervisor, school friend, etc. This type of relationship can be used in an application to turn on the audio player when friends are present (Biamino 2011), or an application to quantify review quality (Lu et al. 2010), or a socially-aware phone call application (Kabir et al. 2014a).

A smart socially-aware *phone-call application* uses the social relationship information available from online social networks to determine the type of the relationship between the caller and the callee and consequently decide whether to vibrate (for calls coming from family), or keep silent but automatically send a message to the caller (for calls from close friends) or without sending a message (for other calls), when the user is in a situation such as meeting. On the other hand, using the application a caller can obtain the situation of an intended callee to check whether it is a suitable time to call.

To develop such a data-centric socially-aware application needs to fulfill the following key requirements:

- *First*, an application should *acquire* its user's social context information. An application may need social context information that is not directly available from external sources but can be derived from the available basic information. For instance, users may want to filter phone calls based on situation categories such as "busy" that may not be acquired from sources but can be *inferred* from collected data by specifying rules (*e.g.,* meeting or seminar being in busy). Similarly, users may want to filter phone calls based on relationship categories such as "family" and "best-friends" that are not provided directly but can be inferred from the semantics of the relationship categories. Thus, it is required to collect, classify, infer and manage different social context information.
- *Second*, an application may need to allow its user to share social context information with other users. For example, allowing a caller to know the status of the callee before calling. In this regard, the application should also allow its user to specify her *privacy* preferences to retain control over who has access to her situation information under which conditions.

In *interaction-centric* socially-aware applications, interaction-oriented social relationships among collaborative actors dominate the applications' behaviour. The interaction-oriented relationships represent agreements and constraints regarding collaborative interactions among users, which are used in developing interaction-centric socially-aware applications. Such applications can assist users in their daily activities and ultimately enrich their social interactions and well-being (Lukowicz et al. 2012).

A socially-aware *telematics application* (Kabir et al. 2014a), for example, can make travel safer and more convenient by allowing drivers to form a cooperative convoy, collaborate and interact with each other based on their interaction relationships. In a cooperative convoy, a vehicle interacts with other vehicles, service providers and infrastructure systems. Through these interactions a vehicle's driver can share information (acquired from the service providers and infrastructure systems) with other vehicles' drivers in performing their tasks. Some interaction examples include— vehicles should notify each other of their positions every 10s, if a vehicle experiences

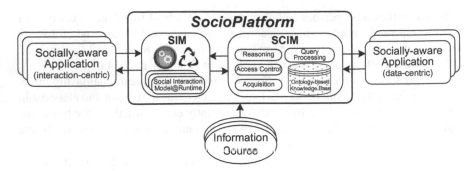

Fig. 19.1 SocioPlatform architecture overview

mechanical problems (*e.g.,* flat tyre, engine issue) it needs to notify the other vehicles as well as the road side assistance, etc.

To develop such an interaction-centric socially-aware application needs to fulfill two major requirements:

- *First,* the application should support interactions complying with the agreed interaction relationships (*i.e.,* constraints and obligations). Thus, a *runtime environment* is required to facilitate interactions.
- *Second,* the application needs to support *runtime adaptation,* as the interaction relationships evolve over time and thus need to adapt with the changes in requirements and environments. For instance, a third vehicle could join when the convoy is on the way; or the break-down of a vehicle might result in its leaving the convoy before reaching the destination.

In the next section we present SocioPlatform that addresses the above mentioned requirements of developing data-centric and interaction-centric socially-aware applications.

19.3   SocioPlatform Overview

The SocioPlatform (see Fig. 19.1) consists of social context information management and social interaction management. Collectively these two parts provide supports to building socially-aware applications with two different focuses: data-centric and interaction-centric.

Social context information management (SCIM) provides a number of functionalities to fulfill the requirements (as discussed above) of developing data-centric socially-aware applications.

Acquiring and Storing Information   The advent of social media such as online social networks, blogs, and instant messaging, have radically changed the way people interact with each other and share information about their lives and works. Such use of social media platforms produces an unprecedented amount of social context information as people specify their relationships, update their status, share interests and contents. Thus, it is now possible to acquire users' social context information from various sources such as Facebook, LinkedIn, Twitter and Google Calendar (Rosi et al. 2011, Lovett et al. 2010). SCIM acquires and integrates social context information from such diverse sources, and stores it in a knowledge base.

Deriving Information SCIM allows application developers to define and obtain derived relationships (at different abstraction levels) based on the basic relationships (*e.g.,* father-daughter and close-friend) and their semantics (*e.g.,* father-daughter being in family) and attributes (*e.g.,* strength and trust). For example, a *best-friend* could be specified as a specially *close* and *trusted* friend, *i.e.,*, *BestFriend* $\equiv$ *CloseFriend* $\sqcap$ (*trust* > {0.0}). A person's relationship with another person can be derived from their social roles and gender, for example, a '*Father-Daughter*' relationship between two persons can be derived from a person's corresponding social role, *e.g.,* '*Father*' and the other person's gender information, here '*female*'.

Inferring Situations To further enhance the services provided by the data-centric socially-aware applications, it might be required to infer *situations* based on users' social interaction events. These events can be identified from users' interaction activities in various social interaction applications (*e.g.,* Facebook, email and socially-aware telematics application). Therefore, SCIM supports *inferring* situations by observing and analysing current and past interaction events, and utilising ontological knowledge about such events.

Access Control The user's social context information is inherently sensitive. The scenarios of emerging socially-aware applications require users to share their information for greater benefits but this may also compromise their privacy. For example, allowing a caller to know the status of the callee before calling might reduce interruptions, but may also raise serious concerns regarding the privacy and access control over users' situation and other data (Khalil and Connelly 2006). Thus, users should be able to retain control over who has access to their personal information under which conditions. In addition, a user may want to fine-tune the granularity of the answer provided to a given query, depending on the context of that query such as who is asking, what is asked for, and the user's current situation. Thus, SCIM provides efficient *access* to this social context information while respecting information owners' *privacy*.

Social interaction management (SIM) provides the *runtime environment* and *adaptation management* of social interactions for the interaction-centric socially-aware applications.

Runtime Environment In interaction-centric socially-aware applications, interactions among collaborative users are based on predefined agreements and constraints that characterise the interaction-oriented relationships among users. We model such interaction-relationships among users from domain- and player-perspectives. The interested reader is referred to (Kabir et al. 2011, 2012, 2014a) for a more detailed description of this modelling approach. The *domain-centric social interaction*

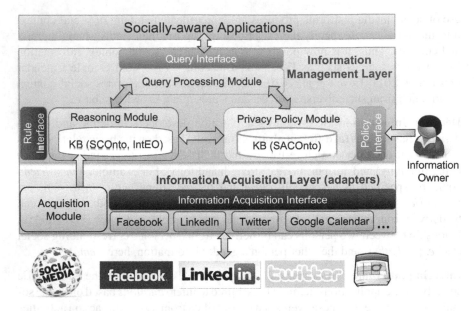

Fig. 19.2 Architecture of the social context information management (SCIM)

model *(DSIM)* captures a *collaborative* view of the interaction relationships among the users/actors, whereas the *player-centric social interaction model (PSIM)* captures an individual's *coordinated* view of all its interactions (across different domains), and thus supports their coordination. SIM provides the runtime environment for the application to instantiate these domain- and player-centric social interaction models. These instantiated runtime models mediate and coordinate social interactions among collaborative users according to their agreements.

Runtime Adaptation The (runtime) domain- and player-centric social interaction models typically evolve and many aspects of these models such as topology, interaction constraints and non-functional quality properties need to be modified frequently in response to changes in user requirements and environments. Thus, it is necessary to support adaptation in such runtime social interaction models. SIM implements an adaptation protocol (Kabir et al. 2014a) that ensures safe and consistent changes of the runtime models.

19.4   Social Context Information Management Architecture

The SCIM architecture comprises two layers: (i) information acquisition layer and (ii) information management layer, as shown in Fig 19.2.

The *information acquisition* layer is responsible for acquiring social context information from various sources such as Google Calendar, Facebook, LinkedIn, Twitter and other social media. A common information acquisition interface is provided so that application developers can build different adapters based on that interface to collect data from various sources. The acquisition module is responsible for managing and operating adapters to fetch raw data from the different sources, make the data consistent (*i.e.,* remove irrelevant data and integrate data of interest) and store it into the knowledge base. The acquisition module keeps the list of the available adapters and their implemented APIs. After a certain time interval, which is configurable, the acquisition module executes the fetching and processing steps to update the knowledge base with users' recent social context information. The frequency for such information update, however, is not the same for all types of social context information. For instance, a user's situation information may need to be updated more frequently compared to his/her family relationship. To fulfil this requirement, we allow users to schedule the execution of different acquisition functions. Moreover, it is also possible to trigger the execution of these functions manually (*i.e.,* on demand).

The *information management* layer is responsible to store users' social context in formation as acquired and to preserve their privacy when this information is accessed. This layer consists of three main modules:

Reasoning Module It classifies users' social data collected by the information acquisition layer, and stores them into the social context ontology (SCOnto) knowledge base. SCOnto (Kabir et al. 2014b) defines general concepts such as social role, social relationship, social interaction and social situation, and extends these concepts to incorporate domain-specific concepts for domain such as Facebook, LinkedIn and Twitter. Interaction event ontology (IntEO) (Kabir 2013a) incorporates SCOnto to capture the properties about users' interaction activities in social media. Reasoning module provides a reasoning functionality to infer abstract social context information that is of interest to applications by exploiting these SCOnto and IntEO knowledge bases. The rule interface allows application developers to develop a mobile- or desktop-based graphical user interface application which can be used by the users (e.g., domain experts) to add, delete, retrieve and update reasoning rules.

Privacy Policy Module It provides a policy interface to allow users to specify and manage their privacy preferences. Users' privacy policies are stored in their socially-aware access control ontology (SACOnto) knowledge base (Kabir et al. 2014b). Like the rule interface, the policy interface allows application developers to develop a graphical user interface application which can be used by the users to add, delete, retrieve and modify their polices. The policy module automatically checks inconsistency in policy specifications and only allows users to add consistent privacy policies. It also automatically enforces the specified privacy policies while users' social context information is accessed.

Query Processing Module It allows different applications to access users' social context information and provides a query interface so that application developers can build applications without the need to deal with the details of information representation schema and management.

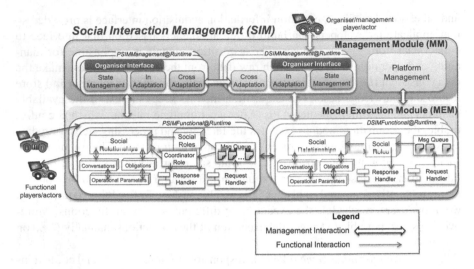

Fig. 19.3 Architecture of the *social interaction management (SIM)*

19.5   Social Interaction Management Architecture

The *Social Interaction Management (SIM)* architecture comprises two main modules: the Model Execution Module (MEM) and the Management Module (MM), as shown in Fig 19.3.

The *Model Execution Module* supports the instantiation of both the domain-centric social interaction models (DSIMs) and player-centric social interaction models (PSIMs). As described in the Sect. 19.3, these interaction models capture interaction-oriented relationships among collaborative actors in an interaction-centric socially-aware application. Therefore, at a given moment, multiple social interaction model instances may exist in parallel.

The MEM maintains a representation of all the functional elements of the domain-centric and player-centric social interaction models, called DSIMFunctional@runtime (in short, *DSIMfun*) and PSIMFuctional@runtime (in short, *PSIMfun*), respectively. The DSIMfun represents Social Roles, Social Relationships, Interactions, Conversations, Obligations and Operational Parameters. In addition, it contains a request handler, a response handler and a message queue. The DSIMfun is able to (1) handle requests received from players (*i.e.,* applications); (2) allocate requests into a message queue; (3) forward messages to corresponding social roles; (4) evaluate conditions (*i.e.,* conversation and obligation) specified in the relationships; (5) send request to relevant social roles and then to players.

The PSIMfun contains all the components of the DSIMfun. In addition, it contains a special type of social role, called the coordinator role. The PSIMfun bounds to one or more social roles in the DSIMfun(s). In the PSIMfun, all the incoming messages are first forwarded to the coordinator role. After evaluating the conditions specified in the relationships, the request message is forwarded to the coordinator player. The message is processed further based on the decision of the coordinator player, *e.g.,* generating a reply message and sending it to the player from which the message has come. Both the PSIMfun and DSIMfun maintain the *state* of their corresponding entities such as social roles, social relationships and the social interaction model (as a whole).

The *Management Module* supports the runtime adaptation of the instantiated social interaction model. Thus, the management components, called DSIMManagement@Runtime (in short, *DSIMman*) and PSIMManagement@Runtime (in short, *PSIMman*), are instantiated for each of the DSIMfun and PSIMfun. Both of these management components implement basic management operations provided by the organiser interface. We classify these operations as structure, parameter and state related operations. The *InAdaptation* sub-component of the management component implements the structure and parameter related management operations, while the *State Management* sub-component implements state related operations. In addition to these sub-components (*i.e.,* *InAdaptation* and *State Management*), the management component contains the *Cross Adaptation* sub-component which supports the adaptation across social interaction models. The MM also supports the platform-level management, *i.e.,* to create, retrieve, delete, deploy and undeploy social interaction models dynamically. These APIs allows application developers to build a graphical user interface application for a user to perform administration level management.

19.6   Prototype Implementation

We have implemented a SocioPlatform prototype (see Sect. 19.6.1) and demonstrated its applicability and feasibility by developing both data-centric and interaction-centric socially-aware applications (see Sect. 19.6.2). We have also quantified the adaptation overhead and efficacy of the platform by conducting a series of experiments. The experimental results, as reported in (Kabir et al. 2014b), show that the platform is robust and efficient.

19.6.1   SocioPlatform Prototype Implementation

The SocioPlatform prototype is implemented in Java. As part of SCIM, we have written adapters for Facebook, LinkedIn, Twitter, and Google calendar using restfb 1.6.7[2], linkedin-j 1.0.415[3], twitter4j 2.2.4[4], and gdata-calendar 2.0 [5], respectively, to fetch users' social data. We have implemented *SCOnto*, *IntEO* and

---

[2] http://restfb.com/
[3] http://code.google.com/p/linkedin-j/
[4] http://twitter4j.org/en/index.html
[5] http://code.google.com/p/gdata-java-client/

SACOnto knowledge bases using OWL API 3[6] to store and manage users' social context information and their privacy policies. We adopt a description logic (DL) based query language, namely SPARQL-DL (Sirin and Parsia 2007), and have used the *derivo 1.0*[7] SPARQL-DL query engine with the TrOWL[8] DL reasoner for reasoning about social context information, executing users' privacy policies and processing applications' query.

We have implemented SIM by adopting and extending the ROAD4WS (Kapuruge et al. 2011) which is an extension to the Apache Axis2[9] web service engine for deploying adaptive service compositions. SIM exploits JAXB 2.0[10] for creating DSIMs and PSIMs runtime from their XML descriptors. JAXB helps the generation of classes and interfaces of runtime models automatically using an XML schema. It exposes each *social role* as a *service*, the associated *interactions* of the role as operations of that service. The constraints specified in the *interaction-oriented social relationship* are evaluated as *event-condition-action* rules and implemented using Drools engine[11]. The *runtime adaptations* are supported by the Java reflection mechanism and the Drools engine. To cope with the changes in environments and requirements, at runtime, Javassist[12] allows generation of *new* classes and *modification* of existing classes, which helps to add new social roles/relationships and change existing roles/relationships, respectively. Drools engine allows the SIM to inject new rules and delete existing rules from the working memory which facilitates the addition and deletion of constraints (conversations, obligations and parameters) in the relationships.

19.6.2   Developing Socially-Aware Applications

To demonstrate the real-world applicability and feasibility of our approach, we have developed a data-centric socially-aware applications for Android mobile devices, named socially-aware phone call application (SPCall) (Fig. 19.4a shows a screen-shot), and an interaction-centric socially-aware application for Android mobile devices, named socially-aware telematics application (SocioTelematics) (Fig. 19.4b shows a screen-shot), using our SocioPlatform.

The *SPCall* application aims to reduce phone call interruptions and considers both the caller and callee perspectives. The application allows the caller to know the situations of the intended callee to check whether it is suitable time to call. Accessing the callee's situations is also subject to the callee's privacy policies. In this regard,

---

[6] http://owlapi.sourceforge.net/
[7] http://www.derivo.de/en/resources/sparql-dl-api/
[8] http://trowl.eu/
[9] http://axis.apache.org/
[10] http://jcp.org/en/jsr/detail?id=22
[11] http://www.jboss.org/drools/
[12] http://www.jboss.org/javassist

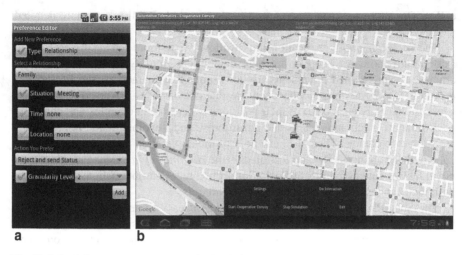

Fig. 19.4 Socially-aware applications **a** SPCall **b** SocioTelimatics

the application allows a person to specify access control polces considering his/her situations at the time of access request and the social relationship with the requester. On the other hand, the application allows a callee to specify her filtering preferences on incoming phone calls such as ring, vibrate, reject, or reject and send situation, considering her current situations and the relationships with the caller. For example, if my situation is *meeting* or *seminar*, and a call comes from *family*, the action is to *reject* and forward my situation at granularity level 2 (Busy). The application exploits social context information provided by the SocioPlatform to support social context-aware behaviour, *i.e.,* filter incoming phone calls and inform situations of the intended callee based on social context information.

SocioPlatform (*SCIM* component) assists the application developer in developing socially-aware phone call applications by collecting and representing the users' social context information from different sources and providing a set of query APIs for the applications to access that information based on the users' privacy preferences. In developing the *SPCall* application we, from the caller perspective, have used the `getSituation(callee)` query API to obtain the situation of an intended callee and then provide that information to the caller. From the callee perspective, to implement the call filtering functionality, we have used the `getAllRelationshipsName(me,inComingCallNum)` and `getSituation(me)` query APIs to obtain the relationships between the caller and callee, and the current situation of the callee. Then, based on the specified filtering preferences in the application, it decides whether to ring, vibrate, reject, or reject and send situation information at a specific granularity. In the case of a "send situation at a specific granularity" decision, the application invokes the `getSituAtGranularity(me,gLevel)` query API to obtain the situation information of the callee at the specified granularity level and then sends it to the caller. The interested reader is referred to (Kabir et al. 2014b) for a more detailed description.

The *SocioTelematics* application aims to allow two or more vehicle drivers to form a cooperative convoy by supporting their social interactions. Such social interactions are based on predefined agreements and constraints that characterise the *interaction-oriented social relationships* between the players, such as drivers. For example, cars should notify each other of their positions every 10s. In complex and changing environments, such agreements and constraints, and thus interaction relationships are subject to change. Thus, the behaviour of the application needs to be adapted to cope with the changes. The application uses the *runtime environment* and *adaptation management* functionalities of SocioPlatform to facilitate interactions and to cope with the changes in requirements and environments.

The SocioPlatform (*SIM* component) makes it easy to develop this application based on their supposed interaction-oriented social relationships and without worrying about the underlying message communication (*i.e.,* social interactions) and the evaluation of the messages, as these interaction-oriented social relationships are modeled and represented in DSIMs and PSIMs, the runtime support and adaptation of these models are externalized to and managed by the SIM component of the SocioPlatform. Moreover, the runtime adaptation capability provided by the platform allows the application to respond to changes in requirements and environmental factors, without any change in the application code. The interested reader is referred to (Kabir et al. 2012, 2014a) for a more detailed description.

19.7 Related Work and Discussion

19.7.1 Platforms for Managing Context Information

Much research in the area of context-aware software systems has investigated the development of context management infrastructure, so as to reduce the complexity of engineering such systems. It advocates pushing as much as possible the acquisition, management and dissemination of context information from the application into a context management infrastructure. Dey et al. (2001) developed a basic framework to support acquisition and interpretation of context information from sensors. Hong and Landay (2001) advocated using a service infrastructure approach to deploy context-aware applications. In this approach, the tasks of gathering, processing and managing context information are encapsulated as services that are accessible to any context-aware devices and applications. While having such supporting infrastructure is important, we argue that the current infrastructure is highly restrictive in addressing the dynamicity and complexity of social context.

Some efforts, such as Kourtellis et al. (2010) and Xing et al. (2011), have already recognized the need to externalize the social context management functionalities and have taken steps towards systematically managing users' social context information. Prometheus (Kourtellis et al. 2010) collects user's social data from different OSNs and represents it as multi-edged graphs, where vertices correspond to users and edges correspond to interactions between users. The interactions are described with a label (*e.g.,* football, music) and a weight specifies the intensity of an interaction, and essentially represents an object-centric relationship. Like Prometheus, PocketSocial (Xing et al. 2011) also collects social data from different sources. But unlike Prometheus, it represents social data in JSON objects and supports only REST based APIs like Facebook, and does not provide any inference functions. Neither Prometheus nor PocketSocial represent both the object- and people-centric relationships with their semantics, and as a consequence they are not able to infer richer information or fine-tune the granularity of information access.

Our work significantly differs from the above noted approaches in that it not only collects users' social relationship information (both object- and people-centric) from multiple sources and stores it in richer ontologies, but also considers the owners' status information and their semantics, allowing information representation and derivation at different levels of abstraction and consequently facilitating fine-grained access control and query processing.

19.7.2 Platforms for Managing Interactions and Adaptation

Much research has been carried out into middleware support for runtime adaptation in context-aware systems (*e.g.,* MADAM (Geihs et al. 2009) and 3PC (Handte et al. 2012)) and service-oriented systems (*e.g.,* MUSIC (Rouvoy et al. 2009) and MOSES (Cardellini et al. 2012)). These middleware solutions mainly target the tasks of individual users/applications and have focused on reconfiguring applications' settings (rather than *interaction relationships*) based on physical context information (*e.g.,* place, time)/quality of service requirements (*e.g.,* performance, reliability), rather than interaction relationships. Moreover, their proposed runtime models are application-specific and cannot be used to model interaction relationships among collaborative users.

In contrast to these solutions, our social interaction management component targets interaction-centric socially-aware applications, and focuses on executing adaptation by explicitly modelling and realising interaction relationships using a social interaction model and providing an organiser interface to change such model. On the other hand, we do not address the monitoring of environment changes (*i.e.,* physical context information), acquiring and analysing such physical context information to make adaptation decisions. In that sense, our adaptation management approach is not a substitute for existing middleware solutions that manage physical context information, rather can be built on top of those solutions as appropriate, in order to manage social interactions and runtime adaptation in interaction-centric socially-aware applications.

19.8 Conclusion

In this chapter, we have presented SocioPlatform to provide high-level platform support for developing socially-aware applications. The platform implements a set of adapters to acquire social data from Google Calendar and different online social networks such as Facebook, LinkedIn and Twitter, and stores the consolidated social context information in an ontology-based knowledge base. It provides a number of functionalities including management and querying of social context information, an environment for executing social interaction models and managing their runtime adaptation, and a set of APIs for developers to build socially-aware applications.Overall, the platform hides the complexity of managing social context, and thus provides better support for the development of socially-aware applications.

References

Bauer, M.W., Gaskell, G.: Towards a paradigm for research on social representations. J. Theory Soc. Behav. **29**(2), 163–186 (1999). doi:10.1111/1468-5914.00096. http://dx.doi.org /10.1111/1468-5914.00096

Biamino, G.: Modeling social contexts for pervasive computing environments. In: IEEE International Conference on Pervasive Computing and Communication Workshops, pp. 415–420 IEEE Computer Society, Washington, DC, USA (2011)

Cardellini, V., Casalicchio, E., Grassi, V., Iannucci, S., Lo Presti, F., Mirandola, R.: Moses: A framework for qos driven runtime adaptation of service-oriented systems. IEEE Trans. Softw. Eng. **38**(5), 1138–1159 (2012)

Dey, A.K.: Understanding and using context. Pers. Ubiquit. Comput. **5**(1), 4–7 (2001)

Dey, A.K., Abowd, G.D., Salber, D.: A conceptual framework and a toolkit for supporting the rapid prototyping of context-aware applications. Hum. Comput. Interact. **16**(2) (2001)

Dourish, P.: What we talk about when we talk about context. Pers. Ubiquit. Comput. **8**(1), 19–30 (2004). doi:10.1007/s00779-003-0253-8. http://dx.doi.org/10.1007/s00779-003-0253-8

Endler, M., Skyrme, A., Schuster, D., Springer, T.: Defining situated social context for pervasive social computing. In: IEEE International Conference on Pervasive Computing and Communications Workshops (PERCOM Workshops), 2011, pp. 519–524 (2011). doi:10.1109/PERCOMW.2011.5766945

Eugster, P.T., Garbinato, B., Holzer, A.: Middleware support for context-aware applications. In: Middleware for Network Eccentric and Mobile Applications, pp. 305–322. Springer Berlin Heidelberg(2009)

Ferscha, A.: 20 years past weiser: What's next? IEEE Pervasive Comput. **11**(1), 52–61 (2012)

Geihs, K., Barone, P., Eliassen, F., Floch, J., Fricke, R., Gjorven, E., Hallsteinsen, S., Horn, G., Khan, M.U., Mamelli, A., Papadopoulos, G.A., Paspallis, N., Reichle, R., Stav, E.: A comprehensive solution for application-level adaptation. Softw. Pract. Exp. **39**(4) (2009)

Gummadi, K.P., Mislove, A., Druschel, P.: Exploiting social networks for internet search. In: Proceedings of 5th Workshop on Hot Topics in Networks, pp. 79–84. Irvine, CA (2006)

Han, L., Jyri, S., Ma, J., Yu, K.: Research on context-aware mobile computing. In: 22nd International Conference on Advanced Information Networking and Applications—Workshops, 2008. AINAW 2008, pp. 24–30 IEEE Computer Society, Washington, DC, USA (2008). doi:10.1109/WAINA.2008.115

Handte, M., Schiele, G., Matjuntke, V., Becker, C., Marrón, P.J.: 3pc: system support for adaptive peer-to-peer pervasive computing. ACM Trans. Auton. Adapt. Syst. **7**(1) (2012)

Henricksen, K.: A framework for context-aware pervasive computing applications. Ph.D. thesis, The School of Information Technology and Electrical Engineering, The University of Queensland, Sept (2003)

Henricksen, K., Indulska, J.: Developing context-aware pervasive computing applications: models and approach. Pervasive Mob. Comput. 2(1), 37–64 (2006)

Hong, J.I., Landay, J.A.: An infrastructure approach to context-aware computing. Hum. Comput. Interact. 16(2), 287–303 (2001)

Kabir, M.A.: A framework for social context-aware pervasive computing applications. Ph.D. thesis, Swinburne University of Technology (2013a)

Kabir, M.A.: Modeling, managing and reasoning about social contexts for socially-aware applications. In: IEEE International Conference on Pervasive Computing and Communication Workshops (2013b)

Kabir, M.A., Han, J., Colman, A.: Modeling and coordinating social interactions in pervasive environments. In: Proceedings of the 16th IEEE International Conference on Engineering of Complex Computer Systems, pp. 243–252 IEEE Computer Society, Washington, DC, USA (2011)

Kabir, M.A., Han, J., Colman, A., Yu, J.: Sociotelematics: Leveraging interaction-relationships in developing telematics systems to support cooperative convoys. In: Proceedings of 9th International Conference on Ubiquitous Intelligence and Computing, pp 40 47 IEEE Computer Society, Washington, DC, USA (2012)

Kabir, M., Han, J., Colman, A., Yu, J.: Scaas: A platform for managing adaptation in collaborative pervasive applications. In: Meersman, R., Panetto, H., Dillon, T., Eder, J., Bellahsene, Z., Ritter, N., Leenheer, P., Dou, D. (eds.) 21st International Conference on Cooperative Information Systems (CoopIS 2013). Lecture Notes in Computer Science, vol. 8185, pp. 149–166. Springer, Berlin (2013a)

Kabir, M., Han, J., Yu, J., Colman, A.: User-centric social context information management: an ontology-based approach and platform. Pers. Ubiquit. Comput. 18(5), 1061–1083. (2014)

Kabir, M.A., Han, J., Colman, A.: Sociotelematics: Harnessing social interaction-relationships in developing automotive applications. Pervasive Mob. Comput. 14, 129–146 (2014)

Kapuruge, M., Colman, A., King, J.: ROAD4WS—Extending apache axis2 for adaptive service compositions. In: Proceedings of the 15th IEEE International Enterprise Distributed Object Computing Conference, pp. 183–192 IEEE Computer Society, Washington, DC, USA (2011)

Khalil, A., Connelly, K.: Context-aware telephony: Privacy preferences and sharing patterns. In: Proceedings of the 20th Conference on Computer Supported Cooperative Work, pp. 469–478 ACM New York, NY, USA (2006)

Kourtellis, N., Finnis, J., Anderson, P., Blackburn, J., Borcea, C., Iamnitchi, A.: Prometheus: user-controlled p2p social data management for socially-aware applications. In: Gupta, I., Mascolo, C. (eds.) Middleware 2010. Lecture Notes in Computer Science, vol. 6452, pp. 212–231. Springer, Berlin (2010)

Li, J., Dabek, F.: F2F: reliable storage in open networks. In: Proceedings of the 4th International Workshop on Peer-to-Peer Systems (IPTPS) URL: http://iptps06.cs.ucsb.edu/(2006)

Lovett, T., O'Neill, E., Irwin, J., Pollington, D.: The calendar as a sensor: analysis and improvement using data fusion with social networks and location. In: Proceedings of the 12th ACM International Conference on Ubiquitous Computing, pp. 3–12 ACM New York, NY, USA (2010)

Lu, Y., Tsaparas, P., Ntoulas, A., Polanyi, L.: Exploiting social context for review quality prediction. In: Proceedings of the 19th International Conference on World Wide Web, pp. 691–700. ACM New York, NY, USA (2010)

Lukowicz, P., Pentland, S., Ferscha, A.: From context awareness to socially aware computing. IEEE Pervasive Comput. 11(1), 32–41 (2012)

Raychoudhury, V., Cao, J., Kumar, M., Zhang, D.: Middleware for pervasive computing: a survey. Pervasive Mob. Comput. 9(2), 177–200 (2013)

Rosi, A., et al.: Social sensors and pervasive services: Approaches and perspectives. In: Proceedings of the IEEE PerCom Workshops, pp. 525–530 IEEE Computer Society, Washington, DC, USA (2011)

Rouvoy, R., Barone, P., Ding, Y., Eliassen, F., Hallsteinsen, S., Lorenzo, J., Mamelli, A., Scholz, U.: MUSIC: Middleware Support for self-adaptation in ubiquitous and service-oriented environments. Software Engineering for Self-adaptive Systems, pp. 164–182. Springer, Berlin (2009)

Schilit, B.N., Theimer, M.M.: Disseminating active map information to mobile hosts. Netw. Mag. Global Internetwkg. **8**(5), 22–32 (1994). doi:10.1109/65.313011. http://dx.doi.org/10.1109/65.313011

Schmidt, A., Belgl, M., Gellersen, H.W.: There is more to context than location. Comput. Graph **23**(6), 893–901 (1999). doi:10.1016/S0097-8493(99)00120-X.

Schuster, D., Rosi, A., Mamei, M., Springer, T., Endler, M., Zambonelli, F.: Pervasive social context-taxonomy and survey. ACM Trans. Intell. Syst. Technol. (TIST)4(3), Article No. 46 (2012)

Sirin, E., Parsia, B.: Sparql-dl: Sparql query for owl-dl. OWL: Experiences and Directions Workshop (OWLED)Vol 258, CEUR-WS, RWTH Aachen, Germany (2007)

Wang, G., Gallagher, A., Luo, J., Forsyth, D.: Seeing people in social context: Recognizing people and social relationships. In: Proceedings of the 11th European Conference on Computer vision: Part V, ECCV'10, pp. 169–182. Springer, Berlin (2010).

Xing, B., Gronowski, K., Radia, N., Svensson, M., Ton, A.: Pocketsocial: Your distributed social context now in your pocket. In: IEEE International Conference on Pervasive Computing and Communication Workshops, pp. 322–324 IEEE Computer Society, Washington, DC, USA (2011)

Zheng, Y., Li, L., Ogata, H., Yano, Y.: Support online social interaction with context-awareness. Int. J. Contin. Eng. Educ. Life Long Learn. **17**(2), 160–177 (2007)

Chapter 20
Context and User-Centered Approaches: Icons in Cross-Cultural Context

Anneli Heimbürger and Yasushi Kiyoki

Abstract Culture is embodied in how people interact with other individuals and with their environment. It is a way of life formed under specific historical, natural and social conditions. Cross-cultural communication environment, user/actor and task/situation is the key triplet in our context research. In this chapter, context is discussed as a multidimensional concept and icons in cross-cultural environments are introduced. The authors present Kiyoki's semantic associative search method, and introduce an example of applying an icon-based platform for cross-cultural communication with Kiyoki's method for searching and creating context-dependent cross-cultural information. This cross-cultural communication platform realizes mutual understanding between two cultures by contextual data structuring and computing.

20.1 Introduction

Globalization is one of the main trends in our world. Increasingly, eastern and western cultures meet each other through business, governmental and environmental issues, research, education and tourism. Professionals, including business executives, project managers and project team members, are finding themselves in uncertain situations due to culturally dependent differences in the communication protocol, language and value systems. Cross-cultural communication is a current topic in many multicultural organizations and companies. In cross-cultural world, many collaborative activities take place in virtual and physical environments: teleconferences and workshops, web meetings, virtual spaces, face-to-face meetings and email, among others. Some of the differences between Eastern and Western cultures that we may come across are related to various meeting protocols, formality and rituals, orientation to time, communication style and decision-making process.

A. Heimbürger (✉)
University of Jyväskylä, Seminaarinkatu 15, Jyväskylä 40014, Finland
e-mail: anneli.a.heimburger@jyu.fi

Y. Kiyoki
Keio University SFC, 5322 Endo, Fujisawa, Kanagawa Prefecture, 252-0882, Japan
e-mail: kiyoki@sfc.keio.ac.jp

© Springer Science+Business Media New York 2014   309
P. Brézillon, A. J. Gonzalez (eds.), *Context in Computing*,
DOI 10.1007/978-1-4939-1887-4_20

Cultural competence has become an important dimension for success in today's international business and research. Cultural computing is an emerging, multidisciplinary computer science field, as discussed by Fei-Yue Wang in his Letter from the Editor in IEEE Intelligent Systems Special Issue for AI and Cultural Heritage (Wang 2009). In the near future, cultural computing will have several important applications in our knowledge societies in the fields of business, environment, health care, education and research, for example.

What is culture? Culture is embodied in how people interact with other individuals and with their environment; it is a way of life formed under specific historical, natural and social conditions (Wang 2009). Culture can be considered as one example of context and cultural computing as a subset of context computing. A computational method, a computer system, or an application is context-sensitive if it includes context-based functions and if it uses context to provide relevant information and services to the user, their relevancy depending on the user's task or situation.

Humans can quite successfully express their thoughts and ideas to each other and react appropriately to them. There are several factors that have an effect on this such as the versatility of the semantics in the language people use, the common culture and common understanding of how the world works, as well as a tacit understanding of everyday situations. Situational knowledge is knowledge that is specific to a particular occasion (Brézillon 2003). Some methods of generating knowledge, such as trial and error, or learning from experiences, tend to create highly situational knowledge. Situational knowledge is often embedded in language, culture, or traditions. Humans are able to use implicit situational knowledge, when they interact with each other. By means of the implicit situational knowledge humans can increase the conversational dimensions. Situational knowledge is also called as *context* (Brézillon 2003, 2013).

According to Dey et al. (2005) "context is any information that can be used to characterize the situation of an entity. An entity can be for example a person, a place, or an object that is considered relevant to the interaction between a user and a computer application" (Dey et al. 2005). A computer system is context-aware if it uses context to provide relevant information and services to the user, where relevancy depends on the user's task. Contextual computing research aims to study and develop models, methods and systems that include awareness of user's context and the ability to adapt to it (Dey 2001). In contextual computing, context should include information to enable systems to achieve precise understanding of users and their situations.

Since we are social beings, one of our basic needs is to communicate with other humans. Communication usually happens within a context. A communicated piece of information always has some relevance to another piece of information or to a specific situation. Links express the relation of one information unit to others and thus express the context in which this information unit is relevant. Without context, it is difficult to absorb a piece of information and as a consequence, it probably will not reach the status of knowledge.

In our paper we discuss contextual computing that increases the richness of communication in human-computer interaction, especially in cross-cultural situations. Cross-cultural communication environment, user/actor and task/situation is the key triplet in our context research. Our approach is similar with Brézillon (2003, 2013). We introduce icons as a mean for cross-cultural communication. Our focus on icons is related to computer systems and user interactions in cross-cultural environments. We apply Kiyoki's semantic associative search method to create context-dependent knowledge in cross-cultural environments (Kiyoki et al. 1994, 2009). Our case cultures are those of Japan and Finland.

We introduce an example of applying an icon-based platform for cross-cultural communication with Kiyoki's method for searching and creating context-dependent cross-cultural information. The platform realizes mutual understanding between two cultures by contextual data structuring and computing. The essential concepts used in our paper are summarized in Table 20.1.

The rest of our paper is organized as follows. In Sect. 20.2, we discuss context as a multidimensional concept. In Sect. 20.3 we introduce icons in cross-cultural communication environments. Semantic associative search method is presented in Sect. 20.4. In Sect. 20.5, we give a forward-looking application of icons and semantic associative search method for searching and creating context-dependent cross-cultural information. Section 20.6 is reserved for our conclusions.

20.2   Context—A Multidimensional Concept

The notion of context is a fundamental concern in cognitive psychology, linguistics and computer science (Bazire and Brézillon 2005). Our focus is on computer science. Computer science community has initially perceived the context as a matter of user's locations. During the last few years this notion has been considered not simply as a state but part of a process in which users are involved. Almost any information available at the time of an interaction can be seen as context information. Some examples are: identity, spatial information, temporal information, and environmental information, social situation, nearby resources, physiological measurements, feelings and impressions.

In order to use context effectively, we must understand what context is and how it can be used. Existing research on context can be classified into two main categories: (a) context-based delivery of knowledge and (b) the capture and utilization of contextual knowledge. An understanding of context will enable application designers to choose what context to use in their applications.

There are several definitions of context (Brézillon 2013; Dey 2001; Bazire and Brézillon 2005). Many definitions of context are done by listing examples or by choosing synonyms for context. We focus on operational definitions of context according to Dey et al. (2005) and Heimbürger et al. (2007). "Context is all about the whole task or situation relevant to an application and its set of users. Context is any information that can be used to characterize the task or situation of an entity. An entity can be a person, place, object or an environment that is considered relevant to the interaction between a user and an application (Dey et al. 2005)." "Context should be seen as a function of interaction between users/objects and environment, and a

Table 20.1 The essential concepts used in our paper

Concept	Definition
Culture	Culture is embodied in how people interact with other individuals and with their environment; it is a way of life formed under specific historical, natural and social conditions. Other cultural levels also exist, such as organization and team cultures; these are out of scope of our paper
Cross-cultural	Concerns comparative studies and knowledge between two cultures. In case of several cultures we talk about multi-cultural studies
Cross-cultural communication	Consists of human-to-human, human-to-machine, and human-to-environment communication in cross-cultural environments. The environment can be physical or virtual or hybrid
Cultural computing	Research, development, design and implementation of computational models, methods, functions and algorithms for cultural applications
Context	Cross-cultural communication environment, user/actor and task/situation is the key triplet in our context research
Context-sensitive	A computational method, a computer system, or an application is context-sensitive if it includes context-based functions and if it uses context to provide relevant information and services to the user, where relevancy depends on the user's situation
Context computing	Context computing can be defined as the use of context in software applications, where the applications adapt to discovered contexts by changing their behavior. A context-sensitive application presents the following features: context sensing, presentation of information and services to a user, automatic execution of a service, and tagging of context to information for later retrieval
Icon	Icons are small-sized isolated signs. The collections of icons usually are context-specific, as in case of an airport, hotel, maps, traffic signs and crisis situations. The focus of our icon research relates to computer systems and user interaction
Semantic associative search method	The basic principle in Kiyoki's semantic associative search method is that each media data item, which can be text, image, animation, music, or movie, includes various meanings. That is, the meaning of a media data item is not fixed statically. The meaning of a media data item is fixed only when we know the context for explaining the content of a media data item. The method defines semantic functions for performing the semantic interpretation of content and for selecting semantically related media data items, according to the given context (Kiyoki et al. 1994, 2009).

consequence of focus or attention. Context can emerge in the moment and it can change quickly. Contexts can be static, dynamic, discrete, continuous, individual or collective (Heimbürger et al. 2007)."

Brèzillion (2003) has introduced the concepts of contextual knowledge and proceduralized contexts. Contextual knowledge is background knowledge, whereas proceduralized context is immediately useful for the task at hand. An interesting issue is the transitional stage from contextual knowledge to proceduralised context. This transition is context's dynamic dimension. According to Brèzillion (2003) links between knowledge and context can be described as follows: (a) context is knowledge and knowledge is context, (b) context is defined and structured with respect to a focus of attentions, (c) context granularity depends on the distance to the focus of attention, (d) context structure evolves dynamically with the evolution of the focus of attentions and (e) context is relative to an observer.

Context-oriented knowledge management provides a structured approach for knowledge transformation, by means of (a) the knowledge context that models the characteristics of the explicit knowledge, (b) the conceptual context that models the structure of the implicit knowledge and (c) the physical context that determines the physical environment in which the knowledge transfer take place (Nonaka and Takeushi 1995; Studer and Stojanovic 2005). Context must be modeled and defined as specific entities, in other words as contextual elements (Brézillon 2013), at some point, but this decision should be deferred to the design of concrete applications or perhaps even to run-time where users should be free to specify the nature and format of context objects.

Brynskov et al. (2003) classify context into three domains: physical, digital and conceptual. Physical context includes the physical surroundings of an entity. This includes physical location, physical objects, physical interaction, absolute time and space, and other physical measurements. Computer systems may be aware of the physical context by using sensors. Digital context includes computer models, infrastructure, protocols, devices, resources and services, logs and relative time and space. Conceptual context describes user activity, intention, focus and understanding of surroundings. Each perspective is defined by the space in which it exists.

With understanding of what context is and the different ways in which it can be used, application builders can more easily determine what behaviors or features they want their applications to support and what context is required to achieve these behaviors. A system is context-aware if it uses context to provide relevant information and/or services to the user, where relevancy depends on the user's task. Context-aware application can support the three following features: (a) presentation of information and services to a user, (b) automatic execution of a service for a user and (c) tagging of context to information to support later retrieval. Sophisticated and general context models have been proposed to support context-aware applications which use them to (a) adapt interfaces, (b) tailor the set of application-relevant data, (c) increase the precision of information retrieval, (d) discover services, (e) make the user interaction implicit, or (f) build smart environments (Bazire and Brézillon 2005). Context-aware applications should capture both immediate context such as environment and

Table 20.2 Summary of essential context definitions

Bazire and Brézillon (2005)	The context acts like a set of constraints that influence the behavior of a system (a user or a computer) embedded in a given task. The definition is based on the analysis of a collection of 150 context definitions from several fields of applications [8].
Coutaz et al. (2005)	Context is not simply the state of a predefined environment with a fixed set of interaction resources. It is part of a process of interacting with an ever-changing environment composed of reconfigurable, migratory, distributed, and multi-scale resource.
Dey et al. (2005)	Context is any information that can be used to characterize the situation of entities that are considered relevant to the interaction between a user and an application, including the user and the application themselves."
Leppänen (2005)	A context is a conceptual or intellectual construct that help us understand, analyze and design the natures, meanings and effects of more elementary things in the concerned environment or circumstances. It is a whole which is determined by the focal thing(s) of which making sense is important. It is composed of highly related things, each of which represents certain contextual domain.
Winograd (2001)	Context is an operational term: something is context because of the way it is used in interpretation, not due to its inherent properties.

distant context such as weather forecasts. This is a context granularity issue. Context granularity can be used as a function of the distance to the focus of attention.

Some essential context definitions in the field of computer science are summarized in Table 20.2.

The concept of context is still a matter of discussion, and through the years several different definitions have been proposed. Coppola et al. (2009) in divide the definitions into extensional and intensional definitions.

Extensional definitions present the context through a list of possible context dimensions and their associated values. The context is represented by the location of the user, the surrounding objects, proximity to other people, temperature, computing devices, user profile, and physical conditions and time. Intensional definitions present the concept of context more formally. Extensional definitions seem to be useful in practical applications, where the abstract concept of context has to be made concrete. However, from a theoretical point of view they are not properly correct, as the context cannot be outlined just by some of its aspects. On the other hand intensional definitions are of little use in practice, despite being theoretically satisfying.

Context modelling approaches can be classified by the scheme of data structures which are used to exchange contextual information in the respective system. Context models can be divided into seven categories: key-value models (Strang and Linnhoff-Popien 2004), markup scheme models (Strang and Linnhoff-Popien 2004), graphical models (Bauer 2003; Halpin 2001; Henricksen et al. 2002), object-oriented models (Coppola et al. 2009), logic based models (Strang and Linnhoff-Popien 2004), ontology based models (Strang and Linnhoff-Popien 2004; OWL 2009) and SECI (Socialization, Externalization, Combination, Internalization)/Shared Context Model (Nonaka and Takeushi 1995; Nonaka and Konno 1998).

Based on context related research, we can summarize that context is a multidimensional concept and a complete and comprehensive model is still missing. Some of the main reasons may be the absence of a comprehensive international standard or at least a recommendation by the World-Wide Web Consortium (W3C) as well as the lack of a reusable reference model that could be applied to manage context in various application domains. In our context research cross-cultural communication environment, user/actor, task/situation is the key triplet.

20.3   Icons

Culture is embodied in how we interact with other individuals and with our environment in different situations; it is a way of life formed under specific historical, natural and social conditions (Wang 2009). Cultural computing is an emerging, multidisciplinary computer science field. We are living in many different cultural spaces. For example, Japanese are living in Japanese cultural space and Finns in Finnish cultural space. The question is how our different cultural spaces could effectively communicate with each other. Broadly speaking, the question concerns all aspects of human life: technological, environmental and social, among others. We need a common language to create, discover and share cross-cultural knowledge as well as to exchange experiences about our environments.

Cross-cultural communication consists of human-to-human (for example, Finnish to Japanese), human-to-machine (for example, Japanese to a train ticket machine in Finland), and human-to-environment (for example, a Finn at a train station in Japan) communication. The environment can be physical, virtual or hybrid, such as a train station, groupware and Skype, respectively. In these environments, we face different kinds of situations and tasks in our everyday life.

Pictorial symbols or *icons* are small-sized isolated signs (Heimbürger 2013; Khanom et al. 2015). We come across icons for example at airports, in traffic, in hotels and in emergency situations (Fitrianie et al. 2007). Icons have also become quite common as interfaces in modern technological devices. There exist two interesting dimensions related to culture and icons. *Speed of messages* refers to the speed with which people decode and act on icons. Time is an important and complex dimension of cultures. It consists of two types. Polychronic time (P-time, many-things-at-once) is characterized as simultaneous and concurrent. Monochronic time (M-time, one-thing-at-a-time) is characterized as being sequential and linear. Context includes high and low context (Hoft 1996). These refer to the amount of information given in a communication. In a high-context communication, most of the meaning is in the context and very little is in the transmitted message itself. In a low-context communication, most of the meaning is in the transmitted message. In a high-context culture, information is implicitly stated, whereas, in a low-context culture, information is explicitly stated.

There is always some cultural interpretation involved in all human activities, even in something as seemingly trivial as finding a meaning for icons. The way we understand icons is affected by culture through learned meanings of phenomena, items and actions, such as reading direction and symbolic meanings. Among other things, our conception of time is presumed to flow to the reading direction and is, thus, affected by it. Context also plays a central role in cultural interpretation. Different contexts lead people to associate different meanings with same icons. The same context may be different for people from different cultures.

Imagine a person at a train station in a foreign country. An icon that probably is important for that person in her/his situation can be observed. The meaning of the symbol is fixed, but the person does not understand it. Being embedded for example in maps, icons typically indicate points of interest or other discrete object classes. Icon-based geocommunication can thus be seen as a part of cartographic communication. In an increasingly globalized world, geocommunication between different cultures has become more intense. Problems arising from this new situation are tradition-ally solved with the lowest common denominator approach—often a standardized symbol set that has to be learnt by those involved. Standardization has three main dis-advantages which are also valid more generally, not only in cartography. (1) The most standardized symbol sets so far have been developed in western countries. Therefore, it is harder for people with other cultural backgrounds to comprehend and learn them. (2) The plurality of existing geo-objects cannot be adequately represented by stan-dardized symbol sets. (3) Little flexibility is left to accommodate innovative designs, which tends to reduce the importance given to the artistic component of cartography.

Examples of Japanese and Finnish map icons are shown in Fig. 20.1. Icons can be used for cross-cultural knowledge browsing and discovery, and for knowledge searching in situations or tasks at hand. Knowledge searching has a twofold mean-ing. Firstly, cross-cultural knowledge can be searched in situations at hand by means of icon recognition: for example, the meaning of a traffic sign in Japan and its coun-terpart in Finland. In this case, knowledge searching is mapping between a user, constraints (image or sketch given by a user) and knowledge itself (icon/pictorial symbols database). Secondly, cross-cultural knowledge, such as knowledge of na-tional traditional musical instruments *koto* in Japan and *kantele* in Finland, can be browsed and similarities or differences between the instruments' sounds can be dis-covered by means of semantic computational functions embedded in icons. The semantic associate search method is presented in the next section.

Icons can be used for cross-cultural knowledge browsing and discovery, and for knowledge searching in situations or tasks at hand. Knowledge searching has a twofold meaning. Firstly, cross-cultural knowledge can be searched in situations at hand by means of icon recognition: for example, the meaning of a traffic sign in Japan and its counterpart in Finland. In this case, knowledge searching is map-ping between a user, constraints (image or sketch given by a user) and knowledge itself (icon/pictorial symbols database). Secondly, cross-cultural knowledge, such as knowledge of national traditional musical instruments *koto* in Japan and *kantele* in Finland, can be browsed and similarities or differences between the instruments' sounds can be discovered by means of semantic computational functions embedded in icons. The semantic associate search method is presented in the next section.

Fig. 20.1 Examples of Japanese (top) and Finnish (bottom) map icons. Top: volcanic crater, fire station, government office building, place of historic, cultural, or scenic interest, hospital, police station and shinto shrine. Bottom: hut, camping place, observation tower, sight, fire place and boat launching place

20.4 Cross-Cultural Computing with Semantic Associative Search

Cross-cultural computing is a new research area for sharing, comparing and analyzing cultural information resources among different cultures. In cross-cultural computing, it is important to manipulate multimedia data, such as icons, images and music expressing cultural contexts. In the design of multimedia computing systems for realizing cross-cultural computing, one of the most important issues is how to search and analyze media data (images, music, movies and documents) according to human's impressions and contexts. The field of "Kansei" information was originally introduced with the word "aesthetics" by Baumgarten in 1750 (Harada 1997). The aesthetics of Baumgarten was established and succeeded by Kant with his ideological aesthetics (Harada 1997). In the research field of multimedia computing systems, it is important to deal with "Kansei" information for defining and extracting media data according to impressions and senses of individual users. The concept of "Kansei" includes several meanings on sensitive recognition, such as "impression", "human senses", "feelings", "sensitivity", "psychological reaction" and "physiological reaction". The Multimedia Database Laboratory at Keio University has constructed "Cross-Cultural Multimedia Computing Systems" for sharing and analyzing different cultures, as a new platform of cross-cultural computing, in the joint research project with the University of Jyväskylä and Tampere University of Technology in Finland (Fig. 20.2). The environment is used to realize a remote, interactive and real-time cultural communication and exchange among different countries and cultures from the viewpoint of cultural contexts. Kiyoki's semantic associative search method (Kiyoki et al. 1994) is applied to similarity calculation and metadata extraction for media data, as functions for finding common impressions and contexts.

In this method, the acquisition of information or knowledge is performed by semantic computations. Context-dependent interpretation means that information is dynamically extracted by a semantic computation with context-recognition. The method realizes the computational machinery for recognizing the meaning of contexts and obtaining the semantically related information to the given context. Several

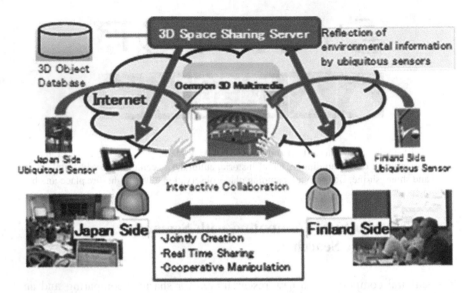

Fig. 20.2 Basic concept of the Japan–Finland cross-cultural collaborative environment

information retrieval methods, which use the orthogonal space created by mathematical procedures like the Latent Semantic Indexing (LSI) method, have been proposed (Berry et al. 1995, 1999; Deerwester et al. 1990; Salton et al. 1975). Kiyoki's method is essentially different from those methods. The essential difference is that this method provides dynamic recognition of the context. That is, the "context-dependent interpretation" is realized by dynamically selecting a certain subspace from the entire semantic space. The other methods do not provide the context dependent interpretation, that is, their space is fixed and static.

The outline of Kiyoki's semantic associative search method (Kiyoki et al. 1994) is briefly summarized as follows:

1. A set of m words is given, and each word is characterized by n features. That is, an m by n matrix M is given as the data matrix.
2. The correlation matrix $M^T M$ with respect to the n features is constructed from the matrix M. Then, the eigenvalue decomposition of the correlation matrix is computed and the eigenvectors are normalized. The orthogonal semantic space MDS is created as the span of the eigenvectors which correspond to nonzero eigenvalues.
3. "Context words" and "a media object" such as an image, sound, video or animation are characterized as "context" by using the n features and representing them as n-dimensional vectors.
4. The context words and "a media object" are mapped into the orthogonal semantic space by computing the Fourier expansion for the n-dimensional vectors.
5. A set of all the projections from the orthogonal semantic space to the invariant subspaces (Eigen spaces) is defined. Each subspace represents a phase of meaning, and it corresponds to "context."

6. A subspace of the orthogonal semantic space is selected according to the given "context" expressed in n-dimensional vectors, which are given as "context" represented by "a sequence of words" and "a media object."
7. The most correlated information resources to the given "context" are extracted as the selected subspace by applying the metric defined in the semantic space.

The advantages and original points of this method are as follows:

- The semantic associative media search based on semantic computation is realized by a mathematical approach. This media search method surpasses the search methods which use pattern matching for associative search. Users can use their own words or images for representing impression and data contents for media retrieval, and do not need to know how the metadata of media data of retrieval candidates are characterized in databases.
- Dynamic context recognition is realized using a mathematical foundation. The context recognition can be used for obtaining multimedia information by giving the user's impression and the contents of the information as "context." A semantic space is created as a space for representing various contexts which correspond to its subspaces. A context is recognized by the computation for selecting a subspace.
- The essential advantage is that this method provides the important function for semantic projections which realizes the dynamic recognition of "context." That is, the "context-dependent interpretation" is dynamically performed by computing the distance between different media data, information resources and words in a context-dependent way. The context-dependency is realized by dynamically selecting a subspace from the entire orthogonal semantic space, according to "context."
- In this method, the number of phases of contexts is almost infinite (currently 2^{2000} in the general English word space and 2^{180} in the color-image space, approximately). For semantic associative computations of "Kansei" information, this method constructed several actual semantic spaces, such as the general English-word space in 2115 dimensions, the color-image space in 183 dimensions, and music space in eight dimensions in the current implementations.

20.5   An Example of Implementation in Cross-Cultural Contexts: Cross-Cultural Virtual Museum

The semantic associative search method has several application areas (Kiyoki et al. 2009; Kiyoki Laboratory 2010). In this section, we focus on a cross-cultural application between Finland and Japan: cultural-images and simplified icons of images. We have created a 183-dimensional color-space for mapping Finnish and Japanese cultural-images. In addition to cultural-images, we have mapped impression words to search those images. These impression words are used to express Finnish and Japanese "Kansei". That is, those impression words are submitted as a "Kansei−query," and highly correlated cultural images to the query are selected from Finnish and Japanese cultural-image databases by using the semantic associative search method. We have also applied the semantic associative search method to cross-cultural icons of Finnish and Japanese musical contexts. This application compares Finnish "*kantele*" and Japanese "*koto*" in a sound-based space with the sound-features such as tones. In addition to sound-features, we have characterized musical cultures with image-icons for those instruments. The cross-cultural communication (CCC) environment is a virtual museum, user/actor is a museum visitor and task/situation is art comparison.

The "Cross-Cultural Multimedia Computing Systems" promotes cross-cultural understanding and communication by using cultural images and simplified icons of images. It consists of image analysis, search and visualization functions, characterized by three main features: (1) a culture-dependent semantic metadata extraction method, which extracts both image elements and impression metadata (e.g., sad, happy and dreamy) corresponding to properties of each image, (2) a cross-cultural computing mechanism to represent differences and similarities among various images, and (3) easy-to-use interfaces designed for helping users to join the image database creation process. This system extracts the features of image-based-cultural aspects and expresses cultural-dependent impressions by interpreting images in the semantic image-space, and makes it possible to compare cultural difference and similarity in terms of impressions among various cultural image resources.

The important objective of this cross-cultural computing system is to evoke impressions and imaginations including the cultural diversity by representing various impression-based responses to cultural image resources from different cultures. There are two main scenarios designed to allow users to attain impressions and imaginations: (1) how images would be interpreted among different cultures and (2) how impressions to images would be composed in different cultures. The system realizes metadata extraction, search, visualization, and search functions which have been designed in a culture-oriented way. Two image-domains, impressions (e.g., sad, happy and dreamy) and images elements (e.g., color, shape and structure) are utilized to compare cultural-differences or similarities. In the system implementation, it is important how to deal with semantic heterogeneity when impressions are variously expressed among different image-based aspects. The system realizes a culture-dependent impression metadata extraction to tackle this challenge with participation of users.

We have designed 3D Cross-Cultural Museum system architecture and implemented the prototype systems for Finnish and Japanese art paintings and scenery photos with their iconic simplifications as examples. Figure 20.3 shows the overview of the system. In this system, we have implemented two image databases (Japanese image database and Finnish image database) from Japanese and Finnish cultures, respectively. The system executes the following processes:

- When a user submits "context-query" as a set of keywords (e.g. "bright and light"), the system retrieves images with the high correlation to this query from Japanese and Finnish image databases, respectively, by means of the semantic associative search system.

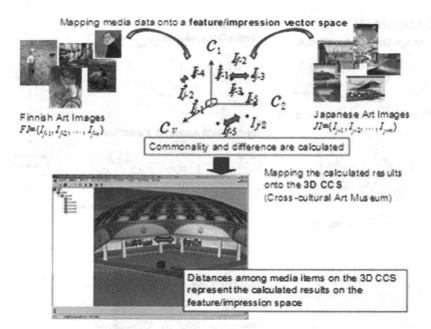

Fig. 20.3 Cross-cultural multimedia museum

- The retrieved Japanese and Finnish images are ranked up along the correlation, and highly related images to the given context are mapped as icons (thumbnail images) onto the walls of the 3D Cross-Cultural Museum. Various aspects among culture, for example color space, are visualized with some specific context.
- Two different cultures are visualized and compared by means of the retrieved images.

To realize cross-cultural collaboration, we must know the differences and similarities between cultures. We have included the functionality of finding common and different features because we need to collaborate beyond culture gaps. We have defined typical use cases of the system as follows:

- Users upload an image, music, or video art work onto the museum walls from different cultures.
- Users can browse and operate these works of art in the museum. The operation includes searching, ordering (sorting by various features), zooming, etc.
- When a certain two objects are placed close to each other, the defined functions are applied automatically.
- When any common and different features are found by the functionality, the art works are highlighted.

We have applied the museum system to Finnish and Japanese paintings as examples (Fig. 20.3). In the prototype, we use a 3D space sharing tool, and the semantic associative search method for similarity calculation and metadata extraction methods for media data as functions for finding common impressions and contexts.

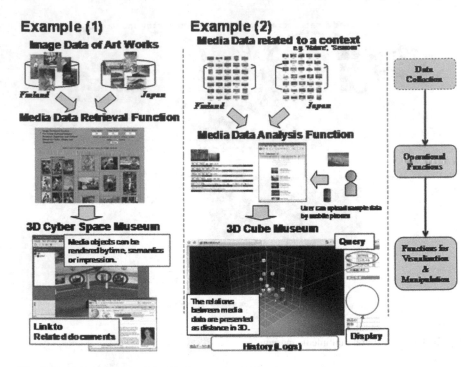

Fig. 20.4 Main functions of the 3D Cross-cultural Museum

In this museum system, we have implemented three types of functions: (a) data collection in context, (b) operational functions and (c) functions for visualization and manipulation (Fig. 20.4). By means of data collection in context users can set any type of multimedia data such as images, music and movies as target, data according to their interests. The data collection, however, is expected to be set by a specific topic for culture-related discussions, for example, "art", "nature", "food", "annual event", "custom" etc.

The context is needed to select a subset from super sets of media data. Operational functions provide several functionalities for each type of media. These functions are used for feature extraction, element analysis, retrieval, calculation of relationships, and sorting/rendering of target media. The functions are listed and classified for each type of media in detail in (Barakbah and Kiyoki 2009; Sasaki et al. 2009). For example, the element analysis functions for image data are provided for treating color, shape, texture and structure as elements of images with cultural backgrounds, and element analysis functions for music data are provided for treating wave pattern, key, tempo, pitch, rhythm and harmony as musical elements (Ijichi and Kiyoki 2005). With the functions for visualization and manipulation, users can manipulate multimedia data as 3D media objects. 3D scenes are provided as shared spaces for remote users as shown with Examples 1 and 2 in Fig. 20.4 (Sasaki et al. 2009; Kiyoki et al. 2012; Sasaki et al. 2010; Suhardijanto et al. 2012).

Example 1 is designed as an analogy of a real-world museum. Data collection (e.g. images, music, movies) represented as 3D media objects are rendered in this 3D scene by the time of publication (time/day/year), by relevance in elements, by impression, by topics, by authors etc. There are links to external related documents such as Wikipedia describing the cultural and historical background of the data. Any user can treat multimedia data like a curator in a real-world museum. Example 2 is designed for deeper analysis of data collection. The relations between each data of data collection (e.g. images, music, movies) are represented as distances between 3D media objects in 3D cube scene. 3D media objects are allocated in 3D cube by the time of publication (time/day/year) or by relevance in elements according to a user's query. The axes of 3D cube are variable so that users can select the type of axis such as time, topics and media feature. Because this 3D Cube scene equips high visibility, scalability and possibility of operation expansion as UI, it is suitable for use cases in ubiquitous situation.

Each user can also upload sample media data as a query icon, for example by a mobile phone, submit queries such as time or impression words, and share the histories (logs) of his/her and other users' manipulations.

20.6   Conclusion

In our paper we discussed contextual computing that increases the richness of communication in human-computer interaction, especially in cross-cultural situations. Our case cultures are those of Japan and Finland. Cross-cultural communication environment—user/actor—task/situation is the focus in our context research. We discussed context as a multidimensional concept and introduced icons in cross-cultural environments. Our focus on icons is related to computer systems and user interactions in cross-cultural communication environments. We presented Kiyoki's semantic associative search method and applied it to create context-dependent knowledge in cross-cultural environments. We introduced three examples of applying an icon-based platform for cross-cultural communication with Kiyoki's method for searching and creating context-dependent cross-cultural information. Our platform realizes better mutual understanding between the two cultures by means of contextual data structuring and computing. Our near future collaboration concentrates on global environmental issues and ICT. We apply the 5D World Map concept (Kiyoki et al. 2012; Sasaki et al. 2010) with time, 3D space and semantic dimensions to information visualization, image and iconic information processing.

References

Barakbah, A., Kiyoki, Y.: A pillar algorithm for K-means optimization by distance maximization for initial centroid designation. Proceedings of the IEEE international symposium on computational intelligence and data mining (CIDM) Nashville, Tennessee, USA, March 30–April 2 2009
Bauer, J.: Identification and Modeling of Contexts for Different Information Scenarios in Air Traffic, Diplomarbeit (2003)

Bazire, M., Brézillon, P.: Understanding context before using it. In: Dey, A., Kokinov, B., Leake, D., Turner, R. (eds.) Modeling and Using Context (LNAI). vol. 3554, pp. 29–40. Springer, Berlin (2005)

Berry, M.W., Dumais, S.T., O'Brien, G.W.: Using linear algebra for intelligent information retrieval. SIAM Rev. 37(4), 573–595 (1995)

Berry, M.W., Drmac, Z., Jessup, E.R.: Matrices, vector spaces and information retrieval. SIAM Rev. 41(2), 335–362 (1999)

Brézillon, P.: Focusing on context in human-centered computing. IEEE Intell. Syst. 18(3), 62–66 (2003)

Brézillon, P.: Context-based development of experience bases. In: Brézillon, P., Blackburn, P., Dapoigny, R. (eds.) Modeling and Using Context (Lecture Notes in Computer Science series), vol. 8175, pp. 143–156. Springer, Heidelberg (2013)

Brynskov, M., Kristensen, J.F., Thomsen, B., Thomsen, L.L.: What is context? Technical report, Department of Computer Science, University of Aarhus. http://www.daimi.au.dk/brynskov/publications/what-is-context-brynskov-et-al-2003.pdf (2003). Accessed 10 Jan 2014

Coppola, P., Della Mea, V., Di Gaspero, L., et al.: AI techniques in a context-aware ubiquitous environment. In: Hassanien, A.-E., Abawajy, J.H., Akraham, A., Hagras, H. (eds.) Pervasive Computing. Innovation in Intelligent Multimedia and Applications, pp. 157–180. Springer, London (2009)

Coutaz, J., Crowley, J., Dobson, S., Garlan, D.: Context is key. Commun. ACM 48(3), 49–53 (2005)

Deerwester, S., Dumais, S.T., Landauer, T.K., Furnas, G.W., Harshman, R.A.: Indexing by latent semantic analysis. J. Am. Soc. Inform. Sci. 41(6), 391–407 (1990)

Dey, A.K.: Understanding and using context. Pers. Ubiquit. Comput. 5(1), 4–7 (2001)

Dey, A., Kokinov, B., Leake, D., Turner, R. (eds.): Modeling and Using Context (LNAI). vol. 3554. Springer, Berlin (2005)

Dublin Core Metadata: Dublin core metadata initiative. http://dublincore.org/ (2014). Accessed 29 Jan 2014

Fitrianie, S., Datcu. D., Rothkrantz, L.J.M.: Human communication based on icons in crisis environments. In: Aykin, N. Usability and Internationalization (Lecture Notes in Computer Science) vol. 4560, pp. 57–66. Springer, Berlin (2007)

Halpin, T.A.: Information Modeling and Relational Databases: From Conceptual Analysis to Logical Design. Morgan Kaufman, San Francisco (2001)

Harada, A. (eds.): Report of Modeling the Evaluation Structure of KANSEI. University of Tsukuba, Japan (1997)

Heimbürger, A.: Context meets culture. In: Brézillon, P., Blackburn, P., Dapoigny, R. (eds.) Modeling and Using Context (Lecture Notes in Computer Science series), vol. 8175, pp. 143–156. Springer, Berlin (2013)

Heimbürger, A., Ojansuu, K., Multisilta, J.: Time contexts in document-driven projects on the web: From time-sensitive links towards an ontology of time. In: Duzi, M., Jaakkola, H., Kiyoki, Y., Kangassalo, H. (eds.) Frontiers in Artificial Intelligence and Applications, Information Modelling and Knowledge Bases XV, vol. 154, pp. 136–153. IOS Press, Amsterdam (2007)

Henricksen, K., Indulska, J., Rakotonirainy, A.: Modeling context information in pervasive computing systems. In: Mattern, F., Naghshineh, M. (eds.) Proceedings of 1st International Conference on Pervasive Computing (Lecture Notes in Computer Science), vol. 2414, pp. 167–180. Springer, Heidelberg (2002)

Hoft, N.: Developing a cultural model. In: Del Galdo, E., Nielsen, J. (eds.) International User Interface, pp. 41–73. Wiley, New York (1996)

Ijichi, A., Kiyoki, Y.: A Kansei metadata generation method for music data dealing with dramatic interpretation. In: Kiyoki, Y., Wangler, B., Jaakkola, H., Kangassalo, H. (eds.) Frontiers in Artificial Intelligence and Applications: Information Modelling and Knowledge Bases XVI, pp. 170–182. IOS Press, Amsterdam (2005)

Khanom, S., Heimbürger, A., Kärkkäinen, T.: Icon-based language in the context of requirements elicitation process. In: Tokuda, T., Kiyoki, Y., Jaakkola, H., Yoshida, N. (eds.) Frontiers in Artificial Intelligence and Applications: Information Modelling and Knowledge Bases XXIV. IOS Press, Amsterdam (2015)

Kiyoki, Y., Kitagawa, T., Hayama, T.: A metadatabase system for semantic image search by a mathematical model of meaning. SIGMOD Rec. **23**(4), 34–41 (1994)

Kiyoki, Y., Heimbürger, A., Jaakkola, H., Takahashi, Y.: Contextual computing of multi-dimensional educational knowledge based on Kiyoki's semantic associative search method. In: Isomäki, H.-K., Häkkinen, P., Viteli, J. (eds.) Future Educational Technologies (University of Jyväskylä, Publications of Information Technology Research Institute 20/2009), pp. 148–170. University Printing House, Jyväskylä (2009)

Kiyoki, Y., Sasaki, S., Nguyen Trang, N., Thi Ngoc Diep, N.: Cross-Cultural Multimedia Computing with Impression-Based Semantic Spaces, Conceptual Modelling and its Theoretical Foundations (Lecture Notes in Computer Science). Springer, Heidelberg (2012)

Kiyoki Laboratory: Multidatabase Laboratory, Keio University SFC, Japan. http://www.mdbl. sfc.keio.ac.jp. (2010). Accessed 10 Jan 2014

Leppänen, M.: An Ontological Framework and a Methodical Skeleton for Method Engineering—A Contextual Approach. Jyväskylä Studies in Computing 52. University Press, Jyväskylä (2005)

Nonaka, I., Takeushi, H.: The Knowledge-Creating Company. Oxford University Press, New York (1995)

Nonaka, I., Konno, N.: The concept of "Ba": Building foundation for knowledge creation. Calif. Manage. Rev. **40**(3), 40–54 (1998)

OWL.: Web Ontology Language. http://www.w3.org/2004/OWL (2009). Accessed 9 Jan 2014

Salton, G., Wong, A., Yang, C.S.: A vector space model for automatic indexing. Commun. ACM **18**(11), 613–620 (1975)

Sasaki, S., Itabashi, Y., Kiyoki, Y., Chen, X.: An image-query creation method for representing impression by color-based combination of multiple images. In: Kiyoki, Y., Tokuda, T., Jaakkola, H., Chen, X., Yoshida, N. (eds.) Frontiers in Artificial Intelligence and Applications: Information Modelling and Knowledge Bases XX, pp. 105–112. IOS Press, Amsterdam (2009)

Sasaki, S., Takahashi, Y., Kiyoki, Y.: The 4D World map system with semantic and spatiotemporal analyzers. In: Druzovec, T.W., Jaakkola, H., Kiyoki, Y., Tokuda, T., Yoshida, N. (eds.) Information Modelling and Knowledge Bases, XXI, pp. 1–18. IOS Press, Amsterdam (2010)

Strang, T., Linnhoff-Popien, C.: A context modeling survey. Workshop on Advanced Context Modeling, Reasoning and Management, UbiComp 2004, The 6th International Conference on Ubiquitous Computing, Nottingham, England (2004)

Studer, R., Stojanovic, N.: Context-oriented knowledge management: An outlook. J. Know. Manag. **9**(5), 150–159 (2005)

Suhardijanto, T., Kiyoki, Y., Ridho Barakbah, A.: A term-based cross-cultural computing system for cultural semantics analysis with phonological-semantic vector spaces. In: Breuker, J., Guarino, N., Kok, J.N., Liu, J., López de Mántaras, R., Mizoguchi, R., Musen, M., Pal, S.K., Zhong, N. (eds.) Frontiers in Artificial Intelligence and Applications: Information Modelling and Knowledge Bases, pp. 20–38. IOS Press, Amsterdam (2012)

Wang, F.-Y.: Is culture computable? A letter from the editors. IEEE Intell. Syst. **24**, 2–3 (2009)

Winograd, T.: Architectures for context. Hum.-Comput. Interact. **16**, 401–419 (2001)

Chapter 21
Context and Collaborative Work: A Context-Sensitive Intervention Approach for Collaboration in Dynamic Environment

Stefan Werner Knoll and Stephan G. Lukosch

Abstract The context of complex design and engineering processes is characterized by dynamic requirements, like changing process goals or group constellations. To deal with these dynamics in a virtual environment, a context-sensitive collaboration support system needs to consider a changing context and provide virtual teams with the support they need. Such elastic collaboration support can range from a fixed process and tool configuration to an open collaboration environment that enables groups to interact in a self-organized way. In this chapter, research about a context-sensitive intervention approach is described that intends to support elastic collaboration in dynamic environments. Based on a review of existing theories on collaboration performance, the use of contextual process information to monitor group performance during collaboration is discussed. Thereby, a rule concept is introduced to derive interventions for elastic collaboration processes compared to existing approaches for context modeling in collaboration.

21.1 Introduction

As systems and products become more complex, organizations work collaboratively in virtual teams across-organizational borders to improve their product lifecycles. However, collaboration in virtual teams faces new challenges that make it more difficult to manage them than face-to-face collaboration (Nunamaker Jr. et al. 2009). Besides the loss of non-verbal cues, different work processes and cultures between the team members represent a challenge for the design of technological support. In this context, the use of product data streams to effectively and collaboratively develop and monitor cross-organizational products has become a major research topic (SmartVortex 2014). One major requirement for such developing and monitoring

S. W. Knoll (✉)
Otto-von-Guericke University, Magdeburg, Germany
e-mail: sknoll@isg.cs.uni-magdeburg.de

S. G. Lukosch
Delft University of Technology, Delft, The Netherlands
e-mail: s.g.lukosch@tudelft.nl

© Springer Science+Business Media New York 2014
P. Brézillon, A. J. Gonzalez (eds.), *Context in Computing*,
DOI 10.1007/978-1-4939-1887-4_21

support is to provide intelligent support for the selection and appropriation of collaboration support tools based on a team's current interaction and process phase and the availability and accessibility of information (Janeiro et al. 2012a).

An application of such an intelligent support tool could be a cross-organizational product like a wheel loader that contains sensors to monitor the performance of the engine. Telemetric data such as the position of the machine, fuel level measures, engine vibrations and temperature could be analyzed to detect a machine degradation. To avoid a machine breakdown, an intelligent collaboration support tool can mobilize a cross-organizational expert team to quickly analyze and understand machine problems, and to identify solutions during the machine runtime. The virtual team has to identify machine failures, malfunctioning components, its causes and consequences, and define action plans. As telemetric data can change during the maintenance process, virtual teams collaborate in a dynamic environment where the original goal of the session can change, and the time planned and the available data can suddenly vary (Janeiro et al. 2012a). As result, the collaboration process needs to be constantly redesigned during the collaboration session.

In face-to-face collaboration, a team leader can provide process support by monitoring the collaboration process and redefining the goals and objectives of the team as well as to outline the procedures, activities, and tasks to accomplish these goals (Sarin and McDermott 2003). To deal with these types of dynamics in a virtual environment, teams need technological support that provide flexible features to monitor the context of a collaboration process as well as to adapt the process to the new situation. Depending on the expertise of the team members for the collaboration process, such support can range from prescribed collaboration processes and tools for inexperienced teams to emergent collaboration support in which the support system just gives recommendations on how to improve the process or on which tools to use (Janeiro et al. 2012a).

Current context-aware systems for collaboration make use of contextual information to provide awareness support (Ardissono and Bosio 2012; Ferscha et al. 2004) or to adapt the collaborative workspace (Terveen 1995; Haake et al. 2010). However, less research has focused on the relationship between group performance of a collaboration process and the need for process adaptation. In this chapter, it is assumed that contextual information of a collaboration process can be used to monitor the performance of a group in prescribed as well as emergent collaboration support environments. Therefore, a framework of group performance is introduced and its application to derive process adaptations is discussed. Based on a semantic model for dynamic collaboration processes the application of contextual information is illustrated by a rule concept. The resulting context-sensitive intervention approach is compared to existing approaches in collaboration and its application to design context-aware collaboration systems is discussed.

21.2 Background

Different approaches exist to define the concept of collaboration. In the Oxford dictionary collaboration is defined as the 'the act of working with another person or group of people to create or produce something'. From a computer science perspective, collaboration can involve humans as well as computational agents, who use technological support in 'a process in which two or more agents work together to achieve a shared goal' (Terveen 1995). A more specific definition is given in behavioral science, where collaboration 'occurs when a group of autonomous stakeholders of a problem domain engage in an interactive process, using shared rules, norms, and structures, to act or decide on issues related to that domain' (Wood and Gray 1991).

In this chapter, the focus is on collaboration as 'an interactive process in which a group of individual group members uses shared rules, norms, and structures to create or share knowledge in order to perform a collaborative task'. Thereby, collaboration can make use of technological support to provide an environment that supports shared rules, norms, and structures of an organization. In the context of virtual teams and cross-organizational collaboration, it is further assumed that collaboration takes place in a dynamic environment, which is characterized by changing requirements and resources such as a changing process goal, available time or group constellation. As a result, technological support needs to be aware of a collaboration context to provide groups with the support they need. Such technological support can be a context-aware system, which 'uses context to provide relevant information and/or services to the user, where relevancy depends on the user's task' (Dey 2001). Thereby, context-aware applications can support the presentation of information and services to a user, the automatic execution of a service for a user or the tagging of context information to support later retrieval (Dey 2001).

Several context-aware systems focus on physical context elements such as user's location, time and activity (Ardissono and Bosio 2012; Ferscha et al. 2004). However, less research has been done on using context to predict group performance. Research on groupware systems (Dennis et al. 1988; Nunamaker et al. 1991) indicates that a collaboration process and its outcome are affected by different factors like group characteristics, task complexity, technology used or organizational culture. Today, different social psychological theories (Tajfel 1974; Janis 1982; Karau and Williams 1993; Diehl and Stroebe 1991; Gallupe et al. 1992) describe and predict the influence of such contextual factors on group behavior and performance. In this chapter, it is assumed that by monitoring group performance a context-aware system can provide new services to handle negative group behaviors such as groupthink (Janis 1982) or social loafing (Karau and Williams 1993) and thereby improve group performance.

21.3 Group Performance in Dynamic Collaboration Processes

This section introduces a framework for group performance in dynamic collaboration processes. The framework is used to illustrate the complexity of a collaboration process. It discusses the factors that define the context of a collaboration process

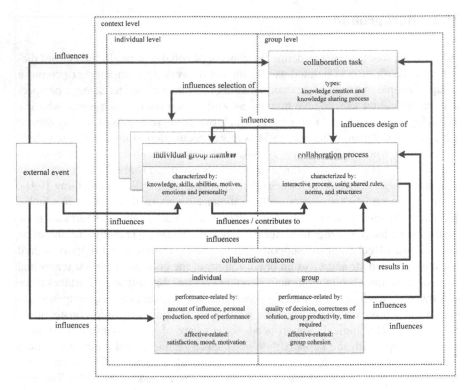

Fig. 21.1 A general framework of group performance in dynamic collaboration processes (adapted from Hackman 1987)

and influence its performance. Based on the input-process-output framework for analyzing group behavior and performance by Hackman (1987), the framework consists of the elements collaboration task, individual group member, collaboration process, collaboration outcome and external event (see Fig. 21.1).

Similar to Hackman (1987), in this chapter it is assumed that performance in collaboration can be observed from an individual and group level. In the center of Fig. 21.1 individual group members form a group for collaboration and represent the individual level. The composition of the group is influenced by the collaboration task, which defines the necessary resources to complete a task. These resources can represent knowledge, skills, and abilities (KSAs) of individual group members as well as their motives, emotions and personality.

During the collaboration process, individual group members interact with the environment by making use of external resources such as task related information or technological support. From a group level perspective, individual group members contribute different resources in an interactive process to the group. The design of the interactive process is influenced by the collaboration task, which defines the shared rules, norms, and structures to generate a collaboration outcome.

The outcome of a collaboration process can be classified into the dimensions performance-related and affective-related. On the individual level, performance of an individual group member can be represented in different ways such as the amount of influence of an individual during a decision-making process, the number of contributions in a discussion or the personal speed of performance. The affective-related outcome can be defined by psychological factors like satisfaction, mood or motivation of an individual group member. On the group level, performance of a group can be represented by factors like the quality of a decision, the correctness of a solution, the group productivity or the time required to achieve an intended goal. The affective-related outcome can be group cohesion.

From the literature, the context of a collaboration process can be defined in different ways. Schilit and Theimer (1994) refer to context as location information that enables context-aware systems 'to adapt according to its location of use, the collection of nearby people and objects, as well as the changes to those objects over time'. Dey (2001) proposes that context is 'any information that can be used to characterize the situation of an entity'. Bazire and Brézillon (2005) define context as a 'set of constraints that influence the behavior of a system (a user or a computer) embedded in a given task'. Thereby, they consider that 'context can be specified for a given situation by the answering of the following questions: Who? What? Where? When? Why? and How?'.

From a context perspective, in this chapter it is assumed that the collaboration context describes the current status of the collaboration task, individual group member, collaboration process, collaboration outcome. During a collaboration process, these elements can influence each other, which lead to a change of the collaboration context over time. From, e.g., a social psychological perspective, the production blocking effect (Diehl and Stroebe 1991) describes the possible negative effect of a process design that hinder the individual group members to share contributions the moment they occur. In this situation, the collaboration process influences the collaboration outcome by reducing the number of contributions as well as the motivation and mood of the individual group members. Another example is given by the social loafing effect (Karau and Williams 1993), which describes the tendency of individual group members to expend less effort in a collaboration process when they believe their contributions to be dispensable and not needed for group success. This effect could increase with the number of individual group members and a collaboration process design that provides anonymity. The composition of the group itself can influence the collaboration process and as a result the performance of the collaboration process. The social identity theory (Tajfel 1974), e.g., proposes that individual group members tend to classify themselves and others into various social categories, which represent attitudinal, emotional and behavioral similarities between the self and in-group members. Milliken et al. (2003) argue that individual group members who strongly identify with their group are more likely to participate actively than they would in groups with which group identification is low. In connection with group diversity, the evaluation apprehension effect (Gallupe et al. 1992) describes that the fear of negative evaluation may further cause individual group members to withhold their contributions during the collaboration process.

With regard to virtual teams and cross-organizational collaboration, a change in the collaboration context can stem from different external events that are not traditionally considered in collaboration process design. These events originate in the complexity and unpredictability of a collaboration process, which can lead to a change of the collaboration task, the group constellation and the process design itself (Janeiro et al. 2012a). During, e.g., a collaborative maintenance process of an industrial machine, the detection of changed machine parameters, such as a critical temperature rise of the machine, can lead to a change of the collaborative task. Instead of identifying the failure cause, the individual group members now need to prevent a breakdown of the machine. In such a dynamic situation, the resources such as the time available might change, which requires process adaptation. As a collaboration process is designed for a specific group of individual group members, a change of the collaboration task and the process design might also require different individual group members to achieve an intended goal.

To sum up, the introduced framework illustrates the contextual factors that influence the performance in collaboration. In this chapter, it is assumed that these contextual factors can be used by context-aware applications to provide collaborating teams with the support they need.

21.4   Concept of Interventions

A change in the collaboration context can lead to a need to adapt the collaboration process to the new situation. In face-to-face collaboration, a facilitator can monitor the collaboration process and perform interventions to help the group and solve its problem. A key skill for a facilitator is to make effective interventions to ensure that the collaboration process fits to a given collaboration context. From the literature, an intervention can take place in three stages (Westley and Waters 1988):

- *Stage 1: to recognize symptoms of a process problem*—The recognition process is characterized by analyzing the behavior of the individual group members. In face-to-face collaboration, this can be done by analyzing the contributions, the body language as well as the interaction of the group.
- *Stage 2: to interpret the syndromes*—To identify the underlying pattern of given syndromes, the facilitator needs knowledge about theories on group behaviors as well as expertise with group dynamics. During this identification process, a list of generic problem syndromes can support a facilitator (for example the generic meeting problem syndromes by Westley and Waters 1988)
- *Stage 3: to make an intervention*—To deal with a process problem, a facilitator can choose between action and interpretation interventions. Action interventions directly manipulate the collaboration process (for example to change the group constellation if expert knowledge is needed; or to prevent interruptions of an individual group member). By using an interpretation intervention, a facilitator communicates the observed patterns to the group to improve awareness and help the group to solve the problem on their own.

Compared to face-to-face collaboration, virtual teams face the challenge that the used technology often reduces or eliminates visual communication channels such as facial expressions or body language. To make use of the concept of interventions, a support technology needs to provide services to monitor and analyze contextual information of a collaboration process as well as to adapt the process.

Elastic collaboration support is needed in highly dynamic processes, such as complex design and engineering processes where external events can lead to an unpredictable change in the collaboration context (Janeiro et al. 2012b). Depending on the expertise of the individual group members, such support ranges from prescribed collaboration to emergent forms of collaboration (Janeiro et al. 2012b). On the one extreme, prescribed collaboration supports individual group members with less expertise in collaboration by predefining process as well as support tools. Here, a support technology provides support by monitoring the collaboration context and providing interventions based on predefined rules. On the other extreme, emergent collaboration supports expert groups that do not need guidance and coordination during collaboration. Here, the individual group members use the support technology to monitor the collaboration context and to adapt the process to new situations. A context-aware system can support such elastic collaboration by providing a service to monitor the collaboration context. Based on a rule concept, such a system can further provide services that provide action as well as interpretation interventions. However, to make this possible, a modeling approach is necessary to describe the context of a dynamic collaboration process.

Several context-modeling approaches exist that make use of contextual information to represent awareness information (Reiter et al. 2013) or to recommend services and tools (Wang et al. 2006; Vieira et al. 2005). For example, Reiter et al. (2013) introduce a conceptual context approach that uses data from a business process model to describe the communication context of an individual group member during collaboration. Here, a collaboration context is characterized by the dimensions: Task (the activity in a process model), Location (the workplace of an activity), Presence (the availability of an individual for communication in relation to a location or task), and Relation (the relationship between the individuals). As common business process models are usually not designed in such granularity to provide detailed information about the individual group members or the services, such context modeling approaches are less suitable to monitor the performance of emergent collaboration, where individual group members coordinates themselves. More contextual information about collaboration can be described by an ontological approach (Vieira et al. 2005; Wang et al. 2006). Such approaches divide the collaboration context into subclasses such as Physical Context, Organizational Context and Interaction Context (Vieira et al. 2005) or relate contextual information to Person, Task, Interaction, Artifact, Tool, Collaboration Control, Environment and History (Wang et al. 2006). However, they do not provide a concept to describe the process workflow, which is needed to monitor the performance of prescribed collaboration. Therefore, a new modeling approach is necessary to define a collaboration process as well as to express contextual process information.

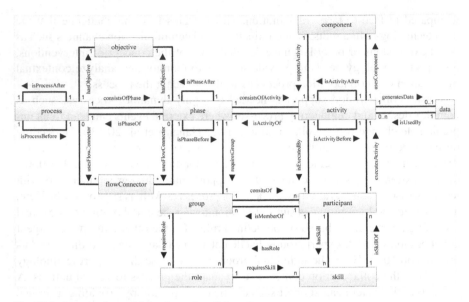

Fig. 21.2 A semantic model for dynamic collaboration processes

21.5 A Semantic Model for Dynamic Collaboration Processes

The following section introduces a semantic model that combines properties of a process definition language to express the workflow of a collaboration process with given ontology-based approaches to capture contextual process information.

Figure 21.2 illustrates a first approach for such a semantic model by the key concepts and their relations. In this model, the concept participant describes an individual group member who participates in a collaboration process. The concept participant has certain skills that can be a prerequisite of a role in a process. Similar to Haake et al. (2010), the concept role is used to abstractly denote a set of behaviors, rights and obligations of a process participant. A participant can be assigned to a group in a specific role. Besides the concept role, the concept skill is used to distinguish different participants and thus to be able to define requirements for the participants of a process. The concept process describes a collaboration process in which a group uses shared rules, norms, and structures to create or share knowledge. Similar to Oliveira et al. (2007), a process has an objective, defining its main purpose or collaboration task. How a group moves through this process to create an intended state in the process can be prescribed by work tactics of a group, similar to the concept of a collaboration pattern (Pattberg and Fluegge 2007). The semantic model represents these stages in a process by the concept phase and relating this concept to a group. During a phase, a group of participants moves through a sequence of activities. Similar to concepts like participation (Oliveira et al. 2007) or action (Haake et al. 2010), the concept activity represents an atomic activity that is executed by a participant using external resources such as a software tool represented by the concept component. To control the collaboration process and allow the representation of parallel phases, the concept flowConnector is used to implement given workflow patterns such as parallel split, exclusive choice or simple merge (van der Aalst et al. 2003).

The resulting semantic model expresses information about a collaboration process in different ways. By using properties of a process definition language, the model can prescribe as well as log the workflow of a collaboration process. The workflow of a problem solving process can, e.g., be prescribed by relating a process entity to phase entities such as 'problem definition', 'solution search', 'solution generation', 'solution evaluation' and 'solution implementation' (Knoll et al. 2013). As each phase can require a different group composition, a phase entity is related to a group entity, which requires participants with specific roles. Each phase itself defines an abstract sequence of possible activities related to predefined components. For example, the activity entity 'to generate a solution' can be related to the component entity 'brainstorming'. An activity sequence defines the possible interaction of a participant with a component. For example, a component entity 'brainstorming' could provide support for the activity sequences AS1: {to view; to create} and AS2: {to view; to create; to comment}. Thereby, the activity sequence AS1 represents a common brainstorming process, whereas the activity sequence AS2 allows brainstorming participants to comment existing contributions.

During a collaboration process, a process log can be created by documenting the executed activities in the process as a relation between the concepts phase, participant, component, activity and data. As it cannot be known before process start, through which phases a group passes, the process log is initialized as a process entity that relates a phase entity to a group entity. During collaboration, the process log relates a participant entity to an executed activity entity, which is defined by the supported activities of a used component. The process log can be refined by searching for patterns or comparing a process log to a predefined collaboration process. Thereby, a specific combination of used components or a specific activity sequence over a period of time can give insights on rules, norms, and structures the group used during collaboration that can be represented as a phase entity.

Besides the workflow of a collaboration process, the semantic model can express contextual process information by using properties of the given ontology-based approach. For example, the semantic model provides contextual information about the individual group members by the properties and relations of the concepts participant and skill. Similar to Wang et al. (2006), this information can be improved by connecting the Friend of a Friend ontology (FOAF 2010) to the concept participant to describe the individual group members, their activities and their relations to each other in more details. Contextual information about a collaborative task is given by the concept objective, which defines the goal for a phase or the whole collaboration process. This information can be improved by relating the concept process to an ontology such as the organization ontology (Organization Ontology 2013) that described organizational structures of an organization in which collaboration processes occur.

21.6 A Context-Sensitive Intervention Approach

In this section, the application of the semantic model to define context-sensitive interventions for context-aware systems that support collaboration in dynamic environments is discussed. Assuming that contextual information of a collaboration processes can be used to monitor the performance of a group during collaboration, such information can be used to define interventions as of event-condition-action (ECA) rules (Goh et al. 2001). The semantics of an ECA rule (ON event IF condition DO actions) is defined as follows.

- *Event*: The concept of an event specifies the situation in which a rule is used to coordinate the use of possible interventions that are related to this situation.
- *Condition*: The concept of a condition defines a logical test that, if satisfied or evaluated to be true, causes the action to be carried out. The expression of a condition can make use of given logical operations and can refer to the concepts of the semantic model. With regard to the concept of interventions (Westley and Waters 1988), a condition combines the stages of an intervention to recognize and interpret symptoms of a process problem.
- *Action*: The concept of an action defines a change or update in a collaboration process. Thereby, the concept of action can support collaboration by adapting the collaboration process (action intervention) or by providing awareness information to the individual group members (interpretation intervention).

Related to Niederman et al. (2008), context-sensitive interventions can be defined at different levels:

- *Design level*: These interventions guide individual group members in choosing appropriate tools, techniques, and participants to structure a collaboration process that is effective in achieving an intended goal.
- *Execution level*: These interventions guide a group step-by-step through the collaboration process and adapt its workflow if needed.
- *Activity level*: These interventions analyze the structure of activities of a collaboration process and provide support to adapt these activities to stimulate effective, efficient and rigorous problem solving.
- *Behavior level*: These interventions focus on behavior of a group during a collaboration process to stimulate positive and prevent negative group behaviors.

A possible application of the ECA rule approach is the design of a context-sensitive interpretational intervention for the social loafing theory (Diehl and Stroebe 1991). This theory describes the tendency of participants to expend less effort when they believe their contributions are dispensable and not needed for group success. The effect increases with increasing group size and can be reduced when participants believe that they are being evaluated as individuals rather than collectively as a group. As group size affects this group behavior, a context-sensitive intervention rule can be related to the number of individual group members in a collaboration process. Furthermore, indicators such as the number of contributions or the time between two contributions can be monitored during the process. A possible condition

```
01   interpretationIntervention reduceSocialLoafing (Activity a)
02   componentset c = a.isActivityOf().consistsOfActivity().usesComponent()
03   ON
04            a.activityType == 'navigate'
05   IF
06   a.isActivityOf().phaseType == 'solutionGeneration' AND
07   a.isActivityOf().requiresGroup().getGroupSize() > 7 AND
08   checkIdeaFlowDeviation(c, 'brainstorming', 2 ) == TRUE
09   DO
10   provideRecommendation( "The system detects a possible social loafing effect.
11   Please keep in mind that every contribution is valuable and needed to find a
12   solution for the problem situation. If a participant needs helps please do not
13   hesitate to ask other participants for help.")
```

Fig. 21.3 Syntax of the context-sensitive interpretational intervention: reduceSocialLoafing

for an intervention can be the situation that a group has a constant contribution flow instead of one individual group member with a high time factor between two contributions. At a certain discrepancy level between individual contribution rate and average group contribution rate, an interpretation intervention can inform the group about this situation and suggest approaches to overcome this situation.

Figure 21.3 represents the syntax of an interpretational intervention rule to monitor and reduce social loafing. The rule makes use of the semantic model for dynamic collaboration processes (shown in Fig. 21.2) to monitor the workflow of a collaboration process and capture contextual process information. During a collaboration session, the relations between the concepts of the semantic model define a collaboration data stream. By monitoring the collaboration data stream the interpretational intervention rule is triggered by the execution of an activity of the activityType: 'navigate' (see Fig. 21.3, Line 04), which represents the situation in the workflow in which the group activates a new phase of a collaboration process. With regard to the introduced semantic model, the rule checks the conditions if the related phase of the event activity is of the phaseType: 'solutionGeneration' (see Fig. 21.3, Line 06) and if the active group involves more than seven participants (see Fig. 21.3, Line 07). Furthermore, the rule uses the function 'checkIdeaFlowDeviation()' (see Fig. 21.3, Line 08) to check whether the group uses the component: 'brainstorming' and if the deviation between the individual idea flow rate and the average group idea flow rate is more than two minutes. In the data stream, the relation between the concepts 'activity' and 'component' (shown in Fig. 21.2) represents the used component. Furthermore, the function uses the relation between the concepts 'participants', 'activity' and 'data' to calculate the idea flow deviation. If the conditions are true, a context-aware system can provides a popup window to the participants with awareness information (shown in Fig. 21.3, Line 10–13).

21.7 Related Work and Discussion

The introduced context-sensitive intervention approach represents a possible application of a semantic model that combines properties of a process definition language to express the workflow of a collaboration process with given ontology-based approaches to capture contextual process information.

In the research field on context, different approaches exist to control the physical actions of a human or computational agent situated in a simulation or in the real world. For example, the context-based reasoning approach decomposes knowledge about human behaviors into a hierarchy of contexts to represent human performance during a process (Gonzalez et al. 2008). At the top of the context hierarchy, a mission context provides knowledge on a process and a sequence of control contexts that could be implemented by an agent during the process. Thereby, a control context contains the actions and procedures relevant to a specific situation as well as transition rules to recognize when a transition to another control context is required. In this context, Gonzalez et al. (2008) introduced a formal description to express the behavior of an agent in a process in a context-based reasoning model. Furthermore, Barrett and Gonzalez (2011) extend the context-based reasoning approach to formalize collaborative behaviors. The resulting collaborative context-based reasoning approach is based on the concepts of the joint intention theory and express the communication among the agents.

As the design process of a context model has to include the experience of human experts to model the necessary knowledge associated, the given approaches seem to be suitable to express well-known collaboration processes. The introduced context-sensitive intervention approach can make use of the hierarchically approach to structure and organize process interventions with regard to the possible collaboration contexts of a process. Thereby, concepts of the semantic model for dynamic collaboration processes can be used to describe a context in a machine-readable description, which can be used by a context-aware system to monitor the collaboration context and adapt the process if needed. However, to monitor collaboration in dynamic environments, where external events can lead to an unpredictable change in the collaboration context, context models need to be adapted and extended to new situation, which evolve during collaboration.

In this chapter, it is assumed that the semantic model can be used to log the context of a collaboration process. Such a process log can be used by experts in collaboration to search for patterns or to compare a given collaboration context to predefined context models. As each collaboration process is unique, context-sensitive interventions must be adapted to be efficient in another collaboration context. Here, the formalism of a contextual graph Brézillon (2007) seems to be a suitable approach to represent and compare similar collaboration processes. To express experience in decision-making, a contextual graph represents a task realizing, and paths correspond to different practices developed by experts for realizing the task. The formalism further allows the incremental enrichment of experience by the refinement of existing practices. This property of a contextual-graph could be used to represent expert knowledge about process interventions. During the analysis of process logs of similar collaboration tasks, experts in collaboration can use a contextual graph to document possible identified process problems. Contextual nodes can be used to express differences between similar collaboration processes such as the initial collaboration context as well as distinctive changes of the collaboration context during the process. Experts can further use action elements to document possible context-sensitive interventions that correspond to a given contextual node. These interventions represent the experience of the experts for a specified context and make use of the introduced ECA approach to define conditions that can be evaluated by a context-aware system. The resulting contextual-graph can be improved over time by the refinement of possible new contextual nodes as well as context-sensitive interventions.

To sum up, in this chapter research about a context-sensitive intervention approach is described that intends to support elastic collaboration in dynamic environments. Based on a review of existing theories on collaboration performance, it is discussed how contextual process information can be used to monitor group performance during collaboration. A first approach of a semantic model is introduced that can be used to capture, share and reuse information about a process definition and contextual information. An application of the semantic model is discussed to define context-sensitive intervention for collaboration processes. Here, the ECA rules concept is used to describe the relation between an intervention and a specific collaborative situation.

Finally, more research is needed to understand the relation between these indicators and the performance of a group in a specific situation. Currently, the semantic model is deployed in a context-aware system for collaboration (Janeiro et al. 2013) to evaluate the semantic model and possible intervention rules. Resulting knowledge can then be used to improve the existing semantic model and to provide new services to handle negative group behaviors in collaboration processes.

Acknowledgments   This work has been partially supported by the FP7 EU Large-scale Integrating Project SMART VORTEX (Scalable Semantic Product Data Stream Management for Collaboration and Decision Making in Engineering) co-financed by the European Union. For more details, visit http://www.smartvortex.eu/.

References

Ardissono, L., Bosio, G.: Context-dependent awareness support in open collaboration environments. User Model. User-Adap. Inter. **22**(3), 223–254 (2012). doi:10.1007/s11257-011-9100-1

Barrett, G., Gonzalez, A.J.: Effective agent collaboration through improved communication by means of contextual reasoning. Int. J. Intell. Syst. **26**(2), 129–157 (2011). doi:10.1002/int.20458

Bazire, M., Brézillon, P.: Understanding context before using it. In: Dey, A., Kokinov, B., Leake, D., Turner, R. (eds.) Modeling and Using Context. Lecture Notes in Computer Science, vol. 3554, pp. 29–40. Springer, Heidelberg (2005)

Brézillon, P.: Context modeling: task model and practice model. In: Kokinov, B., Richardson, D.C., Roth-Berghofer, T.R., Vieu, L. (eds.) Modeling and Using Context. Lecture Notes in Computer Science, vol. 4635, pp. 122–135. Springer, Heidelberg (2007)

Dennis, A.R., George, J.F., Jessup, L.M., Nunamaker Jr., J.F., Vogel, D.R.: Information technology to support electronic meetings. MIS Quart. **12**(4), 591–624 (1988). doi:10.2307/249135

Dey, A.K.: Understanding and using context. Pers. Ubiquit. Comput. **5**(1), 4–7 (2001)

Diehl, M., Stroebe, W.: Productivity loss in idea-generating groups: tracking down the blocking effect. J. Pers. Soc. Psychol. **61**(3), 392–403 (1991). doi:10.1037/0022-3514.61.3.392

Ferscha, A., Holzmann, C., Oppl, S.: Context awareness for group interaction support. In: Proceedings of the 2nd International Workshop on Mobility Management Wireless Access Protocols (Co-located with Mobicom 2004 Conference). Philadelphia, PA, USA, 26 September–01 October 2004

FOAF: The FOAF vocabulary specification. http://xmlns.com/foaf/spec/ (2010). Accessed 03 Oct 2013

Gallupe, R.B., Dennis, A.R., Cooper, W.H., Valacich, J.S., Bastianutti, L.M., Nunamaker Jr., J.F. : Electronic brainstorming and group size. Acad. Manage. J. **35**(2), 350–369 (1992). doi:10.2307/256377

Goh, A., Koh, Y.K., Domazet, D.S.: ECA Rule-Based Support for Workflows. Artif. Intell. Eng. **15**(1), 37–46 (2001). doi:10.1016/S0954-1810(00)00028-5

Gonzalez, A.J., Stensrud, B.S., Barrett, G.: Formalizing context-based reasoning: a modeling paradigm for representing tactical human behavior. Int. J. Int. Syst. **23**(7), 822–847 (2008). doi:10.1002/int.20291

Haake, J.M., Hussein, T., Joop, B., Lukosch, S.G., Veiel, D., Ziegler, J.: Modeling and exploiting context for adaptive collaboration. Int. J. Coop. Inf. Syst. **19**(1&2), 71–120 (2010). doi:10.1142/S0218843010002115

Hackman, J.R.: The design of work teams. In: Lorsch, J.L. (ed.) Handbook of Organizational Behavior, pp. 315–342. Prentice Hall, Englewood Cliffs (1987)

Janeiro, J., Knoll, S.W., Lukosch, S.G., Kolfschoten, G.L., Brazier, F.M.T.: Designing collaboration support for dynamic environments. In: Proceedings of the International Conference on Group Decision and Negotiation 2012, Recife, Brazil (2012a), 20–24 May 2012

Janeiro, J., Lukosch, S.G., Brazier, F.M.T.: Elastic collaboration support: from workflow-based to emergent collaboration. In: Proceedings of the 17th ACM International Conference on Supporting Group Work, Sanibel Island, FL, USA (2012b), 27–31 October 2012

Janeiro, J., Lukosch, S.G., Radomski, S., Johanson, M., Mecella, M.: Supporting elastic collaboration: integration of collaboration components in dynamic contexts. In: Proceedings of the ACM SIGCHI Symposium on Engineering Interactive Computing Systems, London, UK, 24–27 June 2013

Janis, I.L.: Victims of Groupthink: A Psychological Study of Foreign Decisions and Fiascoes. Houghton-Mifflin, Boston (1982)

Karau, S.J., Williams, K.D.: Social loafing: a meta-analytic review and theoretical integration. J. Pers. Soc. Psychol. **65**(4), 681–706 (1993). doi:10.1037/0022-3514.65.4.681

Knoll, S.W., Janeiro, J., Lukosch, S.G., Kolfschoten, G.L.: A semantic model for adaptive collaboration support systems. In: Hussein, T., Paulheim, H., Lukosch, S.G., Ziegler, J., Calvary, G. (eds.) Semantic Models for Adaptive Interactive Systems, pp. 59–81. Springer, London (2013)

Milliken, F.J., Bartel, C.A., Kurtzberg, T.R.: Diversity and creativity in work groups: a dynamic perspective on the affective and cognitive processes that link diversity and performance. In: Paulus, P.B., Nijstad, B.A. (eds.) Group Creativity: Innovation through Collaboration, pp. 32–62. Oxford University Press, New York (2003)

Niederman, F., Briggs, R.O., de Vreede, G.J., Kolfschoten, G.L.: Extending the contextual and organizational elements of adaptive structuration theory in GSS research. J. Assoc. Inf. Syst. **9**(10), 633–652 (2008)

Nunamaker Jr., J.F., Dennis, A.R., Valacich, J.S., Vogel, D., George, J.F.: Electronic meeting systems to support group work. Commun. ACM **34**(7), 40–61 (1991). doi:10.1145/105783.105793

Nunamaker Jr., J.F., Reinig, B.A., Briggs, R.O.: Principles for effective virtual teamwork. Commun. ACM **52**(4), 113–117 (2009). doi:10.1145/1498765.1498797

Oliveira, F.F., Antunes, J.C.P., Guizzardi, R.S.S.: Towards a collaboration ontology. In: Proceedings of the 2nd Workshop on Ontologies and Metamodeling in Software and Data Engineering (Co-located with SBES/SBBD 2007), Pessoa, Brazil, 17 October 2007

Organization Ontology: The Organization Ontology Specification. http://www.w3.org/TR/vocab-org/ (2013). Accessed 03 Oct 2013

Pattberg, J., Fluegge, M.: Towards an ontology of collaboration patterns. In: Proceedings of the 5th International Workshop on Challenges in Collaborative Engineering, Cracow, Poland, 11–13 April 2007

Reiter, M., Houy, C., Fettke, P., Loos, P.: Context-sensitive collaboration in service processes through the integration of telecommunication technology and business process management. In: Proceedings of the 46th Hawaii International Conference on System Sciences, Wailea, Maui, HI USA, 07–10 January 2013

Sarin, S., McDermott, C.: The effect of team leader characteristics on learning, knowledge application, and performance of cross-functional new product development teams. Decision Sci. **34**(4), 707–739 (2003). doi:10.1111/j.1540–5414.2003.02350.x

Schilit, B., Theimer, M.: Dissemination active map information to mobile hosts. IEEE Network **8**(5), 22–32 (1994). doi:10.1109/65.313011

SmartVortex: The SMART VORTEX project. http://www.smartvortex.eu/ (2014). Accessed 01 May 2014

Tajfel, H.: Social identity and intergroup behaviour. Soc. Sci. Inform. **13**(2), 65–93 (1974). doi:10.1177/053901847401300204

Terveen, L.G.: An overview of human-computer collaboration. Knowl-Based. Syst. **8**(2–3), 67–81 (1995). doi:10.1016/0950-7051(95)98369-h

van der Aalst, W.M.P., ter Hofstede, A.H.M., Kiepuszewski, B., Barros, A.P.: Workflow patterns. Distrib. Parallel Dat. **14**(1), 5–51 (2003). doi:10.1023/A:1022883727209

Vieira, V., Tedesco, P., Salgado, A.C.: Towards an ontology for context representation in groupware. In: Fuks H., Lukosch S.G., Salgado A.C. (eds.) CRIWG 2005: Groupware: Design, Implementation, and Use. 11th International Workshop, Porto de Galinhas, Brazil, 25–29 September 2005. Lecture Notes in Computer Science (Information Systems and Applications, incl. Internet/Web, and HCI), vol. 3706, pp. 367–375. Springer, Heidelberg (2005)

Wang, G., Jiang, J., Shi, M.: A context model for collaborative environment. In: Proceedings of the 10th International Conference on Computer Supported Cooperative Work in Design, Nanjing, 3–5 May 2006

Westley, F., Waters, J.A.: group facilitation skills for managers. Manage. Learn. **19**(2), 134–143 (1988). doi:10.1177/135050768801900207

Wood, D.J., Gray, B.: Toward a comprehensive theory of collaboration. J. Appl. Behav. Sci. **27**(2), 139–162 (1991). doi:10.1177/0021886391272001

Chapter 22
The Role of Context and its Elements in Situation Assessment

Odd Erik Gundersen

Abstract This chapter presents an analysis of the concept of context in situation assessment. Situation assessment is the process that develops a situation awareness, which is the basis for deciding which action to perform in a given situation. The contributions of the research documented here include a knowledge level model of situation assessment, a context element ontology and an analysis of the role of context in situation assessment, which are based on models of situation awareness and context found in the literature. The knowledge level model includes a task decomposition, a task description, and a goal analysis. Finally, this view is illustrated in a short example.

22.1 Introduction

Situation awareness represents the degree to which someone understand a given situation. Although situation awareness has been termed *"ill-defined"* by Sarter and Woods (1991), lately, Endsley's view on situation awareness (Endsley 1995) has more or less been adopted by the research community (Breton and Rousseau 2003). Another concept that is ill defined is *context*. One of the reasons that a definition of context is hard to nail down is that *what context is changes with its context*. Thus, the concept of context is more easily analyzed in relation to something else.

The goal of the research presented here is to understand and describe the role of context in situation assessment, while the contributions are three-fold: (1) A knowledge level model of situation assessment in the form of a task decomposition, task description, and goal analysis. (2) An ontology of the context elements of situation assessment that is used to analyse the role of context in situation assessment. (3) A simple example that illustrate this view. This research is based on the work documented in Gundersen (2013).

O. E. Gundersen (✉)
Verdande Technology AS, Stiklestadveien 1, 7041 Trondheim, Norway
e-mail: odderik@verdandetechnology.com

Department of Computer and Information Science,
Norwegian University of Science and Technology (NTNU),
Sem Sælands vei 7-9, 7491 Trondheim, Norway

© Springer Science+Business Media New York 2014   343
P. Brézillon, A. J. Gonzalez (eds.), *Context in Computing*,
DOI 10.1007/978-1-4939-1887-4_22

The rest of this paper is structured as follows: In Sect. 22.2, we present related reseach in situation awareness, while related research in context is presented in Sect. 22.3. Some aspects of the concept situation is discussed in Sect. 22.4. Then, we model situation assessment in Sect. 22.5, and analyse the elements and roles of context in situation assessment in Sect. 22.6. An example is presented in Sect. 22.7, and finally, in Sect. 22.8, we conclude and provide some future work.

22.2 Situation Awareness

Several models of situation awareness exist, and Rousseau et al. (2004) distinguish between descriptive and prescriptive models. Descriptive models describe the cognitive processes related to situation awareness, while prescriptive models are used to simulate situation awareness. Salmon et al. (2008) did a systematic review of situation awareness models, and their focus was on the three most cited ones. Apart from Endsley's model, these are models proposed by Smith and Hancock (1995) and Bedny and Meister (1999). All three models are descriptive. Smith and Hancock take an ecological approach to defining situation awareness while Bedny and Meister use activity theory to describe situation awareness.

According to Smith and Hancock, situation awareness *is adaptive, externally guided consciousness*. They insist that the agent's behavior, which is guided by the situation awareness, is shaped by the agent's interaction with the environment. Thus, situation awareness can only be analysed in context of the agent's environment, but only given *a specified task and concrete performance criteria*. These observations provide insight into situation awareness. However, as their situation awareness framework can only be analysed in the context of the agent's environment, it does not provide good support in analysing situation awareness in general nor in specific domains.

Endsley's three level information processing model (Endsley 1995) has received most attention. She defines situation awareness as *"the perception of the elements in the environment within a volume of time and space, the comprehension of their meaning, and the projection of their status in the near future"*, (Endsley 1995 p. 36). The process of achieving this state of knowledge, situation assessment, is comprised of three sub-processes, called levels, which are illustrated in Fig. 22.1. Level 1 concerns perception of situation elements, while level 2 concerns comprehension of the current situation. Finally, when the situation elements are perceived and the situation is comprehended, one can project the future state of the elements constituting the situation. The main strength of the model is its intuitive description of situation awareness, as also is noted by Salmon et al. (2008), and the three layers that specify the main processes of situation assessment. Our model is based on Endsley's, and the situation assessment task tree has Endsley's three levels as child nodes, which are decomposed further.

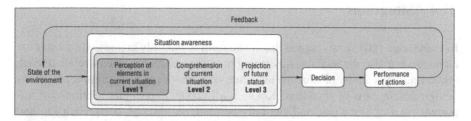

Fig. 22.1 The three levels of situation awareness according to Endsley. (Source: Endsley and Hoffman 2002)

22.3 Context

There is a distinction between the context of a situation element and the situation. The context of a situation element can be other situation elements, as pointed out by Manilla and Moen (1999), but the context of the situation itself is another matter. For example, a situation might exist as part of a simulation, a training exercise or a real-world scenario. Which one of these that applies is a highly important bit of information. This distinction is not made by Day and Abowd. They define context as *any information that can be used to characterize the situation of an entity [. . .]* (Abowd and Dey 1999). Given that a situation is made up of situation elements and relations between them, Day and Abowd's definition include all relations and situation elements except for the target entity as context information. This means that properties of the target entity is not context, such as the color of the shoes a patient is wearing in a diagnostic task where a patient is the target. The definition is too broad to help in structuring information.

Kofod-Petersen and Mikalsen (2005) extends the above definition of context to *"the set of suitable environmental states and settings concerning a user, which are relevant for a situation sensitive application in the process of adapting the services and information offered to the user"*. However, while being more specific, this definition restrict context to environmental states and settings, which again makes the color of the shoes not context information.

There is a distinction between the *role* and the *elements* of context in problem solving according to Öztürk and Aamodt (Öztürk and Aamodt 1997; Öztürk 1999). The context elements can belong to the generic context ontology or the domain knowledge. The generic context ontology distinguishes between the problem solver and the external situation, and it is defined from the point of view and emphasizes the active role of the problem solver. Hence, context can be divided into internal and external context, where internal relates to the problem solver and external relates to the external situation. They argue that the roles of context when solving a problem are to choose the most relevant solution and focus the problem solving process. The work enforces structure on context as it distinguishes between the roles and elements of context. Furthermore, it structures the elements in an ontology, which supports context analysis. Our research is based on Öztürk and Aamodt's view on context.

22.4 Situations

In Gundersen (2013), we argued that a situation is not only comprised of situation elements, but also the relations describing how the situation elements relate to each other. Endsley's theory of situation awareness does not explicitly consider relations being relevant parts of situations. Kokar et al. (2009) argues that relations are important parts of situations, and can only be analysed through comprehension and thus at the second level of Endsley's situation awareness theory. The only situation elements that are considered are physical and palpable elements existing in the real-world that can be perceived. Hence, immaterial situation elements such as goals, dreams and hopes that can be extremely important in order to understand a situation are not considered at all. This excludes what Kolodner called intentional situations (Kolodner 1993). Our analysis of situations include immaterial situation elements, and we discussed events and different definitions of these in detail. We consider events as situation elements in themselves, although they can be interpreted in many ways. For example Baclawski et al. (2002), treats events as a type of relations, but we have found it fruitful to consider events as situation elements. See our work on case-based reasoning for decision support for further details on the advantages this position provides (Gundersen et al. 2013; Gundersen and Sørmo 2013).

Our previous treatment of situations did not discuss in detail the aspect of time and space. Situation is defined quite loosely in Wikipedia (2014) as *"a concept relating to a position (location) or a set of circumstances."* A more meaningful definition is provided by Merriam Webster's Dictionary (2014), which states that a situation is *"all of the facts, conditions, and events that affect someone or something at a particular time and in a particular place."* In this context, "in a particular place" does not mean a point in a volume of space. It can mean a room, a building, the city of London, the planet Earth or this part of the known universe, so it is not necessarily a point in space, but a part of a volume of space. "A particular time" can clearly be interpreted as a point in time, but when talking about a situation one can mean a period of time, such as the Early Middle Ages. So, the expression does not have to mean a point in time in the same way as a particular place does not mean a point in a volume of space.

As part of the definition of the first level of situation awareness, Endsley touches on upon the definition of situation that is used implicitly in her work. The first level of situation awareness is "the perception of the elements in the environment within a volume of time and space," so the elements relevant for the situation is confined in a volume of time and space. Another definition of situation is the one proposed by McCarthy and Hayes (1969), which is that a situation is *"the complete state of the universe at an instant of time"*. This definition is not just only highly impractical to reason with, as open systems are not fixed and possibly not completely available, which is noted by Baclawski et al. (2002), but it defies the commonly acknowledged definition which confines a situation to a part of the universe. Situation semantics attempts to narrow down the definition of a situation to "parts of the world, clearly recognized (although not precisely individuated) in common sense and human language." This is a quotation from Devlin (2006), which again quotes Barwise (Barwise and Perry 1980).

Consider a situation in which something explodes. This situation does not change at every time step, although the explosion expands continuously; it is more like the situation stretches out. A situation description enforces a certain level of detail, and this level of detail typically is held constant during the description of a situation. The situation is also relevant only to parts of the world around the explosion. The part of the world that the explosion is relevant for can be smaller or bigger based on the energy released by the explosion.

Our definition of a situation is focused on the elements forming the situation, *the situation elements*, and the relations between them. Hence, a situation can be described by the situation elements and relations forming the situation at any given point in time. A situation can stay the same over a period of time, and its volume is defined indirectly by the situation elements. Hence, one can say that a situation is defined by the situation elements and the relations between them contained within a volume of time and space. The context of a situation is intrinsic to observers and their situation assessment and will differ for each. The context include properties of the observer of the situation, the observer's environment, some elements and properties of the situation as well as the environment of the situation.

22.5 Situation Assessment

In order to get a better understanding of the role of context in situation assessment, the process of situation assessment itself has to be understood better. Hence, we have done a knowledge level analysis of situation assessment. First, the results of this knowledge level analysis, which are a task tree decomposition, a goal analysis and a detailed task description, are presented. Then, further detail is provided through a formal description of situation assessment.

22.5.1 Situation Assessment at the Knowledge Level

In order to enable a detailed discussion of what situation assessment constitutes, a model of situation assessment has been developed at the knowledge level (Newell 1982). Parts of this model is presented here and includes goals, a task model and task descriptions. Uschold (1998) notes that the purposes of knowledge models fall into two categories. The purpose of this model is first and foremost to (1) *enhance human understanding and communication* for enabling a discussion, which hopefully will lead to (2) *system engineering benefits* during development of decision support systems.

The knowledge model combines Endsley's three level information processing model with the above definition of situation, and it is described from the view of

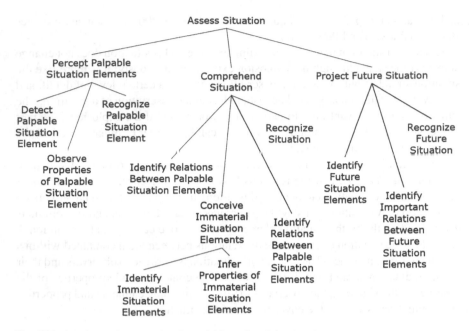

Fig. 22.2 A task tree decomposing the task hierarchy of the situation assessment process

an observer. Thus, as illustrated in Fig. 22.2, situation assessment is decomposed into tasks mirroring the three levels of situation awareness. Their subtasks again specify which components of a situation can be realized in each of the three levels. A detailed description of all the subtasks is beyond the scope of this paper, and we restrict our description to *Assess situation, Perceive Palpable Situation Elements, Comprehend Situation* and *Project Future Situations*. A summary of this description is provided in Table 22.1. The analysis does not consider memory, so the result is a stateless information processing model. Memory does clearly play a role in situation assessment. Although a complete analysis should consider memory, not considering it simplifies the situation assessment analysis while providing new insights. Hence, it is a sensible first step.

Our interpretation of the task *situation assessment* is that it is to *become aware of the situation and its probable future outcomes*, which we interpret as its goal. The task requires input external to the observer, which is not restricted to being human, so the input data can come from sensors or senses. A subset of the external data is the situation context, but we think of it as an essential part of situation assessment so we emphasize it, and thus the input is external data and the situation-related context. The situation is dynamic while the context is static for the situation. The situation can be described in many different contexts, so the context will influence a decision even though two situations are completely similar. For example, given a specific situation, a more risky decision can be made if the context is a training simulation compared to if it is a real-world scenario. In a training context, an action can be made that will

Table 22.1 A summary of the tasks *Assess situation*, *Perceive Palpable Situation Elements*, *Comprehend Situation* and *Project Future Situations* from Fig. 22.2

	Level 0: Assess situation
Goal	Become aware of the current situation and its probable future outcomes
Input	External data, situation-related context
Output	Subjective situation description, subjective future situation descriptions containing the operations leading to the future situations, subjective situation context
Description	Signals external to the observer that include the situation context are interpreted by the observer to develop an internal description of the current situation, the evolution into possible futures and the situation context

	Level 1: Perceive palpable situation elements
Goal	Identify all relevant palpable situation elements and their properties
Input	External data, situation-related context
Output	Subjective descriptions of palpable situation elements, subjective situation context
Description	Detect and describe palpable situation elements and their properties from the external data

	Level 2: Comprehend situation
Goal	Map out relations between situation elements and identify immaterial situation elements that influence the situation
Input	External data, subjective decriptions of palpable situation elements, subjective situation context
Output	Subjective situation description
Description	Make a complete situation description by analysing the palpable situation elements and the external data and identify immaterial situation elements and infer the relationships between all the situation elements

	Level 3: Project future situations
Goal	Identify the most probable and relevant futures that can be evolved from the current situation
Input	Subjective situation description, subjective situation context
Output	Subjective future situation descriptions containing the operations leading to the future situations
Description	Infer the possible future situations evolving from the current situation that are relevant for understanding of the current situation

increase the learning experience without considering the consequence. Furthermore, a situation will be assessed differently by two different observers, as they have different context, such as different experiences and goals.

As is shown in Endsley's three level information model, see Fig. 22.1, the output of situation assessment is the input for the decision process. Thus, the product of situation assessment is used for making a decision about what to do in a situation, so it is not a decision nor an action, but information that can be used to make a decision about an action. An important property of this output is that it has to be detailed enough to inform the decision making. This rules out an output of the situation assessment to be of the type *"bad situation"* or *"good situation,"* as this will not provide enough information to decide which action to select in order to get out off or maintain status quo. So, situation assessment requires an observer to build an internal representation of the current external situation. Furthermore, it requires the observer to project the future state of the current situation. The current situation can lead, not only to one, but many possible future situations or futures. The futures can be described by situation elements and relations that have evolved from the current situation. A future state, described by a set of situation elements and relations, together with the operations that evolved the current situation to that specific future is a future description. Also, the observer is required to recognize the context of the situation. Given all this information, a decision about which action to perform can be made.

The subtasks of *situation assessment* are the three levels of Endelsy's situation awareness model. The first level of situation awareness is about perception, which is internalizing the external world through signals interpreted by the senses. Hence, the goal of the task *perceive palpable situation elements* is to identify all relevant palpable situation elements as well as their properties from the external data. The output of this task is a description of the identified situation elements. However, not all situation elements can be perceived. Only elements that have observable representations in the physical world can be, which exclude dreams and intentions that have not been communicated. Thus, events, physical objects and communicated information can be perceived in the first level. Immaterial objects, such as dreams and intentions can only be identified through comprehending the situation and the relationships between palpable situation elements. Therefore, the goal of the task *comprehend situation* is to map out relations between situation elements and identify immaterial situation elements that influence the situation. This is done through analysing the external data as well as the palpable situation elements that have been identified. The output of comprehend situation is the observer's description of the current situation, which is the set of situation elements and relations that the observer believes to constitute the current situation, which of course can be wrong. The third level of situation awareness is projecting the future state of the situation, and thus the goal of the task *project future situations* is to identify the most probable and relevant futures that can be evolved from the current situation. By forwarding the current situation or making what-if scenarios, the future can be projected, which can result in a set of futures and the operations leading to these futures. The futures and the operations leading to them are the output of this task. All the subtasks of situation assessment will benefit from knowing the situation-related context, as this information will inform the search for situation elements, relations and immaterial situation elements.

22.5.2 Situation Assessment: A Formal Treatment

A situation, S_i, at a given point in time, i, is the set of situation elements, E_i, and the relations between them, R_i, that exist at that time (note that the volume of the situation is defined by the situation elements):

$$S_i = \{E_i, R_i\} \tag{22.1}$$

Situation elements can be both palpable, p, and immaterial, a. Palpable situation elements are elements that exist in the real-world and can be observed directly by an observer, such as physical situation elements and events. Hence, the set of all situation elements, E, is defined as follows:

$$E = \{p, a\} \tag{22.2}$$

The perceived and comprehended situation, S_i^o, which is the observer's, o, overview of the actual situation, S_i, is comprised of a set of situation elements, E_i^o, and relations, R_i^o, that might and might not overlap with the actual situation:

$$S_i^o = \{E_i^o, R_i^o\}, \tag{22.3}$$

$$E_i^o = \{I_i + N_{E,i}\}, \tag{22.4}$$

$$R_i^o = \{J_i + N_{R,i}\}, \tag{22.5}$$

where $I_i \subset E_i$ and $J_i \subset R_i$. Thus, I_i and J_i are correct observations of situation elements and relations, respectively, while $N_{E,i}$ and $N_{R,i}$ are errors.

D_i is the external data the observer receives, i.e. visual images, sounds or data in the computational sense. The tasks *perceive palpable situation elements*, *comprehend situation* and *project future situation* can be represented as functions, *Perceive*, *Comprehend* and *Project*, respectively:

$$Perceive : D_i, C_i \rightarrow p_i^o, C_i^o \tag{22.6}$$

$$Comprehend : D_i, p_i^o, C_i^o \rightarrow S_i^o, \tag{22.7}$$

$$Project : S_i^o, C_i^o \rightarrow F_i^o, \tag{22.8}$$

where p_i^o is the set of palpable situation elements perceived by the observer, C_i^o is the observer's understanding of the actual situation context, C_i, and F_i^o is a set of descriptions of possible futures deemed relevant by the observer.

$$F_i^o = \{F_{1,i+\Delta t_1}^o, F_{2,i+\Delta t_2}^o, \ldots, F_{n,i+\Delta t_n}^o\}, \tag{22.9}$$

where the range of Δt is $[1, \infty]$.

The set of descriptions of possible futures, as projected by the observer, might and might not overlap with the actual set of descriptions of possible futures, F_i, at a given point in time, i:

$$F_i = \{F_{1,i+\Delta t_1}, F_{2,i+\Delta t_2}, \ldots, F_{n,i+\Delta t_m}\} \tag{22.10}$$

A future description, such as for example $F_{1,i+\Delta t_1}$, is a future situation, comprised of situation elements and relations that are evolved from the current situation S_i, and the set of operations, $O_{1,i+\Delta t_1}$ that evolved the current situation to the future situation, such that $F_{1\,i+\Delta t_1} = \{E_{1,i+\Delta t_1}, R_{1,i+\Delta t_1}, O_{1,i+\Delta t_1}\}$.

Then, the task *assess situation* can be represented as a function as follows:

$$Assess : D_i, C_i \rightarrow S_i^o, F_i^o, C_i^o \tag{22.11}$$

The situation awareness, A_i^o, at a given time, t, that an observer, o, has obtained of the situation, S_i, can be defined as follows:

$$A_i^o = \{S_i^o, F_i^o, C_i^o\}, \tag{22.12}$$

The degree of awareness that an observer has of a situation, S_i is a metric for measuring the similarity between A_i^o and $A_i = \{S_i, F_i, C_i\}$, the actual situation, future and context:

$$AwarenessDegree : similiarity(A_i, A_i^o) \tag{22.13}$$

Hence, the observer's degree of situation awareness is said to be complete if the following three conditions hold:

1. $S_i^o \cap S_i = S_i^o = S_i$,
2. $F_i^o \cap F_i = F_i^o = F_i$,
3. $C^o \cap C = C^o = C$,

and non-existent if:

$$S_i^o \cap S_i = F_i^o \cap F_i = C^o \cap C = \emptyset \tag{22.14}$$

In all other cases, the degree of situation awareness is said to be incomplete.

22.6   Context in Situation Assessment

A knowledge level model of context for situation assessment will bring clarity to how context influences situation assessment. Here, we present a knowledge level context ontology for situation assessment (*situation assessment context ontology*), which is founded on the knowledge level context ontology (Öztürk and Aamodt 1997; Öztürk 1999) (*context ontology*). Our ontology clearly specifies the elements of context that are related to situation assessment, which are based on the definitions of situations and situation assessment presented above. The presented ontology is used as a basis for a discussion on the role of context in situation assessment. Finally, both the elements and the role of context in situation assessment are illustrated in a short example.

22.6.1   A Situation Assessment Context Ontology

The context ontology is defined from the point of view of the problem solver. Thus, internal context is internal to the problem solver and the external context is external to the problem solver. The external context is related to the target of the problem solving process and the environment, where the environment is the environment of both the target and the problem solver. This ontology applies for context in general. However, by following the same train of thoughts, a similar ontology specialized for situation assessment can be developed.

Our attempt at capturing an ontology for situation assessment is defined from the view of the observer, and the target is the situation. The situation assessment context ontology is detailed further than the context ontology by specifying which elements of a situation assessment process can be regarded as context elements. It can be more detailed, as it is specific for context elements of situation assesment and not for context in general. Similar to the context ontology, all context elements can further be classified as *interactive* or *independent*. However, the ontology does not capture this aspect. The situation assessment context ontology emphasize the four main components of a situation assessment process, which are the observer, the environment of the observer, the situation and its environment, and the ontology indicates the specific elements of these components that can provide context. It is an ontology of context elements. However, the term "context element" is not used in the ontology, except at the top level, because of readability of the figure. So, except for the leaf nodes in the ontology, all nodes should be read as if the term "context element" is appended.

As can be seen in Fig. 22.3, the top component is *situation assessment context elements*, which is divided into context related to the observer and to the observed situation, *observer-related* and *situation-related* respectively. The observer has internal and external context, where the *internal observer* is related to the internal state of the observer, and the *external observer* is related to the physical properties of the observer and the environment of the observer. Furthermore, the external observer context is comprised of the *observer* and the *observer environment*. The *situation-related* distinguishes between the *situation* and the *situation environment*. Situation can be *situation elements*, *relations between situation elements* and *properties* of these. Finally, the *situation environment* contains *elements*, relations between them, *relations between elements* and the properties describing them, *properties of situation elements and relations*.

The environment of the observer is not necessarily the same as the environment of the situation, which is emphasized by the ontology. Consider the situation in which a car driver observe a situation outside the car. Then the car driver's environment is the inside of the car, maybe with loud music, while the observed situation's environment is the street with the surrounding buildings where no music can be heard. If the car driver leaves the car to walk in the street, then the two environments suddenly overlap.

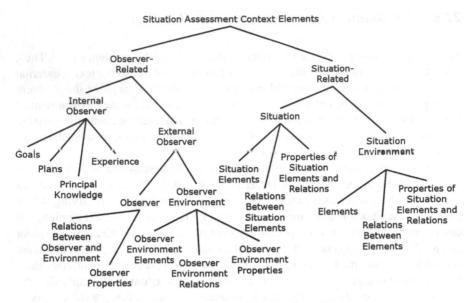

Fig. 22.3 An ontology that categorize the context elements of situation assessment

22.6.2   The Role of Context in Situation Assessment

Öztürk distinguishes between the context elements and the role of context (Öztürk and Aamodt 1997; Öztürk 1999). The analysis of context is performed in relation to problem solving, and two roles are identified: (1) Focus and (2) relevance. Context focuses the problem solving process so that it becomes more efficient and ensures the relevance of the solution. In situation assessment, context plays similar roles for the observer.

As problem solving, situation assessment is a process, which can be both slow and fast. A proper understanding of the situation context will increase the efficiency of the situation assessment. Typically, an expert with long experience will assess a situation faster than a novice. However, the efficiency of an expert can be reduced, if the goal of the expert is not specific to the assessment, but related to something else. Thus, the internal observer-related context elements affect the efficiency of the situation assessment. Also external observer related context elements can reduce the efficiency, which loud music in the car is an example of. Correspondingly, situation-related context elements can affect the efficiency. An act of violence against someone is generally a violation of the law. However, the penalty of the same act will increase if the target of the violence is a police officer. Thus, a property of a situation context element can influence the situation assessment. For a drilling engineer that monitors the drilling process remotely by reading graphs of real-time measurements, the situation can be assessed more efficiently if the geology is known. The geology can be considered a property of an element of the situation environment.

The outcome of the situation assessment process was specified in Sect. 22.5.2 as the situation awareness, which included the situation context. A false conception of the situation context can lead to a situation description that includes too many or too few situation elements and relations, which will make both the situation description and the possible futures less accurate or maybe even completely wrong. Finding a pet when assessing the container contents becomes easier when you know that you are looking for a stick animal. Here, stick animal is a property (the class) of the situation element pet, and the situation description depends on the perception of the situation element. Likewise, a false conception of the situation context can also lead to less relevant projected futures. For example, the context information that person A is the national champion in Karate might change the future projections made by person B considering person A.

22.7   Driving Past the School of Mischief

The following situation has to be assessed by a car driver, the observer, o, driving a car on a street: A child stands on the sidewalk in front of a building, and a paper bag is lying in the middle of the road. The driver, o, has to make a decision about whether to drive over the paper bag or not. Note: Time is omitted in this example. The situation elements, E, include the child and the paper bag, while the building is part of the situation environment:

$$E^o = \{child, building, paperbag\} \tag{22.15}$$

The driver infers that the paper bag might belong to the child, which is a relation between the situation elements:

$$R^o = \{child\_stands\_on\_the\_sidewalk, child\_owns\_the\_paper\_bag\} \tag{22.16}$$

So, the driver's situation description, S^o, is as follows: $S^o = \{E^o, R^o\}$. Based on this situation description, the driver projects two futures. One in which the child runs into the street to pick up the paper bag, F_1 and another where the child stands still on the sidewalk, F_2. Thus, $F^o = \{F_1, F_2\}$. The context is empty except for the building, $C^o = \{building\}$. Hence, the situation awareness is:

$$A^o = \{S^o, F^o, C^o\} \tag{22.17}$$

In this situation, the driver might choose to slow down to see whether the child runs into the street, but drive over the paper bag if not.

In a slightly different situation where the driver has some context information the decision might be another one. If the driver knows the building as the *School of Mischief* and recognizes the child as bob, the school's star pupil, the situation context can influence the assessment. Now, the context contains one property describing the building and another property describing a situation element:

$$C^{o,1} = \{building : \{school\_of\_mischief\}, child : \{bob, infamous\_pupil\}\} \tag{22.18}$$

The following relations might be inferred:

$$R^{o,1} = \{bob\_owns\_the\_paper\_bag, paperbag\_contains\_a\_large\_stone\}, \quad (22.19)$$

and thus, $S^o = \{E^o, R^{o,1}\}$. The set of futures might now include bob standing still on the sidewalk to watch the driver ruin his car when he drives over the big stone concealed in the paper bag, F_3. So, $F^{o,1} = \{F_1, F_2, F_3\}$. The alternative situation awareness then is:

$$\Lambda^{o,1} = \{S^o, F^{o,1}, C^{o,1}\}, \quad (22.20)$$

which might make the driver to decide not to overrun the paper bag.

22.8 Conclusion and Future Work

In this paper, a knowledge level model of situation assessment in the form of a task decomposition, task description, and goal analysis is presented and given a more formal treatment. An ontology of the context elements of situation assessment is presented and is used to analyse the role of context in situation assessment. Finally, a simple example that illustrates how context influences the situation assessment is presented.

In our future work, we will detail the knowledge level model further with detailed descriptions of all subtasks in the task decomposition tree and provide the formal description of these tasks. The model will be the foundation of a conceptual reference architecture for decision support systems that assess situations in real-time based on streaming data.

References

Abowd, G.D., Dey, A.K.: Towards a better understanding of context and context-awareness. In: H.W. Gellersen (ed.) Handheld and Ubiquitous Computing, Lecture Notes in Computer Science, vol. 1707, pp. 304–307. Springer, Berlin (1999)

Baclawski, K., Kokar, M., Letkowski, J., Matheus, C., Malczewski, M.: Formalization of situation awareness. In: Proceedings of the Eleventh OOPSLA Workshop on Behavioral Semantics, pp. 1–15 (2002)

Barwise, J., Perry, J.: The situation underground. Stanford Working Papers in Semantics, vol. 1, pp. 1–55 (1980)

Bedny, G., Meister, D.: Theory of activity and situation awareness. Int. J. Cogn. Ergon. 3(1), 63–72 (1999)

Breton, R., Rousseau, R.: Situational awareness: A review of the concept and its measurement. Technical Report (2003)

Devlin, K.: Situation theory and situation semantics. Handbook of the History of Logic, vol. 7, pp. 601–664 (2006)

Endsley, M.R.: Toward a theory of situation awareness in dynamic systems. Hum. Factors 37(33), 32–64 (1995)

Endsley, M.R., Hoffman, R.R.: The Sacagawea principle. IEEE Intell. Syst. **17**(6), 80–85 (2002)

Gundersen, O.E.: Situational awareness in context. In: Brézillon, P., Blackburn, P., Dapoigny, R. (eds.) CONTEXT. Lecture Notes in Computer Science, vol. 8175, pp. 274–287. Springer, Berlin (2013)

Gundersen, O.E., Sørmo, F.: An architecture for multi-dimensional temporal abstraction supporting decision making in oil-well drilling. In: Hatzilygeroudis, I., Palade, V. (eds.) Combinations of Intelligent Methods and Applications, Smart Innovation, Systems and Technologies, vol. 23, pp. 21–40. Springer, Berlin (2013)

Gundersen, O.E., Sørmo, F., Aamodt, A., Skalle, P.: A real-time decision support system for high cost oil-well drilling operations. AI Mag. **34**(1), 21–32 (2013)

Kofod-Petersen, A., Mikalsen, M.: Context: Representation and reasoning. Representing and reasoning about context in a mobile environment. Rev. Intell. Artif. **19**(3), 479–498 (2005)

Kokar, M.M., Matheus, C.J., Baclawski, K.: Ontology-based situation awareness. Inf. Fusion **10**(1), 83–98 (2009)

Kolodner, J.L.: Case-based reasoning. Morgan Kaufmann Series in Representation and Reasoning Series. Morgan Kaufmann, San Francisco (1993)

Mannila, H., Moen, P.: Similarity between event types in sequences. In: Mohania, M., Tjoa, A. (eds.) Data Warehousing and Knowledge Discovery, Lecture Notes in Computer Science, vol. 1676, pp. 271–280. Springer, Berlin (1999)

McCarthy, J., Hayes, P.J.: Some philosophical problems from the standpoint of artificial intelligence. In: Meltzer, B., Michie, D. (eds.) Machine Intelligence 4, pp. 463–502. Edinburgh University Press, Edinburgh United Kingdom (1969) (reprinted in McC90)

Merriam Webster's Dictionary. http://www.merriam-webster.com. Accessed 17 Jan 2014 (2014)

Newell, A.: The knowledge level. Artif. Intell. **18**(1), 87–127 (1982)

Öztürk, P.: Towards a knowledge-level model of context and context use in diagnostic problems. Appl. Intell. **10**(2–3), 123–137 (1999)

Öztürk, P., Aamodt, A.: Towards a model of context for case-based diagnostic problem solving. In: Proceedings of the interdisciplinary conference on modeling and using context (CONTEXT-97), pp. 198–208 (1997)

Rousseau, R., Tremblay, S., Breton, R.: Defining and modelling situation awareness: a critical review. In: Banbury, S., Tremblay, S. (eds.) A Cognitive Approach to Situation Awareness: Theory and Application, pp. 3–21. Ashgate Surrey (2004)

Salmon, P.M., Stanton, N.A., Walker, G.H., Baber, C., Jenkins, D.P., McMaster, R., Young, M.S.: What really is going on? Review of situation awareness models for individuals and teams. Theor. Issues Ergon. Sci. **9**(4), 297–323 (2008)

Sarter, N., Woods, D.: Situation awareness: A critical but ill-defined phenomenon. Int. J. Aviat. Psychol. **1**, 45–57 (1991)

Smith, K., Hancock, P.: Situation awareness is adaptive, externally directed consciousness. Hum. Factors **37**(1), 137–148 (1995)

Uschold, M.: Knowledge level modelling: Concepts and terminology. Knowl. Eng. Rev. **13**(3), 5–29 (1998)

Wikipedia—The Free Encyclopedia. http://www.wikipedia.org. Accessed 17 Jan 2014 (2014)

Chapter 23
Context and Community Awareness in Support of User Intent Prediction

Nikos Kalatzis, Ioanna Roussaki, Nicolas Liampotis, Pavlos Kosmides,
Ioannis Papaioannou and Miltiades Anagnostou

Abstract Proactive behaviour of pervasive computing systems cannot be realised without the establishment of suitable and reliable user intent prediction facilities. Most of the existing approaches focus on an individual end-user's history of interactions and context in order to estimate future user behaviour. Recent trends in pervasive systems allow users to form communities with other individuals that share similar profiles, habits, and behaviours. Pervasive Communities set new challenges and opportunities regarding proactivity and context management. This chapter presents a context aware user intent learning and prediction framework that is able to exploit the knowledge available at the community level. Community knowledge, if appropriately managed, can significantly improve proactivity behaviour of individual users' systems.

23.1 Introduction

Context awareness, combined with learning and inference mechanisms, contributes greatly to establishing the proactive behaviour of pervasive systems, thus minimising the necessary human-machine interactions and providing an improved user experience. Various research outcomes indicate that repeated patterns can be usually

I. Roussaki (✉) · N. Kalatzis · N. Liampotis · P. Kosmides · I. Papaioannou · M. Anagnostou
National Technical University of Athens, Athens, Greece
e-mail: ioanna.roussaki@cn.ntua.gr

N. Kalatzis
e-mail: nikosk@cn.ntua.gr

N. Liampotis
e-mail: nicolas.liampotis@cn.ntua.gr

P. Kosmides
e-mail: pkosmidis@cn.ntua.gr

I. Papaioannou
e-mail: jpapai@cn.ntua.gr

M. Anagnostou
e-mail: miltos@cn.ntua.gr

© Springer Science+Business Media New York 2014   359
P. Brézillon, A. J. Gonzalez (eds.), *Context in Computing*,
DOI 10.1007/978-1-4939-1887-4_23

detected in human behaviour (Magnusson 2004). People follow their own routines of actions to perform everyday tasks. Modelling, recording and applying learning algorithms on datasets representing user interaction histories along with the corresponding context information can lead to the discovery of user behaviour models.

Most current pervasive computing systems have been designed mainly to address the requirements of individual users. This approach, however, does not consider the need of humans to communicate and socialise with others. To this end, the notion of pervasive communities (Doolin et al. 2012) is introduced that aims to bring together pervasive computing systems and social media, in order to support various interactions among users, communities, resources and smart environments. This notion is modelled based on the Cooperating Smart Space (CSS) and the Community Interaction Space (CIS) paradigms that have been introduced (Doolin et al. 2012). Each individual user is represented by a CSS that may consist of several nodes (devices). Each CIS on the other hand corresponds to exactly one pervasive community and may contain multiple CSSs. Individual users (CSSs) may be part of various communities (CISs) simultaneously. CSSs and CISs aim to support the formation of dynamic physical or virtual pervasive communities of users that demonstrate commonalities for a non-trivial period. The formation of communities can be based on various criteria, which are context-related in most cases (e.g. location, interests, preferences, beliefs, ideas, goals, experiences, etc.) Thus efficient context representation and management on a user and community level is one of the most important features of CSSs/CISs in properly adapting the services provided to users, but also in orchestrating the pervasive communities (Roussaki et al. 2012).

In order to support the proactivity and personalisation-related facilities of pervasive communities, a suitable user intent model is necessary. Thus, the Context Aware User Intent (CAUI) data model has been introduced to capture the common behaviour patterns that may exist for a single user or for a community of users. The CAUI data model primarily describes the actions that a user performs and the possible sequences across those actions along with the accompanied context.

Currently, predicting the future behaviour of humans in pervasive systems has been limited to individual user level. Very few research initiatives have dealt with applying such techniques to communities of end-users in order to extract collective behaviour models regarding interactions with pervasive computing services. This introduces several research challenges, as it needs to take into account social aspects, user similarities and more personal goals, thus having the potential to support both communities and individuals in multiple ways. Knowing the typical behaviour of a community member allows new members to benefit from the existing community's experience. The community behaviour model can be used as an intermediate measure for the time period in which more accurate data are gathered and until a user behaviour model has been generated. Therefore, long learning periods are avoided and predictions are feasible even in situations that the user has not been in the past. On the other hand, serious shortcomings are arising as it is not always safe to predict user behaviour based on community knowledge. It is necessary to develop decision mechanisms that indicate whether community originated knowledge is useful.

This chapter researches the issue of community and context awareness in sup-port of user intent prediction for users interacting in pervasive computing environments. More specifically, the chapter is structured as follows. Initially, a state of the art review is presented. Then, an illustrative use-case scenario is described and the most important user and technical requirements are extracted. The next section elaborates on user and context modelling and the context-based user/community intent learning and prediction mechanisms that have been established are presented. The evaluation of the proposed mechanisms is presented in the next section and finally, the chapter's conclusions are drawn and the respective future plans are discussed.

23.2 Related Work

Various successful paradigms exist where community knowledge is utilised in support of the individual. Authors in Thakor et al. (2004) examined the interaction of users with simple software systems (e.g. web browsers) and concluded that user characteristics affect the way of interaction. Thus, users demonstrating profile similarities tend to interact in a similar manner for achieving certain tasks allowing the proactive adaptation of services according to user characteristics. Collaborative recommender systems, known as Collaborative Filtering (CF) (Adomavicius and Tuzhiin 2005), are another successful paradigm of community knowledge extraction and exploitation. These systems estimate users' unknown ratings over items based on known ratings of similar users.

Pervasive computing systems understand and describe user intent as the tool employed to assist a user to perform a certain task or achieve a specific goal (Sousa et al. 2006). Several areas of pervasive computing, where user intent has been presented include but are not limited to Smart Home environments (such as MavHome; Gopalratnam and Cook 2007 and Aware Home; Abowd et al. 2002), elderly assistive living (Ni et al. 2011), smart applications (Garlan et al. 2002) etc. To this purpose, user intent is subject to advanced prediction methods, as on deciding on the "next step(s)" of a user based on his/her preferences and the surrounding context information, in an effort to maximise the performance of a system and the overall user experience.

There have been some research efforts that utilise multiple users' interaction histories in support of individual user. Intention prediction of user interactions with information systems is the purpose of the research work presented in (Antwarg et al. 2012). Several personal static profile attributes, like user's age, gender, and other demographic data are incorporated in the model, as the user intent accuracy is highly affected by his/her preferences. As the authors indicate, a user's attributes and context (such as age or the operating system) indicate which sequence of actions the user will eventually perform. The authors model the unique characteristics of the end user in relation to the sequence of user actions with the information systems in order to provide accurate predictions. The mechanism employed is based on hidden Markov models (HMM) on the sequence of observations of the actions that the end-user does, as the sequence of actions is not always observable. The model ends up with attribute-driven HMM trees for intention prediction, while the authors are planning to overcome the limitation of their algorithm with regards to the multitasking capabilities of most concurrent devices and applications. Another user intent prediction approach that resembles common sense reasoning is presented in the LifeNet project (Singh and Williams 2003). This large scale system collected common sense actions/situations from human users, represented the knowledge gathered as a graphical model, allowing the execution of user intent predictions for the short future and only for statistical methods. For example if a user declares she is thirsty then she should possibly seek something to drink. Thus, depending on the user's location, the system can predict the user intent and propose the most convenient action. Similarly, another large dataset has been presented in Eagle et al. (2008), where physical proximity and emotions were combined with 3,30,000 hours of continuously recorded mobile phone data on the actions of real users, self-reports and plain logs. These data along with the recorded behaviour of the user can be employed as pattern for user intent prediction, although much work has to be done in order to be easily maintainable and usable from real applications. In Tang and Liu (2009) the authors collect data to allow for online behaviour prediction of users in social media. The "training" dataset is the information provided by other actors with similar characteristics and preferences, along with affiliations of these sample actors with the subject users. The k-means variant algorithm is employed to handle scalability issues, as the social network is a connected graph with areas of various densities with regards to affiliations of users. The approach is promising but further improvements should be performed in order to provide reliable and rapid user intent predictions.

23.3 Scenario and Requirements

In this chapter a use case scenario is presented based on which specific architecture requirements will be extracted regarding the user behaviour modelling and system's proactivity functionality.

23.3.1 Scenario

Scene 1 The main actor of the scenario, Tom, is living in a "smart home" environment and interacts with various intelligent devices, services, sensors, actuators etc. Tom is currently working on a desktop PC and is about to leave home. He sets the

PC in sleep mode, turns off the radio, turns off room lights and is heading out of the house.

Scene 2   As he approaches his car, he unlocks the door, enters the driver seat, and starts the engine, the navigator, and the radio.

Scene 3   Tom aims to drive at **his** workplace but the navigation system notifies him that a significant number of other drivers with similar profiles (similar origin-destination, similar vehicle type, driving profiles) that are currently in the same area are following an alternative route than the usual. Tom is checking social media messages posted by people in the area and he finds out that the last two days construction works are causing delays. Tom agrees to follow a set of actions followed by other users including the alternate route selection, driving related actions regarding route parts that demand special attention, etc.

Scene 4   Tom makes a stop at the gas station, alarm lights are turned on and mutes the car radio

Scene 5   When he arrives at work, he turns off all car systems following the usual sequence of actions.

Scene 6   During weekends he usually takes the bus in order to visit a nearby park. While he is at the bus station he checks the time table, purchases an electronic ticket for the short trip and validates it upon entering the bus via his smart phone.

The described interactions, along with the respective context data, are recorded on a personal history log which is maintained on the user's CSS. The Proactivity component provided by the CSS platform exploits recorded data in order to discover Tom's interaction model and provide services with dynamic behaviour features. According to the frequency of occurrences for each action or group of actions, respective probabilities are calculated and the prevailing patterns are included in the interaction model. A graphical representation that reflects the actions described in the scenario is presented in Fig. 23.1. Six groups of actions have been illustrated, each consisting of a task, while user friendly names have been assigned. Task formation is based on context criteria (e.g. time, location) and sequence of actions frequency of occurrence.

It is obvious that certain actions described in the scenario are context depended while others are not. As it is illustrated in Fig. 23.2 the probability of occurrence for some actions contained in the task labelled as "Leaving home", in the first scenario scene, is differentiating according to current context, such as human presence. In case another person is still in the room, the transition probabilities to action labelled as "Turn off lights" are zero.

Scenario scenes 2 and 5 describe driving related sequences of actions that can be similar over a wide spectrum of drivers and context. Starting or stopping a car includes a set of actions that are more or less the same regardless of the context. On the other hand, in scene 6, the task is mainly context based but does not depend on the sequence of previously performed user actions or tasks. Whenever the user stands in a bus station it is highly probable that he will check the bus time table and purchase a bus ticket.

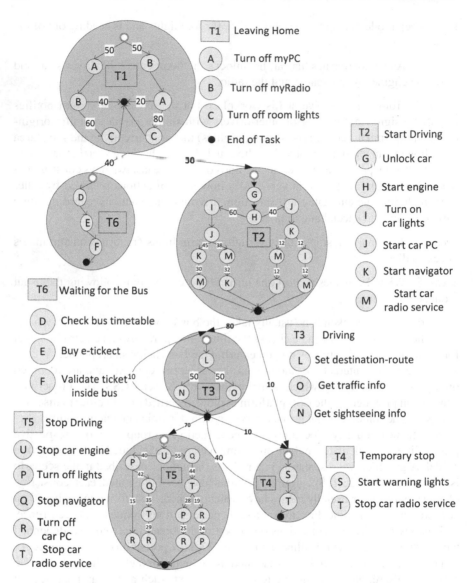

Fig. 23.1 A graphical representation of a single user's actions routines according to the described scenario

In scene 3, Tom is receiving recommendations to follow a set of actions that he does not usually perform. This sequence of actions has been constructed based on routines followed by a significant number of other users with similar profiles that have been on the same situation in the recent past.

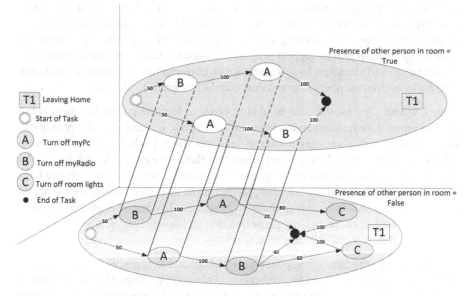

Fig. 23.2 Task "Leaving Home" is differentiated based on context (in this example context regarding the presence of other person in room is considered in the action prediction process)

23.3.2 Requirements

Based on the described scenario, the most important requirements that a proactive system should satisfy are specified hereafter:

User Interaction Modelling and Management User actions and context should be modelled in a manner that will allow the efficient management of data (e.g. to support creation, retrieval, update and deletion operations), to accommodate prediction mechanisms and be easily comprehensible by users.

Discovery of User Intent Model (including community knowledge) Learning algorithms should be able to process recorded data sets of interactions in order to extract user intent models. Data mining techniques and other statistical methods may be applied in order to discover often occurring patterns of actions and context. Classification algorithms, association rules mining, clustering techniques are some of the most common methods used in current state of the art approaches. In a similar manner, the learning algorithm should be able to process history logs or existing prediction models derived from various users in order to discover community-wide recurring patterns of interactions.

Predicting User Actions Discovered interaction models are utilised in order to provide predictions. Predictions should be accompanied by a metric representing the confidence level which will be used by services or humans in order to take further actions. Behaviours of humans may demonstrate significant variations. A person's routines may change over time or even not exist at all, in a significant and tractable level (Horvitz et al. 2002). Hence, it is not feasible to expect that a user interaction predictor will present high success rates in all kinds of situations. As ubiquitous computing systems aim to support persons in everyday tasks, inaccurate prediction should be carefully handled. In a similar manner, community knowledge is not always eligible in user intent prediction and thus should be carefully utilised.

User Control The user should be able to observe learned interaction models but also recorded data sets containing histories of actions. Control over the proactivity system increases user's acquaintance and hence reassures further system's utilisation (Gallacher et al. 2011). It is also important that the user can enable and disable the overall monitoring and prediction system. Community interaction models are built on various users' interaction data. Thus, privacy protection mechanisms should apply. In addition, user should be able to revise (e.g. add, modify, remove) prediction rules. User defined rules, encompassing the notion of goal knowledge, greatly enhance and at the same time simplify models of action.

User feedback Prediction components should be able to recognise and utilise possible successful or unsuccessful predictions. This can be achieved in an automated (implicit) way by monitoring the performed action and comparing it with the predicted or based on explicit user feedback. The latter demands user interference and can be highly distractive if it is not properly handled. Recorded feedback is a useful source of information for improving future learning procedures.

Smoothing on Routines Change Previously learned patterns may no longer reflect the current user interaction routines. People often change their life patterns under certain circumstances (holidays, job change, moving to another place, etc.). The system should be able to detect and adapt based on this changes in a seamless fashion. Furthermore, it should be able to detect and handle appropriately extreme or unexpected recorded values.

Context Selection It is important to select the appropriate accompanying context types in order to construct situation snapshots. It is common to precede learning with an attribute selection stage that aims to eliminate all but the most relevant attributes of the training dataset. As stated in Witten et al. (2011), the best way to select relevant attributes is manually, based on a deep understanding of the learning problem and what the attributes actually mean. As this in not always efficient various statistical and data mining methods have been developed.

23.4 Behaviour Modelling

The introduced Context Aware User and Intent (CAUI) model aims to describe actions that a user performs and possible sequences that arise among those actions. The often occurring sequences of actions are modelled as tasks. The previous sections presented various examples and requirements regarding actions and tasks. The CAUI model is generic enough to model any kind of user action. However, the current framework aims to model and support the prediction of actions that are related with the use of services provided by the CSS platform or third parties. These actions have previously been monitored by software or hardware agents that are part of the CSS platform. A description of the most important data classes of the CAUI model follows:

IUserIntentAction This interface and the respective realisation class models the action that a user performs. The data object contains, among others, information regarding the actual action, the targeted service, user friendly names and unique identifiers.

IUserIntentTask This interface and the respective realisation class models a set of actions (each modelled as IUserIntentAction) that a user performs in order to achieve a certain Task. Additional information captured by this class is related with context (including time) information, user friendly names reflecting goal knowledge, targeted services, and task identifiers.

ITransitionData This interface and the respective realisation class contain all necessary information in order to associate actions or tasks. It refers to a unique transition among actions or tasks. Each instance of this class is related to one source (i.e. a single action or task or groups of these) and exactly one destination.

ICommIntentAction This interface and the respective realisation class model a community action. The CommIntentAction class extends the UserIntentAction class with attributes describing the level of commonality of the performed action among the community members.

ICommIntentTask In a similar manner, the CommIntentTask extends the UserIntentTask with additional attributes referring to the commonality of task.

The UML diagram depicted in Fig. 23.3 illustrates the described Context-Aware User Intent data class model along with the community related extensions.

23.5   Architecture

In this section the main functional parts of the Proactivity component will be presented, as depicted in Fig. 23.4. The provided functionality includes discovery, management and evaluation of user intent models and eventually estimation of the actions that need to be taken. The Proactivity component interacts with the Context Management (CM) component and with potential third party (3P) services that adapt their behaviour according to provided predictions. User interactions with 3P services are monitored, modelled and stored in a history data set by the CM system. The data set is then used for discovering the CAUI model. Finally, a GUI allows users to directly interact with the underlying mechanisms.

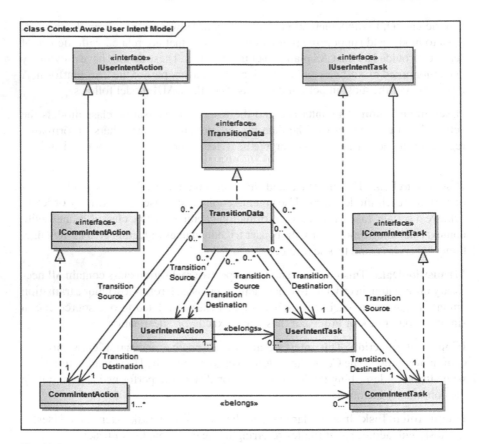

Fig. 23.3 Context-Aware User Intent (CAUI) Data class model

Fig. 23.4 Functional architecture of the Proactivity component block

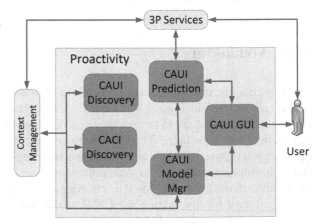

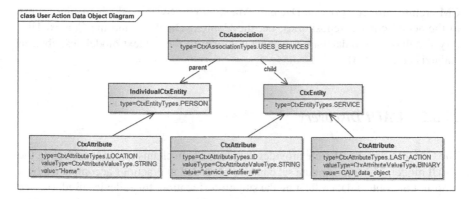

Fig. 23.5 Context model usage for user and services interactions

23.5.1 Context Management and Modelling

The CM component provides features for modelling and managing context information within the CSS framework. The context model, detailed in Kalatzis et al. (2014), includes all the necessary concepts in order to efficiently represent, retrieve, exchange, maintain and manage context information in a CSS environment. The context model comprises the following core informational classes: CtxEntity, CtxAttribute, CtxAssociation and CtxHistoricAttribute. Additionally to these classes there is the CtxIdentifier class hierarchy, which enables the identification of context data items in a privacy-aware manner and the CtxQuality class, which further augments the model with Quality of Context properties. The CtxEntity is the core concept upon which the context model is built and corresponds to an object of the physical or conceptual world. Essentially, the CtxAttribute class identifies an entity's status in terms of its static and dynamic properties and it therefore captures all context information items that are used to characterise the situation of the owner CtxEntity.

Persons and communities are modelled based on IndividualCtxEnity and CommynityCtxEntity which are extending the CtxEntity class. To address the requirements regarding context semantics, a taxonomy has been introduced that includes the various context types as tags and dictates how these can be combined (Roussaki et al. 2012). Figure 23.5 illustrates an example of the context model utilisation for modelling user context and interactions with services. In the current example, user actions modelled as CAUI data objects are stored as a CtxAttribute of type "LAST_ACTION" while additional context (e.g. user location) is stored as a CtxAttribute assigned to IndividualCtxEntity of type "PERSON".

Regarding the CM architecture a detailed description can be found in Roussaki et al. (2012). The provided functionality includes the management of current, historic and future context data in a synchronous and/or asynchronous way; inference of high-level context information based on raw sensor data and/or context history; management of context sources and collection of monitored data. In addition, the

CM architecture comprises a Database Management System which enables access to the actual context repositories, i.e. the Context Database and the Context History Database. Both database schemata conform to the context model described in Kalatzis et al. (2014).

23.5.2   CAUI Discovery

The CAUI Discovery module provides the learning mechanisms for constructing the CAUI model. The training data set contains recorded interactions accompanied by a snapshot of context data reflecting the situation (location, time, device used, service type, user status, ambient parameters, etc.) in which the action was performed. The number of data types included in the snapshot, influences the learning process in terms of time and computational resources consumption but also in terms of the prediction model completeness, thus a balance must be maintained.

Representing high-level context information based on captured low-level data may include uncertainty. However, state-of-the-art sensing technologies and inference mechanism allow the accurate estimation for some context types. For example, location and time, which are significantly related with users' actions, can be monitored with high accuracy. In addition, there are several solutions for dynamic identification and assignment of user friendly tags for places of interest. Regarding time, recorded timestamps allow the extraction of additional information such as hour of day, day of week, month, season, weekends, etc.

The learning algorithm should be able address the requirements above and to discover both recurring sequences of actions but also actions that occur in certain situations. We assume that a user interacts with various resources in a pervasive computing environment and his/her interactions are monitored for time $T = t_k$. Let a^{t_k} express the user interaction at time t_k ($k = 1,2, ..., K$), which was observed when the user was in situation $s^{t_k} = \{c_1{}^{t_k}, c_2{}^{t_k}, ..., c_n{}^{t_k}\}$ where $c_i{}^{t_k}$ is the value of context information of type i, ($i = 1,2, ..., n$). Given all the observed/recorded tuples (a^{t_k}, s^{t_k}) for $k = 1,2, ..., K$, the CAUI Discovery component aims to build a behaviour model to identify the most probable interaction $a^{t_{k+1}}$ that the user will perform. To this end, the learning algorithm processes history logs to extract user action patterns. In the proposed approach, the following cases are targeted: (i) user performs actions in forms of sequences, (ii) user performs actions when certain situations occur, (iii) a combination of (i) and (ii).

23.5.2.1   Sequences Discovery

Based on the described requirements, discrete time Variable Order Markov Chains (VOMC) (Begleiter et al. 2004) has been selected as an appropriate algorithm for modelling and predicting sequences of actions. Prediction of future states of a Markov model depends only on current state, while predictions of a VOMC model depend also on the history of a number of states defined by the model's order. This algorithm is applicable as the system is fully observable and actions are represented as a finite alphabet of possible states $A : \{a^{t_1}, a^{t_2}, ..., a^{t_n}\}$. Discrete time is also supported as data derived from software or hardware sources/sensors and hence distinct updates of context data are occurring. During the learning phase, conditional transition probabilities for all symbols $a^{t_k} \in A$ are estimated by counting the number of action occurrences appearing after a sequence of actions $d \in A$ where $[d : \{a^{t_{k-1}}, a^{t_{k-2}}, ..., a^{t_{k-1}}\}$ and l denotes the length of d. In the proposed framework, the maximum length of dis specified based on a predefined significance threshold that is calculated taking into account the transition probability value and the actual number of recorded actions occurred. The learned sequence predictor maintains several Markov models grouped based on their order.

23.5.2.2 Situations Discovery

The aim of this process is to identify recurring patterns where specific context value combinations are accompanying a certain action. It is possible to handle this issue as a classification problem, where input instances are the observed context values and the outcome is the category of action. According to Witten et al. (2011), Naive Bayes is an algorithm that fulfils the requirements set earlier and has worked quite well in many complex real world situations. It follows a supervised learning approach for estimating parameters of the classifier, such as means and variances of the variables. The algorithm requires a small amount of training data and provides quantifiable probability distributions for each possible class. In addition, it handles well missing values and automatically ignores irrelevant attributes in a process that resembles attribute selection. Finally there is no need for domain expert interference in designing dependencies between input attributes, something necessary for Bayesian Networks. On the other hand, it assumes that attributes are independent from each other with respect to the classification outcome, something that it is not always the case, while the computing resources consumption can get significantly high. Bayes' rule for calculating prediction probabilities according to the defined problem becomes:

$$P\left[a^{t_k}|s^{t_k}\right] = P\left(a^{t_k}\right) \times \frac{\prod_{j=1}^{n} P\left(c_j^{t_k}|a^{t_k}\right)}{P\left(s^{t_k}\right)} \tag{23.1}$$

where a^{t_k} is the expected classification outcome and $s^{t_k} = \{c_j^{t_k}\}$, $j = 1..n$ is the current evidence input.

23.5.3 CACI Discovery

This module aims to create a context-aware community intent (CACI) model by combining common interaction patterns and situations among a group of users. The learned model can then be made available to individual users in order to improve accuracy of user interaction predictions. History logs containing user interactions along with accompanying context are collected to a common repository. To this end, data are pre-processed before being fed into the learning algorithms, in order to apply community-wide semantics. As the community dataset is expected to contain contradicting, incomplete or extreme data, a cleaning phase is necessary in order to drop those tuples. The same learning algorithms used for user intent model discovery are applied for sequences of actions extraction and situations identification.

23.5.4   CAUI Prediction

This module exploits learned models in order to perform next action predictions. Each prediction is accompanied by a confidence level that acts as an indicator for further handling of prediction by users or services. Utilising different prediction methods can be particular useful in cases where one of the predictors fails to provide predictions with high confidence, or in cases where the system has not detected a performed action or any context input. The following main categories of prediction approaches are identified according to available input:

User-Performed action(s)   In this case, system is requested to provide a prediction of next user actions based on one or more performed actions. According to the number of actions, the appropriate Markov model is selected and probabilities are extracted. Given a sequence of actions $d : \{a^{t_{k-1}}, a^{t_{k-2}}, ..., a^{t_{k-l}}\}$ where l is the sequence length, the most probable next action is identified by maximizing the respective probability:

$$a^{t_k}_{seq} = \arg \max_{a^{t_k} \in A} \{P[a^{t_k}|d]\}$$

$$a^{t_k}_{seq} = \arg \max_{a^{t_k} \in A} \left\{ \frac{N(a^{t_k} \ldots a^{t_{k-l}})}{N(a^{t_{k-1}} \ldots a^{t_{k-l}})} \right\} \tag{23.2}$$

Situation Update   In this case, a situation is monitored and the respective context action values are used as instances of the Naive Bayes classification model. Actions demonstrating the highest prediction probabilities are returned. For a situation snapshot described by $s^{t_k} = \{c_j{}^{t_k}\}$, $j = 1..n$ and given the Eq. (23.1) the optimal action category is requested based on the respective probability maximization:

$$a^{t_k}_{sit} = \arg \max_{a^{t_k} \in A} \left\{ P\left[a^{t_k}|s^{t_k}\right] \right\}$$

$$a^{t_k}_{sit} = \arg \max_{a^{t_k} \in A} \left\{ P(a^{t_k}) \times \frac{\prod_{j=1}^{n} P(c_j^{t_k}|a^{t_k})}{P(s^{t_k})} \right\}$$

For every action $a_{sit}^{tk} \in A$ the value of $P\left(s^{tk}\right)$ is a constant, so it can be omitted and the equation becomes:

$$a_{sit}^{tk} = \arg\max_{a^{tk} \in A} \left\{ P(a^{tk}) \times \prod_{j=1}^{n} P(c_j^{tk} | a^{tk}) \right\} \tag{23.3}$$

User-Performed Action and Situation Input In this case, both methods are combined. The adopted approach weights each outcome based on the number of occurrences contributed in probability calculation. Given (23.2) and (23.3) the action predicted based on both inputs is estimated by:

$$\alpha_{comb}^{tk} = \arg\max_{a^{tk} \in A} \left\{ w_{sit} \cdot P\left[a^{tk} | s^{tk}\right] + w_{seq} \cdot P[a^{tk} | d] \right\} \tag{23.4}$$

The amount of history records used for the situation based action prediction is reflected in:

$$w_{sit}(a^{tk}, s^{tk}) = \frac{N_{sit}^{a_j^{tk}}}{N_{seq} + N_{sit}}$$

$$N_{sit}^{a_j^{tk}} = \frac{\sum_i N_{cil}^{a_j^{tk}}}{\sum_i N_{cil}} \cdot N_{sit} \quad \text{and} \quad N_{sit} = [N - N_{\cup \overline{c_{il}^{tk}}}]$$

where $\sum_i N_{cil}^{a_j^{tk}}$ is the sum of recorded context instances c_{il} occurred along with the predicted action and $\sum_i N_{cil}$ is the sum of all recorded context instances c_{il} regardless of the action. Finally, N_{sit} is the number of history tuples $\left(a^{tk}, s^{tk}\right)$ where at least one context value c_{il} of current situation is contained in vector s^{tk} and hence participated in prediction process. The amount of history records used for the particular action prediction based on a sequence of performed actions is reflected in:

$$w_{seq} = \frac{N(a^{tk} \ldots a^{tk-l})}{N(a^{tk-1} \ldots a^{tk-l}) + N_{sit}}$$

where $N_{seq}^{a_j^{tk}}$ is the number of sequences containing the action a^{tk} and N_{seq} is the number of sequences that the user has currently performed.

Community Assisted It is possible that all described methods do not provide adequate results or that a prediction model does not even exist. In this case, community knowledge can be similarly exploited and the provided results can be compared and combined in order to improve future action estimation.

23.5.5   CAUI Model Manager

This module provides the necessary functionality for instantiating and managing CAUI models. It provides methods for creating, retrieving, updating, and removing data objects referring to CAUI model classes. Retrieval of model objects is performed based on various criteria such as IUserIntentAction or IUserIntentTask identifiers, user action details, service type, maximum probability of occurrence etc. This module is utilised by CAUI Discovery component during model generation or update in order to construct the structure of actions, tasks and the respective transitions among them, or to remove an obsolete model. CAUI Prediction mainly utilises retrieval methods in order to identify actions and tasks that meet specified criteria.

23.5.6   CAUI User Interface

The scope of this module is to enhance the user's trust in the overall framework by making it transparent and easy to control. As already stated, user should be able to know what the system has learned, why it proceeds to certain decisions and to enable and disable it at any given time. To this end, CAUI GUI allows user to control various aspects of Proactivity components functionality. The GUI is implemented as a web interface that visualises CAUI model aspects and provides options for manipulating actions and tasks. The GUI supports prediction rules creation and also prompts for user feedback when prediction confidence level is low. It also allows the enabling and disabling of user monitoring, future action prediction functionality and the discovery of new intent models. Finally, it provides a log of performed and predicted actions along with accompanied context.

23.6   Evaluation

The proposed user intent prediction mechanism has been evaluated based on a data set originally collected for the needs of the Reality Mining project (Eagle et al. 2008) of the MIT Media Laboratory. The data set includes data collected by 94 individuals that were using mobile phones with pre-installed software capable of recording various context attributes such as location, voice and data calls, mobile phone application usage, etc. Their activities and interactions with their mobile devices have been monitored for a 10 month period (i.e., from September 2004 until June 2005) and have been recorded. Additional information such as friendship and proximity among subjects has been recorded as well, also based on questions answered by participants. The datasets of these individuals contain tuples of the following context attributes: ApplicationID, Day of Month (DoM), Hour of Day (HoD), location cell ID. To this extent, it has been decided to use the data collected in the first weeks of the 10 month user monitoring period for training purposes that led to a training data set of about 5,00,000 tuples and use the remaining 10 % for evaluation.

Three sets of experiments have been conducted for evaluating user action prediction. Initially, only the sequence of previously performed user actions was used as input. Then, situation-based predictions were tested, exploiting current context data (i.e. location, HoD, and DoW). Finally, the proposed hybrid approach was tested coupling sequence- and situation-based results. For the second set of experiments, an iterative process has been adopted, where users' training data have been collected in a common data set and fed to the three learning algorithms. In Kalatzis et al. (2014), the authors utilised a heuristic algorithm to identify groups of users demonstrating common characteristics in terms of context and friendship connections. For the needs of this paper, the user group carrying the strongest similarity among its members has been selected. This user group contains 22 individuals. The discovered prediction models were evaluated using the same evaluation data set as in the first experiments. The common data set repository did not contain the training data set of the user under evaluation, thus resembling a community assisted prediction process for situations that the user has never encountered.

The results of both experiment sets are illustrated in Fig. 23.6, where the average prediction success rations (*left axis*) and prediction attempt ratios (*right axis*) for the three strategies are provided. In both the community-unaware, as well as the community assisted approaches (presented in Fig. 23.6a, b respectively), the hybrid mechanism clearly outperforms the other two strategies regarding the percentage of attempted predictions, as it delivers 18–22 % more predictions in (a) and 11–97 % more predictions in (b) in average. On the other hand, regarding the prediction success ratios, the sequence-based mechanism slightly outperforms the hybrid mechanism, as it achieves about 4 % higher success rate in average for (a) and 3 % for (b). However, comparing these two dominant strategies, as the success rates achieved are comparable, we may conclude that the hybrid mechanism is preferable, in case the user values greatly the proactive behaviour of the system. Regarding the context-based predictions, one can easily observe that the achieved results are always outperformed by the other two strategies. This is mainly due to the nature of the data set, where the user actions were minimally depending on the user situation, thus forcing our mechanism to build Bayesian graphs of numerous edges with very low probabilities. Finally, it should be highlighted that the proposed approach delivers quite satisfactory results in the community-assisted case (Fig. 23.6b), managing to correctly predict the user actions in two out of three cases, attempting to make predictions in about one out of two cases in average, using the hybrid mechanism. This is of high value, given the fact that zero user historic data are assumed, and all user action predictions are performed based on the user intent models built for the specific user's fellow community members.

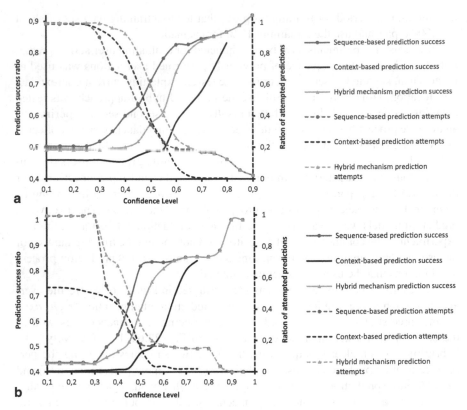

Fig. 23.6 Average prediction success and prediction attempt ratios for the three strategies for the **a** community-unaware and **b** community-assisted approaches

23.7   Conclusions and Future Work

The described framework is part of an open scalable service architecture and platform that aims to realise the concept of Pervasive Communities. A Pervasive Community demonstrates features related with context-awareness, self-organisation, self-improvement, and proactive behaviour in order to optimise and personalise the pervasive experience of an entire community (www.ict-societies.eu). Proactive behaviour is inherently related with user intent prediction, as for any system, to react appropriately for a given end-user, it needs to be aware of what that end-user is attempting to achieve. The presented approach aims to realise this by monitoring end-user behaviours and the context in which these behaviours occur. Observing temporal sequences of end-user actions and context cliques or snapshots can permit the discovery of past goals, and the prediction of future. This process is supported by knowledge originating from other community members. In a nutshell, the described framework aims to exploit recorded histories of users' interactions and context that are taking place in pervasive computing environments, in support of user intent prediction.

Future plans include further evaluation of the proposed mechanisms with additional datasets demonstrating diverse characteristics. To improve the performance of context-based user intent prediction, the adaptation and evaluation of alternative algorithms (such as Bayesian Networks) is planned. Regarding the community knowledge extraction, additional approaches will be evaluated such as the merging of individual user intent models. In addition, methods for the dynamic selection of action's escorting context will be researched. Currently, recorded context types are predefined and the same context escorts all actions. Selecting the attributes that better contribute on a per action base will improve prediction performance, but will also increase the volume of recorded data. In a similar manner, adapting dynamically the granularity of the discrete time-representation will improve the quality of prediction. Recorded timestamps can be refined in variable time intervals adapted to action and task duration.

References

Abowd, G.D., Bobick, I., Essa, I., Mynatt, E., Rogers, W.: The aware home: Developing technologies for successful aging. In: Proceedings of the 18th National Conference on Artificial Intelligence, Edmonton, Canada, 28 July–1 Aug 2002

Adomavicius, G., Tuzhiin, A.: Toward the next generation of recommender systems: A survey of the state-of-the-art and possible extensions. IEEE T. Knowl. Data En. **17**(6), 734–749 (2005)

Antwarg, L., Rokach, L., Shapira, B.: Attribute-driven hidden Markov model trees for intention prediction IEEE. Trans. Syst. Man. Cybern. C. **42**(6), 1103–1119 (2012)

Begleiter, R., El-Yaniv, R., Yona, G.: On prediction using variable order Markov models. J. Artif. Intell. Res. **22**(1), 385–421 (2004)

Doolin, K., Roussaki, I., Roddy, M., Kalatzis, N., Papadopoulou, E., Taylor, N.K., Liampotis, N., McKitterick, D., Jennings, E., Kosmides, P.: Societies: Where pervasive meets social. In: Alvarez, F., Cleary, F., Daras, P., Domingue, J., Galis, A., Garcia, A., Gavras, A., Karnourskos, S., Krco, S., Li, M.-S., Lotz, V., Müller, H., Salvadori, E., Sassen, A.-M., Schaffers, H., Stiller, B., Tselentis, G., Turkama, P., Zahariadis, T. (eds.) Future Internet Assembly Book. pp. 30–41. Springer, Heidelberg (2012)

Eagle, N., Pentland, A., Lazer, D.: Inferring social network structure using mobile phone data. In: International Workshop on Social Computing, Behavioral Modeling, and Prediction, Phoenix, Arizona, 1–2 April 2008

Gallacher, S., Papadopoulou, E., Taylor, N., Blackmun, F., Williams, H., Roussaki, I., Kalatzis, N., Liampotis, N., Zhang, D.: Personalisation in a system combining pervasiveness and social networking. In: Proceeding of 20th International Conference on Computer Communications and Networks, Hawaii, USA, 31 July-4 Aug 2011

Garlan, D., Siewiorek, D., Smailagic, A., Steenkiste, P.: Project aura: Toward distraction-free pervasive computing. IEEE Pervasive Comput. **1**(2), 22–31 (2002)

Gopalratnam, K., Cook, D.J.: Online sequential prediction via incremental parsing: The active LeZi algorithm. IEEE Intell. Syst. **22**(1), 52–58 (2007)

Horvitz, E., Koch, P., Kadie, C.M., Jacobs, A.: Coordinate: Probabilistic forecasting of presence and availability. In: Proceeding of the 18th Conference on Uncertainty in Artificial Intelligence, Edmonton, Alberta, July 2002

Kalatzis, N., Liampotis, N., Roussaki, I., Kosmides, P., Papaioannou, I., Xynogalas, S., Zhang, D., Anagnostou, M.: Cross-community context management in cooperating smart spaces. Pers. Ubiquit. Comput. 18(2), 427–443 (2014)

Magnusson, M.S.: Repeated patterns in behavior and other biological phenomena. In: Oller, K.D., Griebel, U. (eds.) Evolution of Communication Systems: A Comparative Approach, pp. 111–128. MIT Press, Cambridge (2004)

Ni, H., Abdulrazak, B., Zhang, D., Wu, S.: CDTOM: A context-driven task oriented middleware for pervasive homecare environment. Int. J. UbiComp. 2(1), 34–53 (2011)

Roussaki, I., Kalatzis, N., Liampotis, N., Frank, K., Sykas, E.D., Anagnostou, M.: Developing context-aware personal smart spaces. In: Alencar, P., Cowan, D. (eds.) Handbook of Research on Mobile Software Engineering: Design, Implementation, and Emergent Applications, pp. 659–676. IGI Global, Hershey (2012)

Roussaki, I., Kalatzis, N., Liampotis, N., Kosmides, P., Anagnostou, M., Doolin, K., Jennings, E., Bouloudis, Y., Xynogalas, S.: Context-awareness in wireless and mobile computing revisited to embrace social networking. IEEE Commun. Mag. 50(6), 74–81 (2012)

Singh, P., Williams, W.: LifeNet: a propositional model of ordinary human activity. In: Workshop on Distributed and Collaborative Knowledge Capture, Sanibel Island, FL, 23-26 Oct 2003

Sousa, J.P., Poladian, V., Garlan, D., Schmerl, B., Shaw, M.: Task-based adaptation for ubiquitous computing. IEEE. Trans. Syst. Man. Cybern. C. 36(3), 328–340 (2006)

Tang, L., Liu, H.: Scalable learning of collective behavior based on sparse social dimensions. In: Proceedings of 18th ACM Conference on Information and Knowledge Management, Hong Kong, China, 2–6 Nov 2009

Thakor, M.V., Borsuk, W., Kalamas, M.: Hotlists and web browsing behaviour: An empirical investigation. J. Bus. Res. 57(7), 776–786 (2004)

Witten, I.H., Frank, E., Hall, M.A.: Data Mining: Practical Machine Learning Tools and Techniques. 3rd edn. Morgan Kaufmann, Burlington (2011)

Part V
Context in Formal Representation

Chapter 24
Multi-context Logics—A General Introduction

Chiara Ghidini and Luciano Serafini

Abstract Multi-context logics (MCLs) constitute a family of formalisms that allow one to integrate multiple logical theories (contexts) into an articulated structure, where different theories can affect one another via so-called bridge-rules. In the past 20 years multi-context logics have been developed for contexts in propositional logics, first order logics, description logics and temporal logic. Each of these logics has been developed, in an independent manner, for representing and reasoning about contextual knowledge in a specific application domain instead of originating from a single general formal framework. The absence of such a general formal framework for Multi-Context Systems (MCS), from which to extract tailored versions for the different application domain, has led to the development of a rather heterogeneous family of formal systems, whose comparison is sometimes very difficult. Being able to represent all these systems as specifications of a general class would be very useful as, for instance, one could reuse results proven in one MCS in another one. In this chapter, the authors provide an a-posteriori, systematic, and homogeneous description of the various MCSs introduced in the past. The authors do this firstly by providing a general definition of the MCS framework with its main components, which is general enough to capture the various versions of MCSs. Then, an account of the main logical specialisations of the MCS framework is provided, with an explanation of the domain of application they have been developed for.

24.1 Introduction

Multi-context logics (MCLs) are a family of formalisms for the integration of multiple logical theories (contexts) in an articulated composite structure. They are based upon two key principles of contextual knowledge, named principle of *locality* and principle of *compatibility* (Ghidini and Giunchiglia 2001). The principle of locality states that a context represents (or, in a more technical fashion, axiomatizes in a

C. Ghidini (✉) · L. Serafini
Fondazione Bruno Kessler, via Sommarive 18, 38123 Trento, Italy
e-mail: ghidini@fbk.eu

L. Serafini
e-mail: serafini@fbk.eu

© Springer Science+Business Media New York 2014
P. Brézillon, A. J. Gonzalez (eds.), *Context in Computing*,
DOI 10.1007/978-1-4939-1887-4_24

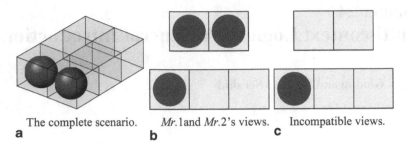

The complete scenario.   *Mr.*1 and *Mr.*2's views.   Incompatible views.

a   **b**   **c**

Fig. 24.1 The magic box. **a** The complete scenario. **b** *Mr.* 1 and *Mr.* 2's views. **c** Incompatible views

logical theory) a portion of the world, and that every statement entailed by such a representation is intended to hold within that portion of the world. The principle of compatibility instead states that different contexts that describe overlapping portions of world are represented by compatible logical theories, which are constrained to describe compatible situations. To illustrate these principles, and the idea of context underlined by MCLs we recall here the magic box example originally introduced in Ghidini and Giunchiglia (2001).

Example 1 Consider the scenario of Fig. 24.1a. Two observers, *Mr.* 1 and *Mr.* 2, are looking at a rectangular glass box from two different perspectives, one from the front, and one from the side. The box consists of six sectors, each sector possibly containing a ball. The box is "magic" and observers cannot distinguish the depth inside it. Figure 24.1b shows what *Mr.* 1 and *Mr.* 2 can see in the scenario depicted in Fig. 24.1a.

In this example we have two contexts, each context describing what an observer sees (its viewpoint) and the consequences that it is able to draw from it. The content of the two contexts is graphically represented in Fig. 24.1b. Notice that here the term context does not refer to a particular circumstance, or state of affair, but it refers to the point of view of each agent. Indeed we use the expression "the context of agent 1 (or 2)" to indicate his/her point of view.

Concerning *locality*, both *Mr.* 1 and *Mr.* 2 have the notions of a ball being on the right or on the left. However there may be situations in which there is a ball which is on the right for *Mr.* 1 and not on the right for *Mr.* 2. Furthermore *Mr.*2 has the notion of "a ball being in the center of the box" which is meaningless for *Mr.*1.

Concerning *compatibility*, the partial representations of *Mr.* 1 and *Mr.* 2's contexts are obviously related. The relation is a consequence of the fact that *Mr.* 1 and *Mr.* 2 see the same box. Figure 24.1b shows a pair of two compatible representations (contexts), while Fig. 24.1c shows a pair of incompatible representations (contexts). In this simple example we can synthetically describe all the compatible representations using a narrative like: "if *Mr.* 1 sees at least a ball then *Mr.* 2 sees at least a ball".

The MCL representing the magic box scenario is composed of:

- Two logical theories T_1 and T_2, each of them containing the logical representation of the context that describes one of the observer's viewpoints over the box. Each logical theory T_i will be described using an appropriate, and possibly different, logic L_i, interpreted in its own set of local models.
- A description of how to constrain the individual logical theories (and similarly the underlying logical models) in pairs that represent compatible viewpoints.

By generalising from the above example, the basic framework of MCLs is constituted by a number of logical theories T_i, each of them used to represent a context by means of an appropriate logic L_i, plus a description of how to combine/constrain the individual logical theories in compatible sequences that represent the entire multi-context structure. In the past 20 years this basic framework of MCL has been developed to model contexts described by means of different types of logic. In this chapter we provide an account of the main logical specialisation of MCLs, namely propositional logic and first order logic Multi-context Logics with an explanation of the types of applications they have been used for.

The chapter is structured as follows. In Sect. 24.2 we introduce the general definition of Multi Context Logic with its basic components, namely: syntax, semantics, logical consequence and deductive system (in literature called Multi Context System). MCLs can be categorized in two main families, namely: propositional MCL and quantificational MCL. In Sect. 24.3 we introduce the general definition of propositional MCL and some of the MCL that have been proposed in the past. In Sect. 24.4 we introduce quantificational MCLs and its two main important instances: Distributed First Order Logics and Distributed Description Logics.

24.2 Multi-context Logics

It its more general form, a *multi-context logic* (MCL) is defined on a family of logics $\{L_i\}_{i \in I}$ where each L_i is a logic used to formalize the i-th context. We assume that each logic L_i is equipped with a formal language, a class of structures in which this language is interpreted, a satisfiability relation (denoted by $\models_i$) which defines when a formula is true or false in an interpretation structure, and a logical consequence relation (also denoted by $\models_i$), that states when a formula is a logical consequence of a set of formulas of the language of L_i.

Languages of MCL

We distinguish two main categories of MCL: propositional and quantificational MCL, depending on the fact the languages associated to each context, are only propositional or quantificationals. By propositional languages we refer to logical languages that contain only expressions that express that a certain state of affair has a certain truth value (independently from the specific truth value). Quantificational languages extend propositional languages with the possibility of specifying objects of the domain, by means of special expressions usually called terms. In the case of quantificational multi-context logic we extend the language of L_i (with $i \in I$) with a set of terms called *arrow variables*, denoted as $x^{\to j}$ and $x^{j \to}$, (with x variable and $j \in I$). Arrow variables are used to point to objects to other domains. The formal semantic will be clarified later.

Multi-context Structure

The set I of context indexes (aka context names) can be either a simple set, or a set equipped with an algebraic structure such as, for instance a partial order, a lattice, a linear order, and possibly a set of operations on context indices. For instance, a partial order structure $\langle I, \prec \rangle$ can be used to represent a set of contexts which are organized according to a general-specific relation. For instance if FOOTBALL is the context (theory) that formalizes the domain of football, while SPORT is the context (theory) that formalizes the more general domain of sport, the fact that the football domain is more specific than the sport domain can be captured by imposing FOOTBALL≺SPORT in I. A discrete linear order can be used to represent the evolution of the knowledge of one or a group of agents, where each context formalizes the agents' knowledge state at a given stage. For instance if ICD10 is the context that describes the international classification diseases - version 10, and ICD11 is the context that describes the the next version of the same classification, then ICD10 $\prec$ ICD11 states that ICD11 is the subsequent version of ICD10. Finally a lattice structure can be adopted to represent knowledge which holds in convex time intervals (represented by pairs of time points $\langle start, end \rangle$). The containment relation between intervals, represents the fact that the temporal span of a context covers the temporal span of another context.

Multi-context Model

A *model* for a multi-context logic $\{L_i\}_{i \in I}$ is a class of functions C where each function $c \in C$ assigns to each element $i \in I$ a set of interpretations c_i for the logic L_i. Each element of c_i is called a *local model* of L_i, and every $c \in C$ is called a *chain*[1]. Figure 24.2 provides a graphical illustration of a chain for a set of four contexts. A multi-context model is also called *compatibility relation* to emphasize the fact that it describes a class of compatible combinations of local models that mimic the type of relation that is assumed to hold between the original contexts they represent.

Some additional definitions are necessary to define the semantics for quantificational MCL. Quantificational logics extend propositional logics with the capability of predicating properties of objects of a universe, by introducing a class of expressions that denote objects of a domain. These expressions are usually called terms. As happens for propositional formulas, terms in different contexts can have different

---

[1] The term "chain" is slightly misleading, as it suggests that the set of contexts are structured in a total order (i.e., a chain) which might not be the case. Historically total ordered context structure was the first form of multi-context logic that has been studied. This made it natural to use the term "chain" for $c \in C$. For the sake of notation this terminology was maintained also in more complex MCLs with different context structures as the one depicted in Fig. 24.2.

Fig. 24.2 A multi-context model. Each language is interpreted in a set of models. Each combination of sets of local models defines a chain and belongs to a compatibility relation. Graphically (and formally) this can be thought as an iper-arc on the graph of a set of sets of local models

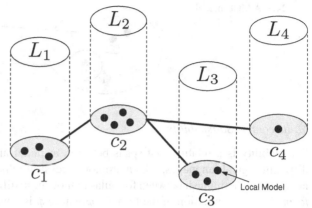

meaning. Classical examples of terms with context dependent meaning taken from the area of formal linguistics are indexicals (like "here", "now", "me"); other examples can be found in the area of heterogeneous information integration, where a term can be used differently in different information resources (e.g., "Trento" in a database can be used to denote the province of Trento, while in another one is used to denote the city of Trento). Conversely, meaning of terms in different contexts can be related. To capture the relations between elements of different domains of interpretation we introduce the notion of *domain relation*. More precisely, let Δ^m be the domain of a local model m, and $\Delta_i = \bigcup_{m \in c_i} \Delta^m$, $\Delta_j = \bigcup_{m \in c_j} \Delta^m$ be the domains of interpretation for the models in c_i and c_j respectively, then a *domain relation* r_{ij} from i to j is any subset of $\Delta_i \times \Delta_j$.[2]

For instance suppose that A is the context corresponding to the database of books available on a web catalogue (say Amazon), and B is the database of the physical copies of books available in a library (say Biblioteca di Trento). A chain for the MCL composed of A and B is a pair $\langle c_A, c_B \rangle$. To represent the correspondence between the books titles available on Amazon and the book copies available in the Library of Trento, we can use the r_{AB}, that contains each pairs $\langle a, b_1 \rangle, \ldots, \langle a, b_k \rangle$ where $b_1, \ldots, b_k$ are the $k \geq 1$ copies of the book a sold by Amazon, which are available in the library of Trento.

---

[2] The domain relation is used to represent the overlapping between the domains of two contexts. Usually, in databases, or in ontology integration scenarios, the overlapping between two domains Δ_i and Δ_j is represented by imposing that $\Delta_i \cap \Delta_j$ contains a set of elements which are supposed to exists both in the domain of the ith context and of the jth context. The usage of a domain relation turns out to be more flexible than assuming domain intersection since it allows to integrate knowledge defined over overlapping but heterogeneous domains of interpretation. The typical case is the one of two databases that adopt a different level of abstraction to represent a specific domain. For instance, time at the level of day, and time at the level of hours.

Fig. 24.3 A MCL model

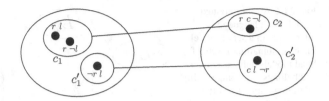

Multi-context Satisfiability

Satisfiability is a relation that spans between a model and formulas belonging to different logical languages, which are not necessarily disjoint. This introduces the necessity to distinguish between formulas that occur in different contexts. A *labelled formula* is an expression of the form $i : \phi$ where ϕ is a well formed formula of L_i. The intuitive meaning of $i : \phi$ is that ϕ holds in the i-th context.

Local satisfiability, that is, the satisfiability of a formula ϕ in a context i, is defined w.r.t. the local models and, possibly, the assignments to the free variables occurring in ϕ in case of quantificational contexts. Intuitively, a labelled formula $i : \phi$ is satisfied by a model C if all the local models $m \in c_i$ for all the chains $c \in C$ satisfy ϕ.

To make a simple example, consider the MCL model C for the magic box scenario depicted in Fig. 24.3. As explained in the introduction, this scenario can be formalized with two contexts 1 and 2 that formalise the points of view of *Mr.* 1 and *Mr.* 2, respectively. The two contexts are associated with two propositional logics L_1 and L_2 respectively, defined over the sets of propositional atoms $\{l, r\}$ and $\{l, c, r\}$[3]. Intuitively, we aim at introducing a definition that says that C satisfies the formula $1 : \neg r \vee l$ as the two elements c_1 and c'_1 belonging to the (only) two chains c and c' in the model C satisfy the formula $\neg r \vee l$ (where, in turn, the fact that c_1 and c'_1 satisfy $\neg r \vee l$ means that all the local models they contain satisfy that formula according to the notion of satisfiability in the appropriate logic, propositional in this case).

The above definition is sufficient for propositional contexts and also for quantificational contexts, if ϕ does not contain free variables. However, the general definition should also take into account the case in which ϕ contains *free and arrow variables, which need to be assigned* to the elements of the domains of the models in c_i. Notice however the models of c_i could have different domains of interpretation, so variables need to be assigned so that they are meaningful in all the models $m \in c_i$. i.e., to the intersections of the domains of the models in c_i. So if a is an assignment for the variable x, since we want to maintain the definition that $c \models i : \phi(x)[a_i]$ if $m \models \phi(x)[a_i]$ for all $m \in c_i$, then x should necessarily be assigned by a_i to some element which is in the intersection of the domains of each $m \in c_i$. More formally, a *local assignment* a_i should map every (arrow) variable x in an element of $\bigcap_{m \in c_i} \Delta^m$, where Δ^m is the domain of interpretation associated to the model m. We make the additional assumption that such an intersection is non-empty.

---

[3] Where l, c and r stand for *left*, *center* and *right*, respectively.

Formally, for any formula $i : \phi$, for every multi-context model C, for every chain $c \in C$ and for every assignment a_i that assigns the free variables occurring in $i : \phi$ to the intersection of the domains of interpretation of the locals models in c_i, we say that C *satisfies* $i : \phi$ w.r.t. the assignment a_i if for all $c \in C$, $c \models \phi[a_i]$, where $c \models \phi[a_i]$ means that $m \models_i \phi[a_i]$ for all the local models m of the i-th element $c_i \in c$, and $\models_i$ is the satisfiability relation defined in the logic L_i. We indicate that C models $i : \phi$ with the symbol $C \models i : \phi[a_i]$. When we have to evaluate a set of labelled formulas Γ that span over multiple contexts free variables, as all the other symbols, are locally interpreted, and therefore we need to have an assignment a_i for each context $i \in I$. This is called *local assignment*. An *MC-assignment* (or simply an assignment) is a family of assignments $a = \{a_i\}_{i \in I}$ such that for each $i \neq j \in I$, a_i assigns every variables of L_i which is not an arrow variable, and if L_i and L_j are quantificational logics, there is a domain relation r_{ij} such that: if $a_j(x^{i\rightarrow})$ is defined then $\langle a_i(x), a_j(x^{i\rightarrow}) \rangle \in r_{ij}$ and if $a_i(x^{\rightarrow j})$ is defined then $\langle a_i(x^{\rightarrow j}), a_j(x) \rangle \in r_{ij}$.

Multi-context Logical Consequence

In MCL the notion of logical consequence is defined over labelled formulas. In particular, if Γ is a set of labelled formulas and $i : \phi$ a labelled formula, then $i : \phi$ is a logical consequence of Γ if and only if,

1. there is a model C, a chain $c \in C$ and a family of assignments $a = \{a_i\}_{i \in I}$ to the free variables of $\Gamma \cup \{\phi\}$ such that $c \models \Gamma \cup \{i : \phi\}[a]$, and
2. for all models C, for all $c \in C$ and for all family of assignments $a = \{a_i\}_{i \in I}$ to the free variables of the formulas in Γ if $c \models \Gamma$ then there is an extension a' of the assignment a, to the free variables of ϕ such that $c \models i : \phi[a_i']$[4].

Information Flow Across Contexts via Bridge Rules

In a MCL every context is interpreted in a set of local models, possibly arranged into chains. Local interpretation is the way to relate the truth and the falsity of the formulas to each context. However, only certain combinations of local interpretations are possible. Those are the ones admitted by the class of compatibility relations associated to a MCL. At the level of formulas, this means that there is a dependency between the truth of a (set of) formulas in a context and the truth of different formulas another context. To go back to our magic box scenario, this means that if a formula l (there is a ball in the left sector) is true in the context of Mr.1, then the formula $l \vee c \vee r$ (there is at least one ball in the box) must be true in the context of Mr.2.

From this perspective we can say that (classes of) compatibility relation(s) determine an information flow across contexts: the truth of a certain formula in a context

---

[4] In the definition of multi-context logical consequence there is an implicit existential quantification of the free variables in ϕ which are not free in Γ. This is similar to what happens for the semantics of rules in logic programming, where variables that appear in the head of a rule (the consequence) which are not contained in the body are usually interpreted existentially.

affects (imposes) the truth of another formula in a different context. *Bridge rules* are expressions over the languages of different contexts that enable the formalisation of this information flow. They are of the form:

$$i_1 : \phi_1, \ldots, i_n : \phi_n, \text{not } i_{n+1} : \phi_{n+1}, \ldots, \text{not } i_m : \phi_m \rightarrow i : \phi \qquad (24.1)$$

with $0 \leq n \leq m$, $i_k \in I$ and ϕ_k a formula in the language of L_{i_k}. The intuitive reading of (24.1) is: "if $\phi_1, \ldots, \phi_n$ hold in $i_1, \ldots, i_n$ respectively and $\phi_{n+1}, \ldots, \phi_m$ do not hold in $i_{n+1}, \ldots, i_m$ respectively, then ϕ holds in i." Thus, a simple bridge rule that represents the propagation flow in the magic box example discussed above is

$$1 : l \rightarrow 2 : l \vee c \vee r. \qquad (24.2)$$

Multi-context System

We are now ready to define an axiomatic system for multiple contexts. A *multi-context system MCS* in a multi-context logic $L_I = \{L_i\}_{i \in I}$ is a pair $\langle \mathbb{T}, \mathbb{BR} \rangle$ where $\mathbb{T}$ is a family of theories $\{T_i\}_{i \in I}$, with T_i a set of closed formulas in the logic L_i, and $\mathbb{BR}$ is a set of *bridge rules*. Intuitively, each T_i axiomatizes what is true in the logic L_i, while the bridge rules $\mathbb{BR}$ axiomatize the constraints imposed by the compatibility relations and act like cross-logic axioms.

Reasoning in Multi-context Systems

There are multiple reasoning systems for MCL. Depending on the local logics, different reasoning systems have been developed in the past. Often, reasoning methods for specific MCL are the result of the combination via bridge rules of local reasoning methods. The work in Giunchiglia and Serafini (1994), Ghidini and Serafini (1998) propose an extension of Natural Deduction for reasoning in propositional and first order MCLs; in Serafiniand Roelofsen (2005) the SAT decision procedure for propositional logic is extended to a context SAT (or C-SAT) procedure to check for satisfiability in propositional multi-context systems; in Ghidini (1999), Borgida and Serafini (2003) tableaux methods for reasoning in modal and description logics have been extended for MCLs based on modal/description logics; Brewka et al. (2007) extends answer set programming to deal with propositional MCLs with non-monotonic bridge rules; finally, Bozzato and Serafini (2013) shows how SROIQ2-RL rule based forward reasoning can be extended to deal with multi-context logics in which each context is associated to a semantic web language OWL2RL. In the remaining of the chapter we will briefly recall and describe the most important reasoning methods that have been developed for MCLs along with an explanation of their main usages.

Local and Global Inconsistency

The fact that in MCL knowledge is split in multiple theories, makes MCL a flexible framework for modelling various types of inconsistencies. A first form of inconsistency arise when a proposition is assumed to hold in a context and the negation of the same proposition is assumed to hold in another context. This is easily represented in MCL with the two formulas $i : \phi$ and $j : \neg\phi$, which, in general, can be managed without generating any form of inconsistency. This is similar to what happens in multi modal logic where the two propositions $\Box_i \phi$ and $\Box_j \phi$ do not interfere, unless there are specific axioms that connect the two modalities $\Box_i$ and $\Box_j$. In addition to this, in MCL we can define two forms of inconsistency. One is called *local inconsistency* and refers to the fact that in a particular context it is possible to derive contradictory statements, i.e., *for some* $i \in I$, $i : \phi$ and $i : \neg\phi$ are both derivable; the second is called *global inconsistency*, which refers to the fact that a contradiction is derivable in all the contexts, i.e., *for all* $i \in I$, $i : \phi$ and $i : \neg\phi$ are both derivable. In general local inconsistency does not entail global inconsistency. So it is possible that one context is locally inconsistent, while others are consistent. From the semantic perspective, local inconsistency in a context i corresponds to the fact that there are chains in the compatibility relation of an MCL where i is interpreted in the empty set of local model, while other contexts are associated with a non empty set of local models.

24.3 Propositional Multi-context Logic

The fisrt, and simplest, family of MCLs that was developed is based on an unstructured set I of contexts, where each context is described by means of a propositional logical language. Following the general definition, a *propositional multi-context logic* (PMCL) is defined starting from a family $\{P_i\}_{i \in I}$, where each P_i is a set of propositional variables. Each logic L_i is therefore described using a propositional language defined on P_i. A model (compatibility relation) C for PMCL is composed by a set of chains $c \in C$ where each c_i is a set of truth assignments to the propositional variables in P_i (that is, each c_i is a set of propositional models defined over P_i). Depending on the constraints one imposes on C it is possible to define various types of PMCS. In the following we provide three important examples of PMCS present in literature.

Partitioning Propositional Theories

One of the simplest ways of looking at multi-context logics is in terms of a partition of a (propositional) theory into a set of interacting *microtheories*. In this case the entire MCS is the (propositional) theory, the different contexts are the microtheories, and the compatibility relations (or analogously bridge rules) express the way microtheories are connected one to another. As explained in Amir and Mcilraith (2000), one of the main reason for partitioning a large (propositional) theory into a set of smaller interacting microtheories is efficiency of reasoning.

Partitioned propositional theories correspond to a *specific class* of compatibility relations for PMCL, which we indicate with C_{part}, that contain chains c defined as follows:

$$\text{for all } i \in I, \quad |c_i| = 1 \tag{24.3}$$

$$\text{for all } p \in P_i \cap P_j, \quad c_i(p) = c_j(p) \tag{24.4}$$

Condition (24.3) states that all the elements c_i of a chain contain exactly one local model and intuitively represents the fact that each chain can be considered as composed of different contexts (the different c_i) that have a *complete* representation of a scenario (from their point of view). For instance, the chain $c' = \langle c_1', c_2' \rangle$ in Fig. 24.3 satisfies this requirement and correspond to the scenario in which Mr. 1 sees a ball in the left sector, and no ball in the right sector, and Mr. 2 sees a ball in the center and left sectors and no ball in the right sector. Condition (24.4) states that the different elements c_i contained in a chain agree on the interpretation of the propositional variables that are common to the two elements. Intuitively this means that the two contexts described by, say, c_i and c_j agree on the truth value of the knowledge they have in common.

If we denote with $\models_{part}$ the logical consequence defined w.r.t. C_{part}, then we can state the following correspondence between a partitioned PMCL and propositional logic.

Theorem 1 *Let $T = T_1 \uplus \cdots \uplus T_n$ be a propositional theory on the set of propositions P, which is partitioned in n theories $T_i \subseteq T$ (for $1 \leq i \leq n$) defined on the set of propositional variables P_i, then: for every formula ϕ that contains only propositions in P_i, we have that*

$$T \models \phi \text{ if and only if } 1 : T_1, \ldots, n : T_n \models_{part} i : \phi.$$

Partial Views

Relaxing conditions (24.3) and (24.4) enables to obtain a more general (that is, weaker) class of MCLs where each context can be considered as describing a partial view on the world. For example, in Fig. 24.3 element c_1 corresponds to a partial view of the two sector's box where Mr. 1 can state that there is a ball in the right sector but is uncommitted on whether there is a ball in the left hand side sector (e.g., because the sector is behind a wall as in an example shown in Ghidini and Giunchiglia (2001).

As shown in Roelofsen and Serafini (2004), this general formulation of PMCL is embeddable in the propositional multi-modal logic S5, with one modal operator $\Box_i$ for each context label $i \in I$. Local formulas of the form $i : \phi$ are translated in $\Box_i \phi$, and bridge rules of the form (24.1) are translated in the implication

$$\Box_{i_1} \phi_1 \wedge \cdots \wedge \Box_{i_n} \phi_n \rightarrow \Box_i \phi \tag{24.5}$$

The correspondence between this PMCL and multi-modal S5 is not an equivalence since modal logics has a *global language* allowing formulas that express relations between local models which are more complex that the one representable in terms of propagation rules. For instance the modal formula $\Box_i \phi \vee \Box_j \phi$ does not correspond

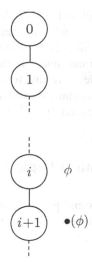

Fig. 24.4 A hierarchical meta structure

to any bridge rule between i and j as it cannot be represented as a propagation pattern. Another example is negated modal formulas like e.g., $\neg\Box_i\phi$, which is not expressible in MCL, as it states that a proposition does not hold in a context. This limitations in the expressivity reflects the fundamental assumption of MCL, i.e., that every formula should be stated in a context. This expressivity limitation turns out to be of great help in the definition of modular reasoning systems, since they prevent to express global inconsistency, since there is no global formula. The assumption of not permitting global logical operators, has been relaxed in the formulaization of non-monotonic MCL (Brewka et al. 2007), where the negation (as failure) operator is applicable to a labelled formula, obtaining **not**$(i : \phi)$.

Hierarchical Meta Logics

In the work on propositional multi-context logics, a special effort was devoted to investigate the usage of these formalisms to formalize the "object and meta relation" between contexts, that is, the situation in which for each context one can define a meta context that predicates on what holds in the object context.

In this case I is the set of natural numbers with the usual total linear order, and each language L_i is a propositional language, such that for every formula ϕ in the language of L_i there is a propositional variable $\bullet(\phi)$ in the language of L_{i+1}, as depicted in Fig. 24.4.

The compatibility relation C_{OM} for a hierarchical meta logic satisfies the following constraints:

1. CLOSURE W.R.T. UNION: If $c, c' \in C$, then $c \cup c' \in C$ (where $c \cup c' = \{c_i \cup c'_i\}_{i \in I}$).
2. INTERPRETATION OF META-FORMULAS: For all $c \in C$, $i \in I$ and ϕ in L_i, $c_i \models \phi$ if and only if $c_{i+1} \models \bullet(\phi)$.

The work in Giunchiglia and Serafini (1994) shows that this logic is equivalent to the modal logic K, when the "•" operator is translated in the modal operator $\Box$, while further works (see, e.g., Ghidini 1999) prove that by further restricting C it is possible to obtain the other normal modal logics, such as B, K4, K45, S4 and S5, and have applied these equivalence results to model propositional attitudes and multi-agent systems by means of a context-based approach (see, e.g., Cimatti et al. 1994; Benerecetti et al. 1998a; Benerecetti et al. 1998b; Fisherand Ghidini 2010).

24.4   Quantified Multi-context Logics

Quantified multi-context logics extend propositional MCL with the possibility of predicating object properties in different contexts and relations between objects. The two principles of MCL of locality and compatibility are extended to the contextual interpretation of terms. In details: according to the locality principle, each context is associated with a local domain. According to the compatibility principle, only certain combinations of local domains are admitted. For instance, if A and B are the contexts associated to two databases DB_A and DB_B, respectively, then the universe of A (i.e., the set of constants that appear in the relations of DB_A) can be completely distinct from the universe of DB_B. For instance, the two databases might use different identifiers, and different ways to denote attributes, and so on. On the other hand, if the intended domains of both DB_A and DB_B overlap, i.e., they contain information about a common subset of objects, say books, then the identifiers of books used in the two databases should be somehow related. As explained in the introductory section, the relation between local domains is modelled via the, so-called, domain relation.

Specific instances of quantified MCL have been developed with the scope of formalizing heterogeneous database integration, ontology integration, and ontology matching. They are all monotonic logics, and the local logics are either first order logic, or description logics. In the following subsections we introduce the two main quantified MCLs: Distributed First Order Logics (Ghidini and Serafini 1998) and Distributed Description Logics (Borgida and Serafini 2003).

24.4.1   Distributed First Order Logics

DFOL is a family of MCL that has been defined with the objective of formalizing contextual knowledge expressed in first order languages. One of the main motivation for DFOL is the formalization of heterogeneous relational database integration (Serafini and Ghidini 2004) and to provide a formal semantics for heterogeneous schema and ontology mapping (Serafini et al. 2007).

A DFOL is defined on a family of first order logics $\{L_i\}_{i \in I}$. A DFOL model is any compatibility relation $\{c\}$ composed of a single chain c where c_i, for all $i \in I$ is a (possibly empty) set of interpretations of L_i on the same domain $\Delta_i \neq \emptyset$. With respect of the original formalization described in Ghidini and Serafini (1998) we also admit the arrow variable $x^{i\to}$ and $x^{\to i}$ in the language L_i and the domain relation r_{ii}. This results in a more uniform treatment.

Consequently, this simplify the general definition on assignment, as this implies that the intersection of the domains of all the local models associated to the context i, is the same as the domain of each local model. The representational hypothesis which derives by assuming shared domain for all local models in c_i is the fact that at each context there is *complete knowledge on the size of the local domain*. Formally this corresponds to the fact that every formula ϕ that does not contain, constant symbols, functional symbols, and predicate symbols with the exception of the equality symbol, is such that $C \models i : \phi$ or $C \models i : \neg\phi$. i.e., all the ith local models agree on the evaluation of ϕ[5]. Examples of such formulas, are the those that allow to state bounds on the dimension of the domain. as, $i : \forall x_0, \dots, x_m \bigvee_{0 \le i < j \le m} x_i = x_j$, which states that ith domain contains at most m elements, and $i : \exists x_1, \dots, x_n \bigwedge_{0 \le i < j \le n} x_i \ne x_j$ that states that ith domain contains at least n elements. The assumptions, of constant local domains does not imply full constant domains, i.e., the fact that every domain in every context has the same dimension. Indeed, for instance the set of labelled formulas $\{1 : \forall xy.x = y, \ 2 : \exists xy.x \ne y\}$ is satisfiable, and they state that the domain of context 1 contain one element and the domain of context 2 contains at least two elements.

DFOL is the first example of MCL described in this chapter where logical consequence relation involves the assignment to variables. Under the assumption of constant local domains, we can simplify the definition of logical consequence as follows:

$\Gamma \models \phi$ if for every chain c and every assignment a for all the variables in Γ, if c

$\models \Gamma[a]$ then there is an extension of a to a' such that $c \models i : \phi[a']$. \hfill (24.6)

24.4.1.1 Representing Cross Domain Constraints in DFOL

In the general case, i.e., when no constraints are imposed on the compatibility relation, the logical consequences across contexts is extremely week, and it is such that $\Gamma_{\ne i} \models i : \phi$ iff $\models i : \phi$ (where $\Gamma_{\ne i}$ is a set of labelled formulas with index different from i). As in all the other MCL's, also in DFOL it is possible to impose restrictions on the compatibility relation and on the domain relation by means of bridge rules. In the following we present some of the properties involving quantificational contextual information that can be formalized by means of DFOL bridge rules:

Absolute names. In general, in different contexts a constant (or a term) can have different meanings, however, it is also possible that the meaning of a term in a context is related to the meaning of another term in another context. An extreme

---

[5] Notice that, if $|c_i| > 1$, i.e., there is more than one local model, it is possible that $C \not\models i : \phi$ and $C \not\models i : \neg\phi$.

situation is when a constant is an *absolute/global name*. I.e., a constant that have the same meaning in all the context. Absolute names can be modelled by imposing the following bridge rule to be valid for every $i, j \in I$.

$$i : a = x^{i\rightarrow} \qquad i : a = x \rightarrow j : x^{i\rightarrow} = a \qquad i : a = x^{\rightarrow i} \rightarrow j : x = a \quad (24.7)$$

The first of the above bridge rules imposes that the constant a is interpreted in a unique element by all local model in c_i. Indeed if c_i contains two models m and m' that interpret a in two different objects, then it is not possible that $m \models a = x^{i\rightarrow}[a]$ and $m' \models a = x^{i\rightarrow}[a]$, and therefore $c \not\models i : a = x^{i\rightarrow}$. The other two bridge rules in (24.7) do not impose that a is interpreted in the same object in i and j, since Δ_i and Δ_j can be different (possibly disjoint) domains, but they state that the interpretation of a in contexts i and j corresponds via the translation defined by the domain relation among the domains of the two contexts. If the bridge rules in (24.7) are imposed for two individual constants a and b in the intersection of the languages of L_i and L_j, then we have that the following logical consequences hold.

$$i : a \neq b \models j : a \neq b \qquad i : a = b \models j : a = b$$

Imposing bridge rules (24.7) on the set of constants contained in the intersection of the universes of two databases DB_A and DB_B, corresponds to assume that the intersection of the universes of the two DBs are isomorphic, and therefore this allow to safely join informations about the intersected domain available in both DBs.

Constraints on the domain relation. Bridge rules can be used to formalize relations between domains in different contexts. For instance, in some situation it is useful to assume that the domains of two contexts (say i and j) are isomorphic. This can be forced by the bridge rules

$$\rightarrow j : \exists y . y = x^{i\rightarrow} \qquad \rightarrow i : \exists y . y = x^{\rightarrow j} \qquad i : x^{\rightarrow j} = y^{\rightarrow j} \rightarrow j : x = y$$

The first two of the above bridge rules imposes that for every element x of the domain of context i, there is a corresponding element of the domain of context j and, vice-versa for every element of the domain of context j, there is a corresponding element of the domain of context i. The third one states that the domain relation between i and j must be a function. In Ghidiniand Serafini (1998) we describe how many other properties can be formalised by bridge rules containing just the equality symbol and arrow variables.

Join among heterogeneous domains. Bridge rules can be used to express the fact that a certain knowledge in a database DB_C can be obtained by joining the information available in two heterogeneous databases DB_A and DB_B. As an example, suppose that we want to represent that the ternary relation $R(x, y, z)$ in the database DB_C is obtained by a join between the relations $P(x, y)$ in DB_A, and $Q(y, z)$ in DB_B over the argument y. But we know that the three databases have three heterogeneous representation of the values in the attributes, and therefore before doing the join it is necessary to perform a translation. There are three possible ways to proceed,

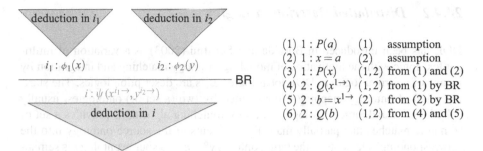

Fig. 24.5 A DFOL proof

- Translate the tuples of P from DB_A into the DB_B, do the join in B and translate the result into C. This is represented by the bridge rules

$$A : P(x,y), \; B : Q(y,z) \land y^{A\rightarrow} = y \land r^{A\rightarrow} - r \rightarrow C : R(x^{B\rightarrow}, y^{B\rightarrow}, z^{B\rightarrow})$$

- Do the same but starting form DB_B, joining in DB_A and translating in DB_C, which is represented by the bridge rule:

$$B : R(y,z), \; A : P(x,y) \land y^{B\rightarrow} = y \land z^{B\rightarrow} = z \rightarrow C : R(x^{A\rightarrow}, y^{A\rightarrow}, z^{A\rightarrow})$$

- or transfer the tuples of P and Q into DB_C and do the join there. This way of reasoning is represented by the bridge rule:

$$A:P(x,y), \; B:Q(y,z), \; C:x=x^{A\rightarrow} \land y=y^{A\rightarrow} \land y=y^{B\rightarrow} \land z=z^{B\rightarrow} \rightarrow C:R(x,y,z)$$

24.4.1.2 Reasoning in DFOL

Being DFOL an extension of first order logic, reasoning in DFOL is an undecidable task but it is finitely axiomatizable. In Ghidini and Serafini (1998) we proposed a sound and complete Natural Deduction Calculus for DFOL logical consequence parametrized on a set of bridge rules BR. This calculus is sound and complete with respect to the class of DFOL models and the domain relations that satisfies the set of bridge rules BR. Natural Deduction systems for FOL is a set of inference rules, with an arbitrary (finite) number of premises and a single conclusion. A deduction of ϕ form a set of hypothesis $\phi_1, \ldots, \phi_n$ is a tree rooted at ϕ, with leaves $\phi_1, \ldots, \phi_n$, such that the father node is derived by applying an inference rule to it's children. The extension of ND to DFOL with bridge rules BR, is obtained by composing local deductions via bridge rules. Informally, the bridge rule $i_1 : \phi_1(x), \; i_2 : \phi_2(y) \rightarrow i : \psi(x^{i_1\rightarrow}, y^{i_2\rightarrow})$ allows to "plug in" a deduction in context i_1 the two deductions performed in context i_1 and i_2 that infers the premises of the bridge rule. In Fig. 24.5 we provide a graphical representation of local inference composition and an example of a simple proof in DFOL.

24.4.2   Distributed Description Logics

DDL has been introduced in Borgida and Serafini (2003) as a variation of multi-context logic with the motivation of modeling ontology matching and integration by means of a formal logic. In DDL local logics L_i's are description logics. The starting point of ontology mapping is constituted by two (a set of) ontologies, usually called source and target ontology. Ontology matching algorithms provides a set of semantic matches that partially maps the elements of the source ontology into the "corresponding" elements of the target ontology[6]. Once a source ontology is semantically matched with a target ontology, and every heterogeneity in the representation of knowledge by the two ontologies has been resolved, the knowledge contained in the two ontologies can be integrated and combined in a unique (sometimes modular) knowledge base. In many cases ontology matches act as information channels that propagate knowledge from the source ontology to the target ontology that is extended with the additional information coming from the source ontology. This perspective of ontology matching/integration can be naturally represented in multi-context logic, using context based on description logic languages. In DDL each context represents an ontology and semantic matches between a source ontology i and a target ontology j are represented via bridge rules with premises in i and consequences in j. A context i can contain concepts and role subsumptions, namely formulas of the form $i : C \sqsubseteq D, i : R \sqsubseteq S$, and assertions, namely statements of the form $i : C(a)$ and $i : R(a, b)$ where C and D are concept expressions, R and S are role expressions and a and b are individuals. A model for DDL is the same as a DFOL model on the FOL translation of the description logic language (where concepts, are unary predicate, relation binary predicates, and individual constants stays the same) with the restriction that for every chain c, and every $i \in I$, $|c_i| \leq 1$. DDL bride rules are used to represent ontology matches, and they can be defined among concepts, roles and individuals. Heterogeneous bridge rules has also been introduced, which maps concepts to roles and viceversa (e.g., "wedding" to "is-married-to"), but for simplicity we only report homogeneous bridge rules here: Bridge rules between concepts and roles are of two forms

$$i : C \overset{\sqsubseteq}{\longrightarrow} j : D \qquad i : C \overset{\sqsupseteq}{\longrightarrow} j : D \qquad\qquad (24.8)$$

where C and D are concept expressions in L_i and L_j respectively. The above bridge rules are satisfied by the DDL model c if there is domain relation r_{ij} such that

$$r_{ij}(C^{c_i}) \subseteq D^{c_j} \qquad r_{ij}(C^{c_i}) \supseteq D^{c_j} \qquad\qquad (24.9)$$

where X^{c_i} is the extension of the concept C in the unique model $m \in c_i$ or it is the empty set if $c_i = \emptyset$.

---

[6] The most general setting semantic matches are associated with weights (confidence value) but when mappings are crisp (i.e., confidence value is equal to 1) then they can be fruitfully formalized in two valued logics.

The intuitive meaning of DDL bridge rules can be easily induced from the satisfiability conditions (24.9). In particular the $\xrightarrow{\sqsubseteq}$ bridge rule, states that the concept C in i matches with some subconcept of D in j. While the $\xrightarrow{\sqsupseteq}$ bridge rule states that the concept C in i is mapped into some superconcept of D in j. Analogous bridge rules can be defined among roles. Bridge rules among individuals are expressions of the form

$$i : a \xrightarrow{=} j : b_1. \qquad (24.10)$$

The bridge rule (24.10) is satisfied when $\langle a^{m_i}, b^{m_j} \rangle \in r_{ij}$ (where m_i and m_j are local models in c_i and c_j respectively). The intuitive meaning of the bridge rule (24.10) is that b is one of the possible translations in j of a in i.

Similarly to what happens for DL, which is a fragment of FOL, DDL is a fragment of DFOL. Indeed a DDL can be rewritteng into a DFOL by applying the standard translation of DL into FOL for each of the formulas in L_i, and by translating the bridge rule (24.8) into the following DFOL bridge rules:

$$i : C(x^{\to j}) \to j : D(x) \qquad j : D(x) \to i : C(x^{\to j}) \qquad (24.11)$$

and translating the individual bridge rule (24.10) into

$$i : x = a \to j : x^{i \to} = b. \qquad (24.12)$$

The semantics of DDL bridge rules entails a form of information propagation between mapped ontologies. The papers Serafini et al. (2004), Serafiniand Tamilin (2005), Ghidini et al. (2007) investigate on the knowledge propagation patterns between a source and a target ontology mapped with a set of DDL bridge rules. A simple example of such a propagation pattern from i to j induced by a pair of mappings from i to j is described by the following sound inference:

$$\frac{i : A \sqsubseteq B \qquad i : A \xrightarrow{\sqsupseteq} j : G \qquad i : B \xrightarrow{\sqsubseteq} j : H}{j : G \sqsubseteq H}.$$

The above propagation pattern in true for any unrestricted domain relation. However in many cases it's interesting to investigate on DDL models where the domain relation satisfies natural restriction, such as functionality or injectivity or compositionality. The more restricted the domain relation the more information is passed by the bridge rules. Detailed investigation of different propagation patterns depending on the restriction imposed on the domain relation are studied in Homola and Serafini (2010).

24.5 Conclusions

Research and implementation activities around multi context system has been carried out for the last 25 years with a number of significant results that include propositional MCLs, first order MCLs, description logics-based MCLs, and MCL for semantic web languages like RDF and OWL. The research activities have focused to the development of theoretical frameworks as well as a set of prototype implementations, among which DRAGO, a Distributed Reasoning Architecture for a set of ontology linked via ontology mappings (Serafini and Tamilin 2005), and the Contextualized Knowledge Repository (Bozzato et al. 2013), a system that extends standard RDF triple stores with the capability of reasoning with multiple RDF graphs (Contexts) linked via bridge rules.

A number of studies that compare multi context system with other logical formalism that support distributed knowledge representation have also been developed, and mappings between the different formalisms have been proposed. In particular Serafini and Bouquet (2000) presents a formal comparison between propositional MCL and the propositional logic of contexts based on modal logics proposed in Buvac and Mason (1993), while Brockmans et al. (2009) exploits DFOL for encoding and comparing several formalisms for ontology mappings.

In this chapter we have provided an overview of the main families of multi context logics (MCLs), a logical formalism that allow to integrate multiple logical theories (contexts) in a structure of inter-related contexts, a description of their main logical properties and an illustration of the types of applications they have been used for.

References

Amir, E., Mcilraith, S.: Partition-based logical reasoning for first-order and propositional theories. Artif. Intell. **162**, 49–88 (2000)

Benerecetti, M., Bouquet, P., Ghidini, C.: Formalizing belief reports – The approach and a case study. In: Giunchiglia, F. (ed.) Proceedings AIMSA'98, 8th International Conference on Artificial Intelligence, Methodology, Systems, and Applications, *LNAI*, vol. 1480, pp. 62–75. Springer, Sozopol (1998a)

Benerecetti, M., Giunchiglia, F., Serafini, L.: Model checking multiagent systems. J. Logic Comput. **8**(3), 401–423 (1998b)

Borgida, A., Serafini, L.: Distributed description logics: Assimilating information from peer sources. J. Data Semantics **1**, 153–184 (2003)

Bozzato, L., Serafini, L.: Materialization calculus for contexts in the semantic web. In: Proceedings of the 26th International Workshop on Description Logics, Ulm, Germany, 23–26 July 2013, pp. 552–572 (2013)

Bozzato, L., Ghidini, C., Serafini, L.: Comparing contextual and flat representations of knowledge: a concrete case about football data. In: Proceedings of the 7th International Conference on Knowledge Capture, K-CAP 2013, Banff, Canada, 23–26 June 2013, pp. 9–16. ACM (2013)

Brewka, G., Roelofsen, F., Serafini, L.: Contextual default reasoning. In: IJCAI 2007, Proceedings of the 20th International Joint Conference on Artificial Intelligence, Hyderabad, India, 6-12 January 2007, pp. 268–273 (2007)

Brockmans, S., Haase, P., Serafini, L., Stuckenschmidt, H.: Formal and conceptual comparison of ontology mapping languages. In: Stuckenschmidt, H., Parent, C., Spaccapietra, S. (eds.) Modular Ontologies, Lecture Notes in Computer Science, vol. 5445, pp. 267–291. Springer, Heidelberg (2009)

Buvac, S., Mason, I.A.: Propositional logic of context. In: Proceedings of the 11th National Conference on Artificial Intelligence. Washington, DC, USA, 11–15 July 1993, pp. 412–419. AAAI Press/MIT Press (1993)

Cimatti, A., Serafini, L., Cimatti, R., Serafini, L.: Multi-agent reasoning with belief contexts: the approach and a case study. In: Wooldridge, M., Müller, J. P., Tambe, M. (eds.) Intelligent Agents: Proceedings of 1994 Workshop on Agent Theories, Architectures, and Languages, Lecture Notes in Computer Science, number 890, pp. 71–85. Springer, Heidelberg (1994)

Fisher, M., Ghidini, C.: Executable specifications of resource-bounded agents. Autonom. Agents Multi-Agent Syst. **21**(3), 368–396 (2010)

Ghidini, C.: Modelling (un)bounded beliefs. In: Bouquet, P., Serafini, L., Brézillon, P., Benerecetti, M., Castellani, F. (eds.) Modelling and Using Context – Proceedings of the 2nd International and Interdisciplinary Conference, Context'99. Lecture Notes in Artificial Intelligence, vol. 1688, pp. 145–158. Springer, Heidelberg (1999)

Ghidini, C., Giunchiglia, F.: Local models semantics, or contextual reasoning = locality + compatibility. Artif. Intell. **127**(2), 221–259 (2001)

Ghidini, C., Serafini, L.: Distributed first order logics. In: Gabbay, D., de Rijke, M. (eds.) Frontiers of Combining Systems 2 (Papers presented at FroCoS'98), Studies in Logic and Computation, pp. 121–140. Research Studies Press, Baldock (1998)

Ghidini, C., Serafini, L., Tessaris, S.: On relating heterogeneous elements from different ontologies. In: Kokinov, B., Richardson, D., Roth-Berghofer, T., Vieu, L. (eds.) Proceedings of the Sixth International and Interdisciplinary Conference on Modeling and Using Context (CONTEXT'07), Lecture Notes in Artificial Intelligence, Roskilde University, Denmark, vol. 4635, pp. 234–247. Springer (2007)

Giunchiglia, F., Serafini, L.: Multilanguage hierarchical logics, or: how we can do without modal logics. Artif. Intell. **65**(1), 29–70 (1994)

Homola, M., Serafini, L.: Augmenting subsumption propagation in distributed description logics. Appl. Artif. Intell. **24**(1–2), 39–76 (2010)

Roelofsen, F., Serafini, L.: Complexity of contextual reasoning. In: McGuinness, D.L., Ferguson, G. (eds.) Proceedings of the Nineteenth National Conference on Artificial Intelligence, Sixteenth Conference on Innovative Applications of Artificial Intelligence, San Jose, California, USA, 25–29 July 2004, pp. 118–123. AAAI Press/MIT Press (2004)

Serafini, L., Bouquet, P.: Comparing formal theories of context in ai. Artif. Intell. **155**(1–2), 41–67 (2004)

Serafini, L., Ghidini, C.: Context based semantics for information integration. In: Bonzon, P., Cavalcanti, M., Nossum, R. (eds.) Formal Aspects of Context, Applied Logic Series, vol. 20, pp. 175–192. Springer Netherlands (2000)

Serafini, L., Roelofsen, F.: Satisfiability for propositional contexts. In: Principles of Knowledge Representation and Reasoning: Proceedings of the Ninth International Conference (KR2004), Whistler, Canada, 2–5 June 2004, pp. 369–376 (2004)

Serafini, L., Tamilin, A.: Drago: Distributed reasoning architecture for the semantic web. In: Gómez-Pérez, A., Euzenat. J. (eds.) The Semantic Web: Research and Applications, Second European Semantic Web Conference, ESWC 2005, Heraklion, Crete, Greece, 29 May -1 June 2005, Proceedings. Lecture Notes in Computer Science, vol. 3532, pp. 361–376. Springer, Heidelberg (2005)

Serafini, L., Tamilin, A.: Instance migration in heterogeneous ontology environments. In: The Semantic Web, 6th International Semantic Web Conference, 2nd Asian Semantic Web Conference, ISWC 2007 + ASWC 2007, Busan, Korea, 11–15 November 2007. Lecture Notes in Computer Science, vol. 4825, pp. 452–465. Springer (2007)

Serafini, L., Borgida, A., Tamilin, A.: Aspects of distributed and modular ontology reasoning. In: IJCAI-05, Proceedings of the Nineteenth International Joint Conference on Artificial Intelligence, Edinburgh, Scotland, UK, 30 July–5 August 2005, pp. 570–575 (2005a)

Serafini, L., Stuckenschmidt, H., Wache, H.: A formal investigation of mapping language for terminological knowledge. In: 19th Joint Conference on Artificial Intelligence (IJCAI-05), pp. 576–581 (2005b)

Chapter 25
Constraint Programming for Context Comprehension

Henning Christiansen

Abstract A close similarity is demonstrated between context comprehension, such as discourse analysis, and constraint programming. The constraint store takes the role of a growing knowledge base learned throughout the discourse, and a suitable constraint solver does the job of incorporating new pieces of knowledge. The language of Constraint Handling Rules, CHR, is suggested for defining constraint solvers that reflect "world knowledge" for the given domain, and driver algorithms may be expressed in Prolog or additional rules of CHR. It is argued that this way of doing context comprehension is an instance of abductive reasoning. The approach fits with possible worlds semantics that allows both standard first-order and non-monotonic semantics.

25.1 Introduction

There is a striking similarity between constraint logic programming and context comprehension. In both cases, a given structure is traversed, and bits of information are accumulated in a growing knowledge base. Constraint programming usually deals with structures that encode complex mathematical problems to be solved, and context comprehension with observed phenomena such as a spoken or written discourse, streaming sensor data from an industrial plant or a transport network, etc. As more knowledge is accumulated, the possible solution space in the constraint logic programming case and the set of possible worlds that represents context, will decrease, i.e., become more and more specific. For each step of computation in either paradigm, the adding of a new piece of information may involve a normalization and consistency check with respect to previous knowledge, and in case of an inconsistency, the overall process may change its control path, e.g., by backtracking.

Constraint logic programming is typically based on a hardcoded set of constraint predicates with a fixed semantics, tailored for a specific class of mathematical problems (as described, e.g., by Apt 2003, Jaffar, J., Lassez 1987) and may not be of much use for context comprehension from, say, linguistic utterances. However, a

---

H. Christiansen ✉
Roskilde University, P.O.Box 260, 4000 Roskilde, Denmark
e-mail: henning@ruc.dk

© Springer Science+Business Media New York 2014
P. Brézillon, A. J. Gonzalez (eds.), *Context in Computing*,
DOI 10.1007/978-1-4939-1887-4_25

declarative programming language for defining constraint solvers such as Constraint Handling Rules (Frühwirth 1998, 2009), for short CHR, changes the picture. With this "white box" approach to constraint solving, it becomes feasible to define constraint domains and solvers for specific knowledge representations, especially tailored for representing context.

In this chapter, we summarize and exemplify how a combination of CHR and Prolog, the latter used for driver algorithms such as linguistic parsers or other structural scanners, can be used to specify and implement different tasks of context comprehension. However, the overall architectural principles are not tied to these specific programming languages, but can be integrated with, say, more advanced systems for linguistic parsing, or—instead of using constraint solvers written in CHR—other knowledge management tools and representation formalisms may be used.

By context, we refer to the set of circumstances in which a particular phenomenon ϕ is observed and to which ϕ may owe its existence. For example, it is difficult to observe a hole in a doughnut (an example of a ϕ) without its context, the doughnut. For a given discourse, its context may be represented as a knowledge base about the particular circumstances explained. References to context in the discourse may be given explicitly in factual form or indirectly assumed. For example "He likes Mary", presupposes that there is a male character in the context as well as a female one named Mary (as "Mary" is usually a female name) plus a fact about the relationship between those two characters. Context may be static when the given discourse describes universal properties (such as a math textbook) or some state of affairs in a stable period of time; in this case, the dynamic aspects are limited to the sequential traversal of the text (i.e., the reader's mental time) during which more and more information is recognized. A discourse may involve further dynamic aspect. It may describe developments in past times as in a history textbook, or the time of each utterance may be essential as in a psychological drama or a running commentary on a football match. In such cases context may be seen as a knowledge base of timestamped facts (as for the history book), or we may be interested in maintaining a representation of a current "now" context, which means that each new observation may give rise to a revision of previous knowledge. The framework and analysis methods introduced below can handle these different modes of context.

The focus on context comprehension, rather than a purely compositional analysis of the observed phenomena, displays a similarity with abductive reasoning (in the sense of C.S. Pierce; see Aliseda (2006) for a modern exposition): the task is to figure out a feasible context in which a given phenomenon has been observed, or in logical terms, that the observation must be deductively derivable from the inherent background knowledge and the context to be identified. As spelled out in more details in Sect. 25.4.1, it can be shown that Prolog with CHR is an instance—and efficient implementation—of so-called Abductive Logic Programming, and in this way our approach to context comprehension confirms the metaphor of "Interpretation as abduction" introduced in the often cited paper (Hobbs et al. 1993).

In Sect. 25.2, we define constraints and constraint solving in a precise way with possible worlds semantics, and Sect. 25.3 introduces CHR and demonstrates how it can be used for defining semantics and solvers. Section 25.4 describes driver algorithms in Prolog, elaborates on the relation to abduction and shows an example of Prolog's grammar notation used with CHR for context comprehension from. Finally, Sect. 25.5 discusses related work and background sources, and Sect. 25.6 provides a summary and conclusions.

25.2 Constraints and Constraint Solving

Traditional constraint programming is concerned with finding values for variables that will satisfy logically specified conditions about those variables. As an informal example, let us consider constraint predicates "$\in \mathcal{N}$" indicating a natural number, and $>$ for the usual ordering relation. The conjunction

$$x \in \mathcal{N} \wedge x > 5 \wedge x < 7 \tag{25.1}$$

is a constraint problem in x, and it has as solution $x = 6$. This short formula is in solved or normalized form: it is accepted as a standard format for delivering solutions. A solved form may express intensional answers, providing a finite representation of a perhaps infinite set of solutions. For example, the constraint problem $x \in \mathcal{N} \wedge x > 5 \wedge x > 7 \wedge x \neq 3$ may have the solved form $x \in \mathcal{N} \wedge x > 7$, that represents the infinite set of solutions $\{x = 8, x = 9, \dots\}$.

When constraints are used for representing context, we also pay attention to variable-free constraints as having important content themselves, being statements about the world. So if "*raining*" is a constraint predicate, we may consider the formula *raining* as being true in any world where it is actually raining, and false in all other worlds. It can be read as an intensional representation of an infinite set of worlds in which it is definitely raining, some in which the sky is densely covered with clouds and yet others with a bit of sunshine and maybe a rainbow. We may still be interested in using variables, so for example "tall-person(x)" may designate a collection of contexts or worlds in which there exists a tall person, although we do not know anything more specific about this person.

What we define below as a standard semantics complies with first-order logic, but we present our definitions in a more general way that also allows for non-monotonicity. A formula or other object is *ground* if it contains no variables; substitutions and grounding substitutions are defined in the usual way.

Definition 25.1 A *constraint framework* $F = \langle \mathcal{C}, \mathcal{W}, W \rangle$ consists of a set of *constraint predicates* $\mathcal{C}$, a set of *possible worlds* $\mathcal{W}$ and a *semantic function* W. The constraint predicates are assumed (without mention) to include the zero-ary predicates *true* and *false*; an atom whose predicate is in $\mathcal{C}$ is referred to as a *constraint*. A *constraint store* is a finite set of constraints, which may be written as a conjunction $c_1 \wedge \cdots \wedge c_n$; the empty store is identified with *true*, and *false* will be used also as a prototypical inconsistent constraint store (below). The symbol $\mathcal{S}$ (with subscript F understood) refers to the set of all constraint stores and $\overline{\mathcal{S}}$ specifically to the ground ones. The semantic function is given by a mapping $W : \overline{\mathcal{S}} \to 2^{\mathcal{W}}$ with

- $W(true) = \mathcal{W}$,
- $W(s_1 \wedge true \wedge s_2) = W(s_1 \wedge s_2)$ and
- $W(false) = W(\cdots \wedge false \wedge \cdots) = \emptyset$.

The semantics is generalized to nonground constraint stores as follows.

$$W(s) =_{\text{def}} \bigcup_{\sigma \text{ a grounding subst. for } s} W(s\sigma) \tag{25.2}$$

In case $w \vDash W(s)$, we may write $w \vDash s$ (F understood). A constraint store s is *consistent* if there is a world w such that $w \vDash s$; any other constraint store is *inconsistent*.

Notice that formula (25.2) corresponds to an implicit existential quantification of a constraint store at the outermost level. In practice, not all conjunctions of constraints will appear as constraint stores in which case we may leave their semantics unspecified or implicitly $\emptyset$.

Definition 25.2 A *standard semantics* W is one in which $W(s_1 \wedge s_2) = W(s_1) \cap W(s_2)$ for any ground constraint stores s_1, s_2.

Standard semantics includes first-order logical theories, in which $\mathcal{W}$ may be identified with a class of first-order models. Non-standard semantics include non-monotonic semantics in which certain constraints can be understood as update instructions, e.g., by deleting or replacing information.

Example 25.1 We consider a constraint framework whose constraints are of the form $in(i, \ell)$, where i is an individual in $\{1, 2, 3\}$ and ℓ a location in $\{a, b, c\}$. A possible world is any set of three ground atoms of the form $\{in(1, \ell_1), in(2, \ell_2), in(3, \ell_3)\}$, $\ell_1, \ell_2, \ell_3 \in \{a, b, c\}$, i.e., each world represents a scene in which each individual is placed in some location. We assume a standard semantics in which a store s is mapped into the set of worlds in which s holds, more precisely $W(s) = \{w \mid s \subseteq w\}$. This yields, for example,

- $W(in(1, a) \wedge in(2, b)) = \{\{in(1, a), in(2, b), in(3, \ell)\} \mid \ell \in \{a, b, c\}\}$,
- $W(in(1, a) \wedge in(1, b)) = W(in(1, a)) \cap W(in(1, b)) = \emptyset$.

In other words, the semantics has the inherent limitation that an individual can only be in one location at a time, but a given location may host any number of individuals, from 0 to 3.

In the following we give a definition of constraint solving that merges one constraint at a time into a developing, normalized store, rather that crunching a huge bunch of constraints in one go. There are several reasons for this.

- It fits well with discourse and text analysis, in which utterances arrive sequentially and the decomposition and translation into constraints of each utterance can exploit the context learned so far (very much like we humans do).
- It corresponds to the way a Prolog interpreter enhanced with constraint solving typically works: A proof is built in Prolog's traditional, recursive and goal-directed

manner, but whenever a constraint is encountered, the constraint solver incorporates it into the growing constraint store, and if this succeeds, Prolog continues in the usual way.

- The sequential order of processing constraints is essential for implementing non-standard semantics.

Definition 25.3 Given a constraint framework $F = \langle C, W, W \rangle$, a set of *normalized* constraint stores is assumed, which includes particularly *true* and *false*. A normalized constraint store s' is a *normalized form of* s whenever, for any substitution σ for variables of s' and s, that $W(s'\sigma) = W(s\sigma)$.[1]

A *constraint solver* for a semantics W is a mapping, denoted $s_1, c \vdash s_2$, from a normalized constraint store s_1 and a new constraint c into a new normalized constraint store s_2 where s_2 is a normalized form of $s_1 \wedge c$. A constraint solver is *sound* if the normalized form of any inconsistent constraint store is *false* (meaning that the constraint solver recognizes inconsistency immediately, signaling this by the result *false*).

We introduce a convenient notation. When a semantics and constraint solver is given, the state s_n following from a sequence of insertions of constraints $c_1, \ldots, c_n$ into an initial store s_0 is denoted $[s_0, c_1, \ldots, c_n]$. More precisely,

$$s_0, c_1 \vdash s_1$$

$$s_1, c_2 \vdash s_2$$

$$\vdots$$

$$s_{n-1}, c_n \vdash s_n =_{\text{def}} [s_0, c_1, \ldots, c_n].$$

When $s_0 = true$, it may be left out.

In the special case of a standard semantics, permuting the constraints may yield syntactically different states which will be equivalent according to the given semantics, i.e., they represent the same set of possible worlds.

Example 25.2 A constraint solver for the constraint framework of Example 25.1 can be described as follows.

$$s, in(i, \ell) \vdash s \cup \{in(i, \ell)\} \quad \text{whenever there is no } in(i, \ell') \in s \text{ with } \ell \neq \ell',$$

$$s, in(i, \ell) \vdash false \qquad \text{otherwise.}$$

---

[1] The mentioning of the substitution σ in Definition 25.3 is necessary in order to preserve the identity of variables in the store and its normalized version.

25.3   Defining Semantics and Constraint Solvers with CHR

Often the possible worlds semantics will be implicit in the definition of the actual constraints and constraint solver. A declarative programming language such as Constraint Handling Rules intended for defining constraint solvers is interesting here. Claiming a programming language to be "declarative" means that its programs can be read as a concise specification of what the program is supposed to accomplish without unnecessary computational details. In the following, we give first a brief introduction to Constraint Handling Rules and show, then, how it can be used for defining constraint solvers that may comply with a standard or a non-standard semantics.

25.3.1   Constraint Handling Rules: A Brief Introduction

Constraint Handling Rules (CHR) is an extension to the logic programming language Prolog that adds mechanisms for forward-chaining reasoning to complement Prolog's standard backward-chaining, goal directed reasoning. CHR is now part of several major Prolog systems, including SWI and Sicstus. Here we give only a very brief introduction; a comprehensive account on CHR and its applications can be found in the book (Frühwirth 2009).

CHR was originally intended as a declarative language for writing constraint solvers for standard constraint domains concerned with numbers, arithmetic, equations and the like. Later it has turned out that CHR is suited for automated reasoning in general as documented by the vast literature on applications of CHR, also summarized in Frühwirth (2009). As shown in, e.g., Christiansen (2009) and the present chapter, the combination of CHR and Prolog is a powerful paradigm for implementing a variety of forms of reasoning and knowledge representations.

A CHR program consists of declarations of constraint predicates and rewriting rules over constraint stores. A simplified explanation of CHR's procedural semantics is that whenever a new constraint is called, it is included in the constraint store and the rules of the current program apply as long as possible. CHR has three sorts of rules of the following forms.

Simplification rules:	$h_1, \ldots, h_n$	<=>	$Guard \mid b_1, \ldots, b_m$
Propagation rules:	$h_1, \ldots, h_n$	==>	$Guard \mid b_1, \ldots, b_m$
Simpagation rules:	$h_1, \ldots, h_k \setminus h_{k+1}, \ldots h_n$	<=>	$Guard \mid b_1, \ldots, b_m$

The h's are head constraints and b's body constraints, and *Guard* is a guard condition (typically testing values of variables found in the head). A rule can be applied when its head constraints are matched simultaneously by constraints in the store and the guard is satisfied. For a simplification rule, the matched constraints are removed and the suitably instantiated versions of the body constraints are added. The other rules execute in a similar way, except that for propagation, the head constraints stay in the store, and for simpagation, only those following the backslash are removed. Prolog calls inside the body are executed in the usual way.

CHR has a logical semantics based on reading a simplification as a bi-implication, a propagation as an implication, and finally considering a simpagation $H_1 \setminus H_2 <=> G \mid B$ as equivalent with the simplification $H_1, H_2 <=> G \mid H_1, B$ (although it is executed in a different way). It is possible to write CHR programs that are inconsistent according to this semantics and non-termination can be an issue as well.

It can be shown (Frühwirth 2009), that if a program is terminating and confluent (roughly: the final result is independent of the order in which rules are applied), then it is consistent. Procedurally, when a new constraint arrives, the interpreter searches for possible rules to apply in the order they appear in the program, and there is also a deterministic strategy for finding companion constraints to form a match with the entire head of a rule. This means that non-confluent and even inconsistent programs may still be both readable and preserve a reasonable semantics, although it may go beyond a standard first-order semantics. This provides a style of programming in which simplifications and simpagations are explicitly used for their effect of deleting or revising constraints in the store. A formal semantics for CHR based on linear logic has been suggested by Betz and Frühwirth (2005) to cope with such programs. In practice, we do not need such apparatus, and in the examples below we can specify a non-standard, possible worlds semantics when relevant.

In the constraint solvers to be shown below, we use the Prolog facility *fail* as a way to indicate an inconsistent state. When used within a larger program, this results in no new store being generated and instead the interpreter backtracks, perhaps leading to a failure of the entire computation.

25.3.2 Constraint Solvers for Standard and Non-standard Semantics

A constraint solver for a standard semantics will typically accumulate the constraints into the growing state, however, taking care to

- avoid adding constraints that are already in, or implied by the current state, and
- detect failure when it occurs.

The following example shows a pattern that can be used for a large class of standard semantics.

Example 25.3 [Standard semantics] The semantics of Example 25.1 and the solver of Example 25.2 can be represented in CHR as follows.

```
:- chr_constraint in/2.
in(I, L1) \ in(I, L2) <=> L1=L2.
```

The first line is necessary to inform the interpreter that the in/2 predicate should be treated in a special way, i.e, as a constraint. The single rule of the program, in case it applies, will ensure that no individual can be registered at two different locations at the same time. If the unification L1=L2 fails, it indicates an inconsistency. Notice that the rule is a simpagation that removes one of the constraints, thus avoiding duplicate constraints to pile up in the store.[2] If the rule does not apply when a constraint is called, it means that the constraint is the first one referring to its particular individual, and it is simply added to the store.

Example 25.4 [Standard semantics] We consider a constraint solver to be used for the analysis of stories about the students at a small university at some fixed moment of time. The university has a number of rooms and other places, where a student can be.

```
lecture_hall_1, lecture_hall_2, reading_room,
student_bar, garden, ...
```

There are two courses going on, programming_course in lecture_hall_1 and linguistics_course in lecture_hall_2. We have constraints in(s,r) indicating that student s is in room r, attends(s,c) that student s attends course c, can_see(s_1, s_2) that student s_1 can see student s_2, and finally reading(s) indicating that student s is reading. A student can only be in one room at a time, and reading can take place in any other room than the lecture halls, and for student x to see student y, they must be in the same room. A constraint solver for this can be expressed in CHR as follows; the constraint diff(x,y) is a standard device indicating that x and y must be different (easily defined in CHR; left out for reasons of space).

```
:- chr_constraint attends/2, in/2, can_see/2, reading/1.
attends(St, programming_course) ==> in(St, lecture_hall_1).
attends(St, linguistics_course) ==> in(St, lecture_hall_2).
in(St, R1) \ in(St, R2) <=> R1=R2.
reading(St) ==> in(St, R),
                diff(R, lecture_hall_1),diff(R, lecture_hall_2).
can_see(St1,St2) ==> in(St1,R), in(St2,R).
```

The first line introduces the constraint predicates, and the rules describe the general world knowledge explained above and at the same time it defines the set of consistent constraint stores. As stated above, we may use ground, consistent constraint stores as possible worlds in a semantics. As an example of running this constraint solver, we observe:

```
[attends(peter,linguistics_course), can_see(mary,peter)]
    ∋ in(mary,lecture_hall_1).
```

---

[2] Most implementations of CHR are based on a multiset semantics; some implementations has an option for switching to a set semantics, but for reasons of efficiency, this is discouraged. It is recommended to use relevant simpagations for duplicate elimination as shown in the example.

This constraint solver is suited for reasoning about a static world, but standard semantics can also capture development over time if world facts are equipped with time stamps or abstract time representations as in the event calculus (Kowalski and Bowen 1988).

Example 25.5 [Non-standard semantics] We consider a robot in a two-dimensional world whose actions are to move forward, to turn left and to turn right. We will use a constraint solver written in CHR to determine the robot's position after a sequence of actions. Constraint predicates are `position/2`, intended to hold the current x and y coordinates, `direction/1` whose argument are expected to be one of `north`, `west`, `south`, `east`, and finally nul-ary constraints for the actions `step_forward`, `turn_left` and `turn_right`. This is defined in CHR as follows.

```
:- chr_constraint position/2, direction/1,
   step_forward/0, turn_left/0, turn_right/0.

direction(north), turn_right <=> direction(east).
7 similar rules
direction(north) \ position(X,Y), step_forward
                      <=> Y1 is Y+1, position(X,Y1).

3 similar rules
```

As normalized constraint stores, we consider in this example only ground ones (for simplicity only[3]) of the form $position(x,y) \land direction(d)$, where x, y are integers and d one of `north`, `east`, `south`, `west`. To define a semantics, we define $\mathcal{W}$ as the set of normalized states, and W as follows.

$W(s) = \{s\}$ for any normalized con. store s

$W(s \land a) = \{s'\}$ for normalized con. store s and action a; s' is a copy of s with

         the `direction` or `position` fact adjusted according to a

$W(s)$ undefined in all other cases.

This is obviously a non-standard semantics as conjunction does not correspond to intersection of world sets. The CHR program above defines a constraint solver for W with $s, a \vdash W(s \land a)$ for normalized state s and action a, and undefined otherwise. To see that the order of normalization steps do matter, consider the following with

---

[3] The constraint solver uses a predicate "`is`" which is a Prolog device for arithmetic that only works when all variables in its right hand side argument are given at the time of the call. Replacing it by a proper constraint solver capable of handling equations concerning the addition and subtraction of the constant one, will make it possible to work with non-ground constraints, corresponding to calculating the robot's position and direction relative to an unknown start position.

```
s₀ = {position(0,0),direction(north).
 [s₀,step_forward,turn_left]
    = {position(0,1),direction(west)}
 [s₀,turn_left,step_forward]
    = {position(-1,0),direction(west)}
```

This is a minimalist example of a dynamically developing context for which each new piece of information (here: a next constraint) results in a revision rather than an addition. The order in which the constraints are encountered is essential and defines a discrete time axis.

25.3.3 Nondeterministic Constraint Solvers

In some cases it may be difficult to represent accommodation of a new constraint in a single new constraint store, and instead we may have the constraint solver produce different, alternative updated stores, corresponding to a disjunction of alternative interpretations. In the setting of CHR embedded in Prolog, this may be handled by backtracking. First a formal definition.

Definition 25.4 Let a constraint framework $F = \langle C, W, W \rangle$ with a set of *normalized constraint* stores be given.

A subset of normalized constraint stores S is called a *normalized form of* a store s, whenever, for any substitution σ for variables of s and S, that

$$W(s\sigma) = \bigcup_{s' \in S} W(s'\sigma). \tag{25.3}$$

A *nondeterministic constraint solver* is a relation, denoted $s, c \vdash s'$, between normalized constraint stores s, s' and constraint c; let $S(s, c)$ denotes the set of all s_i' with $s, c \vdash s_i'$.

It is a solver *for* W whenever $S(s, c)$ is a normalized form of $s \wedge c$. It is *sound* if $S(s, c) = \{false\}$ whenever $s \wedge c$ is inconsistent.

Nondeterminism may be relevant for both standard and non-standard semantics. The notation of Sect. 25.2 for sequences of insertions of constraints is generalized writing "∨" between alternative states. Here we show an example of a constraint framework with a standard semantics and a nondeterministic constraint solver.

Example 25.6 [Nondeterministic constraint solver] We modify the solver shown in Example 25.4 by changing the rule of the form can_see(St1,St2) ==> ... that states consequences of the knowledge that students can see each other. The new rule is as follows, where skypes/2 is a new constraint indicating that two students are having a video chat.

```
can_see(St1,St2) ==> in(St1,R), in(St2,R)
  ; skypes(St1,St2), in(St1,R1), in(St2,R2), diff(R1,R2).
```

The semicolon stands for Prolog's disjunction that is implemented by backtracking. Notice that the rule incorporates a (claimed) world property, that two people will not skype together when they anyhow are in the same room. The semantics is defined as a straighforward extension of the one given in Example 25.4. Considering the steps of this constraint solver, we may possibly have $[\ldots, can\_see(peter, mary)] = s_1 \vee s_2$, where each of s_1, s_2 represents that either Peter and Mary are in the same room or in different rooms and skyping. In case the existing constraint store indicates that both Peter and Mary in fact are in the same room, s_2 will vanish, thus $[\ldots, can\_see(peter, mary)] = s_1$.

25.4   Driver Algorithms

In order to use a constraint solver for automatic extraction of context information from an observed phenomenon (such as a text, etc.) it needs to be combined with an algorithm that processes the phenomenon, converting it into constraints that in turn are handled by the constraint solver.

Here we use the logic programming language Prolog that plays well together with constraint solvers written in CHR. We expect a basic familiarity with Prolog and its grammar notation, Definite Clause Grammars.

We explain first the important result that the combination of Prolog as driver and CHR for context management is provably an instance of abductive reasoning. Second, we show how the special sort of Prolog programs, dressed up as Definite Clause Grammars, works seamlessly together with constraint solvers written in CHR. For reasons of space we leave out other examples of driver algorithms written in Prolog or CHR, but discuss a few options in Sect. 25.4.3 below.

25.4.1   A Close Relationship Between Prolog with CHR and Abductive Reasoning

The term abductive reasoning that stems back to C.S. Peirce, means basically to reason for a best explanation for an observed phenomenon.

While Prolog in itself is a purely deductive paradigm, different approaches to so-called abductive logic programming (ALP) have emerged since the early 1990s, and there is a direct equivalence between Prolog programs using CHR and a class of ALP programs as demonstrated by Christiansen (2009). Here we will give a brief informal background in terms of an example.

   An ALP program consists of a Prolog program in which certain predicates are recognized as abducibles plus so-called integrity constraints, that are restrictions on which combinations of abducibles are allowed. An abductive answer A to a query Q to an ALP is a set of abducible atoms such that

1. if A is added to the program as ordinary facts, Q would succeed according to the traditional logic semantics for Prolog, and
2. A satisfies the integrity constraints.

We can illustrate this in a simplistic example of an ALP program, where we also show its equivalent program in CHR+Prolog.

ALP:	Prolog+CHR:
Abducible pred's: a, b, c	`:- chr_constraint a,b,c.`
Integrity const's: $\neg(a \wedge b)$	`a, b <=> fail.`
`p:- q, a.`	`p:- q, a.`
`q:- b.`	`q:- b.`
`q:- c.`	`q:- c.`

Considering the program clauses as a plain Prolog program, the query q would simply fail, as the predicates a, b and c are false. Switching to abduction, we consider the query q as an observation—we have observed it and insist on it being true—and we need to figure out which yet unkown facts of abducible predicates that should be added in order to make q true in the program. In the example program, obviously a,c is the only possible extension to the program that will make it possible to prove q true and that does not conflict with the integrity constraints.

   Comparing with the program to the right, written in Prolog and CHR, we see that {a, c} is exactly the only final store produced for the query q. We can convince ourselves about the validity of that solution by manually adding the facts a and c to the program.

Prolog and manual editing:
`p:- q, a.`
`q:- b.`
`q:- c.`
`a.`
`c.`

Query q will succeed and the proof includes the newly added clauses.

25.4.2 CHR together with Definite Clause Grammars for Text Analysis

CHR works seamlessly together with Prolog's Definite Clause Grammar (DCG) notation as shown in the following example.

Example 25.7 We consider the nondeterministic constraint solver of Example 25.6, and add to the code, the following grammar rules as driver algorithm.

```
story --> [] ; s, ['.'], story.
s --> np(St1), [sees], np(St2), {can_see(St1,St2)}.
s --> np(St), [is,at], np(C), {attends(St,C)}.
s --> np(St), [is,reading], {reading(St)}.
np(peter)    --> [peter].
np(mary)     --> [mary].
np(jane)     --> [jane].
np(programming_course) --> [the,programming,course].
np(linguistics_course) --> [the,linguistics,course].
```

Traditionally in DCGs, the code inside the curly brackets is used for calculating attributes associated with the grammar symbols, but here we use them also for mentioning those contextual facts that must be a premise for the indicated sentences to be correctly uttered.

These facts are not known in advance, but are abduced on the flight when needed, which is the same as adding them to the constraint store. Consider the query phrase(story, [peter, ⋯]), where the list represents the text *Peter sees Mary. Peter sees Jane. Peter is at the programming course. Mary is at the programming course. Jane is reading.* The resulting constraint store—i.e., the context representation for this text—consists of the following constraints. The variable written as "X" stands for Jane's location which we do not know much about, except that it is not one of the lecture halls.

```
attends(mary,programming_course)     can_see(peter,jane)
attends(peter,programming_course)    can_see(peter,mary)
in(jane,X)                           reading(jane)
in(mary,lecture_hall_1)              skypes(peter,jane)
in(peter,lecture_hall_1)             diff(X,lecture_hall_2)
                                     diff(lecture_hall_1,X)
```

25.4.3   Refinements of Driver Algorithms in Prolog, DCG and CHR

The use of Prolog with CHR allows also for having the driver algorithm to inspect the current constraint store which gives a high flexibility for control. In Christiansen et al. (2007), pronoun resolution has been approached by adding to the constraint store information about position in the text and various attributes (such as gender etc.) for the possible entities that may be referred to by pronouns.

In the so-called CHR Grammars (Christiansen 2005), syntactic parsing is taken care of by CHR rules compiled from a high-level grammar notation with very powerful, context-sensitive rules that also interact with abduction. This means that the constraint store integrates the contextual knowledge base with the grammatical symbols.

The methods we have described extend easily to systems with multiple and perhaps partly shared knowledge bases for different agents' beliefs. Each agent is given an index that is included as an additional arguments to the constraints belonging to its knowledge base. For example, the fact a(k) for agent 7, is made into a(7,k); a general rule a(X)==>b(X) must be written as a(Agent,X)==>b(Agent,X) and if it is specific for agent 7 as a(7,X)==>b(7,X). This should make it possible to model dialogues with exchange of knowledge, but this has not been tested systematically yet.

In Christiansen (2012), a different approach is suggested for use in interactive installations with several concurrent processes and perhaps streaming sensor data. Here each process has its own program, and selected constraint predicates reside in shared files, which thus also serve as communication channels.

25.5   Related Work and Background

The relationship between constraint logic programming and abductive reasoning was observed in an early paper (Maim 1992) from 1992, before CHR was introduced in 1992–1993.

While the recognition of CHR as suitable for general knowledge representation and reasoning emerged through the following decade, its close relationship to abductive logic programming with integrity constraints was first reported in 2000 (Abdennadher and Christiansen 2000). The use of CHR's abductive capabilities for context comprehension was suggested together with CHR Grammars in 2002 (Christiansen 2005). The combination of Prolog and CHR for abduction, including with DCG as featured in the present book chapter, was unfolded in the HYPROLOG framework (Christiansen and Dahl 2005a) in 2005. Its relation to abductive logic programming was formally characterized and proved in Christiansen

(2009). Non-monotonic (i.e., non-standard) semantics[4] and its implementation in CHR were introduced in 2006 by Christiansen (2006) for an implementation of a paradigm called global abduction; similar uses of CHR for knowledge base update is also described by Frühwirth (2009). Probabilistic versions of abduction with CHR and Prolog are introduced by Christiansen (2008), Christiansen and Saleh (2011); here each abductive answer is given a probability and the most probable answer is taken as the best one.

A paper from 2005 (Christiansen and Dahl 2005b) argues that the use of CHR for context comprehension leads to an integration of the traditionally separated levels of semantic and pragmatic analyses (the latter here referring to the mapping of semantic placeholders to indexes of real world entities), motivating a suggestion for a "pragmatic semantics".

The principle of language interpretation as abduction was first formulated (Hobbs et al. 1993) in 1993, and was inherent in earlier and parallel work, e.g., Charniak and McDermott (1985). The paper (Hobbs et al. 1993) introduced also a system for discourse analysis involving a weighting scheme (analogous to, but not the same as, probabilities, cf. above). There is also a clear relation between our work and the flat representation suggested by Hobbs (1985).

Our non-standard semantics is related to the work on so-called belief revision, e.g., Alchourrón et al. (1985), Gärdenfors (1990), Gärdenfors and Rott (1995), in which general heuristics are considered on how to assimilate new observations that conflict with the current knowledge base. The main difference is that with CHR, the developer can define his or her own ways to revise the knowledge base.

In addition to the line of work described here, there is a long tradition for abduction in logic programming with and without constraints, reviewed by Denecker and Kakas (2002), but the identification of abducibles with constraints as in the present work is not made. A detailed comparison shows that the CHR based approach described here is likely the most efficient implementation of abductive logic programming, and the price to be paid for this is a limited support of negation.

25.6   Conclusion

We have exposed the similarity between context representation and a logically based approach to constraint programming, namely Constraint Handling Rules. It has been shown that this gives rise to practical methods for discourse analysis with context

---

[4] Abductive reasoning is often mentioned as a special case of non-monotonicity since conclusions are drawn that may not be a logical consequence of the present knowledge base. However, what we call standard semantics used in relation to abduction is a first-order, monotonic semantics for the constraint stores (knowledge bases) with a knowledge assimilation mechanism that conforms with conjunction. Readers puzzled by this discussion may find the paper (Console et al. 1991) from 1991 interesting, in which the relation between abduction and deduction is investigated in a way that has strong links to the work presented here.

comprehension, and we demonstrated that this can be understood as an instance of "Interpretation as Abduction". The main advantage of the approach is the ease with which a model of the relation between a language syntax and its contextual meaning can be specified, and it can be practiced using standard, implemented tools such as Prolog, Definite Clause Grammars and Constraint Handling Rules. We showed this here only with simplistic syntactic analysis, but it should be kept in mind that we can rely on the large body of experience on using logic programming for syntax analysis and compositional (context-independent) semantics; see, e.g., Pereira and Shieber (1987) or the vast amount of more recent textbooks on this matter.

When used in teaching, the approach indicates a steep learning curve, as has been verified at a number of summer schools and tutorials; this goes for both audiences of linguist and of computer science students. It is well-known for decades that students can learn to write simple Prolog programs and language parsers in a few hours, and extending with CHR does not present any special obstacle—when introduced with language or simple reasoning tasks that everyone can relate to. Interestingly, our mechanisms are essentially abduction and abductive interpretation but presented in this ways, they appear quite natural even for novice students; these subjects are normally considered highly advanced and difficult.

Concerned with efficiency, our methods may give rise to both very slow and very fast language analyzers. As is well known, parsers written in Prolog can easily run into combinatorial explosions due to badly controlled backtracking, but experienced grammar writers (i.e., logic programmers) know how to control that. The addition of a contextual module in the shape of a CHR program may not slow down execution in a noticeable way, as (1) the available implementations of CHR are efficient and fully integrated with the Prolog engine, and (2) the actual CHR rules used in our examples are in most cases quite straightforward and do no give rise to any deep levels of recursion. However, as we have shown in Sect. 25.3.3, it may sometimes be relevant to use disjunction within the body of a CHR rule, represented by Prolog's semicolon operator implemented by backtracking. Used badly, this may also lead to combinatorial explosions. This can to some extent be remedied by additional atomic constraints, that represent the disjunction of other constraints; however, such attempts tend to involve a huge set of strange CHR rules only to deal with disjunctions. This destroys the elegancy and transparency of using CHR for context comprehension and is the reason, why we did not feature this option.

As we have shown, the most obvious and intuitive applications of our approach concern analysis of text describing static sceneries: bits of knowledge are added incrementally, where at each point in the text a few CHR rules may be used to integrate the new knowledge and perhaps using the already found information for disambiguation. To integrate aspects of a dynamic evolution—not only in the acquisition of knowledge, but when the described state of affairs is changing over time—we showed how CHR can represent non-standard semantics, which allow effective knowledge updates, so that the constraint store at any point represents a current "now" knowledge database.

Our approach has been used by Christiansen et al. (2007) to build UML class diagrams from text describing use cases, including with pronoun resolution and other linguistic refinements. The paper (van de Camp and Christiansen 2012) concentrates on using CHR to resolve relative time expression appearing in bibliographical text.

The main practical limitation of the approach is that there is no standard integration with tools such as POS taggers (for the input side) or external knowledge representation systems such as a database (for the output of a discourse analysis). Fragments of such interfaces exist in different applications, but a ready to use environment with these facilities is still lacking. Thus, to use Prolog and CHR for context comprehension in a large-scale practical application, the concise programs we have shown here need to be complemented with a certain amount of detailed interface programming.

References

Abdennadher, S., Christiansen, H.: An experimental CLP platform for integrity constraints and abduction. In: Proceedings of FQAS2000, Flexible Query Answering Systems: Advances in Soft Computing series, pp. 141–152. Physica-Verlag, Heidelberg (Springer) (2000)

Alchourrón, C.E., Gärdenfors, P., Makinson, D.: On the logic of theory change: Partial meet contraction and revision functions. J. Symbol. Logic **50**(2), 510–530 (1985)

Aliseda, A.: Abductive Reasoning: Logical Investigations into Discovery and Explanation (Synthese library). Springer, Berlin (2006)

Apt, K.: Principles of Constraint Programming. Cambridge University Press, Cambridge (2003)

Betz, H., Frühwirth, T.W.: A linear-logic semantics for Constraint Handling Rules. In: van Beek, P. (ed.) Constraint Programming, Lecture Notes in Computer Science, vol. 3709, pp. 137–151. Springer, Berlin (2005)

Charniak, E., McDermott, D.: Introduction to Artificial Intelligence. Addison-Wesley Publishing Company, Reading (1985)

Christiansen, H.: CHR grammars. Int. J. Theory Pract. Logic Programm. **5**(4–5), 467–501 (2005)

Christiansen, H.: On the implementation of global abduction. In: Inoue, K., Satoh, K., Toni, F. (eds.) CLIMA VII, Lecture Notes in Computer Science, vol. 4371, pp. 226–245. Springer, Berlin (2006)

Christiansen, H.: Implementing probabilistic abductive logic programming with Constraint Handling Rules. In: Schrijvers, T., Frühwirth, T.W. (eds.) Constraint Handling Rules, Lecture Notes in Computer Science, vol. 5388, pp. 85–118. Springer, Berlin (2008)

Christiansen, H.: Executable specifications for hypothesis-based reasoning with Prolog and Constraint Handling Rules. J. Appl. Logic **7**(3), 341–362 (2009)

Christiansen, H.: An adaptation of Constraint Handling Rules for interactive and intelligent installations. In: Sneyers, J., Frühwirth, T.W. (eds.) CHR '12: Proceedings of 9th Workshop on Constraint Handling Rules, pp. 1–15. K.U.Leuven, Department of Computer Science, CW 624 (2012)

Christiansen, H., Dahl, V.: HYPROLOG: A new logic programming language with assumptions and abduction. In: Gabbrielli, M., Gupta, G. (eds.) ICLP, Lecture Notes in Computer Science, vol. 3668, pp. 159–173. Springer, Berlin (2005a)

Christiansen, H., Dahl, V.: Meaning in context. In: Dey, A., Kokinov, B., Leake, D., Turner, R. (eds.) Proceedings of Fifth International and Interdisciplinary Conference on Modeling and Using Context (CONTEXT-05), Lecture Notes in Artificial Intelligence, vol. 3554, pp. 97–111. Springer, Berlin (2005b)

Christiansen, H., Saleh, A.H.: Modeling dependent events with CHRiSM for probabilistic abduction. In: Sneyers, J. (ed.) CHR '11: Proceedings of 8th Workshop on Constraint Handling Rules, pp. 48–63. GUC, Technical report (2011)

Christiansen, H., Have, C.T., Tveitane, K.: From use cases to UML class diagrams using logic grammars and constraints. In: RANLP '07: Proceedings of International Conference Recent Advance Nature Language Processing, pp. 128–132. Incoma Ltd, Shoumen, Bulgaria (2007)

Console, L., Dupré, D.T., Torasso, P.: On the relationship between abduction and deduction. J. Logic Comput. 1(5), 661–690 (1991)

Denecker, M., Kakas, A.C.: Abduction in logic programming. In: Kakas, A.C., Sadri, F. (eds.) Computational Logic: Logic Programming and Beyond, Lecture Notes in Computer Science, vol. 2407, pp. 402–436. Springer, Berlin (2002)

Frühwirth, T.W.: Theory and practice of Constraint Handling Rules. J. Logic Programm. 37(1–3), 95–138 (1998)

Frühwirth, T.W.: Constraint Handling Rules. Cambridge University Press, Cambridge (2009)

Gärdenfors, P.: Belief revision and nonmonotonic logic: Two sides of the same coin? In: ECAI, pp. 768–773 (1990)

Gärdenfors, P., Rott, H.: Belief revision. In: Gabbay, D.M., Hogger, C.J., Robinson, J.A. (eds.) Handbook of Logic in Artificial Intelligence and Logic Programming, Epistemic and Temporal Reasoning, vol. IV, pp. 35–132. Oxford University Press, Oxford (1995)

Hobbs, J.R.: Ontological promiscuity. In: ACL, 23rd Annual Meeting of the Association for Computational Linguistics, 8–12 July 1985, University of Chicago, Chicago, Illinois, USA, Proceedings, pp. 61–69. ACL (1985)

Hobbs, J.R., Stickel, M.E., Appelt, D.E., Martin, P.A.: Interpretation as abduction. Artif. Intell. 63(1–2), 69–142 (1993)

Jaffar, J., Lassez, J.L.: Constraint logic programming. In: POPL, Conference Record of the Fourteenth Annual ACM Symposium on Principles of Programming Languages, Munich, Germany, 21–23 January 1987, pp. 111–119 (1987)

Kowalski, R.A., Bowen, K.A. (eds.): Logic programming. Proceedings of the Fifth International Conference and Symposium, Seattle, Washington, 15–19 August 1988 (2 volumes). MIT Press (1988)

Maim, E.: Abduction and constraint logic programming. In: ECAI, pp. 149–153 (1992)

Pereira, F.C.N., Shieber, S.M.: Prolog and natural-language analysis, CSLI Lecture Notes Series, vol. 10. Center for the Study of Language and Information, Menlo Park (1987)

van de Camp, M., Christiansen, H.: Resolving relative time expressions in Dutch text with Constraint Handling Rules. In: Duchier, D., Parmentier, Y. (eds.) CSLP, Lecture Notes in Computer Science, vol. 8114, pp. 166–177. Springer, Berlin (2012)

Chapter 26
Context and Implicature

Luciana Benotti and Patrick Blackburn

Abstract This chapter introduces Paul Grice's notion of conversational implicature. The basic ideas—the cooperative principle, the maxims of conversation, and the contrast between implicature and presupposition—make it clear that conversational implicature is a highly contextualized form of language use that has a lot in common with non-linguistic behavior. But what exactly is its role? The authors invite the reader to view conversational implicature as a way of *negotiating meaning in conversational contexts*. Along the way, the reader will learn something of the theoretical properties of implicatures, why they are tricky to work with empirically, what can be done with them computationally, and (perhaps) where future research on the topic may lead. But the basic message of the chapter is actually quite simple: context and conversational implicature are highly intertwined, and unravelling their interactions is a challenging and worthwhile research goal.

26.1 Introduction

The notion of **conversational implicature** is important in both *philosophy of language* (Grice 1989; Davis 2010) and *pragmatics* (Horn 2004; Levinson 1983), the branch of linguistics which studies how human languages are actually used. The key ideas were first presented in 1967 in Paul Grice's William James lectures at Harvard, and eventually appeared in the paper *Logic and Conversation* (Grice 1975). The paper draws our attention to the fact that in typical linguistic exchanges, many things are *meant* without being explicitly *said*, and attempts to explain how this is possible. Let's start with an example from Grice's paper:

(1) *Man standing by his car: I am out of petrol.*
    Passer-by: There is a garage around the corner.

L. Benotti (✉)
LIIS Team, FAMAF, Universidad Nacional de Córdoba, Córdoba, Argentina
e-mail: benotti@famaf.unc.edu.ar

P. Blackburn
Department of Philosophy and Science Studies, Centre for Culture and Identity,
Roskilde University, Roskilde, Denmark
e-mail: patrickb@ruc.dk

© Springer Science+Business Media New York 2014   419
P. Brézillon, A. J. Gonzalez (eds.), *Context in Computing*,
DOI 10.1007/978-1-4939-1887-4_26

Grice's analysis runs as follows. The utterance made by the passer-by (let's call him B) wouldn't have been relevant (to the conversational exchange) if B knew that the garage was closed or that it had run out of petrol. If B is a local person who knows about local garages, it is thus reasonable to assume that B is directing the man standing by the car (let's call him A) to a garage that is open and currently selling petrol. That is, according to Grice, during the exchange (1), B made the conversational implicature (2):

(2) *The garage is open and has petrol to sell.*

Well, so far, so good. But isn't this just the sort of thing that goes on all the time? Where's the mystery? If this is all there is to conversational implicature, what exactly requires explanation? What makes the concept so important? And why is it considered difficult?

As we hope to make clear, even this little exchange conceals many problems. Conversational implicature involves highly contextualized inferences that draw on multiple sources of information. For instance, in the garage example, presumably the visual information provided by A standing beside his stationary car plays an important role in initiating the exchange. Moreover, by their very nature—we will soon explain what we mean by this—implicatures tend to be resistant to the usual tools of empirical linguistic investigation. Furthermore, they are ubiquitous: get two people talking, and the conversational implicature flies thick and fast. In short, Grice's garage example is the tip of a large iceberg concerning meaning and inference in context. In the pages that follow, we show how deep it extends below the surface, and discuss recent attempts to reveal its contours theoretically, empirically and computationally.

We proceed as follows. In Sect. 26.2 we present conversational implicature as a form of contextualized inference, and make a first pass at explaining why it tends to resist the usual tools of empirical linguistic analysis. In Sect. 26.3 we sketch some of Grice's ideas on the subject, notably his **cooperative principle** and his **conversational maxims**. In Sect. 26.4 we note five key theoretical properties of conversational implicature, and in Sect. 26.5 we discuss further difficulties with empirical work. This leads us to one of the main points we wish to make: conversational implicature is a form of **negotiation**. In Sect. 26.6, we sketch the relevance of **clarification requests** to this conception, and in Sect. 26.7 we briefly note some recent computational work. Section 26.8 concludes with a nod to the future.

Computational implicature is a huge subject, one that has been investigated from many angles. We cannot hope to cover them all, and have opted instead to present a birds-eye-view of relevance to researchers interested in context. But there are many good points of entry to the topic. For a start, Grice's own *Logic and Conversation* is a must: it is clear, accessible and covers many topics we do not have space to consider, but we'd also like to draw the reader's attention to his *Further Notes on Logic and Conversation*; these conveniently appear as Chaps. 2 and 3 respectively of Grice (1989). Moreover, excellent surveys exist: we particularly recommend Chap. 3 of Levinson's textbook *Pragmatics* (Levinson 1983). Furthermore, searching for 'conversational implicature' in the (free) online *Stanford Encyclopedia of Philosophy* will lead to several informative and up-to-date articles (for example, Davis 2010) with detailed bibliographical information.

26.2 Implicature as Contextual Inference

In this section we have two main goals: to convince the reader that conversational implicatures are a highly general form of contextualized inference, and to make a first attempt to explain why conversational implicatures tend to be resistant to standard empirical linguistic techniques. A good way into the discussion is to compare conversational implicatures with what linguists call **presuppositions**.

Presuppositions are another ubiquitous form of inference, one that all known human languages exploit. Consider the following sentence. Imagine it is uttered to you out of the blue, with no prior conversational context:

(3) *Anthony regrets that Brenda is pregnant.*

Now, you know nothing about Anthony or Brenda or who they are or what their life is like. But by reading this sentence (let's assume that you don't have any reason to distrust its source) you have effortlessly internalized a certain piece of information: namely, that Brenda is pregnant. But now consider the following sentence:

(4) *Anthony does not regret that Brenda is pregnant.*

Once again, you have once internalized the information (or: **accommodated** the information, as a linguist would say) that Brenda is pregnant. And this is surprising because it shows that we are dealing with a very strange form of inference indeed. It is certainly not an ordinary logical inference. In ordinary logical inference, replacing a positive premise with its negation will typically destroy the inference. But here replacing 'regrets' with 'does not regret' has no effect: in both cases the inference to Brenda's pregnancy goes through immediately.

Such presuppositions are ubiquitous, and their ability to survive negations is one of their better known characteristics. Consider the following pair of sentences

(5) *Candy knows that Dave is dead.*
    Candy does not know that Dave is dead.

Once again—positive or negative—we infer the same information: Dave is dead.

Now, presupposition is an interesting phenomena. Like conversational implicature it is a ubiquitous fact about language in action. But in at least one crucial respect it is simpler than implicature: *we can point to concrete linguistic triggers that set the presuppositional process in motion, no what matter the context is.* In the first pair of examples, the trigger is the word 'regret'. In the second pair of examples, the trigger is the word 'knows'. Part of the effect of using these words—part of their *meaning*— is that they induce presuppositional phenomena of this sort, and every competent language user instinctively knows how to make good use of this. Now, it should be stressed that presupposition is not a simple phenomena, nonetheless, we now have detailed theoretical accounts of it (Beaver 2001; Geurts 1999) and understand how to incorporate presuppositional phenomena into computational work (Venhuizen et al. 2013; Bos 2003; Blackburn et al. 2001). And much of this understanding stems from the basic fact just noted: we can trace presuppositions to specific linguistic locations, namely, certain trigger words (and grammatical constructions).

But conversational implicatures *can't* be linguistically localized in the same way. As we said earlier, conversational implicatures are highly contextualized inferences, capable of exploiting multiple information sources. Consider Grice's garage example again. First, and most obviously, it rests on an assumed *common knowledge context*: both A and B need to share the knowledge that "petrol can be bought at open garages which have not run out of petrol". Secondly, this example draws on the *situational context*, most obviously on B knowing that the garage is around the corner and that A can walk there. But a lot also hinges on the fact that we are in a *conversational context*. It is quite obvious that the implicature could not have been triggered without considering the immediate conversational context: if A had said "Where do you come from?" instead of "I am out of petrol", B's utterance would have had a quite different meaning. But even more basic components of the *interaction context* are crucial: A and B take for granted that the other is a language user, with intentions and goals, who may be prepared to take part in a cooperative exchange in order to overcome undesired states such as "being out of petrol". In fact, as we shall soon discuss, Grice called one of the central principles driving conversational implicature the cooperative principle. Moreover, other contextual parameters may play a role in how the scenario unfolds, such as information about race, gender and status (is A unshaven, sloppily dressed, and standing by a beat-up old car, or is he wearing a suit and tie and standing by a spiffy new Mercedes?).

So: conversational implicatures are a highly contextualized form of inference. Moreover (unlike presuppositions) there is no simple linguistic trigger with relatively well defined rules which we can analyze to 'solve the implicature problem' in the general case. There is no linguistic trigger in the garage example that sets the implicative process in motion. For example, it would be highly implausible to claim that B's behavior is induced by the word 'garage', or by any other word in the exchange for that matter. Words like 'regrets' and 'know' induce presuppositions, but Grice's little scenario has more complex origins. The same scenario would work if we used the words 'service station' or 'petrol station' instead of 'garage'. Moreover, the initial trigger may well have been non-linguistic: the sight of A (perhaps in his suit and tie) standing forlornly by his new Mercedes may have been the spark that set the little scene in motion.

Conversational implicatures are, in general, not closely tied to the inner-workings of the lexical system in the way that presuppositions are. Rather, they are a type of behavior exemplified by agents with intentions and goals—but special agents, namely human beings, who have a highly refined form of behavior in their arsenal: linguistic behavior. We might say: *conversational implicature constitutes a large part of the meaning conveyed and received by goal seeking, linguistically competent agents when they interact in a given context*. Hopefully this goes some way towards explaining why conversational implicatures are interesting and important—and why they are highly relevant to the study of context. But note the downside: it also tells why they are likely to be resistant to straightforward empirical linguistic investigation. We can't compile a list of trigger words (as we can for presupposition) and explore their effects in a corpus of example sentences. As we have said, in general it is difficult or impossible to point to critical lexical or grammatical triggers when it comes to conversational implicature, because so much of what is going on in conversational implicature is not specifically linguistic behavior; rather, *it's part of the general human behavior displayed by linguistically adept agents.* It spills over into, draws richly on, and is guided by, the surrounding context in all its variety. So empirical investigation will be a tricky business, a point we will return to later.

26.3   Grice on Conversational Implicature

We now outline Grice's account of conversational implicature, and in particular his cooperative principle and the conversational maxims. We draw attention to the possibility of **observing**, **flouting** and **violating** maxims; these are not merely practical distinctions, they are also helpful in understanding Grice's motives. We further note that the conversational maxims are linked to non-linguistic behavior, that they can be used to classify conversational implicatures, and draw the reader's attention to both **relevance implicatures**, the conversational implicatures that embody contextual inference in its most general form, and **scalar implicatures**, those that probably embody it least. Our discussion will establish some standard ideas and terminology and pave the way for our discussion in subsequent sections. Page references here are to the version of *Logic and Conversation* in Grice (1989).

At the heart of Grice's discussion lies the following principle (see p. 26):

> **The cooperative principle:** Make your contribution such as is required, at the stage at which it occurs, by the accepted purpose or direction of the talk exchange in which you are engaged.

In addition, he presents the following maxims (pp. 26–27):

> **Maxims of Quantity:**
> (i) Make your contribution as informative as is required (for the current purposes of the exchange).
> (ii) Do not make your contribution more informative than is required.
>
> **Maxims of Quality:** Try to make your contribution one that is true.
> (i) Do not say what you believe to be false.
> (ii) Do not say that for which you lack adequate evidence.
>
> **The Maxim of Relevance:** Be relevant.
>
> **Maxims of Manner:** Be perspicuous.
> (i) Avoid obscurity.
> (ii) Avoid ambiguity.
> (iii) Be brief (avoid unnecessary prolixity).
> (iv) Be orderly.

Grice calls the cooperative principle a "rough general principle" and it is clear from his discussion on pp. 26–28 that the maxims are a tentative attempt to understand how human beings interact in conversation. But at this point, the reader may have doubts. Aren't the cooperative principle and the maxims far too neat and tidy? They seem to describe an ideal world of effective, rational, maximally cooperative conversational interaction. And, all too obviously, real life just isn't like that at all.

Fig. 26.1 Illustration of the conversational implicature *Not all of the B's are in the box on the left*

But it is a mistake to dismiss Grice and conversational implicature on these grounds. Grice is *not* suggesting that all human conversational interactions live up to these principles, or even that it would be better if they did. Rather, *Grice is trying to indicate the existence of deep-seated norms of conversational interaction.* Humans are social animals. They interact. Moreover they are social animals graced (or cursed) with the power of speech. Grice is suggesting (see p. 29) that assumptions somewhat like the cooperative principle or the maxims must guide this process. And of course—as Grice himself points out—*what is expected of others swiftly becomes a resource to be exploited.* We may communicate by *observing* the maxims, but sometimes we can communicate more effectively by deliberately *flouting* them; we will give examples of both strategies shortly. Indeed, sometimes we may choose to distance ourselves still further from communicative norms and deliberately *violate* the maxims: tricksters and ironists thrive on the socially expected.

Grice views his conversational maxims as direct analogs of norms governing the way we cooperate in *non-linguistic* settings. He is quite explicit on this point. As he says on p. 28:

[O]ne of my aims is to see talking as a special case of purposive, indeed, rational behavior

and then lists analogies between the conversational maxims and physical actions. For example, with regard to the Maxim of Quality, which says we should seek to be truthful, he points out that if we are cooperating to make a cake, and I need sugar, then I expect you to pass me sugar, and not (say) salt, and that if I need a spoon for stirring the cake mixture, I expect you to hand me a real spoon not (say) a trick spoon made of rubber. The strong analogy that Grice draws between linguistic and non-linguistic behavior is important, and we shall return to it when we discuss implicature as negotiation.

The maxims are also useful in that they give us a (somewhat rough-and-ready) way of classifying conversational implicatures. Consider, for example, the maxims of quantity. This has given rise to an extensive literature on what are now called **quantity** or **scalar implicatures** (see, for example, Hirschberg 1985, Geurts 2011). Let's briefly consider an example which we will return to in more detail when we discuss empirical work. Consider the image in Fig. 27.1:

Suppose I then say to you:

(6) *Some of the B's are in the box on the left.*

then I would often be taken as having implicated that

(7) *Not all of the B's are in the box on the left.*

Why? The point is this. If I am observing the maxims, and in particular the Maxim of Quantity that tells us to *make your contribution as informative as is required* then I must be making the strongest claim possible. Logically, the claim that *some* of the B's are in the box on the left is compatible with the (logically stronger) claim that they *all* are. So why did I not make the stronger claim? Well, assuming that I am observing to the maxims, this must be because I was not in a position to (truthfully) do so (and looking at the image we see that I was not, for there is a B in the box on the right). Hence I implicated that *not all* the items are in the box on the left. In short, assuming that conversational agents are *observing* the maxims gives us explanatory power: it enables us to appeal to and reason about communicative goals and intentions.

But so does *flouting*. Stephen Levinson has a nice example involving Maxims of Manner (see p. 104 of Levinson 1983):

(8) A: *Let's get the kids something.*
     B: *Okay, but I veto I-C-E-C-R-E-A M-S*

Why on earth would B spell out the word ice creams? This is not a perspicuous presentation: indeed it's (deliberately) obscure and prolix! And of course, every parent knows why: the maxim has been flouted because B's message is not simply "Yes, I agree we should get the kids something", but the more desperate "For God's sake let's not get them whining for ice creams!"

The logic of flouting is interesting. Once again, it involves appealing to and reasoning about communicative goals and intentions, but in a more subtle way: a flouting seems to function as an *invitation to look beyond the surface level of maxim failure and to search for a deeper vein of cooperativity*. Given such possibilities, it is hardly surprising that many authors have found game theory (and related disciplines which focus on strategic thinking) useful tools for exploring conversational implicature; see van Rooij (2011) for a useful overview.

Finally, we remark that we can now see that conversational implicatures come in all shapes and sizes. For example, the sort of scalar implicature involved in *some of the B's are in the box on the left* example is relatively specific, and is clearly tied to the meaning of the word *some*—though as we shall learn later, this simple example is not as innocent as it looks. Others, such as the garage example with which we started, are more general. This is because the garage example is a **relevance implicature**, governed simply by the splendidly general: *Be relevant!* Some authors (notably Wilson and Sperber 2004) have insisted that the notion of relevance is the real gold in Grice's work. Indeed, Grice himself seems to be partly of this opinion. As he remarks on p. 27:

> Though the maxim itself is terse, its formulation conceals a number of problems that exercise me a good deal: questions about what different kinds and focuses of relevance there may be, how these shift in the course of a talk exchange, how to allow for the fact that the subjects of conversation are legitimately changed, and so on. I find the treatment of such questions exceedingly difficult, and I hope to revert to them in later work.

The problems involving relevance implicature remain exceedingly difficult to this day; some of the hardest problems of contextual inference live there.

26.4   A Little Theory

So far, our discussion has been relatively informal; in this section we make it more precise. We first give a definition of conversational implicature; this won't play a role in our subsequent work, but it will indicate how the role of context is made explicit in formal pragmatics. Following this, we will briefly discuss five basic properties of conversational implicatures; three of them will play a key role in the the concept of negotiability introduced in the following section.

The following definition is adapted from Hirschberg (1985). We have made explicit the role of context and the role of the conversation participants as agents that can modify context:

Definition 1 Proposition q is a conversational implicature of utterance U by agent B in context C if and only if:

(i) B believes that it is mutual, public knowledge in C of all the discourse participants that B is obeying the cooperative principle.
(ii) B believes that, to maintain (i) given U, the hearer will assume that B believes q holds in C, or that C can be modified to bring about q.
(iii) B believes that it is mutual, public knowledge in C of all the discourse participants that, to maintain (i) given U, the hearer will assume that B believes q holds in C, or that C can be modified to bring about q.

What does this mean? Let's return to the garage example, where B implicated *The garage is open and has petrol to sell* (that is, q) by uttering *There is a garage around the corner* (that is, U). If B believes it is common knowledge to all the participants (namely A and B) that B is obeying the cooperative principle, and B further believes that A will assume, on the basis of B's utterance, that the garage is open and has petrol to sell or that the context can be modified to bring those about–for example, B can add, *It is closed now but I know the owner and he can open it for you*, then q is an implicature of U. It's a tricky definition, and we won't pause to discuss it further, but do note the following: the *form* of the definition, with its explicit appeals to an agent's beliefs and to what is mutual public knowledge make it clear that implicature is being modeled as a form of epistemic reasoning that draws on contextual knowledge.

Now let's examine the *properties* of conversational implicatures, for these *will* play an important role in our discussion. Hirschberg argues that we need to insist that conversational implicatures have the following five: (1) deniability, (2) reinforceability, (3) non-lexicality, (4) non-detachability, and (5) calculability.

First, conversational implicatures are **deniable** without contradiction. Let's stick with Grice's garage example. B can append material that is *inconsistent* with the implicature—for example, B can add *but I don't know whether it's open*—and the resulting exchange will *not* be contradictory. Indeed, the resulting exchange would be extremely natural: B would be implicating potentially useful information about the garage, but then expressing a reservation.

Second, note that B can also add material to the exchange that *explicitly asserts* the implicature—*and I know it's open*—without any sense that he is repeating himself.

That is, B can **reinforce** the implicature without redundancy. Indeed, once again, this is very natural language use: we implicate the extra information and then (if it seems important) ram the message home to make sure our conversational partner gets the point.

Third, implicatures are **non-lexical**: they do *not* trace back to particular lexical items. We have already mentioned this. For example, in Grice's garage example, the implicature is not triggered by any particular word in the exchange (such as 'garage') but is a result of the overall semantic content.

Fourth—again something we have discussed—since an implicature is attached to the semantic content of what is said and not to the particular lexical items involved, a conversational implicature **cannot be detached** from the utterance simply by changing the words of the utterance by synonyms. B can replace each word in his utterance with a word with the same meaning—he can say *petrol station* or *service station* instead of *garage*—and the implicature will still go through. Note that non-detachability and non-lexicality are not really two independent properties: non-lexicality can only be tested by evaluating non-detachability. Basically, these two properties are another way of getting at the basic point that conversational implicatures are *not* part of the conventional meaning of the words uttered, but depend on features of the conversational context.

Fifth and last, conversational implicatures are traditionally considered to be **calculable**. Calculability means that the addressee should be able to infer the implicatures of an utterance. For example, in the garage example, A should be able to infer that B conversationally implicates that the garage is open and has petrol to sell.

Three of these properties will shortly return in the guise of *negotiability*. To help motivate this concept, first some intriguing empirical results.

26.5   Towards Negotiability

The empirical literature on conversational implicature is based almost entirely on evidence obtained using the **inference method** (Chemla 2009), a pragmatic-level analog of the introspective method traditionally used in linguistics and philosophy (basically, the introspective approach is to obtain native-speaker judgments on linguistic examples). However, Geurts and Pouscoulous (2009) have shown that the inference method is a biased tool when it comes to gathering data on conversational implicatures. Let's briefly consider the Geurts and Pouscoulous (henceforth G&P) argument.

Consider the scalar implicature example we gave in Sect. 26.3. Experimenters using the traditional inference paradigm might ask experimental subjects whether they think that sentence (9a) implies sentence (9b):

(9) a. *Some of the B's are in the box on the left.*
     b. *Not all of the B's are in the box on the left.*

Now, G&P argue that to ask oneself—or an experimental subject—whether or not (9a) implies (9b) is already to suggest that it *might* be implied. That is, presenting

Fig. 26.2 Illustration of the conversational implicature *Not all of the B's are in the box on the left*

Fig. 26.3 It is the case that *All of the B's are in the box on the left*, the implicature does not go through

these two sentences to an experimental subject signals that whether or not all of the B's are in the box on the left is the significant issue—the *issue at stake*. In conversation, the issues at stake are constructed as part of the exchange and are part of the *conversational context*—for example, A needing petrol is the issue at stake in Grice's example.

Consider the image we used back in Sect. 26.3 and we reproduce in Fig. 26.2. In Sect. 26.3, when we discussed example (9), we carefully placed a B in the right-hand box. Now, this is an effective way of explaining the concept of implicature: it makes the implicature explicit and forces the reader to think about it. But the inference method does much the same thing: it explicitly states the potential implicature (9b) (though it does not show a picture as we did). That is, the implicature is artificially put at stake; it is added to the *conversational context*. Is this really a good way of investigating implicatures empirically? G&P argue that it is not: precisely because it draws attention to what is at stake, the inference method may not tell us much about how (9a) is interpreted in situations where (9b) is *not* at stake; that is, when it is is not part of the *context*.

G&P investigated the matter experimentally. They did so by comparing the inference method with what they call the **verification method**. In the verification version of the previous experiment, subjects simply have to decide whether (9a) correctly describes the situation shown in the picture shown in Fig. 26.3. Notice that the picture is intentionally modified so that the implicature does not hold: all the Bs are in the left-hand box. The experimental subject is simply asked whether *some of the B's are in the box on the left* is a good description of the depicted situation or not. Crucially, the potential implicature *not all of the B's are in the box on the left* is not mentioned to the subject, he only sees the picture and the sentence (9a). In a nutshell, the verification task attempts to minimize signaling of what is at stake. That is, it tries not to alter the conversational context.

Someone who interprets (9a) as implicating (9b) should *deny* that (9a) gives a correct description of the picture (for note: there are no Bs in the right-hand box, all the Bs are in the left-hand box):

G&P's results were striking. Participants detected the implicature that *not all of the B's are in the box on the left* only half as frequently under the verification condition (34 %) as they did twice under the inference condition (62 %). The inference task, which alters the context, *does* increase the rate of detection of conversational implicatures, and the effect is substantial.

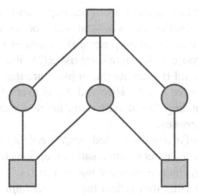

Fig. 26.4 *One of the squares is connected to all of the circles,* the implicature does not go through

G&P show that the effect is even more evident in complex sentences such as (10a) describing the following situation depicted in Fig. 26.4:

Someone who interprets (10a) as implicating (10b) should *deny* that (10a) gives a correct description of the picture (for note: one of the squares is connected to all of the circles).

(10) *a. All the squares are connected with some of the circles.*
       b. All the squares are connected with some but not all of the circles.

Studies carried out using these more complex sentences result in participants deriving the conversational implicature (10b) from (10a) in 46 % of the cases with the inference method, and in 0 % of the cases with the verification method! As we have said before, empirical investigation of conversational implicatures is not easy. G&P's work shows another source of difficulty.

But what is the lesson we should draw? Is it simply that the verification method is better than the inference method? We think not. G&P's experiments show that the inference method does not tell us much about how utterances are interpreted when a certain issue (such as how we use the words 'some' and 'all') is *not* at stake. However the verification method used by G&P has the opposite weakness: it does not tell us much about how utterances should be interpreted when the issue *is* at stake. In our view, what G&P's experiments show is that *whether or not an issue is at stake* is a crucial contextual factor when it comes to implicature.

Another interesting aspect of their work is that it concerns scalar implicatures. Scalar implicatures are usually considered 'better behaved' than (say) relevance implicatures. Clearly the above scalar implicatures have something to do with how we interpret the logical words 'some' and 'all', and such inferences are often felt to be less contextually sensitive than full-blown relevance implicatures such as Grice's garage examples. And this makes G&P's results even more intriguing: *even allegedly simple and well-understood implicatures such as scalar implicatures involving 'some' and 'all' can be dramatically manipulated by playing with the context.* G&P's experiments simply change one pragmatic factor—whether something is at stake or not—and the effects are striking.

And this brings us, at last, to the heart of the paper, and back to the work of Paul Grice. In conversation, whether an issue is at stake or not is naturally determined by what Grice calls "the accepted purpose or direction of the talk exchange". But how is this accepted purpose or direction established? Quite simply, by **negotiation**. Instead of asking "How did B generate the implicature that the garage is open and had petrol to sell?" we need to ask "How did the conversational agents arrive at a state of mutual understanding?" or at least, a mutual understanding sufficient for the contextually relevant purposes.

Recall the properties of of *deniability* and *reinforceability* we noted in the previous section. As we saw, these are natural conversational options for expressing degrees of certainty and uncertainty. Indeed, they are not so much two independent properties as two sides of the same coin: they reflect the fact that *implicatures are often open-ended contributions to an exchange, potential contributions that the speaker can usefully deny or reinforce.*

And it's not just the speaker who can do this. Recall *calculability*: implicatures are meant to be calculable by the hearer. But in conversational interaction, uncertainty abounds. Which potential contributions are on offer? The hearer needs tools to clarify. And what are these tools? The same options of deniability and reinforceability that are available to the speaker. For example, A can naturally continue Grice's garage example with—*I went there, it's closed*—thereby denying the conversational implicature. But A can also continue the exchange by reinforcing the implicature—*oh, and it must be open because it's only 3 pm! I'll go there right away!*

Putting it together: deniability, reinforceability and calculability can be summarized by saying that computational implicatures are *negotiable*. Implicature is not a one way flow of information from speaker to hearer. Rather, speaker and hearer negotiate—they deny, reinforce, calculate, and switch roles as the conversation precedes. In this fashion they explore the issue at stake until (all being well) both are satisfied. Conversational implicature is truly *conversational*. In the following section we will make these issues concrete and see how they give rise to a new way to investigate conversational implicatures empirically.

26.6   Conversational Examples

We argued that deniability, reinforceability and calculability can be summed up by saying that conversational implicatures are negotiable. The hearer can infer the implicatures of an utterance but cannot be completely certain that the speaker meant them (and the speaker knows this) so both speaker and the hearer can talk—negotiate—without redundancy or contradiction.

We find this account theoretically satisfying, but it is of additional interest because it suggests a novel *empirical* approach to conversational implicature. The idea, first suggested in Benotti (2009), is to track the negotiation process by noting what linguists call **clarification subdialogues**. Consider, for example, the clarification request which can naturally follow Grice's garage example:

(11)   A: *and you think it's open?*

B will have to answer and either support the implicature ("yes, it's open till midnight") if he wants to get it added to the common ground, or, if he realizes he was being a little too optimistic, he can reject it without contradiction ("well, you have a point there, they might have closed"). Conversational implicatures are invisible by definition; negotiation subdialogues make them visible.

Let's see some examples of clarification, rejection and reinforcement of conversational implicatures in real dialogues between two players of a multiplayer online game (Stoia et al. 2008). In this game, the player DF (Direction Follower) is collaborating with the player DG (Direction Giver) in order to reach the goal of the game. Since the DG knows the game world and how to reach the goal, most of her contributions come in the form of instructions on how to perform actions in the game world. Situated instructions are a kind of language that maintains a tight link between physical actions and conversational maxims. Recall the analogy Grice drew between his conversational maxims and non-linguistic behavior; situated instructions in this game world offer a concrete scenario in which to investigate the mechanisms governing conversational implicatures and their interaction with non-linguistic and linguistic aspects of context. Moreover, they show that negotiation subdialogues (clarifications, rejections and reinforcements) make conversational implicatures explicit and amenable to empirical studies in their natural context.

26.6.1 Clarifying Conversational Implicatures

In the following dialogue, the players are trying to move a picture from one wall to another. The utterance being interpreted is the one uttered by the DG in (1). Using the *common knowledge context* that "in order to put something somewhere you need to have it in your hands first" and the *situational context* of "DF is not holding the picture", the DF infers a conversational implicature that involves *picking up the picture*. This implicature, foreshadowed by (2) and (3), is finally made explicit as a clarification request in (4):

DG(1): *well, put it on the opposite wall*
DF(2): *ok, control picks the [pause]*
DF(3): *control's supposed to pick things up and [pause]*
DF(4): *am I supposed to pick this thing?*

26.6.2 Rejecting Conversational Implicatures

Here, the players are trying to find a gun that is supposed to be hidden. As in the previous example, the inference of the conversational implicature in (2) is licensed by the *common knowledge context*, here "in order to take something from a container is has to be open". However, the *situational context* of "the cabinet is closed" was unknown by the DG and is an obstacle for carrying out instruction (1). As a result, DF rejects the implicature "the cabinet is open" by uttering (2):

DG(1):   take the gun from the cabinet .
DF(2):   the cabinet is closed

26.6.3   Reinforcing Conversational Implicatures

In this fragment, DG asks DF to go back where he started. This instruction relies on its
previous *conversational context*, indeed it requires the DF to remember the beginning
of the game, which was also the beginning of the conversation. The DF remembers
what was said, and is thus able to infer a sequence of conversational implicatures.
He incrementally grounds them, making them explicit in (2), (4), and (6) while
he simultaneously executes them. Uttering the implicatures of an utterance is a
frequently used method for performing acceptance acts. As before, the conversational
implicatures of (1) are strongly dependent on the *situational context*. In particular,
note that if the DF was already near the steps at the moment of uttering (1), he would
only need to infer (6), not (2) and (4) as well.

DG(1):   let's go back where you started [pause] so
DF(2):   ok [pause] so I have to go back through here [pause]
DG(3):   yeah
DF(4):   and around the corner [pause]
DG(5):   right
DF(6):   and then do I have to go back up the steps
DG(7):   yeah
DF(8):   alright [pause] this is where we started

Conversational implicatures are negotiable, and dialogue provides mechanisms for
carrying out required negotiations of meaning. As these examples show, conversational implicatures are a rich source of negotiation subdialogues. When talking, we
do not make explicit everything in the world that serves "the accepted purpose or
direction of the talk exchange in which we are engaged", but only those parts that
are necessary for the addressees to fill in the details. If the addressee is not sure that
he has filled in the details properly (that is, if he is not sure he had interpreted our
conversational implicatures) a negotiation subdialogue will typically emerge.

A pleasant aspect of this approach is that it brings us closer to modern corpus-
based linguistic techniques: essentially the idea is to find conversational implicatures
in corpora by identifying negotiation subdialogues. The characteristics and functions of clarification subdialogues have been deeply studied by dialogue system
researchers (Gabsdil 2003; Purver 2004; Rodríguez and Schlangen 2004; Rieser and
Moore 2005; Skantze 2007) and sociolinguists. Indeed, in discourse analysis, this
has been a favored theme for almost three decades now; see Schegloff (1987) as a
representative example. As we have emphasized throughout this paper, investigating conversational implicatures empirically is a delicate task; a novel approach here
could be useful.

The approach has the additional merit of anchoring the study of conversational implicatures in their natural habitat, that is, in natural occurring conversation. It can be difficult to decide whether something is a conversational implicature if we simply have a two-line example (often an artificial one) of a speaker saying something to a hearer. But in naturally occurring dialogue, the follow up conversational turns often provides good evidence of the implicatures that have been made, because they reveal what is being negotiated, thereby making the implicatures explicit.

26.7 Recent Computational Work

Recall the five properties of conversational implicature we isolated in Sect. 26.4. Two of them, namely non-detachability and non-lexicality, are closely related and together they tell us that conversational implicatures are not part of the conventional meaning of the words involved but depend on features of the conversational context; Indeed (as the experiments of G&P show) this is true even of seemingly-simple scalar implicatures. This is where conversational implicatures differ from presuppositions. As we pointed out in Sect. 26.2, words like 'knows' and 'regret' carry, as a part of their conventional meaning, the ability to trigger certain presuppositions, but the inferences conversational implicature gives rise too are not so easily localized.

To put it another way, non-detachability (and non-lexicality) have an obvious computational downside. While progress has been made on computing presuppositions, computing implicatures is a heavier task, for work that models the inference of conversational implicatures has to model the (linguistic and non-linguistic) context, and it is often unclear which aspects of it are relevant. However, in spite of the difficulties involved, there has been some recent work on the topic, which we shall briefly note here. These approaches differ not only on the conversational context elements that they model, but also in the inference techniques used.

First, Vogel et al. (2013b) show that a team of interacting agents collaborating to maximize a global reward using only local information reach implicature-rich interpretations simply as a by-product of the way they reason about each other beliefs. The technique used to model the interaction is multi-agent Decentralized POMDP which uses only local information to maximize joint utility. A similar approach is taken by DeVault and Stone (2009) who instead of POMDPs use Maximum Entropy models over abductive interpretations to model the maximization of interpretation success. These two approaches provide a rich representation of the conversational context and the goals shared by the agents. Using such techniques, the cooperative principle and the associated maxims of relevance, quality, and quantity have been shown to emerge from agent interaction because they maximize utility. For instance, agents do not lie to each other and do not give more information than necessary to make collaboration more effective. The main problem of these two approaches is their intractability, although Vogel et al. (2013a) use cognitively-inspired heuristics to simplify the otherwise intractable task of reasoning jointly about actions, the environment, and the nested beliefs of other actors.

An alternative approach is not to explicitly reason about the nested beliefs but to model and reason on the common ground using cheap causal reasoning techniques such as classical planning (Benotti 2010; Benotti and Blackburn 2011). Such have been used to computationally explore the idea of conversational implicature as negotiation, and have also proven to be useful in large scale practical applications (Smith 2012). The main problem with this approach is the limited expressive power offered by the classical planing paradigm which is able to model only some kinds of conversational implicatures. An interesting way around this problem might be to use Dynamic Epistemic Planning (Bolander and Andersen 2011), though, at least at present, the additional expressivity this offers is likely to come with a hefty price in terms of tractability.

26.8 Towards the Future

In this paper we introduced conversational implicature, contrasted this notion with presupposition, explained the cooperative principle and the maxims of conversation on which it rests, and invited the reader to view conversational implicature as a way of *negotiating meaning in conversational contexts*. We discussed theoretical, empirical and computational perspectives, and hope it is now clear that context and conversational implicature are deeply intertwined, and that unraveling their interactions is a worthwhile research goal.

But what of the future? There has been interesting recent work in pragmatics that points towards new research directions. In this paper we simply contrasted conversational implicature with presupposition in an attempt to make clear just how important context is to conversational implicature. But presupposition and conversational implicature are only two examples (albeit important ones) of pragmatic reasoning, and two strands of recent work hint at a more unified view. First, in Simons et al. (2011), Tonhauser et al. (2013) and related publications, a determined attempt has been made to more accurately map the contours of what are called projectable inferences (presuppositions are an important example here, but there are many others). On the other hand, in Beaver and Zeevat (2007) there are signs that linguists are beginning to better understand the process of accommodating new information that is inferred in context. These lines of work both hint at deeper theoretical analyses of some of the key concepts in pragmatics, so the theoretical landscape may well look very different a few years from now.

Nonetheless, despite these new insights, it is clear that Paul Grice got a lot right. We do use language in conversational contexts, this does involve reasoning about the intentions and goals of those we interact with, and this is a norm-governed process open to exploitation. And—above all—when we negotiate with our conversational partners and adversaries, it seems that we draw upon and reason about the information made available by the context in deep and intriguing ways. Paul Grice: still relevant after all these years!

Acknowledgements This work was partially supported by grants ANPCyT PICT-2008-306, PICT-2010-688, PICT-2012-712, and the FP7-PEOPLE-2011-IRSES Project MEALS.

References

Beaver, D.: Pragmatics, and that's an order. In: Barker-Plummer, D., Beaver, D., van Benthem, J., Scotto di Luzio, P. (eds.) Logic, Language and Visual Information, CSLI Publications, Stanford (2001)

Beaver, D., Zeevat, H.: Accommodation. In: The Oxford Handbook of Linguistic Interfaces, pp. 503–539. Oxford University Press, Oxford (2007)

Benotti, L.: Clarification potential of instructions. In: Proceedings of the 2009 SIGDIAL Conference on Discourse and Dialogue, pp. 196–205 . Association for Computational Linguistics (2009)

Benotti, L.: Implicature as an Interactive Process. Ph.D. thesis, Université Henri Poincaré, INRIA Nancy Grand Est, France, supervised by Patrick Blackburn (2010)

Benotti, L., Blackburn, P.: Classical planning and causal implicatures. In: Beigl, M., Christiansen, H., Roth-Berghofer, T.R., Kofod-Petersen, A., Coventry, K.R., Schmidtke, H.R. (eds.) Modeling and Using Context (Lecture Notes in Computer Science), vol. 6967, pp. 26–39. Springer, Berlin (2011)

Blackburn, P., Bos, J., Kohlhase, M., de Nivelle, H.: Inference and computational semantics. In: Bunt, H., Muskens, R., Thijsse, E. (eds.) Computing Meaning, vol. 2, pp. 11–28. Kluwer, Doedrecht (2001)

Bolander, T., Andersen, M.B.: Epistemic planning for single- and multi-agent systems. J. Appl. Non-Class. Logics **21**, 9–34 (2011)

Bos, J.: Implementing the binding and accommodation theory for anaphora resolution and presupposition projection. Comput. Linguist. **29**(2), 179–210 (2003)

Chemla, E.: Universal implicatures and free choice effects: Experimental data. Semant. Pragmat. **2**(2), 1–33 (2009)

Davis W.: Implicature. In: Zalta E.N. (ed.) The Stanford Encyclopedia of Philosophy, Winter 2010 edn. CSLI, Stanford (2010)

DeVault, D., Stone, M.: Learning to interpret utterances using dialogue history. In: Proceedings of the 12th Conference of the European Chapter of the ACL (EACL 2009), Athens, Greece, pp. 184–192. Association for Computational Linguistics (2009)

Gabsdil, M.: Clarification in spoken dialogue systems. In: Proceedings of the AAAI Spring Symposium on Natural Language Generation in Spoken and Written Dialogue, Palo Alto, California, pp. 28–35 (2003)

Geurts, B.: Presuppositions and Pronouns. In: Current Research in the Semantics/Pragmatics Interfaces, vol. 3. Elsevier, Amsterdam (1999)

Geurts, B.: Quantity Implicatures. Cambridge University Press, Cambridge (2011)

Geurts, B., Pouscoulous, N.: Embedded implicatures. Semant. Pragmat. **2**(4), 1–34 (2009)

Grice, P.: Logic and conversation. In: Cole, P., Morgan, J. (eds.) Syntax and Semantics, vol. 3, pp. 41–58. Academic, New York (1975)

Grice, P.: Studies in the Way of Words. Harvard University Press, Cambridge (1989)

Hirschberg, J.L.B.: A Theory of Scalar Implicature. University of Pennsylvania, Philadelphia (1985)

Horn, L.: Implicature. In: Horn, L.R., Ward, G. (eds.) Handbook of Pragmatics, pp. 3–28. Blackwell, Oxford (2004)

Levinson, S.: Pragmatics. Cambridge Textbooks in Linguitics. Cambridge University Press, Cambridge (1983)

Purver, M.: The theory and use of clarification requests in dialogue. Ph.D. thesis, King's College, University of London, London supervised by Jonathan Ginzburg (2004)

Rieser, V., Moore, J.D.: Implications for generating clarification requests in task-oriented dialogues. In: Proceedings of the 43rd Annual Meeting on Association for Computational Linguistics, (ACL 2005), Ann Arbor, MI, pp. 239–246. Association for Computational Linguistics (2005)

Rodríguez, K., Schlangen, D.: Form, intonation and function of clarification requests in german task oriented spoken dialogues. In: Proceedings of 8th Workshop on the Semantics and Pragmatics of Dialogue (SEMDIAL), pp. 101–108 (2004)

Schegloff, E.: Some sources of misunderstanding in talk-in-interaction. Linguistics **8**, 201–218 (1987)

Simons, M., Tonhauser, J., Beaver, D., Roberts, C.: What projects and why. In: Proceedings of 20th Semantics and Linguistic Theory Conference (SALT 2010), vol. 20, pp. 309–327 (2011)

Skantze, G.: Error handling in spoken dialogue systems. Ph.D. thesis, KTII - Royal Institute of Technology, Sweden (2007) (supervised by Rolf Carlson)

Smith, D.: Managing implicit assumptions in natural language interfaces. In: Proceedings of the 2012 ACM International Conference on Intelligent User Interfaces, IUI '12, New York, NY, USA, pp. 383–388. ACM (2012)

Stoia, L., Shockley, D.M., Byron, D.K., Fosler-Lussier, E.: Scare: A situated corpus with annotated referring expressions. In: Proceedings of the 6th International Conference on Language Resources and Evaluation (LREC 2008), Marrakesh, Morocco (2008)

Tonhauser, J., Beaver, D., Roberts, C., Simons, M.: Toward a taxonomy of projective content. Language **89**(1), 66–109 (2013)

van Rooij, R.: Optimality-theoretic and game-theoretic approaches to implicature. In: Zalta, E.N. (ed.) The Stanford Encyclopedia of Philosophy, Dec 1, 2006, substantive revision Feb 17, 2011 edn. CSLI, Stanford (2011)

Venhuizen, N., Bos, J., Brouwer, H.: Parsimonious semantic representations with projection pointers. In: Proceedings of the 10th International Conference on Computational Semantics (IWCS 2013) – Long Papers, Potsdam, Germany, pp. 252–263 (2013)

Vogel, A., Bodoia, M., Potts, C., Jurafsky, D.: Emergence of Gricean maxims from multi-agent decision theory. In: Human Language Technologies: The 2013 Annual Conference of the North American Chapter of the Association for Computational Linguistics, pp. 1072–1081, Stroudsburg, PA, June 2013. Association for Computational Linguistics (2013a)

Vogel, A., Potts, C., Jurafsky, D.: Implicatures and nested beliefs in approximate Decentralized-POMDPs. In: Proceedings of the 2013 Annual Conference of the Association for Computational Linguistics, pp. 74–80, Stroudsburg, PA, August 2013. Association for Computational Linguistics (2013b)

Wilson, D., Sperber, D.: Relevance theory. In: Horn, L.R., Ward, G. (eds.) The Handbook of Pragmatics, pp. 607–632. Blackwell, Oxford (2004)

Chapter 27
Formalizing Context for Domain Ontologies in Coq

Richard Dapoigny and Patrick Barlatier

Abstract While context is crucial for reasoning about ontologies as well as for conceptual modeling, its formal definition is often imprecise and its implementation in standard classical logic-based theories suffers from a lack of expressiveness and leads to ambiguities. In this chapter, it is shown that a two-layered language using the Calculus of Inductive Constructions (i.e., the Coq language) as a lower layer, and an ontological upper layer for giving types their meaning is able to support a clear and expressive semantics for context specification.

27.1 Introduction

Context-based processing plays a key role in many applications in information technology such as context-awareness and context-based reasoning. One of the challenges, from an intelligent application perspective, is to integrate context with other types of knowledge for reasoning, and for decision-making, in the hope building a coherent architecture. There is now a common understanding that achieving desired behavior from intelligent systems will depend on the ability to represent and manipulate information about a rich range of contextual factors. These factors may include physical characteristics of the environment, cognitive factors such as the knowledge states and social factors such as networks, relations, roles, and hierarchies. This representation and reasoning problem presents research challenges to which methodologies derived from areas such as artificial intelligence and knowledge representation (ontologies) can contribute solutions.

In this chapter we discuss in the first part, the requirements that context modeling and reasoning techniques should meet. Context modeling includes the modeling of a variety of context information types and their relationships and of high-level context

R. Dapoigny (✉) · P. Barlatier
LISTIC/Polytech'Annecy-Chambéry, University of Savoie,
Po. Box 80439, 74944 Annecy-le-vieux cedex, France
e-mail: richard.dapoigny@univ-savoie.fr

P. Barlatier
e-mail: patrick.barlatier@univ-savoie.fr

© Springer Science+Business Media New York 2014
P. Brézillon, A. J. Gonzalez (eds.), *Context in Computing*,
DOI 10.1007/978-1-4939-1887-4_27

437

abstractions describing real world situations. For that purpose, an ontological framework appears as a crucial component able to improve the expressiveness of the model. Context modeling has also, by essence, strong connections with conceptual modeling where relevant features are reuse and common agreement on modeling structures. If one expects that these features should be satisfied, then it requires an ontological framework as advocated in Guizzardi (2006). It follows that context representation can gain expressiveness and reuse from an ontological modeling. Alternatively, in order to provide automatic reasoning capabilities, it is important that the context modeling techniques are able to support both consistency verification of the model and context reasoning techniques. The latter can be used to derive new context facts from existing context facts and reason about high-level context abstractions which model real world situations. The compromise between expressiveness and complexity of reasoning has led most of the research in knowledge representation in the last two decades, and Description Logics (DLs) have emerged among logic-based approaches, mostly because they provide complete reasoning supported by optimized automatic tools. However, many questions arise such as the lack of scalability resulting from the limited reasoning performance of expressive integrated reasoning mechanisms (Agostini et al. 2006). Furthermore, reasoning in DL is already computationally expensive and the proper integration of rules makes the resulting language undecidable. In this first part, after a discussion of the main ontology-based context models that have been proposed so far, we explain how reasoning is achieved, and we identify current critical issues.

The second part of the chapter focuses on the representation of context structures in a dependently-typed framework with the purpose of enhancing expressiveness through an explicit introduction of properties characterizing the context. We show that the dependently typed language and more precisely, the Coq language (Bertot and Castéran 2004), easily captures the notion of context with many examples. Viewing contexts as types, and more precisely as collection of properties, each property being described by a (dependent) type then, higher-order reasoning becomes possible while preserving decidability. Collections of properties are dynamic and depend on the domain in which they occur. For example, a laptop has among its properties a set of available wifi connections, each connection standing in a particular relation type with the notepad. It follows that, depending on the location, the collection of properties varies as well (in the previous example, the set of instantiated network connections). Moreover, meta-reasoning about relations can be achieved using part-of relations between appropriate structures called *type classes*. For that purpose we make use of a unified language (Barlatier and Dapoigny 2012), i.e., KDTL (Knowledge-based Dependently Typed Language) able to construct very expressive part-whole hierarchies. In particular, we demonstrate that properties of relations propagate through the hierarchy, resulting in a significant simplification of the reasoning process. We extend the idea of using an ontology (Dapoigny and Barlatier 2013b) for controlling the semantics of formal contexts and show how a well-founded conceptual model can be designed. An evaluation on a case study and many code excerpts illustrates the approach. It is demonstrated that KDTL can model several non-trivial aspects of contexts such as meta-level contextual properties as well as dependent collections of properties. Unlike usual representations of contexts that under-specify the categories of the entity types (relata) involved in the (relational) properties, the KDTL language is able to specify the types of each argument if required, and to control inheritance between the type classes representing distinct property types. Contextualizing the (meta)properties of relational properties solves most challenges inherent in a correct representation. These results are made possible because of the expressiveness of dependent types and type checking allowing to guarantee the consistency of typed expressions (Dapoigny and Barlatier 2010, 2013a).

27.2 High-level Challenges in Context Modeling

There is now a common agreement on the fact that key features of context modeling at a high abstraction level should include (i) an expressive Knowledge Representation (KR) e.g., using ontologies for knowledge sharing and reuse (Wang et al. 2004) and (ii) reasoning skills supporting formal logic inference (Ranganathan and Campbell 2003; Schmidtke 2012). It has been shown that these features reduce the complexity of context-based applications and improve their maintainability and constant evolution (Bettini et al. 2010). In this section, we point out the main challenges resulting from these key features. As a part of a more general modeling paradigm i.e., knowledge representation, a number of critical issues have emerged in context modeling such as (i) the formal context representation, (ii) knowledge sharing, (iii) ambiguity of knowledge, (iv) quality and validity of contextual data, to cite a few. While issues (i–ii) are typically relevant of the knowledge representation domain, issue (iv) rather requires reasoning capabilities.

27.2.1 Ontologies for Context Modeling

There is now a wide agreement that a context representation must address a shared understanding of some domains conceived as a collection of concepts, objects, properties, constraints, etc. This collection can only be made explicit and sharable in intelligent applications when the descriptions share a common reference frame using what is called a domain ontology. Ontologies basically use the description of a domain to capture the meaning of the concepts and their inter-relationships. There exists at least two kinds of ontologies, i.e., foundational (core) ontologies and domain ontologies. Whereas a foundational ontology focuses on abstract relations such as subsumption, part-whole relation, identity and difference, dependence and independence, a domain ontology is rather specific to a particular scientific area (e.g., an ontology of medicine). A significant benefit of ontologies with respect to simple representation formalisms is in the support of reasoning tasks (see next subsection). Ontological models which are well-suited for context modeling through their support for interoperability and heterogeneity, are also able to represent complex relationships and dependencies among context data, which make them appropriate for the recognition of high-level context abstractions. Most ontology-based models of context knowledge exploit the representation and reasoning power of Description Logics (DL) using languages such as OWL-DL. For that purpose, the expressiveness of DL is used: (i) to describe complex context data that cannot be represented with mere ontologies, (ii) to share context among different sources through a formal semantics, (iii) to check for consistency in the set of relationships describing a context scenario, and (iv) to discover that a particular set of instances of basic context information and their relationships corresponds to the proof of a more abstract context structure. It follows that a useful context modeling should require an ontology having at least hierarchies of concepts (i.e., subsumption) and relations for providing a shared semantics together with a minimal expressiveness and a core logic for reasoning. However, OWL-DL alone has only a limited type of reasoning (Krummenacher and Strang 2007) and lack primitives for aggregating contexts in a simple way (Schmidtke 2005). A possible solution to the latter stands in so-called part-whole relation while the former is addressed with a theorem prover like Coq. We will show that using a primitive for the part-whole relation provides a great ability to extend automatically contexts assuming the typed framework of KDTL.

27.2.2 Some Approaches for Reasoning with Context Knowledge

Adding reasoning abilities to context-aware systems has been a long standing challenge of research for several years and a wide range of approaches has been suggested. In a seminal paper, McCarthy (1993) has described contexts as first class objects. The basic relation is $ist(c, p)$ asserting that the proposition p is true in the context c. Context transcendence assumes that a context c can be embedded in a new outer context c' such that the assertion $c' : ist(c, p)$ asserts that the proposition p is true in the context c, itself asserted in an outer context c'[1]. Generally in KR a situation is considered as a set of explicitly known facts. In Ghidini and Giunchiglia (2001), four possibilities are considered to relate a context with a situation: (i) a given situation is described by a set of contexts where each context is considered to be a different approximate theory of the same situation, (ii) contexts are associated to situations in a one to one correspondence, (iii) one context corresponds to many situations (i.e., contexts are not considered in the reasoning process), and (iv) many situations are described by many contexts (i.e., a combination of the cases described above). A model of context that is based on first order predicate calculus has been proposed as part of the *Gaia* middleware (a smart spaces framework for ubiquitous computing) (Ranganathan and Campbell 2003). Ontologies are used to define the semantics of different concepts, such as context information, applications, services, devices,

---

[1] The symbol ":" refers here to an assertion.

file-types, roles, etc. In a predicate model of the Active Space, the state and context information are represented as first order predicates, which are asserted into the Prolog knowledge base. Context-sensitive policies are written as Prolog rules and are checked while choosing appropriate resources. These rules specify constraints on the classes and instances of entities allowed for performing certain kinds of tasks. Using the Region Connection Calculus (RCC-8) (Cohn et al. 1997), a first order theory of spatial regions, several relations between locations or regions can be specified. The relation *external connectedness* (*EC*) holds if two locations or regions are externally connected. To formalize that it may be possible to go from one region to another, a predicate such as $ECNP(a, b)$ is true if $EC(a, b)$ holds and there is no passage to go from a to b. In addition, logic operators, such as quantification, conjunction, negation, and disjunction are used to combine the context predicates into more complex context descriptions. Quantification is limited to finite sets, such as the list of users of the system.

A set of conceptual models designed to facilitate the development of context-aware applications has been developed in the Contextual Modelling Language (CML) provided in Henricksen and Indulska (2006). Modelling constructs are defined for describing types of information in terms of fact types, e.g., *has_channel*[*Michel leWilliams*, +61733654310]. Context information consists of a set of facts expressed in the form of database tuples. Uncertain context information is expressed using a three-valued logic (true, false and possibly true). The situation abstraction is understood as a way to define conditions on the context in terms of the fact abstraction language. Situations are defined as named logical expressions of the form $S(v_1, \ldots, v_n) : \phi$, where S is the name of the situation, v_1 to v_n are variables, and ϕ is a logical expression in which variables $v_1, \ldots, v_n$ occur free. Any logical expression may include a combination of usual boolean connectives ($\wedge$, $\vee$, and $\neg$) as well as quantification over finite sets. Basic expressions include equality, inequality, and assertion. Assertions in the expressions of the situation abstraction restrict the sets of possible values over which the quantification is done. Ambiguity is supported in the form of fact alternatives, and unknowns are represented by null values in the database. If an assertion evaluates to "possibly true" when substituting some constants in a partially matching database tuple with the null value, then it matches with the assertion. In a similar way, assertions that match tuples containing alternative facts are ascribed to the truth-value "possibly true".

A foundation of a theory of contextual reasoning by analyzing its basic principles has been investigated in Benerecetti et al. (2000). The authors have distinguished three types of contextual reasoning w.r.t. the dimensions upon which a context representation may vary, i.e., (i) partial reasoning where reasoning processes only take into account a subset of a more comprehensive state of affairs, (ii) approximate reasoning which abstracts away some aspects of a state of affairs and (iii) perspective-based reasoning which incorporates a spatio-temporal, logical and cognitive point of view on a state of affairs.

In the CxBR approach (Gonzalez et al. 2008), a formal account of tactical knowledge is described by a context hierarchy assuming that a mission context is the highest context level. Using transition rules having the form IF (Conditions) THEN

(`Actions`) between a constellation of contexts, an active context is seen as a triple involving a set of control functions, a set of action rules and a set of transition rules. However, the focus is more on the dynamic aspect of context leading to a planning-like analysis, than on its knowledge representation as a structure on which reasoning is possible.

27.2.3 Requirements for Context Reasoning

Basically, on the basis of asserted knowledge a context-based reasoning system must be able to automatically deduce new knowledge, based on the available context knowledge, and to check for inconsistencies in contextual information. For example, if one asserts a current user context explicitly, then it may entail using reasoning, that the user is also in other contexts. Let us consider a patient in an hospital living in *Room A105* which contains a bed, a TV, a temperature sensor and a dedicated equipment monitoring his vital signs. Here, the whole context of the patient can be an aggregation of a personal context (e.g. name, age and profession), and a physical context (e.g. temperature). Furthermore, the medical unit of the hospital must include the context information of each of its floors, itself aggregating context information for each room. However, in most approaches (and especially in DL) only the subsumption is used to reason about context hierarchies. We will show in Sect. 27.3.3 that partonomic[2] context hierarchies (join semi-lattices) can be also exploited allowing reasoning with specific rules (e.g., overlap of parts, sum of parts, etc.). Another issue in contextual reasoning relates to reasoning mechanisms able to separate information that is relevant for a task from irrelevant information in a given circumstance (Benerecetti et al. 2000). Despite a large amount of work, we must observe that we are still far from a generally accepted theory of contextual reasoning primarily because the diversity of context definitions hampers the specification of a common logical structure of reasoning.

It is a common opinion that deriving requirements for generic context-aware systems using knowledge representation and reasoning methods is a hard task. This task will be coming up with conceptual structures that are broad enough to handle all of the different kinds of context, expressive enough to disambiguate between close situations and computationally decidable in a time consistent with the kind of applications to address. A usual way to solve this foundational problem is to design for the most commonly known situations, that is, to derive requirements from a typical application. Most solutions rely on the so-called Prolog-style logic programming (see e.g., Loke 2004) with the limited expressiveness of the first-order framework.

An important constraint for context reasoning is the support for retraction which depends both on expressiveness and efficiency. In many applications, contexts are

---

[2] Hierarchies using the part-whole relation.

usually captured based on sensor measurements and the challenge is that new measurements may replace previous values. If we assume a discrete time, it means that the measurements at time t and the contexts derived based on measurements at time t should be retracted. Moreover, the context derivation should be repeated at time $t + 1$ which requires computing every conclusion again.

The congruence of inference conclusions is also desirable if interoperability is expected. In other words, similar knowledge must be identified through different abstraction levels. It is worth observing that this constraint strengthens ontological commitments as underlined in Studer et al. (1998) i.e., the more consequences are encoded as axioms in the system, the more its users are ascribed to deal with the represented entities in the same way. If only a part of the entities of the representation are of interest to the user, it constitutes a strong drawback. Some possible way of addressing this problem is the reuse of parts of the whole ontology (modules) using e.g., a Web Ontology Language (OWL) as detailed in Grau et al. (2006).

There is now a common agreement on the fact that formal context representation puts hard requirements primarily on the KR systems in terms of expressiveness. However, the fundamental trade-off between expressiveness of representation on one side and the complexity of reasoning on the other side is still an open challenge. As argued in Perttunen et al. (2009), the lack of systems that meet all these requirements means that future research should investigate this interplay more closely to find suitable solutions. A last challenge is the non-existence of work reporting large scale deployment.

27.3 Formalizing Context in KDTL

In this section we discuss the issue of formalizing contexts in KDTL. We begin by briefly describing the basis of KDTL and then focus on the Coq layer. The main part describes how part-whole hierarchies of context types participate in the reasoning process.

27.3.1 The KDTL Language

Ontological knowledge has been implemented in KDTL which captures the expressiveness required for representing knowledge structures (Barlatier and Dapoigny 2012; Dapoigny and Barlatier 2013b). The language is a two-layered architecture including a higher-order dependent type theory as a lower layer and an ontological layer as upper layer. KDTL is a unifying theory both sufficiently expressive and logically grounded on a higher-order logic. The higher-order typed framework has the ability to reason about numerical information (e.g., statistical values computed from sensor data at a given time-stamp). The higher-order KDTL language permits the definition of new contextual categories and facts on the basis of low-order context. The language also provides the means to support comparability of diverse and non-countable information as well as numeric data. Using a foundational ontology as a core is easily extended within a given domain. It gives rise to a domain ontology which does not restrict the domain of application in any ways. In the following we skip the ontological layer interpreting types and focus on the language.

In KDTL, the basic components of the ontology are first, the *universal* which can be either (i) an atomic kind (usually called *intrinsic property*), (ii) a dependent kind, which stands for what is called *attribute* (or moment) and (iii) ontological (binary) relations further refined in (relational) properties and secondly, the *particular* defined as an instance of a universal which cannot itself have instances. Unlike the FOL-based definition of a property asserting that it is a unary predicate, an atomic kind is considered as a canonical category, an assumption which is in line with the existence of *natural types*, i.e., it can be identified as a type in isolation (Sowa 1988), and also refers to what is called an *atomic concept* in DL. Using kinds instead of unary predicates for the ontological categories (i) gives the possibility of finding an unintended application of n-ary predicates during the type checking (e.g., for non well-typed kinds) and (ii) offers a rich structural knowledge representation by means of partially ordered kinds. Following the latter, kinds are assembled in a taxonomy with a core ontology adapted from the DOLCE taxonomy of (types of) particulars (Gangemi et al. 2002). For example, the root type PT which stands for type of particulars is further refined in ED (endurants) [3], PD (perdurants) [4], Q(qualities) such as a color and AB (abstract entities) such as a space region.

Dependent kinds refer to particular qualities (subcategories of Q in the DOLCE taxonomy) which depend as relational moments (Guizzardi et al. 2002) in some particular. For example, one can define the dependent type Red (x: Boskoop_apple): Q where x stands for an instance of a Boskoop apple. It means that if a1 is an object having the type Boskoop_apple, then Red(a1) is the type describing the redness of a1 and Bright_red is such a color, i.e., an instance of Red(a1). Qualities are defined w.r.t. general quality spaces. A quality space allows qualities to be compared and contrasted, because for instance, the particular color of some object is located within a general color space.

Ontological relations also called associations in conceptual modelling, relate two kinds through either a predicate, i.e., using the basic type: A -> A -> Prop. where A denotes any kind or another kind. Then, such relation types can themselves have (meta)properties e.g., transitivity, asymmetry, etc., which can be checked in the KDTL lower layer. While relations are mathematically described, they can be instantiated as many distinct (binary) ontological relations having appropriate properties. For example, produced_by (a:ED)(a':PRO) is such an ontological relation whose first argument (relata) is any instance of type endurant and whose second

---

[3] All their proper parts are present at any time they are present, such as a person.

[4] Entities that happen in time, and can have temporal parts such as a discussion.

argument is of type PRO (process). Notice that any subtypes of the respective types ED and PRO will be accepted using coercions.

The equality between terms in the ontological layer is ascribed to be coherent w.r.t. the (intensional) Leibniz equality of the lower layer (two types are logically identical iff they have the same properties). It relates to the usual definition of the identity condition for an arbitrary property P, i.e., $P(x) \wedge P(y) \rightarrow (R(x, y) \leftrightarrow x = y)$ with a relation R satisfying this formula. This definition is carried out for any type in Coq (and therefore in KDTL) since equality between types requires the Leibniz equality. The main reason is that identity can be uniquely characterized if the language is a higher-order language in which quantification over all properties is possible (Noonan 2011). This property yields that Leibniz's Law, which is at the basis of identity in the lower layer of KDTL, is expressible in this language. Alternatively, equality can be refined and particularized with equivalence relations for appropriate types through definitions. However using barely the logical context with Leibniz equality is not sufficient (cf. Sect. 27.2.2). We follow the idea of McCarthy by specifying explicitly the context, but giving it a more expressive form through dependently typed variables together with the ability to express and reason about context hierarchies.

27.3.2   Coq Support Language

Coq's type system is built on the Calculus of Inductive Constructions (a dependently-typed lambda-calculus). Dependent types are types depending on values as well as types depending on other types. Dependent types allow, for example, the refinement of the type of a function depending on its behavior (Bertot and Castéran 2004), something which of utmost importance for modeling dynamic contexts. It is based on intuitionistic logic centered on the concept of proof rather than truth. Reasoning in Coq consists of either reducing types to their normal form or finding proofs for reduced types. The language allows to manipulate propositions (*Prop*) and types (*Type*) within propositions. In such a way reasoning is intertwined with conceptual structures mixing in an unifying framework expressive representations and reasoning. A complete introduction to Type Theory and the Coq proof assistant is beyond the scope of this chapter (for more information, refer to Bertot and Castéran (2004). In the following discussion, we restrict the description to relevant features of context modeling and typewriter notation will be dedicated to Coq syntax.

Coq is both a programming language and a proof assistant supporting conceptualization. Using a higher-order polymorphic type theory provides many benefits. First, hierarchical context models can be described by partial-order structures with the expected result that reasoning with hierarchical context models will scale well (Schmidtke 2012). Second, the typed framework enjoys (i) the reduction of the search space by restricting the domains/ranges of functions, predicates and variables to subsets of the universe of discourse, (ii) a structured knowledge representation facilitating both assertions and class-hierarchies and (iii) the detection of type errors with well-typed formulas. The KDTL type system which provides the ability to constrain semantics will give the knowledge engineer the tools to produce models with certain guaranteed properties in terms of ontological transparency, well-foundedness and re-usability.

Coq is designed such that type checking is decidable (evaluation always terminates). All logical judgments are typing judgments. The type-checker checks the correctness of proofs, that is, it checks using proof search that a data structure complies to its specification. The language consists of a sequence of declarations and definitions. A declaration associates a name with a qualification. Qualifications can be either logical propositions that reside in the universe *Prop*, mathematical collections, which are in *Set* or abstract types that belong to *Type*.

Data structures that are relevant for our purpose are `Structure` (a.k.a. dependent `Record` types) and Type Classes (TC) (Sozeau and Oury 2008; Spitters and van der Weegen 2011). A `Structure` is a non-recursive inductive type with a single constructor and projection functions for each field of the type. TCs are just dependent inductive types with one constructor and some fields. These fields are eliminators corresponding to each constructor argument. Coq allows us to specify the rules as fields inside TCs. They allow parametric arguments, inheritance and multiple fields (Spitters and van der Weegen 2011). A strong property of TCs is that parameters can be marked as implicit (i.e., using`) in which case Coq will try to infer them automatically using type inference (instance resolution). The tactic[5] underlying instance resolution for implicit arguments first uses constraint generation and then, resolution using Coq-defined instances. The constraint generation algorithm uses a dedicated tactic. It is linear w.r.t. the term's size and does not interfere with the whole tactic performances. Instance search is a backtracking algorithm using depth-first search. The use of Coq features such as implicit arguments, coercions and overloading through Type Classes renders the formal text close to informal ontological descriptions and makes easy the verification of correct transcription of definitions and statements into the formal language. This appears as a strong argument for the use of TC during context specification.

27.3.3   Context Modeling

In the first section we describe the basic mechanism for fine-grain context reasoning while in the second part, we apply this mechanism in a more concrete example in the medical domain.

27.3.3.1   Basic Principle

The principle of context-based representation is quite simple. In a first step, we design an overall architecture of context using a partonomic hierarchy, i.e., contexts are classified w.r.t. their embedding into others contexts. In a second step, classes describing fragments of knowledge are implicitly indexed on a given context, that

---

[5] Automated sequence transforming a typed expression.

is part of the hierarchy built at the first step. Any instantiation validates a single context and implicitly all knowledge depending on it. The ontology is declared as an instance of the class KDTL[6] having a minimum set of fields that stand respectively for a generic non-dependent type (kind), a generic part-whole relation (PartWhole) assuming its partial-order properties (t_of_PartOf, ant_of_PartOf and ref_of_PartOf), a generic relation (Association) without properties and an instance of the lattice built from the part-whole relation with Overlap as greater lower bound and fusion as least upper bound.

```
Class KDTL : Type := {
    kind :> Type;
    PartWhole : relation kind;
    Association : relation kind;
    Overlap : kind → kind → kind;
    Fusion : kind → kind → kind;
    t_of_PartOf : Transitive (PartWhole);
    ant_of_PartOf : Antisymmetric (PartWhole);
    ref_of_PartOf : Reflexive (PartWhole);
    pwlatt : PWLattice kind PartWhole Overlap Fusion
}.
```

The context appears as the generic class, i.e., the root of the partonomic hierarchy:

```
Class Context : Type.
```

while the DOLCE hierarchy is mapped onto structures with inheritance (coercions):

```
Structure PT := {PTsub :> kind}.
Structure PD := {PDsub :> PT}.
Structure ED := {EDsub :> PT}.
Structure AB := {ABsub :> PT}.
Structure Q := {Qsub :> PT}.
...
Structure AnatomicalEntity := {AnatEntsub :> APO}.
Structure MaterialAnatomicalEntity := {MatAnatEsub :> AnatomicalEntity}.
Structure HumanBody := {HumanBodysub :> MaterialAnatomicalEntity}.
Structure Person := {Personsub :> APO}.
...
```

All these data structures and their derived subsumed structures can be used in context classes to express relevant context types. Any context structure can be derived using parts of the generic context structure and hierarchies of context structures can be

---

[6] The instantiation relation (:) and the subsumption (: > in Structure) are already available in the Coq language and do not require any supplementary modeling structures.

built on the basis of part-whole relations. A context can be constrained either with implicit arguments whose proof is required for validating the context, or with fields representing the ontological context properties. In the latter, we get variables that are usable within this specific context. Let us consider the following example (here, context structures are empty to simplify the discussion).

```
Class ContextC1 : Type := ContextC1_001:>Context.
Class ContextC3 : Type := ContextC3_001:>Context.
Class ContextC2 : Type := {
                        ContextC2_001:>ContextC1;
                        ContextC2_002:>ContextC3.
```

These type classes declarations design a small partonomic hierarchy of context types in which ContextC2 is the aggregation of two simple disjoint context types ContextC1 and ContextC3. In a second step, we introduce three abstract types *PersonC_i*, each of them being accessible only in the scope of a given context using implicit variables: $\{c : ContextC_i\}$. The coercions to *Person* in each respective field means that any instance of *PersonC_i* is also an instance of *Person* within the context C_i.

```
Class PersonC1 {c: ContextC1} := personCont1 :> Person.
Class PersonC2 {c: ContextC2} := personCont2 :> Person.
Class PersonC3 {c: ContextC3} := personCont3 :> Person.
```

The evaluation can be easily assessed through the class Test that requires both an (implicit) instance of the context C1 and an instance of Person. For instance, this test may simulate a decision procedure.

```
Class Test {c:ContextC1}(c1:Person) : Prop.
```

The following code says that when we are in context C3, no instance of C1 is available because C1 and C2 are two disjoint context types. Then, the test fails (Could not find an instance for "ContextC1" in environment).

```
Variable C :ContextC3.
Variable p : PersonC3.
Variable I1 : Test p. ← fails
```

In the second experiment, the context is simply switched to C1. This time, the test class has the right context but the instance of Person is supposed to be in context C3 and the test fails again (Could not find an instance for "ContextC3" in environment:).

```
Variable C :ContextC1.
Variable p : PersonC3. ← fails
Variable I1 : Test p.
```

Now, the context is switched to C2. The backtracking algorithm extracts a proof of C1 (declared as a substructure of C2) and the test succeeds.

Variable C :**ContextC2**.
Variable p : **PersonC2**.
Variable $I1$: **Test** p.

Finally, if the instance of `Person` is now supposed to be in context C3, then the test succeeds again, because an instance of C3 has been created as a substructure of C2.

Variable C :**ContextC2**.
Variable p : **PersonC3**.
Variable $I1$: **Test** p.

With such context definitions, contexts can restrict appropriates classes (here, $PersonC_i$) and switching from a context to another context is filtered by the Coq type checker using the backtracking algorithm. The formalization of context type is close to McCarthy's solution but with a greater expressiveness.

27.3.3.2 A Case Study

Let us consider an example based on Pires et al. (2005) in which use cases have been presented to investigate the usability and applicability of ontologies for context-aware applications. The reasoning process will be based both on subsumption (with coercions) and on the automatic generation of context instances in the partonomic hierarchy of contexts (with type classes). In the context of a personal health assistant, the application is divided into sub processes such as the drug supervision process that is checking for problems related to drug prescriptions and supervising subscription use and renewals. We focus on the decision process about the medical condition, the drugs and their substitutes. In order to model the context information, the given set of prototypical natural language sentences that should be covered by the model is:

i. Paul has a cold.
ii. Paul uses the drug $d1$ against the cold.
iii. The drug $d1$ when used against cold, has a substitute $d2$ with the type *BSDrug*, i.e., a Broad-Spectrum Drug.

The application requires five atomic kinds, i.e., *Person*, *MedicalCondition* (*MC*), *Drug* which subsumes both *TargetDrug* and *BSDrug*. Their respected variables of are inserted into the environment. A given drug can be applied for several medical conditions and therefore it may have different substitute drugs depending on to what medical condition it is targeted. The concepts must also reflect the facts that a person can have a medical condition, that a drug addresses some medical conditions and that a person uses some drug. From these assumptions, and from the domain ontology, the ontological relations can be modeled easily. First, definitions instantiate general statements with particular notions (e.g., instances of associations) in order to use them as instances (proofs) of more specialized properties.

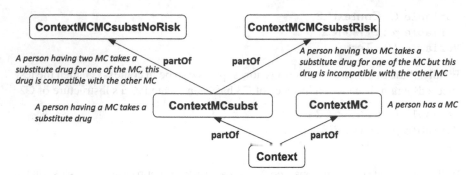

Fig. 27.1 The part-whole hierarchy of contexts

Definition uses_drug (a:**Person**)(a':**Drug**) := Association a a'.
Definition for_condition (m:**MC**)(d:**TargetDrug**) := Association d m.
Definition has_condition (a:**Person**)(a':**MC**) := Association a a'.
Definition has_substitute (d:**TargetDrug**)(d':**BSDrug**) := Association d d'.
Definition incompatible_with (m:**MC**)(d:**Drug**) := Association m d.
Definition compatible_with (m:**MC**)(d:**Drug**) := Association m d.

Axiom *compatible not incompatible* : $\forall$ (m:**MC**)(d:**Drug**), (incompatible with m d) $\rightarrow$ ~(compatible with m d).

The contextual hierarchy formalizes the embedding of contexts using the *partof* relation on the context structures, i.e., at the meta-level (see Fig. 27.1).

Class **ContextMC** := ContextMC_001:> **Context**.
Class **ContextMCsubst** := ContextMCsub_001:> **Context**.
Class **ContextMCMCsubstNoRisk** := ContextMCMCsub_001:> **ContextM-Csubst**.
Class **ContextMCMCsubstRisk** := ContextMCMCsubR_001:> **ContextM-Csubst**.

The strong point here is that properties as well as predicates can depend on the occurrence of a given context. This is possible because using types, properties and predicates are treated on a par. Usual first-order predicates are fully supported and predicates can be only available in an appropriate context. Then we can automatically infer the appropriate contexts using the backtracking algorithm in Coq for type classes which uses local hypotheses as well as declared lemmas. For that purpose, the following type classes built from the set of relation types defined above, are introduced. They represent (relational) properties, i.e., (in)compatibilities of drugs with medical conditions depending on a particular context.

Class **CompatibleDrug** {c:**ContextMCMCsubstNoRisk**} (m:**MC**)(d:**Drug**)
$\qquad\qquad\qquad$:= compatD : compatible_with m d.
Class **InCompatibleDrug** {c:**ContextMCMCsubstRisk**} (m:**MC**)(d:**Drug**)
$\qquad\qquad\qquad$:= incompatD : incompatible_with m d.

The sequence of classes above represents contextualized persons. Their role and their behavior are similar to *PersonC$_i$* classes defined in Sect. 27.3.3.1 with C_i replaced successively by MC, MCsub, MCMCsub,etc.

Class **PersonMC** {c:**ContextMC**} (m:**MC**)(d:**TargetDrug**) := {
$\qquad\qquad$ PersMC_001:> **Person**;
$\qquad\qquad$ PersMC_002: has_condition PersMC_001 m;
$\qquad\qquad$ PersMC_003: uses_drug PersMC_001 d}.

Class **PersonMCsub** {c:**ContextMCsubst**}(m:**MC**)(d:**TargetDrug**)
$\qquad\qquad\qquad\qquad\qquad\qquad\qquad$ (s:**BSDrug**) := {
$\qquad\qquad$ PersMCsub_001:> **Person**
$\qquad\qquad$ PersMCsub_002 : has_condition PersMCsub_001 m;
$\qquad\qquad$ PersMCsub_003 : has_substituted s;
$\qquad\qquad$ PersMCsub_004 : uses_drug PersMCsub_001 s}.

Class **PersonMCMCsub** {c:**ContextMCMCsubstNoRisk**}(m:**MC**)
$\quad$ (m':**MC**) (d:**TargetDrug**)(s:**BSDrug**) {cp:**CompatibleDrug** m' s} := {
$\qquad\qquad$ PersMCMCsub_001:> **PersonMCsub** m d s;
$\qquad\qquad$ PersMCMCsub_002: has_condition PersMCsub_001m'}.

Class **PersonMCMCsubR** {c:**ContextMCMCsubstRisk**}(m:**MC**)
$\quad$ (m':**MC**) (d:**TargetDrug**)(s:**BSDrug**) {r:**InCompatibleDrug** m' s} :={
$\qquad\qquad$ PersMCMCsubR_001:> **PersonMCsub** m d s;
$\qquad\qquad$ PersMCMCsubR_002: has_condition PersMCsub_001 m'}.

From the database, suppose that *Paul* has a cold (*Flu*) and he decides to use the drug $d2$ against the cold. We can easily address the fact that a broad spectrum drug $d2$ when used against a medical condition e.g., *Flu*, can represent a risk in the presence of some other condition (e.g., a liver problem *liverPb*). If the current context (a single context can be proved at a given time) is an instance of *ContextMCMCsubstRisk*, then any instantiation of the class *PersonMCMCsubR* (and its parts) succeeds unlike all structures that depend on the context class *ContextMCMCsubstNoRisk*. For example, the declared instance succeeds:

Instance testrisk : **PersonMCMCsubR** *Flu liverPb d1 d2*

while the following:

Instance norisk : **PersonMCMCsub** *Flu liverPb d1 d2*

leads to the Coq message:

```
Unable to satisfy the following constraints:
?258 : "CompatibleDrug liverPb d2"
?257 : "ContextMCMCsubstNoRisk"
```

27.4 Conclusion

A theoretical core of context structures has been suggested for context-aware systems. The conceptual structures are both generic and modular for supporting different kinds of context, expressive enough to disambiguate between close situations (considered here as proofs) and computationally efficient using a decidable type system such as Coq. In this way, formal and rigorous proofs are provided, preventing the end-user from semantically ill-defined concepts.

Knowing what proofs are available at a given time, automatically determines what context is valid at that time. All proofs can be derived from database requests at a given time-stamp t and the decisions are only valid for that time. This assumption pre-supposes that the context derivation should be repeated in the next time-stamp, which requires (i) collecting every proof again and (ii) that no change can occur in the real world under analysis during proof evaluation.

The idea of building partially-ordered context hierarchies is in line with the work of Schmidtke (2012) who has explained why complexity does not increase, even if arbitrary additional partial ordering relations are allowed. Because sub-relations of pre-orders are also pre-orders, a single pre-ordered relation can be easily extended to a set of sub-relations that do not depend on the dimensions of context.

Finally, cognitive correctness is another aspect of the present theoretical approach. The automatic inference of context-dependent type classes during proof search with a backtracking algorithm is a significant argument for the use of dependently typed system such as Coq. Therefore, KDTL appears as a suitable compromise between expressiveness of representation and the complexity of reasoning with context types.

References

Agostini, A., et al.: Experience report: ontological reasoning for context-aware internet services. Paper presented at the 4th IEEE conference on pervasive computing and communications workshops (PerCom 2006 Workshops), IEEE Computer Society, Pisa, Italy, 13–17 March 2006

Barlatier, P., Dapoigny, R.: A type-theoretical approach for ontologies: The case of roles. Appl. Ontol. **7**(3), 311–356 (2012). doi:10.3233/AO-2012-0113

Benerecetti, M., et al.: Contextual reasoning distilled. J. Exp. Theo. Artif. Intell. **12**(3), 279–305 (2000)

Bertot, Y., Castéran, P.: Interactive theorem proving and program development. Coq'Art: the calculus of inductive constructions. In: Texts in Theoretical Computer Science, An EATCS Series. Springer, Berlin (2004)

Bettini, C., et al.: A survey of context modelling and reasoning techniques. J. Pervasive Mobile Comput. **6**(2), 161–180 (2010) (Elsevier Science Publishers B. V.)

Cohn, A.G., et al.: Qualitative spatial representation and reasoning with the region connection calculus. GeoInformatica **1**, 275–316 (1997)

Dapoigny, R., Barlatier, P.: Modeling contexts with dependent types. Fundamenta Informaticae **104**(4), 293–327 (2010). doi:10.3233/FI-2010-351

Dapoigny, R., Barlatier, P.: Formal foundations for situation awareness based on dependent type theory. Inf. Fus. **14**(1), 87–107 (2013a). doi:10.1016/j.inffus.2012.02.006

Dapoigny, R., Barlatier, P.: Modeling ontological structures with type classes in Coq. Paper presented at the 20th international conference on conceptual structures (ICCS'2013), Lecture Notes in Computer Science, vol. 7735, pp. 135–152. Mumbai, India, 10–12 January 2013b

Gangemi, A., et al.: Sweetening ontologies with DOLCE. In: Gomez-Perez, A., Benjamins, V.R. (eds.) Paper presented at the 13th international conference EKAW'2002, Lecture Notes in Computer Science, vol. 2473, pp. 166–181. Siguenza, Spain, 1–4 Oct 2002

Ghidini, C., Giunchiglia, F.: Local models semantics, or contextual reasoning = locality + compatibility. Artif. Intell. **127**(2), 221–259 (2001). doi:10.1016/S0004-3702(01)00064-9

Gonzalez, A.J., et al.: Formalizing context-based reasoning: a modeling paradigm for representing tactical human behavior. Int. J. Intell. Syst. **23**, 822–847 (2008). doi:10.1002/int.20291

Grau, B.C., et al.: Modularity and web ontologies. Paper presented at the 10th international conference on principles of knowledge representation and reasoning, Lake District, United Kingdom, pp. 198–209, 2–5 July 2006

Guizzardi, G.: On ontology, ontologies, conceptualizations, modeling languages, and (meta) models. Paper presented at the 7th international Baltic conference, DB&IS 2006, Vilnius, Lithuania, 3–6 July 2006. Frontiers in Artificial Intelligence and Applications, vol. 155, pp. 18–39. IOS Press (2006)

Guizzardi, G., et al.: Towards ontological foundations for UML conceptual models. Paper presented at the confederated international conferences DOA, CoopIS and ODBASE'2002 Irvine, California, USA, 30 Oct–1 Nov 2002. Lecture Notes in Computer Science, vol. 2519, pp. 1100–1117 (2002)

Henricksen, K., Indulska, J.: Developing context-aware pervasive computing applications: models and approach. Pervasive Mobile Comput. **2**(1), 37–64 (2006)

Krummenacher, R., Strang, T.: Ontology-based context modeling. Paper presented at the 3rd workshop on context-aware proactive systems, University of Surrey, United Kingdom, 18–19 June 2007

Loke, S.W.: Logic programming for context-aware pervasive computing: Language support, characterizing situations, and integration with the web. Paper presented at the IEEE/WIC/ACM international conference on web intelligence, Beijing, China, pp. 44–50, 20–24 Sept 2004

McCarthy, J.: Notes on formalizing context. Paper presented at the 13th international joint conference on artificial intelligence, Chambéry, France, pp. 555–560, 28 Aug–3 Sept 1993

Noonan, H.: Identity. The Stanford Encyclopedia of Philosophy. In: Edward, N.Z. (ed.). http://plato.stanford.edu/archives/win2011/entries/identity/ (2011). Accessed 7 Nov 2009

Perttunen, M., et al.: Context representation and reasoning in pervasive computing: a review. Int. J. Multimed. Ubiquit. Eng. **4**(4), 1–28 (2009)

Pires, L.F., et al.: Techniques for describing and manipulating context information. Lucent Technologies, Freeband/A_MUSE, Tech. report D3.5v2.0 (2005)

Ranganathan, A., Campbell, R.H.: An infrastructure for context-awareness based on first order logic. Pers. Ubiquit. Comput. **7**(6), 353–364 (2003) (Springer)

Schmidtke, H.R.: Aggregations and constituents: geometric specification of multi-granular objects. J. Vis. Lang. Comput. **16**, 289–309 (2005) (Elsevier)

Schmidtke, H.R.: Contextual reasoning in context-aware systems. Paper presented at the 8th international conference on intelligent environments, Guanajuato, Mexico, pp. 82–93, 27–28 June 2012

Sowa, J.F.: Using a lexicon of canonical graphs in a semantic interpreter. In: Evens, M. (ed.) Relational Models of the Lexicon, pp. 113–137. Cambridge University Press, New York (1988)

Sozeau, M., Oury, N.: First-class type classes. In: Aït Mohamed, O., Muñoz, C., Tahar, S. (eds.) Theorem Proving in Higher-Order Logics, Lecture Notes in Computer Science, vol. 5170, pp. 278–293. Springer, Berlin (2008)

Spitters, B., van der Weegen, E.: Type classes for mathematics in type theory. Math. Struct. Comput. Sci. **21**(4), 795–825 (2011). doi:10.1017/S0960129511000119

Studer, R., et al.: Knowledge engineering: principles and methods. Data Knowl. Eng. **25**(1/2), 161–197 (1998)

Wang, X.H., et al.: Ontology-based context modeling and reasoning using OWL. Paper presented at the 2nd IEEE conference on pervasive computing and communications (PerCom 2004), Orlando, Florida, 14–17 March 2004. Workshop on context modeling and reasoning CoMoRea'04, pp. 18–22. IEEE Press, USA (2004)

Chapter 28
Context and Granularity

Hedda Rahel Schmidtke

Abstract Granularity is one of the core aspects of context. This chapter gives an overview of three perspectives on granularity—size-based granularity, partition-based granularity, granularity in contextual reasoning—and discusses their interrelation. The author identifies three types of granularity: perceptual granularity refers to the fact that any perceptual system has a certain limited resolution; conceptual granularity indicates that the categories in which we think are tied to levels of granularity; physical granularity, finally, refers to the structures, sizes, and densities that exist in the physical world. This chapter discusses the interplay between the three types of granularity and how perceptual granularity could have been fundamental in the evolution of cognition.

28.1   Introduction

Granularity and context are fundamental structuring mechanisms for many reasoning tasks that a human being undertakes. When planning a journey from a place in Paris to a place in Melbourne, we choose a suitable airplane trip between the cities weeks before the journey; then, maybe a day before the trip, select a means to get to the airport in Paris on time. It would be impossible to plan such a journey with a single route planning mechanism, such as A*. In many scenarios of common sense reasoning, we segment reasoning tasks based on a view of the world that employs strata of granularity. Accordingly, an understanding of granularity and mechanisms for handling granularity are fundamental to many applications ranging from automated question answering and text summarization (Mulkar-Mehta et al. 2011) to geographic information science and ontology (Bittner. 2011).

From a computational point of view, we can say that granularity allows us to structure a continuous reality in such a way that we can handle it as a hierarchy of finite domains. Imagine you are sitting at a coffee table (a scenario adapted from Bronowski 1970, Galton 2000), you can see a finite number of objects, including: cups with coffee, spoons, the milk, the sugar, etc. It is then possible to enumerate all the objects on the table, to count them, and to say with certainty: there are 11 objects

H. R. Schmidtke (✉)
Carnegie Mellon University, Kigali, Rwanda and Pittsburgh, PA, USA
e-mail: schmidtke@acm.org

© Springer Science+Business Media New York 2014
P. Brézillon, A. J. Gonzalez (eds.), *Context in Computing*,
DOI 10.1007/978-1-4939-1887-4_28

on the table. We can also look at the scene in more detail: we can talk about the parts of objects, which we previously counted as one whole, for example, a sugar cube; we can say, it is made up of a fixed number of sugar crystals; and with further inspection, we can postulate that a given crystal consists of a fixed number of molecules. Looking at finer and finer levels of detail, we move from the realm of common sense objects, to chemistry, nuclear physics, and particle physics, until we enter domains of science where the part-of relation does not seem to be a good metaphor any more. Even when we handle complex abstract objects, such as field equations, we do this by dissecting them into parts and studying the relations between these parts. Each time, we move from a context to a finer grained context. The notion of granularity, strata of levels of detail or conceptually coherent chunks of reality, is one of the primary ordering schemata of human thinking and an important aspect of context.

To see the fundamental link between granularity and context, consider again the example of the coffee table: we first counted the objects on the coffee table leaving out everything beyond the coffee table, for instance, the cushions on the sofa or the picture on the wall. This is a typical example of reasoning in context. The context in this case is the coffee table. However, we also left out the molecules of the sugar cube when counting the objects on the coffee table. This is an example of granularity-dependent reasoning. The notion of granularity and the notion of context are thus tightly linked, and the main benefit for reasoning is in both cases the same: reduction of complexity. We could say the main distinction is that context restricts the range of reasoning in terms of area covered, while granularity restricts it in terms of detail covered. Generalizing, we can say that granularity-dependent reasoning is one part of contextual reasoning while restriction of the area or scope is another form of contextual reasoning, and both working together define contextual reasoning. The latter perspective is particularly relevant when we assume that the level of granularity in a context depends on the area covered by context, as is the case for the model of size-based granularity, whose cognitive foundations this chapter studies at greater depth.

Structure of this chapter. After a discussion of prominent approaches on granularity (Sect. 28.2), a categorization of three aspects of granularity is presented in Sect. 28.3: granularity appears in perception, cognitive conceptualization, and physical reality. We further study evidence that granularity is pervasive in human cognition in Sect. 28.4, and explore the cognitive complexity of granularity in Sect. 28.5.

28.2 Related Works

As a fundamental mechanism to make reasoning tractable, granularity has received considerable attention. We discuss the main theories of granularity. The concept itself is fundamental for the natural sciences and probably at least as old as the first atomist theories. Galton (2000) distinguishes between representational granularity and intrinsic granularity. Representational granularity regards the available level of detail in a given representation medium, for instance, the resolution of a photographic image. Intrinsic granularity refers to the observation that certain size scales are relevant for the representation of objects while others seem to be irrelevant (Bronowski 1970). We analyzed the sugar cube in the above example, for instance, on the scales of the cube, the sugar crystal, and the sugar molecule, but not on any scale in between (Bronowski 1970).

The models built in the sciences start from smallest granules. Science decontextualizes the world of everyday experience so as to be able to understand the world beyond human perceptual capabilities. Intelligent systems research on the other hand, aims to go into the opposite direction: starting from the advanced computational power of a modern computer, potentially equipped with sensors, it aims to attain the power of human reasoning capabilities. We can distinguish two main thrusts to formalize the notion of granularity: partition-based approaches assume that objects on coarser levels of detail consist of sets of objects of finer level of detail; size-based approaches assume that levels of detail are tied to sizes.

28.2.1 Partition-Based Granularity

Zadeh (1979) was among the first to propose a theory of granularity: information granulation according to Zadeh (1979) is the degree of detail at which a certain set of linguistic variables dissects a certain space of measurable or perceptible attributes. The concept thus is closely related to discretization or quantization, but reflects that boundaries may be fuzzy instead of sharp. In rough set theory (Pawlak 1982), this idea has been developed further (Bittner and Stell 2003). The key idea of the partition-based conception of granularity is to identify certain portions of a domain, e.g. measurement points, spatial regions, or sugar crystals, and consider them indistinguishable with respect to a certain context. An application that detects wild fires from infrared satellite images, e.g., would need to distinguish pixels in a photo that have a very high heat value from those with a lower value, a binary decision. The result is a black-and-white photo with two regions: the fire region and the no-fire region. A more fine-grained analysis of temperature values would yield sub-partitions of the two regions. However, pixels in a satellite image correspond to large regions, and the boundary region between the fire and no-fire region can be critical. Rough set theory approximates the actual fire region with two sets, an upper approximation with a low temperature threshold, yielding a set of pixels covering the fire region, and a lower approximation with a high temperature threshold, yielding a set of pixels covered by the fire region. This allows the theory to handle different conceptualizations of the same reality: the real boundary of the fire is somewhere within the uncertainty region.

Hobbs (1985) developed an overarching framework of granularity connecting different types of granularity-mechanisms. Hobbs' theory builds upon the core notion of an indistinguishability relation. He discusses three different types of granularity that belong to the category of partition-based mechanisms: *abstraction* groups objects into partitions generated by an indistinguishability relation that is an equivalence relation, i.e. transitive, these groups of objects are then conceived as objects of a coarser level of detail; the notion of *simplification* is a mechanism to move between coarser grained and finer grained theories of the world. For the third type of granularity mechanism, which he calls *idealization*, Hobbs (1985) relaxes the previous requirement of a transitive indistinguishability relation, e.g. in indistinguishability relations from measurement or perception, but still requires an equivalence relation, that is, partitions to be constructed. The process of idealization, then is the introduction of such arbitrary boundaries, so as to obtain partitions.

Granular partitions from an ontological point of view are the focus of Bittner and Smith (2003). The notion of size is discussed in Rector et al. (2006).

28.2.2   Size-Based Granularity

Hobbs (1985) also discussed non-transitive indistinguishability relations and the notion of grain-size. Granularity in this sense can be directly related to some measurable dimension, for instance, spatial distance or temporal duration. Human perception of temperatures, for instance, has an accuracy of about 3°F (Hobbs 1985). Metric spaces give rise to a size-based notion of granularity. This notion does not conflict with the partition-based view, rather both highlight a different aspect of granularity. The example of time granularity in calendar systems may illustrate this: seven days partition a week and each day has the same duration, partition-based and size-based granularity are well aligned in this case. When we try to group weeks into months, however, weeks do not partition months well, in general. The months are partitions of the year, but have different duration. It is noteworthy, however, that months have *roughly* the same duration. The deviation of maximally three days, that is, a size around one order of magnitude smaller, can be considered *irrelevant*, making the durations *indistinguishable*. Calendar systems are a prominent area of research for size-based and partition-based granularity (Euzenat 1995; Ohlbach and Gabbay 1998; Montanari et al. 1999; Bettini et al. 2000; Bettini and Montanari 2003; Euzenat and Montanari 2005).

Hobbs (2000) studied, which differences of size or number are relevant, and found that people use half orders of magnitude when giving estimates: 10, 30, 100, or 300 are sizes that can be distinguished well and influence the meanings of words, such as *several*, *about/approximately*, and spatial *where*. He notes that objects of about three times size or groups of about three times size have to be handled in a different manner. Our own physical dimensions thus give rise to size-based granularity as a suitable way for us to structure our environment and to reason about it. Hobbs and Kreinovich (2001) investigated from a statistical and measurement point of view why it makes sense for people to estimate in half orders of magnitude. Perception and measurement of quantitative information is usually restricted to a certain accuracy. The study of limited accuracy in measurement, which appears as a non-transitive indistinguishability relation, is fundamental for measurement theory (Suppes and Zinnes 1963) and any study of the mathematical foundations of perception (Palmer 1999): we might find, that the length of a line of 1 cm may be indistinguishable from that of a line of length 1.1 cm when presented consecutively, and a length of 1.2 cm may be indistinguishable to a length of 1.3 cm, but a length of 1 cm may be well distinguishable from a length of 1.3 cm.

Granularity cannot only be used to distinguish and relate between objects and groups of objects forming the objects of a coarser granularity, but also between relations. The concept of conceptual neighborhood defined by Freksa (1992) describes sets of relations that can be understood as coarsened relations: the set comprised of the relations *before*, *meets*, and *overlaps*, for instance, regards a situation, where the beginning of the first event must be before the beginning of the second. Adding a concept of sizes yields granularity-dependent relations: the temporal relation *meets* between two lectures on a student's schedule, for instance, will rarely be a true *meets*-relation, but rather a *before* relation with a comparatively small distance between the two events, as the student needs to have at least a 10 min break to move from one lecture hall to another. Euzenat (1995, 2001) studied such phenomena and how they can be handled in qualitative temporal and spatial reasoning systems based on the conceptual neighborhood between relations.

28.2.3   Contextual Reasoning Perspective

Granularity-dependent reasoning has been studied from three main perspectives. It is highly relevant for building larger knowledge bases (Hobbs 1985), for understanding how human cognition structures the complexity of the everyday world, and it is interesting by itself as a form of non-classical reasoning. The framework proposed by Benerecetti et al. (2000) is a general framework for contextual reasoning based on an analysis of the main approaches. Benerecetti et al. (2000) describe three types of contextual reasoning: localized reasoning, that is, reasoning within a context, push and pop reasoning which moves parameters outside the current context into the context and parameters inside the context to the outside, and shifting, which changes the perspective taken in a context. They identify three dimensions of context: *partiality* and *perspective* regard what I consider the area or scope of a context, and *approximation*, which I see as most closely related to granularity.

Contextual reasoning in human expert knowledge has been studied by Brézillon (2007, 2011, 2013) using the formalism of contextual graphs. Contextual graphs are directed acyclic graphs that specify the causal structure and contextual conditions under which an action is applicable. Contextual elements in this graph structure form a hierarchical structure that reflects the levels of decision making.

28.2.4   Applications

Applications for the theories of granularity abound, and an appropriate categorization and description would require its own chapter. In fact, any hierarchical representation, be it the organization of a book into chapters, sections, paragraphs, the organization of our calendar systems, the ranks in an organization, or the segmentation of geographic reality into regions, such as countries and cities, is potentially derived from a granularity structure in the respective domain. Granularity is used in a wide range of applications: data bases use time granularity to organize calendar terms (Bettini et al. 2000); web-service composition can benefit from granularity (Niu et al. 2011); context-aware systems use hierarchical structures (Dorn et al. 2006) or size-based granularity (Han et al. 2013) to organize contexts; granularity allows determining causal structures in natural language texts facilitating applications such as text summarization and automatic question answering (Mulkar-Mehta et al. 2011); an understanding of granularity is required to analyze geographic entities with a vague boundary (Bittner. 2011).

28.3 Granularity in Perception, Cognitive Conceptualization, and Physical Reality

The visual experience can be conceived as fundamental to spatial problem solving (Kosslyn. 1994). The visual metaphor itself is often introduced to motivate conceptions and aspects of granularity. The term granularity itself originally refers to the granules of photo paper, which limits how much detail can be visible in a photo. A similar notion is the notion of *resolution*, which refers to granularity of the camera or a digital photo. In both cases, we refer to pictures in raster format. The notion *level of detail*, in contrast, can also be applied to graphics in vector format. The relation between the two is clear: a vector graphic is meaningful on some zoom factors but not on others. The factors where it does make sense determine its level of detail. Figure 28.1 shows a vector graphic at three different scales. The scale in (b) is chosen so that the whole figure fits and can be seen well as a whole, except for the details in the center. The outtake in (d) takes up the same area on the paper, but shows only the detail at the center. The outtake in (c) focuses on a part of the graphic that has a much lower level of detail. The depiction (a) shows a much larger area, of which only a small portion contains details, which are however not well discernable: the graphic becomes point-like.

The complex situations we encounter in reality are inherently multi-granular. As Fig. 28.1 illustrates, even simple depictions already contain multiple levels of granularity, which can vary over the area. An everyday environment, such as a forest or supermarket, contains a multitude of details, which our perceptual system can filter by using several levels of detail. The concrete objects we recognize and name, such as building, bag, apple, or supermarket have a certain range of possible sizes, in fact, our terms are closely tied to a certain size. This allows people to give astonishing estimates, such as, how many students are on average in a school class (Hobbs 2000). If a certain concept exists in several sizes that differ in several orders of magnitude, they have a different name: a landmass that has a diameter of 2 km in size is called an *island*. If it has a diameter of 2000 km, it is a *continent*. If its diameter is 2 m it is a *rock* or *sand bank*. We aim at humoristic or rhetoric effect when we call an island a rock, or vice versa.

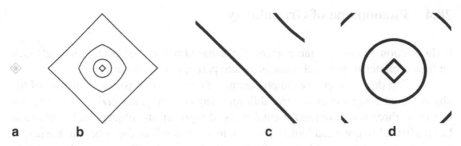

Fig. 28.1 A small vector graphic illustration (model of a non-metric geometry from Schmidtke 2005b) included at three scales. The picture is visible as a whole in (**a**) and (**b**). Details of the same graphic at the same scale are shown in (**c**) and (**d**), but while (c) shows only a non-informative portion of the graphic, (d) shows a relative portion at the same resolution that reveals a relevant detail

Not only nouns are affected by size-dependency: differences in applicability of verbs and prepositions also depend on size-based granularity (Schmidtke 2013). The sentence *Mary ging am Meer vorbei* (*Mary walked past the ocean* or *Mary passed the ocean*) is hard to understand: the verb *gehen* has the granularity of walking associated with it, and this granularity is not compatible with the granularity of the phrase *past the ocean*, as *past* used in this manner indicates that the ground (here: *the ocean*) is conceived as point-like, e.g. like the object in Fig. 28.1a. In order to see an ocean as point-like, the scene we have in mind has to be seen at a very coarse granularity, but an ocean cannot be point-like in a scene where we see a pedestrian walking. The sentence *Mary ging am Meer entlang* (*Mary walked along the ocean*) is much better, since *entlang* is used in a context where the ground is considered to be an extended linear object, such as the boundary of a large object (Fig. 28.1c).

We can classify the types of situations that can occur depending on three different types of granularity involved: the observer can see a certain area at a certain level of detail. What is outside of the scene cannot be seen and what is too small cannot be seen. The categories of objects an observer can name, whether an ocean or a fly, have a certain maximal size and a certain minimal size that depend on their category. Accordingly, we have two types of granularity on the side of the observer: a perceptual granularity and a conceptual granularity. The perceptual granularity can be described as the size of the largest unit or grain contained in the object. A third type of granularity is the physical granularity of the objects in physical reality, size-levels that mark physical properties of the object.[1] Of these three, the perceptual granularity regards the interaction between an observer and the physical reality surrounding it. From a cognitive science point of view, it is interesting to study how the three mechanisms relate.

---

[1] The *representational granularity* of Galton (2000) corresponds to what is called here perceptual granularity, his *intrinsic granularity* is related to the notion of physical granularity employed in this chapter.

28.4 Phenomena of Granularity

In this section, we analyze the concept of size-based conceptual granularity and touch on how it relates to physical granularity and perceptual granularity.

Studying the sugar cube example again, we can find that we can conceive of the object called a sugar cube in three different ways—and, generalizing, we can posit that these three ways are fundamental ways of representing objects (Schmidtke and Beigl 2010). First, we can look at it on the level of detail of the cube: our basic unit then is between 1 mm and 1 cm, in the case of a sugar cube. The sugar cube is clearly a cube. This level gives the cube its name, and it describes its shape. I call this scale of representation of an object, the *level of shape*. We can also have a closer look, seeing the cube in terms of its parts. Staying in the visual metaphor, we *focus* on a part that makes up the sugar cube. We see then, that it is made up of sugar. The first part of the sugar cube's name represents this information. What it is made up of, its substance: I call this range of scales the *level of substance*. For our example, these are the sizes below 1 mm. On a level coarser than the level of shape, in contrast, I can make statements, such as, that the sugar cube is lying next to the spoon. In this case, I am interested in representing the object's relationships with respect to objects in its surroundings. I call this level of representation the *level of position*. For the example, this level is associated with sizes larger than one 1 cm.

When we add the notion of a context area delimiting our representation and reasoning, we can see how the same object can be conteptualized differently in different contexts (Schmidtke 2003): a road is seen as a linear object when planning a trip from a city A to a city B, but the same road is conceived as an extended planar region for a pedestrian trying to cross it. In the first case, the context area could cover a region of a size of maybe 10 km, in the second case it covers an area in the order of magnitude of 50 m. Assuming that we represent maximally one order of magnitude in the same context, we obtain the minimal size represented in the first case as 1 km, in the second case, 5 m. Knowing the size of a context area we can thus assign a certain *size interval* to it as the range of sizes in the context (Schmidtke 2005c). I can limit the grain size of the context, for instance, to an order of magnitude smaller than the context. Any object having a width of less than 1 km—and roads typically have a much smaller width—can therefore be seen as having irrelevant width in the context of route planning, in accordance to our intuition that the width of a road is usually not relevant for planning a trip (Hobbs 1985; Schmidtke 2003).

The sorites paradox and the ship of Theseus paradox are phenomena indicating the boundary between the level of substance and the level of shape. The sorites paradox— *sorites* is Greek for heap—states that the notion of a heap has a contradictory aspect. The argument runs as follows.

- A single grain of sand is not a heap of sand.
- Adding one grain of sand to something that is not a heap of sand, does not make it a heap of sand.
- Therefore by induction, no collection of sand grains can be called a heap of sand.

Size-based granularity can shed light on this paradox: the heap of sand and the individual grains are concepts associated with different levels of granularity. The grains are on the level of substance of the heap, which is irrelevant when we assume a level of granularity suitable to represent the heap, that is, its conic shape. A similar example can be found in the phrase "to not see the forest for the trees." The sorites paradox and the forest-tree incompatibility received some attention from a range of disciplines. It is relevant from a linguistic, philosophical, and computational perspective (Schmidtke 2005a; van Deemter 1995), but also for GIS (Bennett 2001). The notion of clustering is one of the key concepts in data mining (Jain et al. 2000), and we may point to Wertheimer (1923) as the first to illuminate the boundary between substance and shape—German: gestalt.

The above notions of levels of granularity in representation do not only hold for the spatial domain, but can also be applied to other dimensions. We can analyze temporal occurrences, for instance, in the same manner: a symphony is composed of movements and parts of these, and each one is a composition of single notes. Single notes are the *substance* of any musical piece. A particular ordering of notes makes up a melody. As we move to coarser levels of detail, we start to see the musical piece *taking shape*. The ordering of time lets us *position* parts with respect to other parts, notes with respect to other notes. The duration of occurrences generates the levels of granularity: notes have short duration, symphonies have a duration several orders of magnitude larger.

The paradox of the ship of Theseus regards diachronic identity of objects. A version of this argument is the following: assume a famous ship, the ship of Theseus, is located in a harbour. If we replace every plank of it one by one and use the parts to build a ship of the same shape in a museum, then: where is the ship at the end? We can formulate this in a way similar to the above.

- A replacement of one plank does not change a ship.
- If n replacements are irrelevant, $n + 1$ are not relevant, either.
- Therefore by induction, no replacement of planks can be relevant.

The paradox again can be analyzed from the perspective of size-based granularity: no single replacement event regarding a comparatively small part can threaten the diachronic identity or change the position of the ship. Both the spatial extension of the part replaced and the temporal extension of the replacement event are small. A phrase reflecting on spatio-temporal granularity is the proverbial "a journey of a thousand miles begins with one step."

Generalizing, we can transfer these notions to several other domains (Schmidtke 2012; Schmidtke and Beigl 2011): the only requirement is to identify a pre-order relation P, that is, a relation that orders elements we are interested in locally, and a linear extension, that is, a linear order L that extends P, that is, a global relation based on P. In the above, P is a relation that orders some elements locally, such as spatial containment: Paris is in France, and Moskow is in Russia. P is transitive: France is in Europe, so Paris must be in Europe; but not linear, that is globally applicable: we cannot order Paris and Russia, for instance, with respect to P; neither is contained in the other. A linear extension L of P is the relation *smaller than*: it extends P, that is, Paris is smaller than France, but is additionally linear, that is, L represents which one is smaller for any pair, e.g.: Paris is smaller than Russia.

We can apply the same schema, for instance, to temporal ordering in future branching time: at any moment there can be several possible next moments, for instance, as effects of an agent's choices, P is the partial order in a partial order planner, for instance. When analyzing choices of a player in a chess game, we obtain possible configurations as results of choices the player has. Each player will then see what choices the opponent has as a result of each move, and so on. The ordering P in this case is the relation *after* in future branching time. The relation L is the relation *after* with respect to linear, absolute time. The current context in this case is the situation we are thinking about, and granularity delimits how far we look into the future. We then see that there are choices that have more far-reaching consequences, and choices that can be undone easily. We can focus on potential future situations that are reachable from our current position through many paths and explore the future from there. We can also analyze different situations with their possible futures in comparison, determining their position with respect to each other. In a discrete branching time domain, such as chess games, L is very simple. A very interesting case is continuous branching time, which can be combined well with temporal containment. Then, we can represent that an action can consist of sub-actions, each of which, upon completion, triggers the next. It has been shown that reasoning about such combinations of several independent pairs of relations P and L has the same complexity as reasoning about only one pair of relations (Schmidtke 2012).

We can even transfer these notions to domains that are usually not seen as dimensional. Taxonomies, user groups for file access restrictions, social hierarchies, and many other domains can be understood in terms of size-based granularity. The extensional meaning of a class in a taxonomy is a set of objects, the sets higher up near the root of the taxonomic tree contain the sets towards the leaves, e.g.: the set of mammals is a subset of the set of animals. The taxonomic sub-class relation is a pre-order P. The linear extension L can be derived as the cardinality of the sets. User groups having access to many files are closer to the root than groups that have access to fewer files, etc. When we analyze social structures, we can identify human beings, roles of human beings, and human beings in certain roles as the substance of social organizations. We can identify the shape of an organization as pyramidal, and an employee might be concerned about their position with respect to other employees. After restructuring, departments may have a different shape and position within the company.

28.5 Cognitive Complexity of Granularity

In this section we discuss the relation between perceptual and physical granularity, and point at a possible link to conceptual granularity. We start from an analysis of visuo-spatial granularity and audio-temporal granularity, which I suggest to be the evolutionary origin of granularity. We build this theory on the conceptual foundation of the evolution of cognition put forward by Gärdenfors (2005). Gärdenfors (2005) distinguishes three stages in the cognitive evolution of thought. The simplest form of cognition is *transduction*, the direct reaction to perceptual input without internal representation. Examples for this ability are phototaxis or blinking one's eyes as a reaction of something approaching. Cognition then evolved to recognize and react to stored representations of situations or contexts, *cued representations*. In navigation, we use this ability when we retrace a path we went before. The next step in the evolution of cognition was the detachment of representations from concrete situation: *detached representations* are accessible to us independent from perceptual cues or our current context. We use this ability in anticipatory planning.

28.5.1   Visuo-Spatial Granularity

A cognitive system without semantic memory can have visual perception. A simple camera system can follow a moving object based on visual similarity. For this system, a human being in an blue suit moving through a garden, roughly is a blue amorphous spot on a green background. It can be recognized based on perceptual continuity. It is moving, so certain pixels change. The camera can follow these changes. As the person comes closer the changing region will become bigger, but since these changes are step-by-step changes involving adjacent pixels the object can be followed, even if identification is beyond the system's capacity. Our simple algorithm works because human beings have a certain size and move in steps of a certain size. A person who would move faster than the frequency of the camera shots would seemingly disappear. The movement of a person who would be larger than the area covered by the camera would appear as noise, if the human being is smaller than a pixel he/she cannot be followed either. The perceptual granularity of the simple camera application matches the physical granularity of a moving person in a garden.

We can implement the perceptual memory system with very simple means. We only need a processing mechanism for signals that takes a certain time to process the incoming signal, but does not actually process it initially. Delayed synapses (Jakimovski and Schmidtke 2011) are such a mechanism: they implement the identity function in a delayed manner. Given such a delay, we can compare a pixel at time $t - d$ with the pixel at time t, where d is a fixed delay.

This example illustrates two aspects: first, we do not require semantic categories to have a notion of size-based granularity, an observer with visual perception at limited resolution and a physical reality that shows physical granularity are sufficient; second, the observer's perceptual granularity needs to be within a certain range corresponding to a range determined by physical distance and physical granularity in our example. We identified two cases where there is no match: if the object's or movement granularity, that is the pixel change evoked, is too small or when it is too large compared to the perceptual granularity.

The above camera system is static, it cannot move through space. A system that can do this experiences that it can perceive more details of the object in question when moving closer. Perceptually, objects shrink and grow, by its own movements. This experience is caused by the laws of projective geometry. A linear increase in distance leads to a linear decrease of apparent size. An observer of this type can do something to perceive objects that are too large for its visual field or too small for its resolution. It can move away to get a view of the object as a whole, if it is too large, that is if there is just perceptual noise in our example; and it can move closer to get a view of an object that is currently too small to be followed, a blinking pixel in the example. These are physical counterparts to the fundamental steps of contextualizing and decontextualizing in contextual reasoning.

This example still does not need an observer with more memory than to store a couple of images. The only difference to our first observer, was the ability to move through space. More precisely, we can move towards a set of pixels, that is, we can move forward with a turning angle depending on location of the pixels within the image. This ability is assumed to be the cognitively most simple form of navigation (cf. Trullier et al. 1997).

The example illustrates that the fundamental mechanism of changing granularity can be experienced, not yet mentally but physically, by a very simple moving cognitive system without semantic memory. We can assume that visuo-spatial granularity and the ability to change between levels of granularity could be one of the most simple and probably evolutionarily most ancient mental mechanisms. Its foundations are a physical reality in which sizes are roughly stable and perception is subject to the laws of projective geometry.

28.5.2   Audio-Temporal Granularity

The cognitive system sketched above had only visual perception and one-step perceptual memory. If the system also has auditory stereo perception without memory, it can react to sudden sounds and follow continuous sounds, and it will find that the auditory perception matches the visual, with continuous sounds becoming louder as it approaches the sources, and quieter as it moves away.

There are also repetitive sounds, such as footsteps or heart beats, which can be recognized with a memory system that is only slightly more complex and uses adjustable feedback loops, e.g. with sequences of delayed synapses (Jakimovski and Schmidtke 2011) of adjustable length. Using such a system, we can match the past period with the present period, and recognize with the same similarity mechanism as before whether the patterns in the past period match those in the present period. If the moving cognitive system is moving by walking, it may employ such a mechanism for performing periodic movements and may develop the ability for adjusting the frequency of these movements, that is, for shortening or extending the period. This mechanism can be used to adjust the period of the feedback loop. Perceivable patterns of repetitive processes in the physical reality and the leg-based movement mechanism thus give rise to a mechanism for zooming in/out on repetitive processes, so as to detect a match. We can thus bring the temporal granularity of the perceptual system to match a given repetitive signal, and we receive within the bounds of adjustability of the feedback loop a notion of frequency and correspondingly temporal granularity with a perceptuo-motoric mechanism to move closer in on a signal of shorter period or farther away to match a signal of longer period.

Moreover, certain successions of sounds within a repetitive pattern are thus recognized, and the system can observe the relation between its actions and perceived sounds, e.g. of its own footsteps. Irregularities can thus be detected as dissimilarities in the event chain. For instance, we might detect a follower falling back by sounds of steps becoming slower with respect to our own, perceptually they "fall behind" with respect to our own. The steps of a follower moving faster, in contrast, move ahead within the periodic perception aligned to our own step pattern. The steps of the follower become moving pixels on the background of our own periodic step pattern.

It should be noted that this basic mechanism is already very powerful. The principles of temporal granularity embodied by this mechanism underly something as complex and powerful as our calendar system and the prediction of times for farming or making investments, and yet require but a minimum of cognitive capabilities. The main difference separating this simple mechanism and our calendar is scale: a feedback loop cannot store the temporal extension of a year, it is limited to the temporal granularity of seconds and fractions of seconds. However, we already moved beyond the granularity of one-step perceptual memory, and this interval can further be extended as thought is detached from perceptual cues (Gärdenfors 2005) with an advanced memory mechanism that allows for abstraction. Such a system is then also powerful enough to give rise to conceptual granularity.

28.6 Summary and Conclusions

Granularity is one of the core aspects of context. This chapter gave an overview of three perspectives on granularity—size-based granularity, partition-based granularity, granularity in contextual reasoning—and discussed their interrelation. We identified three types of granularity: perceptual granularity refers to the fact that any perceptual system has a certain limited resolution; conceptual granularity indicates that the categories in which we think are tied to levels of granularity; physical granularity, finally, refers to the structures, sizes, and densities that exist in the physical world. We discussed the interplay between the three types of granularity and how perceptual granularity could have been fundamental in the evolution of cognition.

A number of fundamental research questions were outlined. We discussed how granularity and context can be conceived as tightly interwoven mechanisms at the root of cognition. Phenomena of granularity and context abound in language and perception, and recent results suggest that mechanisms of granularity and context can be applied to any structure that can be analyzed as a pre-order. Granularity and context may be assumed to form an evolutionary boundary between cognitive systems without memory and systems with cued representations. Visual recognition of objects or scenes requires abstraction from perceptual size. Thus size and granularity are fundamental to the way we structure our world view. Moreover, size is not only fundamental to perception; we would not be able to abstract from it if it were instable or changing. The fact that things move and change shape rather than change their size makes it an ontologically fundamental notion. The levels of sizes we apply

in our everyday reasoning and any cognitive activity have their foundation in the
levels of sizes that are induced by the fundamental physical forces existing in the
world. Future research should elaborate this tight relationship between the laws of
the physical world and the cognitive systems that were adapted to it by evolution.

References

Benerecetti, M., Bouquet, P., Ghidini, C.: Contextual reasoning distilled. J. Exp. Theor. Artif. Intell.
    12(3), 279–305 (2000)
Bennett, B.: What is a forest? On the vagueness of certain geographic concepts. Topoi **20**(2),
    189–201 (2001)
Bettini, C., Montanari, A.: Temporal representation and reasoning. Data Knowl. Eng. **44**(2), 139–
    141 (2003)
Bettini, C., Jajodia, S., Wang, X.S.: Time Granularities in Databases, Data Mining, and Temporal
    Reasoning. Springer, Secaucus (2000)
Bittner, T.: Vagueness and the trade-off between the classification and delineation of geographic
    regions—an ontological analysis. Int. J. Geogr. Inf. Sci. **25**(5), 825–850 (2011)
Bittner, T., Smith, B.: A theory of granular partitions. In: Duckham, M., Goodchild, M.F., Worboys,
    M.F. (eds.) Foundations of Geographic Information Science, pp. 117–151. Taylor & Francis,
    London (2003)
Bittner, T., Stell, J.G.: Stratified rough sets and vagueness. In: Kuhn, W., Worboys, M., Timpf, S.
    (eds.) Spatial Information Theory: Foundations of Geographic Information Science, pp. 270–
    286. Springer, Berlin (2003)
Brézillon, P.: Context modeling: Task model and practice model. In: Kokinov, B. (ed.) Modeling
    and Using Context, pp. 122–135. Springer, Berlin (2007)
Brézillon, P.: Contextualization of scientific workflows. In: Beigl , M. et al. (eds.) Modeling and
    Using Context, pp. 40–53. Springer, Heidelberg (2011)
Brézillon, P.: Context-based development of experience bases. In: Goebel, R., Tanaka, Y., Wahlster,
    W. (eds.) Modeling and Using Context, pp. 87–100. Springer, Heidelberg (2013)
Bronowski, J.: New concepts in the evolution of complexity: Stratified stability and unbounded
    plans. Synthese **21**, 228–246 (1970)
Dorn, C., Schall, D., Dustdar, S.: Granular context in collaborative mobile environments. In: Meers-
    man, R., Tari, Z., Herrero, P. (eds.) OTM Confederated International Workshops, pp. 1904–1913.
    Springer (2006)
Euzenat, J.: An algebraic approach to granularity in qualitative time and space representation. In:
    Mellish, C. (ed.) Fourteenth International Joint Conference on Artificial Intelligence, pp. 894–
    900. Morgan Kaufmann, San Francisco (1995)
Euzenat, J.: Granularity in relational formalisms—with application to time and space representation.
    Comput. Intell. **17**(3), 703–737 (2001)
Euzenat, J., Montanari, A.: Time granularity. In: Fisher, M., Gabbay, D., Vila, L. (eds.) Handbook
    of Temporal Reasoning in Artificial Intelligence, chap. 3, pp. 59–118. Elsevier, New York (2005)
Freksa, C.: Using orientation information for qualitative spatial reasoning. In: Frank, A.U., Campari,
    I., Formentini, U. (eds.) Spatio-Temporal Reasoning, LNCS, vol. 639, pp. 162–178. Springer,
    Berlin (1992)
Galton, A.: Qualitative Spatial Change. Oxford University Press, Oxford (2000)
Gärdenfors, P.: The detachment of thought. In: Erneling, C., Johnson, D. (eds.) The Mind as a
    Scientific Subject: Between Brain and Culture, pp. 323–341. Oxford University Press, Oxford
    (2005)

Han, J., Schmidtke, H.R., Xie, X., Woo, W.: Adaptive content recommendation for mobile users: Ordering recommendations using a hierarchical context model with granularity. Pervasive Mobile Comput. (2013). doi: http://dx.doi.org/10.1016/j.pmcj.2013.11.002. http://www.sciencedirect.com/science/article/pii/S1574119213001417

Hobbs, J.: Granularity. In: Josh, A.K. (ed.) Ninth International Joint Conference on Artificial Intelligence, pp. 432–435. Morgan Kaufmann, Los Angeles (1985)

Hobbs, J.R.: Half orders of magnitude. In: Papers from the Workshop on Semantic Approximation, Granularity, and Vagueness, pp. 28–38. Citeseer (2000)

Hobbs, J.R., Kreinovich, V.: Optimal choice of granularity in commonsense estimation: Why half-orders of magnitude. In: IFSA World Congress and 20th NAFIPS International Conference, 2001. Joint 9th, IEEE, vol. 3, pp. 1343–1348 (2001)

Jain, A., Duin, R., Mao, J.: Statistical pattern recognition: A review. Pattern Anal. Mach. Intell. **22**(1), 4–37 (2000)

Jakimovski, P., Schmidtke, H.R.: Delayed synapses: An LSM model for studying aspects of temporal context in memory. In: Beigl, M., Christiansen, H., Roth-Berghofer, T.R., Kofod-Petersen, A., Coventry, K.R., Schmidtke, H.R. (eds.) Modeling and Using Context, pp. 138–144. Springer, Berlin (2011)

Kosslyn, S.: Image and Brain: The Resolution of the Imagery Debate. MIT Press, Cambridge (1994)

Montanari, A., Peron, A., Policriti, A.: The way to go: Multi-level temporal logics. In: Gerbrandy, J., Marx, M., de Rijke, M., Venema, Y. (eds.) Liber Amicorum for the Fiftieth Birthday of Johan van Benthem, ILLC, pp. 1–12 (1999)

Mulkar-Mehta, R., Hobbs, J.R., Hovy, E.H.: Applications and discovery of granularity structures in natural language discourse. In: AAAI Spring Symposium: Logical Formalizations of Commonsense Reasoning (2011)

Niu, W., Li, G., Zhao, Z., Tang, H., Shi, Z.: Multi-granularity context model for dynamic web service composition. J. Netw. Comput. Appl. **34**(1), 312–326 (2011)

Ohlbach, H.J., Gabbay, D.M.: Calendar logic. J. Appl. Non-Classical Logics **8**(4), 291–323 (1998)

Palmer, S.E.: Vision Science—Photons to Phenomenology. MIT Press, Cambridge (1999)

Pawlak, Z.:Rough sets. Int. J. Comput. Inf. Sci. **11**, 341–356 (1982)

Rector, A., Rogers, J., Bittner, T.: Granularity, scale and collectivity: When size does and does not matter. J. Biomed. Informatics **39**(3), 333–349 (2006)

Schmidtke, H.R.: A geometry for places: Representing extension and extended objects. In: Kuhn, W., Worboys, M., Timpf, S. (eds.) International Conference on Spatial Information Theory, LNCS, vol. 2825, pp. 235–252. Springer, Berlin (2003)

Schmidtke, H.R.: Aggregations and constituents: Geometric specification of multi-granular objects. J. Vis. Lang. Comput. **16**(4), 289–309 (2005a). doi:10.1016/j.jvlc.2004.11.007

Schmidtke, H.R.: Eine axiomatische Charakterisierung räumlicher Granularität: formale Grundlagen detailgrad-abhängiger Objekt- und Raumrepräsentation. Doctoral dissertation, Universität Hamburg, Fachbereich Informatik (2005b)

Schmidtke, H.R.: Granularity as a parameter of context. In: Dey, A.K., Kokinov, B.N., Leake, D.B., Turner, R.M. (eds.) International Conference on Modeling and Using Context, LNCS, vol. 3554, pp. 450–463. Springer (2005c). doi: 10.1007/11508373_34

Schmidtke, H.R.: Contextual reasoning in context-aware systems. In: Workshop Proceedings of the 8th International Conference on Intelligent Environments, pp. 82–93. IOS Press (2012)

Schmidtke, H.R.: Path and place: the lexical specification of granular compatibility. In: Dimitrova-Vulchanova, M., van der Zee, E. (eds.) Motion Encoding in Language and Space, Explorations in Language and Space. Oxford University Press, Oxford (2013)

Schmidtke, H.R., Beigl, M.: Positions, regions, and clusters: Strata of granularity in location modelling. In: Dillmann, R., Beyerer, J., Hanebeck, U.D., Schultz, T. (eds.) KI 2010, LNAI, vol. 6359, pp. 272–279. Springer (2010). http://dx.doi.org/10.1007/978-3-642-16111-7_31

Schmidtke, H.R., Beigl, M.: Distributed spatial reasoning for wireless sensor networks. In: Beigl, M. et al (eds.) Modeling and Using Context, pp. 264–277. Springer, Berlin (2011)

Suppes, P., Zinnes, J.: Basic measurement theory. In: Luce, R., Bush, R., Galanter, E. (eds.)
    Handbook of Mathematical Psychology, pp. 1–76. Wiley, New York (1963)
Trullier, O., Wiener, S., Berthoz, A., Meyer, J.A.: Biologically based artificial navigation systems:
    Review and prospects. Progress Neurobiol. **51**, 483–544 (1997)
van Deemter, K.: The sorites fallacy and the context-dependence of vague predicates. In: Kanazawa,
    M., Pinon, C., de Swart, H. (eds.) Quantifiers, Deduction, and Context, pp. 59–86. CSLI
    Publications, Stanford (1995)
Wertheimer, M.: Untersuchung zur Lehre von der Gestalt. Psychologische Forschung **4**, 301–350
    (1923)
Zadeh, L.: Fuzzy sets and information granularity. In: Gupta, M., Ragade, R., Yager, R. (eds.)
    Advances in Fuzzy Set Theory and Applications. North-Holland, Amsterdam, pp. 3–18 (1979)

Part VI
Context in Modeling Reasoning

Chapter 29
Context and Case-Based Reasoning

David Leake and Vahid Jalali

Abstract Case-based reasoning (CBR) is fundamentally context-based. CBR's basic principles reflect that reasoning must be done in context, and context is reflected throughout the CBR process. This chapter begins by highlighting how the importance of context is reflected in three key CBR tenets. It then samples two sides of CBR and context. First, it considers the role of context within the CBR process itself, sketching how context drives CBR processing, for internal CBR tasks such as case retrieval, similarity assessment, case delineation and elaboration. Second, it considers applications of CBR for context-aware systems. It then proposes directions for enriching the treatment of context within the CBR process. It closes with a case study of research on one of those directions, increasing the context-sensitivity of case adaptation.

29.1 Introduction

Case-based reasoning (CBR) is the process of reasoning from stored records of specific prior experiences. Given a new problem, a case-based problem-solver retrieves a relevant prior case (or cases), and adapts the prior solution(s) to fit the new situation (e.g., Leake 1996; López de Mántaras et al. 2005). Retrieving and re-using entire solutions from similar prior contexts provides a useful starting point for building context-appropriate solutions, aiding in the choice of solution components which properly reflect context. This chapter discusses some fundamental roles of context in case-based reasoning, highlights how context has been addressed in CBR research, identifies areas of opportunity for increased study, and illustrates with a case study on considering contextual factors when guiding the CBR system's internal reasoning, by increasing the context-sensitivity of the case adaptation process.

D. Leake (✉) · V. Jalali
School of Informatics and Computing, Indiana University,
901 E. 10th Street, Bloomington, IN 47408, USA
e-mail: leake@cs.indiana.edu

V. Jalali
e-mail: vjalalib@cs.indiana.edu

© Springer Science+Business Media New York 2014   473
P. Brézillon, A. J. Gonzalez (eds.), *Context in Computing*,
DOI 10.1007/978-1-4939-1887-4_29

CBR research has often addressed contextual considerations implicitly, without framing them explicitly in terms of context. Consequently, the chapter begins by revisiting the foundations of CBR research to make the context-related tenets and processes of CBR explicit. Early studies of the role of context in CBR focused primarily on the retrieval process. However each step of the case-based reasoning process—retrieval, reuse, revision and retention of cases (López de Mántaras et al. 2005), and each type of knowledge used in CBR—the representational vocabulary, similarity knowledge, case base, and adaptation knowledge (Richter 1995)—can reflect context.

One CBR area in which context has received comparatively little attention is the case adaptation process for fitting prior solutions to new situations. Often, CBR systems adapt cases using general, context-independent rules. However, given a case whose solution must be adapted to a new situation, which adaptation to choose may be strongly context-dependent. For example, in predicting real estate prices, how to estimate the price of one house from another may depend not only on the features of the house itself, but on aspects of the local real estate market. Sometimes the available cases capture that context, and the CBR process exploits that by aiming to retrieve cases from similar contexts. However, sometimes the system must draw on cases from different contexts. In that situation, context-aware case adaptation may be useful for adjusting a previous solution to a new context.

This chapter proposes that case adaptation is a promising frontier for context research and provides evidence to support the potential benefits of case adaptation which reflects meta-level information about the contexts in which previous adaptation rules applied.

To illustrate the benefits of increasing the context-awareness of case adaptation, the chapter presents a case study of context-aware adaptation retrieval by CAAR (Context-Aware Adaptation Retrieval) (Jalali and Leake 2013a). In CAAR, cases are adapted by ensembles of automatically-generated case adaptation rules. The adaptation rules to apply to a particular adaptation problem are chosen based on both the difference to be adapted, and on the similarity of the adaptation context to the context in which each adaptation rule was generated. Experimental results on standard data sets show that CAAR outperforms context-independent baseline methods, and an analysis of results on synthetic data sets (for which domain characteristics can be controlled) shows how the different levels of context-based variations affect CAAR's performance. The chapter closes by discussing some open challenges for context-sensitive case adaptation for a broader range of tasks.

29.2 Cases and CBR

In the case-based reasoning model, reasoning is done by retrieving records of past experiences and adapting the lessons from those experiences to fit new situations. Case-based reasoning has been explored for both problem solving and interpretive tasks. Case-based reasoning has a rich tradition of reasoning based on complex structured cases, as for case-based planning (e.g., Hammond 1989), design (e.g., Pu and Maher 1997), and explanation (e.g., Leake 1992a). For example, for planning, a case might be represented as a trace of a plan, with justifications; for explanation, as a network of beliefs and belief-support links. CBR systems may also manipulate cases in other forms, such as text (Weber et al. 2005) or simple numeric values for case-based regression tasks.

Regardless of task and task representation, the central tenet of CBR is that reasoning is done by retrieving and adapting past cases. Rather than generating solutions from scratch, as a planner might do by applying basic operators, CBR systems generate solutions from experience, fitting old cases to new needs by case adaptation. For structured cases, the case adaptation process may involve replacing, adding, or deleting components of a prior solution structure. Choices of how to adapt cases are often based on domain knowledge encoded in adaptation rules. For example, in the recipe generation domain, the case adaptation process for substituting broccoli for green beans in a recipe might include the structural chance of adding steps for chopping the broccoli and for adjusting cooking time (Hammond 1989). In regression domains, adaptation rules adjust previous case values based on differences in problem descriptions. For example, in the real estate appraisal domain, the problem description could include factors such as location and size. A simple adaptation rule might adjust the sale price of a prior house based on the size difference. For example, for a house x % larger than a prior house, the prior price could be increased by x %.

29.3   Tenets About Context and CBR

Context can be characterized in many ways. For example, Dey frames context as "any information that can be used to characterize the situation of an entity" (Dey 2001); Brézillon describes context as "what constrains a problem solving without intervening in it explicitly," and proposes that sometimes, "contextual reasoning is local reasoning" (Brézillon 1999). In the CBR approach to context, locality plays an important role; cases in the neighborhood of a new problem, as determined by a similarity metric, are considered especially relevant for reasoning about that problem, and often the closest case is considered most relevant.

The development of CBR was strongly influenced by Schank's research on human story understanding, which developed the theory of knowledge structures such as scripts (Schank and Abelson 1977) and MOPs (Schank 1982). According to script theory, standard stereotyped situations, such as eating in a restaurant or doing laundry at a laundromat, are associated with standard schemas, encapsulating the knowledge associated with that context and guiding the generation of appropriate inferences. Psychological studies support the role of such structures in human understanding (Bower et al. 1979).

Like scripts, cases collect information about a situation, and store that information as a whole, resulting in each part being captured with its context. However, rather than capturing generalized knowledge, cases capture the knowledge that applied in the specific context of a single episode. CBR models reasoning from single examples. This reasoning can be done even when the causal factors involved are not explicitly known. Rather than relying on rules to explicitly delineate the relevant factors of a situation, case-based reasoning relies on the principle that "similar problems have similar solutions"—that given a new problem, a solution generated for a similar problem situation is likely to be a good starting point for future reasoning.

The case-based reasoning approach reflects three tenets about context and CBR:

- *The context of past problem-solving is crucial in determining solution relevance:* Real-world reasoning often involves weak theory domains or must be based on imperfect knowledge. A premise of CBR is that successful solutions from similar contexts will implicitly capture relevant causal connections, even if those connections are not explicitly captured in domain knowledge.
- *Reuse of components of old solutions must be done within the context provided by the rest of the case:* In case-based reasoning, the fundamental unit of knowledge is holistic: it is the entire case. Thus each step in a prior solution is captured in the context of the entire solution, and the case only predicts the applicability of the steps as part of the whole.
- *To avoid risking losing context-specific information, cases should not routinely be generalized, and any generalization of cases should only be done in the context of a new problem situation:* Case-based reasoning does *lazy learning*. When a problem is solved, the resulting new case is stored without any generalization. Generalization/adaptation to fit possible new problems is only done when the new problem is known. This enables the use of that contextual information to guide choices about what parts must be generalized/adapted and how much revision must be done. This contrasts to learning methods such as explanation-based learning, which immediately attempt to generalize from new examples, as with machine learning methods which discard examples and only retain generalizations (e.g., decision tree or neural network learning).

The following section illustrates some of the ways in which CBR research has addressed contextual issues as they apply to the CBR process.

29.4   Context-Sensitivity in the CBR Process

Context-Based Retrieval Much early CBR vision grew from studies of human retrieval from memory, and specifically of the phenomenon of human "reminding," in which information about a new episode prompts spontaneous retrieval of information about another episode (Schank 1982). Those studies showed that the reminding prompted by a new event (and whether that event prompts a reminding at all) is not simply a property of the event, but depends on the "understanding context"—the context provided by the state of the understander's internal processing—in which that event was encountered. Remindings are often prompted by anomalies or expectation failures, in which aspects of a new event conflict with normal patterns or with the expectations which were active when the event was encountered.

To illustrate, one example from research on case-based explanation (e.g., Leake 1992a; Schank and Leake 1989) modeled how information about a death would prompt different remindings of prior explanations in an understanding context involving bad health, good health, or old age. If a death was anomalous because of the victim's good physical conditions, the reminding might be that of an athlete who died in peak condition, from a hidden heart defect; if it was anomalous because of how long the victim had lived, it might involve someone who prolonged her life by healthy habits (e.g., eating a daily dose of yogurt). Case-based models of reminding developed *indexing vocabularies* designed to represent summaries of anomalies—how new events conflicted with the understanding context (Leake 1991). The vocabulary was used to index cases in memory. When new anomalies were detected, they were described in the same vocabulary used to index cases in memory, and cases with similar anomaly descriptions were retrieved.

In some cases, the CBR system must elaborate the relevant contextual information to generate indices for retrieval, by a process of *situation assessment* or by a "conversational CBR" process, in which a system-user dialog driven by the information contained in prior cases solicits the information needed to discriminate between candidate cases to retrieve (Aha et al. 2001).

Explicitly considering the context of a new problem situation can reduce the space of cases to consider, helping to focus the system's processing. For example, Marir and Watson (Marir and Watson 1995) demonstrated the value of using local and global context features for classifying cases and focusing on cases within the right context, for building cost estimation. Context can also be used to filter an initial set of cases retrieved by a CBR system, as illustrated for legal case-based reasoning by Hafner and Berman (2002). They analyze aspects of legal context, such as connections between legal precedents and social values or policies they serve, and propose incorporating this context into legal CBR, using a procedural context model to improve similarity ranking of cases and a two-step retrieval process which first retrieves candidate cases without considering context and then filters them based on context.

Context-Aware Similarity Assessment Criteria Context has also been extensively explored in CBR research on similarity assessment. Similarity assessment compares old and new cases to identify similarities and differences, both to estimate relevance (to help in case selection if multiple cases have been retrieved) and to identify needs for adaptation. Similarity assessment procedures often base similarity judgments on a weighted combination of calculated similarities of individual features of a case. However, it has long been known that the right weighting may vary with context (Tversky 1977). Consequently, similarity assessment criteria may be dynamically adjusted to reflect contextual factors, and the contextual constraints themselves may be relaxed to control accuracy and scalability (e.g., Jurisica and Glasgow 1997). Likewise, the context established by the new problem situation may be used to guide elaboration of an old case when doing similarity assessment (Leake 1992b).

Context-Based Case Delineation and Elaboration When humans are reminded, they are reminded of rich episodes, which have unclear boundaries: memories are connected to other events and episodes and reconstructed on demand, from distributed constituent parts (Schank 1982). Consequently, after humans have been reminded, the context can determine what is considered part of the case and the lessons it provides. The experience of buying a house could include many related components, offering different lessons. Early CBR work observed that prior cases could be used to define which aspects of a new situation to elaborate (Leake 1992b), but how to model the use of such cases is a promising and comparatively open area.

29.5   Applications of CBR for Context-Awareness

Beyond investigating fundamental context-related questions for the CBR process, the CBR community has developed numerous applications exploiting the characteristics of case-based reasoning for context-aware systems. We briefly highlight a few examples here. Context-based retrieval has been of special interest in CBR research on ambient intelligence. Zimmermann (2003) illustrates CBR for context-sensitive recommendation (e.g. to provide recommendations when a visitor walks through an exhibition hall wearing wireless headphones) by capturing context in terms of user identity, location, time and environment/activity, and retrieving cases sharing contextual similarities with the current situation. Kofod and Aamodt (2006) study how knowledge intensive CBR can be used to achieve situation awareness for ambient intelligence, by reasoning about personal context, task context, social context, spatio-temporal context, and environmental context; the methods have been applied to tasks areas such as supporting health workers in the patient diagnosis and treatment processes and providing focused guidance for travelers (Mikalsen and Kofod-Petersen 2005). A context layer in their systems collects and maintains data from the environment in a structured format that are primarily used during the retrieval phase.

Another rich application area for context in CBR is medical-based reasoning systems. Montani (2011) surveys this work, pointing to the benefits of using contextual information to reduce the search space in retrieval, to provide the rich knowledge needed to re-interpret prior cases to keep knowledge up-to-date, and for tailoring cases to local constraints. The importance of endowing case-based recommender systems with contextual inputs has also been recognized, including in systems which rely on virtual sensors to make recommendations based entirely on information sensed from the user context (e.g., using information about the music to which a user is currently listening to make concert ticket recommendations) (Coyle et al. 2006).

29.6   Enriching CBR's Treatment of Context

We see two areas as particularly promising for advancing the ability of CBR to exploit context. The first is bringing CBR systems more in line with the original CBR vision of capturing and handling truly rich cases, which will enable a wider range of context-sensitive case processing. In this section, we briefly sketch the challenges this involves. The second is to increase the context-awareness of the case adaptation process, which we explore in the following sections.

CBR applications often assume that cases are clearly delineated to include precisely the relevant information, pre-identified by a knowledge engineer. The more that cases are pre-distilled, the less they enable profiting from lazy context-based processing to focus on different aspects in different situations. Richer cases may provide the depth needed to be able to use cases differently based on context, and as well as increasing the chance of capturing valuable implicit knowledge.

One area of CBR research addressing aspects of rich case issues is trace-based reasoning (e.g., Floyd et al. 2012), which includes work addressing the problem of dynamically elaborating/discovering what to consider within a new situation (Traoré et al. 2013). This work aims to extract information into a fixed case, and an interesting question is how to go further, to model a process in which what is used as a case is extracted/elaborated dynamically from memory as needed, in light of the current problem (Leake 2011), which would enable the scope of a case to be determined by the context. This raises the question of how the distinction between "problems" and "solutions," can be relaxed, for example, enabling the CBR system to be able to index cases flexibly by substructures and use any part of an episode as the retrieval index or solutions (Kendall-Morwick and Leake 2011).

29.7   Context-Sensitive Case Adaptation

The case adaptation process for CBR often relies on global context-independent rules. However, different types of cases may require different types of adaptations, even for differences described the same way. For example, Mille observes that when using CBR to predict the price of apartments, different adaptations may be needed for adapting the price of an old apartment for a given difference, than for adapting the price of a new one (Mille 2006).

A key question is how to integrate such context-awareness into the case adaptation process. Little work has been done on this area. However, the practicality of context-aware adaptation depends not only on ways to characterize contextual relevance—to retrieve the most context-appropriate cases possible—but on endowing the CBR system with a sufficient range of adaptation rules to make context-appropriate adaptations for case differences. Providing the adaptation rules is a special difficulty because knowledge acquisition for case adaptation rules is a classic problem for case-based reasoning.

The remainder of this chapter presents an approach which addresses both the context-based adaptation rule selection problem and generation of adaptation rules in a tightly coupled way: It combines automatic rule generation from prior cases with a rule selection process based on the context of those cases from which each rule was generated. The research uses automatic adaptation rule generation, based on comparisons of prior pairs of cases, to build a large collection of adaptation rules from different contexts. It uses a new method for characterizing the context of an adaptation to select rules generated from adaptations in similar contexts. Thus rather than selecting adaptation rules based only on the differences to adapt, our method considers how the context of the current adaptation problem compares to that of the problem from which the rule was generated.

Our study is done for a numerical prediction task domain, in which the problems to address are represented by a vector of feature values, and solutions are a single numerical value. The goal is to estimate the numeric value associated with the set of input parameters. When case-based reasoning is applied to the regression task, the set of inputs is considered the "problem" to solve, and the "solution"—the output value—is estimated by retrieving similar past problems and combining their solutions, possibly "adapted" according to the differences between the problems they solved and the new problem.

Case-based regression computes the solution value of a new problem based on the values of k "nearest neighbor" cases (for some predefined integer k) retrieved from the case base. Given an input problem description (generally in the form of a vector of feature values), the nearest neighbor cases are those whose problem descriptions are most similar to the input problem, according to a predefined similarity metric. To calculate the solution value, the values of the nearest neighbor cases may be adapted, based on the differences between the problems they addressed and the new problem. The values are then combined by a combination function (e.g., into a weighted average in which the contributions of each case are weighted by the similarity of their problem to the input problem).

Studying context-sensitive adaptation for the regression task enables testing the approach on standard machine learning data sets and facilitates testing on synthetically-generated data sets to explore how variations in problem space characteristics affect the algorithms' performance. The studies demonstrate the importance of considering context during case adaptation for this task. As we describe later, the usefulness of contextual considerations for this task raises the interesting question of how the principle of context-aware adaptation could be applied for the broad class of CBR tasks involving knowledge-rich structured cases. The remainder of this section and Sects. 29.8 and 29.9 are excerpted and adapted from Jalali and Leake (2013a).

Related Work on Generating Adaptation Rules by the Case Difference Heuristic Given the potential difficulty and cost of generating case adaptation rules by hand, it is desirable to generate them automatically. A highly influential approach to automatically generating case adaptation rules for case-based regression is the *case difference heuristic* method, introduced by Hanney and Keane (1997). This approach generates adaptation rules from prior cases, by comparing pairs of cases in the case base (we call these the "composing cases" of the rule). For each pair, the approach compares the problem specifications of the two cases, generating a description of their differences which we refer to as "case difference vector". Often, this vector simply records the numerical differences between the case features. This vector is used as the applicability condition for the new rule; the new rule will be applied when a new input problem and a retrieved case have similar differences in each of their features.

For each pair, the approach also compares the solutions, generating a description of their solution differences. The observed difference becomes the adaptation part of the new rule; the rule adjusts the value of the prior case by this difference when the rule applies. For example, for real estate price prediction, if two apartments' descriptions differ only in that one is 150 ft^2 larger than the other, and the larger apartment's rent is $30 more per month, this suggests the rule that a 150 ft^2 size increase should increase the rent by $30.

We note that this example rule is highly simplified and that alternative rules might apply, e.g., depending on percent changes or corresponding to a more complicated function. How to address these issues is beyond the scope of this paper but is addressed elsewhere in the literature (e.g., Hanney 1997), and the context-based method described here could apply to any rule generation method.

Related Work on Characterizing Context for the Case Adaptation CBR adaptation rules have generally reflected only a few major factors, rather than the rich context in which those differences can occur. For example, in the real estate domain, an adaptation rule might adjust the price of a lot based on size, regardless of other factors. Adaptation rules may also be completely domain-independent, focusing on abstract goal configurations (Hammond 1989). However, in some domains adaptations may vary substantially with contextual details. For example, in the real estate domain, the effect of a change in the size of a lot on price may vary strongly based on whether the property being sold is in a city or a rural area.

When predicting a property price, if cases encode the relevant contextual information, and a similar case is available, the CBR process will automatically take the context into account, by selecting a context-appropriate case. However, if no case from a similar context is available, a case from a different context may need to be adapted to fit. In that situation, having adaptation rules which reflect context could enable bringing in relevant contextual information at the time of case adaptation.

There has been comparatively little attention to the role of context in selection of case adaptations. Some previous research on case-based reasoning for regression has attempted to consider context in case adaptation. McDonnell and Cunningham (2006) define the context of a point in problem space by approximating the rate of change (i.e., the gradient) of the regression system's target value function at that point. We note that their approach only considers the context for the input problem and for the corresponding case used to generate the adaptation rule.

Our own previous work (Jalali and Leake 2013b) introduced EAR (Ensembles of Adaptations for Regression), in which the context of adaptation problems is characterized in terms of covariance vectors for the case to adapt and the corresponding case used to generate an adaptation rule. Our new approach considers both the local situation of the problem to be adapted and the local situation of the cases from which the rules were generated, according to the changes that the gradient predicts in the case solutions, based on their feature differences.

29.8 CAAR

We hypothesize that performance of case adaptation can be improved by refining the treatment of adaptation context in two ways:

1. *Maximizing locality of data used in rule generation:* By restricting the cases used to generate adaptation rules to nearby cases, this aims to draw both cases from the same context, so that the relationship between the cases will give rise to meaningful rules.
2. *Enriching the context description:* By using context information to characterize both the similarity of the input problem and case to adapt, and the similarity of the case pair to the case pair used to generate the adaptation rule, this aims to select more relevant cases to adapt and rules to apply.

CAAR's algorithm respects the first condition by

1. First fixing the cases to adapt, choosing them to be the top nearest neighbors of the input problem, and then
2. Generating the adaptation rules to apply to the cases to adapt on demand, by comparing each case to adapt with its top nearest neighbors, and favoring rules addressing similar contexts.

The following describes how CAAR's contexts are described and compared.

CAAR's Adaptation Rule Selection CAAR selects adaptations to apply by ranking the candidate adaptations based on the similarity of the current adaptation context to the adaptation context in which the rule was generated, as follows. Let Q represent the input problem and C_b a source case whose solution must be adapted to provide a solution to Q. Let C_i and C_j be the composing cases from which two adaptation rules $R_{i,j}$ and $R_{j,i}$ were generated; $R_{i,j}$ is the rule corresponding to adapting C_i to C_j, and $R_{j,i}$ corresponding to adapting C_j to C_i.

CAAR ranks candidate adaptations based on the similarity of two contexts. The first is the relationship between the input problem and the composing case of the adaptation rule corresponding to the input problem. The second is the relationship between the case to adapt and the composing case of the adaptation corresponding to the case to adapt.

Rule ranking is based on $score : cases^3 \times problems \rightarrow R^+$, calculated by:

$$score((C_i, C_j, C_b, Q)) = contextSim((C_i, C_j, C_b, Q)) + contextSim((C_j, C_i, Q, C_b))$$
$$(29.1)$$

As input, *score* takes the two cases used to generate the adaptation rule being assessed, the case to be adapted, and the input problem. Suppose $R_{i,j}$ is the adaptation rule generated from *score*'s first two arguments, C_i and C_j, to adapt case C_b in order to provide a value for Q. *Score* calls the function *contextSim* twice, once in order to assess the appropriateness of $R_{i,j}$ for adapting C_b to Q (based on the similarity of the context in which the rule was generated to the adaptation context defined by the relationship between C_b and Q), and once to assess context-based appropriateness of the reverse rule $(R_{j,i})$, applied to adapt Q to C_b. By considering both directions, the computation takes into account both the context at the query (via the first term) and at the case to be adapted (via the second term). The final score is the sum of both terms.

The function *contextSim* is defined as follows. Like *score*, *contextSim* takes four arguments, the two cases used to generate the adaptation rule $R_{i,j}$, a case to adapt, and a query. Let $\nabla(C)$ represent the gradient vector around the case C, $Diff((C_i, C_j))$ represent the feature differences of the ordered pair of cases C_i and C_j, $\cdot$ be the dot product, and K be a function for tuning the range of results. The *contextSim* function is calculated as:

$$contextSim((C_i, C_j, C_k, C_l)) = K(\mid Diff(C_i, C_j) \qquad (29.2)$$

$$\cdot \nabla(C_i) - Diff(C_k, C_l) \cdot \nabla(C_k) \mid) \qquad (29.3)$$

For example, if it is desired for the ranking score of Eq. 29.1 to generate a higher score given one very high and one very low underlying similarity than given two medium level underlying similarities, K could be set to an exponential function, to scale the raw values such that extremal values have more weight.

Applying the Selected Adaptation Rules   Let Q represent the input problem and R_i represent the ith adaptation rule in the ranked list generated using Eq. 29.1. Then CAAR's case adaptation adjusts the value of the case to adapt, C_b, by the average of the solution changes proposed by the top r adaptations, as follows:

$$adjustedVal(C_b, Q) = \sum_{i=1,r} \frac{1}{r} \times proposedAdjustment(R_i) \qquad (29.4)$$

For k the number of selected cases to adapt to generate the solution, we use the algorithm we introduced in (Jalali and Leake 2013b) to estimate the final solution, as follows:

$$finalEstimate(C_b, Q) = \sum_{i=1,k} \frac{1}{k} \times adjustedVal(C_{b,i}, Q) \qquad (29.5)$$

Algorithm 29.1 summarizes the entire process.

29.9   Evaluation

Our evaluation addressed four questions:

1. How does the accuracy of CAAR compare to that of the baseline methods locally weighted linear regression, k-NN, and EAR?
2. How does CAAR's consideration of both (1) context at the input case and (2) context at the case to adapt, affect its performance compared to considering context only at one or the other?

3. How is the accuracy of the candidate methods affected by increasing the density of case base coverage of the problem space? (Density will normally be correlated to case base size.)

Algorithm 29.1 Case-based regression with context-aware adaptation retrieval's basic algorithm. (Source: Jalali and Leake 2013b)

Input:
Q: input problem
k: number of base cases to adapt to solve query
r: number of rules to be applied per base case
CB: case base
R: set of existing adaptations
Output: Estimated solution value for Q

    CasesToAdapt ← NeighborhoodSelection(Q,k,CB)
    for c in *CasesToAdapt* **do**
        RankedRules ← RankRules(R,c,Q)
        $ValEstimate(c)$ ← CombineAdaptations(*RankedRules*, c, r)
    end for
    return CombineVals($\cup_{c \in CasesToAdapt} ValEstimate(c)$)

---

4. How do changes in domain regularity (i.e., the lack of value fluctuations associated with different contexts) affect the accuracies of the candidate methods?

We expect that either increasing case base size or increased regularity will improve performance of all methods, because increased case base size increases the likelihood of finding cases to adapt from regions with similar characteristics. On the other hand, we expect increasing the rate of fluctuations in the context to make it harder for all methods to generate accurate estimations. However, we expect this to affect locally weighted learning more drastically than CAAR, especially for sparser case bases: We predict that when there is a shift in the changes of the target function (e.g. descending and then ascending), taking the average of the training data will be more accurate than fitting a locally learned linear model. Therefore, we expect to see an increase in the accuracy of CAAR compared to that of locally weighted linear regression for higher frequencies.

29.9.1 Data Sets and Experimental Design

We tested CAAR's method on both synthetic and real world data sets. Synthetic data sets were used to enable precise control over the data characteristics for addressing questions 3 and 4. Standard data sets were Automobile (A), Auto MPG (AM), Housing (H), Computer Hardware (HW) from UCI Machine Learning Repository

(Bache and Lichman, 2013) and Stock (S) and CPU from Luís Torgo's Regression data sets (Torgo 2013). For Automobile, the task was to estimate price, for Auto MPG, to estimate miles per gallon, for housing, to estimate median value of homes, in thousands of dollars, for computer hardware, to estimate relative performance, for stock, to estimate price, and for CPU, to estimate the portion of time that a CPU runs in user mode.

Synthetic data sets were generated artificially by a sinusoidal model, which was chosen because its behavior in different regions corresponds to different contexts (given our treatment of context in terms of gradient and the changes in the gradient of the sine function over the X axis), and because—due to its repetitive pattern of context changes—rules generated from different parts of the domain space can still have similar contexts.

The experiments estimate the target value for an input query. Mean Absolute Error is used for assessing accuracy. Leave-one-out testing and ten fold cross validation are used for conducting the experiments on the synthetic and real world data sets respectively. Methods compared are k-NN, locally weighted linear regression (LWLR), EAR and CAAR. The k-NN procedure and locally weighted linear regression were implemented using WEKA's (Hall et al. 2009) classes IBk and locally weighted learning (using the linear regression class as the base learner). EAR is the method "EAR4" introduced by Jalali and Leake (Jalali and Leake 2013b). All models are compared with optimal parameter settings for the models, as determined by hill climbing. For reasons of space we do not provide further details about the data sets, parameter tuning and other experimental design details, but this is available elsewhere (Jalali and Leake 2013a).

29.9.2 Experimental Results

Standard Data Sets Experiments on standard data sets were used to address evaluation question 1, how the accuracy of CAAR compares to that of the baseline methods locally weighted linear regression, k-NN, and EAR, and question 2, how the consideration of context of both input query and case to adapt affects performance, versus only considering context at one or the other, as in previous work. Table 29.1 lists the mean absolute error for the six methods and six data sets, for which the data were normalized as described previously. CAAR1 and CAAR2 are ablated versions of CAAR, respectively considering only the context of the input problem or only the context of the case to adapt.

CAAR has the highest accuracy in all data sets, and outperforms its ablated versions, demonstrating the value of CAAR's more extensive consideration of context. k-NN has the lowest accuracy in four of the six domains. For four of the six data sets EAR outperforms locally weighted linear regression.

Figure 29.1 shows the percent of improvement in MAE for CAAR, EAR and LWLR over k-NN. Improvement of CAAR over k-NN ranges from 9 to 30 %. Using a one side paired t-test with 95 % confidence interval, and null hypothesis that the

Table 29.1 MAE of EAR, k-NN, LWLR and LR for the sample domains

Method	Domains					
	Auto (A)	MPG (AM)	Housing (H)	Hardware (HW)	Stock (S)	CPU
k-NN	1.6	2.1	2.72	31.5	0.47	2.1
LWLR	1.64	1.87	2.22	26.4	0.51	1.9
EAR	1.43	1.93	2.14	25.64	*0.43*	1.93
CAAR1	1.44	1.78	2.01	26.4	0.53	1.98
CAAR2	1.58	1.82	1.98	28.2	0.54	2
CAAR	*1.35*	*1.77*	*1.91*	*25.24*	*0.43*	*1.87*

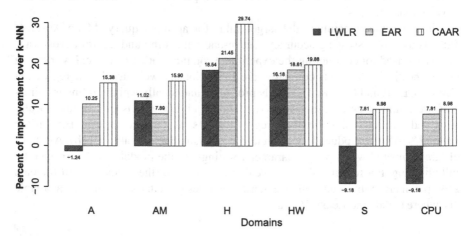

Fig. 29.1 Percent improvement in MAE of CAAR, EAR and LWLR over k-NN for the real world data sets

MAE of LWLR is less than that of CAAR, in the Auto domain $p < 0.001$, in the MPG domain $p < 0.038$, in the Housing domain $p < 0.001$, in the Hardware domain $p < 0.3$ (not significant), in the Stock domain $p < 0.001$ and in the CPU domain $p < 0.001$.

Synthetic Data Sets Tests on synthetic data sets were used to explore Question 3, how the accuracy of the candidate methods is affected by increasing the density of case base coverage of the problem space, and Question 4, how changes in domain regularity (i.e., the level of fluctuations across different contexts) affect the accuracies of the candidate methods. Figure 29.2 shows the MAE of CAAR's estimates for the synthetic domains as a function of the frequency of domain changes and case base size. To show the whole spectrum of MAEs, a logarithmic scale is used. Figure 29.2 shows that increasing case density decreases MAE, and increasing frequency increases MAE. The explanation is that increased case base coverage increases the likelihood of CAAR being able to select prior cases within a similar context, and that higher frequencies decrease the size of regions with similar context, increasing likelihood of generating new adaptation rules from cases in different contexts.

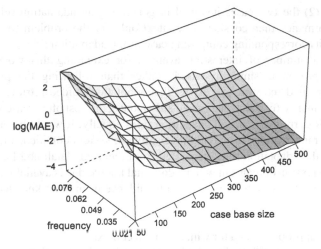

Fig. 29.2 MAE of CAAR on the synthetic data sets

We also tested the effect of increasing density when frequency is fixed and vice versa. Increasing case-base size increased accuracy of all methods compared to k-NN, with CAAR's performance always best, followed by LWLR and EAR. Results also showed that increasing frequency (for a fixed case base size) decreases the relative advantage of EAR, LWLR and CAAR over k-NN, but the loss for CAAR is less than for the other two methods. Full details are available elsewhere (Jalali and Leake 2013a).

29.10   Conclusion and Future Research

In case-based problem solving, cases record not only the prior solution, but also the context in which it was applied—the context of past problem-solving. When new problems arise, CBR attempts to retrieve cases from similar contexts. Thus addressing contextual issues is fundamental to CBR. This chapter highlights major aspects of the role of context in case-based reasoning, how context has been reflected in CBR research, and new opportunities for context-sensitive delineation of rich cases and reflecting and exploiting context in the case adaptation phase of CBR, as illustrated by CAAR.

CAAR's case adaptation selects ensembles of context-appropriate case adaptation rules from a collection of case adaptation rules generated automatically in different contexts. When ranking candidate adaptation rules, the approach considers two types of context, the local neighborhood context of the input problem, and the context in which candidate case adaptation rules were generated. Our experimental evaluation compared CAAR to three baseline methods and two ablations, in 200 synthetic and six standard domains, and showed that CAAR generally improves performance. It also showed that considering the context of both (1) the problem and the case to adapt, and (2) the two cases involved in generating an adaptation rule, provides better performance than considering context only for the problem (or the case to adapt) and its corresponding composing case of the adaptation rule.

We see a number of interesting avenues for extending this work. CAAR's retrieval approach is similarity-based, rather than following the principles of adaptation-guided retrieval; we expect that adaptation-guided retrieval would improve performance (cf. Jalali and Leake 2014), but at the cost of increased processing time. CAAR currently treats all adaptation rules equally; it would be interesting to explore the ramifications of making it sensitive to system confidence in stored solutions and the adaptation rules generated from them (cf. Jalali and Leake 2013c). Also, for regression domains in which additional knowledge is available, integrating CAAR's "knowledge-light" approach with guidance from other knowledge sources could be worthwhile.

CBR is often applied to complex structured cases, for which knowledge-rich methods are appropriate, and for which domain context plays an important role (e.g., Öztürk and Aamodt 1998). Developing context-based adaptation methods which consider both domain context and adaptation context for rich structured domains is an important challenge. For domains in which an explicit model of context can be generated, reasoning from that model might be used to identify contextual factors and generate context-based applicability conditions for adaptation rules. For domains in which it is harder to precisely codify context, an interesting possibility is to build on work on case-based reasoning for adaptation (e.g., Leake et al. 1997; Leake and Powell 2007; Minor et al. 2014), bringing context-sensitive CBR to bear on the case adaptation task.

References

Aha, D., Breslow, L., Munoz-Avila, H.: Conversational case-based reasoning. Appl. Intell. **14**, 9–32 (2001)

Bache, K., Lichman, M.: Machine Learning Repository. University of California, School of Information and Computer Sciences, Irvine. http://archive.ics.uci.edu/ml (2013)

Bower, G., Black, J., Turner, T.: Scripts in memory for text. Cognit. Psychol. **11**, 177–220 (1979)

Brézillon, P.: Context in problem solving: a survey. Knowl. Eng. Rev. **14**(1), 1–34 (1999)

Coyle, L., Balfe, E., Stevenson, G., Neely, S., Dobson, S., Nixon, P., Smyth, B.: Supplementing case-based recommenders with context data. In: Proceedings of the 1st International Workshop on Case-Based Reasoning and Context Awareness at ECCBR 2006 (2006).

Dey, A.K.: Understanding and using context. Pers. Ubiquit. Comput. **5**(1), 4–7 (2001)

Floyd, M., Fuchs, B., Leake, D., Ontanon, S., Rubin, J. (eds.): Proceedings of the ICCBR-2012 Workshop TRUE: Traces for Reusing Users' Experience (2012)

Hafner, C., Berman, D.: The role of context in case-based legal reasoning: teleological, temporal, and procedural. Artif. Intell. Law **10**(1–3), 19–64 (2002)

Hall, M., Frank, E., Holmes, G., Pfahringer, B., Reutemann, P., Witten, I.H.: The WEKA data mining software: an update. SIGKDD Explor. Newsl. **11**(1), 10–18 (2009)

Hammond, K.: Case-Based Planning: Viewing Planning as a Memory Task. Academic, San Diego (1989)

Hanney, K.: Learning adaptation rules from cases. Master's thesis, Trinity College, Dublin (1997)

Hanney, K., Keane, M.: The adaptation knowledge bottleneck: how to ease it by learning from cases. In: Proceedings of the Second International Conference on Case-Based Reasoning. Springer, Berlin (1997)

Jalali, V., Leake, D.: A context-aware approach to selecting adaptations for case-based reasoning. In: Brézillon, P., Blackburn, P., Dapoigny, R. (eds.) Modeling and Using Context, pp. 101–114. Springer, Berlin (2013a)

Jalali, V., Leake, D.: Extending case adaptation with automatically-generated ensembles of adaptation rules. In: Delany, S.J., Ontañón, S. (eds.) Case-Based Reasoning Research and Development, ICCBR 2013, pp. 188–202. Springer, Berlin (2013b)

Jalali, V., Leake, D.: On deriving adaptation rule confidence from the rule generation process. In: Delany, S.J., Ontañón, S. (eds.) Case-Based Reasoning Research and Development, ICCBR 2013, pp. 179–187. Springer, Berlin (2013c)

Jalali, V., Leake, D.: An ensemble approach to adaptation-guided retrieval. In: Proceedings of the 2014 Florida AI Research Symposium, AAAI Press, pp. 295–300 (2014)

Jurisica, I., Glasgow, J.: Improving performance of case-based classification using context-based relevance. Int. J. Artif. Intell. Tools 6, 511–536 (1997)

Kendall-Morwick, J., Leake, D.: A toolkit for representation and retrieval of structured cases. In: Proceedings of the ICCBR-11 Workshop on Process-Oriented Case-Based Reasoning (2011)

Kofod-Petersen, A., Aamodt, A.: Contextualised ambient intelligence through case-based reasoning. In: Proceedings of the 8th European Conference on Advances in Case-Based Reasoning, ECCBR'06, pp. 211–225. Springer, Berlin (2006)

Leake, D.: An indexing vocabulary for case-based explanation. In: Proceedings of the Ninth National Conference on Artificial Intelligence, Menlo Park, CA, pp. 10–15. AAAI Press, July 1991

Leake, D.: Evaluating Explanations: A Content Theory. Lawrence Erlbaum, Hillsdale (1992a)

Leake, D.: Constructive similarity assessment: using stored cases to define new situations. In: Proceedings of the Fourteenth Annual Conference of the Cognitive Science Society, pp. 313–318. Lawrence Erlbaum, Hillsdale (1992b)

Leake, D.: CBR in context: the present and future. In: Leake, D. (ed.) Case-Based Reasoning: Experiences, Lessons, and Future Directions, pp. 3–30. AAAI Press, Menlo Park. http://www.cs.indiana.edu/~leake/papers/a-96-01.html (1996)

Leake, D.: Assembling latent cases from the web: A challenge problem for cognitive CBR. In: Proceedings of the ICCBR-11 Workshop on Human-Centered and Cognitive Approaches to CBR, Greenwich, UK (2011)

Leake, D., Powell, J.: Mining large-scale knowledge sources for case adaptation knowledge. In: Weber, R., Richter, M. (eds.) Proceedings of the Seventh International Conference on Case-Based Reasoning, pp. 209–223. Springer, Berlin (2007)

Leake, D., Kinley, A., Wilson, D.: Learning to integrate multiple knowledge sources for case-based reasoning. In: Proceedings of the Fourteenth International Joint Conference on Artificial Intelligence, pp. 246–251. Morgan Kaufmann, San Mateo (1997)

López de Mántaras, R., McSherry, D., Bridge, D., Leake, D., Smyth, B., Craw, S., Faltings, B., Maher, M., Cox, M., Forbus, K., Keane, M., Aamodt, A., Watson, I.: Retrieval, reuse, revision, and retention in CBR. Knowl. Eng. Rev. 20(3), 215–240 (2005)

Marir, F., Watson, I.: Representing and indexing building refurbishment cases for multiple retrieval of adaptable pieces of cases. In: Proceedings of First International Conference on Case-Based Reasoning, Sesimbra, Portugal, pp. 55–66, October 1995

McDonnell, N., Cunningham, P.: A knowledge-light approach to regression using case-based reasoning. In: Proceedings of the 8th European Conference on Case-Based Reasoning, ECCBR'06, pp. 91–105. Springer, Berlin (2006)

Mikalsen, M., Kofod-Petersen, A.: Representing and reasoning about context in a mobile environment. Rev. Intell. Artif. (RIA) 19, pp. 479–498 (2005)

Mille, A.: From case-based reasoning to traces based reasoning. Technical Report 2281, LIRIS, University of Lyon (2006)

Minor, M., Bergmann, R., Gorg, S.: Case-based adaptation of workflows. Inf. Syst. **40**, 142–152 (2014)

Montani, S.: How to use contextual knowledge in medical case-based reasoning systems: a survey on very recent trends. Artif. Intell. Med. **51**(2), 125–131 (2011)

Öztürk, P., Aamodt, A.: A context model for knowledge-intensive case-based reasoning. Int. J. Hum.-Comput. Stud. **48**(3), 331–355 (1998)

Pu, P., Maher, M.L.: Issues and Applications of Case-based Reasoning to Design. Lawrence Erlbaum, Mahwah (1997)

Richter, M.: The knowledge contained in similarity measures. Invited talk, the First International Conference on Case-Based Reasoning, Sesimbra, Portugal, October 1995

Schank, R.: Dynamic Memory: A Theory of Learning in Computers and People. Cambridge University Press, Cambridge (1982)

Schank, R., Abelson, R.: Scripts, Plans, Goals and Understanding. Lawrence Erlbaum, Hillsdale (1977)

Schank, R., Leake, D.: Creativity and learning in a case-based explainer. Artif. Intell. **40**(1–3), 353–385 (1989). [also In: Carbonell, J. (ed.) Machine Learning: Paradigms and Methods. MIT Press, Cambridge (1990)]

Torgo, L.: Luís Torgo - regression data sets. http://www.dcc.fc.up.pt/~ltorgo/Regression/Data Sets.html (2013). Accessed 5 May 2013

Traoré, A., Tattegrain, H., Mille, A.: A trace analysis based approach for modeling context components. In: Brézillon, P., Blackburn, P., Dapoigny, R. (eds.) Modeling and Using Context (Lecture Notes in Computer Science), vol. 8175, pp. 101–114. Springer, Berlin (2013)

Tversky, A.: Features of similarity. Psychol. Rev. **84**(4), 327–352 (1977)

Weber, R., Ashley, K., Brüninghaus, S.: Textual case-based reasoning. Knowl. Eng. Rev. **20**, 255–260 (2005)

Zimmermann, A.: Context-awareness in user modelling: Requirements analysis for a case-based reasoning application. In: Proceedings of the 5th International Conference on Case-based Reasoning: Research and Development, ICCBR'03, pp. 718–732. Springer, Berlin (2003)

Chapter 30
Tactical Reasoning Through Context-Based Reasoning

Avelino J. Gonzalez

Abstract This chapter describes and discusses *Context-Based Reasoning* (CxBR), a human behavior representation paradigm based on context and designed for use in modeling tactical reasoning. This chapter describes CxBR both formally and informally, and discusses experiences in developing and applying this concept, its advantages and its opportunities for improvement.

30.1 Introduction

There is little need to point out to this audience the virtues of using context to model human activities. As the reader of this edited volume can see, there are indeed many areas where context has been used to great advantage, either as a modeling paradigm, or simply as the underlying concept behind the models. Therefore, I will dispense with the traditional introduction and discussion of context-related research, and point to the contents of this volume as evidence of that.

Nevertheless, one interesting application of context that has largely eluded the attention of most researchers in the literature (Turner's Context-Mediated Behaviors being the notable exception—see Chap. 32 of this book) has been for modeling and implementing tactical reasoning. Tactical reasoning can be said to involve a time-based decision-making process, where multiple decisions are made sequentially as an agent seeks to complete a task or a mission over time. These decisions almost always involve the execution of some actions prescribed by the decisions made. Consequently, the actions will inevitably change the environment, either a lot or a little, which will have an effect on the agent's subsequent decisions. While some of these actions may be reversible, others are not. It can take an arbitrary length of time to complete such a mission or task—from several seconds to several days. We assume here that tactical reasoning is always made in the context of an environment that may be unknown, uncertain and possibly hostile. An agent reasoning tactically must move through time and space (physically or virtually), and must make decisions that are more often than not time critical.

A. J. Gonzalez (✉)
Computer Science Division, University of Central Florida, Orlando, FL, USA

© Springer Science+Business Media New York 2014
P. Brézillon, A. J. Gonzalez (eds.), *Context in Computing*,
DOI 10.1007/978-1-4939-1887-4_30

Thorndike and Wescourt (1984) assert that tactical reasoning *involves (1) assessment of the situation at hand, (2) selection of a plan to most properly address the present situation, and (3) execution of that plan.* This plan may be an explicit plan formally described and decided after discussions among the stakeholders, or it may simply be decisions made instinctively on the spot by the decision maker in the heat of the moment. This depends on the context of situation faced.

In tactical reasoning, decisions may have to be made on a frequent (possibly continual) basis, and at different levels. Some decisions can be made subconsciously as part of a motor skill (e.g., keeping a car within a lane of traffic) while others may be more complex and require careful consideration (e.g., how best to attack an opposing team in football).

In this chapter, I describe and discuss the *Context-Based Reasoning* (CxBR) paradigm that uses context as the basis on which to build agents that reflect human performance when undertaking a tactical task or mission. CxBR was specifically designed to be simple, intuitive, and efficient. This was in reaction to the complex, hard to use and inefficient tools and languages that existed at the time. This complaint was something I continually heard from my students while teaching my courses the University of Central Florida (UCF).

30.2 Background

The concept of context is very familiar to us. Everyone believes he/she knows what is meant by "the context." Yet, when asked to define it, we often struggle to do so. This is reflected in the research literature by the perceived need to always define context whenever we write about it. In fact, Brézillon (1999) once canvassed the literature of the time and found many different definitions of context. Most of the definitions revolve around the concept of "situation." So, we continue with the tacit admission that there is no commonly-accepted definition of context, and resist the urge to define it here yet again.

CxBR is not a new concept—the first papers appeared in 1993, over 20 years ago (Gonzalez and Ahlers 1993) even though it wasn't called CxBR at that time. Many papers on CxBR have been written since that time and some aspects of it have changed over the years. These papers include those introducing the concept informally (Gonzalez and Ahlers 1998) as well as formally (Gonzalez et al. 2008) There have been several papers describing direct applications of CxBR to tactical reasoning. Automobile driving has been a common theme (Gonzalez et al. 2000) simply because most of us know how to drive a car, so access to expertise is not an issue. Patz et al. (2008) used CxBR as the main control scheme in the UCF autonomous car entry in the DARPA Grand Urban Challenge of 2007. Their vehicle came in seventh place overall Patz et al. (2008) in spite of having by far the lowest budget of any finalist. This has been one of the very few applications of CxBR to the physical world. Hu and Liu (2007) used CxBR to model the pilot's behavior in a helicopter simulation. Luotsinen et al. (2005) used CxBR for computer games.

Trinh et al. (2004) implemented CxBR in a robot performing a fight or flight decision in the physical world. Gallagher and Gonzalez (2000) used CxBR to model the behavior of a military vehicle under various degrees of degraded states. Barrett and Gonzalez (2011) expanded CxBR to represent teams of agents. He called his extension *Collaborative Context-based Reasoning* (CCxBR). He reasoned that the use of commonly available contexts gave the agents a common basis with which to communicate in the process of collaboration. Saeki and Gonzalez (2000) conceived the idea of the *competing context concept* (ccc) and extended the basic CxBR concept to include this. More about ccc later in this chapter. Finally, the Norwegian Defense Research Institute (FFI) is using CxBR to model command and control in their training simulators.

Other papers have described the use of CxBR in applications not directly related to tactical reasoning such as construction management (Gonzalez et al. 2010) dialog management (Hung and Gonzalez 2013) planning (Grama et al. 1998) intent recognition (Drewes et al. 2000) context identification from observation of task performance (Trinh and Gonzalez 2013) automated after-action review in military training (Fernlund et al. 2009) and a smart home (Fazenda et al. 2012). In this chapter, I base the discussion about CxBR on tactical reasoning—its original intent. Rather than repeat the contents of these other papers, I seek here to provide a high-level overview of CxBR, its original inspiration, the thinking behind it and how it has been used in its most notable applications. Nevertheless, for the sake of completeness, brief formal and informal descriptions of CxBR are included in this chapter.

My first encounter with context came in the early 1980s when I was working in industry, developing the knowledge base for the GenAID system (Gonzalez et al. 1986) for Westinghouse Electric Corporation (now part of Siemens). The GenAID system (stands for Generator Artificial Intelligence Diagnostics) was designed to autonomously diagnose in real time the performance of large turbine generators located throughout the country. GenAID first came on-line in 1983 to remotely monitor and diagnose seven large generators in east Texas and one in upstate New York from one central location (Orlando, Florida). GenAID is still in operation to this day, and although modernized in many important ways, the basic rule-based core that reflects its diagnostic knowledge remains largely unchanged from the early 1980s. Its objective was (and still is) to identify incipient faults. GenAID also decides when these incipient faults become serious enough to warrant a costly unit shutdown, thereby avoiding even costlier repairs and longer downtimes later if the unit were to remain in operation and subsequently fails catastrophically. One could argue that such diagnostic reasoning in real time has some elements of tactical reasoning—assess, plan and execute—making this application relevant to tactical reasoning.

Generators are equipped with many sensors that monitor the critical signs of their performance. However, generators have several different operating conditions that can make the expected readings quite different. One could consider these conditions as *operational contexts*. These could include (1) full normal operation (connected to the grid and generating full or nearly full power); (2) floating (generator at full speed and connected to grid, but not generating power); (3) startup (generator not connected to the grid while rotational speed gradually increases); (4) turning gear (generator off line and slowly rotating to keep rotor from sagging); and (5) down (generator is shut down and disassembled for repair). At all these times (except possibly the last), the condition of the generator is continually monitored, but the meaning of the readings can vary widely depending on the operational context. For example, temperature readings that would be considered normal under normal operation could be cause for concern if the generator is in the floating context.

GenAID was a first generation rule-based knowledge-based (expert) system. At one point, it had upwards of 10,000 diagnostic rules that were always "on", regardless of context. The unstructured nature of this system made it difficult to manage, yet our focus was on making the rules execute very fast. However, it became obvious that there were better options than having thousands of unstructured rules. McDermott had come to a similar conclusion in his work on R1 (McDermott 1982) So, the rules were organized by activating those whose context was active. That permitted only a subset of the entire collection of rules to be "on" at any particular time. This made the system's operation more efficient. More importantly, it first exposed me to the power of context as a natural tool for dividing-and-conquering

There is ample evidence in the cognitive psychology literature that humans do think in terms of context (Parker et al. 2013) However, I make no claim to CxBR being cognitively correct, only that it provides an organization for the knowledge of the agent to perform the mission in a way consistent with what a human would do in the same series of situations. Nevertheless, speaking strictly for myself, I find that the recognized context in situations I face triggers in my mind a set of concepts, ideas and protocols that until that context emerged, remained hidden deeply in the recesses of my mind. One informal example I like to give my students is that of the automobile mechanic who is also an amateur chef. Let's call him Peter.

When Peter is ready to go to work on any normal morning, he gets in his car for the commute to his shop and drives there. At this time, his mission is to reach his destination safely and on time. Therefore, during this time when this mission is actively pursued, his knowledge about how to drive an automobile is forefront in his mind as a result of the context he faces. All other knowledge (e.g., how to repair cars, how to cook a roast) can be said to be in the background. For the sake of simplicity in this example, we will neglect our sometimes-dangerous habit of daydreaming while doing other things.

Upon reaching his destination, his context has changed to where he now must begin his job of repairing automobiles. His knowledge about automobile engines, transmissions etc. now comes to the forefront, while the knowledge about driving cars recedes to the background. At the end of his day, he drives home, once again activating his knowledge about driving. Upon reaching his home, his new objective is to cook a nice dinner for his family, thereby causing a third set of knowledge to rise to the surface, so to speak, while the others recede. Now his focus is on preparing the sauce, roasting the meat, cooking the vegetables, etc. This knowledge is unrelated to the other knowledge he used earlier in the day,

Turner (1993) similarly and more succinctly uses the example of how people instinctively lower their voices upon entering a library, as that behavior is normally required when in that context. That is, knowledge about how to behave in a library "rises" rather instinctively when one enters the library.

Meta-rules in rule-based systems have been used to provide a means to select what I call a "bucket of rules" that are applicable to the current issue while ignoring the others. This could be considered similar to CxBR, as the reader will see in the next section. The same could be said about finite state machines and meta automata. While similarities exist between CxBR and these, CxBR makes an intuitive distinction with the use of context. In other words, a context knows what to do, how to do it and what to expect. It also provides a structure to the knowledge organization that rule-based systems do not do, even in the presence of meta rules.

I next describe CxBR informally in Sect. 30.3, followed by a more formal description of it in Sect. 30.4.

30.3 Informal Description of CxBR

As human beings, it is important that we know how to act properly at all times. If we assume that life is a never-ending (or at least until we die!) sequence of end-to-end contexts, then if we know how to behave in each context and we correctly identify the context present at any time, then our behavior should always be correct and appropriate. Likewise, CxBR seeks to make the agent behave appropriately by decomposing its "life" into a series of contexts for which knowledge on how to behave in each is organized and stored. Informally, Context-based Reasoning can be said to be the codification of Peter's (and everyone else's') ability to call up the contextually relevant knowledge when needed, and let it recede when no longer contextually relevant. This, I believe, permits us to efficiently manage and use the vast amounts of knowledge that we have collected over our lifetimes. Therefore, we define two basic types of knowledge:

1. Knowing how to behave (what to do and not do) while in a context.
2. Knowing how to identify the context faced, as well as when it changes.

Both elements require knowledge. CxBR organizes this knowledge as a hierarchically structured set of *contexts* that control the actions of the agent. CxBR requires that one and only one context be *active* at any point in time during the tactical mission.[1] The active context is the one that controls the actions of the agent.

30.3.1 Knowledge About How to Behave

This knowledge relates to how to behave when in a context. While equally important as being able to identify the context, it is generally more voluminous. The representational format for this knowledge is not specified by CxBR ... on purpose ... to

---

[1] A mission need not be military in nature. I refer to *mission* as the process of an agent seeking to achieve a simple or complex objective. I think it has a more appropriate connotation than *task*.

provide flexibility to the developer. Most applications have used functions, but others have used production rules (Brown 1994) while yet others have used embedded neural networks (Gonzalez et al. 2007; Sidani and Gonzalez 2000) A discussion of which works better for which application is beyond the scope of this article.

Contexts also contain an expectation of what is likely to be present when the agent is in that context. The behavioral knowledge in a context, therefore, must take such expectations into account, either implicitly or explicitly. My preferred example of a CxBR application is that of an agent that drives an automobile, whether in the virtual world (Gonzalez et al. 2000) or in the physical world, as in (Trinh et al. 2004) In this application, the agent's CxBR knowledge could be decomposed as to the type of road environment it would have to navigate to accomplish its mission. For example, driving the car in the urban core of a city might require some knowledge that would be different from driving in the more pastoral suburbs. In the former, one would expect heavy traffic, many pedestrians, many traffic lights, loud noises, etc. One would need to drive slowly, carefully and looking for pedestrians crossing in front of the car. In a suburb, traffic would be lighter, with fewer traffic lights, but with the possibility of children playing on or near the streets. Other contexts in this application would include driving in high speed, access-controlled highways (i.e., autoroute, autobahn or interstate highway), in a two-lane country road and in a parking lot. Again, these require knowledge and skills that are different, depending on the situation faced.

30.3.2 Knowledge to Identify Context Faced

The second important type of knowledge contained in the context is how to tell when the situation has changed enough that the context is no longer present. In the automobile driving example, maybe the agent exited the freeway and is now in a city street. This is critical, as inability to do this could preclude the correct behavior of the agent. Imagine our driving agent racing down a city street at 70 mile/h because it still thinks it is in a freeway.

Figure 30.1 depicts what we refer to as the *Context Map*. This represents the admissible transitions for this particular mission of driving one's car safely. Note its directionality.

The context identification knowledge can be handled in different ways: The original approach taken in CxBR, and still the preferred one, was to have each context know when it was no longer applicable, and select the new applicable context based on the external environment as well as possibly internal considerations (e.g., need to refuel). Thus, a context would have knowledge about when it should *phase itself out*. This was done through *transition rules* that would be actively looking at the environment (internal and external) every cycle. The advantage of this was that it was a distributed form of control—the active context always decided to which other context it would "pass the baton," so to speak. This passing of the "active" baton would be unambiguous—it would only be one. The problem was that the transition

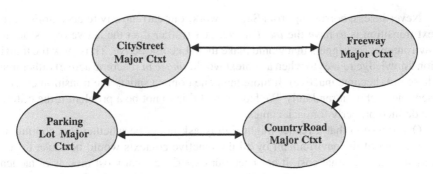

Fig. 30.1 A Context map

knowledge needed to be built-in a priori, and if a new context were added, the transition rules for all other contexts would have to be examined and possibly modified, making additions rather inefficient.

Turner, in his Context-Mediated Behaviors (Turner 1993) used a centralized control process, where a central manager would determine the context to be activated (although he does not use that same terminology). We prefer distributed control to central control because the transition rules would be truly context-sensitive. In this vein, Saeki and Gonzalez (2000) devised a clever combination of central vs. distributed control and built what they called the competing context concept (*ccc*) mentioned briefly above. Borrowing from Selfridge's shrieking demons (Selfridge 1959) in the *ccc*, each of the *inactive* contexts continually evaluates the environment to determine whether it has the best tools to address the emerging situation. As the situation changes and the case for a context transition becomes stronger and stronger, each context *shrieks* in a volume proportional to how well it can match the needs of the situation. When the shrieking becomes loud enough, the context that shrieks the loudest takes the baton, so to speak, from the de-activating context, and the process continues.

If more than one competing context is equally (or nearly-equally) viable at the time the transition is to be made (i.e., the intensity of their shrieking does not clearly separate them), then Saeki proposed a super-real-time (faster than real time) process in which the system quickly simulates what could happen in the immediate future if each one of those contexts were to be activated, and evaluates the projected result. The context with which the "best" outcome is predicted wins. This is akin to the *what-if* mental simulations we often make when deciding between several alternatives.

While conceptually elegant and clever, the competing context concept has proven to be difficult to implement in practice for all but some relatively simple applications. Specifically, it has been hard to implement in complex applications where the needs of the situation cannot be easily defined quantitatively, at least not in a general manner. This is because defining the metrics to be used in determining the volume of the shrieking (a weighted factor), can be difficult. Nevertheless, we continue to investigate this intriguing approach.

Nevertheless, borrowing from Saeki's work, our current way to accomplish context transition is to have the *inactive contexts* (rather than the active one) scan the environment for triggers that would make them become active. Thus, now the transition knowledge relates to when a context would *phase in* (become active) rather than phase out (become inactive). If more than one context satisfy the transition criteria, then one is chosen randomly. We have found this to not be a problem if the criteria are defined properly for each context

One question that a reader might rightly ask could be whether this continuous monitoring of the environment by all the inactive contexts would be cause for extensive computational cost. It has been our experience that most models of tactical missions require between 10 and 15 contexts that would vie for the chance to become active—in some applications only seven or eight. If we assume that there are two or three transition rules per context (which is typical), this would make a maximum of 45 rules continually monitoring the environment. This is not a significant computational load and we have never seen this to be a problem.

Another issue that has stirred up considerable debate in our research group has been the current dictum that only one context must be active at any one time. While developers that adopt CxBR as their modeling paradigm can do as they please with respect to this, I have managed to fend off my students and remained steadfast on this conceptual requirement. This is because the alternative (having multiple concurrently active contexts), while intellectually interesting and certainly not without merit, gives rise to several complexities that go against the simple and intuitive grain of CxBR. The argument has been made that different contexts can control different variables in the agent's platform. For example, one context could control the accelerator and brake pedals while another could control the steering wheel. The difficulty has been to find an application where the contexts control two (or more) completely independent variables, whose actions will not affect the actions of the other. Such has been hard to find. In most tactical reasoning applications, the agent must act in a holistic manner, considering many aspects of its environment and the cause-and-effects relationships among the variables it controls. Yes, of course, the controlling contexts could be made to keep the actions of the other(s) under consideration and negotiate the application of decisions. However, the complexity this would add to CxBR would counter its intuitive nature.

30.3.3 Context Organization

Contexts in CxBR are defined in three hierarchical levels: *Mission Context, Major Context*, and *Minor Contexts*. Mission contexts are called *defining contexts* while Major are the *control contexts*. Minor Contexts are considered *auxiliary contexts*. Mission and Major Contexts occupy the top two levels of the hierarchy. However, Minor contexts can occupy several levels in the hierarchy. These can be labeled as Sub-Contexts, Sub-sub-Contexts, Sub-Sub-Sub-Contexts, etc., depending on the level they occupy. While there is no conceptual limit to the number of levels possible

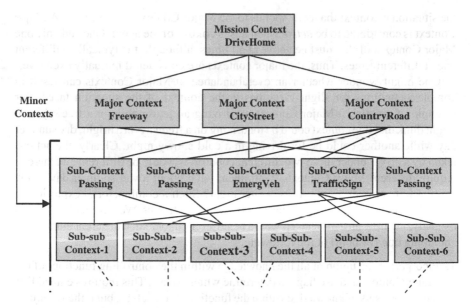

Fig. 30.2 Hierarchical context organization

for Minor Contexts, in practice, we have never needed more than two levels—most often only one. Figure 30.2 depicts a simple hierarchy for an agent in CxBR. A similar version of this figure was originally published in (Gonzalez et al. 2008).

30.3.4 Mission Contexts

The Mission Context defines elements of the mission or task, and the agent's role in it. It defines the objective of the mission, the criteria for completing the mission successfully, and any constraints that may be imposed on the mission execution (e.g., travel by daytime only, use expressways only, etc.). It is not absolutely necessary to use a Mission Context in a CxBR agent implementation, as the objectives and constraints could be inherently built directly into the Major and Minor Contexts. However, we have found it very useful to explicitly define the mission and requirements, not only for the benefit of the agent, but also for the benefit of the human later modifying the CxBR system code.

30.3.5 Major Contexts

The Major Contexts are the most important, as well as an essential, element of CxBR. They contain the knowledge about how the agent can and should behave while in that context. They are the basic control modules for the agent while the agent is in the situational context that corresponds to the Major Context controlling it. A Major Context is considered to be *active* when it is in control of the agent. One and only one Major Contexts of the must be active at all times, although it is typically a different one at different times. Thus, the major contexts are considered mutually exclusive.

One might wonder whether an overabundance of Major Contexts can result in complex situations for slight variations in the context of the situation faced. For example, if creating a Major Context for driving an automobile in a freeway, one might think that one context could be for driving on a freeway on a bright, dry summer day while another could be for driving in a cold snowy night. Clearly, the actions taken by a driver under these two different conditions would be different and thereby require different Major Contexts. Well, then, what about a wet summer day? How about a wet summer night? A dry winter night? Such a combinatorial explosion of possible contexts could indeed make CxBR very inefficient. We have addressed this by analyzing how an action taken would be different under such different conditions, and doing one (or both) of the following:

1. Incorporate the union of all the knowledge within the controlling functions of the Major Context and use flags to determine which to use. This requires embedding the various sets of knowledge within the functions themselves, but if the variations in behavior are small (e.g., slow down in snowy conditions), it is acceptable.
2. Use Minor Contexts to hold the appropriate knowledge. This approach is more desirable for variations that are more complex and it is more explicit. More about this when we discuss Minor Contexts next.

In general, our experience has been that this has not been a problem when approached in either one of the two manners above.

30.3.6   Minor Contexts

Minor Contexts are similar in nature to Major Contexts, except that they are not essential. One could place all the knowledge on how to behave in a situation into a function in the corresponding Major Context. However, in many cases, there is benefit derived from abstracting functionality. For example, in the mission of driving home, while in the context of driving in a freeway, an agent may face the need to pass a slow moving truck. There is a commonly accepted procedure for doing this. While the agent is in a **freeway** Major Context, a Sub-Context that knows how to pass another vehicle in expressways is called[2]. The Sub-Context leaps into action, performs the passing function, and then returns control to the calling function, in this case, the **freeway** Major Context. In effect, Minor Contexts are exactly that—minor situations that are part of the Major Context, but require complex behavior in order

---

[2] We do not use the term *activate* a Minor Context to avoid confusion with the Major Context. We assume that the Major Context that calls the Sub-Context remains active.

to be addressed. Therefore, Minor Contexts play an auxiliary role in addressing situations encountered while in a larger context. They also permit the re-use of specific behaviors in more than one Major Context.

The calling of Minor Contexts does not result in the de-activation of its parent Major Context. Thus, it could be argued that in fact more than one context is "active" at the same time, which contradicts our earlier requirement. However, while a Minor Context is controlling the agent, the Major Context remains active—their relationship is the same as one function calling another in computer programming. Upon completion, control reverts to the calling function (the Major Context). Thus, we do not see this as inconsistent.

Minor Contexts monitor the environment to determine when their presence is no longer needed (i.e., its task is complete or interrupted) and it can return control to the Major Context. However, they are not charged with determining when they are needed—the Major Context will do that. However, the Major Context can also prematurely wrest control away from the Minor Context before the latter completes its task if something in the environment has changed that makes the task irrelevant or undesirable (i.e., an emergency vehicle coming up quickly behind).

30.4 Formal Description of CxBR

Now that we have described CxBR through an informal discussion, a formal definition of CxBR follows. I refer the reader to (Gonzalez et al. 2008) for a more in-depth and complete discussion of this topic. Because of page limits, what follows is a condensed version of what is contained in (Gonzalez et al. 2008).

We begin with the assumption that all CxBR-controlled agents have an assigned mission **M** to execute. **M** is to be carried out by the agent under the control of a *CxBR model* composed of a *context base* that is specifically defined for that mission. The CxBR model is executed within a *CxBR engine* that knows what to do with the contexts in the context base, (i.e., executes their knowledge, executing rules to activate and de-activate contexts, etc.). The control context is the most important element in the CxBR model. Therefore, we begin with its definition.

30.4.1 Control Contexts

Control contexts are composed of three basic elements:

- The *context logic:* allows the agent to carry out the behavior defined in the context. It represents the agent's *functional intelligence.*
- The *transitional logic:* determines when a transition to another context is warranted. This represents the *situational intelligence.* It is expressed as *Transition Rules* for Major Contexts and *Action rules* for Minor Contexts
- *Declarative knowledge:* describes some aspects of the context that may be useful in decision-making. This is not essential but can be helpful.

We define the set **C** as the *constellation of contexts*—those contexts that are relevant to the assigned mission **M**. This constellation is a subset of the *universe of contexts* X—the set of all possible contexts in the domain **D**. **C**, then, is defined as the subset of X that is relevant to mission **M**. Therefore, X − **C** = the set of contexts not necessary for mission **M**.

$$C_m = \{C_1, C_2, C_3, C_4,, C_n, c_1, c_2, c_3, c_4,, c_m\} \subset X$$

where C_i is a Major Context and c_i is a Minor Context. As discussed earlier, only one Major Context can be in control of the agent at any one time. This one context is the so-called the *active context* and we denote is as C_a. Control of the agent is therefore a function of the active context C_a.

$$\text{Control of agent} = F(C_a)$$

where **F** is the CxBR engine that executes the system and enables agent actions.

The relationship among the contexts in a context base is depicted by the *context map* Δ_M for mission **M**. Δ_M defines the possible transitions of Major Contexts within the constellation C_m. Figure 30.1 describes a generic context map.

30.4.2 Knowledge Representation in Major Contexts

The knowledge contained within each Major Context of a CxBR model is represented by several components. I will assume here that the context logic is represented by functions, although as I stated before, other paradigms can be used if the CxBR engine being used permits it. In addition to the context logic, the agent has a local memory in the form of a *local fact base*, or **LFB**, whose contents come directly from the agent's input stream. The **LFB** can also serve as the place where internal memory is kept, and which is not accessible to other agents. An inference engine, accessible to each agent can use the *action rules* to draw conclusions from these facts using traditional forward chaining inferencing, adding new assertions to the fact base in the process. The context logic for a Major Context is composed of the control functions (cf's). Formally, we define **CF**$_{MC}$ as the set of functions:

$$CF_{MC} = \{cf_1, cf_2, cf_3,, cf_n\}$$

Furthermore, we define the set of action rules (*ar*'s) for a specific Major Context as **AR**$_{MC}$. Action rules are general purpose productions used for, among other things, calling Minor Contexts. They can use facts located on the local fact base, or local variables in the functions that form part of **CF**$_{MC}$. Some implementations of CxBR may additionally contain a *global fact base* **GFB**, whose facts are accessible to all agents (e.g., weather conditions, the score of the game, etc.). Action rules may also use facts on the global fact base as antecedents. Thus, we can formally define **AR**$_{MC}$ as:

$$AR_{MC} = \{ar_1, ar_2, ar_3, ar_4,, ar_k\}$$

Lastly, we define *declarative knowledge* as that relevant to the mission, but not directly in control of the agent. This knowledge is typically represented as frames or classes. We refer to this knowledge, for lack of a better name, as *Knowledge Frames* or KF_{MC}. Therefore, the Context logic which controls the actions of the agent while under the control of a Major Context is formally defined as:

$$Context\text{-}logic = [CF_{MC}, AR_{MC}, KF_{MC}]$$

The other important part of the Major Context is the transitional logic. For this, we have used *transition rules,* or TR (formerly called *sentinel rules*). TRs define when the conditions for an applicable transition hold true. If, for instance, the mission provides a context-transition pair for Major Context C_1 to C_3, a transition rule will be present within C_1 that monitors the fact base(s) for the conditions warranting a transition to C_3. If the condition(s) exist(s), then TR will fire and a transition will be effected (phase-out). Alternatively, the TRs of inactive contexts can be used to detect when the Major Context to which they are attached should become active (phase-in). Transition rules are unique to the context to which they belong.

Each Major Context C_i includes a set S of transition criteria. There can exist multiple TRs for transitions involving the same context pair. Therefore, we define the set S_{ij} to represent the set of criteria that can effect a transition from Major Context i to Major Context j. Thus, S_i is the combination of all S_{ij} where $<i, j>$ exists as a valid transition within mission M. We can think of $TR_i = \{tr_1, tr_2, tr_3, \ldots tr_n\}$ as the set of all TRs for C_i that incorporate the transition criteria in S_i.

Therefore, a Major Context C_i, when implemented within a Mission M for an agent A, includes a set of transition rules TR_i, and context logic that determines the action of the agent when operating in C_i.

$$C_i = < Context - logic_i Transitional - logic_i, > = [TR_i, CF_i, AR_i, KF_i]$$

I should note that in many tactical scenarios there exist conditions that require the agent to perform a certain task or behavior irrespective of its current context. To account for such conditions, *universal transition rules* are encoded within the Mission (Not the Major or Minor Contexts!). These rules dictate that the agent should immediately change its context when certain criteria are met, and they hold precedence over the normal transition rules. One example is that when we should see another car aiming straight at us, regardless of the reason or context, it would be most beneficial to first get out of the car's way and avoid a collision. Universal transition rules are important because they represent instinctive behavior that must be represented in the model.

30.4.3 Knowledge Representation in Minor Contexts

Minor Contexts, as mentioned earlier, share logical similarities to Major Contexts, but lack some of their attributes. In effect, Minor Contexts have the same structure for Context-logic, but do not have the Transitional-logic. A Minor Context is called upon, like a function, to perform a subtask deemed necessary by a Major Context. Unlike Major Contexts, however, one Minor Context (let's say, a Sub-Context so we can pin-point its hierarchical level) need not be active at any given moment. Furthermore, when a Sub-Context has finished executing, control shifts back to the Major Context that called it. Sub-Contexts can be used by any Major Context in **C**. This enhances re-usability of components in the model. Nevertheless, we can represent the Sub-Context by a vector function—whose input is an *action rule* of the calling Major Context.

$$Sub - Context = F\ (AR_{SCi}, CF_{SCi}, KF_{MCi})$$

30.4.4 Descriptive Contexts—Mission Contexts

A Mission Context contains a description of the mission to be accomplished, and it is assigned to its agent prior to run-time. Included within the Mission description are the goals, any imposed constraints, and the *context topology* that will dictate the high-level behavior of the agent.

The goals provide the agent with the end-game criteria. For example, if we were to provide an agent with our now-familiar **Drive-Home** mission, the goal would likely be for the agent to reach a specific destination (i.e., home). That goal slot in the Mission would then be represented by the label of the destination, and a Boolean variable indicating whether the agent has reached it. We can formally define the Mission goal as a function g of a set of environmental and physical conditions **E** and **P** that exist at the time of mission.

$$Goal = g\ (E\ (t_0), P\ (t_0))$$

In tactical missions, often the end of 'goal' cannot be defined or is not applicable. More specifically, it is not uncommon to assign an agent the mission of performing a certain behavior repeatedly for an indefinite amount of time. In this case, the goal is the task itself. For example, an agent is a scout plane assigned the mission of reconnaissance in a specific area. So, as long as the reconnaissance mission is in effect, its goal is to patrol and the end criterion is the time when the agent is ordered to discontinue the mission, is shot down, or runs out of fuel (hopefully the first).

The constraints on the mission can be used to provide the agent with a set of guidelines for operation. These constraints can be in the form of physical limitations placed on the sensing faculties of the agent (e.g., snowy day), scenario-specific entities (such as obstacles or enemies), or even map boundaries within which the agent is ordered to operate. We can consider the constraints on the mission **M** to be the union of the set of physical, environmental, and scenario-specific constraints (denoted **co**$_p$, **co**$_e$, and **co**$_s$) placed on the agent as required by its Mission. In this definition, a constraint c can provide the agent with either a constant value or a range of valid values for a certain variables within the simulation.

$$Constraints = \{co_p, co_e, co_s\}$$

The Mission is also responsible for indicating the *default major context* that the agent will use during its mission. This context serves as the initial context for the agent when it begins a scenario, as well as a safe behavior when it doesn't know what else to do because of gaps in the context model. Lastly, the Mission Context may also have Knowledge Frames to describe aspects of the mission that are not otherwise described. These are also called **KF$_M$**.

The constellation of contexts **C**, along with the Default Major Context (**DMC**), and the scenario's *Universal Transition Rules*, make up the context topology of mission **M**.

$$\text{Context-Topology}_M = < C_M, DMC_M, \text{Universal-transition-rules}_M >$$

After combining this with the mission constraints and goal, the definition of mission **M** can now be:

$$M = [\text{Goal}_M, \text{Constraints}_M, \text{Context-Topology}_M]$$

30.4.5   CxBR Engine

In 1998, Norlander (1998) developed a CxBR Framework that provided an infrastructure optimized for executing tactical agents in CxBR. The Framework provided the mechanism to execute a context model. Since that time, several other such engines have been built in our lab by different students that have taken advantage of modern features. However, at the moment there is no standard CxBR engine, and possibly never will be—at least not from us.

30.5   Summary and Discussion

There has been very much written about CxBR, both by our research group as well as by others. It is impossible to cover it all in these pages. This chapter represents a summary of CxBR and points to other publications that contain a more detailed description. In concluding this paper, I should add that I believe that the main strength of CxBR is its intuitiveness. We have had countless students run through our lab over the last 20 years, and without exception, they pick up on the concept very quickly, and can start writing models sometimes only within a few hours of being initially introduced. Secondly, the fact that we do not have a defined language to restrict a developer on how to build a CxBR system gives a developer much flexibility in how to implement it. Most developers have added features that are relevant to their particular application. Therefore, we consider CxBR to be more of an organization of knowledge rather than a language. In fact, even the CxBR Framework described above gives the user much latitude in how to design the context model and how to execute the transitions.

What is next for us in CxBR? Well, for one, the concept of finding a general measure of the needs of the situation—any situation—would go a long ways towards enabling the competing context concept described above. This would relieve us from the need to hardcode transition rules into the contexts. Perhaps the place to look is in Case-based Reasoning (CBR), where selecting the most appropriate case among many is always one of its main concerns. CBR defines similarity measures as a way to do this. While similarity measures tend to be very domain dependent, there may still be very much to learn from that body of research.

An area of much more interest to us has been how to acquire the knowledge to build the contexts. This is an age-old problem, ever since the beginning of AI when Feigenbaum coined the term "knowledge engineering bottleneck" (Feigenbaum 1979) Traditionally, the context base has been built by hand. While the raison d'ê tre of CxBR is specifically to facilitate this very process of building models of tactical behavior, it nevertheless cries out for automation. We have responded by investigating two approaches. The first of these was the CITKA system (Context-based Interactive Tactical Knowledge Acquisition tool) (Gonzalez et al. 2006) CITKA could be classified as automated knowledge engineering. CITKA took advantage of the structure of CxBR and its highly intuitive nature to interact with an expert to elicit the knowledge and directly convert it into a useable context base. In tests, it succeeded in significantly reducing the involvement of a knowledge engineer.

More intriguing to us has been the use of CxBR to facilitate machine learning. Our work centers on learning from observation of a human performing a task in a simulator. Conceivably, we can also learn from observing a human perform a task in the physical world, but it is much harder to do because of the difficulties in acquiring and (more importantly) interpreting the data necessary for the learning algorithm. We have undertaken several projects that investigated this approach to building context bases for tactical missions. Sidani and Gonzalez (2000) modeled driver behavior at a traffic light. Although he did not use the term Context-based Reasoning in his work, the structure he used greatly resembled CxBR and was our original implementation of these concepts. Fernlund et al. (2006) took the idea one step further and built a CxBR model of a driver using Genetic Programming. Stensrud and Gonzalez (2008) built a system to learn the transition rules from observing poker players. Johnson and Gonzalez (2014) built a system to learn team behaviors using CxBR as the base paradigm for the tactical agents. Lastly, Stein and Gonzalez (in print) directly showed the value of CxBR in machine learning by recasting in CxBR a failed learning from observation system that sought to learn the behavior of a crane operator. The recast system was able to learn the tasks automatically from observation where the original system was not.

All these machine-learning systems succeeded in automating a significant part of the model building process. However, they did not achieve full automation, as it was still required that the contexts be defined a priori as well as the data that belonged to each defined context be also identified a priori. Thus, the context building effort was still burdensome. Trinh and Gonzalez (2013) solved most of this problem by conceiving a system that can discover the contexts in a trace of data of arbitrary length and partition the data trace into the identified contexts for use in these systems, in particular, in Fernlund's GenCL system.

One problem shared by all these systems was their computational inefficiency. The systems, particularly Fernlund's and Stein's systems, required several weeks of computation time construct the contexts required by the agent to do its thing. Therefore, our current research thrust is to conceive an algorithm that can build such CxBR agents in a more realistic time frame.

References

Barrett, G.A., Gonzalez, A.J.: Effective agent collaboration through improved communication by means of contextual reasoning. Int. J. Intell. Syst. **26**(2), 129–157 (2011)

Brézillon, P.: Context in problem solving: a survey. Knowl. Eng. Rev. **14**(1), 47–80 (1999)

Brown, J.C.: Application and evaluation of the context based reasoning paradigm. Master's Thesis, Department of Electrical and Computer Engineering, University of Central Florida, Orlando (1994)

Drewes, P.J., Gonzalez, A. J., Gerber, W.: Interpreting trainee intent in real time in a simulation-based training system. Trans. Soc. Comput. Simul. **17**(3), 120–134 (2000)

Fazenda, P., Carreira, P., Lima, P.: Context-based reasoning in smart buildings. Proceedings of the First International Workshop on Information Technology for Energy Applications, vol. 923, pp. 131-142. Lisboa (2012)

Feigenbaum, E.A..: Themes and case studies of knowledge engineering. In: Michie, D (ed.) Expert Systems in the Micro-Electronic Age, pp. 3-25. Edinburg University Press, Edinburg (1979)

Fernlund, H., Gonzalez, A.J., Georgiopoulos, M., DeMara, R.F.: Learning tactical human behavior through observation of human performance. IEEE Trans. Syst. Man Cybern. B. Cybern. **36**(1), 128–140 (2006)

Fernlund, H., Gonzalez, A.J., Ekblad, J., Rodriguez, A.: Trainee evaluation through after action review by comparison. J. Def. Model. Simul. **6**, 135–150 (2009)

Gallagher, A., Gonzalez, A.J.: Modeling platform behaviors under degraded states. Proceedings of the Inter-service/Industry Training Systems and Education Conference (I/ITSEC), Orlando (2000)

Gonzalez, A.J., Ahlers, R.H.: Concise representation of autonomous intelligent platforms in a simulation through the use of scripts. Proceedings of the Sixth Annual Florida Artificial Intelligence Research Symposium, Ft. Lauderdale (1993)

Gonzalez, A.J., Ahlers, R.H.: Context-based representation of intelligent behavior in training simulations. Trans Soc Comput. Simul. **15**(4), 153–166 (1998)

Gonzalez, A.J., Osborne, R.L., Kemper, C.T., Lowenfeld, S.: On-line diagnosis of turbine-generators using artificial intelligence. IEEE Trans. Energy Convers. **EC-1**(2), 68-74 (1986)

Gonzalez, F.G., Grejs, P., Gonzalez, A. J.: Autonomous automobile behavior through context-based reasoning. Proceedings of the International FLAIRS Conference, Orlando (2000)

Gonzalez, A.J., Castro, J., Gerber, W.E.: Automating the acquisition of tactical knowledge for military missions. J. Def. Model. Simul. **3**(1), 145–160 (2006)

Gonzalez, A.J., Georgiopoulos, M., DeMara, R.F.: Maintaining coherence among entities' states in a distributed multi-agent system. J. Def. Model. Simul. **4**(2), 147–172 (2007)

Gonzalez, A.J., Stensrud, B.S., Barrett, G.: Formalizing context-based reasoning-a modeling paradigm for representing tactical human behavior. Int. J. Intell. Syst. **23**(7), 822–847 (2008)

Gonzalez, A.J., Tsuruta, S., Sakurai, Y., Nguyen, J.V., Takada, K., Uchida, K.: Using contexts to supervise a collaborative process. Int. J. Artif. Intell. Eng. Desi. Anal. Manuf. **25**(1), 25–40 (2010)

Grama, C., Pollak, E., Brasch, R., Wartski, J., Gonzalez, A.J.: Automated generation of plans through the use of context-based reasoning. In: Proceedings of the International Florida Artificial Intelligence Research Society Conference. Sanibel Island, FL (1998)

Hu, Z., Liu, J.: The research of ASW helicopter ACGF construction based on CXBR. International Conference on Computational Intelligence and Security Workshops (2007)

Hung, V.C., Gonzalez, A.J.: Context-centric speech-based human-computer interaction. Int. J. Intell. Syst. **28**(10), 1010–1037 (2013)

Johnson, C.L., Gonzalez, A.J.: Learning collaborative behavior by observation. Expert. Syst. Appl. **41**, 2316–2328 (2014)

Luotsinen, L.J., Ekblad, J.N., Wu, A.S., Gonzalez, A.J., Bölöni, L.A.: Two-stage genetic programming approach for non-player characters. FuturePlay, The International Academic Conference on the Future of Game Design and Technology, East Lansing, Michigan (2005)

McDermott, J.: R1: A rule-based configurer of computer systems. Artif. Intell. **19**(1), 39–88 (1982)

Norlander, L.: A framework for efficient implementation of context-based reasoning in intelligent simulations. Master's Thesis, Department of Electrical and Computer Engineering, University of Central Florida (1998)

Parker, J.E., Hollister, D.L., Gonzalez, A. J., Brézillon, P., Parker, S.T.: Looking for a synergy between human and artificial cognition. CONTEXT Conference, Annecy (2013)

Patz, B., Papelis, Y., Pillat, R., Stein, G., Harper, D.: A practical approach to robotic design for the DARPA Urban Challenge. J Field Robot. **25**(80), 528–566 (2008)

Saeki, S., Gonzalez, A.J.: The competing context concept for CGF's: experimental results. Proceedings of the Inter-service/Industry Training Systems and Education Conference (I/ITSEC), Orlando (2000)

Selfridge, O.: Pandemonium: A paradigm for learning. Proceedings of the symposium for mechanization of thought and processes (1959)

Sidani, T.A., Gonzalez, A.J.: A framework for learning implicit expert knowledge through observation. Trans. Soc.Comput. Simul. **17**(2), 54–72 (2000)

Stein, G., Gonzalez, A.J.: Learning in context: Enhancing machine learning with context-based reasoning. Appl. Intell. (in print)

Stensrud, B.S., Gonzalez, A. J.: Discovery of high-level behavior from observation of human performance in a strategic game. IEEE Trans. Syst. Man Cybern. B. Cybern. **38**(3), 855–874 (2008)

Thorndike, P.W., Wescourt, K.T.: Modeling time-stressed situation assessment and planning for intelligent opponent simulation. Office of Naval Research. Technical Report PPAFTR-1124-84-1 (1984)

Trinh, V.C., Gonzalez, A.J.: Identifying contexts from observed human performance. IEEE. Trans. Hum. Mach. Syst. **43**(4), 359–370 (2013)

Trinh, V.C., Stensrud, B.S., Gonzalez, A.J.: Implementation of a prototype context-based reasoning model onto a physical platform. Proceedings of the Second Swedish-American Workshop on Modeling and Simulation, Cocoa Beach (2004)

Turner, R.M.: Context-sensitive reasoning for autonomous agents and cooperative distributed problem solving. Proceedings of the 1993 IJCAI Workshop on Using Knowledge in Context, Chambery (1993)

Chapter 31
Representing Experience-Based Reasoning by Contextual Graphs

Patrick Brézillon

Abstract Experts' experience concerns the progressive elaboration of a context-specific model during the decision-making process. However, context modeling generally stays implicit because experts focus on the result of the decision-making. Modeling context within a decision-making process supposes a uniform representation of knowledge, reasoning and contexts. In the Contextual-Graphs formalism, a decision-making episode is represented as a contextual graph in which each path represents a practice developed by an actor in a specific working context for reaching the decision. By incremental accumulation of the practices developed by experts, a contextual graph becomes a living experience base with the decision-making process. Such an experience base may be used by experts for collaborative decision-making, or by future experts for training how to behave in the different ways to make a decision according to the variants of the working context. The experience base can be exploited by an intelligent assistant system for proposing an effective support to decision makers by a new type of simulation, compared to previous knowledge-based systems. Several applications have been developed in the last 10 years, including the last two being a project in medicine for supporting pathologists in breast cancer diagnosis, and a project for decision-makers in a command and control room.

31.1 Introduction

Experts rely on a highly compiled experience. They are few and generally act under temporal pressure because they are very concerned about the consequences of their decision, not the contextualization process leading to it. As a consequence, their expertise appears as chunks of contextual knowledge that never can be reused directly because each context in decision-making is unique. Thus, any experience must be adapted to be efficient in another context. This supposes (1) identifying how the initial experience was contextualized, (2) isolating the reusable part of the experience, and (3) applying the process of contextualization in the new working

P. Brézillon (✉)
Laboratoire d'Informatique de Paris 6 (LIP6),
University Pierre and Marie Curie (UPMC), Paris, France
e-mail: patrick.brezillon@lip6.fr

© Springer Science+Business Media New York 2014

P. Brézillon, A. J. Gonzalez (eds.), *Context in Computing*,
DOI 10.1007/978-1-4939-1887-4_31

509

context (Brézillon 2011). Conversely, the executive board of an enterprise develops procedures by decontextualizing practices that are accumulated in a flat way (e.g. as in incident reports). A procedure tries to cover a class of problems, while an actor develops a practice by adapting the procedure to the specific working context (a recontextualization process) in which the actor makes a decision. Procedures are described in pairs {problem, solution}, while practices suppose a triple {problem, context, solution} representation.

Real experience reuse requires a management of the process of contextualization, decontextualization and recontextualization. This supposes a formalism that provides a uniform representation of elements of knowledge, reasoning and contexts. For exploiting such experience bases, a support system must be equipped with powerful functions, such as simulation and learning.

Hereafter, the paper is organized as follows. Section 31.2 discusses the need to make context explicit for representing experience and the details of the Contextual-Graphs formalism. Section 31.3 presents the specifics of simulating experiences. Section 31.4 compares our approach to other works. Section 31.5 ends this paper with a conclusion.

31.2 Context-Based Acquisition of Experience

31.2.1 Making Context Explicit

A practice represents how work actually gets done, not what is supposed to happen (i.e. the procedure). Contextual cues in a practice rely on actors' preferences, the particular of the task realization, the situation where the task is realized and the local environment where resources are available. As a consequence, there are as many practices (or activities) as actors and contexts.

Context depends on the actor's focus, but, conversely, the focus determines what is contextual knowledge (important knowledge for the focus) and what is external knowledge at a given moment. At each step of the decision-making process, a subset of the contextual knowledge is proceduralized for addressing the current focus. This "proceduralized context" is built from elements of the (highly heterogeneous) contextual knowledge that are invoked, assembled, organized, structured and situated according to the given focus.

A contextual element corresponds to an information piece that must be analyzed. The value taken by the contextual element when the focus is on it—its instance—is taken into account as long as the situation is under analysis. The distinction between a contextual element and its instance is important for the reuse of experience because the difference between the two contexts may come from different instantiation of a given contextual element. Otherwise, a past context and the working context may differ on a contextual element (e.g. a contextual element only exists in one of the contexts). For example, most car accidents occur on the way from home to work, a well-known way that leads the driver to rely on past experience, say, for crossing an intersection. An accident occurs when the driver does not pay attention to the

Table 31.1 A classification of opposed terms

Level/Context	Decontextualized	Contextualized
Strategic	Logic of functioning	Logic of use
Tactical	Task	Activity
Operational	Procedure	Practice

specificity of the current context at hand where there is a new contextual element (e.g. oil poured from a truck on the pavement) or a change in the instantiation of a contextual element (e.g. the traffic light is off). Experience management involves considering explicitly the working context as well as the decision-making process.

31.2.2 A Problem Appearing in All Disciplines

The difference between procedure and practice appears in different approaches for modeling human behaviors: procedures and practices (Brézillon 2007), task and activity (Leplat and Hoc 1983; Clancey 2002), logic of functioning and logic of use (Richard 1983). The reuses of decision-making can be put in the light of these different perspectives for modeling human behaviors. In one perspective (procedure, task, logic of functioning), one considers, from an external viewpoint, only the task, while according to the actor's viewpoint, one considers the actor, the task, the situation in which the actor realizes the task, and the local environment with its resources available. Brézillon (2011) proposes an interpretation of this dichotomy in terms of {decisional levels (policy, strategy, tactics, operation), contexts} as illustrated in Table 31.1. Links with the decisional levels are discussed in (Brézillon 2011) and results are applied in (Fan 2011). This paper discusses the dichotomy in terms of context and the consequence for experience modeling.

A procedure is the (formal) translation of a task realization at an operational level. The translation takes into account task realization and the constraints imposed by the logic of functioning at the strategic level. Conversely, a practice is the expression of an activity led by an actor accomplishing a task in a particular situation with the available resources in the local environment. The actor's experience appears as an accumulation of practices based on activities developed in logic of use. Thus, experience can be discussed in terms of activities and, concretely represented in terms of practices.

A decision-making episode is an activity that starts with the analysis of the working context (identification of the relevant contextual elements and their instantiations) to have a picture of the problem as complete as possible before any action. Brézillon (2011) speaks of a two-step decision-making. The instantiated contextual elements are then assembled, organized and structured in a proceduralized context that allows the actor to make his decision and continue his activity. Then, making a decision consists of the assembling and execution of actions in a sequence. Indeed, these steps constitute a unique process.

31.2.3   A Representation by Contextual-Graphs Formalism

Brézillon (2007) introduces the Contextual-Graphs (CxG) formalism for obtaining a uniform representation of elements of knowledge, reasoning and context. Contextual graphs are acyclic because of the time-directed representation and guarantee of algorithm termination. With a series–parallel structure, each contextual graph has exactly one root and one end node because the decision-making process starts in one state of affairs and ends in another state of affairs (generally with different solutions on the different paths) and the branches express only different contextually dependent ways to achieve this goal. A contextual graph represents the realization of a task, and each path corresponds to a practice developed by an actor in a given context. Thus, a contextual graph represents the accumulated experience of one or several actors.

Contextual elements—the key concept of the CxG formalism—organize experiences differently from knowledge bases of expert systems, in which knowledge was represented in a flat way because context was not made explicit. Contextual elements, which concern the actor, the task, the situation and the local environment, have a heterogeneous nature.

The notion of chunk of knowledge proposed by Schank (1983) has a clear implementation in contextual graphs as the proceduralized context, i.e. an ordered series of instantiated contextual elements. However, a proceduralized context is either static when attached to an item in the CxG, or dynamic when attached to the practice development (Brézillon 2007). Moreover, a particular action (or an activity) may exist on two different paths, thus with different proceduralized contexts (i.e. two different contexts). Brézillon (2007) give the example of a driver that brakes hard when arriving at an intersection because another car approaches it from the right side. It is a context of correct driving if nobody is behind the driver, and a dangerous context if there is another car just behind. Thus, the proceduralized context specifies the quality of an action or activity. The main point here is that the simulation of a practice development requires to take into account the working context.

The CxG_Platform (Brézillon 2011) contains an editor with the usual functions for managing a contextual graph. The piece of software is available at cxg.fr under GNU license. It is an interface used by an actor wishing to edit a contextual graph, reading practices for selecting the best one in his working context, browsing alternatives of a practice, exploring a contextual graph at a different granularity (by representing an activity by an item or by the contextual graph representing this activity), analyzing contextual information attached to each item (date of creation, comments, etc.). Design and development of the software is user-centered for an intuitive use by non-specialists in computer science and mathematics. An interesting function of the CxG_Platform is the possibility to link an item to an external document (Word, PDF, Web page, etc.), to run an external piece of software, etc. (This was used in the medical application, see Attieh et al. 2013). The behavior of the platform itself can be described in a contextual graph (see Brézillon 2014).

31.3 Experience-Based Simulation

31.3.1 Introduction

Previously, expert systems were considered as "model based" and introduced a means of modeling processes qualitatively (Clancey 1989). The CxG formalism provides an organization of practices structured by contextual elements. Each path corresponds to a practice development in a specific context. Thus, a support system exploiting a CxG has to develop and execute a practice at the same time. This introduces a new approach in the use of the simulation.

31.3.2 Model-Based Versus CxG-Based Simulation

31.3.2.1 Model-Based Simulation

Usually, a simulation describes the evolution of a (formal) model, starting from a set of initial conditions. The model expresses a statement about a real system that is based on formalized concepts and hypothesis about the functioning of the real system. Such a model is given by a structure that is specified by parameters that appear in the relationships between variables (a typical formalism for representation is differential equations). A model-based simulation gives a description of the evolution of the variables with respect to an independent variable, generally time, given a set of values for the parameters and a set of initial conditions for the variables. The evolution of some variables is then compared to temporal observations of the real system. (We will not discuss here the time-based or real time aspect of the representation).

In a formal model, time appears through the evolution of the variables from the model structure and relationships between variables (e.g. $y(t)$ in a model expressed in the formalism of differential equations like $dy/dt = -ay + b$). The working context in a model-based simulation (initial conditions and parameter values) only concerns the initial state of the simulation: The initial conditions $y(0)$ specify the initial state of the model, and the parameter values generally are not modified during the simulation. There is no "unpredicted event" during an experiment.

"Browsing" a model is exploiting its mathematical properties for predicting variables' evolution (number and stability of steady states, self-oscillations, exponentially decreasing curve, etc.) for different sets of parameter values that verify some constraints, such as the conditions to have an unstable steady state.

At a quantitative level, model-based simulation is used to find the best set of parameter values and initial conditions describing a set of real-world observations (generally by optimization methods). Here, the formal model is used for the prediction of any behavior of the real system in other contexts, assimilating this context to constraints and initial conditions. In a model-based simulation, the working context describes the initial state only, while variables evolve during the entire model-based simulation.

Formal models address the evolution of a system, and the corresponding trajectory is unique because the model structure is unique (parameter values are constant during the entire simulation). Thus, a model-based simulation relies on {model structure, parameters, initial conditions on variables} where model structure, parameter values and initial conditions are fixed during all the simulation.

31.3.2.2 CxG-Based Simulation

At a qualitative level, a contextual graph is a structure of practices organized by context-specific models that correspond to all the working contexts already faced by actors. A CxG-based simulation supposes the joint building (through instantiation of contextual elements) and development of a practice (i.e. the equivalent of a model structure).

At the quantitative level, a CxG simulator needs to know only the instantiations of the contextual elements that will be used in the development of the practice (i.e. the contextual elements belonging to the developed practice), and the effects of action execution. The execution of an action may modify the instantiation of a contextual element. The change in working context (i.e. the change in instantiation of a contextual element) leads the simulator to consider another practice with different consequences: the halting of the simulation (e.g. the required resource is no longer available), the simulation must be restarted in the new working context, a routine action in the practice development must be executed several times, and a contextual element not yet met during the current practice development. In the last situation, the simulation can be pursued because there is no divergence because the change of context does not impact the practice development.

31.3.2.3 Assessment

Table 31.2 gives a comparison of model-based simulation and CxG-based simulation according to seven characteristics.

31.3.3 CxG-Based Simulation Management

A practice that is developed in the working context is the "best practice" because the practice is built at the same time it is used, thus taking into account all that occurs during this process. For example, action execution may modify the instantiation of a contextual element because of, say, to lack of availability of a resource. This change of the working context is visible if we consider the activity represented by the practice development, not the task realization.

The working context has two parts. First, a static part contains the list of the contextual elements in the contextual graph and their known values. Second, a dynamic part gives the list of the known instances, i.e. the value taken by contextual elements at simulation time.

Table 31.2 Comparison of model- and CxG-based simulations

	Model-based	CxG-based
Goal	Represent a real system	Represent a task realization on the real system (a level above the real system)
Real system	An internal viewpoint	An external viewpoint
Tactical level	A model structure	A graph of model structures (practices)
Operational level	Simulation from an initial state	Simulation and building of a context specific model
Working context	Initial values of variables and parameters (constant during the simulation)	Contextual elements and instantiations (may vary during the simulation)
Simulation	Evolution of the variables in the model	Building and use of a model specific of the working context with practice development
Type of support	Prediction, interpretation of deviation (real-system centered)	Task realization on the real system (use-centered)

A contextual element allows the management of context-dependent methods for a step of the task realization according to the working context. The instantiation can be known prior to the practice development or provided by the actor to the system during the practice development or found by the simulator in the local environment.

During a CxG-based simulation, the instantiation of contextual elements may be altered by either an external event or an internal event. The external event corresponds to an unpredicted event, i.e. not represented in the contextual graph. For example, an external resource stops to be available. An internal event occurs as the result of an action execution. An action (or an activity) is executed at the operational level (e.g. execution of an external program or a service). The way in which an action is executed matters at the operational level, but consequences impact practice development at the tactical level. The most obvious consequence is the duration of the action execution that may delay the practice development.

The alteration of an instantiation implies a change of the working context. The first type of change may concern a contextual element already crossed. Then, the simulator must decide (1) to stop the development of the current practice and re-start the simulation (for the building of a new practice) in the new working context; (2) to redo the part of the practice that is concerned (e.g. for a routine action); or (3) to finish the development of the practice at hand and then analyze the need for a new simulation in the new working context (e.g. as long as the working context evolves). The second type of change concerns a contextual element not yet reached by the focus, and the simulator can continue its simulation to progress in the contextual graph because this change of instantiation does not affect the part of the practice already built. The lesson here is that the working context must be intimately associated with the simulation.

31.3.4   Related Functionalities

31.3.4.1   Knowledge Acquisition Management

A contextual graph allows the incremental enrichment of experiences by the refinement of existing practices. The introduction of a new practice generally corresponds to a contextual element that was not considered explicitly up to now because always having the same value, but with a different value in the working context at hand. Thus, this contextual element is introduced in the contextual graph with the value implicitly considered up to now (with the action used previously), and the value taken in the working context with the action(s) corresponding to this new instantiation. It is possible because experience is organized in a contextual graph as practices structured by contextual elements. The knowledge is acquired in its context of use, when needed.

31.3.4.2   Learning Management

Conversely to the old image of an expert system as an oracle and the user as a novice (Karsenty and Brézillon 1995), actors are experts in their domain. Thus, a decision support system must follow (as a "novice") what the expert (the "oracle") is doing, and benefits of the opportunity to learn incrementally new practices developed by experts during their interaction (and stored in the base of experience). Generally, discriminating between two methods (i.e. two practices) is often a problem of missing knowledge. However, there is an eventual more drastic change of the experience base when the expert decides that it is not a simple action that is concerned but a sub graph. For example, consider in Fig. 31.1, action 1 "Take water" in coffee preparation. Implicitly, the actor considers that he is speaking of running water, i.e. this contextual element "Type of water" does not appear in the representation. Now, suppose that the same actor is in a hurry one morning and decides to use "hot (running) water" to make his coffee more rapidly. A decision support system that will observe the actor's behavior will fail to follow the actor reasoning because it does not know the difference between the choices "cold water" and "hot water". Then, the actor will have to provide the system (see Fig. 31.1) with the contextual element CE1 "In a hurry?" with the two values, namely "No" for the previous action 1 "Take (cold) water" and the value "Yes" for the new action 2 "Take hot water".

Now, suppose that the decision support system helps another actor in the same task of coffee preparation, and that this new actor only uses mineral water instead of running water to prepare his coffee. Then, when the system will ask him "Are you in a hurry?", and the actor will have to explain that this question may be relevant for running water, but not for mineral water in a bottle. The system will need to add a new contextual element CE2 "Type of water?" with the value "running water" for the previous practices (toward CE1 in Fig. 31.1) and the value "mineral water" for a new action 3 "Take your bottle of water".

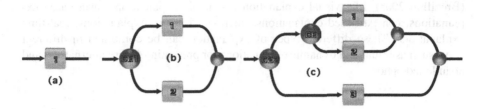

Fig. 31.1 The two types of learning in coffee preparation

A decision support system may learn in two ways. In the first learning, the system learns by assimilation of a new practice (refinement of an existing practice). It is a practice-based learning. In the second learning, the structure of the experience base is modified for integrating a new method for preparing coffee (i.e. use of mineral water versus running water). It is a procedure-based learning and the system must learn by accommodation.

31.3.4.3 Explanation Generation

More than 20 years ago, Artificial Intelligence was considered as the science of explanation (Kodratoff 1987), but few concrete results were obtained at that time (e.g. see PRC-GDR 1989, in French) because explanations were generated from domain knowledge, not contextual knowledge. With Contextual Graphs, a decision support system may be an explainer for actors not quite familiar with practices for realizing a task. The training here consists of explaining the elements used during a practice development, especially contextual elements and their possible instantiations in a chunk of contextual knowledge (i.e. the proceduralized context). Note that a contextual element corresponds to a piece of "surface knowledge" (e.g. take hot water) representing a more complex "deep knowledge" (e.g. the goal of the coffee machine is to make hot the water before to pour it on the coffee, and using hot water will speed up this long process).

The explicit representation of context at the same level of knowledge and reasoning provides now a new insight on explanation generation. Previously, we showed that a proceduralized context is attached to each item in a contextual graph. Its representation (in the CxG formalism) is an ordered sequence of instantiated contextual elements that can be used for explanation generation.

A decision support system, which exploits a contextual graph, applies a human expert's reasoning, and not an "automated reasoning" constrained by control knowledge hidden in the inference engine (e.g. fire the first rule f the list). In the previous example, the type of water (running water versus mineral water) appears in first on the path, but its justification relies on the next contextual element (in a hurry or not).

The uniform representation of elements of knowledge, reasoning and contexts allows the generation of different types of expressive context-based explanations

(Brézillon 2008), like visual explanations, dynamic explanations, user-based explanations, context-based explanations, micro- and macro-explanations, real-time explanations. These different types of explanation can be combined in different ways such as visual and dynamic explanations for presenting future alternatives and abandoned options.

31.3.5 Discussion

The contextual-graph representation puts in the front stage different interesting findings for working on an experience base.

First, a contextual graph is the representation of a task realization by one or different actors. The realization of a task by actors that have different roles are represented in different contextual graphs because they do not use the same methods. For example, a physician and a computer engineer analyze bio-images differently. This implies a new step for representing collaboration of actors through contextual-graph interaction.

Second, a contextual graph gives a representation of a task realization at a given level of granularity at which actions are the building block of the representation. Thus, requirements for action execution do not matter. However, some aspects may have some effects on the representation. For example, time for an action execution may modify the instantiation of a contextual element and thus the practice development. This means that for developing a practice in the contextual graph like in a simulation, we need to consider it within the working context.

Three, for interacting intelligently with an actor that is an expert in his domain, the decision support system, on the one hand, adheres to expert's viewpoint, and, on the other hand, makes explicit the needed tools for the management of context, actions, the contextual graph, learning, explanations, etc. We are working on such an architecture in a companion paper in this book (Brézillon 2014). The key point here is that domain knowledge and expertise are only in the experience base. Globally, a contextual graph (i.e. "optimal" practices in their working contexts) is a better solution than the "best practice" that is generally consider with the few contextual elements found in a large number of practices.

31.4 Related Works

In a classical case-based reasoning (CBR) scenario, a case consists of a problem description and a solution. A case contains a set of (structured) information entities, and optional artifacts. Structured information is represented as attribute—value pairs, while the optional meta-information contains unstructured textual information. Atzmueller (2007) uses stored cases (experiences) for selecting an appropriate task and method, reusing those stored task-configurations that are similar to a (partially) defined characterization. The process of capturing and reusing complex task-experiences is done in four main steps: Experience Retrieval, Task Instantiation, Task Evaluation and Deployment, and Experience Maintenance. Thus, a case is re-called as a whole and its characterization is then adapted to the context at hand. There are now extensions of this formalism towards process-oriented CBR[1] and trace-based reasoning (Mille 2006). In the CxG formalism, the practice, the equivalent of the case, is identified jointly with its use. In the CBR, the approach is "result-oriented" while in Contextual Graphs, the approach is "reasoning-oriented."

Clancey (2002) proposed that solving a particular problem (e.g. diagnosing a patient) involves creating situation-specific models. "Situation-specific" refers to a particular case, setting, or scenario. "Situation-specific" is not "situated cognition" that refers to how people conceive and thus coordinate their identity, values, and activities in an ongoing process enabled by high-order consciousness. In the CxG approach, context is concerned an actor accomplishing a task in a particular sit-uation in a specific local environment. A practice development is associated with the progressive building of a "context-specific model." For Clancey, the "situation-specific model" is embedded in the problem solving as a static description that is fixed initially and filled progressively during the problem solving. Conversely, the context-specific model (i.e. the proceduralized context) is built in parallel with the practice development with the movement of contextual elements entering and leav-ing the proceduralized context. Note that we consider also situation as a part of the context.

A model-based simulation is a top-down (deductive) modeling, while a CxG-based simulation corresponds to a bottom-up (inductive) modeling. In a model-based simulation, the whole working context is defined at the start of the simulation and stays constant during the simulation, while in a CxG-based simulation, the working context evolves during practice development. A formal model is given initially (its structure is confronted to observations), while a practice (the contextualized model of a task realization) is built progressively from the contextual graph and evolves with its working context. In that sense CxG-based simulation is a particular type of simulation. The behavior of a CxG simulator is comparable with the usual model-based simulator's behavior, supposing that (1) contextual elements in the contextual graph can be compared to the parameters in the formal model (a change of parameter values impacts the model behavior as a change of instantiation modifies the practice developed), and (2) variables in a model-based simulation are related to the result of the progressive building of the practice corresponding to the working context.

These approaches also can be discussed with respect to decisional levels: Case-based reasoning approach is at an operational level and model-based simulation at a tactical level. A decision support system, which uses an experience base, plays the role of a CxG Browser at the tactical (qualitative) level and of a CxG Simulator at the operational (quantitative) level. The CxG Browser allows working on the experience base. The CxG Simulator is a tool at the tactic level or the operational level because it takes into account the specificity of the working context to find the best practice.

---

[1] www.iccbr.org/iccbr12/ICCBR-12_WS_proc.pdf.

31.5 Conclusion

Our goal is to develop an intelligent assistant system (IAS, as a new generation of decision support systems) for users that have a high level of expertise in a domain that is not well known or overly complex. Experts' experience is highly compiled, like chunks of contextual knowledge built mainly by incremental enrichment of their experience. Such expertise is generally used in a decision-making process leading to a critical and definitive decision. In the MICO project, the export is an anatomo-cyto-pathologist that analyzes digital slides (coming from biopsies) to diagnose whether or not a patient in a surgery has breast cancer.

The consequences are:

1. An IAS follows what the expert is doing, how he is doing it, and anticipates potential needs. This supposes that the IAS possesses a representation of the experts' reasoning, may fix alone all the simple problems, and prepare a complete folder on complex situations letting experts make their decision. It is the role of an experience base.
2. The IAS must work from practices developed by experts in different working contexts. The line of reasoning of the system is drawn from lines of experts' reasoning described in the experience base, which gives a user-centered representation of the task realization.
3. The IAS must be able to develop the decision-making process in real time to analyze the associated diagnosis and action built by experts during their reasoning. Indeed, the IAS simultaneously develops the decision-making process and its context-specific model like experts.
4. The decision-making process is highly contextual. The IAS must benefit of its interaction with the expert to learn new practices and acquire incrementally the missing knowledge in its context of use, and thus enriching its experience base.
5. Making context explicit in the experience base leads to the possibility of generating relevant explanations for presenting the rationale behind a practice with alternatives abandoned; training (future) experts on the different practices developed; facilitating experience sharing among experts in a kind of dynamic corporate memory; allowing a first step towards the certification of their protocol. An example in anatomo-cyto pathology is given in (Attieh et al. 2013).
6. The main tool of an IAS is the CxG simulator. Its originality is to build and apply at the same time the practice. Indeed the CxG simulator is the key element of a real-time decision making because it is possible to account for unpredicted events, thanks to an explicit modeling of context as contextual elements covering, the user, the task realization, the working situation, the local environment with its available resources (Brézillon 2014). All the items are interdependent and also time-dependent. Thus, IASs cover a more general problematic than context-aware applications. This seems to us also the key point for mobile decision making because the instantiations of contextual elements are taken into account at the moment it is necessary.

Acknowledgments This work is supported by grants from ANR TecSan for the MICO project (ANR-10-TECS-015), and we thank partners (IPAL, TRIBVN, UIMAP of Service d'Anatomie Cytologie Pathologie at La Pitié, Thalès, Agfa) for fruitful discussions, and from the TACTIC project funded by the ASTRID program of Délégation Générale aux Armées.

References

Attieh, E., Calvo, J., Brézillon, P., Capron, F.: Modélisation informatisée des étapes d'un examen anatomo-cyto-pathologique: "Graphes contextuels". Poster presented at 36es Assises de Pathologie Versailles, 23 & 24 mai (2013)

Atzmueller, M.: Experience management with task-configurations and task-patterns for descriptive data mining. KESE, 2007. http://ceur-ws.org/Vol-282/02-AtzmuellerM-KESE-Paper CRC.pdf (2007) Accessed 18 Sept 2014

Brézillon, P.: Context modeling: task model and model of practices. In: Kokinov B., et al. (eds.) Modeling and Using Context (CONTEXT-07), LNAI 4635, pp. 122–135. Springer, Heilderberg (2007)

Brézillon, P.: Explaining for contextualizing and contextualizing for explaining. In: Proceedings of ExaCt 2008, CEUR Workshop Proceedings, ISSN 1613-0073, online CEUR-WS.org/Vol-391/00010001.pdf (2008)

Brézillon, P.: Contextualization of scientific workflows. In: Beigl M., et al. (eds.) Modeling and Using Context (CONTEXT-11), LNAI 6967, pp. 40–53. Springer, Heidelberg (2011)

Brézillon, P.: Chapter 7: Intelligent assistant systems. In: Gonzalez A.J., Brézillon. P. (eds.) Context in Computing: A Cross-disciplinary Approach for Modeling the Real World through Contextual Reasoning, Springer, Heidelberg (2014) (to appear)

Clancey, W.: Viewing knowledge bases as qualitative models. IEEE Expert: Intell. Syst. Appl. **4**(2), 9–23 (1989)

Clancey, W.J.: Simulating activities: relating motives, deliberation, and attentive coordination. Cognit. Syst. Res. **3**(3), 471–499 (2002)

Fan, X.: Context-oriented scientific worlflow and its application in medicine. Ph.D. Thesis, University Pierre and Marie Curie, Paris, France (2011)

Karsenty, L., Brézillon, P.: Cooperative problem solving and explanation. Expert Syst. Appl. **8**(4), 445–462 (1995)

Kodratoff, Y.: Is artificial intelligence a subfield of computer science or is artificial intelligence the science of explanation? In: Bratko, I., Lavrac, N. (eds.) Progress in Machine Learning, pp. 91–106, Sigma, Cheshire (1987)

Leplat, J., Hoc, J.M.: Tâche et activité dans l'analyse psychologique des situations. Cah. Psychol. Cogn. **3**, 49–63 (1983)

Mille, A.: From case-based reasoning to traces-based reasoning. Ann. Rev. Control **30**, 223–232 (2006)

PRC-GDR: Actes des 3e journées nationales PRC-GDR IA organisées par le CNRS (1989)

Richard, J.F.: Logique du fonctionnement et logique de l'utilisation. Rapport de Recherche INRIA no 202 (1983)

Schank, R.C.: Dynamic memory, a theory of learning in computers and people, Cambridge University Press, Cambridge (1983)

Chapter 32
Context-Mediated Behavior

Roy M. Turner

Abstract Context-mediated behavior (CMB) is an approach to giving intelligent agents the ability to recognize their context at all times and to behave appropriately for it. It is based on the idea that contexts—classes of situations—should be represented explicitly as first-class objects. These representations (contextual schemas) are then retrieved based on a diagnostic process of context assessment. Contextual schemas contain descriptive knowledge about the context, including predicted features and context-dependent meaning of concepts. They also include prescriptive features that tell the agent how to behave in the context. This approach has been implemented in several systems, including an intelligent controller for autonomous underwater vehicles (AUVs), and the author is now exploring distributing the process in multiagent systems.

32.1 Introduction

Context-sensitivity is a hallmark of intelligent adaptive behavior. As the context changes, an agent may find that goals that were important are now not, or vice versa. It may encounter unanticipated events that can only be understood and responded to appropriately by considering the context in which they arise. Different actions may be more appropriate for achieving goals in one context than in another. And some routine aspects of behavior, such as how loudly to talk or how close to get to obstacles, may be modulated by knowledge about the context.

Animals and humans are adept at fitting their behavior to their context (e.g.,Glass and Holyoak 1986; Mantovani 1996). Artificial agents also need to be aware of and adapt to their context if they are to perform well or, in the case of some real-world agents, if they are to survive. Not only that, but the process of acting within the context should be effortless, so that cognitive resources can be devoted to the agent's problem-solving effort.

R. M. Turner (✉)
School of Computing and Information Science, University of Maine,
Orono, ME 04469, USA
e-mail: rturner@maine.edu

© Springer Science+Business Media New York 2014
P. Brézillon, A. J. Gonzalez (eds.), *Context in Computing*,
DOI 10.1007/978-1-4939-1887-4_32

Unfortunately, until recently, context-sensitivity in artificial agents has for the most part been an afterthought, or at best, a second-class concern. Most work has instead been focused—and for very good reason—on achieving agents' goals. This is challenging enough, and without this, the agents can do nothing. Context has traditionally been taken into account only implicitly during goal achievement, for example as plan preconditions or rule antecedent clauses, and its impact on other aspects of behavior has not been the subject of much work at all until recently (as discussed in this volume, for example).

However, much can be gained by focusing attention on context. If an agent's context can be explicitly reasoned about and examined, then it can more effectively and efficiently be taken into account during goal achievement. General knowledge about aspects of goal achievement that rely on context can be grouped together with a representation of the context, then used whenever the context is encountered.

One aspect of this is deciding which goals should be pursued in the context. For example, an ambulance driver en route to the hospital with a patient, even if he or she has the goal of picking up the laundry, should not pursue that goal in that context; it should not even come to mind. Recognizing the context can also quickly tell the agent how to achieve goals appropriately in the situation. For example, in a city, getting to one's destination might be best done by taking a taxi, while in the context of being in a rural area, driving might be best; satisfying thirst in one's home is best done by getting a drink of water from the kitchen, while in a restaurant, asking a server is more appropriate. While regular scheduling and planning methods can be used to determine which goal to work on and how to achieve them, both of these are computationally-intensive (and intractable in the worst case). By using knowledge about the context, the agent can potentially save time and avoid expending this computational effort, instead quickly and automatically determining on which goal to focus and how to achieve it.

Recognizing the context can also let the agent know how to appropriately set behavioral parameters. For example, an autonomous underwater vehicle (AUV) entering a harbor should, upon recognizing the context, automatically turn on its obstacle avoidance sonar and tighten its depth envelope to avoid surface traffic and the bottom.

Handling unanticipated events is also context-dependent, where "unanticipated" means here events that are not necessarily novel, but for which it is not possible to predict the exact time of occurrence, or even if they will occur at all. When driving, the event of someone stepping in front of the car is unanticipated in this sense. In this context, this is immediately identifiable as an important event that must be quickly handled by stereotypical actions: braking, swerving, etc. On the other hand, while walking across a university campus, if someone steps in front of the same person, the event is perceived and handled quite differently. In both cases, identifying the event from environmental and sensory queues, assessing its importance, and choosing a response, all have to be done quickly and correctly for the context.

In order for an artificial agent to behave in a context-appropriate way, it needs to be able to represent knowledge about contexts in such a way that it can determine which context it is in, then easily use the associated contextual knowledge. This means that contexts themselves need to be explicitly represented, so that the agent can reason about them and compare them to the current situation, associate contextual knowledge with them, and explicitly commit to the context it is in.

Context-mediated behavior (CMB) (Turner 1998) is an approach to context-sensitive reasoning that represents contexts explicitly as first-class objects and associates related contextual knowledge with them. These objects are called *contextual schemas* (c-schemas). A context manager works in tandem with the agent's usual reasoning system (the *performance element* (Russell and Norvig 2003)) to provide it with contextual knowledge as needed. The context manager assesses the situation via a differential diagnostic process, resulting in a commitment to one or more of the c-schemas to represent the current context. Contextual knowledge from these c-schemas is then merged and given to the performance element. The context manager monitors the situation as it changes, updating its assessment of the context as needed. The context manager can set behavioral parameters and assess how to respond to events, and the performance element simply operates as usual, but always with highly context-dependent information.

In the remainder of this chapter, we first describe what we mean by "context" and the representation of contexts and contextual information in CMB. We next focus on the CMB process, including context assessment, event handling, and disseminating contextual knowledge. We then review related work, followed by conclusions and future research directions, including new work on decentralizing CMB for multiagent systems.

32.2   Representing Context

We make a distinction between the situation and the context. An agent's complete *situation* consists of all the features of the world that could potentially affect its behavior. This includes the agent's own internal physical states, its goals, plans, and beliefs, features of the environment, and what it may know about other agents. Note that this means that the situation is potentially infinite (cf. McCarthy (1993). However, we are more interested in the portion of the situation that can be observed or produce effects on the agent's behavior, what we call the *observable situation*; this is what "situation" will mean in this chapter.

For many authors, a situation *is* the agent's context (see, e.g., (McCarthy 1996) in artificial intelligence, and the general definition of "context" in psychology). However, to us, a situation is observed without regard to how it may or may not impact an agent's behavior, while a context is different.

To us, a *context* is a recognized class of situations that has implications for the agent's behavior. A given situation is thus an instance of one or more contexts.

This is a useful distinction: it allows an agent to generalize over a range of different instances of what is, to the agent, the same context. Thus an autonomous underwater vehicle performing a search mission in Portsmouth (NH) Harbor, in Boston Harbor, or in San Francisco Bay is, in each case, in the context of being in a harbor as well as the context of performing a search mission. Knowledge the agent has about how to behave in a harbor or on search missions can thus be brought to bear in each situation. This can help the agent predict unseen features of the situation as well as know how to behave appropriately.

32.2.1   Contextual Schemas

Contextual schemas (c-schemas) are the knowledge structures used in CMB to represent contexts. They grew out of earlier work in schema-based reasoning for medical diagnosis (Turner 1994) which, in turn, grew out of case-based reasoning (CBR) (e.g., Kolodner 1993). A contextual schema both represents a context and serves as the organizing point for all knowledge about how to behave in the context.

The knowledge contained in a c-schema can be divided into descriptive knowledge and prescriptive knowledge.[1] *Descriptive knowledge* has to do with describing the context being represented. *Prescriptive knowledge*, on the other hand, has to do with telling the agent how to behave in the context. Figure 32.1 shows a c-schema from our AUV domain, and an ontology for contextual knowledge is discussed elsewhere (Turner et al. 2014).

32.2.1.1   Descriptive Knowledge

A c-schema's descriptive knowledge consists in part of the salient features of the context it represents: features of the world that are expected as well as features that *have* to be present for the situation to be considered a member of the context. For example, a c-schema representing "search mission in a harbor" would include information such as: the agent has a search goal; the water column is shallow; there is likely to be surface traffic; and shore is nearby.

Some features predicted may not have yet been seen. C-schemas can thus help make sense of new sensor information. For example, a c-schema representing operating in a hostile harbor could predict that mines are present, thus providing an important hypothesis for a new sonar contact.

C-schemas can also provide context-dependent semantics of concepts. For instance, in prior work (Turner 1997), c-schemas provided context-dependent definitions of fuzzy linguistic values (e.g., "nominal", "too-deep") simply by specifying their membership functions for the context, which allowed context-independent rules (e.g., "if too deep, go up") to be used in a context-dependent way (e.g., by having the meaning of "too-deep", and, indirectly, the resultant meaning of "up", specified by the context). Similarly, in another project a neural network's "semantics" were changed to fit the context by allowing c-schemas to specify the net's weights and

---

[1] In some work related to CMB, a third type, predictive knowledge, was identified (Whitsel 2013); however this can be viewed as a subtype of descriptive knowledge.

Fig. 32.1 A portion of the c-schema c-harbor, representing the context of being in a harbor, with annotations. (From Turner (1998); copyright 1998 Elsevier, reprinted with permission)

connections (Arritt and Turner 2003). When the context is recognized, the neural network automatically assumes the correct structure and weights for the context. This also has the potential to overcome some of the over-generalization to which neural networks are prone. Any learning done in the context is stored for later use in that context.

32.2.1.2 Prescriptive Knowledge

A c-schema's prescriptive knowledge tells an agent how it should behave in the context. This includes both goal-directed behavior (e.g., planning) as well as non-goal-directed behavior, such as arises from setting behavioral parameters and handling unanticipated events.

Goal-Directed Behavior Knowledge about goals that are important in a context is stored in the corresponding c-schema. This includes both how to focus attention on appropriate goals and how to achieve the goals.

An agent's focus of attention is governed by which goal or goals it chooses to work on at any given time. Goals will have different priorities based on their relationship to other goals, who assigned them (internal source vs. exogenous, e.g.), the likely result of *not* achieving them (especially for so-called *preservation* or *maintenance* goals), and, in some cases, convention (Albert et al. 2007).

A c-schema can influence the focus of attention for a context by changing goal priorities, by indicating a goal should not be pursued, or by suggesting a goal that was not active until the context was entered. As shown in Fig. 32.1, c-schemas store description of goals important in the context, along with whether or not the goals should be pursued and their priorities, either in absolute terms or relative to other goals that may be active. For example, a c-schema representing a rescue mission context would dictate that handling a leak is less important than rescuing a human.

C-schemas can also provide knowledge about threats to active goals. For example, a c-schema representing a context in which a magnetometer has failed would predict that any plan requiring the sensor would also fail, even if those plans are not yet nearing execution. This can help the agent anticipate future problems.

C-schemas also provide knowledge about how to achieve goals, which is highly context-dependent. The form of this knowledge differs depending on the kind of performance element the agent uses. Most work on CMB has involved schema-based reasoners (Turner 1994) that use *procedural schemas* (p-schemas) to achieve goals. P-schemas are similar to hierarchical plans, with steps that can be executable actions, subgoals to achieve, or other p-schemas. If a goal is best handled differently in a context than usual, then the c-schema will have a link from that goal to a context-specific entry point in the p-schema memory.

Other kinds of performance elements can be supported, too. For example, in prior work, we have used c-schemas to supply context-appropriate rules to rule-based systems (Whitsel 2013), different meanings for concepts in fuzzy rule-based systems (Turner 1997), and appropriate weights and structure to neural networks (Arritt and Turner 2003).

An important benefit of having ready access to context-specific knowledge about how to achieve goals is speed. For example, if an AUV's mission has to be aborted because of power loss, the correct action depends on the context: in the open ocean, surface and radio for help; in a harbor, avoid surface vessels by landing and releasing a buoy. The decision is critical to agent's survival, and it must be made very quickly. CMB lets the agent choose the right action automatically.

Standing Orders Contextual schemas also provide knowledge about "background" behavior, such as actions related to homeostasis and behavioral parameter settings to modulate ongoing (goal-directed) behavior, as well as activating or deactivating goals based on the context. This knowledge is called "standing orders".[2] Examples include changing an AUV's depth envelope when entering a harbor, decreasing the

---

[2] Term thanks to D.R. Blidberg.

frequency of GPS fixes on covert missions, and activating an obstacle avoidance goal when entering a harbor or deactivating it when docking.

Event-Handling Knowledge There are three aspects to handling unanticipated events: detecting/diagnosing the event, evaluating its importance, and responding (or not) to the event. Contextual schemas provide context-specific knowledge about each of these.

The first step in handling an event is detecting that it has occurred. Some events can be trivially detected: a leak detector can signal a leak, or a power sensor a power failure. Other events, however, have no simple herald: an AUV will not have a "current detector", for example. Detecting these events requires analysis of simpler events (e.g., changes to speed or direction); that is, diagnosis is required.

C-schemas representing the current context provide context-specific diagnostic knowledge about events to increase the speed and accuracy of event detection. For example, in some implementations of CMB (Turner 1997) that use a fuzzy rule-based system, the rules used as well as the membership functions of the fuzzy values appropriate for the context are provided by c-schemas. In current work, a differential diagnostic approach similar to that used for context assessment (see Sect. 32.3.1) is being developed. Here, c-schemas provide context-dependent, weighted links between features of the environment and potential events and vice versa.

The next step after detection is determining the importance of the event to decide whether to respond. This is highly context-dependent; e.g., when driving, hearing a nearby car horn is much more important than when eating lunch on a park bench. Importance often depends on the what the impact would be on the agent's goals if the event were *not* handled.

In CMB, importance evaluation knowledge is part of event descriptions in c-schemas (see Fig. 32.1). This can include information about an event's likely impact on goals and/or an overall estimated importance level (e.g., "critical" for the event of "power failure"), which can be used if no other goal information is known or if the event affects many goals.

If an event is important enough, a response needs to be selected, and this depends on the context. For example, if an AUV detects an object dead ahead during a mine-hunting mission, it should investigate the object carefully; if it is rendezvousing with a support vessel, on the other hand, then it should consider initiating docking.

Event responses are also associated with event descriptions in contextual schemas. These consist of goals that should be activated in response to the events. Goals can be general, such as "identify possible mine", or quite specific, such as "perform the action abort to surface". The priority of the response is set based on the event's importance and other goal-handling knowledge about the context. By providing this kind of knowledge, c-schemas allow an agent to quickly implement a response to an event, which can be critical to the mission or the agent's survival.

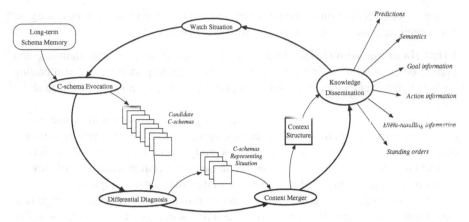

Fig. 32.2 Overall context-mediated behavior process

32.3   The CMB Process

Figure 32.2 shows context-mediated behavior process as implemented in a context manager, which we refer to here as ConMan.

ConMan constantly watches the evolving situation to assess the current context. C-schemas are found that represent various facets of the context, then these are merged to form a knowledge structure, the *context representation* (CoRe), which is a coherent representation of the entire context. ConMan then disseminates contextual knowledge from this to the rest of the agent (the performance element) as needed.

ConMan consists of several parts, as shown in Fig. 32.3. EMMA (Event Monitoring and Management Agent) is responsible for accepting sensor data and other input from outside the agent well as monitoring ConMan's own working memory to detect and respond to unanticipated events. EMMA is also responsible for looking for events predicted to occur by the performance element; in that case, it will inform the performance element when they are detected. Knowledge inferred as part of the event-handling process is added to working memory as well.

The context assessment module (CAM) is responsible for diagnosing the current context and creating a context representation. The long-term memory (LTM) and CAM work tightly together. As in our earlier work, ConMan's LTM is an active, associative memory that constantly watches the working memory and produces c-schemas that the situation evokes. These then become grist for CAM's differential diagnosis process. We will discuss these modules' actions in more detail in the next section.

Working memory (WM) and the CoRe are two parts of a unified view of the current situation, with the CoRe representing the context and WM holding facts/beliefs that describe the situation as sensed. Information in WM can affect ConMan's confidence in its context assessment, and they indicate differences between the CoRe's predictions and the actual situation.

Fig. 32.3 A current view of the structure of the ConMan context manager

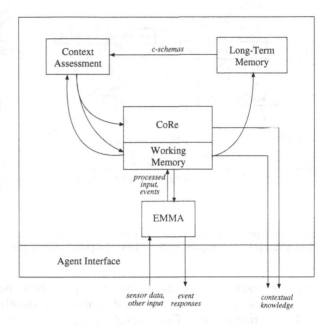

The final module in ConMan is the agent interface. This is responsible for handling communication with the rest of the agent, with respect both to sensor data as well as the output of event responses and contextual knowledge as needed.

32.3.1 Context Assessment

Context assessment entails finding a set of c-schemas that best represent the current situation, then merging them to form a representation of the context. Finding the c-schemas is a diagnostic problem. Features of the situation can suggest c-schemas, and c-schemas predict features of the situation. The task is finding a parsimonious set of c-schemas that in some sense explains all the features of the situation. There are many ways of doing this, from rule-based reasoning as was done in early medical diagnostic reasoning to formal methods of doing abductive set covering (e.g., Reggia et al. 1985).

In CMB, we use an abductive differential diagnosis approach based on work in the INTERNIST-I/CADUCEUS project (Miller et al. 1982) and related medical diagnostic work in AI (e.g., Feltovich et al. 1984). Differential diagnosis allows different hypotheses about the context to be directly compared and contrasted, unlike, say, rule-based approaches.

The process starts when the long-term memory is "reminded" of c-schemas by the current situation (cf. Kolodner 1984); these are said to be *evoked* by features of situation. For example, if an AUV detects that the water column has become shallow and that there is evidence of multiple sonar contacts overhead, the evoked c-schemas

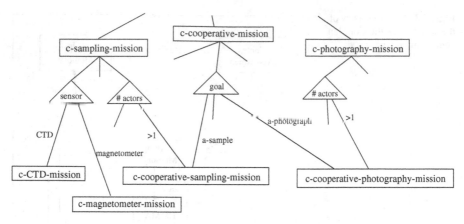

Fig. 32.4 A portion of a long-term schema memory; triangles are indices, rectangles are c-schemas. (From Turner (1998); copyright 1998 Elsevier, reprinted with permission)

might include those representing being in a harbor, being near the beach, being near an underwater plateau (e.g., the Grand Banks), and possibly others.

Long-term memory (LTM) is based on research on content-addressable, *dynamic memory* (Schank 1982), in particular, of the kind often used in case-based reasoners (Kolodner 1984). It consists of multiple discrimination nets that link the c-schemas in a specialization hierarchy based on their features, with each node being a c-schema, and the leaves being records of actual situations (*cases*) encountered.[3] Figure 32.4 shows a diagram of part of a schema memory.

To find c-schemas, LTM uses part or all of working memory as a *probe*, which is compared to the topmost c-schema. Differences from salient features predicted are used to traverse the c-schema's *indices*, feature/value pairs that link it to more specialized c-schemas.[4] This process repeats at the new c-schemas, spreading throughout memory, until finally c-schemas are reached that have no salient differences from the probe; these are the ones evoked and given to CAM. (Cases are not returned in CMB, but are available for case-based reasoning or as the basis of new c-schemas.) Each c-schema returned is marked with an *evoking strength* that measures how strongly it was "brought to mind" by the situation (Lawton et al. 1999). When the situation changes, the process repeats, possibly leading to a new set of evoked c-schemas, which may cause a new round of context assessment.

The evoked c-schemas are initial hypotheses about which contexts the situation is a member of, and although they match the situation along some axes, they may not truly fit the situation well. For example, when an AUV is in a harbor on a sampling mission carrying a camera that is not currently in use, with a strong magnetometer

---

[3] In the original dynamic memories, the internal nodes were memory organization packages (MOPs), of which c-schemas are one kind.

[4] The process is more complex than this; see Kolodner (1984) or Lawton et al. (1999).

signal and hearing dolphin sonar clicks, CAM might retrieve c-schemas representing being in a harbor, being on a sampling mission, taking photographs of underwater structures, using a magnetometer in mine hunting, and being around dolphins. Not all of these are good matches. Consequently, further diagnosis is needed.

Differential diagnosis first groups the context hypotheses into logical competitor sets (LCSs; Feltovich et al. 1984), which roughly hold all c-schemas that account for the same set of the situation's features. Strategies are then applied to "solve" the highest-scoring LCS—i.e., to find the best c-schema—by looking for additional evidence (see Miller et al. 1982). With new evidence, new c-schemas may be evoked and the set of LCSs may change. Features explained by the LCS' c-schema are then removed from consideration, and the process continues for the remaining features and c-schemas. The result is a set of c-schemas that together represent the context.

A problem is that gathering evidence can require inference or additional actions, and taking diagnostic actions can interfere with ongoing goal-based behavior. For example, impeded forward progress might be predicted by both a c-schema representing being in a current and one representing being in a kelp forest; which is accurate can be determined by turning off the vehicle's thrusters, but this is likely to impact mission goals. A good solution may be to activate the diagnostic action as a goal for the agent to carry out and let the normal attention-focusing mechanism decide when and how to schedule it. However, this, too can cause problems: what if the diagnostic goal is ignored? and what should ConMan do about diagnosing the situation while waiting for the results of the action? We will address this issue in future work.

The set of c-schemas found are next merged to create the context representation (CoRe). Note that this is a way that novel contexts can be handled, i.e., by combining knowledge about several known contexts. Context merger is a difficult problem, and one that is the focus of continuing research. In the best case, only one c-schema will contain each piece of knowledge needed, and so no real merger will be necessary for that piece. However, it may be that several c-schemas provide a particular kind of knowledge, and what is provided is mutually exclusive. In this case, one solution is to use the knowledge from the c-schema that is most similar to the current situation, as determined by CAM's diagnosis. A second approach might be to use a weighted voting mechanism if multiple c-schemas offer the same knowledge, but some do not. Or, third, the agent could simply ignore the contextual knowledge and fall back on whatever from-scratch reasoning mechanisms the performance element may have.

A more interesting case is when knowledge from multiple c-schemas about something is not mutually exclusive and itself can be merged. For example, if c-schema κ_1 prescribes that an AUV's depth should be in the range [1,10] while κ_2 specifies [5,15], the ranges could be merged in at least two ways, [1,15] and [5,10]. Deciding which to do may itself be context-specific; for example, if the agent needs to be cautious in the current situation about being outside its depth envelope, the latter merger may be preferred. Other kinds of information can be merged, as well. For example, fuzzy linguistic values could be merged by combining their membership functions (Turner 1997), and concepts in an ontology could be "merged" by using a common ancestor in an inheritance hierarchy.

Unfortunately, there will rarely be a single best way to merge the knowledge: ConMan could use the maximum versus the minimum values for membership functions, for example, or there may be several common ancestors when the ontology has a tangled isa hierarchy. In some cases, the merged value may be so vague as to be meaningless: the combined membership function may degenerate to values of all 0 or 1, for example, or the common ancestor may be too far up the hierarchy to be of use (e.g., "physical object"). It may be better in some cases to list alternatives (multiple ranges, membership functions, or concepts) than to try to merge them, then let ConMan or the performance element decide what to use at runtime as needed. Much more work remains to be done in this area in the future.

32.3.2   Using the Contextual Knowledge

After context assessment, the contextual knowledge can be used. Some of the knowledge is used by the context manager itself, i.e., to handle unanticipated events. Most, however, has to do with the performance element's behavior, and so the information has to be made available to it. This includes predictions about possibly unseen features of the situation, context-specific semantic information, attention-focusing (goal-priority) information, knowledge about how to solve goals, and standing orders.

In past work, the context manager was an integral part of the agent's design and specific to it, and so it was hard-coded with knowledge of where to distribute contextual knowledge and when. In the current incarnation of ConMan, which is self-contained, this will not be the case.

There are two general ways the performance element can get contextual knowledge from ConMan. First, it can request the information as needed. A scheduler could request goal priority information, for example, or a planner could request information about appropriate actions for its goals. Second, it could register its needs with ConMan, and then ConMan would "push" the knowledge to it as it becomes available. In either case, a language is needed to allow the performance element to tell ConMan what it needs and when. In the push version, the performance element will also need to be able to receive knowledge from ConMan asynchronously, or a buffer will be needed between the two. This entire issue is the subject of ongoing research.

32.4   Related Work

Artificial intelligence systems have always taken context into account, but for most of the field's history, this has been done implicitly by preconditions in planners, antecedents in rules, etc. Some early reasoners had simple notions of context (e.g., Chandrasekaran et al. 1979), but the representations were generally quite limited.

Work on explicitly modeling context essentially began with work in logic (e.g., McCarthy et al. 1995). However, work in that area (e.g., Giunchiglia 1993) does not group contextual knowledge together as is done in CMB, and so cannot benefit from having all knowledge about a context represented explicitly in one place, nor can such work easily handle uncertainty or conflicting or incomplete knowledge.

Guha's microtheories (Guha 1991) did group contextual knowledge and are superficially similar to our c-schemas. However, whereas he was most interested (as was Chandrasekaran et al. 1979) in partitioning domain knowledge, we are interested in performance (prescriptive) knowledge and representing the agent's context itself.

The context-aware applications area shares our goal of making systems context-sensitive. Dey (2001), for example, defines context similarly to CMB as information that can be used to characterize the situation. However, although some recent work has begun to look at richer contexts (e.g., Adomavicius and Tuzhilin 2011), research in context-aware applications is often more concerned with simple first-order properties of the context, such as location, the user's current focus, etc., whereas CMB is concerned with a wider range of contextual features needed for intelligent autonomous agents.

Much work on modeling context has been done in the community that coalesced around the CONTEXT conference series.[5] Leake et al. (2005), for example, have developed a notion of context that is used for and based on concept maps, informal node-and-link structures used in (e.g.) education and knowledge acquisition. Akman (Akman and Surav 1995) makes a distinction similar to ours between situation and context; to him, a context is a situation type that contains constraints and *infons*, situational information, that are either *saturated* (agent has complete knowledge about the infon) or *unsaturated* (partial knowledge). However, this approach is more tailored toward theory than use in intelligent agents. van Wissen et al. (2013) have recently proposed representing contexts as sets of constraints on the agent.

Brézillon and colleagues (Brézillon et al. 1997, 2002; Brézillon and Brézillon 2007; Tahir and Brézillon 2013) have developed a model of context whose primary knowledge structure is the *contextual graph* (CxG), an acyclic graph representing appropriate actions to take in a context. A CxG's *contextual nodes* are decision points in the graph, with branches being taken based on information from the environment or user; a path through the CxG has associated actions that are appropriate for the context. This is similar to the prescriptive knowledge contained in c-schemas, although CxG's seem not to contain much descriptive or explicit event-handling or attention-focusing knowledge; however, since they prescribe the agent's actions, this latter may be a moot point.

Gonzalez and collaborators (e.g., Gonzalez et al. 2008) have developed a model of human reasoning they call *context-based reasoning* (CxBR) that is similar in many ways to CMB. A context in CxBR is a module that contains actions relevant to a situation, which is broadly similar to c-schemas. In CxBR, an agent has multiple active contexts (mission context, major context, and minor contexts), with links

---

[5] International and Interdisciplinary Conference on Modeling and Using Context.

between them. Goals arise from the contexts themselves. One difference between this and our approach that CMB's notion of context is more fluid in the sense that c-schemas do not directly specify their relationship to other c-schemas that may be appropriate; instead, the memory and the diagnostic process together find them during context assessment. However, CxBR has the advantage that where important linkages between contexts are known or are necessary, they can be specified, unlike the case with c-schemas. C-schemas are somewhat more comprehensive than CxBR's contexts in the sense that they provide, at least potentially, more knowledge about the features of the context (especially after merger) and goal priorities. CxBR is, however, in a way a complete reasoning *style*, similar to schema-based reasoning (Turner 1994) itself, of which CMB is a part. For example, goals arise exogenous to ConMan as well as endogenously, and it is not clear this is the case for CxBR: goals seem to arise primarily if not solely based on the context itself.

CxBR has also recently been extended to the multiagent case in CCxBR (Collaborative Context-Base Reasoning) (Barrett and Gonzalez 2010). This is based in large part on joint intentions, and thus is somewhat different than CMB as used in multiagent systems (Turner et al. 2014). For example, we make no claim for necessarily achieving joint intentions, but instead focus on agents arriving at a joint context representation, from which joint goals may arise or be recognized.

Recently, work has begun to combine CxG and CxBR into a new context-based architecture (tentatively) called CDMAHI (Context-Driven Modeling Architecture for Human Intelligence) (Gonzalez and Brézillon 2008). It will be interesting to see how this combined approach compares to CMB. Indeed, combining all three approaches is likely to be desirable.

32.5   Conclusion and Future Work

Context is critical to the intelligent behavior of agents, both natural and artificial. By recognizing a new situation as an instance of a known context, an agent can quickly bring to bear knowledge about how to behave appropriately. Context-mediated behavior is our approach to realizing this in intelligent agents. Contexts, represented as contextual schemas, serve as organizing points for all knowledge about how to behave while in them, including both descriptive/predictive and prescriptive knowledge. The result is an agent that automatically adjusts its behavior to its context, and that can make decisions about how to behave very rapidly once the context has been assessed.

Over the years, CMB has been refined and used in a variety of systems, including its original use in MEDIC (Turner 1994), a medical diagnostic reasoner in the area of pulmonology; Orca (Turner 1994, 1995), an intelligent controller for autonomous underwater vehicles and other agents; CoDA (Turner and Turner 2001), an approach to multiagent systems control for autonomous oceanographic sampling networks and other MASs; CA-SLAM (Whitsel and Turner 2011), which explores context-based trust strategies in open multiagent systems; and a new project focused on assistive technology for the cognitively impaired. Currently, the approach has been well worked-out and tested in general, and there is empirical support for its efficacy (Whitsel 2013), but much still remains to be done in future work.

One ongoing project focuses on making the context manager more independent of the agent using it, as discussed in this chapter. Another focuses on creating explicit ontologies both for contexts and for contextual knowledge; some work has already been done in this regard (see Turner et al. 2014). Work continues as well on merging contextual knowledge in a principled manner.

An important area of future work is using CMB in multiagent systems. We have already applied CMB in a limited way in the CoDA project for organization design. In that project, the agent selected to create an organization for the MAS assesses its context (which includes the other agents, etc.), then uses knowledge in c-schemas about appropriate organizational designs for the context to design an organization for the MAS that fits the context. In current work (Turner et al. 2014), we are expanding the role of CMB in multiagent systems by distributing the CMB process itself, so that context-aware agents are able to cooperatively assess the joint context. This will allow a MAS to use CMB to always behave appropriately for its context.

As work progresses, we anticipate CMB continuing to benefit our own intelligent agent controllers and multiagent systems. We also anticipate ConMan becoming something that others can include in their agents and MASs, as well, to add automatic context-sensitivity to their behavior.

Acknowledgements   The author thanks the members of the Maine Software Agents and AI Laboratory (MaineSAIL) for their work on projects described here. This work has been supported by ONR grants N000—14–00–1–00–614, N0001–14–98–1–0648, and N0001–14–96–1–5009, and NSF grant BES–9696044.

References

Adomavicius, G., Tuzhilin, A.: Context-aware recommender systems. In: Ricci, F., Rokach, L., Shapira, B., Kantor, P.B. (eds.) Recommender Systems Handbook, pp. 217–253. Springer, New York (2011)

Akman, V., Surav, M.: Contexts, oracles, and relevance. In: AAAI Fall Symposium on Formalizing Context, AAAI Technical Report Series, No. FS-95-02, pp. 23–30. AAAI Press, Menlo Park (1995)

Albert, E., Turner, E.H., Turner, R.M.: Appropriate commitment planning for AUV control. In: Proceedings of the 2007 International Symposium on Unmanned Untethered Submersible Technology (UUST'07). Durham, NH (2007)

Arritt, R.P., Turner, R.M.: Context-specific weights for a neural network. In: Proceedings of the Fourth International and Interdisciplinary Conference on Modeling and Using Context (CONTEXT'03), Stanford, CA, pp. 29–39. Springer, New York (2003)

Barrett, G.C., Gonzalez, A.J.: Effective agent collaboration through improved communication by means of contextual reasoning. Int. J. Intell. Syst. **26**(2), 129–157 (2010)

Brézillon, J., Brézillon, P.: Context modeling: context as a dressing of focus. In: Proceedings of the Sixth International and Interdisciplinary Conference on Modeling and Using Context. Springer, Berlin (2007)

Brézillon, P., Gentile, C., Saker, I., Secron, M.: SART: a system for supporting operators with contextual knowledge. In: Proceedings of the 1997 International and Interdisciplinary Conference on Modeling and Using Context (CONTEXT–97), Rio de Janerio, pp. 209–222 (1997)

Brézillon, P., Pasquier, L., Pomerol, J.C.: Reasoning with contextual graphs. Eur. J. Operat. Res. **136**(2), 290–298 (2002)

Chandrasekaran, B., Gomez, F., Mittal, S., Smith, J.: An approach to medical diagnosis based on conceptual structures. In: Proceedings of the Sixth International Joint Conference on Artificial Intelligence. Stanford, CA (1979)

Dey, A.K.: Understanding and using context. Pers. Ubiquit. Comput. **5**(1), 4–7 (2001)

Feltovich, P.J., Johnson, P.E., Moller, J.A., Swanson, D.B.: LCS: the role and development of medical knowledge and diagnostic expertise. In: Clancey, W.J., Shortliffe, E.H. (eds.) Readings in Medical Artificial Intelligence, pp. 275–319. Addison–Wesley, Reading (1984)

Giunchiglia, F.: Contextual reasoning. Epistemologia (special issue on I Linguaggi e le Macchine) **16**, 345–364 (1993)

Glass, A.N., Holyoak, K.J.: Cognition, 2nd edn. Random House, New York (1986)

Gonzalez, A.J., Brézillon, P.: Comparing two context-driven approaches for representation of human tactical behavior. Knowl. Eng. Rev. **23**(3), 295 (2008)

Gonzalez, A.J., Stensrud, B.S., Barrett, G.: Formalizing context-based reasoning: A modeling paradigm for representing tactical human behavior. Int. J. Intell. Syst. **23**(7), 822–847 (2008)

Guha, R.: Contexts: a formalization and some applications. Ph.D. thesis, Stanford University (1991)

Kolodner, J.L.: Retrieval and Organizational Strategies in Conceptual Memory. Lawrence Erlbaum Associates, Hillsdale (1984)

Kolodner, J.L.: Case-Based Reasoning. Morgan Kaufman, San Mateo (1993)

Lawton, J.H., Turner, R.M., Turner, E.H.: A unified long-term memory system. In: Proceedings of the International Conference on Case-Based Reasoning (ICCBR'99). Monastery Seeon, Munich, Germany (1999)

Leake, D., Maguitman, A., Reichherzer, T.: Exploiting rich context: an incremental approach to context-based Web search. In: International and Interdisciplinary Conference on Modeling and Using Context, CONTEXT'05, pp. 254–267. Springer, Berlin (2005)

Mantovani, G.: Social context in HCI: a new framework for mental models, cooperation, and communication. Cogn. Sci. **20**, 237–269 (1996)

McCarthy, J.: Notes on formalizing contexts. In: Bajcsy, R. (ed.) Proceedings of the Thirteenth International Joint Conference on Artificial Intelligence, pp. 555–560. Morgan Kaufmann, San Mateo (1993)

McCarthy, J.: A logical AI approach to context (1996). http://steam.stanford.edu/jmc/logical.pdf. Accessed 14 Oct 2014.

McCarthy, J., Buvac, S., Costello, T., Fikes, R., Genesereth, M., Giunchiglia, F.: Formalizing context (expanded notes), Technical Report. Stanford University, Stanford, CA (1995)

Miller, R.A., Pople, H.E., Myers, J.D.: INTERNIST–1, an experimental computer-based diagnostic consultant for general internal medicine. New Engl. J. Med. **307**, 468–476 (1982)

Reggia, J.A., Nau, D.S., Peng, Y.: A formal model of diagnostic inference. I. Problem formulation and decomposition. Inf. Sci. **37**, 227–256 (1985)

Russell, S., Norvig, P.: Artificial Intelligence: A Modern Approach, 2nd edn. Prentice Hall, Englewood Cliffs (2003)

Schank, R.C.: Dynamic Memory. Cambridge University Press, New York (1982)

Tahir, H., Brézillon, P.: Contextual graphs platform as a basis for designing a context-based intelligent assistant system. In: Akman, V., Bouquet, P., Thomason, R., Young, R.A. (Eds.)Modeling and Using Context, pp. 259–273. Springer, Berlin (2013)

Turner, R.M.: Adaptive Reasoning for Real-World Problems: A Schema-Based Approach. Lawrence Erlbaum Associates, Hillsdale (1994)

Turner, R.M.: Intelligent control of autonomous underwater vehicles: the Orca project. In: Proceedings of the 1995 IEEE International Conference on Systems, Man, and Cybernetics. Vancouver, Canada (1995)

Turner, R.M.: Determining the context-dependent meaning of fuzzy subsets. In: Proceedings of the 1997 International and Interdisciplinary Conference on Modeling and Using Context (CONTEXT-97), Rio de Janeiro (1997)

Turner, R.M.: Context-mediated behavior for intelligent agents. Int. J. Hum. Comput. Stud. **48**(3), 307–330 (1998)

Turner, R.M., Turner, E.H.: A two-level, protocol-based approach to controlling autonomous oceanographic sampling networks. IEEE J. Oceanic Eng. **26**(4), 654–666 (2001)

Turner, R.M., Rode, S., Gagne, D.: Distributed, context-based organization and reorganization of multi-AUV systems. J. Unmanned Syst. Technol. (JUST) **2**(1), 1–9 (2014)

van Wissen, A., Kamphorst, B., van Eijk, R.: A constraint-based approach to context. In: Brézillon, P., Blackburn, P., Dapoigny, R. (eds.) Modeling and Using Context, pp. 171–184. Springer, Berlin (2013)

Whitsel, L.T.: A context-based approach to detecting miscreant agent behavior in open multagent systems. Ph.D. thesis, School of Computing and Information Science, University of Maine, 346 Boardman Hall, University of Maine, Orono, ME (2013)

Whitsel, L., Turner, R.M.: A context-based approach to detecting miscreant behavior and collusion in open multiagent systems. In: Proceedings of the Seventh International and Interdisciplinary Conference on Modeling and Using Context CONTEXT'11, Karlruhe, Germany (2011)

Chapter 33
Context-Awareness in Multi-agent Systems for Ambient Intelligence

Andrei Olaru

Abstract There is a large body of research that lies at the intersection of the domains of context-awareness, multi-agent systems (MAS) and Ambient Intelligence (AmI)/Ubiquitous Computing (UbiComp). This is because, while multi-agent systems are an appropriate architecture for AmI implementations, one essential requirement for AmI is to be aware of the user's context and to act accordingly. In order to implement context-awareness in a MAS for AmI applications, one must on the one hand choose an appropriate representation for context, that is suitable for agents of all sizes and functions, and, on the other hand, create an agent-based architecture that facilitates communication between agents that share context. This chapter presents a model, mechanisms and methods for integrating context-awareness in multi-agent systems for AmI. The model is based on experience with several implementations of MAS dealing with various aspects of context-awareness.

33.1 Introduction

Ambient Intelligence—or AmI—is a pervasive electronic environment that will assist people in their daily lives, in a pro-active but non-intrusive manner (Augusto and McCullagh 2007; Ducatel et al. 2001). In order to be able to take the appropriate action at the right time, AmI must consider the situation—or context—of the user, in order to help the user, potentially by means of proactive action, without disrupting the user's focus. Context-awareness is therefore a central element in Ambient Intelligence, being instrumental in AmI appearing as "intelligent". An AmI system must "understand" the context of the user before acting upon it.

In context-aware AmI applications, context is many times viewed as set of pieces of information that originate outside the AmI system, and that the system can perceive and manage in order to provide it to the various algorithms involved in decision. However, only so much context information will come from the outside of the system.

A. Olaru (✉)
Department of Computers, Faculty of Automatic Control and Computers,
University "Politehnica" of Bucharest, 313 Splaiul Independentei, 060042
Bucharest, Romania
e-mail: cs@andreiolaru.ro

© Springer Science+Business Media New York 2014   541
P. Brézillon, A. J. Gonzalez (eds.), *Context in Computing*,
DOI 10.1007/978-1-4939-1887-4_33

Applications in the system will also produce information that is relevant to other applications, essentially creating more complex elements of context. We therefore view applications and agents in an Ambient Intelligence system as both consuming and producing context information.

Moreover, there are a few processes related to context information that can be found in most context-aware applications: the application must be able to detect the context information that is relevant to it; it must detect the appropriate action to take, considering the context; and it must share new context information that it has perceived or aggregated (if any), in order to make it available to other components of the system.

The purpose of this chapter is to present a model that makes possible the isolation of application-independent context-related processes in a specific layer—a middleware that relies on a simple, flexible and generic context representation in order to perform tasks such as situation detection, decision, and sharing of context information.

Moreover, in order to enable simple situation detection and action without the need for domain-specific processes, context information and recognized situations should be easy to view, edit and manage by the user directly.

Throughout this chapter we will be using, as example, an Ambient Assisted Living (AAL) scenario: Emily is an elderly woman that lives alone. Most of her activity happens indoors, but some days she goes shopping outside of the house. Her caretakers have configured an AmI system that uses motion sensors, RFID tags and AI to detect potential emergency situations and assist Emily in her daily life.

After discussing some related work in the fields of MAS for Ambient Intelligence, and of context-awareness in AmI, we elaborate on our perspective on the problem in Sect. 33.3. Section 33.4 will present the model of a context-awareness layer for AmI. The practical experience with implementing this model is detailed in Sect. 33.5. The last section draws the conclusions.

33.2   Related Work

In the field of agent-based Ambient Intelligence platforms, there are two main directions of development: one concerning agents oriented toward assisting the user, based on centralized repositories of knowledge (ontologies) and complex platforms (Lech and Wienhofen 2005; Tapia et al. 2010), and one concerning the coordination of agents associated with devices, sometimes using agent mobility, in order to resolve complex tasks that no agent can do by itself, also considering distributed control and fault tolerance (Cabri et al. 2005; Rogers et al. 2009). In both approaches context-aware reasoning is lacking, or is performed in centralized repositories, away from the agents in need of the reasoning process. We propose a model in which reasoning can be done in the agent, close to the user, not depending on centralized components.

In context-awareness for pervasive computing, infrastructures for the processing of context information (Henricksen and Indulska 2006; Perera et al. 2013) contain several layers, going from sensors to the application. This type of infrastructures is useful when the context information comes from the environment and refers to environmental conditions such as location, temperature, light or weather, also having a simpler representation. Our approach is directed towards an infrastructure that is decentralized, in which each entity/agent has knowledge about the context of its user (Olaru et al. 2013).

The research group of Diane Cook working on activity detection proposes a method that bears much similarity to our own, in the sense that textual pattern detection is used to detect behavioral patterns in activity data recorded as text (Cook et al. 2013). By comparison, this work is directed towards activity recognition (rather than detection) and proposes a representation for context/situation information that is easier to read and handle by the carer of the assisted person.

Modeling of context information uses representations that range from tuples to logical, case-based and ontological representations (Perera et al. 2013). These are used to determine the situation that the user is in. However, these approaches are not flexible throughout the evolution of the system—the ontologies and rules are hard to modify on the go and in a dynamical manner. Moreover, a less informed user is unlikely to be able to modify an ontology or a set of rules based on FOPL, as opposed to a visual representation based on graph. The work of Sowa (2008) on conceptual graphs is interesting with respect to our research, but in our work we focus on graph matching for situation detection.

33.3   Context-Awareness from an Application-Independent Perspective

We position this work at the intersection of Ambient Intelligence, context-awareness and multi-agent systems.

Software agents (and multi-agent systems (Ferber 1999)) are an appropriate paradigm for the implementation of AmI (Ducatel et al. 2001; Tapia et al. 2010), as agents are autonomous, therefore more reliable in a dynamic environment and more capable of focusing on just one user or one functionality. Moreover, there is a large amount of research that can be used from the fields of multi-agent platforms and agent reasoning and communication. Even if an AmI system does not use agents, reliability and robustness concerns call for distributed, autonomous application components that are much like software agents.

As most of the agents in an AmI system need to access context information that is relevant to their activity, many features of context-aware behavior can be integrated in a generic, application-independent layer below the main application functionality, to serve as component in a middleware for context management. Such a *context-awareness middleware* would handle context information transfer, detection of information that is relevant to the application, a certain range of context-aware decisions, and sharing of new context information with other agents. This approach is directed towards a decentralized solution (supporting robustness and dependability)

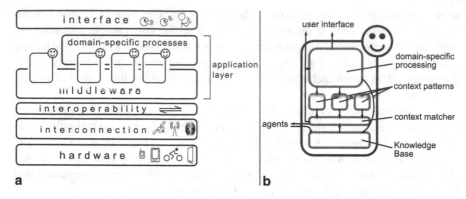

Fig. 33.1 a A layered view of an Ambient Intelligence system, dividing the application layer into context-awareness middleware and domain-specific processes. **b** A schematic view of an agent's internals, presenting the context graph (KB), matcher and patterns, and domain-specific processing

in which all context information is stored in the agents to which that information is potentially relevant at the current time (the context is the "dressing" of the agent's focus (Brézillon and Brézillon 2007)).

An Ambient Intelligence system can be modeled as having several layers (see Fig. 33.1a; El Fallah Seghrouchni 2008): the devices that compose the system; the pervasive network connecting the devices; an interoperability layer ensuring uniform representations throughout; the application layer, concerned with intelligent behavior and application logic; and the multi-modal natural user interface. In this model, the context-awareness middleware fits inside the application layer, underlying domain-specific processes. Ideally, the middleware handles all incoming and outgoing communication between agents, providing applications the information relevant to their activity. There may be agents that don't even have any application-specific logic, and rely only on the functionality offered by the middleware to provide data to the interface.

By using the underlying middleware, the application must be able to *access context information* (e.g. know about the activity of the user), must *understand the context* (e.g. understand the relations between the different facts and to evaluate the relevance of a piece of information) and must be able to *decide upon correct context-aware action* (e.g. know about the user's experience and expectations, detect appropriate action and also be able to perform the action). Most of these features can rely on the functionality of the middleware. Its architecture is presented in the next section.

33.4   The Context-Awareness Layer

The middleware presented in this chapter offers to AmI applications that use it a possibility of integrating context-awareness, by providing them with storage of context information, detection of situations specified by the application, suggesting potential action, and sharing with other devices and applications context information that is potentially interesting to them.

In order to make these processes generic, an appropriate representation for context information is needed, such that it is possible to represent the user's situation and also to be able to say if the user is in a specified situation or not. For this purpose, the model that we propose uses context graphs to represent information and context patterns to represent interesting situations (Olaru et al. 2013). Context graphs and patterns have been developed specifically for a general, non-restrictive representation of information that allows matching patterns against graphs. Context matching can be used to compute the relevance of incoming information, to detect situation and appropriate action, and to extract information potentially relevant to other agents.

Beside the internal representation of context, the model also specifies that agents only communicate with other agents that share some context, creating a topology of the agent system that is an overlay of the actual network topology. This helps efficiency and privacy.

33.4.1   Formal Model

This section presents the model that the context-awareness middleware—integrated in a multi-agent system—relies on. In this model, the multi-agent system is organized on three levels (see Fig. 33.2): containers (or machines), agents, and knowledge/context information. Each of these levels is modeled as a graph: the Container Graph shows what containers can communicate directly with each other; the Agent Graph specifies which agents share context (see Sect. 33.4.3), and what is their relation; and each agent contains a ContextGraph with the information relevant to its activity).

The *Tri-Graph* is formed by the reunion of *ContainerGraph* = (*Containers, Connections); AgentGraph* = (*Agents, AgentRelations*); and agents' context graphs CG_{Agent} :

$Tri\text{-}Graph = (Nodes, Edges)$, where

$$Nodes = Containers \cup Agents \cup \bigcup_{A\ agent} CG_A.V$$

$$Edges = Connections \cup AgentRelations \cup AgentLocations \cup \bigcup_{A\ agent} CG_A.E$$

$CG_A = (V, E)$, where $V \subseteq Concepts$ and $E = \{edge(from, to, value, persistence) \mid from, to \in Concepts, value \in Relations, persistence \in (0, 1] \}$.

In a *context graph* CG_A, the elements of *Concepts* and *Relations* are strings or URIs; *Relations* also contains the empty string, for unnamed relations. The *value* attribute is the label of the edge. The *persistence* attribute specifies how long the edge will persist after it has been added to the context graph.

Situation recognition is done by means of *context patterns*. A pattern represents a set of associations that are specified by the user, the applications, or are extracted by the agent from the history of context information.

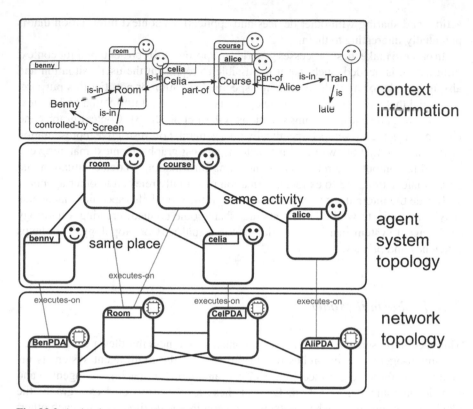

Fig. 33.2 A visual representation of the various graphs, in the modeling of an example scenario involving five agents and four machines

A pattern is also a graph, but there are several additional features that make it match a wider range of situations. For instance, some nodes may be labeled with "?" and are generic; also, edges may be labeled with regular expressions (matching series of edges in the context graph).

Each agent has a set of context patterns that it matches against its context graph and against the information that it receives, in order to determine relevant situations and solve potential problems:

$Patterns = \{(G_s^P, relevance, persistence) \mid s \in PatternNames, G_s^P$ a graph pattern, $relevance, persistence \in (0, 1]\}$.

A *graph pattern* is a graph $G_s^P = (V_s^P, E_s^P)$ with:

$V_s^P = \{v_i^P \mid v_i^P.label \in Concepts \cup \{?\}\}$

$E_s^P = \{(from, to, label, characteristic, actionable) \mid from, to \in V_s^P, label \in Regexps(Relations), characteristic, actionable \in (0, 1]\}$,

The *characteristic* feature of a pattern edge influences the measurement of how well a pattern matches a subgraph. Its *actionability* feature measures how correct it would be for the agent to infer the existence of this edge in case of a partial match between the pattern and the context graph. The *relevance* of a pattern shows how important is an information matching the pattern; *persistence* shows for how long new information will persist after being matched by the pattern. Once a pattern has been matched, its *persistence* value will be assigned to all edges in the matched subgraph. Labels in both context graphs and patterns are unique (with the exception that there may be more than one generic node in a pattern).

A *match i* between a pattern G_s^P and an agent A's context graph CG_A is defined[1] as $M_{A\text{-}si}(G'_A, G_m^P, G_x^P, f, k_f)$.

G'_A, G_m^P, G_x^P are graphs[2], with $G'_A \subseteq CG_A$, $G'_A = (V', E')$, $G_m^P = (V_m^P, E_m^P)$, $G_x^P = (V_x^P, E_x^P)$, where $V_m^P \cap V_x^P = \emptyset$, $V_m^P \cup V_x^P = V_s^P$, $E_m^P \cap E_x^P = \emptyset$ and $E_m^P \cup E_x^P = E_s^P$.

That is, $G'_A \subseteq CG_A$ is a full match for the *solved part* G_m^P of pattern G_s^P. What is left of the pattern is the *unsolved part* G_x^P (also called *the problem*). There is no intersection between the solved and unsolved parts of the patterns (no common nodes or edges).

The matching function $f : V_m^P \to V'$ establishes a correspondence between the vertices of the solved part and the match in the graph with the conditions that every non-generic vertex from the solved part must match a different vertex from G'_A; every non-*RegExp* edge from the solved part must match an edge from G'_A; every *RegExp* edge from the solved part must match a chain of edges from G'_A; and G'_A does not contain other nodes or edges than the ones that are matched by the pattern (G'_A is minimal).

The number $k_f \in (0, 1]$ indicates how well the pattern G_s^P matches G'_A in match $M_{A\text{-}si}$, and is given by the normalized sum of the *characteristic* factors of matched edges, i.e.

$$k_f = \sum_{e_i^P \in E_m^P} e_i^P.characteristic \, / \sum_{e_j^P \in E_s^P} e_j^P.characteristic.$$

Equivalently, we can define the match of any 2 graphs G_X and G_Y—where G_Y is the "pattern"—as $M_{G_X\text{-}G_Y i}(G'_X, G_m^P, G_x^P, f, k)$, since a graph is a particular case of graph pattern.

33.4.2 Reasoning

Based on the formal model presented in the previous section, there are three processes that occur constantly in the context-awareness component of the agent: the agent is able to *integrate new information* coming from other agents (e.g. an RFID reader notifies Emily's activity manager that Emily has her keys with her); the agent is able to *detect situation and act upon it* (e.g. Emily's activity manager infers that Emily is going to go out and notifies her she should take a shopping bag); and the agent is able

---

[1] There may be multiple matches between the same pattern and graph.
[2] G_x^P is not a proper graph, as it may contain edges without containing their adjacent vertices.

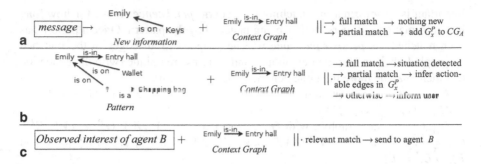

Fig. 33.3 Processes happening in a context-aware agent: **a** integrating new information; **b** detecting situation; **c** sharing information with other agents. The matching has been marked with ||·

to *share information with its neighbors* (e.g. Emily's activity manager informs her caretaker that she will go shopping). We have previously shown that these processes (behaviors) are essential and sufficient to ensure that interesting information reaches the potentially interested agents.

Whenever the agent receives a message from which a graph can be extracted, the graph is matched against the context graph of the agent. If there is no match, it means that the information has no relevance with respect to the agent's activity, and it is discarded. If there is a full match, the agent already has the information, so no change occurs. If there is a partial match, the new information is integrated with the agent's context graph, by simply adding the unsolved part of the match to the context graph. This way, the agent acquires new information (see the example in Fig. 33.3a).

Whenever the context graph of the agent changes, related patterns of the agent are matched against the context graph, to detect if the situation of the agent has changed. In case of a full match, the situation is considered as current. In case of a partial match, the actionability of the edges in the unsolved part is checked, and if it is greater than the k_f of the match, the edges are added to the context graph. This is how the agent infers new information. Otherwise, depending on the k_f, the user may be notified of the partial match, as user action may be needed and action cannot be taken by the agent autonomously (see the example in Fig. 33.3b).

As the agent receives information from other (neighbor) agents, it forms an "observed interest" record for the agents. Since agents send only information that is interesting to them, extracting interest indication from received messages may be useful. This indication can be represented as patterns of the agent that may be interesting for the other agent. Whenever information matching those patterns is found, it will be sent to the other agent, as it may be potentially interesting to it (see the example in Fig. 33.3c).

An important process in the agent is the removal of parts from the context graph— *forgetting outdated information*. For example, if the system detected that Emily was in the kitchen 5 min ago and her position has not been reconfirmed since, it may well be that she has moved elsewhere and that information can be considered as obsolete, as a new detection should take its place. When new edges are added, their *persistence* is set according to the indications of the pattern that contains the edge. With time, persistence of the edges in the context graph of the agent (CG_A) fades, and as it reaches zero, the edge is removed (along with any resulting isolated nodes).

All actions that an agent can take are related to matched patterns and added edges (creation of relations between concepts). The actual actions that are connected to the addition of edges are performed by attached procedures that are part of the application-specific part of the agent, allowing the agent to actually change its environment accordingly. This is why the only edges that are "actionable" should be the ones that correspond to effects that the agent can actually create.

33.4.3 Dynamic Agent Topology

Our approach is directed towards the context-aware transfer of information in a distributed, decentralized MAS for Ambient Intelligence. But to achieve communication efficiency, and to deal with privacy concerns, we have devised for our model an agent topology that is induced by context. In this *context-based topology*, if two agents share context, then they should be neighbors. The topology becomes an overlay on the actual network that the agents use to communicate. Shared context can be a common activity, a common place, etc.

There are five types of context that we consider for the agent hierarchy, four being identified by Chen and Kotz (2000), and the fifth being activity, an important aspect in the association-based model of Henricksen and Indulska (2006). The five types are *spatial context, temporal context, computational context, activity context and social context*. For each aspect of context we introduce agent types and relations between agents. The possible relations between agents are presented in Table 33.1. While temporal context is an aspect of context that we consider, we do not have a specialized agent for time intervals (which would be the hierarchical element of temporal context), as an agent that manages a time interval does not make much sense: since the internal context representation, as well as the relations between agents, reflect the present situation—therefore shared temporal context is already achieved. The temporal aspect is further discussed in Sect. 33.4.4.

Using such a topology has several advantages: the agents only send information to agents that share context with them—an agent would not find any interest in information received from an agent with absolutely no common context with it; and when looking for information, the search will be kept local (in terms of context), there where it makes more sense (and is more likely to yield results).

Moreover, in previous work we have explored the idea of mapping context structure to agent hierarchies (Olaru et al. 2013). Most aspects of context are hierarchical: places are parts of other places, activities are part of more general activities, computational resources belong to places or are related to certain activities, social structure is hierarchical, etc. Using hierarchies not only helps us organize the system, but

Table 33.1 The possible relations between different agent types, resulting from the mapping of context to system topology

Agent type (context type)	Possible incoming relations (and their sources)	Possible outgoing relations (and their destinations)
Place (spatial)	*is-in* ($\leftarrow$ *Activity, User, Device, Service, Place*)	–
Activity (activity)	*part-of* ($\leftarrow$ *User, Group, Activity, Service*)	*of* ($\rightarrow$ *User*)
Device (computing)	*executes-on* ($\leftarrow$ *Service*)	*is-in* ($\rightarrow$ *Place*), *controlled-by* ($\rightarrow$ *User*)
Service (computing)	–	*executes-on* ($\rightarrow$ *Device*), *is-in* ($\rightarrow$ *Place*), *part-of* ($\rightarrow$ *Activity*)
User (social)	*controlled-by* ($\leftarrow$ *Device*), *of* ($\leftarrow$ *Activity*), *connected-to* ($\leftarrow$ *User*)	*part-of* ($\rightarrow$ *Activity*), *in* ($\rightarrow$ *Group*), *connected-to* ($\rightarrow$ *User*)
Group (social)	*in* ($\leftarrow$ *User*)	*part-of* ($\rightarrow$ *Activity*)
Organization (social)	*part-of* ($\leftarrow$ *User, Group, Place, Activity*)	*part-of* ($\rightarrow$ *Organization*)

allows us to use hierarchical mobility—in which a mobile agent moves together with its subtree of agents.

Whenever the context of an agent changes, the relations with the other agents change as well—the topology of the system is dynamic. In some cases, mobile agents may be used. For example, the *Shopping List* agent may normally execute on the same machine as the kitchen agent, but when Emily goes shopping, it should move, as a part of her *Shopping* activity, to Emily's personal device, which will stay with her. It makes sense that an agent managing an activity should reside closer to the place where the activity takes place.

The choice of the presented types of context and relations is not random, as they cover the types identified in the literature. The use of specific types of agents and relations does not reduce the generality of the model, as these types may be used for any Ambient Intelligence application. The context-aware topology is not claiming to be a complete implicit representation of context—it only helps organize the system and keep information transfer between the agents local in terms of shared context.

33.4.4 The Temporal Aspect

Using context graphs and patterns is very useful when working on the *current* situation. If the Context Graph represents context information about the present, then patterns can identify the situation(s) that the user is in *right now*. However, some situations depend on the passage of time. For example, if the system knows Emily is in the bathroom, it cannot tell if any problem has occurred. If Emily has been in the bathroom for 5 min, it is alright; if she has been there for 1 h, then it is likely that

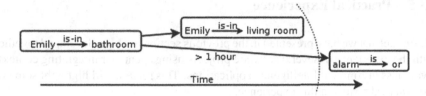

Fig. 33.4 Example of *Timeline* of an agent. The *dotted line* represents the current moment of time

there is a problem. Time-related situations such as this may be handled by introducing time moments or time intervals as nodes in the context graph, and can be handled by specialized processes in the application specific part of the agent. However, as time-related situations are frequent in all types of AmI scenarios, we have developed a generic solution. This is our most recent research.

Beside the "instantaneous" patterns already presented in Sect. 33.4.1, an agent can also contain *Timelines*. A timeline is a second-order graph pattern: $T_s^P = (V^P, E^P)$, with $V^P \subseteq$ *Patterns* and $E^P = \{$ *(from, to, value, characteristic, actionable)* | *from, to* $\in V_s^P$, *characteristic, actionable* $\in (0, 1]\}$. The label of an edge can take values that are time lengths (e.g. "5 min", "more than 1 h", etc), special values (e.g. *next*) or the empty string. Timelines are restricted to be single root directed acyclic graphs, so that they can represent branching paths of temporal events. Once a timeline is activated, its nodes and edges describe a sequence in which patterns should be matched.

A particular timeline becomes active when the pattern in the root of the timeline is matched. The edges going out from the root become *enabled*. Enabled edges can become active depending on their value. When the pattern at the destination of an active edge is matched, all other edges are inactivated and disabled and the edges outgoing from the matched node are enabled. The process continues until no edges are enabled or active, in which case the timeline is inactivated. Edges with no value are activated immediately and remain so indefinitely (until they are disabled by external events); edges labeled with "less than *time*" become active immediately and are inactivated after *time*; edges labeled with *next* become inactive when their source node is not matched anymore and their destination node is not matched immediately after; edges specifying precise times, or lower limits on times ("more than 30 min") become active only after the specified amount of time passes.

In the example in Fig. 33.4, the simple timeline specifies that if Emily entered the bathroom and has not come back to the living room (which is next to the bathroom) in under 1 h, then the alarm must be activated. Using timelines is a simple and easy to visualize method to specify possible sequences of events.

33.5   Practical Experience

The model that we have presented in the previous section has been developed together with the experience of several software projects using agents for integrating context-awareness in Ambient Intelligence applications. This section will highlight some of the practical results in this experience.

33.5.1   Agent Behavior and Topology

The described agent behavior and topology have been designed through experiments using platforms described in previous work (Olaru et al. 2013).

Agent behavior has been studied through a large number of simulations using the AmIciTy:Mi platform, that allows for fast simulations of large numbers of agents, using scenario files that completely specify the evolution of the simulation[3]. Simulations of up to over 1000 agents have been used to study the context-aware dissemination of information based on local communication, relying on self-organization mechanisms. The leading principle of the best behavior was that agents should send information that is interesting to them to neighbor agents that are potentially interested in that information.

The context-based hierarchical *agent topology* described in Sect. 33.4.3 improves the one in AmIciTy:Mi experiments and has been validated through experiments using the agent-oriented programming (AOP) language CLAIM, based on ambient calculus, that supports hierarchical mobile agents. A distributed AmI scenario has been publicly demonstrated (Olaru et al. 2011).

33.5.2   Context Representation and Matching

As all of the processes in the context-awareness middleware that we present rely on matching graphs, we have developed a purpose-build, efficient graph matching algorithm, dedicated especially to directed graphs in which most edges are labeled[4] (Olaru 2013).

The *context-matching algorithm* is focused on matching edges. It works with valid partial matches of various sizes and merges them in order to form larger (better) matches. The algorithm has two phases. First, it generates a set of all possible single-edge matches. Then, it selects pairs of compatible matches that it merges in order

---

[3] We thank Cristian Gratie, Guillaume Masson, Alexandre Hocquard and Sofia Neață for their contributions to the project.
Code is open source at https://github.com/andreiolaru-ro/AmIciTy-Mi.

[4] Code is open source at https://github.com/andreiolaru-ro/net.xqhs.Graphs.

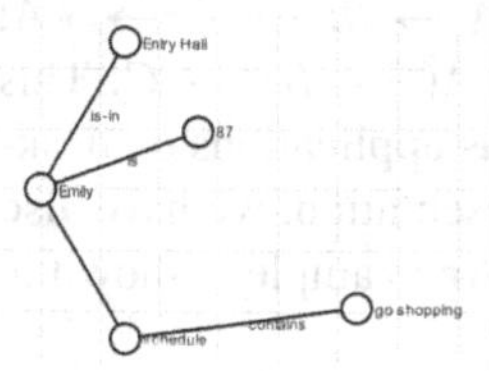

$$Emily(\rightarrow schedule \xrightarrow{contains} go\ shopping\ )(\xrightarrow{is} 87)\xrightarrow{is\text{-}in}$$
$$Entry\ Hall$$

b

```
Emily (-> schedule-contains -> go shopping)
      (-is-> 87) -is-in-> Entry Hall
```

a   **c**

Fig. 33.5 Various representation of a graph: **a** graphical; **b** textual; **c** ASCII

to create new matches. The search for new matches is close to a depth-first search, in order to get better matches faster. The gist of the algorithm is that it does not test the compatibility (from the point of view of merging) of the matches before each merger, but instead uses for each match a set of data structures (a frontier, a set of adjacent, "immediate", merger candidates and a set of non-adjacent, "outer" merger candidates) that allow the algorithm to know precisely if two matches can be merged or not.

Single-edge matches are compatible if their pattern edges have any common vertices and if those vertices correspond to the same node in the matched graph. The match could be potentially merged, later, with any other match that is not adjacent to it. In the second phase of the algorithm, for each match, new matches are created by merging it with immediate merger candidates (guaranteed to be compatible). When matches M_1 and M_2 are merged, the newly created M match has candidate sets that are guaranteed to be correct without actually checking them. The set of immediate merger candidates of M is the union of immediate merger candidates for both M_1 and M_2, immediate candidates for M_1 that are outer candidates for M_2 and immediate candidates for M_2 that are outer candidates for M_1. The outer merger candidates are candidates that were acceptable by both M_1 and M_2 but were not immediate merger candidates for any of the two.

Both the experimental results and the complexity analysis (Olaru 2013) have shown that the algorithm is particularly appropriate for the problem of context matching, yielding good results for graphs that come from AmI scenarios. As an additional feature, the algorithm can be stopped at any time, as with time it builds better and better matches. Not waiting for the algorithm to complete does not mean that no results are obtained, only that they may not be the best.

Representation Features have been developed so that context graphs and patterns in the agent can be visualizable and editable by the user directly, even without application-specific processes. First, we have developed a linear textual representation of directed graphs, for the purpose of displaying a human-readable form of graphs in the output console and to easily input graphs from the keyboard. It uses vertex and edge names, arrows, stars and parentheses to completely display a graph. Each edge is shown once, and nodes are repeated once per graph cycle. For instance, a graph that is formed of three nodes (A, B, C) linked by two edges a and b is represented as $A \xrightarrow{a} B \xrightarrow{b} C$; the cycle ABC is represented as $A \rightarrow B \rightarrow C \rightarrow *A$; a tree with root A and children B and C is represented as $A(\rightarrow B) \rightarrow C$. This representation is also easy to copy and paste between various applications on desktop PCs or mobile devices. Based on the linear textual representation, we have also built a graphical representation for graphs and for matches. An example is shown in Fig. 33.5.

A *Continuous Context Matching Platform* has been developed, that allows for one context graph to be matched against a large set of graph patterns, but avoiding that a full graph matching process is carried out at every change in the graph. Instead, intermediate matches are kept in memory so that at any modification to the context graph the algorithm creates only new matches that are based on an added edge, or removes matches that include a deleted edge. This platform can be used by an agent to assist it in its context-aware behavior (as presented in Sect. 33.4.2).

33.5.3 Context-Based Agent Platform

In order to further test the model that we have developed for a context-awareness middleware for AmI applications, we have integrated context-awareness features in a platform for building and running AmI applications—the tATAmI platform (towards Agent Technologies for Ambient Intelligence)[5] (Baljak et al. 2012). The platform was implemented using a modular structure, and features tools for the visualization and tracking of agents, as well as for the realization of repeatable experiments, based on scenario files. The platform is underpinned by JADE[6] for communication, management and mobility features.

The platform allows the implementation of various AmI applications and is meant to validate the model presented in Sect. 33.4 through the integration of all of its components. The platform uses an evolved version of the CLAIM language, called S-CLAIM, which is simpler and easier to use. The definition of agents is based on behaviors, which can be reactive or proactive. The agents use Context Graph Knowledge Bases for context information that are accessed by means of a small number of functions that use patterns represented in text to locate information in the Knowledge Base. Agents also feature hierarchies and hierarchical mobility is implemented, allowing for the definition of the context-aware topology.

---

[5] We thank Thi Thuy Nga Nguyen, Marius-Tudor Benea, Emma Sevastian, prof. Amal El Fallah Seghrouchni, and Cédric Herpson for their contributions to the project. The code is open source and can be found at https://github.com/tATAmI-Project.

[6] Java Agent Development Framework http://jade.tilab.com/.

33.6 Conclusions and Future Work

This chapter presents a model in which generic functionality related to context-awareness in AmI applications can be isolated to a layer below domain-specific processing. In an agent-based architecture, the context-aware middleware lives in the 'lower' part of the agent, handling incoming context information, situation detection and context information sharing.

The model relies on a representation for context that is based on graphs, and patterns that are matched against the current context to detect interesting information and current situation. Outside the agent, an agent topology can be defined that reflects the actual context of the agent. The model of context patterns can be extended to handle temporal relations and sequences of events.

Practical experience with the model includes an algorithm for persistent context matching involving multiple patterns, graphical and textual representations for graphs and patterns that are easy to read and to input, as well as a platform for context-aware AmI applications.

Future work involves the implementation and simulation of more complex scenarios, as well as the deployment of the tATAmI platform in the Ambient Intelligence Laboratory of our Faculty, to serve as a context-aware middleware for AmI applications. Temporal elements in context matching are still at the beginning, and more work is required to cover a wider range of time-related issues and scenarios.

Acknowledgements The work has been funded by the Sectoral Operational Programme Human Resources Development 2007-2013 of the Ministry of European Funds through the Financial Agreement POSDRU/159/1.5/S/134398.

References

Augusto, J.C., McCullagh, P.J.: Ambient intelligence: Concepts and applications. Comput. Sci. Inf. Syst. (ComSIS) **4**(1), 1–27 (2007)

Baljak, V., Benea, M.T., El Fallah Seghrouchni, A., Herpson, C., Honiden, S., Nguyen, T.T.N., Olaru, A., Shimizu, R., Tei, K., Toriumi, S.: S-CLAIM: An agent-based programming language for AmI, a smart-room case study. In: Proceedings of ANT 2012, The 3rd International Conference on Ambient Systems, Networks and Technologies, 27–29 August, Niagara Falls, Ontario, Canada, Procedia Computer Science, vol. 10, pp. 30–37. Elsevier (2012). doi: 10.1016/j.procs.2012.06.008. http://www.sciencedirect.com/science/article/pii/S1877050912003651

Brézillon, J., Brézillon, P.: Context modeling: Context as a dressing of a focus. In: Kokinov, B., Richardson D.C., Roth-Berghofer, Thomas, R., Vieu, L. (eds) Modeling and Using Context (Lecture Notes in Computer Science), pp. 136–149. Springer, Berlin (2007). doi: 10.1007/978-3-540-74255-5_11

Cabri, G., Ferrari, L., Leonardi, L., Zambonelli, F.: The LAICA project: Supporting ambient intelligence via agents and ad-hoc middleware. Proceedings of WETICE 2005, 14th IEEE International Workshops on Enabling Technologies, 13–15 June 2005, Linköping, Sweden pp. 39–46 (2005)

Chen, G., Kotz, D.: A survey of context-aware mobile computing research. Technical Report TR2000-381, Dartmouth College (2000)

Cook, D.J., Krishnan, N.C., Rashidi, P.: Activity discovery and activity recognition: A new partnership. IEEE Trans. Cybern. **43**(3), 820–828 (2013)

Ducatel, K., Bogdanowicz, M., Scapolo, F., Leijten, J., Burgelman, J.: Scenarios for ambient intelligence in 2010. Technical Report, Office for Official Publications of the European Communities (2001)

El Fallah Seghrouchni, A.: Intelligence ambiante, les defis scientifiques. Presentation, Colloque Intelligence Ambiante, Forum Atena (2008)

Ferber, J.: Multi-Agent Systems: An Introduction to Distributed Artificial Intelligence, 1st edn. Addison-Wesley Longman Publishing Co., Inc., Boston (1999). isbn = 0201360489

Henricksen, K., Indulska, J.: Developing context-aware pervasive computing applications: Models and approach. Pervasive Mobile Comput. **2**(1), 37–64 (2006)

Lech, T.C., Wienhofen, L.W.M.: AmbieAgents: a scalable infrastructure for mobile and context-aware information services. Proceedings of the 4th International Joint Conference on Autonomous Agents and Multiagent Systems (AAMAS 2005), 25–29 July 2005, Utrecht, The Netherlands, pp. 625–631 (2005)

Olaru, A.: Context matching for ambient intelligence applications. In: Björner, N., Negru, V., Ida, T., Jebelean, T., Petcu, D., Watt, S., Zaharie, D. (eds.) Proceedings of SYNASC 2013, 15th International Symposium on Symbolic and Numeric Algorithms for Scientific Computing, 23–26 September, Timisoara, Romania, pp. 265–272. IEEE CPS (2013). doi: 10.1109/SYNASC.2013.42

Olaru, A., Nguyen, T.T.N., Benea, M.T., El Fallah Seghrouchni, A.: Ao dai: Agent-oriented design for ambient intelligence. Sixth joint NII-LIP6 WorkShop on Multi-Agent and Distributed Systems, Paris, France (2011). http://herpsonc.eu/6workshopNii/index.htm

Olaru, A., Florea, A.M., El Fallah Seghrouchni, A.: A context-aware multi-agent system as a middleware for ambient intelligence. Mobile Netw. Appl. **18**(3), 429–443 (2013). doi: 10.1007/s11036-012-0408-9. http://link.springer.com/article/10.1007

Perera, C., Zaslavsky, A., Christen, P., Georgakopoulos, D.: Context aware computing for the internet of things: A survey. IEEE Commun. Surv. Tutorials **16**(1), 414–454 (2013)

Rogers, A., Corkill, D., Jennings, N.: Agent technologies for sensor networks. IEEE Intell. Syst. **24**(2), 13–17 (2009)

Sowa, J.: Conceptual graphs. Found. Artif. Intell. **3**, 213–237 (2008)

Tapia, D., Abraham, A., Corchado, J., Alonso, R.: Agents and ambient intelligence: Case studies. J. Ambient Intell. Humanized Comput. **1**(2), 85–93 (2010)

Chapter 34
Contextual Reasoning in an Intelligent Electronic Patient Leaflet System

Hedda R. Schmidtke, Haixia Yu, Pie Masomo, Andrew Kinai
and Alain Shema

Abstract This chapter discusses that contextual reasoning enables a wide range of novel intelligent e-health systems. The ability to represent a user's context—health situation, spatio-temporal circumstances, as well as medical proficiency and other parameters—allows a reasoning system to provide information from medical or pharmaceutical expert knowledge that is suitable for the situation. The claims are illustrated with the example of a mobile electronic patient leaflet application called Pharma+, which was developed to provide pharmaceutical product information to illiterate patients visiting a pharmacy in Rwanda. The authors outline a minimal framework for contextual reasoning in the health domain. This context logic framework is formalized as a labeled deductive system. It allows one to represent the three forms of context dependency (partial representation, perspective, and approximation), but is limited in the type of relations that can be represented: context logic is able to handle partial order relations over several domains, and can be implemented in an efficient manner using directed acyclic graphs (DAGs). The authors investigated main relations required for formalizing patient leaflets and whether these can be realized within this simple framework.

H. R. Schmidtke (✉) · A. Kinai · P. Masomo · A. Shema
Carnegie Mellon University, Kigali, Rwanda and Pittsburgh, PA, USA
e-mail: schmidtke@acm.org

H. Yu
Ricoh Innovations Corporation, Menlo Park, CA, USA
e-mail: hyu@ric.ricoh.com

A. Kinai
e-mail: akinai@rwanda.cmu.edu

P. Masomo
e-mail: pmasomo@rwanda.cmu.edu

A. Shema
e-mail: ashema@rwanda.cmu.edu

© Springer Science+Business Media New York 2014   557
P. Brézillon, A. J. Gonzalez (eds.), *Context in Computing*,
DOI 10.1007/978-1-4939-1887-4_34

34.1   Introduction

The health domain is one of the most interesting domains of application for context research. E-health systems, that is, information systems for the health domain, benefit considerably from a correct representation and handling of context. The term e-health has a wide variety of definitions (Oh et al. 2005). In this chapter, we focus specifically on intelligent e-health systems, that is, intelligent systems that are able to provide medical or pharmaceutical information and support to patients, care givers, or health care professionals. We discuss that contextual reasoning plays an important role in this domain: what is the correct action to take for a health care provider at any given moment depends on the circumstances and background information about the patient and the situation.

Three areas of research are of particular concern for intelligent e-health applications: decision support for processes in hospitals and general health care, ambient intelligence and context-awareness for making hospitals as smart environments and mobile health support more efficient and safe, and finally, biomedical ontologies supporting research and practitioners in managing a rapidly growing body of knowledge. Context-dependency is a key concern for this interdisciplinary effort. We motivate requirements for a minimal compendium of contextual reasoning mechanisms for an example e-health application and position these requirements within an overarching framework for contextual reasoning based on labeled deductive systems.

The framework distinguishes two types of context mechanisms: contextualization—with its inverse decontextualization—and granularity or level of detail mechanisms. In the e-health domain, the former is of particular relevance whenever expert knowledge is to be applied in a given situation, the latter is of particular importance when medical knowledge is to be communicated to lay persons. To illustrate our claims, we will use an application example of an e-leaflet, a pharmaceutical assistance application, which combines information about a person and other information about the context with pharmaceutical knowledge and leaflet contents to generate appropriate warnings and display these at the right level of detail for a patient, care giver, or a pharmacist.

Structure of this chapter. After a discussion of related works (Sect. 34.2), we outline the logical framework for describing context-dependent information (Sect. 34.3). We then introduce the application scenario of an e-leaflet in Sect. 34.4 and analyse key aspects of context-dependency in this scenario (Sect. 34.5). We conclude this chapter with a summary and discussion of research questions (Sect. 34.6).

34.2   Related Works

A number of frameworks have been developed to formalize and analyze contextual reasoning. An excellent overview and categorization was put forth by Benerecetti et al. (2000). Benerecetti et al. (2000) define three dimensions that characterize a contextual representation: to what part of the world it relates (*partiality*), which *perspective* it expresses, and at what detail it represents the world (*approximation*). *Bridging axioms* relate local theories expressed in different contexts, allowing for three types of contextual reasoning: *localized reasoning*, that is, reasoning within a part of the world, *push and pop reasoning* as contextualizing and decontextualizing, and *shifting*, that is, changing perspectives. We show a simplified framework in which change of perspective can be modeled as a form of contextualization or decontextualization. Also, we have only one set of rules, that is, there are no special rules for different contexts or dimensions of context.

The context logic framework used in this article extends the language of Schmidtke et al. (2008) and is described in this chapter using the more general formalism of labeled deductive systems of Gabbay (1996). Gabbay (1993) showed that this formalism is suitable to encode a wide variety of contextual formalisms including situation theory.

Context research has its roots in a range of disciplines, likewise, e-health applications involving some form of contextual reasoning mechanism are proposed with a range of approaches. Three particular domains are particularly relevant for intelligent e-health: decision support, ambient intelligence, including ambient assisted living, and medical ontology research. In general, any intelligent e-health system can be understood as a decision support system that uses both information about the context, which can be obtained from sensors but also from other sources, and medical knowledge.

Clinical research indicates that practitioner performance can be improved by decision support systems (Garg et al. 2005). Contextual graphs have been shown to be a valuable tool in situational decision support and collaboration support for experts (Brézillon 2005; Brézillon et al. 2002; Brézillon and Pomerol 1999). Contextual graphs span a space of contexts and potential actions in a directed acyclic graph (DAG). Brézillon et al. (2002) show that this structure covers both temporal and other context-based reasoning. A key difference between DAGs and the traditional decision trees is DAGs' allowing context-dependency and dynamics of human decision making to be reflected more correctly. The partial orders and Boolean algebra that form the core of the context logic formalism in this article are implemented using DAGs in the prototype reasoner.

The medical domain is one of the primary application domains for context-aware computing research (Bricon-Souf and Newman 2007). Context-aware application frameworks, such as Aura (Garlan et al. 2002; Sousa and Garlan 2002) or the Context Toolkit (Salber et al. 1999), can provide situation critical information, derived from sensory information and other distributed data sources to provide information about the context. In the health domain, such information can save lives. Consequentially, specialized application frameworks for the medical domain have been put forward. Bardram (2004) shows one of the most detailed studies about a real-world deployment in a hospital. His system includes a basic context-aware infrastructure, a location tracking system, an interactive display system, and a mobile phone based system for facilitating social awareness among clinicians. Three parameters of context were collected through the system: location, status of an operation, and activity

(Bardram 2004). Bardram highlights three important factors for context-aware computing particularly relevant for safety in the health domain: the accuracy of the context recognition mechanism, the confidence of the decision-making algorithms, and the cost of consequences if an action is taken.

Uncertainty of information plays a key role in context-aware e-health systems. Accordingly, the reasoning systems at the center of context-aware health support systems require careful handling of uncertainty. The reasoning system RIMER (Augusto et al. 2008) supports a combination of event-condition-action (ECA) rules with spatio-temporal reasoning and uncertainty, where the events and conditions as well as the rules themselves can be uncertain. The resulting rule-based system combines spatio-temporal reasoning—a classical domain of contextual reasoning—with a special uncertainty reasoning formalism. A granularity mechanism allows handling of uncertainty (Schmidtke and Woo 2006) and can also be used to control information disclosure in medical applications (Rashid et al. 2007). In our example application of an e-leaflet, we use granularity only in the sense of explanation detail. A detailed discussion of granularity can be found in Chap. 28.

The most critical component of intelligent e-health applications is medical knowledge. Biomedical ontologies contain large amounts of such knowledge. These ontologies are often constructed by medical experts who are not ontologists. The biomedical ontology Gene ontology (Blake et al. 2001), for instance, has been criticized for being actually comprised of three independent ontologies that are intermingled, an impediment for ontology integration (Smith et al. 2007). Contextual reasoning can be a key component to alleviating this, as integration of sources of knowledge regarding different perspectives on a domain—*bridging* in the terminology of Benerecetti et al. (2000)—is one of the key points of contextual reasoning.

34.3 Types of Context-Dependency

Benerecetti et al. (2000) point out three different types of context mechanisms, which depend on three different basic relations between context worlds. First, we can move from a representation of a world to a part of this world, or, in the opposite direction, move from a part of the world to a larger part containing it. The relation to describe this is a part-of relation, formally a partial order relation. Second, we can move between worlds, for instance, from the present to a future time point or to a past time point, the relation here is related to a movement with respect to some reference system. Generally, this entails that the relation is a linear or partial ordering relation. We notice that in both cases the relations between contexts are partial order relations.[1] Third, we can increase or lower the degree of detail. The relation, in this case, is more complicated and can regard the structure of the situations or worlds we are

---

[1] A linear order is a partial order that fulfills the additional constraint of linearity, that is: any two elements can be ordered with respect to each other.

studying or the logical structure itself. The framework of context logic allows us to model all three cases in a unified way.

A labeled deductive system is defined by a logical language L, a classical theory $\mathcal{M}$, and a term algebra $\mathcal{A}$ on labels (Gabbay 1993). We define the basic infrastructure of context logic (Schmidtke et al. 2008) within this framework. The key idea of context logic is that it integrates labels—intuitively denoting worlds, situations, or circumstances—with variables—intuitively denoting entities about which propositions are formulated. The key idea is to take the notion of Dey and Abowd (2000), that everything is context, literally. Accordingly, the only basic entities in the logic are context variables. Context variables can be combined to form context terms, which, as we will see, can serve as labels, entities about which propositions are formulated, and relations with which propositions are formulated. Formally, all propositions about contexts are formed with a single relation $\sqsubseteq$, which represents in different contexts the different core partial ordering relations that relate contexts as entities.

34.3.1 Context Logic Language

We keep the description of the syntax of the context logic language close to its original description (Schmidtke et al. 2008). The set of context terms *CTerm* is defined based on a set of context variables *CTVar*, together with two additional symbols 1, for the *universal context*, and 0, for the *empty context*. The set *CTerm* of *context terms* is the smallest set that fulfills:

1. The context variables $a \in CTVar$, and the special symbols 1 and 0 are atomic context terms.
2. If c and d are context terms, then the *complement* $-c$, the *sum* $(c \sqcup d)$, and the *intersection* $(c \sqcap d)$ are also context terms.[2]

The algebra $\mathcal{A}$ for the labeled deductive system is the Boolean Algebra over context terms with $\sqcap, \sqcup, -$, etc. taking the roles of *and, or, complement*, etc. as one would expect. The relation $\leq$, holds between two context terms $c, d \in CTerm$ iff we can prove $c \leq d$ in the algebra for each valuation of the context variables in c and d. For any given terms c, d, for instance, we know $c \leq 1$ and $0 \leq c$ and $c \sqcap d \leq c$ and $c \leq c \sqcup d$, etc.

The logical language L of context logic formulae is defined recursively as the smallest set containing the following expressions:

1. If c and d are context terms, then $[c \sqsubseteq d]$ is an atomic context formula.
2. If ϕ and ψ are formulae, then the negation $\neg\phi$, the disjunction $(\phi \vee \psi)$, and the conjunction $(\phi \wedge \psi)$ are also formulae.

---

[2] To improve readability, we omit brackets, in particular outer brackets, if no ambiguity can arise.

For a context term c other than the special symbols 1 and 0, the formula $[1 \sqsubseteq c]$ is called the *positive atom* of c, and $[c \sqsubseteq 0]$ is called the *negative atom* of c. We abbreviate $[1 \sqsubseteq 0]$ as $\perp$ and $[1 \sqsubseteq 1]$ as $\top$. We define a *contextual knowledge base* (CKB) formally as a set of labelled context formulae.

34.3.2 Context Logic Theory

The key advantage of labeled deductive systems is that they unite proof theory and semantics for a logical language in one formalism, the system of rules M, which also lends itself to the implementation we used to realize the reasoning system. We assume rules for the propositional connectives to be given and just state rules for $\wedge$ introduction and elimination 34.1 and modus ponens 34.2 as examples.

$$\frac{c : \phi \quad c : \psi}{c : \phi \wedge \psi} \qquad \frac{c : \phi \wedge \psi}{c : \phi \quad c : \psi} \tag{34.1}$$

$$\frac{c : \phi \quad c : \phi \to \psi}{c : \psi} \tag{34.2}$$

The interesting contribution comes from the rules for atomic formulae.

$$\frac{c : \phi \quad d \leq c}{d : \phi} \tag{34.3}$$

$$\frac{}{x : [1 \sqsubseteq x]} \qquad \frac{x : [1 \sqsubseteq y]}{x \leq y} \tag{34.4}$$

$$\frac{x : [c \sqsubseteq d]}{x : [1 \sqsubseteq c] \to [1 \sqsubseteq d]} \tag{34.5}$$

$$\frac{x : \neg[c \sqsubseteq d]}{\text{create} y, y \leq x, y : [1 \sqsubseteq c] \wedge \neg[1 \sqsubseteq d]} \tag{34.6}$$

Additional rules are needed for decomposing context terms within formulae. We give an example for the complement, which is relating positive atoms to negative atoms.

$$\frac{x : [1 \sqsubseteq -c]}{x : [c \sqsubseteq 0]} \tag{34.7}$$

This simple language is surprisingly powerful (Schmidtke 2012) and capable of capturing an interesting portion of the pharmaceutical and medical domain. In order to show this, we prove a core result for this language, showing that the language is able to move objects suitably between the label position and internal context positions.

$$x \leq y \vdash x : [1 \sqsubseteq y] \tag{34.8}$$

$$x : [c \sqsubseteq d] \vdash x \sqcap c : [1 \sqsubseteq d] \tag{34.9}$$

$$x \sqcap c : [1 \sqsubseteq d] \vdash x : [c \sqsubseteq d] \tag{34.10}$$

We first prove that $x \leq y \vdash x : [1 \sqsubseteq y]$ 34.8. By 34.4, $y : [1 \sqsubseteq y]$. With the assumption $x \leq y$ by 34.3, we infer $x : [1 \sqsubseteq y]$.

To prove $x : [c \sqsubseteq d] \vdash x \sqcap c : [1 \sqsubseteq d]$ 34.9, we assume $x : [c \sqsubseteq d]$ and derive 34.5 $x : [1 \sqsubseteq c] \rightarrow [1 \sqsubseteq d]$. Now, $x \sqcap c \leq x$ clearly holds by $\mathcal{A}$ and we can conclude with 34.3 that $x \sqcap c : [1 \sqsubseteq c] \rightarrow [1 \sqsubseteq d]$. Since $x \sqcap c \leq c$, we also know $x \sqcap c : [1 \sqsubseteq c]$ 34.8 and thus by 34.2 $x \sqcap c : [1 \sqsubseteq d]$.

We prove $x \sqcap c : [1 \sqsubseteq d] \vdash x : [c \sqsubseteq d]$ 34.10 by contradiction. Assume that $x \sqcap c : [1 \sqsubseteq d]$ and not $x : [c \sqsubseteq d]$. In this case, we would have to assume 34.6 there is a context $y, y \leq x, y : [1 \sqsubseteq c] \wedge \neg[1 \sqsubseteq d]$, that is 34.1, $y : [1 \sqsubseteq c]$ and $y : \neg[1 \sqsubseteq d]$. We conclude $y \leq c$ 34.4, and with $y \leq x$, we can infer $y \leq x \sqcap c$ from $\mathcal{A}$. But this entails by the assumption $x \sqcap c : [1 \sqsubseteq d]$ and 34.3 that $y : [1 \sqsubseteq d]$, a contradiction.

34.3.3   Types of Context in Context Logic

With this formalism, it is now easy to describe basic types of contextual reasoning that can be built upon notions of Boolean algebra. We look at three examples to make this discussion more illustrative. An example for reasoning about and between partial views of the world is the language of spatial regions as contexts. Assume spatial regions are given as sets of spatial points, the Boolean algebra of sets with $\sqcap, \sqcup, -$ interpreted as intersection, union, and complement can be used to represent focussing on a spatial part of the world. With the intuition of the algebra of point sets as $\mathcal{A}$, the relation $\leq$ is the subset relation. But we are not limited to spatial parts, we can also represent other partial order relations. The subsumption relation is_a, for instance, can also be endowed with a set theoretic interpretation. More surprisingly, we can have both:

- (In terms of location), Bugesera is in Rwanda.
  $loc : [Bugesera \sqsubseteq Rwanda]$
- Bugesera is a province.
  $is\_a : [Bugesera \sqsubseteq province]$

Decontextualizing yields:

- The location Bugesera is in Rwanda.
  $1 : [loc \sqcap Bugesera \sqsubseteq Rwanda]$
- Bugesera is a province.
  $1 : [is\_a \sqcap Bugesera \sqsubseteq province]$

From there, we can again contextualize and obtain:

- (Speaking about Bugesera), it is located in Rwanda.
  $Bugesera : [loc \sqsubseteq Rwanda]$
- It is a province.
  $Bugesera : [is\_a \sqsubseteq province]$

We can also represent *shifting* in this framework. In order to move along the axes of reference frames, such as moving along the time axis between past and future, we only need to think of the relation ≤ as an ordering relation, such as before and after in branching time. Again, a set-theoretical formalization is possible, but not as intuitively applied.[3] It is easier in this case to think of ≤ simply as a partial order relation, such as a causal relation in future branching time. A causal relation useful in many context-aware applications is the relation describing possible reactions of the system. In our example application we are particularly interested to make the application cause different warnings depending on medications and information from the patient record:

- Milk-sugar interacts (causes an allergy warning) with lactose-intolerance.
  has_warning ⊓ *allergy* : [*milk_sugar* ⊑ *lactose_intolerance*]
- Sugar interacts (causes a condition warning) with diabetes.
  has_warning ⊓ *condition* : [*sugar* ⊑ *diabetes*]

The example also illustrates that we can represent sub-relations and compound relations in a natural manner.

We can represent a hierarchy of levels of detail, by delimiting details explicitly in different domains. In order to provide information to a patient, for instance, we might want to restrict explanations to exclude more specific medical terminology in a taxonomy:

- Expert terminology has more detail than common sense terminology.
  detail : [*common_term* ⊑ *expert_term*]
- *Antipyretic* is in terms of detail (higher or equal to) an expert taxonomic term.
  detail : [*expert_term* ⊑ *antipyretic*]
- *Against-fever* is in terms of detail (at most) a common taxonomic term.
  detail : [*against_fever* ⊑ *common_term* ⊑]

We can infer that *against_fever* has less detail than *antipyretic*.[4] When choosing between the terms, e.g. for generating answers, we can then take into account to which level of explanation detail a term belongs. The hierarchy of contexts with respect to detail can thus be stratified. Rashid et al. (2007) showed how coarsening levels of detail can also be used to increase a user's control over privacy of his or her health data and other context data, generalizing the approach taken by Duckham and Kulik (2005) for using level of detail control for increasing location privacy.

---

[3] The future of a time point t can be understood, for instance, as the potentially branching time in the interval $[t, \infty]$ and the past of a time point can be denoted by $[-\infty, t]$.

[4] Note that we cannot infer from the above that the terms have a similar meaning, we only know from the above how they are related with respect to complexity of terminology.

34.4   Scenario: Contextual Reasoning for a Pharmaceutical Assistance Application

To make the discussion more concrete, consider the scenario of the pharmaceutical assistance system: should Mr Smith take a certain medicine M at a given time t? Context parameters that should be taken into account in this example are (with currently implemented relations in brackets):

- Taxonomic/partonomic circumstances of M (relations is_a and has_part)
  - Does this medicine interact with other medicines that Mr Smith is taking? (has_warning ⊓ medicine)
  - Does this medicine or any of its parts interact with specific health conditions of Mr Smith? Maybe the medicine contains sugar and Mr Smith has diabetes? (has_warning ⊓ condition and has_warning ⊓ allergy)
- Personal circumstances of Mr Smith
  - What is the correct dosage for Mr Smith? What is his age, weight?
  - Who is giving Mr Smith the medicine? Is he taking it himself, or is he dependent on caregivers?
  - Did he already take the medicine? When did he take the last dosage?
  - Is Mr Smith in severe danger? We might allow a higher dosage or otherwise contra-indicated medicine if the patient is suffering under severe conditions.
- Temporal circumstances of t
  - Is it the right time to take the medicine? During a meal, after a meal, in the morning, in the evening?
  - Did he already take the medicine? When did he take the last dosage?
- Spatial circumstances (location)
  - Is this medicine given in a hospital? Administered at home? We might allow a higher dosage or otherwise contra-indicated medicine if the patient is within the reach of medical emergency measures.
  - Globalization brings people into unknown contexts: is Mr Smith in a region he does not know well, maybe trying to cure the wrong disease? Does he think he has a cold, but, in fact, caught malaria? (has_warning ⊓ location)

Figure 34.1 shows the basic architecture for the knowledge base derived from theses considerations together with some example terms.

While the core concern for this application, which is addressed by the patient leaflet in traditional paper-based health information provision, is the second point of taxonomic/partonomic aspects of the medicine itself, this list illustrates that many other aspects of context also have to be taken into account. We developed an electronic patient leaflet as an application scenario to investigate the expressiveness and usefulness of the context logic framework in a relevant and important domain. Such an application can be a core of a more comprehensive intelligent e-health system, since correct administration of pharmaceutical products is a key step in health care process support and health information systems in general. But, the e-leaflet is also a paradigmatic example of an intelligent e-health application by itself: it provides decision support based on medical knowledge and using context information.

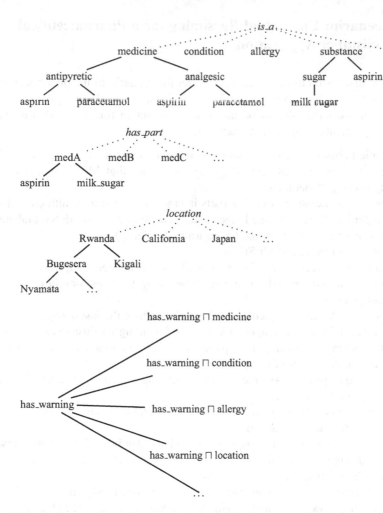

Fig. 34.1 Architecture for a pharmaceutical knowledge-base comprising a basic vocabulary of types (taxonomy, is_a), parts (partonomy, has_part), and a location hierarchy of regions, but also hierarchies of relations, such as specific subrelations that can be used to distinguish warnings to be issued

Figure 34.2 shows screenshots from the application Pharma+, a prototype electronic leaflet application for Android devices.

A small knowledge base with taxonomic, partonomic, and location information is shown in Fig. 34.3 and graphically illustrated in Fig. 34.4. We can see that milk sugar is a sugar and that medA contains milk sugar. From the knowledge base (Fig. 34.3) we know that

$$[\text{sugar} \sqcap \text{has\_warning} \sqcap \text{condition} \sqsubseteq \text{diabetes}],$$

Fig. 34.2 Screenshots from an electronic leaflet application for the Android OS: Pharma+ provides patients with knowledge about pharmaceutical products that is particularly relevant to them given their medical record. Depending on context—here: spatial context—health warnings are issued when the context and the chosen medicine indicate that a patient might have symptoms of a serious disease

that is, that sugar causes a condition warning for diabetes. Assume Mr. Smith has diabetes and wants to buy medA. His medical record contains diabetes as an entry. We check that diabetes is a condition and try to prove whether any part of medA belongs to a category that conflicts with this condition

$$[medA \sqcap \text{has\_part} \sqcap \text{is\_a} \sqcap \text{has\_warning} \sqcap \text{condition} \sqsubseteq diabetes],$$

where the italics show the schema instantiations we make in this case.

34.5 Modeling Context-Dependent Information for an e-Leaflet

We developed Pharma+ to study context-reasoning for intelligent e-health systems with a concrete use case. An important contribution of intelligent systems technologies is that they allow to structure and prepare expert knowledge so that it becomes accessible to a larger proportion of lay persons. Health related information is known to be particularly hard to access for a lay person, which has led to a range of studies on the phenomenon and consequences of *health literacy* levels. Parker et al. (1995) found that "15 % of the patients [participating in their study] could not read and interpret a prescription bottle." *Health literacy* is defined as "the degree to which individuals can obtain, process, and understand the basic health information and services they need to make appropriate health decisions" (Berkman et al. 2011). Even presumably simple prescription medication warning labels can be misunderstood

Example queries:

$[medA \sqcap has\_part \sqcap is\_a \sqcap has\_warning \sqcap condition \sqsubseteq diabetes]$?

$[medA \sqcap has\_part \sqcap is\_a \sqcap has\_warning \sqcap allergy \sqsubseteq galactose]$?

$[medA \sqcap has\_part \sqcap is\_a \sqcap has\_warning \sqcap medicine \sqsubseteq medB]$?

$[medA \sqcap has\_part \sqcap is\_a \sqcap has\_warning \sqcap location \sqsubseteq Bugesera]$?

Knowledge base:

$[milk\_sugar \sqcap is\_a \sqsubseteq sugar]$;

$[analgesic \sqcap has\_warning \sqcap medicine \sqsubseteq medA]$;

$[analgesic \sqcap has\_warning \sqcap medicine \sqsubseteq medB]$;

$[sugar \sqcap has\_warning \sqcap condition \sqsubseteq diabetes]$;

$[milk\_sugar \sqcap has\_warning \sqcap allergy \sqsubseteq galactose]$;

$[aspirin \sqcap is\_a \sqsubseteq analgesic]$;

$[aspirin \sqcap is\_a \sqsubseteq antipyretic]$;

$[paracetamol \sqcap is\_a \sqsubseteq analgesic]$;

$[paracetamol \sqcap is\_a \sqsubseteq antipyretic]$;

$[analgesic \sqcap is\_a \sqsubseteq medicine]$;

$[antipyretic \sqcap is\_a \sqsubseteq medicine]$;

$[medA \sqcap has\_part \sqsubseteq (aspirin \sqcap milk\_sugar)]$;

$[medB \sqcap has\_part \sqsubseteq aspirin \sqcap paracetamol]$;

$[is\_a \sqcap antipyretic \sqcap location \sqcap has\_warning \sqcap has\_part \sqsubseteq malaria]$;

$[malaria \sqcap location \sqsubseteq Bugesera]$;

$[diabetes \sqcap is\_a \sqsubseteq condition]$;

$[malaria \sqcap is\_a \sqsubseteq condition]$;

Fig. 34.3 Example: fictitious medications medA and medB and their interactions modeled as contexts in a knowledge-base for pharmaceutical product assistance, and examples of the four types of queries used by Pharma+ to determine whether a user can take a medicine. The terms in italics are the medicine in question (here medA) and information from the user medical record file

(Davis et al. 2006). The importance of health literacy for public health and international development is recognized widely, e.g. by the World Health Organization[5] (Nutbeam 2000).

Patient information in electronic format was proposed early as a chance to improve access to health information (Kenny et al. 1998), and a number of web sites are now providing leaflet information. To our best knowledge however, a knowledge based system for personalized medication information provision, as we propose, does not exist.

A number of relations are important for an electronic patient leaflet: patients have diseases, special conditions, symptoms and allergies; pharmaceutical products are used to treat certain symptoms and diseases, have side effects, interact with other

---

[5] http://www.who.int/healthpromotion/.

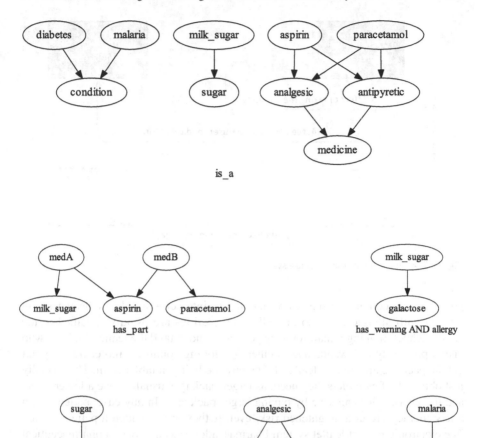

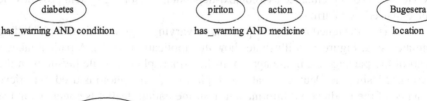

Fig. 34.4 Selected relations in the knowledge base shown in Fig. 34.3. In context logic, everything is context, including relations. It is therefore easy to construct complex relations such as "has_warning ⊓ condition"

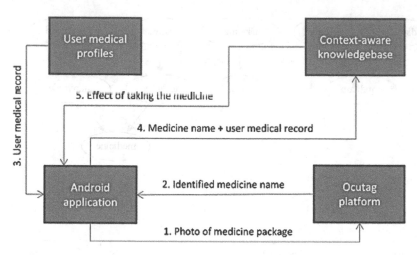

Fig. 34.5 Architecture of the Pharma+ system

products, and contain substances, which in turn interact with other substances, can interact with allergies, and so on. All these relations are usually specified in the patient leaflet, making it hard for a lay person to understand the leaflet. Patients who visit a pharmacy in Rwanda and in other developing countries, moreover, may not get the package and patient leaflet if they buy medicine in tablet form. They usually just obtain the few tablets they need, as larger packages usually have a lower price, and the pharmacies can save by buying larger packages. In any case, patients with a low literacy are at a heightened risk, even if they are provided a patient leaflet. The electronic patient leaflet system Pharma+ addresses this risk: a pharmaceutical knowledge-base implemented as a context-dependent reasoning system provides the back end used by Pharma+.

Pharma+ is designed to support patients of varying degree of literacy, including illiterate users. Figure 34.5 illustrates how the application works. A patient takes a photo of the package using the app on his/her smart phone, while he/she is in the pharmacy. Using the Ocutag visual search platform,[6] this photo is used to retrieve the name of the medication. Information from the patient leaflet is contained in the knowledge-base; information about the patient is stored in a medical record system. The query is then formulated by asking whether any of the conditions, diseases, allergies, or pharmaceutical products recently taken by the patient interacts with the medication the person is about to buy.

The core component is a reasoning system implemented so as to provide expert knowledge about medications. It provides the expert knowledge to Pharma+ as described above. A simple context logic reasoner implementation based on DAGs was used in this project for a fragment of the language that allows atomic formulae with

---

[6] https://www.ocutag.com/.

arbitrarily complex context terms. The decontextualized formulae in Fig. 34.3, for instance, can be handled efficiently by the implemented reasoning engine. Other components include the medical record system and the Ocutag repository which provides the name of the medication when provided with a photo of the box.

34.6   Conclusions

We demonstrated that the e-health domain gives rise to a wide range of applications for contextual reasoning. For the example of an electronic leaflet application, we demonstrated that pharmaceutical and medical knowledge are highly dependent on context. All three variants of context-dependency described by Benerecetti et al. (2000) were shown to be necessary for a proper formalization of medical knowledge and for making this knowledge accessible to patients. We demonstrated how an e-health application, such as Pharma+ can employ this knowledge and available context information. We conclude that automatic systems for decontextualization of knowledge could further the usefulness of publicly available formalized or semi-formal knowledge.

Knowledge-based systems can be a key enabler for making life saving health information accessible to a wider range of people. Context is key for these applications, as people need to be made aware of exactly the facts that apply to them to avoid the overload of information and the complicated structure and terminology of traditional patient leaflets. However, quality of information is crucial for the medical and pharmaceutical domains (McClung et al. 1998). We identify intelligent, context-dependent e-health assistance as an important area for future research in contextual reasoning applications, alleviating the burden of rising health system costs and addressing a key concern of international development in the health sector. However, work on such systems requires an interdisciplinary effort involving medical and pharmaceutical expertise, ontology engineering expertise, as well as expertise in natural language production and understanding to ensure quality of information provision. Future work should include construction of a large-scale knowledge base and extensive expert evaluation.

Acknowledgements   The research described in this article was partially funded by Ricoh Innovations Corporation. The Pharma+ application was developed by Andrew Kinai, Pie Masomo, Alain Shema, and Bonaventure Twagirimana.

References

Augusto, J.C., Liu, J., McCullagh, P., Wang, H., Yang, J.B.: Management of uncertainty and spatio-temporal aspects for monitoring and diagnosis in a smart home. Int. J. Comput. Intell. Syst. **1**(4), 361–378 (2008)

Bardram, J.E.: Applications of context-aware computing in hospital work: examples and design principles. In: Proceedings of the 2004 ACM Symposium on Applied Computing, pp. 1574–1579. ACM, New York (2004)

Benerecetti, M., Bouquet, P., Ghidini, C.: Contextual reasoning distilled. J. Exp. Theor. Artif. Intell. 12(3), 279–305 (2000)

Berkman, N.D., Sheridan, S.L., Donahue, K.E., Halpern, D.J., Viera, A., Crotty, K., Holland, A., Brasure, M., Lohr, K.N., Harden, E., Tant, E., Wallace, I., Viswanathan, M.: Health literacy interventions and outcomes: an updated systematic review. RTI International–University of North Carolina Evidence-based Practice Center, Rockville (2011)

Blake, J., Corradi, J., Eppig, J., Hill, D., Richardson, J., Ringwald, M., et al.: Creating the gene ontology resource: Design and implementation. Genome Res. 11, 1425–1433 (2001)

Brézillon, P.: Task-realization models in contextual graphs. In: Dey, A.K., Kokinov, B.N., Leake, D.B., Turner, R.M. (eds.) International Conference on Modeling and Using Context, LNCS, vol. 3554, pp. 55–68. Springer, Berlin (2005)

Brézillon, P., Pomerol, J.C.: Contextual knowledge sharing and cooperation in intelligent assistant systems. Le Travail Humain Théor. Méthodol. 62(3), 223–246 (1999)

Brézillon, P., Pasquier, L., Pomerol, J.C.: Reasoning with contextual graphs. Eur. J. Operat. Res. 136(2), 290–298 (2002)

Bricon-Souf, N., Newman, C.R.: Context awareness in health care: a review. Int. J. Med. Inf. 76(1), 2–12 (2007). doi: http://dx.doi.org/10.1016/j.ijmedinf.2006.01.003. http://www.sciencedirect.com/science/article/pii/S13865056060 00098

Davis, T.C., Wolf, M.S., Bass, P.F., Middlebrooks, M., Kennen, E., Baker, D.W., Bennett, C.L., Durazo-Arvizu, R., Bocchini, A., Savory, S., Parker, R.M.: Low literacy impairs comprehension of prescription drug warning labels. J. Gen. Intern. Med. 21(8), 847–851 (2006). doi: 10.1111/j.1525-1497.2006.00529.x. http://dx.doi.org/10.1111/j.1525-1497.2006.00529.x

Dey, A.K., Abowd, G.D.: Towards a better understanding of context and context-awareness. In: Workshop on The What, Who, Where, When, and How of Context-Awareness. CHI 2000, The Hague (2000)

Duckham, M., Kulik, L.: A formal model of obfuscation and negotiation for location privacy. In: Gellersen, H.W., Want, R., Schmidt, A. (eds.) Pervasive Computing, pp. 152–170. Springer, Berlin (2005)

Gabbay, D.: Labelled deductive systems and situation theory. In: Aczel, P., Israel, D., Katagin, Y., Peters, S. (eds.) Situation Theory and Applications, vol. 3, pp. 89–118. CSLI, Stanford (1993)

Gabbay, D.: Labelled Deductive Systems, vol. 1. Clarendon, Oxford (1996)

Garg, A.X., Adhikari, N.K., McDonald, H., Rosas-Arellano, M.P., Devereaux, P., Beyene, J., Sam, J., Haynes, R.B.: Effects of computerized clinical decision support systems on practitioner performance and patient outcomes. JAMA 293(10), 1223–1238 (2005)

Garlan, D., Siewiorek, D.P., Smailagic, A., Steenkiste, P.: Project aura: toward distraction-free pervasive computing. Pervasive Comput. IEEE 1(2), 22–31 (2002)

Kenny, T., Wilson, R., Purves, I., Clark, J., Newton, L., Newton, D., Moseley, D.: A pil for every ill? Patient information leaflets (pils): a review of past, present and future use. Fam. Pract. 15(5), 471–479 (1998)

McClung, H.J., Murray, R.D., Heitlinger, L.A.: The internet as a source for current patient information. Pediatrics 101(6), e2–e2 (1998)

Nutbeam, D.: Health literacy as a public health goal: a challenge for contemporary health education and communication strategies into the 21st century. Health Promot. Int. 15(3), 259–267 (2000)

Oh, H., Rizo, C., Enkin, M., Jadad, A.: What is ehealth (3): a systematic review of published definitions. J. Med. Internet Res. 7(1), e1 (2005)

Parker, R.M., Baker, D.W., Williams, M.V.: The test of functional health literacy in adults. J. Gen. Intern. Med. 10(10), 537–541 (1995)

Rashid, U., Schmidtke, H.R., Woo, W.: Managing disclosure of personal health information in smart home healthcare. In: Stephanidis, C. (ed.) International Conference on Universal Access in Human-Computer Interaction, Held as Part of HCI International, pp. 188–197. Springer, Heidelberg (2007)

Salber, D., Dey, A.K., Abowd, G.D.: The context toolkit: aiding the development of context-enabled applications. In: CHI, pp. 434–441. ACM Press, Pittsburgh (1999)

Schmidtke, H.R.: Contextual reasoning in context-aware systems. In: Workshop Proceedings of the 8th International Conference on Intelligent Environments, pp. 82–93. IOS Press, Amsterdam (2012)

Schmidtke, H.R., Woo, W.: A formal characterization of vagueness and granularity for context-aware mobile and ubiquitous computing. In: Youn, H.Y., Kim, M., Morikawa, H. (eds.) International Symposium on Ubiquitous Computing Systems, pp. 144–157. Springer, Heidelberg (2006). doi: 10.1007/11890348_12

Schmidtke, H.R., Hong, D., Woo, W.: Reasoning about models of context: a context-oriented logical language for knowledge-based context-aware applications. Rev. Intell. Artif. 22(5), 589–608 (2008)

Smith, B., Ashburner, M., Rosse, C., Bard, J., Bug, W., Ceusters, W., Goldberg, L.J., Eilbeck, K., Ireland, A., Mungall, C.J., et al.: The obo foundry: coordinated evolution of ontologies to support biomedical data integration. Nat. Biotechnol. 25(11), 1251–1255 (2007)

Sousa, J.P., Garlan, D.: Aura: An architectural framework for user mobility in ubiquitous computing environments. In: Bosch, J et al. (eds.) Software Architecture: System Design, Development, and Maintenance (Proceedings of the 3rd Working IEEE/IFIP Conference on Software Architecture. Springer, New York (2002)

Printed in the United States
By Bookmasters